Understanding Human Geography

People and their changing environments

People and their
changing
environments

Understanding Human Geography

People and their changing environments

Michael Bradford and Ashley Kent

Oxford University Press

Oxford University Press,
Walton Street,
Oxford OX2 6DP

Oxford New York Toronto
Delhi Bombay Calcutta
Madras Karachi Kuala Lumpur
Singapore Hong Kong Tokyo
Nairobi Dar es Salaam Cape Town
Melbourne Auckland Madrid

and associated companies in
Berlin Ibadan

Oxford is a trade mark of
Oxford University Press

© Oxford University Press 1993
ISBN 0 19 913310 7

Editorial and Design by
Hart McLeod, Cambridge

Printed and bound in Great Britain by
Butler & Tanner Ltd, Frome and London

ACKNOWLEDGEMENTS

We would like to thank Sheila Bradford, Gill Mellor (Carney) and Fiona Smyth for their help and comments. We appreciate very much the cartographical work and advice of Graham Bowden and Symone Faulkner of the Drawing Office in the Department of Geography, University of Manchester. Some other figures are based on originals from K. Jones and G. Moon (1987) *Health, Disease and Society*, W. Lever ed (1987) *Industrial Change in the United Kingdom* and D. Herbert (1982) *The Geography of Urban Crime*. We would also like to thank Peter Dicken, of the same Department, for his permission to use some figures from *Global Shift* (1986). Finally we would like to thank our families for their patience and support while we completed this work and for the 'North-South Divide' Trophy and Plate which added spice to our squash matches. Both our families and squash helped to keep us sane.

The publishers and authors would like to thank the following people for their permission to use copyright material:

The Associated Press Ltd., 164; Barnaby's Picture Library, 36, 178; Geoffrey Berry, 119; BFI Stills, Posters and Designs, 9; Michael Bradford, 22, 23, 118, 268, 289; Camera Press Ltd., 41, 48, 105, 152; J. Allan Cash Ltd., 19, 132, 172, 175, 181, 239; Collet, Dickenson, Pearce & Partners Ltd, 302; Nicholas Frazer, 281; Sally & Richard Greenhill, 210; Ashley Kent, 29, 128, 129, 171; Magnum Photos, 112, 123, 278; Popperfoto, 48, 141, 144; Rex Features Ltd., 51, 124, 238; J. Sainsbury plc, 88; Sipa Press (Paris), 233; Sony Man. Co. Ltd., 154; Stockbridge Village Trust, 75; John Edward Unden, 33; Wind Energy Group Ltd. (British Aerospace plc & Taylor Woodrow Construction Ltd.), 44.

The cover photograph is reproduced by permission of Rolf Richardson, Ace Photo Agency.

Dedicated to the ones we love

Just when you thought it was safe,
Bradford and Kent II: the sequel's revenge.

CONTENTS

Chapter 1   Introduction: Setting the scene   1

Part I   Environmental 'goods': resources, goods and services

Chapter 2   Competition and conflict over the use of a resource   16
Chapter 3   What resources should be used?   36
Chapter 4   Organising production and services   58
Chapter 5   Access to goods and services   85

Part II   Environmental 'bads': hazards and threats

Chapter 6   Hazards   112
Chapter 7   External threats   127

Part III   Changing environments

Chapter 8   Changing economic actors and environments   148
Chapter 9   Changing technological actors and environments   168
Chapter 10   Changing social actors and environments   196
Chapter 11   Changing political actors and environments   223

Part IV   Synthesis: home and work

Chapter 12   The changing geography of work   248
Chapter 13   Urban renewal policies and access to housing   273

Chapter 14   Overview   294

PREFACE

This entirely new Bradford and Kent is aimed at 16-20 year olds as well as more mature students who are studying Geography. It complements our previous book, *Human Geography: theories and their applications* in that it takes a very different approach to Geography, as 'sequel's revenge' suggests. It establishes a new framework and emphasises principles, themes and concepts that will contribute to an understanding of Human Geography and the human aspects of the interactions between people and their environments. It concentrates on the processes that influence spatial outcomes.

It will assist those studying new syllabuses, developed to follow on from the National Curriculum, such as NEAB's A and AS syllabuses, as well as those doing established A and AS syllabuses, such as the Geography 16-19 Project (A219). It also provides a wide-ranging text to support introductory Human Geography courses in the first year of higher education, especially in the United Kingdom and North America.

The book aims to enable readers to achieve: a better understanding of the changing environments in which people live and work, and of the growing interdependence of places and areas of the world; an ability to interpret and evaluate contemporary events and issues and to realise their geographical effects; an awareness of varying strategies towards geographical issues and problems; and an informed and critical perspective on the world around them.

We consider ideas at scales from local to global. Examples are drawn from a variety of areas but most are from the western world, particularly the UK and North America, in order to allow a better understanding of how all the processes discussed interact and to provide an overall view of cities, regions and countries.

The organisation of the book is rather new, so to help those who are more familiar with traditional topics, we provide a table on page 305 as well as an index to assist their use of the book.

Michael Bradford and Ashley Kent,
November 1992

The Authors

Both have worked in geographical education and research for over 20 years. Michael Bradford is a Senior Lecturer at the University of Manchester where he lectures in Urban Geography and researches into the Geography of education, housing and urban policy. At present he is on the Council of the Institute of British Geographers and is the Secretary of its Education Committee. He is also the Chair of IBG's Urban Geography Study Group. He has recently been elected as Honorary Vice-President of the Geographical Association. Ashley Kent is a Senior Lecturer at the Institute of Education in the University of London, where he is engaged in the professional development of teachers. He is the director of various curriculum projects. These include projects on Humanities and Information Technology (HIT), Geography 16-19 TVEI and Remote Sensing in the Geography Curriculum. He is on the Council of the Geographical Association and is National Coordinator of the Geography 16-19 Project. Both authors have been actively involved in syllabus development and examination at AS and A level.

The authors met at St. Catherine's College, Cambridge and both spent a year of postgraduate study at the University of Wisconsin, Madison. While Michael Bradford returned to Cambridge for his PhD research, Ashley Kent undertook a PGCE year at London University. After this, Ashley taught at Haberdasher Aske's, Elstree, where he was part of the Oxford Geography Project team. He became Head of Geography at John Mason School, Abingdon before moving to the Institute of Education as the Associate Director of the Geography 16-19 Project. After Cambridge, Michael obtained a lectureship at the University of Manchester, where currently he is Senior Tutor of the Faculty of Arts and, as a research member of Spatial Policy Analysis, is evaluating Inner City Policy.

Chapter 1

INTRODUCTION: SETTING THE SCENE

1.1   Environments

Look around you. You might be at home, school or college. If you are not at home, imagine for a few moments that you are. What is the physical environment like? Is it raining now? Does it rain a lot? Is it sunny or dull? Do you get much sunshine? Is the ground wet or dry? Does the ground slope or is it flat? Is it covered with vegetation or is it very bare? Is it well drained or does water stand for some time? These aspects of the environment – the weather and climate, the characteristics of the surface, its slope, drainage and vegetation and the type of soil and underlying rock – are included in the *physical environment*. The physical environment of your home will have some characteristics in common with many other homes but there may also be some important differences that distinguish your home from others: a silver birch or a pond, for instance.

Your family may have modified the physical environment considerably, by building a wall or a patio which along with the house and paths contributes to the built environment of your home. What kind of house is it? Is it a terraced (town house), a semi-detached (duplex) or a detached, with either two storeys or one (bungalow/ranch style)? Or is it a flat or apartment? Notice the language is different for Britain and the USA; so too are the building materials and styles. The materials are more likely to be brick in

Britain, while wood is used more often in the USA than in Britain. The architecture, style or design may reflect the physical environment; for example, in some parts of the USA the roofs are constructed so that they can withstand heavy layers of snow and angled so that some of it falls off. The architecture may also reflect the age of the building and the fashion of the time, although some styles are borrowed from the past, such as Georgian windows.

Your home may be very similar to those of your neighbours but different in particular ways. It might have a new style of windows, using aluminium or plastic (PVC) rather than wood. If you have a garden, you might have a rather different layout of paths to that of your neighbours. The materials, for instance, with which the garden fences, the furniture and fireplaces as well as the house itself are made may differ. The waste products of the home may be disposed of in different ways. You might have a cesspit for sewage and a compost heap for garden and vegetable waste, whereas other houses may be connected to a sewer system and take garden waste to a tip. The buildings, the layout of paths or routeways above and below the ground, the materials with which things are made and the waste produced in various processes are elements of what we call the *built environment*. The particular combina-

tion of these gives a distinctive character to your home.

The physical and built environments are two important components of the concept of 'home' but they are not sufficient. The human context or environment should be included. Different people could live in the same physical and built surroundings and create a different atmosphere and a different way of life. The number of people and their relationships contribute to such an atmosphere; so do their work and recreational activities. In time they might also modify the physical and built environments in numerous ways: clearing some trees or a hedge; draining a pond; extending the house; or creating one room out of two. In these ways human activity may make a relatively permanent imprint on the physical and built environments.

Your household may be composed of a different set of people to those of your neighbours. Yours may include a grandparent and therefore consist of three generations rather than two. There may be no children next door and only one person, an elderly widow, in the home beyond that. Life within these households, although similar in many ways, will also be rather different. Even if the composition of the households were identical, two adults and three children say, life may still be rather different if the cultural or social backgrounds of the families are dissimilar. Compare the lives of a British Asian family, more specifically a Sikh family, in Bradford living alongside a family which has Yorkshire ancestors stretching back over many centuries; or a richer Swedish American family and a poorer Italian American living in adjoining neighbourhoods in Rockford, Illinois. The relationships within the households and the activities carried out may show some interesting differences despite their proximity. The human environment may be considered in part therefore as a *demographic and social environment*.

Economic as well as social activities within the home may be different. These involve work within the home, even though most of it may be unpaid. The work might be shared in different ways. In some households a man might cook, while in others a woman may do so. Children might be paid to help with some chores or be expected to do so as part of their household duties. Two adults might share tasks such as cleaning and decorating or they may divide them in some way. In larger houses they might each have their own studies where they carry out tasks related to their paid employment. Some may even work from home. In some households the income gained from paid work will be shared among the adults in an equal way, while in others it may be controlled by one earner and allocated for particular tasks to other members of the household. Some households may spend much of their money on material possessions while others may be inclined to spend it on special holidays or many short breaks. How they allocate their scarce resources, whether the resources are money or time, is a key economic question for members of a household. Production, distribution and consumption form part of the *economic environment* of the home and all may vary across households. It also includes the economic status and financial state of the household: whether they have less coming in and more going out of the home and therefore are in debt, for instance.

Whether people work from home and the way they do so may depend upon the type of technology that is available there. A telephone and answering machine may be absolute necessities for external communication, while a fax may make communication of documents much faster than mail. A computer linked to the telephone system through a modem, so that it can send and receive information as well as analyse it within the home, may again form an important external link. It may make working at home more possible. Housework may also be made easier by washing machines, vacuum cleaners and the like. The type of technology available within the home does not affect only work. The possession of a video recorder (VCR) or a barbecue may affect how leisure time is spent. Living conditions may well be enhanced by the installation of central heating or air conditioning, or particular types of insulation. The way that scientific knowledge is applied to such areas as communication, leisure, energy and work processes and the new products it yields may be called the *technological environment*.

Finally, though more abstractly in this context, the political environment may vary. In some households the distribution of power may be very concentrated, with one particular member taking most of the decisions and making most of the policies on the way the home is run: for example, the amount and type of television watched by the children, the times teenagers should be home by, the degree to which teenagers have control over the use and decoration of their rooms, and the location and types of holidays. In other households, power may be more diffuse with, for example, less inter-generational differences in the degree of influence on what is done. More obviously the political environment may vary in terms of the attitudes and values of particular members and the political parties that they support. The distribution of power, the policies, the political values and attitudes and party and pressure group support are elements of the *political environment*.

These four components of the human environment – the demographic and social, the economic, the technological and the political – all interact with one another; for example, the technological environment affects the way work is done in the economic environment. The technological environment affects the way materials are used and indeed what new materials are used to produce elements of the built environment. Social, economic and political activities are identified with the buildings in which they take place, be they recreational centres, factories, offices, shopping centres, town halls or the White House. The human environments then also interact with the built environments. They also affect the physical environments as well as being affected by them; social and economic activities can produce soil erosion, for example, while policies or lack of them on 'environmental issues' may influence the degree of air, water and soil pollution.

For any one person the physical, built and human environments combine together to contribute to the idea or concept of 'home'. Homes in Britain and the USA will have many features in common. There may be some differences between the countries and some among regions within each of the countries. Although there may be many similarities about which we can generalise at the scale of the country or the region within a country, there may also be differences produced by the particular way the component parts of the environment interact. The interaction of the component parts may in some ways make the individual home unique. Consider ways, if any, in which your home is unique.

The home is one example, at a particular scale, of the important geographical concept, *place*. It is the particular combination of these environments in one part of geographical space. The ideas of home and place also have a historical dimension. They are not just what exists now. Both home and place embody past activities, some of which have left their mark in tangible ways – for example the laying of a lawn or the planting of some trees, or at another scale, the draining of the fens and the clearing of the woods. Others remain only in the memories of the households or people to whom the place has meaning. In the same way that we have described the home then, at a different scale, we can describe the local area where you live, its physical, built and human environments. The features, we emphasise, may be somewhat different, but the general ideas will be similar. The local area where you live is more usually the scale at which we talk of place. Think about its physical, built and human environments and their meaning to you. The diagram in Figure 1.1 may be useful for you in organising your thoughts and discussion. It helped us to organise our thoughts in writing this book. The framework presented in the diagram is repeatedly used to organise chapters within the book and to discuss ideas within chapters. They form the components of the 'changing environments' in the title of the book. Please note that we are using 'environment' in a

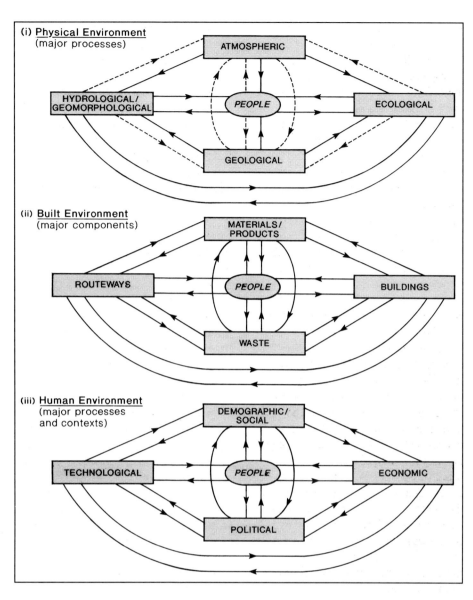

1.1 The conceptual framework

rather different way from how it is used in common speech, where sometimes it means only the physical environment or perhaps both the physical and built. Often it is a word that is used loosely. We hope our diagrams portray our meaning more precisely.

1.2 People

Before extending our discussion of the home in order to introduce other important geographical concepts, it is worthwhile spending some time commenting on the idea of 'people' in the book's title. Sometimes we simply mean a person, you as a member of your household for example, with your home as part of your immedi-ate environment. People may mean a group such as a household with their local environment being the neighbourhood in which they live. At a different scale it could be the set of people that make up the neighbourhood or community and their environment might be the town in which it is situated. In these examples it is residence which ties the people together. Note that what is considered as part of the environment at one scale can become the 'people' for another.

In another situation it may be employment that groups the people together. People work in *organisations* such as manufacturing companies, local government departments or banks. These groupings of people again have environments to which their organisations respond and which they affect. Part of their environment may include other organisations such as retail companies, which may buy their manufactured goods, or the national government which may make regulations that affect a company's activities or produce guidelines or directives for local government. The environments of organisations may be different but they may also overlap – for example the national government being part of the environment of both manufacturing companies and local government, and indeed banks.

These organisations where people work operate at different scales. The very large ones, such as transnational corporations, as their name indicates, operate in more than one country. Part of the environment of people running one of their plants is the rest of the transnational organisation, particularly the corporation's headquarters which sets the policy of the organisation. This can be in a different country from that of the plant. As with the residential examples above then, what may be part of the environment of people at one scale may form the organisation at another: for the plant, the rest of the corporation is part of its environment while at another scale the whole corporation may be considered as the organisation with an environment which includes its competitors, its suppliers and customers, and national governments that may offer inducements for its investments or put controls on its activities.

People belong to other organisations or institutions that are not where they work. There is a whole series of social and political organisations that again have their particular environments to which they respond and which they affect. There are institutions where they are educated such as schools, colleges and universities. Two important parts of the environments of such institutions are the demographic and political components: if birth rates are declining then the educational establishments face the possibility of falling rolls; if the local, state or national government changes educational policy or its financial contribution then, again, the educational institutions have to respond.

People may also feel they belong to other social groupings such as social classes, ethnic groups or religious groups, some of which may have distinct geographical identities. Some may occur in many areas but share similar types of environments. If we return to the example of the home, people belonging to the same social class (whether defined according to, for example, birth, occupation or length of education) may have homes that are very similar from one region of the country to another. Indeed, similar social classes in two countries may share as many or more features as different social groups within one of the countries.

'People' in the title of the book, then, refers to individuals, households, neighbourhoods, other groupings based on residence up to the scale of the country, all kinds of business, social and political organisations and institutions and all types of social groupings which may have similar cultures, values, attitudes, interests and/or activities. Some of these are easily identified geographically. They occupy a 'territory', such as that of a nation state. Others may cluster in space, such as some ethnic and religious groups. Others, such as large business organisations, may occupy centres or nodes over a wide area of space which are connected by a network of communications and transport routes.

We have now discussed in outline 'people and their environments' and have seen how, what at one scale may be regarded as part of an environment may at another be regarded as 'people' in an organisation or social group. We shall often make the analogy between people and their environments and *actors* and their stage. This conveys the idea that people play roles: as parent, as salesperson or as supporter of a particular sports team or pressure group. Sometimes their roles conflict; as a car worker they might want to limit choice to their own country's car to ensure their continued employment, whereas as a consumer they might want a wider range of cars, including foreign imports from which to choose. We shall refer to actors' roles and indeed their possible viewpoints. The analogy of the environment as a stage on which actors play roles has its limitations. People influence their environment or, by moving home for example, change it. We wish to convey the idea that people as individuals, as groups, in organisations and en masse change their environments in intended and unintended ways, to produce new environments that then influence their activities and behaviour. There is a continual interaction between people and their environments, in the same way that there is between you and your home. Thus the subtitle of the book is 'people and their changing environments'. We will now return to the concepts of home and place in order to convey some other basic geographical concepts that will be employed in the book and to use further our framework for the environment.

opportunity to another; for the potential victim crime is a hazard, while for the criminal it may be an opportunity. It depends on through whose eyes you are seeing things. The problems that we discuss are generally viewed as 'bads' by a set of people in the area, often the majority.

Chapter 6 discusses various *hazards* to which an area may be susceptible, arising from its physical, built and human environments. We examine the degree to which hazards may be predicted, prevented and managed and discuss the organisations involved in hazard management and relief. Chapter 7 discusses the ways an area can be considered under threat from external sources or events and the ways in which its people can respond to such external threats. Here, in particular, it is important to note the point of view. To some people from outside the area there is an opportunity within the area, a new land use or activity perhaps, but that opportunity is viewed by at least some of the people within the area as a threat.

In Parts III and IV recent changes in component parts of the environments and their key actors and organisations are considered.

Part III: Changing environments (Chapters 8–11)

Chapter 8 examines recent changes in the *economic actors, organisations and environments*, with particular attention being paid to transnational organisations and the changing spatial division of labour at an international scale. Chapter 9 studies changes in the *technological environment*, particularly communications and information technology and the organisations involved with such developments. Chapter 10 analyses *demographic and social changes* and their effects on the need and demand for social provision. Chapter 11 studies changes in *political organisations and environments*, changes in local, national and supra–national government and important developments in policies. In all four chapters the effects on and the influences of the other parts of the human environment are discussed. So too are the effects on and influences of the physical and built environments.

Part IV: Synthesis: home and work (Chapters 12–13)

In this part we attempt to synthesise some of the changes in the various environments in the way they influence work, housing and more generally geographical change, in terms of urban–rural, regional, national, international and global change. Chapter 12 discusses various changes in access to *employment* and patterns of *work*, both paid and unpaid. It reviews changing policies on employment, unemployment and development. Chapter 13 analyses the problem of *housing decay* and various responses to it. In doing so, it reviews the changes in access to housing by various groups. By discussing central issues about where people work and reside, we can begin to bring together some of the different parts of the environment that we have identified and separately discussed.

Finally, Chapter 14 presents an overview of the most significant recent geographical changes that have been discussed in the book.

1.6 The standard format of chapters

Although there is a very clear structure to the book, we realise that readers will use it in their own way, so we have written every chapter so that it can to a large extent stand alone. To assist the reader we have adopted a standard format.

1 Case study
2 General problem
3 Other examples
4 Alternative strategies
5 Perspectives
6 Exercises
7 Further reading

Every chapter is based on an issue or problem. The chapter begins with a case study of the problem in order to involve the reader and to illustrate the problem. It should always be read along with the second section, which develops the general problem from the case study and identifies important concepts, key actors and major effects upon the various types of environment. The third section examines other examples to show other situations in which the problem occurs and to a lesser extent to illustrate some of the strategies by which the problem is tackled. The fourth section discusses alternative strategies to resolving the general problem. The fifth places the problem and strategies in perspective. This is followed by various exercises that require readers to apply the ideas of the chapter, examine further examples and extend the ideas of the chapter. The exercises include discussion questions, data response and stimulus questions, role playing and decision–making problems, practical questions and essays. Finally there is a set of further reading that will help readers to gain greater depth on some of the material discussed and extend their awareness.

1.7   **Changing approaches to geography**

This book reflects and to some extent projects changes in the study of geography. There have been many recent changes in the subject in all levels of geographical education from the research level through to primary school teaching. These reflect the changing geography of the world around us, changing geographical and wider academic thinking, and changing educational ideas and practices. For example, a recent change in the geography of the world around us in the UK and USA has been greater investment from overseas and greater competition from foreign corporations in a greater variety of goods and services. The study of geography has reflected these changes by giving more attention to the impact on a country or certain regions within it of particular countries and transnational corporations in the wider world economy. It has also directed more attention at the scale of the global economy as more corporations operate at that scale. As education has become more enquiry based and student centred, so geography has included such ideas as role playing and decision–making exercises. Changes in academic thinking will be illustrated by two major changes in the 1970s and a number of developments in the 1980s.

Radical Left

Two major changes can be identified in the 1970s: the influence of the Radical Left and their critique of capitalism and capitalist institutions; and Humanistic Geography with its concern for the individual. Instead of seeking government intervention to correct or prevent failures of the market, the Radical Left sought to change the structure of society. The profit motive, the dri-ving force of capitalism, was not to be a key concern. They thought there should instead be a greater emphasis on *equality* and *social justice*. Their ideas went further than those of wider academic and political thought of the 1960s when equality of opportunity to education and employment were of prime concern. Then in the USA the issue of equality centred on that between races. In Britain it was discussed in relation to social classes.

The Radical Left made clear their own values and their intent to change society, and criticised much previous geographical analysis which was supposedly 'value free', that is the researchers wrote as though they were objective with none of their own values influencing their research. The Radical Left also suggested that much geographical research tended to accept and maintain the society of the time and not advocate change.

They also criticised much of the work on locational analysis for paying too much attention to seeking generalisations across time and

David Harvey, Professor of Geography at the University of Oxford, is a leading figure of the Radical Left. He has published many challenging and influential books, including "Social Justice and the City" in 1973, "The Limits to Capital" in 1982 and "The Urban Experience" in 1989.

space. They emphasised that the structure of society changes over time and is different from one part of the world to another. Any generalisations that can be made will therefore be both time and place specific.

The Radical Left not only challenged much previous analysis, they discussed new issues and led geographers to study previously ignored institutions such as the financial institutions, for example the effect of building societies/savings and loans on the geography of housing. They also concentrated much of their attention at the national scale or the impact of the national level on local issues. The structure of society, for example its capitalist nature, was seen as all–important in influencing and constraining people's behaviour. Individuals were not viewed as being particularly important.

Humanistic Geography

Humanistic Geography, in contrast, shares with the Behavioural Geography of the late 1960s its emphasis on the individual, but it focuses less on the behaviour of the individual and more on an individual's *feelings, experience* and *values*. It also uses very different methods of enquiry and analysis. Behavioural Geography had challenged the assumptions of many of the earlier locational models, such as central place theory, that were based on a rational, all–knowing 'economic being'. It suggested people had limited information and used it in different ways, according to their motives and attitudes to risk, for instance. It also suggested that there were numerous types of rationality, not just one. Humanistic Geography was and is less concerned with the mind, and more interested in feelings. Whereas behavioural geographers were still concerned with questions of spatial interaction or location, such as why people shopped where they did or why they located their small businesses where they were, humanistic geographers were concerned with the meaning that a place conveyed to an individual or, as it has been called, *'a sense of place'*.

Most humanistic geographers have been concerned with the individual but it is possible to think of sets of people for whom the same place or landscape may have a very different meaning. Consider, for example, a very large city. For some, its buildings are seen as threatening, particularly at night. There is an association with danger and crime. There is much uncertainty. Such feelings of the city are created and reflected in films such as Fritz Lang's *Metropolis*, in Batman's Gotham City and in some advertisements. For another set of people or even the same people at a different time, the city may feel exciting but not menacing, and full of positive possibilities. In the book we shall

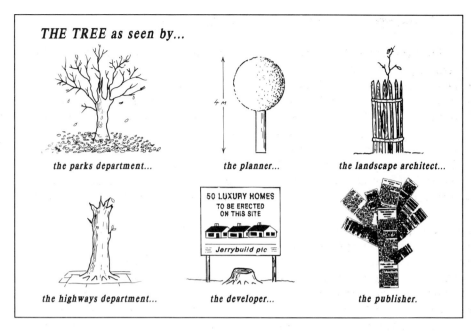

1.2 Perspectives on a tree

encourage you to explore your feelings about places as well as to attempt to understand those of others. (Figure 1.2)

Your values and ours

Similarly we shall seek to make you think about and develop your own values as well as be aware of those of others. In that we shall reflect the importance of Humanistic Geography, that is discovering the values of the people you are studying. Sometimes we shall suggest different people's viewpoints in order to contrast them. In doing this, ensure that you do not simply accept them as stereotypes. Challenge our assumptions and consider other possible viewpoints.

In writing such a text as this, we are also aware of a major contribution of the Radical Left. As writers we have our own values and although we present varying approaches and ideas to a number of issues so that you can form your own conclusions, we do not pretend to be 'value free'. No doubt our values

Batman's Gotham City

Yi-Fu Tuan, Professor of Geography at the University of Wisconsin, Madison, is a leading figure in Humanistic Geography. He has published many thought-provoking books, including "Topophelia: a study of environmental perception, attitudes and values" in 1974, "Space and Place" in 1977 and "Landscapes of Fear" in 1979.

have affected what we have included and what we have omitted. Where it is obvious to you that our ideas are reflecting our values, then critically assess them and use that process to clarify your own values. Where our values are less obvious to you, then perhaps it is even more important that you think through the possible values that underlie the issues discussed. It might help you to know that although we the authors have many values in common, we do have some differences. One of us is more to the left of the other, or one is more to the right, depending on how you wish to look at it. Neither person belongs to either extreme.

We have briefly outlined two major directions in Geography in the 1970s that have informed our work. In some ways our concern with environments reflects the Radical Left's interest in the structure of society, while our concern for people follows a humanistic tradition. This book tries to show the continual interaction between people and their environments, or *human agency* and *structure*. It is not so easy to identify

directions in the 1980s but we suggest a few developments, the discussion of which allows us to introduce key ideas that occur within the book.

Geography and Gender

During the 1980s a number of books and papers appeared about the Geography of Gender. They discussed mainly the geography of women, which had been neglected in previous work. In fact much earlier work in locational analysis and systems theory discussed people as though they were particles, not beings. Much also implicitly or even explicitly treated all people as though they were men or was written from an entirely male perspective. Some of the work on women shows how they behave and the constraints on their choices. Some concerns their access to particular types of employment, housing and social provision and reflects an interest in Welfare Geography in the 1970s. This approach posed the question: who gets what, where (when and why)? – the latter two parts sometimes being included. This approach, which studied many different types of social groups, not just gender, suggested that some form of *intervention* was needed to improve access of particular groups to jobs, housing and social provision to make a fairer society. In this they shared an interest in social justice with the Radical Left.

It was from the Radical Left, though, that much of the work on the Geography of Gender arose. They were already interested in power relations, between labour and management and between social classes. They went on to study gender relations in the home, at work and more generally in the private and public arenas of life. They compared gender relations and roles in different societies and examined the effects of living in a patriarchal society.

This work makes us consider our discussion of people in a new light. We shall not simply examine different scales of organisations and social groups; we shall also consider the gender relations within them and other aspects of the Geography of Gender. More generally we shall consider *power relations* and *access, social justice* and *forms of intervention* in society that aim to improve access and bring about a fairer world.

Global scale

In the 1980s there were also two significant changes in the geographical *scale* that people studied: an interest in the *global* scale and in much smaller areas within regions called *localities*. Both to some extent arose from the work of the Radical Left. They had been interested in the power relations between the developed (first) and developing (third) world, indicating the depen-

David Smith, Professor of Geography at Queen Mary and Westfield College, the University of London, is a leading figure of the Welfare Geography school. "Human Geography: a Welfare Approach" in 1977 and "Where the Grass is Greener: living in an unequal world" in 1979 illustrate the approach very well. He has also written on the geography of South Africa.

dence of the latter on the former. They argued that there were many forces maintaining the dependence and that in itself prevented or at least constrained economic develop-

Classifying the countries of the world is problematic. Whatever terminology is used may be regarded by some as offensive. We have used a common classification into First, Second and Third Worlds. This is based on the economic and political circumstances of countries. The First World includes North America, Western Europe, Australia, New Zealand and Japan. These are sometimes called the 'advanced nations'. The Second World includes the former USSR, Eastern Europe, China, N. Korea, Vietnam and Cuba. These were or are command economies. Although many of these countries are changing rapidly, they have a similar past organisation and it is difficult to foresee their future. They are likely to be different from the First World for some time yet. The Third World includes most of Africa, Latin America and Asia. These countries are sometimes referred to as 'developing' or 'less economically developed'. Both terms can be criticised, as can the term, 'Third World', which some take to be representing an order of importance rather than a category. The classification can also be attacked because of the great variation among the countries within the categories. For example, the Third World includes oil-rich as well as poorly resourced countries. Readers should consider other classifications, their terminology and the degree to which countries within a class are similar and classes are different from one another (non-overlapping).

Doreen Massey, Professor of Geography at the Open University, a leading figure of the Radical Left, has made a major impact on the subject in a number of ways. Her work on localities and on gender are just two of her contributions. Such books as "Spatial Divisions of Labour" and with Richard Meegan, "Geography Matters! a reader", both published in 1984, demonstrate her approach.

ment of the Third World. One of the major mechanisms by which dependence was maintained was the activity of transnational corporations which some compared to past colonial powers in their empire building and in the way they spread the new religion, capitalism rather than Christianity. This work stimulated interest in both economic and political geography at a global scale.

Many other geographers became involved, identifying a major *global shift* in economic activity with the rise of Japan and the emergence of the Newly Industrialising Countries. They studied relations between transnationals and host countries and cast more light on the simplistic picture painted above. More research examined investment flows and the emerging international finance system based on New York, London and Tokyo. Both radical and other writers identified a changed international division of labour with, for example, the First World no

longer being the main source of some manufactured goods. They directed attention at the ways in which this new global economy, transnationals and international financial institutions were having major effects on the regions of the First World countries.

Localities

This interest in the global scale has been paralleled, particularly in Britain, by concern for small areas or localities. It was felt that the geography of the economic changes that were occurring within Britain was better studied at the scale of these smaller areas than at that of the old industrial regions. So research centred on places like Lancaster rather than the North West and Middlesbrough rather than the North East. These best approximated to the size of labour market areas (crudely areas within which people commuted to work). These had become the preferred scale of studying employment change. Even in the same old industrial region they responded differently to changes in the wider economy and in government policy.

Many were also at a similar scale to that of local government and so the relationship between local economic and political processes could be observed. The main emphasis though was on the impact of global and national change, either economic or political, on these localities. More recent work has tried to put more emphasis on the interrelationships between the locality and the wider world, so that the relationship was not always seen as being in one direction. Research at both the global and locality scales emphasises the *interdependence of places* and the *interdependence of places at different spatial scales*. These ideas are discussed in many parts of the book, as are the global and local scales.

Environmentalism

A further major change in the 1980s also occurred at a global scale. The concern over global warming (the depletion of the ozone layer and the increased greenhouse effect) reinforced peoples' interest in the 'environment'. There had been concern over the growth of the world population and resource depletion for over a century but along with such issues as acid deposition (commonly called 'acid rain'), nuclear power, forest depletion and saving the whale, these major concerns stimulated research and made people become more environmentally aware. Green parties and environmental pressure groups became more influential. In Human Geography issues related to resource use and to the landscape became more dominant. They are considered in the next two chapters.

In this book we shall also be interested in *environmental values*, particularly the priority put on them relative to *economic* and *social values*. In sections 4 and 5 of chapters (alternative strategies and perspectives), priority among these values will often be addressed. It is clear that priority changes over time within a country and may be different from one country to another at any given time. The relative prominence of such values forms part of the human environment within which people and organisations operate. Some people, some organisations and some events also influence the values and their priority.

The New Right

The final change that we observed in the 1980s was the rise, in both the academic and political worlds, of radical right or 'New Right' thinking. This was a wide movement in that it covered a number of disciplines and was reflected in some of the legislation passed in both the USA and the UK. Whereas the Radical Left in Geography clearly identified themselves, New Right thinking in Geography is not usually so obvious. There are a number of papers and books emerging, however, that reflect some New Right thinking in their advocacy of the market and wealth creation and their abandonment of state intervention and attempts to reduce inequality. Such thinking tends to emphasise choice in both private and public services without considering the unequal constraints on people and their unequal abilities of making choices. It advocates private rather than public solutions to issues and individual rather than collective responsibility. In the book, market solutions are contrasted with ones based on forms of intervention; privatisation is reviewed as a strategy; and the priority of economic over social values and individual over collective solutions are discussed. New Right policies have different geographical effects from other policies. As with other policies and strategies, they help to create new geographies.

The changes that we have identified in Geography in the 1980s are varied to say the least. Many traditions continue, though perhaps in new forms – Regional Geography, locational analysis and Welfare Geography for instance. Here we have given a taste of recent changes in geography in order to introduce some basic concepts and perspectives that are included in the book.

1.8 Summary

The book then considers the interactions between people and their environments. People are viewed at different scales in varying groups and organisations. They play many different roles, for example consumers, producers, entrepreneurs, managers, managed, decision makers, innovators, implementers, planners, voters, governors, parents, carers. They share many different forms of relationships with other people, groups and organisations, which can be seen as forming part of their environment.

The environment offers opportunities and choices but it also constrains and limits them. It is a source of 'bads' as well as 'goods', hazards and threats as well as opportunities. Both 'goods' and 'bads' are dependent on how the people view them. They are not good or bad in themselves.

The environment is not constant. It is a source of change, a source of uncertainty. There are some parts of the environment an individual or organisation can affect and to some extent control. Uncertainty can then be reduced. A business organisation can acquire one of its competitors, for example. There are other parts of the environment over which one individual or organisation has little or no influence; for example, the economic or political climate, prevailing values, or indeed the capitalist or socialist nature of their country. These still change though, and like other changes in the environment influence an individual or organisation.

The environment is a source of change but so too is the individual and the organisation. People respond to changes in their environment. They also produce changes in their environment by their actions, particularly their aggregate actions. Sometimes these are intentional, at other times unintentional. They are often complex with both intended and unintended effects.

It is sometimes in order to tackle the unintended effects of actions or to reduce uncertainty that policies are made. These too can have intended or unintended consequences. Different strategies or groups of policies have varying geographical effects, some foreseen, some unforeseen. This applies whether it is a market-based strategy with limited state intervention or one based on much state intervention or control. Sometimes the strategies in themselves are geographical, for example centralisation or decentralisation. Such strategies may be responses to a changing environment but when implemented they change it, often producing further need to respond.

This constant interaction between people and their environments produces a dynamic, changing geography. It is the *processes* producing these changes, this interaction between people and their environments, that this book is all about. We hope it will stimulate you to look around you in a somewhat different way.

1.9 **Further reading**

P. Cloke, C. Philo and D. Sadler (1991) *Approaching Human Geography: An Introduction to Contemporary Debates,* Paul Chapman Publishing

P. Haggett (1965) *Locational Analysis in Human Geography,* Edward Arnold

D. Harvey (1973) *Social Justice and the City*, Edward Arnold

D. Harvey (1989) *The Urban Experience*, Basil Blackwell

P. Jackson and S. Smith (1984) *Exploring Social Geography*, George Allen and Unwin

D. Massey (1984) *Spatial Divisions of Labour: Social Structures and the Geography of Production,* Macmillan

D. Massey and J. Allen (eds.) (1984) *Geography Matters*, Cambridge University Press

D.M. Smith (1977) *Human Geography: a Welfare Approach,* Edward Arnold

Yi-Fu Tuan (1977) *Space and Place: The Perspective of Experience,* Edward Arnold

Also see the periodicals *Geography, Geography Review, Geographical Magazine, Geofile, Area and Progress in Human Geography.*

PART I

ENVIRONMENTAL 'GOODS': RESOURCES, GOODS AND SERVICES

Chapter 2
Competition and conflict over the use of a resource

2.1 Case study: Conflict over resources in a National Park – Topley Pike and the Peak District
2.2 General problem
2.3 Other examples
    2.3a Conflict in a wilderness area: wild beauty versus a mass of wattage
    2.3b Conflict over land in the city: the Ealing Broadway Centre
    2.3c Development pressures in the metropolitan rings
    2.3d Conflict over the use of coastal land: the south coast of England
    2.3e The ownership and use of a huge mineral, eco-logical and strategic resource: Antarctica – the last great wilderness
2.4 Alternative strategies
2.5 Perspectives
2.6 Exercises
2.7 Further reading

Chapter 3
What resources should be used?

3.1 Case study: Possible sources of energy – Sizewell B Nuclear Power Station and the Severn Barrage
3.2 General problem
3.3 Other examples
    3.3a Two other energy alternatives – sun and wind
    3.3b Agribusiness or permaculture? – or how best to produce food?
    3.3c Alternative ways of crossing the Channel
    3.3d Alternative methods of building and heating houses
    3.3e Changed ways of making cars
3.4 Alternative strategies
3.5 Perspectives
3.6 Exercises
3.7 Further reading

Chapter 4
Organising production and services

4.1 Case study: Different ways of organising and finaning local transport
4.2 General problem
4.3 Other examples
    4.3a Inter-city bus travel
    4.3b Public and private health systems
    4.3c Alternative ways of organising housing
4.4 Alternative strategies
4.5 Perspectives
4.6 Exercises
4.7 Further reading

Chapter 5
Access to goods and services

5.1 Case study: New shopping for all?
5.2 General problem
5.3 Other examples
    5.3a Education for some?
    5.3b Access to health
    5.3c Where you live and who you are!
5.4 Alternative strategies
5.5 Perspectives
5.6 Exercises
5.7 Further reading

"Thank God we got rid of that eye-sore of a 'nuke' plant."

"Thank God we kept that alternative mob out with their infernal wind machines."

Chapter 2

COMPETITION AND CONFLICT OVER THE USE OF A RESOURCE

In 1983 Tarmac, a British-based international company concerned mainly with building and construction, sought to extend Topley Pike (Figure 2.1), one of its four limestone quarries in the Buxton area of the Peak District, a British National Park. The 7.7 hectares of required land could be used in many ways. It was already grazing land, part of Sterndale Green Farm, and as part of the Peak District could be used for tourism, or conserved for ecological reasons. Should such land be used

2.1 *Topley Pike Quarry*

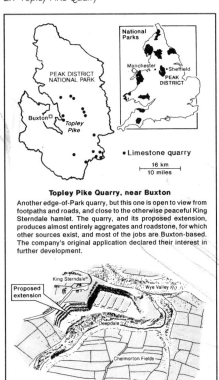

Topley Pike Quarry, near Buxton
Another edge-of-Park quarry, but this one is open to view from footpaths and roads, and close to the otherwise peaceful King Sterndale hamlet. The quarry, and its proposed extension, produces almost entirely aggregates and roadstone, for which other sources exist, and most of the jobs are Buxton-based. The company's original application declared their interest in further development.

for limestone extraction? What and whose are the conflicting viewpoints and how should they be resolved?

The Peak District already produces considerable quantities of crushed rock, much of it limestone. The existing Topley Pike Quarry specialises in limestone aggregates and coated roadstone mainly for the markets of North West England. The quarry, plant and tipping area consists of 31 hectares. Forty-nine people are employed within the quarry and about sixty lorry drivers transport the stone. The quarry's 1983 approved resources will last at least until the early 1990s. The proposed extension would have a life of about sixteen years and a total output of about 7 million tonnes.

This example is typical of the conflicting uses and users within the Peak District National Park. On the one hand this proposed development can be seen as beneficial. For instance, supporters pointed out that limestone has been quarried in the Park since before the First World War, and steady expansion of workings has been allowed. It has brought employment to the area and proponents argued that environmental impacts have been minimised. They also stated that the proposed extensions would use existing roads and bring only a small increase in road traffic. At the same time 30 per cent of the rock would be transported on the existing British Rail system. The quarry edge would be land-

scaped and a tree screen planted concealing the quarry from King Sterndale, the local hamlet (Figure 2.1).

The noise, blast and dust pollution would be subject to stringent controls and the hole created could be filled by refuse from Greater Manchester, which is in great need of tipping space. Furthermore, proponents argued that the quarry is right on the western edge of the National Park and therefore would have less impact on recreational users. It would also safeguard 1983 employment levels until 1998. Supporters of the proposal included existing quarry employees, lorry drivers and the local farmer whose land would be purchased.

On the other hand, the opponents of the proposal argued that there is no overriding national or local need for this stone and that it would eliminate one of the last islands of 'natural' landscape around Buxton. In particular Deep Dale (Figure 2.1) is a Site of Special Scientific Interest (SSSI) because of its particular botany. The area is also covered by an extensive network of public footpaths which would be truncated if the quarry went ahead. Furthermore it was argued that King Sterndale would effectively be encircled by the quarries and several trees would have to be felled. Opponents included local residents, tourists, conservationists, the Council for the Protection of Rural

England (CPRE), Friends of the Earth (FoE) and the Countryside Commission. For them environmental and social values had priority over economic ones.

The Peak Park Planning Board (PPPB) was the body faced with the task of resolving this issue. When the Peak District National Park was established in 1951, the PPPB was created as the overseer of its 1400 square kilometres. It has representatives from the Department of the Environment (DoE) and six counties with land in the Park. The Board's objectives were defined by the 1949 National Parks Act as: to preserve and enhance the landscape; to provide facilities for public open air recreation; to preserve wildlife and historic buildings; and to ensure that the local economy continues to function. The PPPB has the unenviable task of balancing the needs of conflicting uses and users. In the Topley Pike case, it applied the four tests at the heart of the Board's policy: Will the quarry cause unacceptable damage to the qualities of the National Park? Will it generate traffic problems? Is there an overriding national need? Are there practical alternatives? In February 1984 the Board refused planning permission for the extension because the proposal did not fully satisfy the four tests.

In general the Park provides many cases of resource use conflict. The Park is 69 per cent privately owned; 15 per cent by the water authority; 11 per cent by the National Trust; 4 per cent by the local authority and the PPPB; and 1 per cent by the Forestry Commission. One of its major uses is recreation, especially for day trippers by car or by bus. Eighteen and a half million visitors have been estimated to use the Park each year, not least because the three major conurbations of Merseyside, West Yorkshire and Greater Manchester are within 100 kilometres of the Park– indeed, 27 million people live within three hours' driving time. Recreational use can conflict particularly with uses in the privately owned sections of the Park. Much of this land is used for farming. There are 2436 mainly small farms which rear dairy cattle and/or sheep. Extractive industries, as in the Topley Pike case, can also be the source of significant conflict with 6 million tonnes of limestone produced a year as well as shale fluorspar. Further conflict is generated by the processing of limestone into cement within environmentally obtrusive

2.2 Actors and viewpoints

Actors	Probable views on developments in the Peak District	Possible views of physical environment
Householders		
Residents working within Park	Maintain and increase local employment	Place to live and work
Residents' commuting outside Park	Maintain scenic character of area as a place to live	Place to reside
Second-home owners		Scenic value. Closer to nature
Local business		
Farmers and their workers	Minimum interference with farm activities	Husbandry Natural resource for profit
Extractive industry employers and employees	Want access to economically workable minerals and stone	Natural resource for profit
Tourist oriented retailers and hoteliers etc	Encourage activities leading to more tourism	Scenic value for profit
Non-residents		
Car drivers	Improved access and parking	Access through to views
	Ease of passing lorry drivers	
Lorry drivers	Gentler, straighter roads	
Hill walkers	Conservation of landscape but good access and rights of way	Experience of scenery and open air
Wildlife enthusiasts	Preservation of wildlife and wild areas	Preserve and conserve ecology
Hang-gliders, climbers, skiers	Preservation of suitable landscapes for activities	Sites for sport and recreation
Tourists - day trippers	Rapid access to scenery and tourist activities	Scenic value
- stayers	Variety of accommodation and amenities	Contrasts to city life
User organisations		
Forestry Commission	Obtain best returns per hectare	Natural resources
Water Boards	Maintain and develop the quantity (and quality) of water	Natural resources
National Trust	Preservation and conservation of landscape, historic buildings and estates	Heritage
Council for Protection of Rural England	Preservation of rural way of life	Heritage
Friends of the Earth		Conserve and live in harmony with environment
Ramblers Association	Maintenance of rights of way	Scenic beauty
Management and planning organisation		
Peak Park Planning Board	Manage and develop the Park according to criteria/legislation for National Parks	

works. The adjoining large cities increasingly demand water and so there are already fifty-five reservoirs within the Park, which have flooded settlements and farmland. These have changed the ecology and landscape including many stands of commercial timber which are managed by the Forestry Commission.

Finally it must not be forgotten that settlements in the Park house 38,000 people. Most are permanent residents who live and work in the Park. Many commute to the conurbations, while some use the Park for second homes. There is a possible conflict in the use of some houses between those people who have been brought up and perhaps work in the Park and outsiders who want a second home there.

Figure 2.2 summarises the viewpoints of these and other actors involved in conflict over resource use in the Park. It is clear from this figure that although an area may be attractive in the sense of presenting many alternative uses of its resources, this, in itself, may produce many potential conflicts.

2.2   General problem

The case study illustrates some of the factors involved in determining how a particular resource, Topley Pike, or set of resources, the Peak District, is used.

Resources

A resource may be a piece of land, water or even air, material that is organic such as timber or inorganic such as iron ore, or animals, for example whales. These are all part of the physical environment. The built environment may also be regarded as providing resources such as urban land and buildings. Various parts of the human environment may also be seen as resources, such as people's entrepreneurial, technical, manual and social skills, which may all be used in various ways. In this chapter, however, the resources considered are mainly from the physical and built environments, but their uses have impacts on all the types of environments.

The set of resources in the case study is an area of land, the minerals and the rock under it, the character of the landscape, the flora and fauna which it sustains, the quantity and quality of water associated with it, and its agricultural and recreational potential. Some wish to see the Peak District National Park as a repository for wildlife and retained as part of our landscape heritage, while others want it to make a contribution to the economy as a major food factory. Others view it as an area of 'recreation for all' while some see it as a major source of stone, minerals and water. While a few of these uses may be to some extent complementary, for example water supply and water-orientated recreation, many are conflicting and some way of resolving the balance of uses has to be found.

The resource may be at different spatial scales. Consider the conflicts which can arise over the use of a back garden, as play space for children, ornamental lawns and flower beds, a wild natural area or as a vegetable patch. If there is enough room, a compromised partitioning of the space may be made. Otherwise how may its use be determined? At a very different spatial scale, there is the growing conflict between the super-powers over the use of outer space. Usually the greater the scale, the more people there will be that are affected by the decisions over the resource's use.

Every proposed use of a resource is seen as beneficial to at least one individual or organisation, because they are the ones who are prepared to invest capital or time in its development. As the diagram (Figure 2.2) shows, the types of benefit in the case study relate to experiencing and valuing the physical or built environment, living in harmony with it, deriving economic returns from it or making it the focus of some social activity. One facet of the general problem is whether priority of use should be given to environmental, economic, social or political interests.

Indirect effects of resource use

The benefits, and indeed losses, are felt not only by those using the resource directly. There are indirect effects of resource use which occur in the various types of environments and these in turn influence other actors. Figure 2.3 shows how the *physical environment* may be changed by farmers and mining companies both in the Peak District and more generally. Their activities change, if not spoil, people's experience of the landscape, and yet they provide primary products which are used to support people and their built environment.

Some of these activities, such as quarrying, may affect the *built environment* too, not only by new buildings but by heavy lorries using roads and perhaps causing damage to existing buildings through vibration, as well as slowing other traffic on the roads. Many activities may lead to demands for new housing to accommodate employees, visitors or second-home owners and more buildings and routeways to provide the services for these.

These *multiplier effects* present further investment and employment

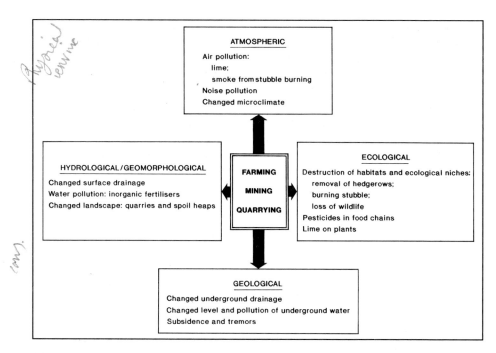

```
                    ┌─────────────────────────────┐
                    │         ATMOSPHERIC         │
                    │                             │
                    │  Air pollution:             │
                    │    lime;                    │
                    │    smoke from stubble burning│
                    │  Noise pollution            │
                    │  Changed microclimate       │
                    └─────────────────────────────┘
                                 ↕
┌──────────────────────────────────┐   ┌─────────┐   ┌────────────────────────────────────────┐
│  HYDROLOGICAL/GEOMORPHOLOGICAL    │   │ FARMING │   │              ECOLOGICAL                │
│                                   │   │         │   │  Destruction of habitats and ecological │
│  Changed surface drainage         │ ← │ MINING  │ → │  niches:                                │
│  Water pollution: inorganic       │   │         │   │    removal of hedgerows;                │
│  fertilisers                      │   │QUARRYING│   │    burning stubble;                     │
│  Changed landscape: quarries and  │   │         │   │    loss of wildlife                     │
│  spoil heaps                      │   └─────────┘   │  Pesticides in food chains              │
└──────────────────────────────────┘                 │  Lime on plants                         │
                                 ↕                    └────────────────────────────────────────┘
                    ┌─────────────────────────────────────────┐
                    │                 GEOLOGICAL                │
                    │                                           │
                    │  Changed underground drainage             │
                    │  Changed level and pollution of underground water │
                    │  Subsidence and tremors                   │
                    └─────────────────────────────────────────┘
```

2.3 Possible effects of farming, mining and quarrying on the physical environment

opportunities in the *economic environment*, maybe attracting immigrants to the area and thus changing the *social* and perhaps *political environments*. The arrival of second-home owners may also bring contrasting life styles as well as affecting property values, which, while benefiting estate agents, does not help prospective buyers from within the area. At a different scale, use of home-grown or extracted material may substitute for imports, which benefits the nation's balance of payments (the difference between the value of exports and imports). Certain uses of resources may stimulate new or evolved technologies which in themselves may be exported; for example, the extraction of oil and natural gas from the North Sea led to the manufacture and export of oil rigs from Scotland. Change in the *technological and economic environments* is thus stimulated. Finally the *political environment* may be changed, for example the establishment of the British National Park Planning Boards and the Environmental Protection Agency in the USA.

These changes in the various

types of environments obviously interact; for instance, a new economic opportunity, such as processing limestone, presented by the use of the resource, such as quarrying, may lead to change in the built environment, for example a cement works, and further alteration to the physical environment, in this case in the form of a spoiled view and air pollution. The general problem does not then just involve questions about the use of the resource. Whatever that use, it stimulates many other changes which in themselves benefit some but not all people. The conflicts created by these ramifications are as great as those presented by the

Cement works near Hope in the Peak District

direct use, the resolution of which they make even more difficult.

Conflict and scales

Both sets of conflicts involve actors at different *spatial scales*. For example, in the Peak District and Utah (Chapter 2, Section 3a) what degree of say as to what happens in the park should go to: those who live and work there; those who live there and work elsewhere; those who visit there; and those, like managers of some multinational mining companies, whose headquarters may well be outside the country?

The conflicts also involve different *time scales*. Some users of resources lead to short rather than long-term gains; for example a mine may bring some local employment as well as jobs and profits for the mining company and of course benefits to the users of the mineral. The mine, however, may be open for a relatively short time, depending on the amount and quality of the ore, the world markets in that mineral and technological change which may lead to a substitute being discovered. Other uses of the land may be of longer term benefit. Even the same type of use can vary as to whether it is for short or long-term gain, whether it is *speculative* or not, and whether it is *exploitative* or *conservationist*; for example, some farmers may work the land for a short period without attempting to maintain or improve fertility, speculating that they can sell the land for some other more profitable use in the future. Agricultural land on the edge of cities may well be used in this way, with little investment of capital or time, as urban development is anticipated. Other farmers may practise better husbandry and aim for returns over a much longer period. Many argue that the present use of tropical rain forests as in Amazonia is exploitative and can only be short term because it will disturb the balance of the ecosystem and lead to long-term decline. Whether the eventual use of a resource is dominated by short or long-term gains very much influences the degree of stability of the area, that is whether it is subject to many rapid changes or slow gradual change. The exploitative farming of the American 'Dust Bowl' in the 1930s, for example, rapidly led to soil erosion, a dramatic change in the ecosystem, as the phrase implies, and out-migration.

Externalities

Figure 2.2 summarises some of the key actors and their viewpoints in such decisions over resources. Benefits accrue not only to the users. Other groups and organisations may gain or receive what are called *positive externalities* from the use of the resource. These are external events (in this case the use of the resource) that are advantageous; for example demand for their service may increase or their land and property may gain in value. Equally, some may experience *negative externalities* (Chapter 7). Their view may be spoiled or their access hindered by increased road traffic. Individual actors may be supported by pressure groups or movements, as for example the Friends of the Earth or the Ramblers Association in promoting or preventing some uses. The power of such groups depends on the size of their membership, their financial resources, their ability to publicise their views and their access to the ears of the eventual decision-makers (Chapter 7). Finally, local, regional or national government may help make the decision, even though sometimes one of their departments may be one of the potential users; for example, in Britain the Departments of Energy or Agriculture may be subject to decisions taken by the Department of Environment.

Context

The behaviour of the actors and the eventual use of the resource are not independent of the economic, social and political context of the time or the place (the *spatial* and *temporal contexts*). In the 1970s the environmental lobby in the USA and some parts of Western Europe had grown in influence, and decisions over resources then were much more likely to reflect environmental priorities and values than they were in the 1950s and early 1960s, when economic growth was the major consideration. In the early 1980s economic priorities again became relatively dominant, especially in Great Britain. Often it is argued that a particular decision has been made in the 'public or national interest', but this may vary from time to time and place to place and it is not always clear how it is determined. Consider, for example, the different interests involved in a decision over an application for housing on a piece of semi-rural land that is part of the London Green Belt. At one time it may be refused because access to open space, retention of agricultural land and freedom from urban sprawl are highly valued. At another time, it may be granted because more people are moving to the South East, a stimulus is needed for the house-building industry which in turn increases demand for consumer durables, and the particular piece of semi-rural land is said not to be attractive or well cared for. Who establishes the 'public interest' and on what criteria is it based? These are major questions to answer.

Summary of general problem

The general problem then is to what use should the resource be put, and how should that be resolved? If a decision is to be made, who makes the decision, based on which set of values, and considering which benefits and losses?

2.3 Other examples

Definition of a resource

A resource is anything that people in society value and can use. Resources are then socially defined in particular places at particular times. Uranium, for example, became a resource only when knowledge of nuclear reactions became available and appropriate technologies were developed to apply it to purposes of armaments and power supply. The resources may be defined by economic, technological, social, political and ecological values. *Economically* a resource is a source of profit and employment, through its discovery, exploitation, processing and marketing. *Technology* may make a resource available. It can also make it redundant by finding cheaper or better substitutes. *Certain groups* in society may give value to wilderness areas or wildlife, and politically express that value through pressure groups. *Political value* may also be imparted at a different scale, as a country sees strategic value in being self-sufficient rather than dependent on imported resources. It may also see *strategic value* in a piece of territory because it controls access, say, between two oceans – the Panama and Suez Canal zones were particularly important for this reason. Finally, some people express the *ecological value* of resources by emphasising the interdependence in the ecosystem between plants, animals and parts of the physical environment. They try to ensure that resources are not used in a way that disrupts those interdependencies in order that, for example, the 'carrying capacity' of an area – the extent to which a renewable resource may be cropped while still sustaining its renewability – is not exceeded. These people emphasise living in harmony with nature rather than controlling or exploiting it. These different values are illustrated in the case study and the following examples.

Resources also have geographical value. A resource may come from any part of the physical environment; for instance clean air (atmospheric), energy or scenic value from a waterfall (geomorphological/hydrological) timber (ecological) and minerals and fossil fuels (geological). Parts of the built environment may be valued as a resource as indeed may human beings themselves. Characteristically resources are not evenly distributed in space. They are concentrated in particular areas (for example mineral ores in particular rock formations), or they can grow, or grow better, in some areas rather than others (a crop has biological limits to the areas in which it can be grown, while within those limits it will give higher yields in certain places because of their particular combination of physical characteristics). The location of resources then affects their value. In the past, though to a much lesser extent today, the location of the resource limited the uses to which it could be put. Now, in many cases, modern transport technology permits its distribution and use far away from its original locations. The relative accessibility of a resource, however,

still affects its value. One location of the resource may be developed before another because of its greater accessibility to its market. However, such resources as clean air, landscape and wilderness are place specific and their absolute as well as their relative location becomes part of their value. Their relative location is important, for instance their proximity to cities so that people can easily visit them to relax. Their absolute location is also part of their value because it is a particular combination of physical and often human processes that have produced them in a way which cannot be replicated elsewhere.

Land

Although the principles developed in this chapter apply to such problems as competing uses for timber – fuel, building material, paper, cellulose, etc. – the core of the argument is to

what use we should put a piece of land which is valued for at least two, but usually a whole series of resources, as in the case of Tople, Pike. The land can be viewed as a resource in itself in a number of ways (Figure 2.4).

It is different from many other resources because it is immobile, with both its absolute and relative location being part of its value. The buildings, plant, routes and waste disposal may be valued in economic, social or historical terms. The problem of this chapter, which is illustrated in a number of ways in this section, occurs when the piece of land, or indeed water, has a number of potential uses. The uneven geographical distribution of resources and people which lends value to them as resources ensures that there are many pieces of land that can be used in many ways. This section begins with an area of dramatic scenery, a wilderness area which

2.4 Land, air and water as resources

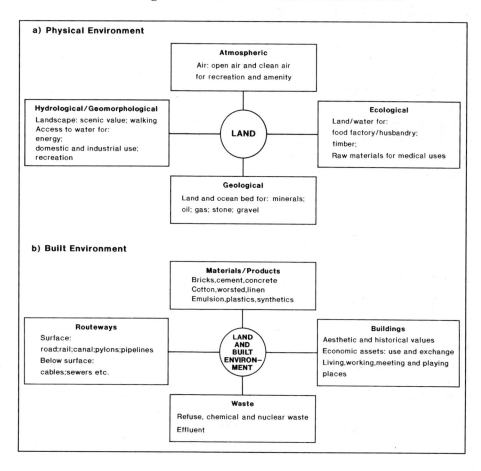

has geological resources (2.3a). This contrasts with conflict over land within the city (2.3b). Conflict over the use of land within the metropolitan rings and along the coast (2.3d) highlights the question of whether the physical or built environment should have priority. Finally, at a much greater scale, the land and sea areas of Antarctica (2.3c) are viewed as the scene of international conflict over their resources and their strategic value.

2.3a Conflict in a wilderness area: wild beauty versus a mass of wattage

Southern Utah is located near to some of the world's finest scenery: all or part of six national parks and five national forests, the Glen Canyon National Recreational Area, three national monuments, plus primitive and wilderness study areas. From Kanab (Figure 2.5), seat of Kane County with a population of 4250, it is 43 miles to Zion National Park, 75 miles to the Grand Canyon's North Rim and 80 miles to Bryce Canyon National Park.

This region is considered an incomparable landscape of high plateaux and deep canyons. At present it is a scantily populated region relying on tourism for employment alongside some jobs in forestry and ranching. Its wilderness environment offers beauty, peace, solitude and remoteness.

This region however is underlain by rich deposits of coal, uranium and oil bearing tar sands. A proposal has been made for the Kanab area to develop a large open-cast coal mine with a 7-mile trench and two coal-fired power plants, in the so called Allen/Warner Valley Energy

Bryce Canyon National Park : Landscape under threat

System. The plants would be served by a slurry pipeline system in which coal would be ground and mixed with water pumped from local wells. Such technological developments have made possible the exploitation of this substantial resource. Three hundred million tons of mineable, fair quality coal would be strip mined from 4000 hectares of land very close to a viewing point in Bryce Canyon National Park. This proposal has been put forward by a variety of Electricity Corporations in South West USA and in particular by Utah International, a subsidiary of General Electric. These proponents justify the development because of the energy needs of the USA and quell potential environmental critics by guaranteeing land reclamation after having mined the coal. Other institutions support the proposal, including the California Public Utilities Commission, the Department of the Interiors Office of Surface Mining and the US Bureau of Land Management, owner of much of the local cattle ranching land which is irrigated and supports alfalfa. The proponents point to the scheme's impact of reducing national dependence on imported oil, a likely reduction of the then 16 per cent local unemployment rate and the encouragement of local industry of which there is little at present.

2.5 Coal versus the environment

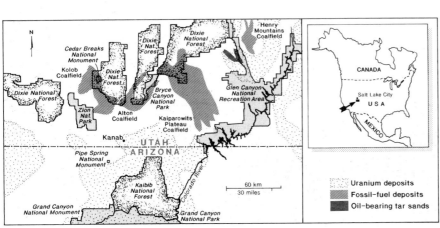

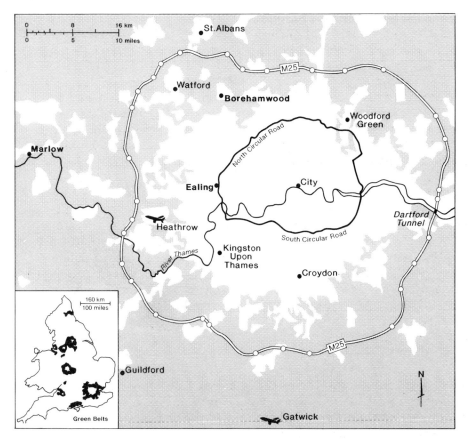

the orbital motorway around Greater London, has made it the prime target for development of jobs and homes especially near the intersections with radial motorways. In both cases there is considerable pressure to build offices, as modern information technology, for many types of offices, no longer necessitates expensive central London locations. Rank Xerox, for example, has recently moved from central London to Marlow (Figure 2.8). Office development growth has already been particularly rapid on the south-western part of the M25 orbital corridor, where there was a 27.3 per cent growth in office floor space between 1978 and 1983. This is the direction in which many of the key London office workers live, so moves in a south-westerly direction lead to less costly and less time-consuming commuting.

The national government itself has even encouraged development at one of the intersections, the M25/M1 interchange. Here the adjoining agricultural area was compulsorily purchased in 1982 at £1200 per hectare, but was put on sale three years later, reportedly at £1,000,000 per hectare, as a zone for industrial development, which could include warehousing, distribution and retailing as well as manufacturing. National government, through the Department of the Environment, also has to respond to the consortium's pressure since most local governments will oppose it in order to maintain the status quo and retain their local green environments. Developers are then likely to appeal to the higher body for a decision. These metropolitan rings are then major foci of conflict because of their present functions and future potential.

Britain during the 1940s and 1950s to give breathing space to cities and to halt the urban sprawl of the 1930s. Therefore new housing and centres of employment were prevented in the Green Belts which were to act mainly as recreational and food-producing areas for the cities. Since their establishment, residential development in particular has leapfrogged the Belts. In some ways this indicates their success in that little development has taken place within them, while in other ways it represents their failure to halt the spread of the metropolis in functional terms, since people now commute across the Belt to the central city. Given this functional extension of the cities beyond their Green Belts, it is not surprising that developers have exerted great pressure on the planning authorities to allow them to create homes and jobs within and on the edge of the Belts. They see them as areas of great

growth potential, particularly the London Green Belt. In brief, the conflict is whether the Belts remain green or become grey.

Until now they remain generally intact, despite there being some erosion particularly at the edges, but they are beginning to face increasing pressure. Past erosion has occurred as certain towns have expanded. For example, Borehamwood in Hertfordshire, since its establishment as a London County Council overspill estate in the late 1940s, has gradually penetrated the Green Belt.

Present pressure comes in two major, not unconnected forms: a building consortium, consisting of major developers such as Barratt and Wimpey, has applied to construct fifteen or more 'private new towns' by expanding existing villages within and just outside the Green Belt; and the changing accessibility of the zone along the M25,

2.3d Conflict over the use of coastal land: the south coast of England

Who Cares for the Coast?

The British coastline is under threat. Pollution from a variety of sources – oil spills, sewage and industrial effluent – has affected many kilometres of land at the sea's edge ... The coast is also affected in more visually obvious ways by people. Tourism, housing and industry have all led to a growing number of building at the coast, changing the landscape to concrete ... Of the 4800 kilometres of coastline in England, Wales and Northern Ireland, 1600 kilometres have already been developed beyond redemption.'

(*Geographical Magazine,*
September 1984)

2.9 Coastal conflict

Another general area where there are often conflicts over use is coastal land, which is attractive for such uses as housing, transport, industry, recreation and farming. Under particular threat is the coastline itself (see insert).

The stretch of 25 kilometres or so between Southampton and Portsmouth on the south coast of England has been in particular demand (Figure 2.9).

In a short distance there is a remarkable mixture of uses, few of which are in harmony with one another. The rich farming land and woodland are under great pressure from retail, office and housing development, particularly on the edge of the two cities, and from recreational activities such as golf courses as at Gosport and Stokes Bay and holiday cabins at Solent Breezes. A number of industries benefit from access to raw materials imported through the

ports but the oil refinery, chemical manufacturing plant and power station at Fawley, while providing vital services and employment, are environmentally incompatible with most other uses. Finally, complexity is added to this mosaic of not always complementary land uses by transport-related activities such as pleasure boating, marinas, the ferry terminals at Southampton and Portsmouth, the container terminal at Western Dock, Southampton and the M27 south coast motorway. It is not only the coastal land over which there is conflict, it is also the coastal water. For example, Southampton Water experiences a similar range of competing uses, and as the insert and table (Figure 2.10) suggest, suffers from various kinds of pollution as side effects of some of these activities.

Users	Uses	Possible Impacts
Householders Developers	Housing	Increasing pressure fro housebuilders on the edges of the cities. Danger of urban sprawl. Pressure on coastal land
Industrial workers and managers Transport workers Travellers	Industry such as ship repairing, oil refining, power generation. Container, ferry and hovercraft terminals	Potential pollution - visual, noise, water and air Need coastal access Conflict with recreational traffic. Provides employment
Motorists Construction and Maintenance Workers	Motorways	Potential pollution Division of communities Increased access
People engaged or employed in recreation	Golf courses, holiday cabins sailing, hotels, swimming beaches	Access to coast needed Congestion. Possible pollution

2.10 Conflicting users, uses and impacts

2.3e The ownership and use of a huge mineral, ecological and strategic resource: Antarctica - the last great wilderness

The armed conflict between Britain and Argentina over the Falkland Islands in 1982 was partly a reflection of the wider international conflict engendered by Antarctica, since possession of the Falklands

2.11 Antarctica: national interests; conflict or cooperation?

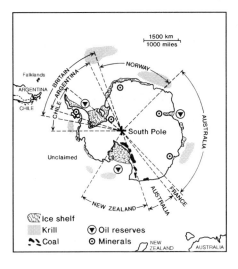

affects claims on Antarctica.

Not only did the Falklands have a historical and cultural value to both Britain and Argentina, they also possessed mineral, ecological and strategic value. Similarly for Antarctica as a whole, various nations have competed for ownership, control and use of its largely untouched resources. Coal, iron ore, platinum, gold, silver and oil are present in commercial quantities, as are fish and whale stocks. Finally its strategic and military value has not been overlooked by the international community, because parts of it, like the Falklands, provide excellent surveillance points for observation of naval movements from one ocean to another.

In 1959 the Antarctic Treaty was signed by sixteen developed world nations. This encouraged scientific research and froze disputes about sovereignty. Non-participating

nations would argue, however, that signatories have gained invaluable 'access' to unlimited resources by a relatively cheap commitment to scientific research. One signatory, for instance, has extracted huge quantities of krill, the basic food of baleen whales and a key component of the marine ecosystem. This scale of exploitation flies in the face of the 1959 treaty which suggested that Antarctica should be the 'common heritage of humanity'. Recent debate in the UN has centred on how this huge and unique set of resources can be managed. At present it does seem that the sixteen signatories, via a commitment to scientific research, have reserved valuable access to wide ranging resources denied to most countries. The 1959 treaty offered the opportunity of unparalleled cooperative action on an international level – so far this has not materialised.

2.4 Alternative strategies

There are two major types of strategies which are employed in first world countries today to determine the use to which a resource is put; one allows market forces to operate, the so-called 'invisible hand', while the other involves some intervention which may be called *planning* in its broadest sense, with some kind of decision-making body resolving the conflict over the resource.

The market

In a classical market situation the forces of supply and demand operate so that more will be paid for a scarce than a common resource and more

for one in great rather than in limited demand. The use of a particular resource will be determined by the highest price bid, which will reflect the greatest demand for the resource. The market strategy obviously means that economic priorities are uppermost or, at least, all other interests are reduced to economic terms. The basic process is *competition*, which is legitimised conflict, regulated by a set of rules to which actors generally adhere. It is agreed, for example, that the actor who bids most for using the resource will win. The decision-making body in the planning strategy is needed partly because there is no agreed way of deciding priorities between the actors wishing to use the resource.

Intervention planning

Social and environmental factors need to be considered as well as economic ones and some body is needed to adjudicate between the various uses. This can be done case by case, or by laying down some guidelines. The zoning of various pieces of urban land for particular uses is a rather rigid example of the latter. The decision-making body often consists of elected or appointed representatives, with local or national government employees advising it. It has some legal powers, given to it by government, in order that its final decisions are backed by the force of law. For very important decisions it may involve a government minister or the government as a whole. The planning strategy then is a bureaucratic and/or political intervention in the market system which involves some legal powers.

One owner of a resource

The two strategies may be illustrated by the simplest form of the problem which involves the owner of a resource, say a piece of land, deciding how to use it. This is the basic problem analysed by von Thunen concerning farm land use. In his analysis the best land use is decided purely in economic terms as to which brings the greatest returns after production and transport costs have been met. In the present day these simple market forces do not act alone. The farmer would have to consider national and supra-national grants, subsidies and price support schemes such as those for US agriculture, and the Common Agricultural Policy of the European Community. The decision would still be made in economic terms though. At first sight the farmer seems an independent decision maker but pressure may be applied by large suppliers of seeds, fertilisers and equipment and consumers of the potential products. The farmer may not then be a very powerful part of what has been loosely described as 'agribusiness'. In the present context the actions of governments and large business organisations complicate the processes of the first strategy, the operation of the market.

The second strategy may also enter this simple situation because decisions to plough rough pasture, to drain wetlands, remove hedgerows or to set up factory farming may bring protests from environmental and animal rights protest groups, some of which may result in government intervention to resolve the conflict over the use of the land. In

Britain the government, using the Wildlife and Countryside Act 1981, has tried to stop the draining of some wetlands which have ecological importance (Halvergate Marshes in Norfolk and parts of the Somerset levels for example) by offering the farmers financial incentives not to use them. In other instances regulations affecting the use of land are already in existence, for example tree preservation orders and public rights of way, both of which, if ignored, can result in legal action against the farmer. So even in this simple situation both strategies are involved in quite complex ways.

Competition over land for the same use

Both strategies come into effect in the slightly more complex situations where more than one actor wants the resource for the same type of use. A number of building companies such as Wimpey and Barratt, for example, might want a piece of land for housing. The amount they are prepared to pay for it will depend on the location of the land, particularly how that affects the type of houses they think they can build and sell there, the anticipated house prices and the building costs. By subtracting the building costs from the price, they know how much they can afford to bid for the land, given the amount of profit they wish to make. As building companies often need to buy land some time ahead of building, called 'land banking', they obviously have to estimate costs, prices and potential profits for some future date. Sometimes the purchase of the land will be by auction when it will go to the highest bidder. At other times the landowner will sell to the first person to offer the desired price, as in most transactions of private house sales in England and Wales.

Even this relatively simple competitive process can become more

complex if, as in the housing case, at either the local or national level there are social pressures to restrict the areas where housing may be built or control the type or density of the development. In Britain the town and country planning system operates to control many forms of development. Before housing, for example, can be built in an area, planning permission has to be given. This is given in two stages: *outline planning permission* which establishes the use and approximate overall density, and *detailed planning permission* when exact maps and drawings are submitted for each part of the development. Potential developers have to take the likelihood of planning permission into consideration when deciding on the exact use and making their bids – for example whether to build four storey apartment blocks or many single dwellings.

Competition and conflict over land for different uses

The competitive process can operate in a situation where there are many potential uses of a resource but this is often where *conflict* rather than competition occurs. In competitive situations there is a set of actors playing to an agreed set of rules, the demand and supply mechanisms of the market determining the bid prices and the highest bidder winning. Where there is conflict, there is no agreed set of rules for resolution. Conflict can result where there is no agreed owner of the resource to whom bids can be made, as is the case for the ocean bed, Antarctica, or whales. It can also result where elements or the whole of society decides that value and use should not be assessed simply in the narrow terms of the potential returns to the owner or user of the resource. Other people are affected by the use, because there are gains and losses to them as well as to the owner. The ploughing up of wetlands, which has become profitable to individual farmers because of subsidies from the Common Agricultural Policy of the European Community, removes in some cases areas which due to their flora and fauna are designated Sites of Special Scientific Interest (SSSI). These are areas that conservationist bodies such as the Nature Conservancy Council wish to remain in their wild state. This is not a question that can be resolved by the market. Local planning bodies such as the Norfolk Broads Authority in the case of Halvergate Marshes and national government through the Department of the Environment have had to intervene. In this case the other people involved are not clearly identified because it refers to retaining our heritage for future as well as present generations.

In the example of the proposed development of about fifteen small towns in or near the Green Belt around London by a consortium of leading house-builders (see Chapter 2, Section 3c), some of the people affected are more easily identified. The residents of areas in the vicinities of the new towns, such as Tillingham Hall in south Essex and Hook in north-east Hampshire, are mostly against such proposals because they would change, for the worse as far as they are concerned, the environment to which they are accustomed. The local councils, who represent the residents, also foresee that the developments will necessitate future public expenditure, even though the developers are offering to provide community facilities and schools. The Council for the Protection of Rural England sees such new building as perpetuating the draining of development from the cities at continuing cost to the countryside. Others, on the other hand, see these protests as representing a conservative pressure to maintain an unequal situation in which the countryside is enjoyed by a privileged few to the exclusion of many less well-off within London.

The builders point to the demand for new housing in the South East, which their New Homes Marketing Board helps to create as well as to monitor. Yet the Standing Conference of Local Planning Authorities suggests that if development is to go ahead in the South East then there is enough land in London, particularly in the old dockland areas, for the housing needed this century. It would prefer, however, that new development should go to other regions which are in need of new jobs as well as better housing. Planning applications for these private new towns are likely to be turned down by local councils, to go to a public inquiry as the developers appeal against the decision and eventually to be settled by the Secretary of State for the Environment, who will review the advice of his inspector who chairs the inquiry. Since a recent Secretary has said that a balance must be struck between development and conservation in the Green Belt, the outcome is not obvious. In the Tillingham Hall case, permission was not granted. Clearly such decisions involve more than just conservation. They affect the future geography of population, housing and employment both within the South East and between it and the other regions. They also influence the relative growth of cities, the metropolitan fringes and rural areas.

They are not then just local issues. They set precedents and have ramifications for many other areas.

Planning bodies and inquiries

The examples of the wetlands and the Green Belt developments are just two of a whole range of conflicts over resource use which involve both local and national planning bodies, using the term planning in the sense that these bodies will have to make the decision over use. Some people suggest that the planning bodies act as referees in settling disputes, which implies that they are neutral. This is a difficult argument to sustain because the decision-makers can be subject to intense lobbying by interested parties and of course have their own set of values which may give economic considerations priority over say environmental ones or vice versa.

What distinguishes these planning decisions is the degree to which they are open or closed to public scrutiny and involvement. For example, compare the open Sizewell public inquiry on a nuclear power plant (Chapter 3, Section 1) with the

Planning blight in Ealing

behind closed-doors decision over the Channel Tunnel (Chapter 3, Section 3d), both of which are discussed in the next chapter. The briefs for such decisions and inquiries vary, for example as to whether they are considering the need for something, or accepting that it is needed and deciding the narrower question of where it should go or what form it should take. They also vary in their scope, as regards the range of the benefits and costs that are taken into account. The question of building in the Green Belt, for instance, could involve whether new houses are needed or accept that they are, and limit the decision to where they should or should not go. The Third London Airport Inquiry, the Roskill Commission (1968–70), evaluated only possible locations. These were eventually narrowed down to four: the use of marshland at Foulness (Maplin Sands), an area near a middle-income village, Cublington (Bedfordshire), Thurleigh near Bedford and Nuthampstead, about 10 miles north west of Stanstead. Its recommendation of developing Foulness was never followed, partly because air traffic did not grow at the predicted rate. The decision was then made not to have a third airport, an option which the costly inquiry was not asked to consider. Since then traffic has grown and

Stanstead has effectively become the third London airport, despite the recommendations of Roskill. The hundred-day decision on the Channel Tunnel did not debate whether one was needed; it just decided what form it should take.

Generally speaking, the wider the scope of and the more the public participation in the inquiry, then the more evidence there is presented, the longer it will take and the more it will cost. There are opportunity costs too; these are partly the benefits that would have accrued from the eventually favoured use if it had occurred from the beginning of the inquiry. Sometimes they may also include the cost of using some other resources elsewhere while the decision is being made. The uncertainty about the decision may also produce *planning blight*, as in the case of Ealing Broadway Centre where some housing deteriorated because people refused to invest in property that might be demolished. It can also produce *speculative gains* as people buy up land or property in the vicinity of the potential development in anticipation of the land/property increasing in value once the decision has been made. So just as the market mechanism may have consequences for other than the direct users of the resource, so can the planning procedures.

There are ways other than planning for conflicts to be resolved. Overt displays of power in illegal action or war may produce an outcome; for example Greenpeace, has used illegal action to draw attention to the dumping of radioactive waste on the sea floor off the coast of Cumbria. Conflicts over use of the ocean floors and areas like Antarctica, in general, need international agreement. It is lack of agreement between nations over the use or often the ownership of resources that may result in various scales of armed conflict from, for example, the dispute over fishing rights between Iceland and Britain in the early 1970s – the so-called 'cod war' – to the wars between the indigenous Indians and the white settlers in the USA during the nineteenth century. In such conflicts it is often the strategic rather than the economic value of the resource that is being fought over. Although there are international bodies like the United Nations and the International Court of Justice at The Hague, in the Netherlands, these need the support and recognition of all countries to be able to resolve such disputes without armed conflict.

2.5 Perspectives

Exchange value and use value

So far we have considered the question of what happens to resources from the viewpoint of the relative demand for particular uses. At first sight this seems very reasonable but in economies like those of the USA and UK where the market is a major force the value of a resource may be related to its *exchange value* as

much as its use. Areas of land in the middle of cities, for example, where buildings have been demolished, may be used temporarily as car parks. This land use would not occur on the basis of bid-rent principles alone. It is the gains to be made from the expected increase in value of the land that attract ownership. The returns on the use of the land while it is owned is of secondary importance to the potential returns from selling it. Similarly there are commodity markets, for example in

minerals like tin or crops like coffee, which work not on adding value by processing or using the resource but on the potential profits of ownership, buying at one price and as demand increases selling at a higher one, without ever seeing the resource. In both the land and commodity cases it is speculative behaviour because the exchange value may fall as well as rise. It is therefore in the interests of the speculators to do everything possible to ensure that there is a rise. Speculative house builders will therefore not only build houses, they will design the estates so that they can market them in a way that enhances their value. In the USA and Britain, for example, developers have bought relatively cheap agricultural land, emphasised its rural qualities through the house and estate names such as Cotswold and Constable Lee Park, and presented it as an exclusive residential area that only the rich can afford. Here the developers are trying to create differences in space, and to create scarcity, and if they are successful they will gain substantially from it.

Radical and traditional views

This *radical view* of understanding the land and resource use is very different from the *traditional* one which emphasises use rather than exchange values and suggests that there are inherent differences between areas to which people respond according to their evaluation of the areas at different times. As society, the economy and technology change then particular resources and areas will take on different use values and different geographies will result. For example, in the USA as people became more affluent and lived longer, buying a retirement home became more popular and Florida with its warm winters seemed suitable for this relatively new land use. Changing geographies are interpreted partly through changing comparative advantages. In contrast, the radical view suggests that certain groups in society help to create the differences between areas, by for example making resources or particular types of land scarce, and then profiting from that scarcity. One group therefore gains at the expense of others. Developers of retirement areas in Florida then, by this view, would have bought land cheaply, packaged it as desirable, marketed it and gained considerably from the

exchange. In this view, rather than land values resulting from competition for different uses, the creation of the land value is what brings about the use.

The traditional view emphasises the users rather than the developers in determining the resource or land use. For many years geographers have suggested that office blocks were built in proximity in particular areas because users were central to a large labour supply and needed agglomeration economies of linkages through informal and formal contact, were near to competitors and so knew what they were doing, and enjoyed the prestige associated with having an office in a known quarter. Yet it is the developers who build the offices, and only occasionally are these the eventual users. Research in the UK, USA and Canada indicates that many new office concentrations arise from a leading developer investing in an area, which others see, expect success and therefore imitate, follow and develop nearby. Often the eventual users are unknown during development, and the office blocks may remain empty for some time after completion. In these circumstances it seems unreasonable to explain their existence and location, and the land use, simply on the basis of demand. Too often we seek explanation from what is there now, rather than understand the history of how what is there came about.

We have previously discussed the impacts of different uses of a piece of land on the surrounding area, for example Topley Pike. It should also be clear that the use and exchange value of the surrounding area affect the use and exchange value of the piece of land. When railways, for example, were built into the countryside around large cities, the land close to, if not adjoining the stations increased in value as it could potentially become a commuter village or town. For this land the railway is a *positive externality*. Equally the use as a refuse tip of an open area adja-

cent to some housing will devalue the housing. Although this may not lead to a change in use, it may trigger a change of occupants to those of lower income. The widening of a road, such as the North Circular in London, may have a similar effect, a *negative externality*.

In the same way that the value of one piece of land is affected by another, one resource may have relatively little value until it is used with something else. Molybdenum, for example, takes on a greater value because it acts as a hardener for steel.

Intensity of use

Although the type of use of a resource or piece of land is an important question to resolve, so too is the intensity of use. Increasing the *intensity of use* of land can increase its exchange value and produce greater returns from the increased use. Demolishing a three-storey block in the centre of a city and replacing it with a high rise office block will bring greater rents from the additional floor space, given that the demand exists, so that much higher returns are obtained for the same area of land.

Some increases of intensity, however, can destroy the perceived value of the land and produce lower returns and a lower exchange value, if owned. Some people argue that some forms of agriculture, through increased use of inorganic fertilisers, are producing higher yields now but are changing the long term characteristics of the soil so that future returns will be lower. Recreational use of open spaces, such as the Peak District in the case study, also illustrates the point. The intensity is the increased use by people who contribute to the erosion of the landscape (Chapter 6) and limit one another's enjoyment of the scenery by their presence. In some areas, such as the Goyt Valley in the Peak

District, there have been suggestions of limiting the numbers travelling into the area, especially on Sundays, because of the rapid erosion associated with 'honeypots', the points where many people congregate. In Tarn Hows in the Lake District, use of some areas was prevented until the vegetation regenerated.

Global resources

The *intensity* and *rate of use of world resources* by its growing population is a more fundamental problem at a greater scale. Those who view the world's resources as finite foresee a crisis when demand will far exceed supply.

Tragedy of the Commons

The problem has been conveyed in the parable of the 'Tragedy of the Commons'. In this there was some common land on which all farmers had the rights to graze their cows. While the number of cows or indeed farmers with cows was low, there was not any problem of overgrazing. When one farmer decided to increase his stock and graze more cows, and others followed suit, the commons rapidly became overgrazed. Since all had a right to the commons (free access), the common land was finite, and all farmers followed their own self-interest (short-term, self-interested rationality), nothing was done, the commons declined and the local economy and society collapsed. Our present rate and increasing rate of use of resources is expressed by the growing number of cows, the commons is the world, and the local society the world's population.

Some optimistic writers offer a *technological solution*. This includes increasing efficiency in the use of resources, increased recycling, and the conservation and substitution of resources. These optimists also suggest that people's ingenuity, particularly in creating new technologies, will overcome the resource constraints. Others propose *social* and *governmental solutions* which restrict access or attempt to change people's rationality from short to long-term and from self interest to group interest. These suggest that changing the organisation of society will affect use. The point to be emphasised here, since this debate will be taken up in the next chapter, is that whether and how a resource is used now influences future generations and their quality of life as well as present ones.

Attitudes to rural land

The problem of resource use obviously involves people's attitudes and priorities. They are at the root of the question as to which strategy is used to resolve the problem. The use of rural land provides a good illustration. People have pointed to the inadequacies of the 1981 British Wildlife and Countryside Act which, among other things, in recognising the need to conserve Sites of Special Scientific Interest (SSSI) offers compensation to landowners for not farming them. As European Community subsidies and the market change, new farming opportunities arise and by threatening to plough up such land, farmers can obtain compensation for their loss of potential. For many people the priority is production, the resources are seen as raw materials, and rural areas are viewed as food factories. Maximum output may be the goal with increased inorganic fertilisers, greater use of chemicals in feed in order to fatten the livestock, and large-scale farming techniques entailing the removal of hedgerows to enable the use of machinery over larger fields. This can result in irreversible ecological damage and the presence in our meat and vegetables of chemicals that may have harmful effects. For others the priority is *good husbandry*, living with rather than using the physical environment. The emphasis is on appropriate ways of working the land to conserve it as a resource, for future leisure as well as farming, together with providing satisfying work practices and livelihoods for all farm workers and health-giving food for consumers. One difference is between maximum and optimum land use, the 'most out of' as against 'the best use of' the land for present and future generations. The first indicates the economic and technological imperatives. The second does not go to another extreme and argue a purely conservationist/environmentalist imperative. Rather, it establishes a more balanced approach to the environmental, economic and social priorities with the use of technologies appropriate to this balance. It takes account of the effect of farm methods not only on the physical environment but also on farm workers, consumers of farm products and other uses of the land. Indeed, instead of seeing one land use as dominant, it allows for the possibility of a *multifunctional environment* where farming is just one of a number of complementary rather than competing uses.

Even between government departments there may be differences in priorities over resource use. The Department of Agriculture, for example, is more economically minded while the Department of the Environment is more open to other considerations for rural land. Interdepartmental conflict may then result. Between countries there may also be considerable differences in priorities, notably between the First and Third World, with the latter paying little attention to environmental factors as the economic drive for development dominates almost everything. While the First World has exported this economic prerogative, it has not at the same time exported its environmental concern. Often Third World environments and indeed social systems are being damaged to satisfy the needs of the First World. There is then a continual need to identify and assess our attitudes and priorities worldwide as well as in our own country.

Different cultural views of land

There is also a need to appreciate that our thinking and feeling towards resources and land reflect our spatial and temporal context. At different times and/or places the land has been viewed in rather different ways. Elements of it may have, for example, religious significance or even magical meaning, reflecting the particular culture of the people in that time and place. The cultural contrasts in attitudes towards nature, land ownership and land value are well illustrated in the conflict between the aborigines and international mining companies in Australia. The mining companies want to exploit the rich reserves of, particularly, bauxite and uranium and thus see this vast area and indeed 'nature' as a whole as a source of riches and resources which should be extracted and used. The aborigines view nature as a living thing of which they are part, and as a renewable storehouse with which they must live in balance. They see mining as harming nature and destroying their land and the landscape, every feature of which is related to their own origin as a people and many features of which have everlasting sacred significance. The mining companies show that they have legal right to the land by processing the title deeds. The aborigines do not recognise this form of land and property ownership, which can be bought and sold. They have lived there for 40,000 years. The

St Paul's Cathedral overshadowed by surrounding offices

land is them; they are inseparable from it. Whereas the mining companies say the land belongs to them, the aborigines say they belong to the land. The aborigines will thus assess land value in a very different way from mining companies who determine value in terms of productivity and profitability. For them this particular piece of land has meaning based on their history and religion. It cannot be exchanged for land elsewhere.

Similar cultural contrasts can be made about the *built environment*. Whereas in the First World countries private ownership of property is dominant with the market and planning forces working in various combinations to determine its development, use and exchange, in the second or socialist world, property is at present mostly publicly owned with state planning deciding its development and use. The different social, economic and political organisations of the First and Second Worlds are reflected in the spatial structure of their cities. In the First World the commercial dimension occupies the prominent position in the form of the central business district with its major shops and often high-rise office blocks. In the Second World the centre of the city is dominated by state administrative and cultural buildings. Built-form is symbolic and indicates much about the society in western cities: the towering cathedrals of the religious past are now overshadowed by insurance and banking institutions of the more secular present. So although various combinations of market forces and planning dominate the use and exchange of physical and built-form resources in the First World countries now, that has not been so in the past and is not the case in other societies today. Spatial and temporal variations occur then in people's attitudes towards resources. There are also similar variations in their approach to settling conflicts over resource use.

Changing strategies for urban and rural land

In Britain at present, there are interesting changes occurring to attitudes and priorities towards strategies of resolving use of different types of land. Over time, as economic specialisation has occurred, it has been accompanied by a separation of functions in space, and different attitudes towards planning and market forces have come about in different functional areas. For many years planning has attempted to control market forces in towns (initially from the 1947 Town and Country Planning Act). Recently there has been a reversal of this trend, with, for example, the establishment of enterprise zones in some cities, in order to allow freer play of market forces and reduce the time taken in making decisions; while in the countryside, where planning controls have been less widely used, there are pressures to increase them to prevent what are seen as misuses of the land, as discussed above.

These contrasting tendencies, as applied to different types of land, demonstrate the continual tensions between market forces and planning or bureaucratic control of varying kinds. Here we just highlight the situation within one country. In Chapter 4 we discuss the debate at greater length showing the contrasts between countries as well as within. The bureaucratic controls or planning strategies have usually been used in part to reassert the importance of environmental and social considerations as against the economic ones of market forces. Controls or laws, however, work successfully in the long run only if they reflect and reinforce generally agreed attitudes. If the economic is

the dominant attitude, then the successful controls will be the ones reflecting and reinforcing it.

Summary

The use to which a resource will be put in First World countries today then, is influenced by market forces related to either use and/or exchange value, and to the relative dominance of these economic factors as against environmental and social considerations that may be reflected in the bureaucratic control and political intervention of planning strategies.

2.6   **Exercises**

1. Note any parts of your home, school or college, or resources within them for which there are conflicting uses. Discuss the benefits and beneficiaries and the ways in which conflict is resolved.

2. A cement works has been proposed for the old quarry (now disused) at Topley Pike (Figure 2.1). The following raw materials will be required each year:
   • local limestone 1314 tonnes;
   • local shale 305,000 tonnes;
   • coal for kiln 173,000 tonnes;
   • small amounts of gypsum.
   Transport would involve:
   • 30 per cent of the cement carried by road – 80 lorries deliver locally;
   • 70 per cent of the cement carried by rail and delivered to distant markets;
   • 400 tonnes of coal per day arrives.
   A total of 450 people would be required to run the works. Landscaping suggested includes:
   • 30,000 trees planted;
   • open areas paved chippings;
   • local Topley Pike Quarry does not break skyline.

Also special equipment is required to suppress large emissions of dust. The scale of the cement works would be similar to that in Hope Valley.
   (a) Who would hold strong views for and against the development?
   (b) What would their views be?
   (c) As a member of the Peak Park Planning Board, say whether or not you would agree to this development taking place. State your reasons.

3. The name Greenpeace was coined in 1971 by a group of people on their way by chartered ship to protest against USA nuclear tests in the Aleutian Islands. 'Deeds not words' is the philosophy upon which Greenpeace groups work. Later, Greenpeace groups turned their attention, and their unique tactics, to the issue of commercial whaling.
   Study Figure 2.12 which is an extract from a Greenpeace

2.12 Greenpeace on whaling

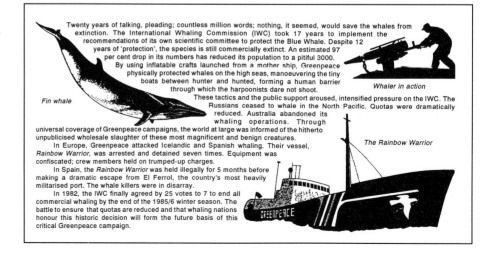

Twenty years of talking, pleading; countless million words; nothing, it seemed, would save the whales from extinction. The International Whaling Commission (IWC) took 17 years to implement the recommendations of its own scientific committee to protect the Blue Whale. Despite 12 years of 'protection', the species is still commercially extinct. An estimated 97 per cent drop in its numbers has reduced its population to a pitiful 3000.

By using inflatable crafts launched from a mother ship, Greenpeace physically protected whales on the high seas, manoeuvering the tiny boats between hunter and hunted, forming a human barrier through which the harpoonists dare not shoot.

Whaler in action

Fin whale

These tactics and the public support aroused, intensified pressure on the IWC. The Russians ceased to whale in the North Pacific. Quotas were dramatically reduced. Australia abandoned its whaling operations. Through universal coverage of Greenpeace campaigns, the world at large was informed of the hitherto unpublicised wholesale slaughter of these most magnificent and benign creatures.

In Europe, Greenpeace attacked Icelandic and Spanish whaling. Their vessel, *Rainbow Warrior*, was arrested and detained seven times. Equipment was confiscated; crew members held on trumped-up charges.

The Rainbow Warrior

In Spain, the *Rainbow Warrior* was held illegally for 5 months before making a dramatic escape from El Ferrol, the country's most heavily militarised port. The whale killers were in disarray.

In 1982, the IWC finally agreed by 25 votes to 7 to end all commercial whaling by the end of the 1985/6 winter season. The battle to ensure that quotas are reduced and that whaling nations honour this historic decision will form the future basis of this critical Greenpeace campaign.

publicity pamphlet.
(a) What is unique about Greenpeace tactics?
(b) What groups would question the Greenpeace interpretation of commercial whaling?
(c) Discuss the arguments for commercial whaling.
(d) After considering opposing viewpoints, what is your view about whaling?

4. Discuss the opposing viewpoints on the proposed development of Green Belts.

5. Using examples, distinguish between the alternative ways of resolving competition or conflict over a piece of land.

6. (a) Describe an area of land that has special meaning to you and explain its significance.

(b) How would you respond or have you responded to changes in the use of that land?

7. Evaluate the pessimistic and optimistic viewpoints on world resources. (Use this chapter and other sources.)

2.7   Further reading

J. Fernie and A.S. Pitkethly (1985) *Resources: Environment and Policy*, Harper and Row

P. Haggett (1983) *Geography: a Modern Synthesis*, Harper and Row (3rd ed)

J. Herington (1984) *The Outer City*, Harper and Row

Geography 16-19 Project Booklet (1986) *Impacts of Mineral Development*, Longman

J. Rees (1990) *Natural Resources*, Routledge 2nd ed.

I.G. Simmons (1991) *Earth, Air and Water: Resources and the Environment in the Late 20th Century*, Edward Arnold

Chapter 3

WHAT RESOURCES SHOULD BE USED?

3.1 Case study: Possible sources of energy – Sizewell B Nuclear Power Station and the Severn Barrage

The Sizewell B Nuclear Power Station and the Severn Tidal Barrage Scheme are two large scale examples of how different combinations of resources and technology can be employed for the same basic use, in this case the generation of electrical energy. Nuclear power relies on the application of sophisticated technology to small amounts of non-renewable resource (uranium),

Sizewell A nuclear power station

3.1 Britain's nuclear power stations

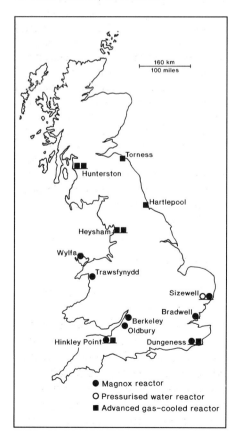

● Magnox reactor
○ Pressurised water reactor
■ Advanced gas-cooled reactor

whereas tidal power is a renewable source of energy. The two schemes would have different impacts on the physical, built and human environments.

Sizewell B

A major debate in the 1980s concerned the pros and cons of the UK developing more nuclear power stations and centred on whether or not Sizewell B should be commissioned. By the early 1980s the UK had fourteen nuclear power stations on stream with two under construction. The Sizewell B proposal was for the construction of a pressurised water reactor (PWR). A twenty-six month long inquiry began in January 1983.

Its findings could influence the government's long-term energy policy. If it found in favour this could lead to an extensive nuclear power programme as the cornerstone of future electricity production. Such a development in the UK could add strength to the nuclear power lobby in other countries. It could also increase the chances of the spread of nuclear power to developing countries, as the British nuclear industry seeks to increase its export orders.

The length of the inquiry and its cost (the Central Electricity Generating Board (CEGB) spent £20 million) pointed to the wide-ranging dispute over the value of such a reactor. The supporters of the scheme included: the CEGB who regarded it as an essential, cheap and safe element of their overall energy policy; the nuclear 'industry' which included British Nuclear Fuels Ltd (BNFL); the United Kingdom Atomic Energy Authority

(UKAEA); the Atomic Energy Research Establishment (AERE); the construction industry; related research agencies such as the Culham Laboratory south of Oxford, and high energy-using industries such as aluminium smelting.

On the other hand, the detractors of Sizewell's expansion included: those who pressed for other more economic and less dangerous alternatives, such as the Electricity Consumers Council who questioned the CEGB's 'value for money' assertion, particularly as other energy sources had recently become more competitive; the Council for the Protection of Rural England (CPRE) which, alongside other conservation groups, is against such schemes in remote and unspoilt areas of high landscape value; the National Union of Mineworkers (NUM) who wished to see, in contrast, the expansion of the coal industry; and the Friends of the Earth (FoE) who stressed the potential damage, danger and pollution to an area brought about by such a scheme and had the evidence of the Mayor of Harrisburg to support their case.

The Campaign for Nuclear Disarmament pointed to the military aspects of such a nuclear plant, and the East Anglian Water Authority pointed to the possible pollution of local fresh water.

Critics not only referred to the dangers of leaks from the reactors, they pointed to the Achilles heel of nuclear technology, the need for reprocessing, waste management and decommissioning. Reprocessing plants (for example Thorp plant at Sellafield) also present dangers of radiation leakage, accident and fire. The disposal of nuclear waste also produces potential hazards both at the disposal sites and near the routes along which the waste is transported. Indeed, many countries including Germany (West), Sweden, Belgium and Holland have paid large amounts to be relieved of the responsibility, exporting their irradiated fuel to France and Britain.

Mayor whose town neared brink of disaster warns Sizewell locals

In 1979 Harrisburg almost became a nuclear catastrophe. Its mayor spoke to a British public inquiry yesterday.

The Mayor of Harrisburg, whose local Three Mile Island nuclear power station suffered a near catastrophic accident in 1979, told the Sizewell public inquiry yesterday that had the town known what it knows now it would actively have resisted the plant's construction instead of welcoming it.

Mr Stephen Reed's advice to local Suffolk parish councils was that no community should be asked to accept the risk of a plant which had the potential, however slight, to annihilate that community and create a radioactive wasteland for thousands of years.

Mr Reed, accompanied by his fire chief and emergency management director, said that before the accident this community was trusting, docile and conservative.

People believed assurances from the electricity company and the nuclear experts that "it couldn't happen here".

Even since the accident there had been expert assurances that the fuel in the damaged reactor had not melted, but in recent months samples removed from the core showed that it had been within moments of a complete meltdown.

The Babcock and Wilcox pressurised water (PWR) nuclear plant near the Pennsylvania town is similar in principle, but quite different in detailed design, to the Westinghouse PWR the Central Electricity Generating Board proposes for Sizewell.

Counsel for the board, Lord Silsoe, emphasised such differences in his cross-examination of the United States, witnesses, suggesting that the board had already learned the lessons of Three Mile Island.

Mr Reed said he distinctly remembered "the metallic taste of radioactive iodine" as invisible plumes of gas drifted downwind from the over heated reactor.

Mr Reed's team criticised Harrisburg's inadequate evacuation plans and said that from what had been seen of the Sizewell plans similar problems could arise if there were an accident there.

Theoretical plans for a three, five or 10-mile evacuation zone were useless.

In a real emergency people from a much wider area who were frightened for themselves or their children, would get up and go – just as he, his family, and 140,000 people did three hours before the state Governor gave the order in 1979.

Mr Reed said the basic "fall-out" of the 1979 accident had been "a deep-rooted sense of betrayal and resentment".

The change in public perception, combined with new safety regulations, had prompted the cancellation of nuclear power station orders throughout the US.

Owners of the Three Mile Island station had sharply increased their electricity prices, partly to pay for a cleaning up operation that would require a further billion dollars over the next three years.

Harrisburg had developed less centralised forms of energy – burning rubbish to supply steam to a nearby steelworks and a district heating scheme, using methane gas from sewerage treatment to generate electricity.

The American witnesses complimented the planning inspector, Sir Frank Layfield, QC on the exhaustive nature of the Sizewell inquiry – Mr Reed suggesting it was something the US nuclear regulatory commission should have been doing years ago.

3.2 Lessons from Three Mile Island

The debate concerning nuclear power is very much alive around the world, particularly after the Chernobyl disaster in the USSR in 1986. Even before Chernobyl the growing opposition to nuclear energy in the USA, augmented by such incidents as Three Mile Island, had a major impact on orders and cancellations of PWR reactors. Over the same period in France, on the other hand, there was a massive commitment to nuclear energy.

Opposition there had been limited partly because of a powerful French bureaucratic machine and financial inducements to local communities in the form of compensation, reduced energy tariffs and a rating levy for affected communes. There have also

	1973 (75% imported) %	1981 (65% imported) %	1990 (projected) (50% imported) %
Oil	66	48	32
Natural gas	8.5	13	13
Coal	17	17	16
HEP	6	8	6
Nuclear	1.5	12	28
Renewables	1	2	5

Source: EDF (1982) Energies at Environment (based on two-year energy plan, 1982-1984, November 1981)

3.3 The evolution of French energy consumption

been construction contracts for local firms and the encouragement of new businesses because the French have a policy of making nuclear plants the focus of regional growth centres. Opposition has frequently been ill organised, diluted and fragmented. Only Plogoff in 1981 was a success for the French anti-nuclear campaigners, not least because of the powerful regional feeling in Brittany.

Severn Barrage

The Severn Barrage (Figure 3.4) is one of the developments of renewable resources which could act as an alternative to nuclear power. The

3.4 The proposed Severn Barrage, 1989

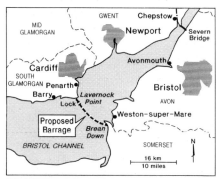

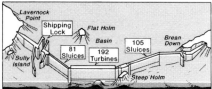

Severn Estuary was considered as the site for a barrage as long ago as 1933, and more recently interest has been revived. Apart from the small-scale scheme at St Malo, France, there are no large-scale precedents.

The Severn Barrage could supply 12 per cent of the electricity requirements of England and Wales but, like Sizewell, has an uncertain future. The advantages tend to be economic and the disadvantages ecological. On the negative side there would be a reduction in tidal volume and velocity leading to less salinity in upper layers, higher water temperatures in summer and possible winter icing. Arguably the reduced flushing action of tides would lead to the accumulation of pollutants, not least metal pollution, particularly mercury from Avonmouth, and crude sewage (the Severn Estuary at present copes with 47 million gallons of such sewage a day, more than any other estuary in England and Wales). Furthermore, there would probably be a major alteration of sedimentation and erosion patterns with silt accumulation upstream.

On the positive side the barrage could give a spur to regional development through better access provided by the barrage road and local availability of electric power. The Bristol area is at present already attracting more industry and population, and this could be maintained as well as bringing growth to depressed South Wales. Some have also argued that given suitable lock facilities, 250,000 tonne vessels

could have permanent access to Portishead docks at the mouth of the Avon. There could also be a boom in tourism and recreation, particularly water sports behind the barrage.

Much more research is needed to predict the likely ecological impact, as apparently no small-scale prototype can be built. This contrasts with the Bay of Fundy, where in 1984 a 20 MW pilot plant was opened at Annapolis Royal, North America's first tidal generating station. This pilot scheme is intended to throw light on likely effects on fish stocks, river hydrology and nearby fresh-water marshes.

At present the Department of Energy in the UK remains unconvinced that the £4000 million cost and fifteen to twenty years' construction time would be worth the 10 million tonnes of coal equivalent in energy produced annually.

Agreement over the Severn Barrage is still a long way off, not least because of the irreversibility of such large scale, capital-intensive schemes. The Sizewell B inquiry, however, decided in favour of the development. This gave a fillip to the British nuclear industry with more proposals coming under consideration, including one at Hinkley Point in Somerset, another PWR at an existing nuclear power site (Figure 3.1).

3.5 Tidal power in the Bay of Fundy

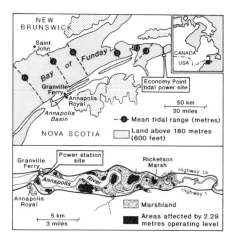

3.2   General problem

In the last chapter, the competition and conflict over alternative uses of a resource were studied. Here the focus is on a particular use or objective, for example the production of electricity as in the case study. The problem is which set of resources to use to achieve that end. In the case study two of the many alternative resources, nuclear and tidal power, were considered as possible ways of obtaining electricity. This section illustrates the arguments involved in the general problem by widening the discussion from electricity to the harnessing of energy in general.

Sources of Energy

Figure 3.6 displays various sources of energy from the three environ-

3.6 Sources of energy

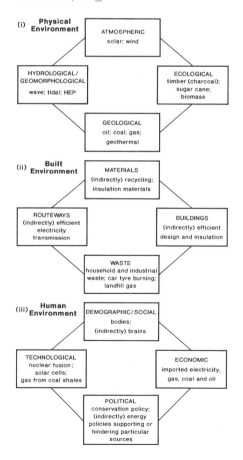

ments. At this point in the chapter the physical environment is being examined as a set of potential resources, some of which are renewable and others non-renewable. It is the latter, particularly oil, coal and gas, which are most used for energy at present. These *geological* resources are clearly being used up faster than they are being formed. They occur in variable quantities and qualities in sedimentary rocks and involve differing costs of exploitation, depending on the site conditions, location and available technology. Although new deposits are continually being found, it is very unlikely that the supply could meet the demand in the long term without the development of alternatives.

The *atmospheric* and *geomorphological/hydrological* sources, in contrast, are renewable. Their potential, however, varies in both time and space. Some areas, such as mountainous ones with precipitation all year like the Alps, have considerable hydroelectric power (HEP) potential. Wherever rain, wind or sun is variable over time then the suitability for HEP, wind and solar energy is less. In addition, the most favourable locations for supply reasons may be very far from concentrations of demand. Since these sources are immobile and have to be harnessed on site and then the electricity transferred to the demand areas, their location relative to demand is more important than for oil, gas and coal. These are more cheaply transported per equivalent therm than electricity and can be used directly as well as being converted into electricity at power stations that can be located closer to demand.

The *ecological* sources of energy have been used in the past. Although they are renewable, there are biological limits on their replacement rate, and there is often competition for the

use of land. The too rapid use of timber for fuel and charcoal and indeed for the competing uses of ship and house building contributed to the disappearance of much of the woodland in England and Wales before 1750. Clearance for agriculture was the major competing land use. In countries where there is less competition for land, ecological supplies may have greater potential; for example, in Brazil processed sugar cane is providing an alternative to petrol as car fuel. The ecological sources involve areal production that is spread over an area of space, whereas geological sources, in particular coal, usually involve production at a point on the surface or punctiform production. In Britain the change from areal to punctiform production of fuel in the eighteenth century contributed significantly to the geographical changes of the industrial revolution, especially for the iron and steel industry. This changed from being small scale and charcoal based in areas like the Forest of Dean and the Weald to the larger-scale coal-based smelters of the Black Country (the West Midlands), the North, the Central Lowlands of Scotland and South Wales. Punctiform production of coal together with the new transport technologies of canal and railway permitted economies of scale for the iron and steel industry that developed on or near the coalfields.

The *built environment* also provides a source of energy. Appropriate technology has now been discovered to produce high quality fuel oil from ordinary household waste. The process changes organic matter into oil in ten minutes, a transformation that takes nature millions of years. Although this scheme, a Greater Manchester Council Project, has not yet been implemented, there were about a dozen local authorities in the UK which produced electricity or steam from the incineration of raw waste or refuse-derived fuel pellets. However, the UK lags far behind other countries in using this renewable source. It burns only 6 per cent of its waste while Denmark uses 75 per cent, Sweden 50 per cent and France and Germany 25 per cent of their waste to produce energy.

There are two indirect 'sources' from the built environment. One is the recycling of materials, where recycling not only saves the use of other non-renewable resources, it also may use less energy than processing new resources. The other major indirect 'source' is the more efficient design and insulation of buildings, which may conserve energy. When combined with economic, social, political and technological factors affecting the degree to which people conserve energy, this forms a determinant of energy demand. The argument is that resource conservation is substantially more cost effective than resource development; for example, spending a similar sum on promoting new energy conservation may be as cost effective as investing in a new power station. Returns on conservation investment are certainly more immediate than on power station development, as the Tennessee Valley Authority (TVA), the largest federally owned utility in the USA, discovered. In the USA in general, this direct comparability of conservation and new supply is accepted widely, whereas in the UK the Department of Energy and the Department of the Environment in the Sizewell inquiry stated that investment in conservation and supply cannot be meaningfully compared.

In the *human environment* the use of people's brain power to develop energy-related technology is clearly more important now than the use of their body power. Nuclear fission and more recently fusion provide the best examples of scientific research being applied to energy supply. The Sizewell B reactor is just one of a whole series of technologies within the nuclear arena.

Although the economic, social and political environments do not provide any other sources of energy as such, they are unequally supportive of particular sources in terms of prices, capital investment, employment opportunities, and social and political support. At the local scale, for example, coal-mining communities are likely to favour coal as a source because it is their livelihood and often the reason for the existence of their community. At the national scale, in Britain, much economic and political support is given to the nuclear industry. It has important ties to the military industrial complex, so much scientific research is linked to its development. It is highly capital intensive and the relatively few employees involved in it are not known for their militancy. This is seen as an added advantage by some, compared with the main established alternative, the coal industry. On the global scale, the transnational oil companies and the Organisation of Petroleum Exporting Countries (OPEC) exert considerable power in maintaining oil and gas as major forms of energy. Even they were not able to manage supply in relation to demand well enough to prevent the major fall in oil prices in 1986. OPEC, however, was able to engineer the massive price rise in 1973. Both price movements had an effect on the future supply and demand for oil.

The different sources and their use, then, involve different research, installation, and running costs. They involve different combinations of capital, labour and land as inputs. Present technologies suited to the varying sources entail different scales of production. In some cases energy is converted to electricity at the source; in others, the ecological and particularly geological materials may be transported some distance to the power station. So the impacts on the three major types of environment made by the harnessing of the sources may be very different, the

geographies they produce vary and the direct and indirect costs are difficult to compare.

Effects of the choice of sources: regional

Choice between sources may also involve wider economic, social and political factors. If two different sources are available in different regions of the same country, the use of one rather than the other may stimulate economic development in one of those regions, possibly at the expense of the other. However, particularly in advanced countries there are complex economic interactions between regions so that development in one area may stimulate business in another through the extra demand for goods and services. This, of course, takes time and the initial advantage of the first area may be retained. The French government, unlike the British, have had very little local opposition to their nuclear power plants partly because they have suggested that they will bring economic development to the areas as they are planned as integral parts of growth centres. Whereas in Britain they are seen as potentially dangerous or at least environmentally detrimental, nuclear plants in France are seen by many as ways of stimulating regional growth.

The planned move towards nuclear and away from coal-based electricity in Britain has also accentuated the closure of coal mines. The social and political as well as economic cost of closures has to be borne in mind. If there are no other local job opportunities, unemployment or, if economically feasible, migration to areas where there is a demand for labour will result. The decline in the demand for local services both will bring may result in further job losses, house prices will fall relative to other areas and migration will become even less feasible. In such circumstances social unrest and political action, as in the British miners' strike of 1984/85, are likely to occur. Energy policies, then, can have major economic, social and political effects on the regional geography of a country.

Effects of the choice of sources: national

The choice between sources may involve economic and political factors at a different geographical scale, between countries rather than within them. A country's government may decide to develop home-based energy sources rather than rely on imported ones, so that its *balance of payments* is improved (balance of payments is the difference between the value of exports and imports). One reason for the French investment in nuclear power and in renewable sources such as tidal (at Odeille), solar (at Targasonne), geothermal and bio-mass energy is the desire to be less dependent on imported oil. It has

The miners' strike of 1984/85: confrontation between police and pickets

developed its nuclear fuel from its own uranium ore deposits (3000 tonnes approximately in 1985) in the Massif Central, Hérault and Brittany, as well as importing it, partly in order to conserve domestic resources. A country might also be able to export its energy resources, for example the UK's North Sea oil. It may also export the technology associated with such development, for example oil rigs. In the nuclear case, countries like Britain and France seek to export reactor types and to reprocess other countries nuclear waste, in order to earn revenue. Again the trade balance is positively affected. There may also be political factors influencing choices. The political instability in the Middle East, particularly in the 1973 crisis, has meant that many countries including France and the USA have sought to find substitute energy supplies because they did not want to be dependent on unreliable sources.

Relative costs of distribution

The sources may also involve different costs and kinds of distribution. Transport costs can obviously

change over time but in the 1970s electricity cost more per therm to transmit than oil, coal or gas.

This may affect the choice between types of energy. It is, not, however the only factor in the location of power stations. The efficiency of the conversion process from coal to electricity, for instance, will influence the form in which the energy is transported. The choice of location of a coal-fired power station requires the consideration of the cost of transporting three times the amount of coal equivalent to the electricity produced. It is therefore cheaper to transport the electricity than the coal and power stations are consequently coal-field orientated. Energy is also used and some lost in the transmission process. Pumping oil by pipeline involves less energy use and loss than transporting it by rail. Both methods of transporting oil use and lose less energy than the transmission of electricity. There is also a choice in the transmission of electricity between underground transfer and the cheaper, but environmentally detrimental, above ground transfer using pylons.

At a different geographical scale there may be a choice between pipeline and tanker transport of oil from production in one country to processing plant in another. Tankers are more flexible, but with their increase in size, fewer ports are deep enough to deal with them. They are better when there are many supplying countries and the processing country does not wish to be tied to one producer for strategic reasons. Pipelines are better when there is a long term transfer and where the pipeline crosses friendly, stable countries. Otherwise they are particularly vulnerable to terrorist attack. They can also be environmentally disturbing, witness the furore over the proposed Canadian gas pipeline to the USA (Chapter 7, Section 1), and the leakage from an oil pipeline into the Mersey (1989). The choice of the energy source then, in itself, involves different possible forms of transmission, and for any one source there are also different means of transmission which have different effects on the physical and built environments and therefore help to create different geographies.

Types of demand

The choice between sources is also very much influenced by the amount and type of present and predicted demand. The demand for electricity, for instance, as well as having long-term trends, has cycles which are daily or extend over periods of five to ten days, are typical of UK weather variations, and are seasonal. Different sources are more suited to meet the *peak load* of these cycles as against what is called the *base load*. Nuclear power is usually used for base load while coal and oil-fired stations meet the peaks. This is because of their different running costs; it is inefficient to run nuclear power stations under capacity and try to vary it to meet the peaks. HEP schemes, such as Ffestiniog in North Wales, pump water uphill using power during the low night-time demand in readiness to generate power from its descent during the peak daytime demand. In Third World countries the rapid urbanisation and growth of very large cities, which use much more energy per capita than rural areas, have meant a rapid growth in base demand, which some think can be met only by the development of nuclear power, so presenting a market for the nuclear technology of the First World.

The effect of the type of demand is best illustrated within homes where there is a choice of gas or electricity for cooking and a choice for space and water heating. Although people are influenced by the installation and running costs of the various supplies, they may also have a preference not based on price for a par-

ticular type of cooking or heating. If many more people preferred say gas cooking then this would affect the relative demand for gas over electricity. It is interesting to note that the built environment is having an effect on the type of demand; few new multi-storey buildings are having gas installed because of the risk of explosions.

Changes in demand may lead to increased energy use or more efficient use and conservation of energy. The changing technology of office work with greater deployment of computers, which need environments of constant temperature and humidity, means greater use of energy for the computers and for the maintenance of the environment through heating, air conditioning and humidifying machinery. In this case, the choice is between high energy use and cost, or somewhat less energy use but the added cost of energy conservation through better insulation and ventilation. Better design and materials aid conservation; for example, building office blocks with a central atrium allows passive air conditioning, through the mixture of office and atrium air.

Demand may also be influenced by marketing which may use *product, price, promotion and place (the four P's)* to influence people's expressed preferences. The Gas and Electricity Boards offer examples of such marketing for instance with their advertising of the 'cookability' of gas, and the Economy Seven pricing of electricity. Place means getting the good/service to the place where the consumers want it, at the right time. Demand may also be influenced by government policy, which may increase energy prices as an indirect taxation and/or a means of encouraging conservation activities. It can even increase the price of one form of energy-gas in the UK in the early 1980s – in order to restore competition between oil and gas central heating. Consumer behaviour is not, then, an independent, external factor but something that can be

influenced by marketing and government activity.

Pollution and waste

One of the promotional comments about electric cooking is that it is cleaner. Pollution, then, is a possible disadvantage of some sources even during consumption. Pollution and waste may occur at the stages of extraction, production/processing and distribution as well as consumption. Different sources of energy give different problems of pollution and waste at different stages. Nuclear fuel does not produce either the SO_2 or CO_2 of coal-fired stations which are linked with *acid deposition* (rain) and the strengthening of the *greenhouse effect*, respectively. The disposal of radioactive waste, however, is a problem which has not yet been satisfactorily solved. Again there are various options to achieve this end. Burial at sea or on land or storage on the surface are some of them. Not producing the waste in the first place is another. The environmental and social as well as economic costs of pollution and waste should be taken into account when deciding between different forms of energy supply.

Summary of the general problem

In summary we have considered the direct and indirect effects and costs of extraction, production, distribution, consumption and waste and these need to be considered in full when examining different energy alternatives. It is obvious from the discussion of Sizewell B that there is not one generally agreed view of an energy option. Different interest groups consider somewhat varying sets of factors, and where they are the same factors give them different weights and evaluate their effects and costs in varying ways. Some take a rather narrow view and do not consider all the costs and benefits – for example looking only at transport costs of taking nuclear waste to various sites rather than also considering the population at risk along the transport corridors. Some take an optimistic, others a pessimistic view of the disadvantages such as the dangers of nuclear power. They will also bring their own environmental, social and eco-nomic values to the argument. Some may emphasise small scale technology which may have less environmental costs, though the projects may occur in more areas and may use more labour, while others may press for large scale capital intensive projects which have greater but concentrated environmental effects.

Although it is relatively easy to state the general problem it is not at all easy to answer it, partly because of the varying attitudes and view-points. The problem is which set of physical and human resources to use that will most effectively and efficiently achieve the desired end – in this case harnessing and using energy – with the minimal amount of direct and indirect harmful or negative effects to the physical, built and human environments, and with the maximum benefit to the environment, economy and society.

3.3 Other examples

In the case study and general problem sections, different sources of energy have been discussed. Similar principles and arguments may be applied to the discussion of objectives other than energy. The further examples include food production, transport across the English Channel, building and heating homes and manufacturing cars. The discussion begins, though, with a comparison of some renewable energy resources so that there is a more complete view of energy alternatives.

3.3a Two other energy alternatives – sun and wind

Less controversial, yet less developed than nuclear power is the use of the sun and wind as energy sources. These sources are renewable and waste free. They vary in availability over both time (for example sunless and calm days) and space (for instance some locations would generate little wind power). Some areas, particularly coastal ones, are more exposed to wind, while some receive more sunlight, because of either their southerly aspect or their location relative to the paths of depressions. In 1985 the

Department of Energy increased to 2 per cent its estimate of the share that solar energy could contribute towards the UK total energy demand by AD 2000. This can be from direct or diffuse sunlight. Unsurprisingly the British government has invested least of all developed nations in research and development in solar energy – unsurprising since the British climate is hardly the most suitable (Figure 3.7) and the greatest period of sunlight and diffuse daylight, of course, is the season of least demand for energy. Even so, nearly £4 million was made available by the government in the late 1970s for research and development into domestic solar systems.

The conversion into energy of direct daylight and diffused light can be achieved in three ways. Firstly, the solar energy can be used to heat water for homes, but at present this is about as cost effective an exercise as double glazing for energy saving in a house – not much! Secondly, solar energy can be used for space heating but the problem of thermal storage has not been resolved. Finally, solar electricity probably offers the most potential for the UK since solar cells have been developed which are pollution free, contain no moving parts and require little maintenance. The amount of energy generated, of course, could satisfy only a limited local demand. The problem of storing the electricity, however, has yet to be successfully mastered and two of the largest oil companies are working on producing a methanol-air fuel battery – possibly the battery of the future.

3.7 Variations in insolation among countries

	Midsummer	Midwinter	Ratio	Annual mean
UK	18	1.7	10.0	8.9
Central USA	26	11.0	2.4	19.0
Southern France	24	5.0	4.8	15.0
Israel	31	11.0	3.0	22.0
Australia	23	13.0	1.8	20.0
Japan	17	7.0	2.4	13.0
India	26	14.0	1.9	20.0

(J per m² per day x 10⁶)
(Source: Department of Energy, Energy Paper No. 16, p. 21)

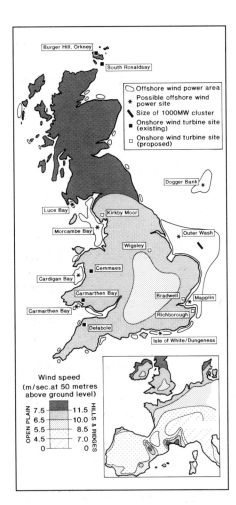

3.8 Wind power potential

Elsewhere, in the USA, France and southern Italy, solar power stations have been developed in which the sun's rays are focused on an array of mirrors converting water into steam to generate electricity.

More interest has been shown in the UK by government and industry in the harnessing of wind energy – unsurprising given the range of potential sites available for climatic and/or topographic reasons.

This is not a new energy alternative since 10,000 windmills were in action in the UK in the nineteenth century. It has been argued that with sufficient government commitment 2000 units per annum could be produced within five years. The present trend is for aerogenerators of 200 ft in diameter or more. North and west Scotland possess many possible sites for such aerogenerators but here there are problems of both transmission and scenic/noise pollution. An alternative location in shallow off-shore waters has been proposed. For example, the Wash offers a suitable shallow, windy area. The average wind speed in this region at a height of 50 m (the centre of the windmill) is 9 metres per second and therefore a cluster of 400 windmills half a kilometre apart would provide a power output of 1000 MW. It has been suggested that the area between 10 and 50 kilometres from the coast in shallow water less than 20 metres in depth exceeds 4000 square kilometres – if one half of this area was zoned for wind-power generation it is estimated that one-third of our present electricity requirement could be supplied. At a very different, more local scale, smaller wind power projects could serve farms and remote areas which are not served by the national grid.

An estimate in 1975 of the capital and running costs of nuclear, solar, wind and wave energy (Figure 3.9) shows the clear advantages of wind power.

Solar and wind power have major environmental advantages in comparison to the relatively damaging (or at least potentially so) coal, oil and nuclear sources of electricity. The political will to support their future development, however, is at present lacking in the UK, not least probably because of the relative

Aerogenerators

abundance of coal and oil. Furthermore, the scale of technological research and capital investment needed for a government seriously to move towards a future based on renewable alternatives may be an additional disincentive, but increased environmental concern and the reduction of non-renewable reserves may lead to a change in direction for energy policy.

3.9 Is nuclear power cheaper?

		Capital cost	Annual running cost	Total for 20 years
Nuclear	(a) no storage	174	3.6	246
	(b) 150-h storage	90	2.1	132
Solar panels		85	0.5	95
Wind		49	0.8	65
Wave		125	3.0	185

The capital and running costs per unit ($) in 1975 (for all non-nuclear systems, costs include storage)

3.3b Agribusiness or permaculture? - or how best to produce food?

The trends of farming in advanced countries are clear. High yields and profits are gained by increasingly industrial and large-scale methods. Such *agribusiness* relies on large doses of organic fertilisers and an array of selected herbicides, insecticides and fungicides, the effects of which on future soil fertility, flora, fauna and human beings are not fully known. Such production consumes enormous quantities of fossil fuels; for instance, in the USA for each unit of food energy produced at least one and a half units of fossil fuels are consumed by agriculture and related activities. The large-scale application of chemicals continues to increase; for example, in the UK in 1974-1975 nitrogen fertiliser consumption was 979,900 tonnes yet by 1980-1981 this had risen to a costly 1,335,000 tonnes. The impact on natural systems of applying large quantities of chemicals has caused increasing concern in recent years. However, this approach to producing food, it has been argued, is financially rewarding to large scale farmers and the food-processing industry.

A radical alternative would be to engage in *permaculture* or *organic farming* – a self-sustaining, cultivated ecosystem pioneered in Australia and characterised by producing more energy than it consumes, which does not destroy its own base through misuse of soil or water resources, meets local needs, and finds all necessary nutrients on site without depending on inorganic fertilisers. The latter would be replaced by crop residues, livestock manure, legumes such as clover, sewage sludge and other waste. These would give sufficient nutrients for growth – mainly nitrogen, phosphorous and potassium. Additional mechanical cultivation would keep weeds at bay and crop rotation would help control insect pests. The savings in chemicals, it is argued, would easily cover the cost of employing more labour. Output would be maintained, employment in farming massively boosted and there would be 70 per cent less energy input.

These two alternatives of producing food, the organic and agribusiness (Figure 3.10), show how different combinations of input – land resources, capital and labour – can lead to the same product but with very different indirect effects. Whether organic farming will ever replace agribusiness depends on convincing a wealthy and powerful lobby of large-scale farmers and the food-processing industry of its economic viability, which is in doubt, and on overcoming the vested interests of the chemical industry. This may be encouraged by an increase in consumer demand for organically grown food, which is slowly occurring as more attention is being paid to connections between diet and health and there is more concern shown about the physical environment. It will, however, need a dramatic change to offset the momentum and power of agribusiness.

3.10 Two ways of producing food

Organic or permaculture	Large scale farming part of agribusiness
Mixed farming	Monoculture
Radical (though not dissimilar to traditional farming)	Economically efficient, established
Conserves	Pollutes
Low fossil fuel energy input	High fossil fuel energy input
Intensive use of land	More extensive use of land
Labour intensive	Capital intensive

(There are many possible ways of producing food. These are but two.)

3.3c Alternative ways of crossing the Channel

More people than ever before cross the English Channel each year and this is likely to continue, particularly as the European Community expands and not least as trade and immigration restrictions are reduced in 1993. Over 20 million people cross the Channel by ferry or hovercraft each year, compared to 5.5 million in 1962. One hundred and fourteen ferries are at present on this 'flexilink' route. There are two major issues: the choice between a new fixed link or retaining the flexilinks with their very different geographical impacts (Figure 3.11); and the choice between the alternative possibilities for a fixed link and their different forms and impacts.

There are certain advantages in retaining and improving existing ferry and hovercraft services, as Figure 3.11 shows. However, since the early nineteenth century when the idea of a fixed link between France and Britain was first mooted, a permanent land bridge has had a continuing appeal. In fact digging began in both 1882 and 1974. With the emergence of a strong European Community, to which Britain now sends over one half of its exports, the development of a fixed link has seemed inexorable. For different reasons, Thatcher and Mitterrand agreed to build such a link in 1985. Since then the pace of development has been hectic, not least because both countries feel it will stimulate

Alternative schemes	Technical and cost details	Points for	Points against	Possible impacts
Scheme 1 Channel Tunnel Group	Technical and cost details £2.6 billion twin-bore rail tunnel. BR and SNCF to share tunnel. Drive on, drive off shuttle service ,'The Chunnel'	December '85 All Commons Committee preferred it. Supported in France partly because of pro-rail policy there. Less impact on ferry traffic, uses existing tunnelling technology	Possibility of rabies brought into GB. Rail unions would have power to close. Potential target for terrorist attack.	Need transfer points from road to rail. Likely concentration of activity at termini. Need for special termini in Paris and London. Dispute over rail route in GB. Motorway traffic in NE France and SE England bound to increase
Scheme 2 Channel Expressway	£2.5 billion twin-bore motorway tunnel with separate twin rail tunnel	74% of people want drive through scheme	Costly technological development needed. Lacked support in France because initially a British suggestion. Potential target for terrorist attack	Need transfer points from road to rail. Likely concentration of activity at termini. Need for special termini in Paris and London. Dispute over rail route in GB. Motorway traffic in NE France and SE England bound to increase
Scheme 3 Euroroute	£5.6 billion bridge and tunnel scheme , road and rail. Bridge then submerged tube, 'Brummel'	74% of people want drive through scheme	Costly technological development needed. Potential target for terrorist attack	Need transfer points from road to rail. Likely concentration of activity at termini. Need for special termini in Paris and London. Dispute over rail route in GB. Motorway traffic in NE France and SE England bound to increase
Scheme 4 Eurobridge	£5.9 billion motorway road bridge scheme	74% of people want drive through scheme	Costly technological development needed. Potential target for terrorist attack.. Pro-Rail lobby in France angered	Even greater expansion of motorway traffic. Possibility of new motorways
Scheme 5 Flexilink	Retain and improve existing ferry and hovercraft services	Existing technology and much cheaper. £1 million fixed link campaign. 40,000 jobs could be secured on ferries and ports. Choice of origins and destinations. Terrorist attack less effective	Less rapid. Subject to seamans' disputes and weather	More dispersed impacts than schemes 1 – 4. More jobs involved in running ferries and hovercraft

3.11 Alternative schemes for crossing the Channel

job creation and economic activity.

The likely environmental and spatial impacts of the alternatives put forward (Figure 3.11) are of great interest to geographers. Indeed, geographical debate over likely consequences has been taking place now for many years since a fixed link became more likely. Four alternative routes were submitted during 1985 and each would lead to three broadly similar types of impact:

(a) effects on physical environments, for instance the extent of damage to the cliff scenery and Sites of Special Scientific Interest (SSSI) such as Folkestone, Warren, and marine ecology generally;

(b) the disruption caused by the building period, which could involve the construction of a temporary harbour at Dungeness and which would lead to noise, dirt and traffic affecting villagers near tunnel or bridge terminals;

(c) the subsequent effects on the location of jobs, settlements and travel patterns.

The likely socio-economic impacts are perhaps the most controversial and could lead to massive negative and positive impacts on Kent (negative on east Kent ports and, from an economic viewpoint, positive for centres such as Maidstone and especially Ashford). Overall a fixed link could lead to a boom for parts of the South East of England and indeed for the depressed Pas de Calais area

in France. On the other hand, northern Britain looks on anxiously as a further boost is given to the relatively prosperous South East.

Yet the four schemes, as Figure 3.11 shows, have distinctive negative and positive impacts. The final choice, Scheme 1, the 'Chunnel', was announced in January 1986. This received much French support and was designed to use existing tunnelling technology. The future possible addition of a road tunnel built into the scheme partly satisfied the British government's preference for a dual link. In some ways it is the government's way of reaching a decision, rather than the decision itself, which is of interest here. There was not a public inquiry as for Sizewell or the Roskill Commission for the Third London Airport. The latter two investigations were wider in scope and the first involved questions about the need for such developments as well as their positive and negative impacts. This decision was narrow – not whether there should be a fixed link, but simply which kind of link. It was closed, the final discussions being in private between the French and British ministers and their teams. It was also rapid, taking only a hundred days rather than Sizewell's twenty-six months. Arguably these were decisions of equal importance, but perhaps they indicate that the choice of strategies for solving them is changing.

3.3d **Alternative methods of building and heating houses**

Housing is a very important part of the built environment and its spatial variation contributes much to the character of places. The type of housing that is built varies over time as well as space and involves the choice of building material, building technology, architecture and the layout and density of the housing. Since housing has quite a long life, these temporal variations can often be seen today juxtaposed within a limited spatial area, giving great variety to the urban landscape. These spatial and temporal variations are influenced by changes in the factors illustrated in Figure 3.12 and discussed below.

The traditional way of building houses in Britain until the industrial revolution was to use local building materials; these still lend much to an area's character, the millstone grit farmhouses of the northern Peak District and the limestone ones of the southern Peak District, for instance. The replacement of stone by bricks and the ability to transport these long distances cheaply by rail and later road led to rather standard brick-built housing nationwide. Similar spatial standardisation has occurred more recently on an even greater scale with the use of concrete and steel to build high-rise apartments in many countries. The rapid discolouring of concrete and more general dissatisfaction with high-rise has brought brick back into prominence.

The choice between materials has much to do with the technology used. In the 1950s and 1960s large building companies, employing concrete and steel, worked with prefabricated sections which could be mass produced in factories and assembled on site. This allowed economies of scale of production and substituted capital for labour. The use of timber frames in the 1970s and 1980s in Britain also allowed rapid assembly on site with the roof being built immediately, so that inside work could begin much earlier than with traditional building techniques. The advent of standardisation of components and mass production has led to a decline in the demand for traditional skills; for instance, the great quantity of plasterboard manufactured means that there is less need for plasterers. Indeed, it can be argued that one of the main reasons for the introduction of these new techniques and materials was the building companies' aim to have greater control over their workforce and be less dependent on expensive skilled labour such as plasterers.

The choice between low- and high-rise building partly involves materials and technology. The boom of high-rise (over five storeys) in many countries in the 1960s was also due to the influence of architectural fashion, following Le Corbusier's vision of 'cities in the sky'. In Britain, local government's adoption of such building in its redevelopment projects was also encouraged by subsidies for high-rise from the national government which wanted to stimulate the building industry and its use of new industrial techniques because it thought that this was a faster and cheaper way of providing much-needed accommodation. Criticisms of the buildings, their standard, their eventual cost and life within them culminated in the gas explosion at Ronan Point, east London in 1968 which triggered the removal of subsidies and local government's withdrawal from high-rise and a return to high-density low-rise public housing.

3.12 Factors affecting house building

Ronan Point after the gas explosion on the nineteenth floor. Five people died

In the owner-occupied market one choice is the varying sizes of estates. The emergence of national building companies such as Wimpey, Barratt and McClean (Tarmac), which seek economies of scale in production and marketing, has led to the building of very large estates with a limited number of house designs which are standard across the country.

Geographical differences in housing are therefore reduced. The search for large areas of cheaper land for these estates has also encouraged decentralisation of population from the cities, because such land does not usually exist within cities. Local government policy on the release of land for building obviously affects the location and rate of construction, while national and local development control influences the density at which housing is built. There are therefore a number of constraining factors on the choice of type of housing built.

As well as considering a number of ways of constructing a house, the builder also has a choice of methods for space heating. Since we began this chapter with a discussion of energy, it is useful to consider this choice at this scale of spatial unit. Gas, electric or coal fires can be installed or more commonly gas, oil-fired, solid fuel or electric central heating systems may be included.

The existing householder also faces these choices together with the possibility of using mobile heating, such as calor gas fires. As with other energy systems already discussed, comparison of both installation and running costs has to be made as well as questions of efficiency, maintenance, comfort and cleanliness. The running costs of any system can be reduced by various forms of insulation to conserve energy use. Legislation ensures that new housing is well insulated but occupants of older housing should consider the benefits and costs of installing loft insulation, with which government grants have assisted in Britain, cavity wall insulation and the least value for money in terms of heat insulation – double glazing. Government advertising in addition to the marketing by companies of their products ensures that many at least consider these energy conserving options. This is especially necessary since British housing has been particularly poor at conserving energy relative to that of other countries, where greater climatic extremes provided the incentive to apply better methods.

3.3e **Changed ways of making cars**

Originally Herbert Morris and other early car makers developed their businesses from coach and bicycle making concerns. They employed small numbers of skilled craftsmen who produced a rather expensive but hand-made product for a select market. Things changed with Henry Ford, who aimed at mass producing a cheap car for a mass market. His Model T Ford benefited from the early writings of Adam Smith on division of labour and redeveloped the car assembly line where car workers specialised to a minute degree on

Henry Ford and his son Edsel in a Model F, 1904 in front of the family house in Detroit. Inset: Model T

small tasks along the line. The benefits for production were outstanding and its cost dramatically declined.

By the early 1960s Henry Ford's methods began to be questioned because people were demanding more satisfaction from their work and wished to be treated less like bits of machinery. Worker unrest was displayed by strike activity. The line system suffers from the problem that the speed of the line determines the entire production process. Work comes along the line at predetermined intervals and the worker has to complete the work in the time available. Each worker was faced with a boring, repetitive, fragmented and low-skilled job. To the manufacturer this system means inflexibility of production whereby one hold-up, whether caused by worker, machinery or component part, can bring the entire line to a standstill.

SAAB and VOLVO in Sweden were the first car manufacturers to explore alternatives, not least because of the social environment of Sweden where its particular system of education has massively affected people's expectations. They began to implement changes in both work organisation and technology. Workers are organised in teams

which produce entire sub-assemblies such as engines or gearboxes. They are given a lot of choice in the way they work given their skill, experience and personal preference. Physical effort has been cut to a minimum, so women can do most jobs, and job cycle times have been increased from 1.8 minutes to 30 minutes in the case of SAAB. Job content was also improved, whereby several stages of assembly could be undertaken in rotation to avoid the monotony of just one task. Furthermore, more choice and consultation are now offered to employees. In addition new wage systems have been introduced, social aspects improved, and health and recreation facilities and training emphasised more. Much of this has been achieved through more constructive union-management relationships. The gains have been substantial and many of these ideas have been taken up elsewhere. They include: a reduced labour turnover; less absenteeism; improvement of productivity and quality; reduced staffing requirements; and fewer grievances such as at Tarrytown near New York, a General Motors plant, which had 2000 grievances in 1970 yet only two in 1978. These innovations have some costs. These have included a

slight rise in wage bills, training bills and the cost of building new plants. Nowadays, however, the newer approaches are considered fully cost effective and are now widespread.

Automation has substituted machines for people. In Sweden such changes have included automatic paint spraying and multi-weld systems. Even more revolutionary has been the introduction of robots and automatic computer-controlled production systems. The Rover Group's Metro, for instance, has a body shell which consists of some eighty-five components brought together into some twenty-six major sub-assemblies by resistance spot-welding and fusion welding. All this is made possible by computerised production management. Essentially these systems allow flexibility to be increased and make quality control more immediate and effective. Also assembly 'islands' can be established, allowing workers to be responsible for a particular module in the production process.

So the ways of making cars in the 1910s, 1950s and 1980s have changed substantially as the relationships between workers, management and machinery have been transformed.

3.4 **Alternative strategies**

The preceding chapter discussed the general alternatives of the market and planning for deciding on the use of a particular resource. Both could be applied to resolve this chapter's problem of which resources to use to achieve an objective. The economic system is now, however, so complexly related to government action that for many objectives there is little possibility of market forces alone resolving the problem. Some may argue that decisions should be made on the prices of varying resources, supposedly reflecting the operation of the market, but those prices in

themselves have often been directly or indirectly influenced by government action. Equally important in this argument is the fact that market forces do not incorporate all the costs or indeed benefits of the development of the alternatives for they penetrate into many aspects of a country's life. Social, political and environmental factors would be ignored along with some economic factors if reference were made to the market alone. In consequence some kind of planning or government policy or strategy is adopted which tries to incorporate the wider ramifica-

tions of particular options. Sometimes these take the form of a widescale, public planning inquiry such as that intended for the Sizewell B proposal. In practice this did not consider the nuclear option in as broad a way as some would have liked. It was, however, more than just an inquiry on the particular site. It contrasts to the closed government decision on the form of the Channel Tunnel. This considered only the alternative forms. It did not debate whether such a link was necessary and what its consequences might be. It did not allow a public inquiry at which different groups could put their views. It is an example of a closed decision taken by a government for which it is accountable only at elections. So what has been called the planning as against the market strategy has a number of forms.

Rather than consider in any greater depth the mechanisms of market forces and planning by which a resolution can be reached (Chapter 2), this chapter discusses alternative strategies that influence which set of resources will be used. These include the use of renewable rather than non-renewable resources, varying scales of development, capital-versus labour-intensive development, and consumer values, whether they be motivated by self-interest or the social good. Again the three major types of environment provide the framework: the natural resources come from the physical environment; the scale of development is most obvious in its effect on the built environment, though of course it affects both the physical and human ones; while capital, and labour and consumer values are arguments within the human environment which affect both the physical and built ones.

Renewable and non-renewable resources

In the debate over energy sources a

change of strategy has recently been observed as more research and capital are going into renewable rather than non-renewable resources.

This is due partly to the more general concern over the rate of use of what some see as the earth's finite resources. *Pessimists* – many of them neo-Malthusians – (modern writers with views similar to Malthus) about future global population and resources argue that the known reserves of fossil fuel and many minerals are being used faster than they are being discovered. They also argue that the use of fossil fuels leads to major pollution which affects atmospheric, hydrological, ecological and physiological processes in a harmful way.

Optimists minimise the problems, emphasising the continual discovery of new deposits, of new technologies for extracting, transporting and processing them, of new production processes that use less resources, and of the development of substitution when through scarcity a particular resource becomes too expensive. The optimists' views clearly emphasise technology and economics. Not only the pessimists, however, would see the long term general need and often possibly short term gains of developing renewable resources and

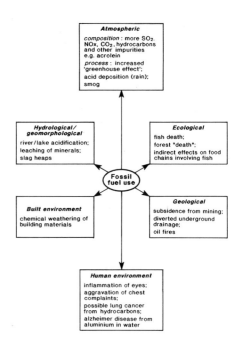

3.14 The effects of fossil fuels in the environment

recycling used products. The arguments for conservation of resources in general, not only energy, are very powerful whether you are an optimist or a pessimist about the world's future resources. *Conservation* makes more effective use of resources. It reduces pollution and waste of many kinds. It releases land for uses other than extraction, for example agriculture or tourism. It necessitates new technologies and

3.13 Renewable and non-renewable energy sources (1986)

	R&D spending on renewables		
	$M	Share of R&D energy budget %	Spending per capita ($)
Sweden	17.3	21.8	2.06
Netherlands	17.0	10.6	1.17
West Germany	65.9	11.6	1.09
Greece	9.7	63.2	0.97
Japan	99.2	4.3	0.82
USA	177.2	7.8	0.73
Spain	19.4	27.6	0.5
UK	16.6	4.4	0.29

Renewable		Energy/mass	Estimated costs (in p/kwh) Wallis Committee 1987
Organic:	wood		
	other biomass e.g. dung	low	
	biofuels e.g. landfill gas		
Inorganic:	solar		
	wind		2.26
	tides		3.23
	waves (on-shore, deep sea)	variable	(3.17, 5.00)
	hydro (small scale)		(1.35)
	geothermal (hot rocks)		3.01
Non-renewable:	coal		
	oil	high	
	natural gas		
Nuclear:	fission (uranium – 235)	very high	
	fusion (hydrogen – 3)		

goods, the production of which provides jobs which might somewhat offset loss of jobs in extraction. *Recycling* also requires extra skills and labour, and in using many home-based products in place of imported raw materials it may improve the balance of payments and reduce dependency on perhaps politically unstable countries. At the same time, however, it could have considerable initial consequences on extractive areas in advanced countries and especially in Third World countries who rely on their export of natural resources in order to fuel their own development.

Scale of development

A further set of alternative strategies that are concerned with this general problem is the scale of development which various technologies involve. For the built environment there is a debate about the desirability of high-rise office and apartment blocks. They can be built to high standards and offer intensive use of land. To some, the glass skyscrapers of the twentieth century are architecturally and culturally the equivalent of the cathedrals of the past. To others they are repugnant as they are not at a human scale and they obscure previously valued skylines. Some extend the argument to the scale of cities. Very large cities have been permitted to grow to that size by twentieth century technology, especially its transportation and communications. Some argue that there are diseconomies of scale for the economy and society of the city as a whole, through inflated land values, traffic congestion, pollution and superficial social contact. For Third World countries in particular, they argue that the infrastructural investment that is needed in these 'parasitic' cities would be more effectively spent on smaller cities and towns elsewhere in the country, which might then intercept the

migrants to the very large cities. Faster and better spatially balanced development, they argue, would then result. Again they argue socially that smaller towns are of a more human scale. Other writers, in contrast, do not think that there is a simple link between spatial structure or city size and social life.

The different scales for the development of nuclear as against solar or wind energy have already been discussed. A conscious decision to develop a few very large scale nuclear reactors in the UK instead of more, somewhat smaller ones, it has been alleged, has been made in order to minimise the amount of local opposition and the number of public inquiries. Paradoxically it is partly the scale of the reactor to which some people object because of the heightened danger if something should go wrong in the plant. It has been clearly shown that any policy to try to keep a low profile for nuclear power can be totally negated by disasters outside the country, the Chernobyl disaster in the USSR in the spring of 1986 being the most recent example. In general, the

objections to large-scale technology in these cases are environmental and social.

Some developmental strategies also oppose large scale, especially imported technology because development becomes concentrated in a few locations, scarce capital is used rather than plentiful labour and the technology is expensive. Some argue that these concentrated developments launch a country towards 'take-off' and that eventually the benefits are spread to other areas, while others suggest that the spread effects do not occur, regional disparities grow and in the extreme political instability may result. Some prefer small-scale simpler technologies which they argue are more appropriate to the level of development, employ more labour and spread skills, even if simpler ones, further afield. Consequently many regions advance together and the home market is developed. An extreme example of this thinking is the manufacture of radios in preliterate areas with little energy resources. A tin

Chernobyl after the explosion

can containing paraffin wax with a wick producing heat via a thermo-couple to operate an earplug speaker can form a radio which can be easily produced on a cottage industry scale. It minimises the use of resources and energy yet maximises the environmental and social benefits.

Capital-intensive or labour-intensive

The argument about capital-intensive investment is very current in advanced countries. In the 1970s and 1980s capital investment has proceeded while unemployment rates have increased. The overt argument for capital intensity is that productivity per capita increases faster and companies are more competitive. Others argue that the main reason for this trend is so that greater control over workers can be achieved. The fewer competing jobs there are, the greater is the control of management over workers. This keeps wage levels and, consequently, costs down and allows greater returns to capital. The latter argument suggests that differences in society are maintained and increased. Very generally those investing capital will gain most, while the employed will obviously be better off than the unemployed. The alternative strategy, then, is more labour-intensive investment in order to create jobs and reduce unemployment. Alongside that could go the advancement of industrial democracy through worker involvement, which has had little backing in capital intensive investment where management control has been strengthened.

Self-interest versus the social and environmental good

These alternative strategies are associated with production. There are fundamental alternatives too involving consumption. One concerns the degree to which individuals are motivated by self-interest as against the social good, for they do not always coincide. Consider someone who has consumed the contents of a bottle of fizzy orange on a beach and on leaving adopts the minimum effort of leaving the empty bottle on the sand. Someone else may be less anti-social, be aware of the danger of glass and place the bottle in a waste-paper bin. Someone with even more environmental awareness might carry the bottle off the beach for later depositing in the bottle bank skips for recycling.

Another example concerns the choice of transport to work. Cars are more flexible in time and space than buses or trains. You can drive almost door to door and leave at any time. You also have charge of your own immediate environment within the car, in terms of temperature, radio or cassette, and company. Yet the car uses much energy and con-tributes to air pollution, congestion and the demand for further road building. On the other hand, buses and trains have set routes and timetables, which may mean walking and waiting times. You share the immediate environment within them with other travellers and have little control over it. Yet, especially when full, they use much less energy and give off less pollution per person transported than cars, and would help to reduce congestion and the need for more roads. By no means everyone has the choice of transport, but for those who do, personal convenience often outweighs other goals. The influence on the individual of direct costs, stress and travel time is usually greater than the often unrealised indirect costs which are borne by society as a whole or sometimes mainly by a particular part of it. The car driving commuters often congest roads in areas where they do not live, which produces demand for wider and faster roads, the building of which can physically divide a community and destroy homes. These accumulated choices of commuting modes influence the built-form and human geography of the city.

The adopted strategies about the use of renewable rather than non-renewable resources, the scale of technology, capital- or labour-intensive investment, and consumption patterns have major effects on the human, built and physical environments. In short, different strategies produce different geographies.

3.5   Perspectives

From the previous discussion it is clear that decisions on the resources used, the organisation and technology of production, the means of distribution and the amount and type of consumption of a good have wide-ranging effects on the physical, built and human environments. In order to obtain an overview of these decisions and their effects, it is useful to establish what has been called the *ecological marketing channel* of the good (Figure 3.15). This shows the routes and institutions involved in the supply, production, distribution and consumption of a good from the original supply points through to the points of consumption and eventual waste.

The ecological marketing channel

The concept is illustrated by the nuclear cycle (Figure 3.16) and the car channels, both of which have been discussed in this chapter.

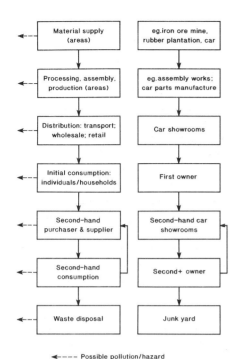

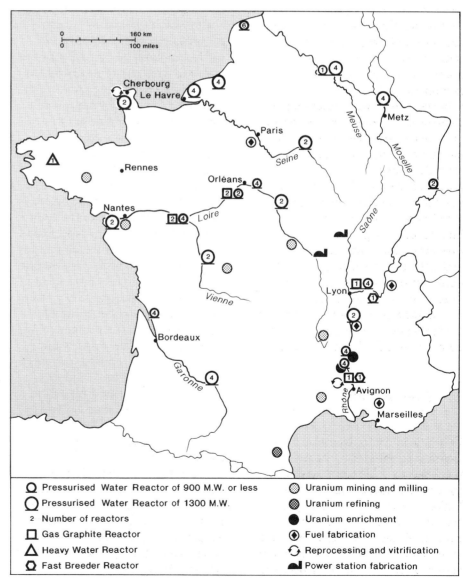

3.15 Cradle to grave: the ecological marketing channel - theory and application

costs and perhaps amounts of inputs at the production points. Improved technology in production, for example, may mean more efficient and less use of a raw material, while increased costs of supply may give the stimulus to improve production technology. Changes in demand may also have reverberations throughout the channel. The rapid increase in petrol prices in the mid 1970s led to a demand for more fuel efficient cars. The car manufacturers' response was lighter, smaller and more streamlined cars. The use of less and different materials to make the cars lighter affected resource supply areas as well as production techniques.

The supply points of all the inputs to a product like a car would indicate the mines for iron ore and other metals for the car body, and the rubber plantations for the tyres. Any substitution of these materials in production would affect these supply areas. So would a change in the relations between owners and labour, or use of capital as against labour in the supply areas, potentially affect

There may also be changes along the channel produced by reactions against the form and/or amount of waste/pollution. In the case of the car the environmental lobby in America applied pressure to remove lead in petrol, which meant that all new car engines had to be manufactured to work on lead-free petrol. This was sold alongside leaded petrol in gas stations much earlier than in Britain. The consumer lobby in the USA, led by Ralph Nader, caused new, more stringent safety regulations to be passed which also affected the design and content of cars. These regulations meant that car manufacturers wishing to export to the USA also had to amend their

3.16 The French nuclear cycle: marketing channel and its spatial expression

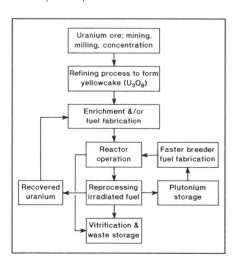

cars for that market. Changes in regulations in one country, then, affect parts of the channel in others. It is the inclusion of these possible environmental effects that distinguishes the ecological marketing channel from the more common concept, the marketing channel.

The ecological marketing channel concept has a number of uses. Firstly, it demonstrates that changes in one part of the channel affect others, so we should not examine any one of raw material supply, production, distribution, consumption of waste, pollution in isolation. Secondly, it emphasises the *interdependence of geographical areas*, whether that is at the interregional scale within a country or at the international scale, with particular regions or nations specialising in one or more of the levels in the channel. Thus it makes us consider the spatial organisation of the channel. Thirdly, it makes us consider the *power relationships* between the levels in the channel, so that we can see whether it is the suppliers, producers, distributors or consumers who dominate the channel. This relates to the second point because we can then determine which regions or countries are dominant within the interdependent relations. If there are dominant regions or nations then the channel is useful to highlight the form and inequality of the interdependence. Finally, these all help us to reach conclusions on the aims of this chapter, since we can compare and evaluate two different ecological marketing channels. We can compare, for example, the nuclear and coal systems, or car/road commuting and rapid transit systems. The debate is then much wider than where we locate a nuclear power station, or low level nuclear waste, or which coal pits we close; consideration of the whole channel permits the evaluation of the consequences of following a particular way of harnessing energy. While this is ambitious, it ensures that social and environmental con-

siderations are made as well as economic ones. It also means that the national and international consequences of our actions and policies are now seen. A number of these points will be developed and illustrated in later chapters.

One point to emphasise here is the consideration of the gains and losses of the whole system, not just a small part of it. When individuals make a choice, say between car and bus for getting to work, usually there are limited criteria on which that choice is based. The consequences of many individuals making the same small decision, say the car, may be major traffic congestion, air pollution, increased road building, more traffic accidents and possibly eventually the loss of the bus service alternative altogether. The aggregate result of all these individual decisions, based on limited criteria, may be something that none of the individuals wants. Such unwanted and unconsidered outcomes result from what is called the *'tyranny of small decisions'*. Individual choice can be short-sighted. Emphasis on this wider view in education, in information from local and central governments and in policy-making may make individual choice less short-sighted.

Changing from one combination of resources or ecological marketing channel to another, to produce or achieve some objective, is not a simple thing. It is not just a question of making individual consumers or producers aware of more and wider implications of operating in a particular way. It is not as though one decision was made at one point in time to operate in a particular way in the first place. It is much more likely a whole series of events, including decisions, which bring about a way of doing things: the build-up of technological know-how or, more formally, research and development in certain fields rather than others (nuclear rather than renewable energy resources for instance); a way of economic think-

ing; a social form and organisation within which production and distribution methods fit; and a political form, all of which support and sustain certain combinations of resources. There is considerable inertia. The momentum from the technological, economic, social and political environments, which are often mutually supporting, produces almost a way of life, certainly a set of value systems, which are difficult to challenge, let alone change. This becomes all the more difficult in an area like nuclear power which, because of its links to nuclear weapons and defence and its susceptibility to terrorist attack, means that in many countries it is shrouded in secrecy. Lack of or poor information is confounded by alternative ways of interpreting what is available. Some experts, for example, point to the clusters of child leukaemia around nuclear sites and assume that association in space implies a causal link, while others indicate the clusters that do not coincide with nuclear sites and suggest that the spatial clusters are random and that the association of some with the sites is fortuitous. The scientific evidence in itself, then, is often debatable and such disputes frequently occur in many levels of the channels. It is no wonder that particular ways of doing things survive for so long.

The uniqueness of place

The ecological marketing channel extends across space and is a useful way of comparing different ways of 'producing' goods, services, power, transport and construction. As geographers we are also interested in how all these combine to make and give the *unique character to a place*. In itself the adoption of a particular combination of physical and human resources rather than another may have major effects on the character of a place. A particular place may also play different roles, that is specialise in different levels of various ecological marketing channels which involve particular processes and functions that contribute to its unique character. Contrast, for example, Stoke and Blackpool, with Stoke's contracting pottery industry, its derelict land from past coalmining and steel industry and its 1986 garden festival on what was derelict land, and Blackpool's consumption-oriented atmosphere of summer holiday-making which has changed its form over the years from traditional boarding houses to guest houses and holiday apartments, extended its season into the autumn by the illuminations and used its large hotels to make it a major conference centre. The history of the places is very important. It is the way that these roles and their associated processes and functions combine and are superimposed upon one another over time that gives a place its uniqueness. Sometimes remnants from past functions and processes can still be seen in the built environment, often playing new functions in the present: the castle, representing defence and control functions in the past, functions now as a tourist attraction which may complement a present role such as a festival of arts, as in Edinburgh. Other processes, such as labour management relations, are less tangible but no less important, in that the way they have been practised in the past influences the roles that the place performs in the present. So while the ecological marketing channel is an important concept in showing the interdependencies between places, the importance of the intersection and interaction of different channels in one place must not be neglected.

Examining how the ecological marketing channels of many goods and services have intersected and interacted in one place enables us to understand the uniqueness of that place. An area may have played the role of raw material supplier in one channel, manufacturer in another and consumer in still more. The North East of England, for example, was a producer and exporter of coal, a manufacturer of steel and a builder of ships. In this example the roles do not just intersect; they interact, as the coal was used in the steel industry and the steel in the shipbuilding. The roles that areas play change over time in a complex way, with past roles influencing, sometimes preventing, present ones. The old, now declining industries of the North East were dominated by male employment. This presented the opportunity of a cheap, unskilled, unorganised female labour force which in the 1960s and 1970s proved attractive for new industries like electrical goods. Female employment thus rose from being 20 per cent of the workforce in 1901, far below the national average of 30 per cent, to just below the national average of 45 per cent in the early 1980s. The area now plays new roles in new channels as well as playing amended roles in old channels, as a result of changing demand for and foreign competition in the old industries.

A place, then, is affected by changes within existing channels and by the advent of new ones. Existing roles it plays, through the built and human environments produced, may affect the possibility of entering new channels and influence the type of role it plays within those channels. Its physical environment is also important, in that new resources may be found or new uses or new technologies may produce a demand for known resources of the area. In this case the area may emerge as a supply area, in the way that Britain has done during the 1970s and 1980s from North Sea oil.

Interdependence between areas

In the above discussion it is implied that what happens in other regions and other countries affects what happens in an area, whether it is changes within a channel in which the area already plays a part, or the arrival in that area of a new channel. So while this chapter poses the question about which combination of resources, technology, capital and labour to use for a good or service, it is clear that people in one area cannot answer that question in isolation of other areas. Just as we are influenced by the tyranny of small decisions, we are also influenced by the interdependence with the wider world. We are affected by actions elsewhere.

Summary

The perspectives that have been emphasised in this chapter revolve around the concept of the ecological marketing channel. The concept focuses attention on the whole system, the interrelationships between the various functional levels of it, their spatial organisation and the often unequal spatial interdependencies between areas that specialise in those functional levels. It also shows how many limited decisions and deep-seated value systems contribute to establishing and reinforcing certain systems rather than others. Finally, the roles that particular areas play within channels have been shown to influence their unique characters.

3.6 Exercises

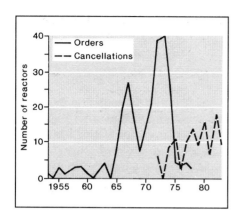

3.17 The impact of Three Mile Island on the US nuclear reactor industry

1. Study Figure 3.17 which shows the changing state of the nuclear reactor market in the USA.
   (a) Describe the trends illustrated.
   (b) Using this chapter and wider research, suggest what factors might explain these trends.

2. The modal split problem for long distance transport: How to get from Calais to Marseilles?
   (i) Student
   (ii) Executive
   (iii) Family with young children
   (a) Fill in the matrix for the roles (i), (ii) and (iii).
   (b) Compare and discuss the results with fellow students.

3. Figure 3.18 shows the regional distribution of electricity generating capacity from different sources. It represents the spatial organisation of one level of ecological marketing channel for electricity.
   (a) Using appropriate techniques, map the regional distributions.
   (b) Describe these distributions.
   (c) Attempt to explain them.
   (d) Using the information in the figure and other sources, including this chapter, discuss the geographical implications of a change in policy on developing nuclear power stations.

4. In this question we are examining the effects of change in one level of the ecological marketing channel of food on its other levels.
   Discuss the geographical effects on agriculture, food processing and retailing of dietary changes by consumers such as less consumption of animal fats (meat and dairy produce).

3.18 Electricity generating capacity

Installed capacity, MW (Megawatts)

Area Electricity Board	Coal pre-1960	Coal post 1960	Oil pre-1960	Oil post-1960	Nuclear	Hydro and pumped storage	Gas turbine	Total
London	–	–	330	345	–	–	140	815
South Eastern	308	1920	–	2691	410	–	318	5647
Southern	–	1820	95	1932	–	–	240	4087
South Western	85	–	–	–	1470	3	–	1558
Eastern	347	2548	248	–	665	–	458	4266
East Midlands	1494	5948	–	–	–	–	338	7780
Midlands	1600	3636	–	–	700	–	314	6250
South Wales	338	2027	–	1900	–	–	151	4416
Merseyside & North Wales	228	1880	–	480	1230	999a	118	4935
Yorkshire	908	6917	–	–	–	–	367	8192
North Eastern	972	1100	–	–	–	–	68	2140
North Western	802	112	–	–	–	–	–	914
Total	7082	27908	673	7348	4475	1002a	2512	51000

a includes 890MW pumped storage

Source: Data from CEGB Statistical Yearbook 1983/4

3.7 **Further reading**

J.E. Allen (1992) *Energy Resources for a Changing World,* Cambridge University Press

A. Blowers and D. Pepper (1987) *Nuclear Power in Crisis*, Croom Helm

J. Blunden and A. Reddish (eds.) (1991) *Energy, Resources and Environment*, Hodder and Stoughton (Open University)

D.R.Cope, P. Hills and P. James (eds.) (1984) *Energy Policy and Land-Use Planning*, Pergamon

B. Ilbery (1992) *Agricultural Change in Great Britain*, Oxford University Press

Geography 16-19 Project Booklet (1983) *Energy and the Environment,* Longman

P. Sarre (ed.) (1991) *Environment, Population and Development*, Hodder and Stoughton (Open University)

Chapter 4

ORGANISING PRODUCTION AND SERVICES

4.1   Case study: Different ways of organising and financing local transport

The history of public transport in London since 1933 is one of changing organisation, finance and control. (Figure 4.1). Most recently control changed from local to central government with the London Regional Transport body (LRT) being established to be directly responsible to the Minister of Transport. Increasingly the way the bus and underground systems are run is determined by the political ideologies of those in control. This has been reflected over time for example in capital expenditure. (Figure 4.2). This new body (LRT), which has been controlled by a Conservative minister, is very different from its predecessor, the London

4.1 The recent history of the organisation of public transport in London

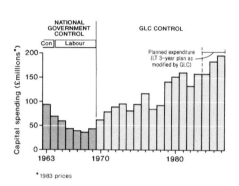

4.2 Capital spending by London Transport 1963-1986

Transport Executive (LTE), which was controlled by a Labour Greater London Council (GLC). The transport strategies associated with these particular political stances have been quite distinctive, as Figure 4.3 shows.

The debate over the 'Fares Fair'

Policy introduced by the GLC in 1981 was an interesting example of a change of financing. Fares were dramatically reduced and as a result passengers using London Transport increased while car traffic decreased.

The London Borough of Bromley, however, took the GLC to the High Court since it objected to the added tax/rate burden for their rate payers, many of whom did not use LTE services, particularly since the underground railway (Tube) system does not extend as far as Bromley. On the other hand, it is worth pointing out that Bromley commuters do benefit from the subsidised Southern Region of British Rail (BR). This action was successful, and 'Fares Fair' was withdrawn in 1982 with clear impacts on the use of public and private transport (Figure 4.4). In 1983, however, LTE was allowed to reduce fares by 25 per cent alongside the introduction of Travelcards, which partly reversed the 1982 changes.

In spite of political posturing there has been considerable common ground, during the last ten years or so, over policies towards London Transport. Whichever body (and related party) has been in power, it has been faced with a large dominance of people travelling to work by car, compared with other modes of transport. In 1981, for instance, within the GLC area, 43 per cent of journeys to and from work were made by car; 16 per cent on foot; 14

The recent history of the organisation of public transport in London	
1933	London Passenger Transport Board, a public body, ran bus, trams, trolleybus and underground services in London and South East
1948	London Transport Executive (LTE) takes over. It is a part of the state owned British Transport Commission
1962	London Transport Board is set up as a separate nationalised industry, responsible to the Minister of Transport
1970	London Transport Executive (LTE) established to operate red buses and the underground. LTE is under the overall financial and policy control of the Greater London Council (GLC). Country Buses and Green Line Coaches are made a subsidiary of the National Bus Company
1984	London Regional Transport (LRT) created. It is responsible to the Department of Transport
1985	London Buses Ltd and London Underground Ltd are established as wholly owned subsidiary companies of LRT

Overall control	Department of Transport (DOT) Conservative	Greater London Council (GLC) Labour
Transport Organisation	London Regional Transport (LRT)	London Transport Executive (LTE)
Strategy	'Value for Money'	'Quality of Service'
	Low subsidy	High subsidy
Policy	Reduce services to viable routes only	Extend services wherever possible
	Raise fares	Lower fares
Impacts	More 'efficient' use of money	Meeting a social need
Critique	Financed by users	Financed by non-users
	Reduced service/system	Increased service/system
	Less labour	More labour
	More congestion/accidents/pollution on roads	Less congestion/accidents
	Less tax burden	Less pollution on roads
	Less safe because lower investment in safety procedures	Higher tax burden
	Run down of service and high fares	Inefficient use of public money (oversubsidised fares)

4.3 Political stances on transport strategies in London in the early 1980s

per cent by bus; 11 per cent by Tube; 9 per cent by British Rail; 3 per cent by cycle; and 2 per cent by motorcycle. Policy can only marginally affect these figures. (Figures 4.4, 4.5).

LTE and LRT, in spite of quite different controlling agencies and underlying political ideologies, have in fact implemented similar policies on:

- Extending the Tube network (Heathrow and Terminal 4)

4.4 Impacts of changing fare structures on modes of commuting into central London

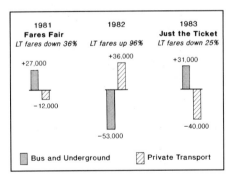

- Building the Docklands Light Railway
- Cleaning up and modernising Tube stations
- Bus services for the disabled
- Simplified ticket issuing, inspection and fare structures including Travelcards now allowing 800,000 people to move between the bus, Tube and railway networks of London.

Contrasts with other cities

British cities have been working their public transport systems with consistently less subsidy support than other European cities. So, for instance, in 1979 figures for the percentage of revenue from fares were as follows:

75 per cent for London
67 per cent for a group of British cities
52 per cent for a group of German cities

44 per cent for Paris
27 per cent for New York

Paris has probably the public transport system most comparable to that of London, being of a similar size and age. In contrast to London, however, throughout the 1970s there was a steady increase in use made of the system. A high quality of service is offered via a modernised integrated (Metro, railway and bus) and extended system. Much earlier than in London, the so-called 'orange' ticket system allowed passengers easily to pay for and transfer between Metro, bus and railway. This was made possible by significant injections of central government's resources into capital costs as well as annual financing by state, regional, local authorities and employers. Nowadays the system is regarded as a success in the achievement of its employment and structural goals.

4.5 Modes of transport to and from work, London 1981

Area of workplace	Car	Motorcycle	Underground	BR train	Taxi	Bus	Cycle	Walk	Other	Row Total (%)
Central	114	14	202	176	4	95	15	44	–	664 (14.3)
Inner	448	24	153	68	5	257	37	250	1	1 243 (26.8)
Outer	1384	67	158	185	6	313	103	444	2	2662 (57.5)
Outside	50	2	–	4	–	3	1	1	–	61 (1.3)
Total	1996	107	513	433	15	668	156	739	3	4630 (100.0)
(%)	(943.1)	(2.3)	(11.1)	(9.4)	(.3)	(14.4)	(3.3)	(16.0)	(.1)	(100.0)

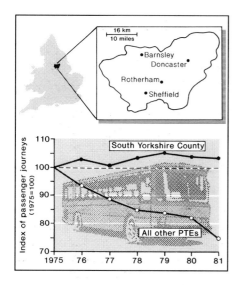

	S Yorks	Manchester	Leeds	Birmingham
2 miles	5	30	30	32
5 miles	10	58	50	40
10 miles	15	70	70	70

4.6 Contrasting use of public transport systems

4.7 Bus fare structures for different conurbations, 1984 (figures in pence)

New York, on the other hand, although its system was equally old and extensive, attempted, through the creation in 1968 of the New York Metropolitan Transportation Authority, to bring 'order and uniformity' to public transport. The new authority unified city subways and buses with suburban railways and bus lines. In the late 1970s total traffic increased, especially on the suburban systems. In principle the authority is self-financing but annually it generates heavy deficits made up by state and federal grants. Unlike the Paris system, New York public transport gives a distinctly run-down impression, not helped by high levels of vandalism.

Within Britain there has been an extreme example of a highly subsidised public transport system that of South Yorkshire, to which the GLC was most attracted. South Yorkshire is an area of contrasts including extensive countryside as well as the four cities of Sheffield, Rotherham, Doncaster and Barnsley (Figure 4.6).

In 1974 South Yorkshire

Transport (SYT) was formed with the main objective of providing everyone in South Yorkshire with access to an adequate range of opportunities for work, shopping and leisure activities.

SYT contrasts markedly with LRT. Its policy for the last ten years or so has been underpinned by the following principles:

- to relieve pressure on roads by encouraging greater use of public transport which saves energy and generates less pollution;
- to allow the system to be affordable by the less privileged in society and this is paid for by the more privileged and wealthy;
- to invest in and improve the system since improvement leads to greater use which in turn leads to more improvements.

This has meant that passenger journeys by public transport have increased in spite of an overall loss of population in South Yorkshire. The biggest increases have been in carrying children and young adults. Special services have been introduced and have proved a success. These include free bus transport for the disabled; very cheap rates for children and students; free off-peak travel for the elderly; the introduction of night buses; early morning and Sunday buses; 'Nipper' buses (smaller buses able to get to less accessible pockets of demand); and 'Clipper' buses (a single deck bus service around the centre of Sheffield linking the bus and rail-

way stations with the City's elongated shopping centre).

Since 1974 bus mileage, bus passengers and the bus fleet have increased. The economics of this system depended on 22 per cent of operating costs (1983) being met by fares and the rest by South Yorkshire County Council whose monies came from county rate payers and a central government grant. Fare structures were simplified and cheaper than similar public transport executives (Figure 4.7). From spring 1984 a simplified fare scale was introduced on all SYT buses with single fares of 5 pence, 10 pence, 15 pence and 20 pence and a maximum of 25 pence.

So, South Yorkshire had an enviable public transport system which was much used and well maintained, but at a cost to rate payers locally and tax payers nationally. Underlying its policy was a political belief in access to public transport, particularly for the less privileged, in contrast to LRT's belief in a public transport system that largely pays its way in a market economy. More recently policy on fares has been affected by the deregulation of buses and the relative reduction of local public expenditure which has been brought about by central government policies. Although South Yorkshire's fares are still lower than those of many other British cities, the difference is no longer so great.

4.2 General problem

The case study has examined different ways of organising local transport. It has shown how local transport is subsidised by national or local taxes to varying degrees, in different places and at different times. When transport is subsidised, people pay through their fares for only part of the real cost of their journey. The degree of subsidy is but one aspect of organisation that may have considerable geographical effects, as will later be shown. The degree of subsidy is part of the *financial* organisation of a service or industry. Other aspects of organisation that will be discussed in this section are *ownership, management, accountability* and the *involvement* of both *workers* and *consumers*.

In the preceding chapter we examined the different ways a set of physical and human resources could be combined to meet an objective and saw the effects of these, from cradle to grave, throughout their ecological marketing channels. In this chapter we are studying a particular combination of resources and seeing the effects of the ways in which they are organised. Every one of the organisational aspects may be spatially variable and have different geographical effects. This chapter aims to show the different direct and indirect geographical effects of the ways in which a service, industry or indeed country can be organised. Its general problem is how best to organise the service or industry in order to meet particular social, economic, political and environmental goals. In this section we shall study the aspects of organisation and mention some of the goals that will be examined in more detail in the perspectives section. We shall pay particular attention to transport but also broaden the argument to include other industries and services. In the alternative strategies section, recent changes in the forms of organisation will be more closely scrutinised.

Ownership

Ownership is considered by some to be the key aspect of organisation. The debates about the form of ownership of a particular service or industry and the amount of public and private ownership in the economy as a whole certainly give that impression. The division is far from simple, though, since there is considerable variation within each sector and there are all kinds of shades along a continuum from public to private. In the case study, for example, cars in cities are mostly privately owned but the roads they use are mostly publicly owned and financed. Private roads with users paying tolls, however, are an option that is further along the private end of the continuum.

Private ownership can vary from a company which is privately owned by a family to a company which has shareholders, with those shares being publicly quoted on the Stock Market. An example of the former is Littlewoods, the British high street store and mail order company. Tottenham Hotspur, the London soccer club, became an example of the latter during the 1980s. An organisation may be owned outright by an individual, and that individual may then *control* the activities of the organisation. Alternatively ownership may be shared by many individuals or bodies with one having a controlling interest or majority share.

An individual or body with more than a 50 per cent share of the company may be said to be in control. In some situations, though, there are so many individuals and bodies, such as insurance companies or pension funds, with shares in the organisation that it is argued that effective control of the organisation's activities lies with the senior management. The management deals with the medium- and long-term strategies of the organisation as well as its day-to-day running. The type of management rather than ownership may then be as important, or more important, in influencing the activities of a company, its geographical decisions and its geographical effects.

Public ownership, where the organisation is owned by some form of government, can also vary; for example, it can be owned at different spatial scales, by different levels of government – local, regional (state in the USA) or national (federal). In both Britain and the USA the library service is a local public service. In the USA non-private education is 'owned' and organised at the local school district level. The British Water Authorities were examples of regional public ownership until 1989 when they were privatised. British Rail, the National Coal Board and the National Health Service are all examples of national level ownership, though they are all organised to some extent at a regional level for administrative purposes. Here again ownership is not necessarily the same as control. The management of a publicly owned body may well exert a strong influence on its activities.

Thus the benefits and profits from these different types of ownership go to different sets of people: the private owners (private companies), the shareholders (public companies), and the whole population at local, regional or national scales for the different forms of public ownership.

The *continuum between private and public* is illustrated by companies which are or were partly owned by the government (the government once owned 51 per cent of British Petroleum for example) and quangos (quasi-autonomous non-governmental organisations). These are semi-public bodies which the government financially supports. The government also makes their senior appointments. British examples include the Arts Council, the Countryside Commission, the Housing Corporation, the Equal Opportunities Commission, the Race Relations Board and the Training Agency (once the Manpower Services Commission, now TEED).

Degree of competition

The debate about private or public ownership often concerns a particular industrial sector rather than an individual company and as such, more often than not, revolves around the *degree of competition* within that sector. Yet private ownership of an industrial or service sector in itself may vary from ownership by many small companies to a *private monopoly* where one company totally controls the market. One of the best examples of a private monopoly is British Gas (privatised in 1986). The degree of competition may be very different along the spectrum from many small companies to a private monopoly.

People often argue for private ownership because of its traditional association with a high degree of competition in some industrial sectors. Where competition is high, consumers can benefit, at least in the short term. Highly competitive price wars in the USA, and to a lesser extent in Britain, between petrol (gas) stations benefit the customer while they are taking place, but the end result is often the disappearance of petrol stations which cannot survive, and consequently less choice for the consumer. In some areas, particularly rural ones, the end result can be that the consumer has to travel further to buy petrol because the local station could not sell in sufficient volume to survive a price war. A similar situation can occur with private bus competition on the same route. Highly intense competition can be used as a strategy to force competitors off the road. During the period of competition

passengers may benefit. When a monopoly results after competitors have been forced out of business, passengers may do less well. In short, competition itself can result in a different industrial structure (that is, fewer companies), which may be less beneficial to consumers. The new industrial structure certainly reduces their power.

In some industries and services, competition can lead to duplication of service and waste of resources. The duplication of private bus companies along profitable routes, and their absence along less profitable ones, can lead to an overall decline in service. The lack of coordination that may result from transport competition may also bring disadvantages, through, for instance, the absence of timetabling of connections between differently owned services. For transport, in some instances, and water, gas and electricity utilities in nearly all cases, the capital investment is too high for anything but a monopoly of supply and distribution, whether it be private or public. The debate between private and public ownership, then, should not be confused with one between a competitive and a monopolistic structure. Both private and public monopolies may exist and a private competitive situation may rapidly change towards a monopolistic one through competition.

Political beliefs

The debate between private and public monopolies, and indeed between private and public ownership more generally, revolves around political ideologies or beliefs. In particular it concerns which sections of the public benefit, who has access to the service, and the degree to which a monopoly is accountable. It can be argued that the efficiency and effectiveness of the service are more likely to depend on manage-

ment, finance, accountability and worker or consumer involvement than on ownership alone.

A number of comments about public and private ownership in general, however, may be made to illuminate the conflicting political beliefs underlying them. Some people argue that services such as transport should be run as businesses to make profit, and think that private ownership is more likely to achieve that. Others regard services, such as transport, as though they were social services. They fear that, if run as a business, some people living near unprofitable routes will cease to receive the service, even though highly profitable routes could subsidise them. Unprofitable routes are clearly ones where there are few potential travellers because either there is a low population density, as in rural areas and to a lesser extent the rural-urban fringe, or there is high car ownership, as in richer outer suburban areas. In these last areas, young people and the elderly are the main users of public transport and would be most disadvantaged by the loss of the service.

The 'social service' argument reflects the importance of meeting 'needs'. A publicly run health service, for example, should be directed towards meeting patients' needs, whereas a privately run health service, it is feared, may tend to serve those who have the ability to pay for it. In short, one argument about public and private services is based on access to them: *'need'* versus *'ability to pay'*. These are discussed further in Chapter 4, Section 3b and Section 5, and Chapter 5.

The geographical importance of the form of ownership, then, concerns the underlying aims of the organisation and the consequent geographical distribution of gains and losses to different sets of people. The form of ownership should not be confused with the degree of competition which may also have geographical effects.

Management

In the past, ownership and management more often coincided: the owners managed what they owned. This is still the case for small businesses, indeed often part of their definition, but now the management of many larger companies is by other than their owners. The management of an organisation involves making such decisions as the target market, the type and price of products, the volume of production, the size and composition of the workforce, the suppliers and the appropriate marketing channels (Chapter 3, Section 5) for the products to reach their target markets. In another organisation the managers may be concerned with identifying the client group, deciding the most appropriate type of service and the best way of ensuring that the clients receive the service. Many of these decisions involve the *allocation of resources* within the organisation. In a private system the criteria for allocation within a company may be based on maximising profits, market share, or return on capital. In a public system, meeting needs, shortening waiting lists or queues may be the rather different criteria.

Conflict within the organisation

In both systems, however, power or influence may be distributed unequally within the organisation. The marketing department of a private company may hold sway over the production side and attract resources for meeting more precisely customers' varying demands in order to gain *market share*. In another company the production department may reign supreme, with standard products being produced in bulk over a long period in order to allow internal economies of scale and so *minimise costs*. If a new location were being considered,

whether a company were trying to maximise its market or minimise its costs would affect its location decision.

In a public system, the administrators may conflict with the professionals as to priorities of allocation. The education and health services in Britain are often contrasted, with administrators (local authority officers) being said to have more power in the education system while professionals (doctors) have more in the health system. So, for example, where school populations are falling, a school may be closed for financial and administrative reasons because of 'vacant places', while the professional (teachers') view might be that it should remain open with smaller classes.

In these two examples, different spatial outcomes have resulted from the distribution of power within the company and within the public service. In the case of the private company, either a standard or variable product would be available where it is supplied, perhaps from differently located plants. In the case of the public service, either a school remains in amended form or it is closed, with all that might mean to the local community.

Sometimes the competing elements within the management of a service may be geographically identified. National and local government in the mid 1980s in Britain were competing strongly over who should manage education, both in terms of who should negotiate and settle teachers' pay and conditions, and who should decide the curriculum.

Decentralisation versus centralisation

This involves a debate about *decentralisation* versus *centralisation* and is echoed at the level of a company in the private sector right through to the way a command economy or

socialist country is run. Some companies are highly centralised with all key decisions being taken in the company headquarters (HQ), while others may be run with many more decisions being taken at the point of production or at some level between that and the HQ.

Since the various levels of a company are often now spatially separated, the locus of decision-making has a geographical meaning (Chapter 8). In centralised companies, decisions are taken well away from the areas in which production occurs, sometimes in a different country. This external control often refers to ownership by people outside the area of production, but more meaningfully should refer to the location of decisions. Again it is the form of management, not ownership, that is important. At the level of a country with a command economy, the decisions about the allocation of resources and production targets can be set from the centre, as was the case in the USSR. On the other hand, major decisions can be taken at the points of production with the national government playing a coordinating role, as occurred in the former Yugoslavia.

The degree of centralisation and decentralisation of a system is well illustrated when comparing educational systems of different countries. In the USA local school districts manage their education, negotiating contracts with teachers and deciding on the curriculum, though in the 1980s some states became more involved. Therefore there is considerable geographical variation of the service within the USA. In France the same decisions are taken centrally by the national government, with consequently much less geographical variation.

In Britain the management of the system is partly local and partly national, with it often seeming as though each level is trying to increase or maintain its power. Indeed, the management in the 1980s was in a state of flux with central government trying simultaneously to increase its control of the curriculum while advocating increased control for school governing bodies and, particularly, parents on those bodies. Such a redistribution of power is at the expense of local authorities and teachers.

Another aspect of the central-local debate may be illustrated by the past management of the economy in the USSR, and on a more local level the management of local authority services. The USSR was usually run from the centre with different ministries in charge of different sectors of the economy, for example agriculture and iron and steel. This sometimes led to poor integration between sectors, particularly at the regional level. In the 1950s

regional planning was tried so that greater integration of sectors could occur, but this led to less efficiency within sectors and indeed loss of central control.

Most English local authorities are run on a departmental/divisional basis, similar to the sectoral approach. This sometimes means that services are poorly coordinated in areas within the authority. Area-based management has been tried in some authorities such as Walsall and Rochdale but, while producing a more locally integrated and responsive set of services, it may increase costs, decrease central control, and lead to inefficiencies within departments. Similar sectoral versus areal management tensions or debates occur within private companies. In all three instances, a further form of management is used, *corporate management*, which straddles the sec-

tors/departments/divisions, trying to ensure their integration and coordination. This can, of course, greatly centralise control.

'Who' makes decisions and 'where' they are made vary then from service to service, industry to industry and country to country. They also vary over time. The criteria used to manage (the 'how') are influenced by the same 'who' and 'where' questions, with those criteria having distinctive effects on varying sets of people in different places. Thus the way a service or industry is managed has major effects on the workers and consumers through the allocation of resources and the establishment of priorities.

Finance

The financial organisation of a service or industry involves such aspects as the ways in which finance is raised, and the ways consumers pay for the service or good. Some comments on access to finance follow in the next chapter. Here we shall illustrate some of the issues involved in financial organisation by the ways payment can be made.

Some publicly provided services are seemingly 'free' but are in fact paid for through local or national taxes. In Britain the education, library and park services, for instance, are mainly free. Others are in part paid for directly and in part subsidised from taxes. These include use of swimming pools, recreation centres and medical prescriptions. Some are totally paid for directly at their full economic cost – for example on-line library services in the late 1980s. There are moves to make rents of local authority housing reflect their approximate economic cost. They used to be highly subsidised to meet a social need. So within the public sector the financing of provision varies enormously, both with the type of service and over time, according to the orientation of policy towards economic or social criteria.

4.8 Organising local authorities

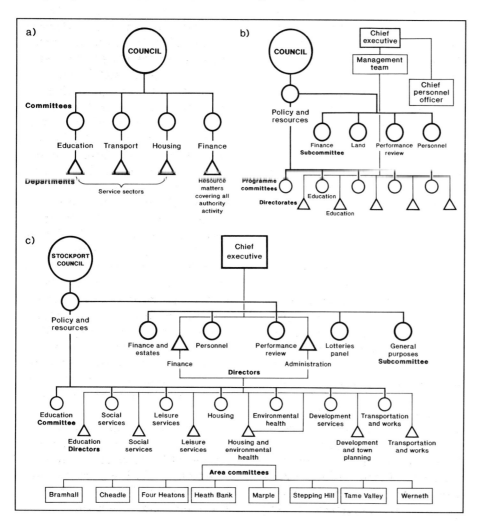

Subsidies

It also varies across space from local authority to local authority, as was illustrated in the case study (Chapter 4, Section 1) for the amount of subsidy given to public transport. Whatever the amount of subsidy, it can be given either to particular users or to the service as a whole. If received by the service, the distribution of the subsidy becomes one of the management decisions. In the transport case it can be used to cut all fares, fares only on particular routes (commuter ones) or at certain times (off-peak), fares for particular categories of people (the elderly), or even to improve the service overall with no cut in fares.

Subsidies can be viewed in part as though non-users are subsidising users of the service, and in part as though one set of users is subsidising another set. Non-users of public transport subsidise users, for example, while long-distance commuters on British Rail were for a long time subsidised by other users.

Whether or not a subsidy is given depends on the political context. For public transport it also depends on the amount of private car ownership. The greater this is, the less the political support for subsidy is likely to be.

As was shown in the case study of London Transport, increased subsidy and lower fares led to greater use of the service and reduced travel by private car. There are other geographical consequences. Traffic congestion and energy consumption are reduced. Since public transport is usually oriented to the city centre, workers and customers of offices and shops located there benefit relatively more from subsidised fares than do workers and customers associated with activities situated elsewhere in the city, where journeys are much more often by car. A removal of subsidy, and thus higher fares, can lead

to increased wage demands by commuters to the city centre. The cost of higher wages may then be passed on to consumers via higher prices. Alternatively it may lead to methods of reducing labour costs via automation and consequent job loss in the city centres. It may even stimulate relocation to the suburbs to reduce commuting distances. The level of subsidy can therefore affect the spatial structure of the city.

Where some routes and areas are subsidised by other routes and areas, people living along the routes and in the areas that are subsidised have, in effect, relatively increased disposable incomes. This extra purchasing power can increase demand for goods and services in these areas. So the economic geography of areas can be indirectly influenced. This can occur in other ways. Subsidies which are targeted on particular people also produce changing geographies. Concessionary fares for the elderly permit them to afford to shop further from home than they otherwise might, thus increasing the potential market of shopping centres by extending their market areas for the elderly. Concessionary fares for the unemployed in Tyne and Wear allow a greater area in which to search for jobs and thus there is an extension of labour market areas (Chapter 12).

Accountability

All organisations, be they companies, public services or governments, are accountable or responsible to some degree to some set of people. They have to justify or account for their decisions and actions. Different forms of organisation are accountable to different sets of people to varying degrees. The directors of a company have to subject the outcome of their decisions and actions to the scrutiny of their shareholders. They should be responsive to the consumers of their products, otherwise they will lose custom. They may also be accountable for the way

they operate their production, both to their workers and to the surrounding community, who may otherwise suffer various forms of pollution, such as air and noise pollution. Accountability can then be direct and indirect.

Local and national governments are accountable to their electorates for the services they run. Not all voters and tax payers, though, necessarily use a particular service; so governments should also be responsive to the consumers of the services, though these are not always so easy to define. Are the consumers of education the pupils, their parents, potential employers or unions, or the wider community? A case can be made for the education service to be responsive to every one of these groups. Sometimes there are special organisations set up to represent consumers and to monitor services; for example, Community Health Councils provide an indirect form of accountability for health authorities in Britain and the Gas Consumer Council acts as a watchdog on British Gas. The reorganisation of local government in 1974 and 1986 changed the accountability of some services. The creation of Regional Water Boards in the 1970s with no direct election of councillors to them meant that the water service was less directly accountable than before. As the case study (Chapter 4, Section 1) indicates, the dissolution in 1986 of the Metropolitan Counties, which were directly elected bodies, newly created in 1974, meant that London and the large conurbations became organised in a less accountable way (Chapter 11, Section 1). Local people can no longer vote for metropolitan county councillors and the policies that they advocate for the conurbation as a whole.

In the new system, there is accountability at the district level but less at the conurbation level. The scale at which services should be organised and the degree to which they should be locally

4.9 The spatial organisation of police forces

accountable are vexed questions. The British police forces are organised at a metropolitan/shire county level (Figure 4.9), with some accountability to the local police authority, which includes some nominated councillors from district councils.

Some would advocate much greater accountability at this level or at an even more local scale, arguing that communities should have more say in how they are policed. In a not too dissimilar way, some argue for greater community involvement and accountability in how their children are educated. The debate here is partly between community/client/consumer on the one hand and the professionals, in this case the police and teachers, on the other. The professionals usually have national unions or professional bodies representing them, so the debate can often take on a local versus national dimension, as well as one between different sets of actors.

Conflicts may also occur over the scale at which a service should be accountable. Some argue, for example, that all police forces, not just the Metropolitan Police of London, should be accountable directly to the Home Secretary, thus tending to increase centralised control. Some advocate that British state education should be accountable more at

the school level than at a local government level, thus tending to increase the power of the local community over that of local government.

Worker involvement

Workers may be involved in their organisations to different degrees, which may vary over time and space as well as among organisations. Even the basic rights of workers are debated and vary. These include health and safety conditions, the presence and level of a minimum wage, redundancy arrangements, pensions and the right to belong to a union, or indeed, not to belong to a union. The European Community's Social Charter, which was debated from the late 1980s, aimed to establish common minimum rights across all member states to accompany the open market arrangements of 1993. This tried to give equal rights to men and women and to full-time and part-time workers. The need for such a charter showed the extent of variation even within this part of the western world.

Worker involvement usually refers to their participation in the decision-making of their organisation and/or their receipt of some part of its profits. Such involvement may or may not be organised through unions, which can have a cooperative as well as a conflicting relationship with employers and managers. In many western societies work is generally organised in ways where workers play little part in decision-making and receive only their wages/salaries for their labour and not any part of company profits. It is argued that worker involvement in decisions increases the incentive to work and improves job satisfaction. Greater incentives in turn increase productivity, while higher job satisfaction minimises absenteeism and staff turnover, which again increases productivity. On the other hand, many companies keep management and decision-making as distinct roles, with their company organised

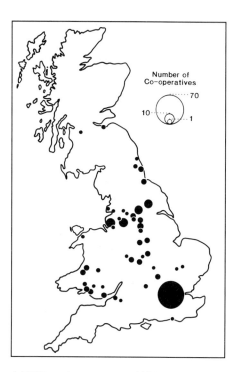

4.10 Women's cooperatives, 1986

in hierarchical tiers. Often these tiers are located in separate places, the HQs being spatially separate from the production units for instance. The location in a small town of a large production unit which needs low skilled labour may allow the company to dominate the local labour market. It can increase management control over labour, with short term contracts and lower wages. This is possible because in small towns there is little competition for labour from similar companies, and workers have to move town to obtain more secure and better paid jobs. In this way, the company may lower its labour costs. It is interesting to note that the first form of worker involvement increases productivity, while this rather different relationship with workers is aimed at lowering costs.

Cooperatives contrast with the hierarchical arrangement of most companies in that all workers are involved in decision-making, and responsibility for success and failure is shared. The distinctions between employer and employee, and manager and managed, do not occur. In Britain in the 1980s, the number of cooperatives rapidly increased. The form of organisation, though, becomes more complex as the cooperatives grow in size.

Cooperatives

There are various levels of financial involvement for workers. In cooperatives, for instance, any profits that are not reinvested to improve the product/service, productivity and output are shared among all the people working in the cooperative. In some companies, such as John Lewis, the British departmental store chain, workers receive a share of the profits, while in others there are bonus schemes related to profits. Recently share ownership by employees has been encouraged, partly through the privatisation of public industries and utilities. Technically this brings a degree of accountability as well as financial involvement. The proportion and amounts of shares owned by employees, however, are usually small, so that employee shareholders have little power in annual general meetings compared with large institutional shareholders.

Cooperatives, profit sharing and employee shareholding not only involve workers to differing extents, they also retain profits to differing degrees within the workers' home areas. Where none of these options operates, profits that are not reinvested in the company may go out of the area, even out of the country. Where profits are localised, there are more likely to be multiplier effects in the local economy through extra consumer spending on goods, services and construction.

The geographical importance of the degree of worker involvement lies in the way that basic rights and labour-management relations vary from locality to locality and country to country, and in the way that profits are spatially distributed.

Consumer involvement

The involvement of consumers also varies between countries and over time, first in the way that they are viewed within the production-distribution-consumption process, and secondly in their individual and group pressure for consumer rights and participation.

Forms of marketing

There are also some cases where consumers receive a share of any profits, as in cooperative societies. In some industries and services, consumers are not regarded as being particularly important. They are just the end point of the production-distribution-consumption process, the receivers of products and services. It is the product or service that dominates the organisation's thinking and activity. This is product-based marketing. For others, consumers are seen as central to the process, their demands or needs have to be met by the product or service, and the right distributional channels have to be chosen to maximise the chances of reaching the appropriate consumers. In such situations, their 'wants' would be reached first to establish whether there was demand as yet unfulfilled, that is, a gap in the market. A product or service would then be developed, with various trials being carried out on a panel, or sample of consumers, to see whether it met the identified demand. Sometimes such trials would occur in one region of a country which was either representative of the national market or particularly suited to the product. The North East of England is often used as a trial region. Such consumer-based marketing is now regarded as being more effective than that which is product-based.

In the early twentieth century, when there were relatively few products, most marketing was product-based. If companies could produce goods of reasonable price and quality, they would sell. As the growth in the number of potential products rapidly outstripped the growth in demand, greater interest was shown in ensuring that products satisfied individual consumer demand.

In the 1960s, especially in the USA, people became more concerned with the type of society in which they lived and the effects that various forms of production, distribution and consumption were having on their physical environments. Some corporations became more sensitive to meeting these wider concerns and responded by adopting 'social marketing' which was oriented more to the wider concerns of society than to satisfying the narrower wants of the individual.

Consumer rights

This was also a time when consumer groups put pressure on corporations and governments to establish consumer rights and protection. In 1962 President Kennedy of the USA identified four rights of the consumer: to safety, to choose, to be heard and to be informed. These referred largely to products, for example testing that drugs were safe, and proper labelling so that consumers could make informed choices. Some consumer groups pressed for more influence on the processes that produced the goods. In response a few corporations introduced consumers on to their boards. Others adapted both their products and processes to make them more socially desirable and environmentally friendly – indeed, they observed marketing opportunities. Cars, for example, were made safer for drivers and passengers, and in the 1970s made lighter so that they did not use so much fuel.

Consumer movement

The pressure of the consumer and environmental movements also resulted in government legislation to ensure that consumers and the environment were protected. Such governmental intervention responded to the right of the consumer to be heard. It also, incidentally, made the contexts or environments in which corporations operate more complex. It had other indirect effects; the testing of drugs meant that they did not appear on the market so rapidly, and the increased costs of research and development meant that only a few large companies could afford it. New companies found entry into the market more difficult and thus competition was limited.

Many of these changes occurred much earlier and to a greater extent in the USA than in Britain, where there was a less developed and less powerful consumer and environmental movement. Some writers argue that these movements grew strongest where there was a greater need to counter the power of large manufacturing and retail corporations. They regarded their growth as part of a *countervailing tendency*. As retail organisations have become more powerful in Britain, it does seem that the consumer movement, in various guises, has also developed, particularly to protect the indi-

vidual. In Italy, in contrast, where there are few very large retail organisations, there is little that can be called a consumer movement.

Increased consumer involvement in the private sector in the late 1960s and 1970s was accompanied by increased citizens' participation in planning. Although it was costly and time-consuming, there was much more consultation of local people in the 1970s about planning decisions. 'Planning' itself did not receive much governmental support in the 1980s so, not surprisingly, people's participation in it became less of an issue. In the public sector in the late 1980s in Britain it was another form of involvement that was given more emphasis: the individual's right to choose. This was introduced through parental choice of schools and an attempt to get local authority tenants to choose their preferred landlord, whether it remained the local authority or became a housing association or a private landlord. These were attempts to introduce the idea of *consumer sovereignty* into the public sector. This suggests that consumers can exercise the choice not to buy or to withdraw their custom. The idea suggests that the consumer is paramount, but it ignores geographical considerations. In some areas there is very little possible choice between goods or services. In a low-density rural area there is very little choice of school. In an urban ghetto, highly

disadvantaged people may have little local choice of shops and little opportunity to travel to shops outside of the ghetto. Geographically and socially, then, choice and sovereignty can be unequal. In these terms, therefore, some consumers can be involved much less than others.

In the late 1980s in Britain, consumer pressure on the private sector was renewed with concern being expressed for the individual consumer, rather than the society, and for the environment. The specific issues changed, for example the safety of food and its additives. The general issues remained – in these cases, safety and information for the individual. The main environmental issue of global warming concerned a different scale and necessitated international action. As was the case with lead-free petrol Britain acted later than some other western countries, though it tried to coordinate international action at a later date.

Summary

In summary, these various aspects of organisation vary over time and space as well as between and within manufacturing and service sectors. Changes in organisation have significant direct and indirect geographical effects, some of which are too often ignored.

4.3   Other examples

The three examples compare different organisations of inter-city bus transport in Britain and North America, private and public health systems, and the changing organisation of housing in Britain.

4.3a   Inter-city bus travel

National Express is a long distance bus company formed in Britain in the early 1970s following the formation of the National Bus Company (NBC) as a result of the 1968 Transport Act. By the end of December 1969, NBC controlled ninety-three bus companies grouped into forty-four operating units, employed 81,000 staff and had a fleet of 21,000 vehicles. The trading name National Express first appeared on vehicles in 1978. The 1980 Transport Act removed licensing restrictions and introduced com-

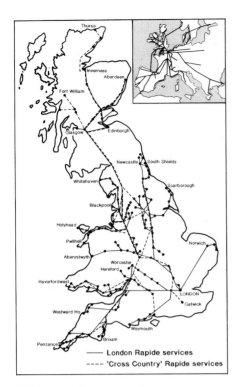

4.11 National Express network

petition on long-distance coach routes. National Express, as a response, introduced a 'Rapide' network of services.

These offered a hostess/steward service of light refreshments to each seat. The coaches were fitted with their own toilet/washroom, air suspension and reclining seats. Refreshment and toilet stops were thereby not needed and journey times were cut by 20 per cent. In 1988 the company was privatised in a management buyout and the company again restructured. Staff directly employed fell to 700 (150 at the headquarters in Birmingham) and only eight coaches were directly owned by the company. Now coaches are hired in on a contract basis from local coach operators and National Express determines the nationwide services and their safety and quality. East Kent and Crosville Wales are two examples of local operators working on contract. In all about fifty operators are employed by National Express. During the summer, 900 or so coaches are in daily use and around 1500 destinations are served nationwide (Figure 4.11).

About 14 million passengers are carried each year, compared with 8.5 million in 1980. There are 160 services offered by National Express and the system has rapidly expanded to include links with continental European cities (Figure 4.11). Understandably their rapidly emerging network has centred on London, with 265 daily journeys in and out of the capital on 67 routes. The non-stop 'Rapide', inter-city services using the motorways and allowing fast, comfortable cheap travel, have been a particular success.

Major competitors of National Express are private cars, British Rail and the airlines. Particularly intense competition exists at and beyond 200-mile journey lengths. So, for instance, London-Edinburgh is served by Rapide services, Inter-City 125 trains and a British Airways shuttle service. As National Express admitted, 'we take commercial decisions on routes, frequencies and fares', so social motivation does not underlie their decision making. What is clear is that the services National Express have offered in the last few years have been welcomed by the public, since growth in customers has been so marked.

Greyhound, the US based inter-city bus company, has a longer and different track record to National Express. It began as long ago as 1914 when a Swedish miner began a bus service between two towns in Minnesota. In the early 1920s the grey buses led to the use of the term 'greyhound' which became the company name in 1930. It is probably the largest inter-city bus company in the world with about 3,100 buses carrying 45 million passengers a year, and each day 90,000 route miles are covered by regular schedule. The buses are manufactured by a Greyhound subsidiary, while other subsidiaries are in such related businesses as food products, restaurants and financial services.

The Greyhound Corporation, itself a subsidiary of a much larger corporation, is divided into operating regions within the USA and Canada each headed by a regional vice-president. Policy is determined by head office in Phoenix, Arizona, by a board of directors which includes the regional vice-presidents. The company's fleet of buses is regulated by the Inter-State Commerce Committee (ICC) which approves tariffs and grants licences. The bus company is geared to making profits for the Greyhound Corporation to whom dividends are distributed. Non-profit-making routes are, wherever possible, franchised. Where this is not possible services are closed, so there is no wider commitment to maintain a network of services. The most profitable routes are those short distances between cities and large towns. Coast-to-coast routes are no longer profitable and cannot compete with the speed and cost of airline travel. They are still used however, by overseas visitors and some US citizens benefiting from concessionary rates. Because of recent deregulation of bus systems in the USA, the company has unlimited flexibility in opening and closing routes.

Continental Trailways offers a similar but smaller network of inter-city bus routes across North America and is a direct competitor. The greatest competition faced by Greyhound, however, is from the airlines, now that air fares in the USA have been deregulated. Also Amtrak, the railway carrier which is partly subsidised by the Federal Government, competes on major inter-city routes especially in north east USA.

Indirectly Greyhound offers a social service (cheap and fast inter-city travel) to the less well-off in American society. In addition, its inner city bus terminals provide a twenty-four-hour facility in many large American cities through selling food and drink. This is used as a focus particularly at night, for a range of people including those seeking shelter.

4.3b **Public and private health systems**

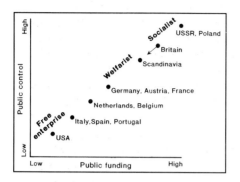

4.12 Private-public continuum for health care

Among western societies the health care systems of the USA and UK are at different poles of the private-public continuum.

The USA has a history of minimal state intervention, with health service delivery operating mostly for profit. Medical personnel tend to make locational decisions according to individual financial reward or prestige. The consumers of health care have little involvement in the regulation of such decisions. They pay for care either personally or through an insurance scheme, with the patient paying for anything costing above the threshold that insurance companies will pay. A 'safety net' system, however, has been provided by federal investment. Medicare and Medicaid help to pay for treatment of the aged and the very poor respectively, while there is a network of public hospitals situated in run-down inner-city areas close to their client populations. In addition, a paternalistic, philanthropic role has been played by corporate capital through, for example, the Carnegie and Rockefeller Foundations. A variety of other non-orthodox forms of health care, such as homeopathy, have also blossomed as medical expressions of *laissez-faire* attitudes and the democratic ideal.

In contrast, in the UK the state has been the overwhelmingly dominant provider of health care through the National Health Service (NHS)

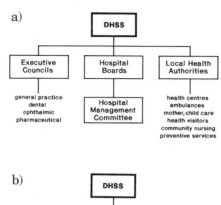

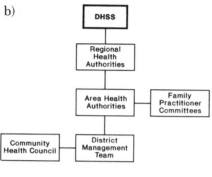

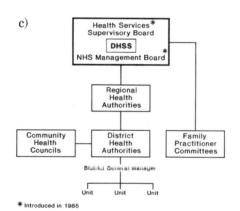

* Introduced in 1985

4.13 Changes in the structure of the National Health Service: a) 1948-74; b) 1974; c) 1982/5

which was established in 1948. The service is paid for from taxes, so patients do not have to pay for hospital treatment or visits to or from doctors, though most pay a charge for prescribed medicine. The original service (Figure 4.13a) had three divisions: family practitioners who were (and still are) paid fees by the NHS for their services; the hospital services; and the local authority services. The family practitioners and most of the local authority services are the points of first contact for most NHS consumers and are called

primary care. The hospital service is called secondary care.

The lack of effective liaison between the three divisions and a parallel reorganisation of local government were major reasons for the reorganisation of the NHS in 1974 (Figure 4.13b).

The resulting three tiered administrative structure of Regional Health Authorities (RHA), Area Health Authorities (AHA) and District Management teams in England and Wales (Figure 4.13c) was rationalised in 1982.

In England this removed the area level which had corresponded to local authority areas and was replaced by 191 district health authorities (Figure 4.14) which were responsible for the planning, provision and development of services

4.14 The spatial organisation of the National Health Service

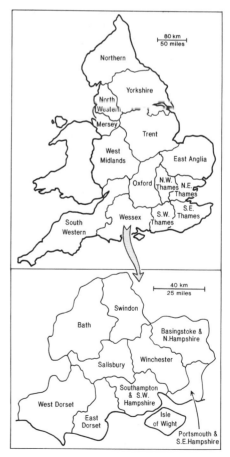

within their boundaries. In Wales it revived the district level, leaving the area authorities (nine) which were renamed as district health authorities, being equivalent in resources used and population served (100,000 – 500,000) to those of England. Scotland and Northern Ireland were reorganised differently in both 1974 and 1982.

Given the differences between the countries and the possibility of the RHAs carrying out their responsibility for overall planning and allocation of resources differently, there is considerable spatial variation in the local organisation and management of the British NHS.

Finance is allocated from central government to the English RHAs which until 1985 had been relatively autonomous. The two boards (Figure 4.13c) created in 1985 overview the RHAs and provide the means for greater central direction.

Historically there had been considerable regional inequality in provision of health care and related resources. In particular the presence of many teaching hospitals in central London where population had fallen reinforced the regional disparity between the South East and other areas. In 1976 the Resource Allocation Working Group (RAWP) was established to '... review the arrangements for distributing NHS capital and revenue to regional

4.15 The changing regional allocation of health resources

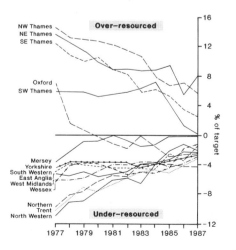

health authorities ...' with the underlying intention of creating equal opportunity of access to health care for people at equal risk. The disparities in levels of service and expenditure per head soon became apparent to the group and its impact has been to divert funds away from the South East to the North and West at the national level. At the regional level it caused funds to be diverted away from inner-city areas to suburban and other outer metropolitan authorities. The extent of the disparities in 1976 can be judged by reference to Figure 4.15 which shows the position of the regional health authorities in relation to the revenue targets suggested by the RAWP group. It also illustrates how the resource allocation procedure has reduced the regional resource disparities over time.

The national reorganisation of the NHS and the regional changes in the allocation of finances have been accompanied by major changes at the local level. In primary care there has been a growth of partnerships of three or more general practitioners into group practices, where they can benefit from economies of scale such as expensive facilities that separately they could not afford. There has also been a gradual acceptance of health centres which are multi-purpose premises where the surgery of a group practice is located together with other primary health facilities such as ante-natal clinics and family planning. They were seen as an appropriate way of upgrading primary health care in deprived areas where needs are high but facilities are below average. Health centres have expanded rapidly in Northern Ireland where over half the population attend them. They have also been developed in many inner cities and rural areas with the exception of Wales. Single handed practices are now most common in rural Wales and in poorer inner city areas where they often have large list sizes. The trend towards larger group practices and health centres and the closure of

outlying surgeries has meant an increase in the average distance people must travel to their doctor.

At the secondary level, there has been a growth in the size of non-psychiatric hospitals as more general district hospitals have been developed and many small cottage hospitals closed. The general district hospitals provide a full range of special facilities while the remaining smaller, more locally based community hospitals provide facilities for chronic illness. This rationalisation has been dominated by the arguments of administration and specialist professionals who want to promote learning and enhance the importance of specialist use. Closure of small hospitals has often been resisted by local general practitioners and the local community who, among other things, do not wish to travel further to facilities or to visit sick relatives and friends.

In secondary psychiatric care the trend has been the opposite. The size of hospitals has decreased and there has been a move towards hospital closure and replacement by more local care within the community. This trend has resulted from changes in the ways mental illness is viewed and treated. It used to be viewed as abnormal behaviour rather than as an inherent problem of society, like other forms of ill-health. Such a view led to the removal of the mentally ill from the rest of society and their isolation in asylums, often located outside large cities in green areas. As attitudes changed these asylums became mental hospitals. Their closure and replacement by day hospitals, community care and half-way houses has meant that these facilities are more accessible to the ill and that they should be more readily integrated into the community. They are often located in inner-city areas where there is least resistance from the host community (Chapter 7, Section 3). There is, however, a degree of reservation about some of the motives for these changes.

Critics argue that a major motive is economy and that insufficient resources are being provided for community care. They cite the increased number of mentally ill among the homeless as a result of this economy drive. In both primary and secondary care, the debate between concentration and decentralisation continues.

In 1976 the Labour government of the time phased out pay beds in NHS hospitals. This was the signal for a major expansion of private health provision and health insurance companies such as BUPA which occurred not least because American insurance companies were looking for investment opportunities. In the UK at that time there was a period of wage control, so private health care was seen as a possible legal way of rewarding employees. London and the South East experienced most growth in private health care (Figure 4.16) with London having in the early 1980s a 38 per cent increase in hospital beds.

The significance of this lay in the regulation that only new hospitals with more than a hundred beds needed the approval of the Secretary of State for Health and Social Services. Part of the boom in the private sector has been in specialist

4.16 The take-up of private health insurance, 1983

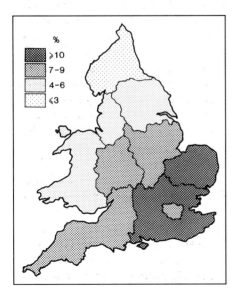

health facilities such as health farms, sports injury clinics and abortion clinics, and these usually require only a small hospital. By 1981 over 4 million people were covered by health insurance, with the South East showing the greatest take-up. A total of £250 million was being spent annually on private health care but this was only 2 per cent of total state expenditure on health.

The expansion of private health has reduced the differences between the UK and the USA health systems. The introduction of market processes into the NHS in the late 1980s is likely to continue that trend. There is an attempt to separate provision and finance. Patients have more choice about where they will receive treatment, with districts paying one another for the care provided. Some hospitals have 'opted out' of control by regional and district health authorities and are funded directly from the government. This began to blur the previously clear distinction between public and private provision. It has also led to a more complex geography of the organisation of health care.

The links between the private and public systems in Britain are subtle and fascinating. Are the two systems symbiotic or parasitic in relation to one another? Which sector is exploiting which, if at all? Who benefits/loses by the system as it stands? Many doctors and surgeons work in both systems. Some doctors in the private system use NHS hospitals for radiology, pathology and highly expensive equipment, arguably a form of hidden subsidy for the private health system. It is no coincidence that new private hospitals have clustered around existing NHS regional hospitals, because high order facilities can be used by local private hospitals, where equipment and staff can cope directly only with low-level needs. For example, Nuffield Hospital in the private system is located in Newcastle under Lyme less than 3 miles from the

North Staffordshire Infirmary, an NHS regional hospital. The NHS system pays for the training of doctors and for the equipment, so why, some argue, should they be accessible to anybody outside the NHS? The NHS also tends to meet the needs of those whose treatment is most expensive, because insurance companies are less prepared to accept people who are ill over a long time and in constant need of treatment.

Private health in Britain cares mostly for acute rather than chronic illness. Chronic illness is long-standing and is either experienced all the time or is recurring. It includes heart disease, respiratory diseases and cancer. Acute illness is short term, being experienced within two weeks or less. It includes infectious diseases and such things as appendicitis. Advocates of private medicine argue that the costs should be borne by individuals and/or by insurance schemes; that many patients do not burden the NHS system if treated privately; that sometimes old hospitals (NHS) are otherwise abandoned; and that available private beds may be used and paid for by a regional health authority when beds are not available in NHS hospitals. Finally, it can be pointed out that often people can be covered by a company's private medical scheme throughout their working life but that after retirement, when the potential need for health care is highest, they are forced back into the public system. The private insurance system does not therefore have to provide for the expensive care of sick elderly people which is left largely to the NHS.

Accountability in the private and public systems is different. In the public health system community health councils, consisting of both lay people and professionals, are the local level watch-dogs. A private hospital has to attract customers by offering a quality of service for which people and organisations are prepared to pay. The competition it

	Private	NHS
Ownership	Limited Company	The National Health Authority – we all own it!
Management	Board of Company	Minister and Regional Health Authorities
Finance	Self financing Private and insurance company payments (arguably publicly subsidised)	Income tax and national insurance
Accountability	To clients To board of directors	To hospital administrators and community health councils
Worker involvement	None but offer good wages and conditions of work	Some, on committees
Customer involvement	Yes a key factor	Less so but increasing
Key objectives	Profit, customer satisfaction, soothing environment, rapid access to service	Fairness, and constant access for all including poor and needy

4.17 Organisational aspects of private and public health care

faces is with both the public system and other competing private hospitals. There is also competition between the private health insurance companies.

One can summarise some differences between the private and public health care systems in the UK by use of a table (Figure 4.17).

In the UK in the 1980s there was much political debate about alternative health systems and strategies. On the one hand, the Conservative Party saw the importance of widening the choices of health care available to the public, whereas the opposition parties pointed to the restricted access of the poor to any private system as well as to the underinvestment, as they saw it, in the NHS by the Conservative government. There has been considerable recent change in the organisation of health care in Britain. Its future position in the private-public continuum is difficult to predict.

4.3c Alternative ways of organising housing

During the 1980s in Britain there were some major changes in the organisation of housing. Owner occupation was promoted as the main form of tenure. Investment in local authority housing or social housing was dramatically reduced by the national government, which put more of its housing expenditure into housing associations. These are voluntary/non-profit-making organisations, many of them charities. They vary in size from the very small and local to the very large and national. They are financed largely through the Housing Corporation, a quango. In the 1970s housing associations were seen as a 'third arm' to housing production, additional to private developers and local authorities. During the 1980s, however, they tended to replace local authorities in the production of housing for rent and, indeed, in many areas were able to offer lower rents than local authorities because they were receiving more government subsidy. Consequently, through their 'fair rent' schemes, they were able to provide housing for many people in housing need, for example poor elderly, single parents, divorced and handicapped.

Housing associations

Housing associations also became involved in the drive for greater home ownership through low-cost home ownership schemes: improvement for sale, shared ownership and leasehold schemes for the elderly. These schemes were also subsidised by national government through the Housing Corporation. Improvement for sale mainly involved improving houses in declared areas of inner cities as part of renewal programmes (Chapter 13, Section 2). Shared ownership was seen as the first step on the owner-occupation ladder, with people part-owning their property through a building society and part-renting it from the housing association. In leasehold schemes for the elderly, they are given a 30 per cent subsidy on the cost of a unit in sheltered accommodation, paying only 70 per cent of its market value. Sheltered accommodation has a number of living units with some communal facilities such as a lounge and a launderette, and has a warden or manager either resident or on call. Housing associations would check that the people applying for these schemes were in need of the subsidy.

In the late 1980s the national government tried to attract private finance into housing and used housing associations as the mechanism. Some of the larger national associations such as Coventry Churches had already attracted private finance to permit them to expand their house building for rent and for sale. The use of private finance has meant that associations now seek returns on investment, that is profit. In order to do so, they have to serve a different market. They serve housing demand rather than housing need. In making this change, they build and acquire houses in different areas of cities.

The fact that the government's view of housing associations changed over the decade is reflected in their inclusion in published statistics under public building at the beginning of the decade and private building at the end.

Local authority housing

Local authority housing also saw many changes in the 1980s. Such housing had been built, especially from 1919 onwards, mainly to accommodate manual workers. It was paid for by local government with central government help, and was usually built by private builders under contract to the local authority. It was seen as a particularly efficient way to provide good-quality housing in periods of housing shortage, for example after 1945. It was also used for people who were displaced by slum clearance. Tenants had to qualify for such housing (Chapter 13, Section 6) and pay rents to the local authority who maintained the property. The rents were subsidised by national and local government. At the beginning of the 1980s about 30 per cent of households were accommodated in such housing, but the proportion varied from area to area with Scotland, in particular, having a much higher percentage in local authority housing.

In the early 1980s, 'tenants' right to buy' was enhanced as part of the drive for greater owner occupation (see Ch 13, Section6) and more generally part of the move towards increased individual rights discussed in Section 4.2. They were

allowed to buy at highly subsidised prices with certain restrictions on resale.

Not surprisingly, the housing stock that was in better condition and in more desirable areas was bought. This left some authorities short of property for rent. Some had only property that was in poor condition and/or in undesirable areas. Some writers regarded local authority housing as becoming 'residualised', that is being used for the relatively few and most disadvantaged, who cannot gain access to other housing.

Some estates had been difficult to let and/or difficult to manage – so-called 'problem estates'. A proportion of these resulted from authorities' allocation policies of placing 'problem families' in such 'sink' estates. Others acquired poor reputations which, whether true or not, deterred people from wanting to live on them. Various approaches have been tried to improve these and other estates rather than demolish them, an option chosen in certain cases. Some, through the 'priority estates scheme', entailed much more intensive management on site. Others involved management or even ownership being taken over by the tenants in some form of tenant cooperative (Chapter 4, Section 2). More recently tenants have been offered a choice of landlord (local authority, housing association or private landlord). Their choice will be affected partly by their knowledge of varying types of management. It will also be affected by the rents charged. Since the government continues to change the degree of subsidy to housing associations and local authorities, it is very difficult to estimate future rents. The decision for tenants is a difficult one.

Cantril Farm

One example of trying to improve a problem estate was initiated in 1982

and involved a partnership or joint venture between public, non-profit-making and private bodies. *Cantril Farm* was built in the late 1960s as a Liverpool overspill estate in Knowsley (Figure 4.18), which, when it became a metropolitan borough council in the local government reorganisation of 1974 (Chapter 11, Section 1), took over the estate from Liverpool.

The 3500 dwellings, 60 per cent of which were in flats and maisonettes, were typical of the higher density developments of the 1960s.

The target population of Cantril Farm was 15,000. It lacked community facilities because most of its residents' social life was concentrated in Liverpool, 8 miles away, where they worked. Its population peaked at only 11,500. This was partly because during the 1970s the local economy declined, skilled workers left, and unemployment rose. The remaining inhabitants became trapped on the estate, where vacancies and inadequate maintenance produced an unattractive built environment which a growing rate of vandalism made worse. Crime rates

4.18 'Cantril Farm' becomes 'Stockbridge Village'

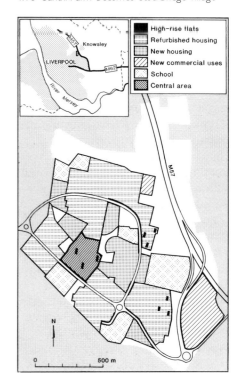

grew, social problems increased, and Cantril Farm became regarded as the worst estate on Merseyside. Locally it was known as 'Animal Farm' and even 'Cannibal Farm'.

In 1983, on the personal initiative of Michael Heseltine, the Secretary of State for the Environment, who was regarded as an unofficial 'Minister for Merseyside', a non-profit making trust was set up to take over the estate from the debt-ridden Knowsley MBC, which did not have the resources to improve the estate. The trust consisted of Barclays Bank, Barratt (builders), Abbey National Building Society and Knowsley MBC. The trust acquired the estate for £7.5 million through mortgages from Abbey National (£3 million), and Barclays (£2 million), with the remainder being left with Knowsley MBC (£2.5 million). Barclays also provided overdraft facilities. The seven year plan was to demolish 728 maisonettes and flats and build 600 houses for sale by Barratt and 400 for rent by a newly set-up housing association. Barratt were to buy the three twenty-two-storey blocks for refurbishment and sale. The six six-teen-storey blocks were to be remod-elled with improved security and amenities and remain for rent. New shopping and recreation centres were to be built and the layout of the estate was to be changed from its Radburn-based design of traffic and pedestrian segregation to one where there were footpaths alongside the roads. Overall, then, there was to be an estate of varied properties and mixed tenure: owner occupied, shared ownership, rented from hous-ing association and rented from local authority. Housing management would be created on the estate and be much improved, in particular the response to necessary repairs. Crime was to be reduced in a number of ways. Security was to be improved by creating more 'defensible space', for instance increasing the degree to which areas are overlooked and strangers easily recognised.

Pedestrian subways, part of the Radburn system, which presented too easy an opportunity for 'mug-gers', were to be closed, and better access to the police was to be provid-ed on the estate. These changes along with the new facilities were to alter the whole image of the estate, which symbolically received a new name, *Stockbridge Village*.

Stockbridge Village

National government provided resources for the remodelling of housing areas and the construction of the recreation centre through Urban Programme monies, and for the housing association's building through the Housing Corporation.

By 1989 there had been many improvements. Most of the 2141 homes had been remodelled, the maisonettes and flats had been demolished, and over two-thirds of the housing for rent and 125 of those for sale had been built. In addition, about 500 tenants had bought their homes. The new shopping centre had been built and let, new path-ways had been added, and subways had been blocked in. Relations

between the police and the commu-nity had improved from the very low point of the early 1980s. To some extent the Trust's aim of making residents feel they wanted rather than had to live in Stockbridge Village had been achieved.

The experiment has been used as a model for the Housing Action Trusts (HATs) which were announced by the national govern-ment in the late 1980s. These will take over a few large estates in dif-ferent parts of the country, change their tenure, and demolish, remodel or rebuild with the help of the build-ing industry, private developers and private finance. Some areas, such as Hulme in Manchester, have fought to avoid becoming HATs. People there, along with many in Stockbridge Village, did not like the idea of privatisation, because owner occupation often means different kinds of residents coming on to the estate and less opportunity for the original tenants.

In Stockbridge Village, privatisa-tion has had its problems. The hous-ing for sale and for shared owner-ship has been relatively unsuccess-ful. Some people could not afford to

Stockbridge Village

keep up their mortgages because interest rates rose and jobs were lost, and they have had their houses repossessed by the building society. A high rate of repossessions tends to lower the value of housing, as does vacant, boarded-up housing in the private development at the heart of Stockbridge. The resulting drop in house values leaves the remaining residents trapped in houses which are of less value than they paid for them. Vacancies and trapped residents echo the situation at the time of Cantril Farm. In this case, changing the tenure and the residents has not made any difference to the underlying economic problems of the area. More, better-paid and more secure jobs have to accompany housing improvements for longer term success.

Stockbridge Village Trust has also battled against cash-flow problems because the £7.5 million valuation was probably too high. Given the poor state of repair of the properties, an economic rent could not be charged, so there is a considerable gap between rental income and running costs. In such areas, where there are major problems in the local economy and local authority housing is in much need of repair, the proposal of the late 1980s that local authorities sell their property to private landlords or developers has little chance of success. In Knowsley, such are these problems that its total local authority housing stock was attributed a negative market value! Housing in disadvantaged areas and housing for the disadvantaged can rarely be provided by the private system without any subsidy.

Views vary on whether Stockbridge Village has succeeded or failed. It is possible that without the Trust the estate would have been completely demolished. In that sense it must be regarded as a success. In other ways it has been less successful. Whether such joint ventures can work better in more favourable economic environments remains to be seen.

4.4   **Alternative strategies**

The discussion of the different dimensions of the issue of how industries and services should be organised conveyed many of the alternative strategies. This section will discuss recent changes in the ways that industries and services are organised in order to examine in greater depth the strategies, the values underlying them and their effects.

Privatisation

Privatisation can take many forms: selling nationalised industries; encouraging private provision and ownership; privatising the delivery of public services by 'contracting out'; deregulation; and introducing business ideas into the operation of public sector organisations. Some people very much advocate returning industry and services partly or wholly from the public to the private sector. This may entail selling shares for the ownership of the whole of a nationalised industry, such as British Gas, or the majority holding (51 per cent) with the government retaining a minority share (49 per cent), as with British Telecom.

It may mean the encouragement of private provision of health, education and social services, or of individual ownership, such as sales of local authority housing. It may also involve putting certain local government services, such as refuse collection, out to tender by private companies, with the responsibility for the service remaining in local authority hands but its delivery being performed by a private company.

Greater competition is also the motive for deregulation, as in the case of bus transport in Britain. Finally, running services as though they were businesses involves such ideas as efficiency, performance,

4.19 Privatisation (see question 4 in 4.6)

The privatisation portfolio 1990				
Company	Date	Min holding	Issue price	Current price
Abbey National	July 1989	100	130	184
Amersham Intl	Feb 1982	100	142	352
Assoc British Ports	Feb 1983	100	56 *	632
	Feb 1984	100	125 *	632
BAA	July 1987	100	245	382
British Aerospace	Feb 1981	50	150	524
	May 1985	100	375	524
BA	Feb 1987	400	125	200
British Gas	Dec 1986	100	135	230
BP	Oct 1987	80	330	349
British Steel	Dec 1988	400	125	137
British Telecom	Nov 1984	200	130	307
Britoil	Aug 1985	200	185	500 **
Cable & Wireless	Oct 1981	100	168	555
	Dec 1985	50	293.5	555
Enterprise Oil	June 1984	100	185	646
Jaguar	Aug 1984	100	165	850 **
Rolls-Royce	May 1987	400	170	173
TSB	Sep 1986	100	100	139

* Adjusted for capitalisation issue   ** Price when taken over

Standard region	No. of councils	One service		Number of authorities contracting:		
			Two services	Three services	Four + services	
GLC	32	3 (9%)	3 (9%)		2 (6%)	
South East	98	16 (16%)	7 (7%)	3 (3%)	2 (2%)	
South West	47	6 (13%)	1 (2%)	3 (6%)		
East Anglia	20	4 (20%)	1 (5%)			
East Midlands	40	3 (7%)				
West Midlands	36	4 (11%)				
Wales	37	1 (3%)				
Yorkshire and Humberside	26	2 (8%)				
North West	37	1 (3%)		3 (8%)	2 (5%)	
North	29	1 (3%)		1 (3%)		

Source: Hardingham, 1983, 1984

4.20 Contracting out, 1984

value for money and cost centres, with competition for clients and resources rather than an allocation; schools, for example, will compete for students rather than be allocated them according to a catchment area.

Privatisation as a strategy involves a belief in the 'market', particularly its competitive element, which is seen as promoting *efficiency* and better '*value for money*', both ideas being associated with more output for a given input. It has accompanied a late 1970s and 1980s desire of many western world governments to reduce public expenditure and promote wealth creation and the private sector, and also to reduce the power and responsibilities of the state while increasing the power and responsibilities of the individual and the family. Privatisation of state-run industries has brought a considerable amount of money into the treasury which otherwise would have had to have been obtained via taxation or borrowing. Taxation would have reduced spending power, while borrowing could have increased inflation. It has seemingly, therefore, lowered public expenditure. On the other hand, it cost the government a considerable sum to market the shares and since the share prices were set at attractive levels, maxi-

mum revenue was not achieved (Figure 4.19).

Since many of the industries were making profits, the government was also losing the returns on previous investment. As a strategy involving sales of public assets to finance present expenditure, it can only be short term. Such assets, or the 'nation's silver' as they have been called, are finite. The gains achieved in the short term must allow, or help to produce, longer term change that will render the policy unnecessary in the future.

The ownership is then transferred from the state (all its citizens) to share-holders. Typically shares have been concentrated in the hands of large institutions like insurance companies, banks, building societies and pension funds, if not initially then after many individual shareholders have made their early gains by reselling. While the growth in share ownership has increased, and thus it could be argued that more people have a more direct interest in the success of the industries, any profits are now concentrated in few hands. These are the individual shareholders, some of whom may work within the industry but who, as a whole, are likely to consist of a disproportionate number of the better-off. These are also investors in the institutions, particularly large-scale investors. Within a country

such as Britain (Chapter 4, Section 6 and Question 3), this means greater profits to the more wealthy areas such as the South East and less chance of the profits being used in the poorer areas, as they might have been under state ownership.

It is argued that privatised industries can be managed better by the people who know the industry, without the interference of civil servants and politicians. On the other hand, the government, which has the final say in the management of publicly owned industries, may have wider goals than the management of an industry or utility. After privatisation the aims may change from those of a public service to that of a business. Will costly rural services of telephones, bus transport and mail still be provided as part of the service to all or will they eventually be cut to improve profitability? The government loses the possibility of controlling the services' prices. It may want to keep them down to control inflation, or to raise them to increase public revenue or, indeed, encourage conservation in the case of energy.

Accountability is more concentrated in privatised industries. It is to institutional and individual investors, particularly the former, rather than to the government and the voters. Though many workers may own shares, there is no guarantee of further worker participation. The privatisation of service delivery has in some cases tended to produce lower wage rates for the job, increase staff turnover and reduce the effectiveness of the service, as in school cleaning. Where the workers remain in direct control of the local authority, they have more security but arguably less incentive. Usually privatisation by contracting out local services reduces the relative power of workers and their unions.

Some consumers will welcome any change from a public service to a business, while others will be afraid that such a change may lead to concentration of service on, and pricing in favour of, the most profitable customers and areas – for example, for British Telecom, business rather than domestic users, and urban rather than rural consumers. Consumers' views on privatisation, then, may be influenced by their values, type of use and location.

Public or social ownership

This may involve nationalised industries, public services, and municipal or social housing. Social ownership like privatisation, reflects a set of political views: that state monopoly is better than private monopoly, because management decisions may encompass wider interests than just that of the company and may generate a greater and fairer distribution of benefits (not necessarily profits, since that depends on the pricing system). Social ownership, or state intervention without full ownership, is common where returns on investment are long term, where national security is involved, and where it is needed to compete with foreign companies whose production is subsidised by their governments. It also occurs when the social and indirect economic costs of closure, such as spatially concentrated unemployment, are greater than public subsidy or nationalisation. State control also gives greater control of any public money that is invested, including the geography of that investment.

Nationalised industries are criticised for being excessively bureaucratic, inefficient and non-responsive to both workers and consumers. Private monopolies and very large companies have similarly been criticised. Such criticisms, if valid, are probably due more to size, internal organisation and monopoly status than to being in public ownership. Innovations in management and worker and consumer involvement could well counter these criticisms.

Social ownership at the national level became unfashionable in the 1980s in the western world. In the late 1980s its extreme form, state planning in the command economies of the Soviet Union and Eastern Europe, came under attack from within. *Glasnost* (openness) and *perestroika* (restructuring) in the USSR paved the way for rapid change in Poland, Hungary, Bulgaria, East Germany, Czechoslovakia, Romania and later in the former USSR itself. At the time of writing, it is not clear what kind of economies and societies will emerge. New more democratic forms of social ownership at the local rather than national levels are possible, as well as extensions of a market system.

The household or domestic economy

There are numerous other ways of organising production and services. One is to concentrate them in the home: the household or domestic economy. Painting and decorating used to be performed mainly by craftsmen, employed by either the owners or landlords of the houses. They were part of the private sector. Nowadays many people perform the tasks themselves, do not cost their own time, and some say this allows scope for creative ideas and satisfaction that are no longer found in many jobs. Some households also produce, process and store their own food. There may be a division of labour within the household to perform these tasks. Indeed, there may even be a spatial division of labour with one member of the household responsible for the garden or part of it, and another for the house, or one for exterior and one for interior decoration. In some cases these tasks have become associated with gender, as have many jobs in the private and public sectors (Chapter 5, Section 2, Chapter 12, Section 3).

Services such as care for the infirm elderly may also be undertaken at the household level. Much of this household-based production and services, however, is secondary to jobs for wages and salaries earned by members of the household in the private or public sectors. The self-sufficient ecology movement, however, is an example where the household economy is the dominant one.

Informal or unenumerated economy

Another form of organisation is the informal or unenumerated economy, where transactions take place without any tax being paid. Bartering is one such method, where someone might construct a garden wall for you in return for you painting their house. No money is exchanged. One person's skills are directly exchanged for another's. Although production and a service have occurred, just as with tasks undertaken in the household economy, they will not enter into the calculation of the gross domestic product (GDP). Informal economies are often recognised in Third World countries, but they exist in western societies too. When the activity infringes on by-passes laws, this part of the economy is often referred to as the 'black economy', an unfortunate and inaccurate term.

Some advocate official encouragement of the informal economy (although not the illegal activities) as part of the self-help ideal, particularly in areas of high unemployment. They see it as a route back into the formal economy. Others fear it would create similar tiers in the economy and labour market to those in many Third World countries, where it is argued that the formal economy exploits the labour of the informal one. Such encouragement is often at the community level, where economies of scale may be gained, as in the investment in a set of appliances which individuals can hire but would not be able to afford to own. At this scale skills may be shared, exchanged or acquired, as in the Information Technology Education Centres (ITECs) of Britain, where inner-city youths learned particularly computer-oriented skills.

Voluntary/non-profit-making sector

Finally there are the voluntary or non-profit-making sectors. These have been encouraged, along with privatisation, in order to reduce public spending, public management and service delivery. There have been, for example, moves to increase the number of social services operated by unpaid volunteers in community/religious organisations rather than those run by workers in local government. Local government would no longer operate the service; instead it would license and oversee it. This would mean less paid employment in an area and thus less local spending power for other goods and services. It also means that the service is performed by non-professional workers, which might reduce its effectiveness.

The increased involvement of housing associations (Chapter 4, Section 3c) in the management of local authority and ex-new town development corporation housing, in addition to their provision of new and refurbished housing for rent and sale, provides a new form of organisation with advantages and disadvantages. They might be able to be more responsive to tenants, because they may be smaller organisations than local authority housing departments. On the other hand, many have less economies of scale and, as with local authorities, their effectiveness will be affected by their level of state funding. If funding is reduced or the service costs more because of lower economies of scale, rents may have to rise and tenants may be less well-off or indeed unable to pay. This may lead to a move out to cheaper property and a replacement by higher-income people, thus changing the consumer of the service or, for those remaining, creating the need for some kind of housing subsidy which increases public spending in a different account. If the housing is managed by the local authority, tenants can always complain about any inadequacies in the service to their local councillor, who represents them on the local authority council. The councillor can take up the complaint with the local authority officers. He or she has no such power to follow up complaints so directly with housing associations.

Organisations of tenants into cooperatives for maintenance and repair, as in Rochdale, and even rent collection, as in Glasgow, are alternative methods which involve tenants much more. In doing so they present greater responsibilities to tenants, such as the handling of rent arrears and non-conforming tenants. Such responsibilities may prove more difficult to fulfil after the originators of the cooperative have moved elsewhere. Continuity is difficult to maintain where there is high mobility.

Partnerships

Many combinations of the above strategies have been recently applied in Britain to various problems where a single strategy has been found wanting. National and local governments combined together to form the Inner City Partnerships in the late 1970s in order to improve the environmental, social and latterly economic conditions of these areas. In this case it is overall development of areas rather than a particular service that is being tackled. Political differences between central and local governments over the use of allocated funds have hindered success.

Central and local governments

Central and local governments have combined to provide funds which will 'lever' or attract private finance to form a three way financial partnership; for example, Urban Development Grants in Britain usually offered one part public money to 'lever' four parts private money to develop, for instance, housing and factories. About three-quarters of the public money came from central government, the rest from local government. Similar public 'pump priming' to attract private finance and interest has been responsible for the revitalisation of many American central cities, such as Baltimore and Philadelphia. In many ways, Britain has borrowed from American experience in revitalisation.

Public and private

Local government on its own has combined with private companies to form joint ventures on various projects, such as shopping centres (Chapter 2, Section 3b) and housing (Chapter 4, Section 3c, Chapter 13, Section 4).

More recently in Britain, central government has sought to exclude local government from a number of its initiatives which link with private finance. City Technology Colleges are one such initiative (Chapter 9, Section 4); so too are Urban Development Corporations (Chapter 11, Section 3d). The City Technology Colleges (Figure 9.24) are funded partly by central government and partly by private finance.

They are not run by local authority education departments but by trusts. Such potential increase in central control and decrease in local accountability are advocated in order to overcome local 'red-tape', to obtain better coordination between government departments at the local level, as in Inner City Task Forces, and sometimes to offset local political opposition.

Private and non-profit-making

The involvement of private investment in what were previously non-profit-making organisations usually means that more attention has to be paid to profitability than to need. Housing associations' search for private funds to replace the reduction in government finance has meant a changed emphasis to higher rents which are needed to ensure sufficient returns on the private investment. Lower-income people cannot afford such rents, whereas they could afford the 'fair rents' housing which associations provided with the help of government funds. This private/non-profit-making combination, then, has changed the market segment provided for and thus the people who benefit.

Finally, in our examples of combined strategies there are those between public and community organisations, such as neighbourhood watch schemes to support the police (Chapter 6, Section 4) and the combination of local authority ownership of housing with tenant organisations being responsible for its

management. All such schemes rely on the continued enthusiasm of the community bodies, which may decline due to perceived lack of success or initial leaders moving out of the area. They also depend on continual support from the other agency, which may decline due to lack of resources or a change in attitude to the schemes.

Summary

This section has discussed the main strategies towards the organisation of industries and services. Some very obviously change the location of production and services, such as more reliance on the household economy (Chapter 12, Section 2 for 'self-service economy'). Others more indirectly produce geographical change. Some, such as many of the partnerships, are specifically aimed at effecting geographical change, for instance by revitalising the inner cities. Support for the various strategies alters over time as well as across space. Partnerships have been a recent favourite, partly because they sound harmonious and less extreme. Yet they may be very unequal, with one partner having much more influence or power and gaining much more than the other. They may also involve conflict between the partners. Some so-called partnerships or joint-ventures are different forms of state intervention in order to support the private sector (Chapter 11, Section 2). Some involve a change of role for local government (Chapter 11 Section 2), with for example, its development control function being minimised when local government is a partner with the private sector over some development (Chapter 2, Section 3b). Thus although the idea of a partnership sounds beneficial, this may not always be the case, nor may it always be beneficial for all people.

4.5 Perspectives

In this chapter the examples have been derived mainly from the built and human environments. The organisational dimensions and strategies for the physical environment could also be discussed (Chapter 4, Section 6, Question 4). The way certain types of land, production and services are organised has direct and indirect effects on all the environments. Their organisation varies over space and time, and in so doing creates different and changing geographies at various scales. In this section, the relationships between the private and public sectors are considered and changes in emphasis between sectors for both production and consumption discussed. Finally, the question of the values and priorities that the different forms of organisation reflect is reviewed.

Relationships between sectors

First, a particular service may be organised in varying ways in different parts of the country. The health service provides an example. In Britain, private hospitals are concentrated in wealthier areas, particularly the South East, where there is a greater proportion of the population covered by private health insurance, some of which is provided by companies as a benefit for their staffing (Figure 4.21).

Private hospitals are also located near the National Health Service (NHS) teaching hospitals of London so that they can employ their consultants part-time. They also cluster near NHS facilities in order to use their radiology units and pathology laboratories. These locational pulls on private hospitals, however, have partially counteracted the objectives of the public health sector, which have been to redistribute resources from acute to primary and community care, and from central London to the more peripheral regions. Since the private sector concentrates almost exclusively on secondary acute medical services, especially in London, it has tended to widen rather than reduce geographical inequalities in overall health care.

The relationships between different types of organisation are important, then, for reasons of policy. The discussion of the growing amount of private investment in what were non-profit-making housing associations illustrated how changing the financial arrangements necessitated altering the objectives and thus resulted in a new range of tenants.

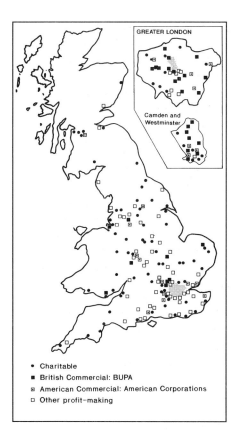

4.21 The spatial organisation of private hospitals

Different sets of consumers benefit from the involvement of private finance.

A change in the way a service is organised, for example a transfer of its production/delivery from one sector of the economy to another, in itself creates new 'niches' for further services to fill and consequently new geographies. The transfer of painting and decorating, for example, from local craftsmen to household labour within the household economy (Chapter 4, Section 4) has generated new niches with its enormous demand for DIY equipment and materials from the private sector, and DIY books from both bookshops and public libraries. The associated growth of DIY superstores has led the move to 'out-of-centre' shopping and thus in itself helped to transform the geography of retailing. The transfer of service provision from one sector to another may therefore generate many further economic, social and geographical changes.

National scale

These sectoral changes within individual services are aggregated at a national level to contribute to the changing proportion of the private and public sectors in gross domestic production. There was certainly an upward trend in the share of the public sector in Britain which was about 10 per cent of GDP in 1890 compared with 45 per cent in 1980. Post-1945, though, in the mixed economies of the western world, there is some evidence that the changing emphasis on the public and private sectors is cyclical. 'Private affluence and public squalor' was coined for the USA in the 1950s and early 1960s, while by the 1970s, after increased state intervention, people were talking of public affluence and private squalor in both the USA and UK, while in the 1980s, particularly in the UK, privatisation was making the private sector much more prominent. In mixed economies the appropriate balance between the social, political and even spatial arguments may give different answers. It is not surprising then that the balance varies between countries at one point of time and over time (Figure 4.22).

Command economies

The extreme of public ownership, exhibited in the socialist or command economies of the USSR and Eastern Europe before 1990, has recently received much criticism from both within and outside these

countries. In each country almost the whole economy had been planned, with targets being set for every point of production and resources allocated to them. When targets were not met for one product, other points of production using that product as an input were prevented from meeting their targets. If targets were exceeded, perhaps an understandable goal of enthusiastic local managers, then more resources had to be used to achieve them. Those resources could not be used elsewhere in the economy, so preventing other places from reaching their targets. Such systems had more chance of success for economies based on heavy industries than for more complex ones based on a mixed range, including consumer goods.

Market economies

These economies are not the only ones to have been criticised for inefficiencies of resource allocation. A market system also has its faults. Speculative production and building, caused by overestimating demand, and in-built obsolescence of goods to maintain levels of consumption, all misallocate resources. Some inefficiencies, probably of both systems, can be reduced. In the market system, demand, for example, is often variable over time and space, whereas production is better organised in long steady runs. This often means that large levels of inventory or stockpiles have to be kept at

4.22 The balance between the private and public sector

	1875	1900	1925	1950	1982	With local regional expenditure
GB	5.5	9.4	15.9	25.6	44.3	(51.1)
Italy	10.7	11.1	12.2	20.6	51.8	
Germany	3.5	6.8	8.4	11.9	32.0	(50.6)
Sweden	5.7	6.7	8.1	17.3	48.3	(69.9)
average	6.4	8.5	11.2	18.9	44.1	

Charitable

■ British Commercial: BUPA

▨ American Commercial: American Corporations

□ Other profit-making

points of production or distribution to meet the fluctuating demand. Instead of using marketing to attempt to smooth out demand, so as to reduce the inefficiency and costs of large inventories, the Japanese and others have changed the organisation of production to 'just in time' (Chapter 8, Section 2, Chapter 9, Section 2) rather than 'just in case' methods. Production is made more flexible to meet rather than exceed demand and to minimise inventories. In command economies more investment in infrastructure would reduce the loss of food through poor storage and transport provision. Some improvements in resource allocations can be made in both market and command systems. Some misallocations, such as exceeding targets in the command economies and over-speculation in market systems, seem to be inherent to the respective systems.

Private or public consumption

The above discussion concerns production. Whether consumption is in the private or public sector is an equally important question. Again there are interesting international comparisons, for example of the consumption of housing (Figure 4.23).

Individual choice between tenures is affected by the international and household context. At the national level, tax and state subsidy systems may present greater advantage to one form of tenure; for example, in the UK mortgage tax relief and untaxed capital gains from house sales make ownership much more financially rewarding than renting. The dramatic reduction in national government's contribution to public housing expenditure since 1976 has also meant a decline in the maintenance and repair of public housing, making it less attractive to tenants. The household context limits the amount of tenurial choice.

Population and dwellings	UK	W. Germany	France	Ireland	EEC
Population (millions)	55.9	61.5	52.9	3.2	258.8
People per dwelling	2.7	2.6	2.4	3.8	2.7
Owner-occupied dwellings (%)	54	39	50	75	49
Public-sector dwellings (%)	33	18	50*	25*	51*
Pre-1919 dwellings (%)	32	27	38	38	31
1919-45 dwellings (%)	22	15	16	18	17
Post 1946 dwellings (%)	46	58	46	44	52

*Rented dwellings – ownership not known

Source: Nationwide Building Society and Housing Finance in the European Economic Community.

4.23 Housing differences among countries

Unemployment or low, insecure incomes drastically limit access to mortgages for ownership, whereas families with two secure incomes have much greater choice.

Whether people consume predominantly in the private or public sector provides a classification which has been shown to be significant in predicting people's political attitudes and voting behaviour and in understanding the structure of society. Production-based classifications, that use occupations, have dominated our interpretation of social structure. 'Consumption cleavages', as they are called, to reflect the private-public sector cleavages in housing, transport, health, education and pensions for example, cut across occupational classifications. It is suggested that people who consume in particular ways develop attitudes based on self-interest. More indirectly, ideas may develop in society about the political interests of consumers of various public or private sector goods and services and the social meaning of public and private property. Political interests, then, are not identified only with class, based on occupation, they are also related to consumption. Both, though, are simplifications and generalisations. Within any occupational or consumption group there is still much individual variation. The geography of political interests, however, needs to examine the spatial organisation of consumption cleavages as well as the spatial division of labour. To some extent the concentration of private health and education in the South East of Britain, where owner

occupation and car ownership are very high, compounds north-south differences in occupational composition and contributes to the growing geographical political divide, as witnessed in the 1987 general election.

Values

These political interests reflect different values and it is these that have underlayed the discussion in this chapter. All the strategies reviewed in the last section have been advocated by some part of society. The objectives behind the strategies are often different. Satisfying need and social or spatial justice (Chapter 5, Section 5) are much more likely to be aims of public and non-profit-making sectors. Increased profitability and productivity may dominate private sector objectives. Goals are often imported from one sector to another. In the 1980s there was a much greater attempt to run public services on business lines, while in other periods, greater concern for the quality of life of workers and community welfare has been shown by the private sector.

The 'success' or 'failure' of a strategy or initiative can be judged in different ways, in part reflecting the values of the assessor. A refurbishment of public housing in an inner city by private builders may upgrade the local built environment and provide reassurance to the rest of the community and potential investors that the whole area may improve. On the other hand, the displacement of the original tenants to other areas and their replacement by somewhat 'better-off' owners breaks up the local community and may not lead to any improvement in the original tenants' quality of life. Similarly the lowering of rates of certain crimes in a neighbourhood watch area may be due to displacement, with those crimes being committed in another, less well protected area. In these cases some people's gain may have been indirectly at the expense of others.

Environmental priorities

In most of the chapter we have contrasted economic and social priorities, but we should not forget environmental ones, which were discussed at length in the last chapter (Chapter 3) when deciding which set

of resources to use. Production, distribution and consumption may be organised in ways which are more or less environmentally friendly. As with worker and consumer involvement, governments can encourage organisations to change their ways, either by exhortation or by financial inducement. They can introduce taxes that are levied on those using processes and products that harm the environment and thus force up their prices. Such ideas suggest that the polluter pays. Environmentally such a strategy relies on competition working well and rapidly to remove the polluters from the market or make them change their ways. In certain situations, however, where a few major suppliers all pollute the environment in various ways, increased costs may simply be passed on to the consumer. Alternatively, instead of reducing pollution and the taxes, they reduce other costs which may be easier to do. Environmental pollution may

then continue. It could be argued that such organisations would be contributing to remedial action against pollution through their taxes, but people who greatly value the environment would advocate the prevention, not the correction, of pollution. Governments could alternatively ban certain environmentally harmful processes and products and thus compel organisations to change. This, of course, means major state intervention in the economy and again raises the issue of the relationship between governments and economies, not just at a national but also at a global scale.

Which strategies you advocate and how you evaluate the different forms of organisation will depend on your perspective. The issue of the organisation of production and services, the general problem of this chapter, is very much concerned with underlying values and people's priorities.

4.6 Exercises

1. (a) What are the advantages and disadvantages of
     (i) owning and
     (ii) renting a house?
   (b) In what ways might these advantages and disadvantages vary among countries?
   (c) Study Figure 4.24 which shows changes in housing tenure in England. Describe the changes and suggest reasons for them.
2. (a) Examine the critical comments below on privatising prisons. In the USA some prisons are privately owned and managed. Discuss the advantages and disadvantages of privately run prisons.

   Gaol sell-offs 'would lead to profiteering' (based according to the Guardian 21.9.87.)

   Profits would come before the

humane treatment of offenders if prisons were privatised, claimed a Fabian Society Report. Privatisation would create a lobby with a vested interest in a high prison population and long gaol sentences, argued the director of the Prison Reform Trust. Law and order should be the responsibility of the state, but privately-run prisons would not be publicly accountable.

'It would be totally unacceptable for private concerns to be involved in decision-making on such matters as prison discipline, home leave

and parole, which directly determine the length of a prison sentence' the report said.

'Applying the profit motive to prisons will mean that financial questions take precedence over considerations of humane regimes, decent standards and staff safety and welfare. The result will be prisons run with the maximum of technology and the minimum of human contact'.

4.24 Housing tenure in England

	Local Authorities	Owner occupation	Private rented and others (Housing associations)
1973	4.6m (28%)	8.9m (54%)	2.9m (18%)
1979	5.1m (29%)	10.0m (56.6%)	2.5m (14.4%)
1983	4.8m (26.1%)	11.2m (61.3%)	2.3m (12.5%)
1988	4.3m (22.6%)	12.8m (66.8%)	2.0m (10.6%)

(b) In England 'difficult prisoners' are dispersed among many prisons. In Scotland they are concentrated into one, Peterhead. Discuss the advantages and disadvantages of these two systems of management.

3. During the 1980s in Britain a number of publicly owned industries and utilities were privatised (Figure 4.19). The privatisation programme was partly to increase the population's investment in shares of companies. Below are figures related to share ownership in general and ownership of privatised companies in particular (Figure 4.25).

Though the value of shares held by private individuals increased in the 1980s, the percentage of shares held privately fell because it was outstripped by institutional share ownership (e.g. insurance companies, pension funds).

(a) Display graphically and cartographically the data in Figure 4.25.

(b) To what extent is Britain becoming a 'shareholding democracy'?

(c) Suggest reasons for the geog-

4.25 Estimated percentage of adult population owning shares (1987)

	% owning shares	% owning shares in privatised companies
Outer metropolitan	29	18
Greater London	30	18
Outer South East	21	18
South West	21	17
East Midlands	19	17
East Anglia	19	18
West Midlands	18	14
North West	18	15
Scotland	17	10
Yorks and Humberside	16	10
Wales	16	16
North	14	12
Britain	21	15

raphy of privatised share ownership.

(d) From the above data and other information available to you, suggest the possible geographical differences in the distribution of 'profits' and dividends from privatised shares.

4. The following questions relate to various aspects of the organisation of the physical environment.

(a) Some people fear that the privatisation of the water indus-

try may reduce access to attractive landscape that was previously owned by the ten Regional Water Authorities of England and Wales. Why may this change of ownership affect access?

(b) Needle loss from trees has been attributed to acid deposition ('rain'). The type of forest management has also been suggested as a cause. Discuss how you might assess the relative importance of acid deposition and forest management in explaining needle loss in a number of forest areas.

(c) Some people advocate that the polluter should pay and want to establish a pollution tax.
(i) How easy is it to establish who pollutes:
the air
a lake
a river?
(ii) What are the advantages and disadvantages of such a pollution tax?

(d) To what extent should local residents be involved in affecting what happens to their local environment? (See also Chapter 2 and Chapter 7.)

4.7 Further reading

M. Boddy and C. Fudge (eds.) (1984) *Local Socialism*, Macmillan

J. Eyles and K.J. Wood (1983) *The Social Geography of Medicine and Health*, Croom Helm

J. Eyles (1987) *The Geography of the National Health*, Croom Helm

R. Haynes (1987) *The Geography of Health Services in Britain*, Croom Helm

J. Le Grand and R. Robinson (eds.) (1984) *Privatisation and the Welfare State* Allen and Unwin

S. Pinch (1985) *Cities and Services:*

The Geography of Collective Consumption, Routledge and Kegan Paul

J. Scarpaci (ed.) *Privatisation of Health Services: An International Survey*, Rutgers University Press

Chapter 5

ACCESS TO GOODS AND SERVICES

5.1   Case Study: New shopping for all?

Some people live in a local environment where there is a wide range of shopping facilities from which they can obtain a set of goods and services at very competitive prices. For each good, there is plenty of choice as to what they buy and where they buy it. Some other people have a very limited range of shopping facilities close by, with a restricted number of goods and services on offer. They have little choice of what and where they can buy and they often pay much higher prices for the same good or service compared with the first set of people. Retailing has changed much since the 1960s but it has changed faster in some countries and in some parts of a country than others. Most retail change has been directed at the more mobile and more affluent, so while shopping behaviour has changed too, not all groups have been able to respond to the retail changes to the same degree; nor have they been able to benefit equally, even when they live in the same area of the country. Since shopping is an important part of people's everyday life and the quality and quantity of goods and services they consume are considered as a significant part of their well-being or 'quality of life', this unequal access to existing and new retail facilities is worthy of consideration. Recent changes in retailing have been regarded by some as a revolution. In Great Britain the 1970s saw the development of many

superstores and some hypermarkets within or sometimes outside existing shopping centres. The early 1980s witnessed a boom in non-food retail parks especially DIY, furniture and carpet stores outside of existing centres; while in the late 1980s there was a surge in applications for major regional shopping centres.

These were at least 250,000 square feet in area and in several cases were planned to be over 1 million square feet. Because of the land required, there were few suitable sites adjacent to existing town centres, so the applications tended to be for out-of-town-centres on large greenfield sites close to motorways within or at the edge of major conurbations (Figure 5.1). One advantage of such sites to the developers and retailers is that there is a large number of affluent car owners with considerable disposable incomes within easy driving distance. With this potential market, developers hoped to attract departmental and specialist stores as well as large food stores and leisure facilities. The emphasis would be on shopping for comparison rather than convenience goods. The flagship for such developments is the innovative Metro Centre in Gateshead, north east England, which opened in 1986 with its 1.5 million square feet of retail floorspace and leisure facilities.

Of the (nearly) seventy proposals for major out-of-town-centre regional shopping centres in Great Britain,

thirteen were concentrated in the Greater Manchester area. The majority were on greenfield sites. Some, like Prestwich, originally the site of a mental hospital, were not. Greater Manchester offered particular advantages to developers of regional shopping centres since over 2.5 million people could reach such a shopping centre within a half hour's car drive. This was made possible by the almost circular motorway system and dense road network.

This boom in proposals for

5.1 Proposed out-of-town centre retail developments

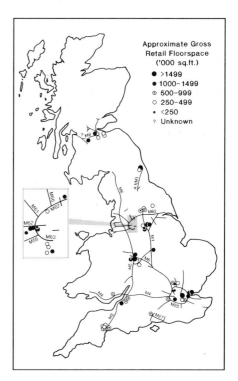

Location	Proposal	Planning gain
1. Etchells Road, Cheadle	A 250,000 square foot Savacentre	A34 by-pass
2. Bradshaw Hall	A 250,000 square foot Asda with additional 50,000 square feet of retail uses	Resources to Health Authority for land
3. Woodford (withdrawn prior to public inquiry, because being on green belt land it was unlikely to receive permission and because it was not considered viable if other 1m sq ft centres received permission	910,000 square feet of retailing, banking, leisure and conference facilities	A34 by-pass contribution Part of East – West airport link
4. Handforth (just outside SMBC in Macclesfield District of Cheshire)	A 240,000 square foot Marks & Spencer and Tesco development	A34 by-pass and East – West airport link (contribution)

5.2 Proposed schemes for the Stockport area

Greater Manchester can be illustrated by those for the Stockport area (Figure 5.2).

In some cases the developers offered to contribute finance, for instance towards the A34 by-pass and for an east-west airport link road that would be needed to facilitate local access. Both Stockport and Macclesfield welcomed the road improvements (planning gain, Chapter 7 Section 5) but were concerned about the new centres' impacts on existing ones. Macclesfield and eventually Stockport supported the Handforth proposal (Figure 5.2). Stockport originally intended to reject the three in its district. In doing so, it would have kept faith with the ten districts of the old Greater Manchester Council, which decided to present a united front against all the proposals. Salford had previously welcomed the developments in its area because of the increased rates revenue and impetus to redevelopment that the proposals would bring, but for a time also joined the other districts. The Secretary of State for the Environment, however, had already declared that he would want to see the proposals whether the local councils accepted or rejected them. Eventually only seven of the districts actively opposed them with Salford, Trafford and Stockport deciding not to do so.

Salford in the end actively supported the proposals. A public inquiry on all the Greater Manchester proposals took place during 1987/88. This was an innovation, since usually such inquiries are restricted to one proposal. The overall impact of all the proposals on the conurbation and its existing centres, and the changed access to shopping for different groups of consumers that would result, made such a combined inquiry necessary. Factors considered included: economic impact on other shopping centres particularly the major town centres; new employment opportunities; impact on traffic; environmental impact, accessibility by public and private transport; and likely catchment populations.

The issue that concerns us for this chapter is that such developments unequally benefit different groups of people. At the national level (Figure 5.1), for instance, such sites generally benefit those residents of metropolitan rings who have cars and live near to the sites. In the case of the districts of Manchester, many people will find it difficult to reach such centres since many do not own a motor car (only 40 per cent of households had a car in 1981). In comparison the generally better-off residents of Stockport (in 1981, 65 per cent of households had a car) would have much better access to the four proposed nearby developments.

The proposals and the areas of greatest social disadvantage in Greater Manchester are shown on Figure 5.3.

These are mainly inner-city areas and peripheral council estates. Not all disadvantaged people live in these areas and not all of those living in them are disadvantaged. There is little doubt that the proximity of one of these large shopping developments could aid the urban regeneration of the environments of the socially disadvantaged. There are four particular benefits which would accrue: firstly there would be the benefits of more convenient and varied shopping combined with the possibility of lower prices; secondly, new jobs would be created by the schemes themselves; thirdly, employment opportunities might arise from any secondary investment effects resulting from the schemes; and fourthly, the symbolic

5.3 Who would benefit in Greater Manchester?

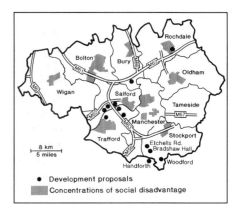

significance of the development in demonstrating confidence in the area might in itself encourage further retailing investment. These probable benefits are unlikely to be felt by the socially disadvantaged if the proposed sites are not adjacent to areas where they live. This is because the residents concerned tend not to have access to a car. Their access to possible centres is limited by public transport routes, which tend to radiate from the town centre of Greater Manchester. Their areas of job search are restricted by cost and public transport routes, and women with young children seeking part-time work can travel only a short distance.

The thirteen proposed developments in the Greater Manchester area are therefore unlikely to benefit the region's socially disadvantaged people, because they are inaccessible to them in a variety of ways. Such new developments claim to offer a wider range and higher quality of goods and services at competitive prices in pleasant traffic-free, enclosed shopping environments. It could be argued that residents of socially disadvantaged areas in and around Greater Manchester, whose movements are more constrained, could well become even more disadvantaged in relation to their more privileged, more mobile suburban neighbours, who have greater access to such new developments. So if these new developments cause trade to decline in existing centres, producing shop closures, they would be further disadvantaged. Thus what may be seen as a major increase and improvement in shopping facilities may be beneficial to one section of the community but may reduce choice for other groups.

5.2   General problem

The case study has shown how different sets of people would have varying degrees of access to proposed new shopping developments. This section will discuss various forms of access and describe how people may be classified into groups which enjoy differential access to private and public goods and services and indeed resources in general. Even though an area or county may have plenty of resources/goods and services, not everyone will have equal access to them. This is due partly to the type of people they are, partly to the region in which they live and partly to where they live within the region. Since particular types of people tend to live in similar areas, the type of people they are and where they live are not unrelated. Since access may be unequal, the take-up or use of private and public goods and services may also be unequal and so too may the benefits enjoyed from using them. The general problem of the chapter concerns the ways in which access to goods and services may be unequal for different sets of people, and how any inequality may be spatially distributed. The alternative strategies section examines ways in which access may be improved and inequalities reduced. The chapter expands on the ideas of spatial and social justice that have been mentioned earlier (Chapter 4, Section 5).

Access includes a number of aspects or dimensions.

(a) The *differential availability* of private and public goods and services in space.
   This is measured on a regional or areal scale. People in one area may potentially have more choice than those in another. In this sense, it is the *potential environment of choice*.
(b) The *awareness* of these goods and services and *access to information* about them.
   This indicates the extent to which individuals or households are aware of the potential environment of choice.
(c) The *spatial access* or *accessibility* of these services.
   This suggests the extent to which individuals and households can travel to those services of which they are aware.
(d) The *financial access* to goods and services.
   This indicates whether individuals or households can obtain finance (money, credit, mortgages, insurance) to benefit from the goods and services.

The characteristics of different types of people, their needs and wants, must also be considered when discussing access.

(e) The *differential needs and wants* of particular groups of people, distinguished by such characteristics as
   gender
   age and life cycle
   social class and socio-economic status
   ethnicity
   and the way these characteristics affect people's accessibility and access to information and finance.
(f) People's *differential access to power* or influence to affect the availability of services and to facilitate access to them. This reflects people's ability to use information, and financial and other resources, in order to obtain influence.
(g) The resulting *degree of match/mismatch* between the goods and services available and the needs and wants of different sets of people living in the area. This is sometimes referred to as *spatial* or *territorial justice*.

The degree of match (g), like availability (a), is measured at the regional or areal scale. Availability is an absolute measure, whereas match, which is clearly similar, is availability relative to the types of people in the region.

Awareness, accessibility and financial access are not independent of one another. Here they are all measured at the individual or household level, to distinguish them from availability which is measured at an areal scale. They can also be discussed for groups of people, grouped either by some social or economic characteristic or by where they live. Access to both information and finance depends partly on other people who control or manage access to them. Estate agents (realtors), for instance, manage access to information about available houses for sale or rent, while building societies (savings and loans) allocate mortgages to certain people for particular houses. Such controllers of access to information and finance are called 'gatekeepers'.

The above dimensions of access are now discussed in detail.

(a) Availability of private and public goods and services

The last chapter (4) showed how goods and services are provided by different sectors (private, public, voluntary) and how different areas have varying mixes of sectoral provision. Areas also have varying

An out-of-town site for Sainsbury

amounts and spatial arrangements of their goods and services. Many other geography books attempt to explain the factors affecting the location of particular goods and services. The argument presented here is that location is just one of many decisions which are made about provision. It is useful to highlight the main reasons why some areas are better provided with goods and services than others, and why there are different spatial organisations of provision within them.

Retail decision-making

For both private and public goods there are methods of allocation which decide the amounts of resources going to particular regions. A major retailing company may decide to extend its market share by investing in new areas, as Sainsbury did moving north in England in the 1970s and 1980s and Asda by moving south during the same period. New spatial markets can be achieved by opening new stores or by acquiring existing companies and their outlets, as Tesco has done with Hillard in Yorkshire (1987). The companies have in these cases decided to allocate some of their capital to new building or to merger. They may have made planning applications for new stores. All these will have been based on locational decisions related to available

land at a reasonable price, a given demand within a particular travel time distance, existing competition and any loss of custom from their existing stores, if there are any in the area. The successful planning applications do not necessarily coincide with the best commercial prospects. Thus it is not always correct to infer that the new stores are in the 'best' locations, however that may be defined. Some local authorities are more welcoming than others because they want to attract activities that contribute to local taxes and employment, while in some areas local opposition from residents and commerce is less organised or influential. In the case study it is the developers' rather than the retailers' choice of locations that is important, particularly for the proposals for 1 million square feet. The major reasons for the developers' choice of locations are the availability and suitability of the land for building, the gain in value of the land by development from which they would benefit, and its access to a large potential market.

Differential availability of retail provision

Private investment will be attracted to regions where there is greatest or, at least, good potential for profit. For the retailing of comparison (higher order) goods, this is associated, among other factors, with concentrations of high disposable income. So areas with large numbers of socio-economic groups 1 and 2 (managerial and professional people) and high-income manual workers will tend to be more attractive and better served. Retail innovations, however, may not always go to such areas first; in the South East of England, for example, hypermarket and superstore development was slower (Figure 5.4) because of the greater difficulty of obtaining planning permission, and perhaps the higher

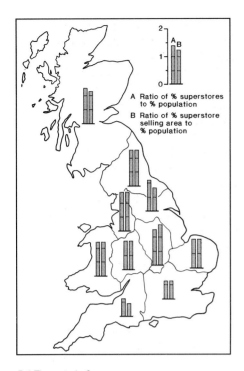

5.4 The arrival of superstores

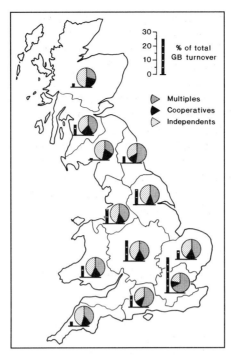

5.5 Retail independents and cooperatives

price and lower availability of land. It is also worth noting that many of the grocery multiples had just invested in large supermarkets in the South East and it is these that feel the greatest effects of hypermarket competition. It needed the competitive edge of Asda's invasion before Sainsbury and Tesco were prepared to build hypermarkets which would also compete with their existing developments. So the North West, the North, the East Midlands, Scotland and Wales were much better served by superstores and hypermarkets in the early period of their development. The cooperative movement and the small independent store tradition are, for historical reasons, both better represented in certain areas (Figure 5.5), Scotland and the North West in particular. The retail opportunities available to people in different areas, as the case study also shows for the most recent shopping centre developments, are rather different even during a time dominated by nationwide multiple stores.

Similar historical and contemporary reasons account for the unequal availability of private health and education. In both cases it is Inner London where the greatest recent growth has been. In some instances the private schools and hospitals have taken over former public facilities.

The availability of public goods

The allocation of public resources, for instance health resources by RAWP (Chapter 4 Section 3b, Chapter 5 Section 3b), may frequently be distributed firstly on the basis of past funding (so again emphasising the importance of the historical dimension) and secondly on assessed current need, to the extent that it is not already included in past funding. The allocation is affected, of course, by the ability of areas, be they health authorities or housing authorities, to make the best cases to demonstrate their need. Location of services, such as a hospital or housing refurbishment, within an area depends upon the distribution of need and the policy towards meeting it. One health

authority may locate one large hospital to serve a large area for specialist needs. Another may put priority on a number of small local hospitals for secondary care. The first centralises services while the other decentralises them. One local authority, such as Salford, may have a 'worst first' policy for refurbishing its housing estates, while another such as Stockport may put relatively more emphasis on investing in estates 'on the downward turn' in order that they do not get worse and are launched on an upward spiral.

Availability of private and public goods and services varies between and within regions, so people in one area may have more potential choice than those in others. Whether they can avail themselves of that choice depends on their awareness of it, their spatial mobility and their financial circumstances.

(b) Awareness and access to information

Often people do not use services because they are not aware of them. The distance they live away from them affects the probability of people knowing of the service. For a given size of shopping centre, for example, they are less likely to know of ones further away from their home. Size of shopping centre is also important; at a given distance the larger the centre the more likely it is to be known. Information about facilities, then, fits a gravity model where the probability of being aware of a facility varies positively with its size and negatively with its distance.

The effect of the social geography of cities

Awareness and use are also affected by the social arrangement of cities. Many cities exhibit social segregation of space – that is, different types of people live in different areas of the city. Often this social differentiation is spatially represented by sectors and rings. The spatial distance between these areas may be accentuated or reduced by the *social distance* between them, that is the degree to which one group feels socially comfortable with another, shares common interests, values and culture. The effect of social distance is that people in a middle-income sector are less likely to know of or use a facility in a low-income sector than a similar sized facility in the middle-income sector that is located further from them. They are less aware of the services because they do not travel very much in an area that is socially different from them. Commuters from middle-income outer suburbs are often unaware of wide areas of the inner city except those parts directly adjacent to their commuter route. Similarly, people from the inner city often know little of the outer suburbs, partly because of their limited spatial mobility and partly because of the effect of social

5.6 Views of Los Angeles: from Boyles Heights, a Hispanic area and Northridge, an outer suburb - note that the view from Boyles Heights is at the same scale as that from Northridge and that it shows that the people are not aware of more distant parts of LA (the areas where the insert map and key have been included are entirely blank)

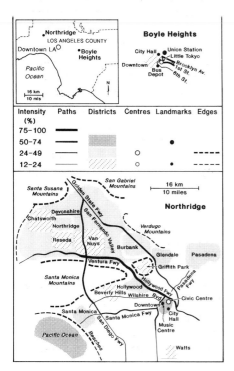

distance. Figure 5.6 shows typical maps of inner- and outer-city residents' awareness space. Note the decline with distance and the sectoral shape which is partly to do with social distance and partly with physical and built form barriers to movement, such as rivers and railway lines. Indeed, these barriers often mark abrupt social changes and therefore the effects of barriers and social distance reinforce one another.

The effect of gatekeepers

People's information about services may be affected in other ways. When searching for a house many people use estate agents (realtors), particularly when moving into a new city or region. It has been shown that realtors in the USA, in particular, 'filter' the information they provide. The agents themselves often tend to specialise in property in particular areas rather than in the whole city. They fit people to areas, that is, they show buyers areas where there are people of similar incomes and social and ethnic characteristics to those of the buyers. The characteristics of the buyers influence the time taken and information provided by the agent. Usually more attention is given to richer people who will buy higher priced property, because the charge for the service is a percentage of the sale price of the property. Hence the higher the price of the house, the greater is their potential profit. *Gatekeepers* such as estate agents, then, may filter the type and amount of information provided to their clients.

'To those that have'

Areas where rich people live are more likely to receive free newspapers and financial magazines with all their information and advice

about goods and services. Such areas are more attractive markets to the advertisers who effectively finance such newspapers. Richer people can afford to buy information more readily. They have better access therefore to data on prices and quality of goods and services from consumer associations, magazines and computerised data systems. Richer people and richer areas attract and receive more information because they form a more profitable market. In addition their greater spatial mobility through a greater degree of car ownership means that they are also more spatially aware of services. In general, then, they are aware of more options from which to make a more informed choice. They can realise more of the potential environment of choice.

(c) Accessibility or spatial access

Private and public goods and services are not evenly distributed across space, and even if they were, some people would live further from them than others. One major geographical assumption about people's behaviour is that it takes time, effort and money to cross space (called the *'friction of distance'*) and thus the probability of people using a service declines the greater the distance away that they live. Because of the friction of distance, people who live relatively far from goods and services are considered to be relatively disadvantaged. It has been shown in East Anglia, for example, that people living furthest from health facilities use them least.

Space should not be considered separately from time because people may use the service as much over a period of time in that they spend the same but visit it less often. Their access to different forms of transport may influence the amount and frequency of use. A car may allow more frequent use but often it facilitates the bulk transport of goods, such as groceries, which means less frequent journeys are needed. Bulk purchasing, multi-purpose trips and the lower frequency of journeys may mean that people are prepared to travel further to the service. Distance is then less of a constraint.

Space-time budgets

People are also constrained in their response to a particular service by their other activities. Their 'space-time budgets' differ. Those who work full time are constrained to shop during their lunch hours or after work. Their environment of choice may be oriented to their place of work or the route to and from work. Those who need to take young children to and from school are also constrained to shopping, or indeed working, within certain periods of time. This may limit the distance they can travel to shop or work, especially if they do not have use of a car.

The friction of distance, the physiological constraint of having to sleep and the constraint of having to fit in with other people's time budgets, whether it is for social interaction and recreation or for work, may all be combined together diagrammatically.

Such a diagram has been called a *time-space prism*. Different people, even within the same household, have different prisms, which reflect the varying constraints on their movement (Figure 5.7).

In summary, accessibility to a particular service is influenced by distance, available transport, the proximity of other services permitting multi-purpose trips and the space-time budgets produced by people's other activities.

(d) Access to finance

Where people live and their individual and household characteristics affect their access to finance. In the past some inner areas of cities were 'red-lined' by building societies, that

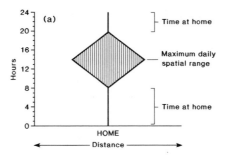

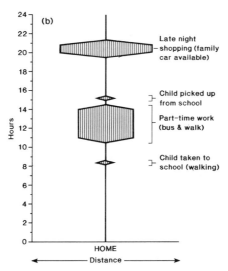

5.7 *Time-space prisms: a) concept; b) example*

is, no mortgages were allocated to houses within them. This was because building societies did not view houses in these areas as secure investments. Insurance companies have refused to give house contents and buildings insurance to certain areas because they assess them to be of too great a risk. Credit facilities too have been withheld from people living at certain addresses. Finally, and perhaps most critically, people have been refused interviews for jobs because of their address. Thus the most crucial access to finance – income – has been affected by place of residence. In all these cases it was the area, not the individual or household, that was the reason for the lack of access to finance. It is therefore possible that, by living in a particular area, people will be less likely to get a job, own a home, get credit to buy goods and insure any that can be bought. People living in such areas are then *multiply disadvantaged*.

Certain types of people also have limited access to finance. In the past women found difficulties in obtaining mortgages and still do have problems getting certain jobs, despite legislation (Chapter 12 Section 3c). Some immigrants and ethnic minorities still find access to mortgages and jobs difficult, again despite legislation. Retired people on small pensions, people with low or insecure incomes and the unemployed also find problems gaining mortgages.

Poor access to one form of finance limits access to others. Those who cannot get a job are less likely to be able to obtain a mortgage. Those who do not own their own home are less likely to receive credit facilities because they have little collateral. Ready access to one form of finance, on the other hand, enables many advantages. Access to what is seen to be a good school may have been obtained through being able to raise a mortgage on a house within its catchment area. A home owner may more easily, and often more cheaply, obtain credit to purchase goods such as home computers and books that help educate their children. More educational qualifications are thought to improve people's chances of better jobs and their associated incomes. They have certainly been shown to affect the type of training scheme that non-employed youths follow, and these in turn influence their chances of gaining employment. There is then a link between owner-occupation and ease of obtaining credit, both of which may influence children's chances of being well educated and consequently having better job opportunities.

(e) The needs and wants of different types of people and their access to goods and services

It is helpful here to summarise the ways in which people may be classified into groups with different needs and wants and to examine how their access to them varies.

Gender

Gender is the socially or culturally defined difference between men and women, while sex is the biologically defined difference. Gender differences are based on socially defined roles of men and women and the relations between them, such as the degree of power they exert over one another. Men and women may have different social as well as biological needs and wants. They may also have different degrees of access, for example, to certain jobs, higher education, and some social and recreational organisations. Such differential access is socially constructed and not biologically based. It has been noted that many women are constrained in the spatial extent of their activities and are limited to the 'private domain' of domestic life, while men dominate the 'public domain' of paid-work and public decision-making. Such observations contribute to the view that women are subordinate to men. The introduction to the international atlas *Women in the World*, states that 'everywhere women are worse off than men: women have less power, less autonomy, more work, less money and more responsibility...... Women in rich countries have a higher standard of living than do women in poor countries, but nowhere are women equal to men.'

Age

Some needs and wants vary with age. Many of these are also socially rather than biologically based, but there are some obvious differences between the needs of children, young adults and the very elderly. People of the same age, however, may be in very different situations; for example, some people between sixty and sixty-five may be economically active, some may be retired but active in voluntary groups, while others may be retired and much less active. Age is therefore only a rough guide. Some areas are relatively under-provided with facilities for children and the elderly. Access for children and the elderly to certain activities may be encouraged by reduced prices, whereas to others it may be restricted or limited; for example, children cannot attend some films, even if accompanied by an adult. Access to mortgages can also be difficult for the elderly.

Life cycle

Some needs and wants may vary more with stage in the life cycle rather than age. One progression, which is too often regarded as typical for everybody, is

single adult → marriage or cohabitation → child breeding → child rearing → children leaving home → widowhood. For many this progression is interrupted or is not completed. Separation and divorce sometimes lead to one parent families with, for some, remarriage and repetition of parts of the cycle.

Some people remain single, while others marry and do not have children. People in different parts of the cycle, or variations from it, often have different needs and responsibilities, and varying access to goods and services to fulfil them. Housing needs, for example, vary during the cycle. Young women, or indeed men, who have responsibility for caring for very young children may find access to jobs difficult or the range of possible jobs within time and distance constraints of the home limited.

Household composition or family size

The number of people in the household and their relationships with one another may be partly related to life cycle stages or their variations, such as one parent families. Households may also be at a similar stage but be of different sizes, for example families with a large rather than a small number of children. Difficulties of access have been associated with household composition. One parent families may have difficulties obtaining mortgages to own a house and often find social/public housing for rent the only type open to them; while the youngest children of large families in general do not achieve as well at school as their older siblings.

Ethnic groups based on religion and/or race

These groups are defined culturally and socially as well as by faith, area of origin and biology. The social definition is based partly on lack of access to goods and services. Many of the 'troubles' in Northern Ireland concern the unequal access to jobs by Protestants and Catholics. People of Afro-Caribbean background have also lacked equal access to houses and jobs in Britain and North America. Racial and religious differences are sometimes combined, as with those of Asian descent who are not Christians living in predominantly Anglo-Saxon areas which have Christianity as the main religion. Religious and cultural differences, though, may be just as significant between the Asians, be they for instance Hindu, Muslim or Sikh, as between Asian and non-Asian. It should also be carefully noted that in one country a particular ethnic group may enjoy much greater access to goods and services than another, while in a different country the same group may find such access more difficult than other groups. The relationships between ethnic groups are not the same everywhere.

Social class

This is a complex concept that may be related to family of birth, position in the division of labour (whether employer or employee, manager or managed, skilled or unskilled) or length of education. Social class then can be related to access to jobs and to income, which then influences other forms of access. The concept is fundamental to major theories of society. Marxist thought puts the class struggle at the centre of the development of society, with the working classes continually trying to overcome the dominance of the owners of capital, who maintain the subordination of the working classes in numerous ways. Other writers see the idea of *social status* cutting across class structures so that the possibility of class consciousness is reduced, because workers of different types are attributed different status, which they reflect in their consumption of goods and services and by their location in housing areas.

Corporate sector

This is a more recent classification that is also based on occupation but not on the horizontal levels of divisions of labour such as manager and manual worker, rather on the vertical slices that divide different sectors of the economy, such as the coal mining industry, the car industry, financial services and education. One sector may have more power than another because of its greater importance in the economy at that time. This permits greater bargaining power for salaries and wages. The coal mining industry in Britain, for example, traditionally wielded much power because of the economy's dependency on it. As nuclear and oil-fired power stations reduced the dependency on coal for electricity and cheaper imported coal became available, the relative position of coal mining declined. Pit closures and the reduced number of miners also weakened the power of the coal mining unions and workers relative to other unions and workers. So coal mining workers as a corporate sector have declined relative to, say, workers in financial services, a growing and increasingly important part of the economy. Because some sectors of the economy are spatially concentrated, the differences in power may

have a spatial expression. The very spatial concentration may in itself lend greater strength to the group in mobilising its resources and organising its actions.

Consumption class

This is also a recent classification. It is based on the degree to which people consume in the private or public sector. Some people own their own house and car and use private health, education and pension schemes. Others rent their house from the local authority and use public transport, health, education and pensions. Some have a mix between the two. Again this is already based on some forms of access but affects other forms. As with social class and the corporate sector, it also affects access to power which can affect the availability of goods and services. People in different consumption classes may have different self-interests and develop different sub-cultures which may be reflected in their voting patterns. These are large classifications and include substantial internal divisions; for example, there is a big difference between the more wealthy owner-occupiers who in Britain obtain considerable benefits from mortgage tax-relief and gains in the capital value of their houses, and the marginalised home owners who struggle to make repayments on the mortgage, obtain relatively little tax relief, and whose houses may appreciate at a much less rapid rate than higher priced houses in the same region. Some writers even see these marginalised owner-occupiers, among whom certain ethnic groups are over-represented, as being more similar to many who are privately renting and to some who are renting the lower standard stock in the poorer areas of local authority housing. They contrast these three groups with the better-off home owners and renters of local authority housing in 'better' estates and higher standard stock. The finer differences within a

consumption group are represented partly by the area of housing within which people live, because status is attributed and signalled partly by the housing area in which people live.

(f) Access to power

Power is a complex concept. For some it is expressed as an attribute possessed by an individual or group while for others it is a relationship between people, with one group being able to influence what another does or decides. Access to power suggests that people have differential influence on decisions about the availability and quality of goods and services in an area. This may arise because they have different degrees of success in getting their case heard or because they are more or less able to mount a case that will convince those making the decisions. The latter situation suggests almost an open competition between groups, which has been called a pluralistic situation. The decision makers are judges or arbiters of the best case. Not all groups have similar access to information and resources in order to make a case. They need access to information and the knowledge to make the best use of it. They need the human and financial resources to gather the information, assemble it and present it in a convincing form.

Successful tactics

Community opposition to school closure (Chapter 10 Section 3b), for example, has been shown to be more successful when the tactics adopted towards a consultation exercise are 'factual' and 'political' rather than based on 'public opinion formation'. The factual is the presentation of an argued, written factual report, in a similar style to that produced by an education authority. The political involves obtaining the support of local councillors. The public opinion formation includes public meetings and letters to the press. Those groups using only the last tactic did not succeed in keeping their schools open. Those using a combination of the first two tactics generally succeeded. There is no guarantee that there would be the same outcome over a different issue, but in this case the differential success is interesting. Groups led by male, middle-income, professional workers, even if it were not middle-income groups they were leading, were more likely to use the successful tactics and retain their schools. They probably spoke the same language as those working on behalf of the authority, who were predominantly male. They probably also knew the best channels of communication with the decision-makers. It is not clear whether professional status or gender was the key factor. Even in this open situation, not all groups shared the same ability to affect the outcome. Some areas lost their schools.

Access to decision-makers is often not so open. Consultation may not take place as it did for these school closures. Some groups may be more aware than others of impending decisions and be able to act in order to affect them. Some may be incorporated into the decision process while others are not. The teacher unions, for example, had already been incorporated into the process before the communities were consulted about their schools.

It is also very possible that the decision-makers are not neutral judges. They often have values and attitudes that are shared more with some groups and areas than others. That is why it is felt that decision-makers should be more representative of the population as a whole and include more of these that are often excluded such as women and certain ethnic groups.

Some groups are able to maintain their access to attractive physical or built environments by preventing construction or redevelopment in

their area. Well- coordinated and focused professional campaigns that emphasise fashionable issues such as conservation of ecological niches or buildings representing an architectural heritage may only conserve the areas for the existing residents. In such cases it is often difficult to distinguish genuine environmentalism from self-interest. Development may be displaced elsewhere where opposition is less articulate or less well organised.

Some groups in society are more able to obtain what they want, retain what they want and repel what they do not want in their local areas (Chapter 7 Sections 4 and 5). They have better access to those who are making the decisions that affect their areas and they are more able to mobilise and organise resources to mount a more effective campaign.

(g) Degree of match between needs and provision: social and spatial justice

The extent that needs are met by provision for different social groups is related to the idea of 'social justice'. Although social groups have varying needs, a socially just situation would meet their needs to an equal degree. The needs and provision of services may be aggregated across social groups for particular areas and compared. The relationship between needs and provision for areas is associated with the idea

of 'spatial or territorial justice'. The concepts of social and spatial justice are not straightforward. It is not easy to decide what is 'just'. The concept of equality on which social and spatial justice are based has many aspects. So too does the idea of need (Chapter 5 Section 5). Some idea of the concepts, however, can be given at this stage.

Figure 5.8a shows an example of spatial justice where expenditure or areal provision of services is positively related to needs. Figure 5.8b indicates the opposite situation which has been called the 'inverse care law'. This so-called law was first applied to health services where the 'availability of good medical care tends to vary inversely with the need of the population served'. It summed up the common observation that 'in areas with most sickness and death, general practitioners have more work, larger lists, less hospital support ... than in the healthiest areas; and hospital doctors shoulder heavier caseloads with less staff and equipment, more obsolete buildings and suffer more recurrent crises in the availability of beds and replacement staff'.

The concepts of social and spatial justice may be applied to services other than health care. They could even be applied to the idea of access to power. If such access is uneven socially and/or spatially and that unevenness coincides with the pattern of provision, then it is unlikely that there will be much change in

5.8 a) spatial justice; b) inverse care

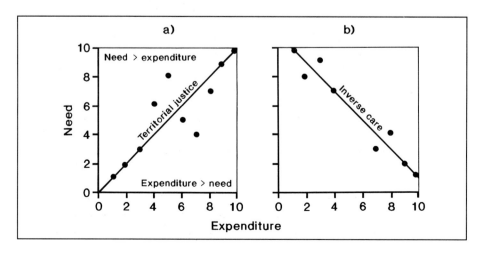

provision. Only where there is an overriding agreement between groups and areas and a willingness that is reflected in government policy will any improvement be made in social and spatial justice in such situations. The degree to which spatial justice is being approached, or indeed departed from, is one major aim of geographical enquiry. This is followed by another main aim of understanding why spatial inequalities are increasing or decreasing.

Summary

The general problem of the chapter is identifying types of inequality of access to goods and services and discussing reasons for them. Underlying the discussion is the question of whether inequalities of access are increasing or decreasing. The section on alternative strategies examines ways in which inequalities may be reduced.

5.3 Other examples

The first two examples discuss access to two major services: education and health. Access to two other major aspects of life, work and housing, forms part of the discussion of Chapters 12 and 13. The final example in this section shows how place of residence influences people's access to a whole series of services and opportunities.

5.3a Education for some?

Throughout recent history, the principle of equality of educational opportunity has pervaded education in the UK. At first sight access to schools may appear to be equal for all pupils, but this is far from the case in reality. From area to area there is a differential availability of types of schools. In many areas all schools are 'comprehensive', that is open to all and catering for the varied needs of a range of pupils. In some regions there are selective schools which take in only pupils of particular abilities, often assessed by some form of examination.

In some areas there are relatively many private schools which have access to them limited by ability to pay (financial access), examination and/or interview. Some schools limit access to particular national or religious groups while others are restricted to a single sex. Even within their local area the awareness and information that parents possess of particular schools, and indeed types of schools, may well be very varied, sometimes being inaccurate, partial and prejudiced. Knowledge of how to gain access to schools is also often very varied,

with only a few parents knowing how to use such knowledge to benefit their own children.

Differential availability of schools obviously affects choice. Inner-city areas, for instance, have particular problems because the local area and pupils are often socially disadvantaged. Their choice of schools is constrained in comparison with parents in higher socio-economic groups who can exert greater pressure to gain entry for their children to popular schools, or purchase a place in a private school, or move house to a particular district where a neighbourhood school has the characteristics they want for their children (Figures 5.9).

Schools and educational systems vary greatly at a variety of scales. At a regional level there is a major difference in the number of places available in private schools.

At a local education authority level there are also big differences. Some LEA's, for instance, have a mixed system of schools with middle schools, 11-16, 11-18 and 16-19 institutions in the same area. Also, different authorities have quite different policies on such issues as

nursery places for under fives (Figure 5.10).

At a more local scale individual schools vary enormously. For instance some may have been part of the first set of TVEI (Technical and Vocational Educational Initiative) schools which might have affected the numbers of microcomputers held by the school. Some might have active parent-teacher associations (PTAs) helping to provide extra resources such as minibuses and

5.9 Private secondary schools

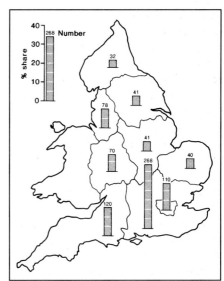

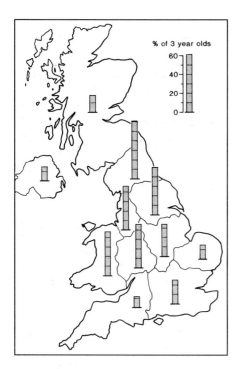

5.10 Access to nursery places in maintained schools for three-year-olds

computers. Some might offer a wide curriculum choice at the 16-19 level, whereas others might offer only a limited range of subjects. Since the introduction of the local management of schools in 1990, such local differences between schools may have increased.

Parents in Britain in the early 1990s may choose between schools in their area. This is in contrast to the 1970s, when most of their children were allocated to schools according to the catchment area in which they lived or, at the secondary school level, according to the primary school they attended. Parental choice, however, is constrained by the capacity of schools which may not be equal. Differential availability of types of schools means it varies between areas. The density of population, and consequently schools, also means that choice will effectively be less in rural than in urban areas. Within the same area, choice will vary according to the awareness, interest, information and spatial mobility of parents. Richer families may be able to afford to send their children further than poor fam-

ilies or have access to a car to ferry them to and fro. Those without private transport may have their choice limited by the pattern of the public transport network. Thus the introduction of parental choice may not have the same effect for all people in all areas.

Within schools certain ethnic groups, for cultural or language reasons, might be faced with inappropriate curricula and resources. They might respond more to the expectations of teachers than their potential ability, as it has been shown that less is expected of some groups. Researchers have found that although educational attainment varies across ethnic groups (Figure 5.11), this does not reflect differences in potential ability.

The under-achievement of Afro-Caribbeans in this example was related to a number of factors, including teachers' expectations. There are gender differences too. Some girls have negative attitudes to maths, science and computers and fail to realise their learning potential because they have been socialised to respond to certain, but not all subjects. In summary, the schools themselves vary from place to place, and pupils' access to them and to success within them is constrained by such factors as cultural background and gender.

The process of education within schools and the output from schools also varies considerably. Some schools have a 'progressive' approach to teaching strategies in which enquiry learning, working in groups and individual responsibility are encouraged. The wide-ranging skills so developed can readily be transferred into later life. In other schools the educational process may be less stimulating and benefit

fewer. Here our values are clear. Variations in teaching methods, of course, also occur within schools.

The educational process is also affected by the pupils with whom children are educated – their peer group. Since most pupils attend their nearest school, especially at primary level, then the composition of pupils in the school is usually closely matched to the socio-economic characteristics of the neighbourhood within which the school is situated. So the attitudes and characteristics of the school peer group are often similar to and reinforced by those of friends in the neighbourhood. Both sets influence children's attitude to education. The larger and more spatially varied in social composition the school catchment area, the greater the chance that the characteristics of school peer group and local friends are different, and that they have separate effects. Where pupils live within a school catchment area, the characteristic of their peer group within school and the school they attend all affect their educational attainment.

The output of schools, in terms of GCSE and A level results, is very much influenced by the social background of the intake of pupils as well as the process of education during their school career. Results reflect catchment areas as well as schools.

Home background, school, qualifications from school and youth training schemes all affect future life chances. Research suggests that the effects of one are compounded rather than offset by the others. There are, then, still great inequalities of educational opportunity.

5.11 Ethnic groups and educational attainment

Mean number of O levels (number in set)

	Asian		Afro-Caribbean		White	
School	2.4	(85)	0.9	(37)	3.3	(95)
College FE	2.9	(22)	2.1	(12)	3.5	(17)
Other	0.2	(34)	0.5	(22)	1.2	(117)

(based on case studies in Bedfordshire, Birmingham, Bradford, Ealing, Hounslow, the Inner London Education Authority)

5.3b **Access to health**

Access to health care may vary from country to country and within countries both regionally and locally, producing inequalities at a number of geographical scales. There may also be inequalities between social groups within a country. These spatial and social inequalities, though, can be of varying types, for example inequality of use and inequality of outcome (Chapter 5 Section 5). Equality of use would ensure that individuals have an equal opportunity to use the health system according to their needs. In the 1980s in Britain use was not equal; for example, the children of fathers of social class 1, compared with those of social class 5, were twice as likely to have visited a dentist, five times as likely to have been immunised against smallpox and ten times more likely to have received polio or diphtheria immunisation. Equality of outcome includes not just the use but the resulting health of the population. At present, health is by no means equal across countries or within them (Figure 5.12).

These two ideals most approximate the goals of the British National Health Service (NHS) as represented by the Resource Allocation Working Party (RAWP) in 1976 (Chapter 4, Section 3b) in their objective of allocating resources so that there was 'equal opportunity of access to health care for people at equal risk'. This is a complex goal because it involves discovering the geographical distribution of risk for different diseases as well as allocating appropriate health care facilities to match needs resulting from the diseases. RAWP developed a formula which allocated resources in proportion to resident populations weighted by standardised mortality ratios (SMR), as a proxy measure of 'need'. Need varied regionally (Figure 5.12) and was not matched by health care provision or resources. One direct impact of this

formula has been the steady reallocation of resources away from the well-served South East to the relatively poorly served other regions (see Figure 4.15).

Within the regions another aspect of access is the accessibility of clients to health resources. Not surprisingly the greater is the distance from health facilities, the less is the likelihood of clients using them. Evidence from East Anglia indicates that outpatient clinic attendances, in-patient admissions and visiting rates are all affected by accessibility to a hospi-

tal. With the trend towards larger centralised district health facilities, any further centralisation could well be exacerbating existing inequalities. Sadly it is often those in greatest need of health care who are the least mobile members of the community, such as some women, some of

5.12 Standard mortality ratios for selected causes of death (SMR = (actual deaths/expected deaths) x 100; actual and expected deaths are by age and sex; expected deaths are based on national deaths applied to the age and sex composition of the area

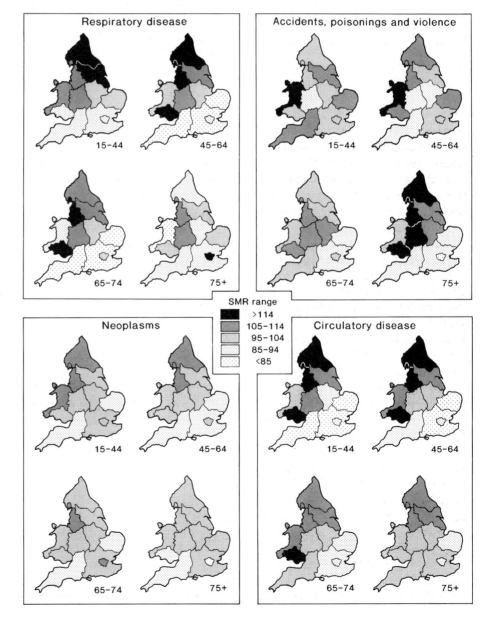

	Social class						
	I	II	IIIN	IIIM	IV	V	All
North	99	110	109	115	109	120	113
Yorkshire & Humberside	115	108	107	103	110	99	105
North West	113	118	114	116	116	114	116
East Midlands	98	95	99	92	98	88	94
West Midlands	97	103	104	104	102	108	104
East Anglia	87	92	95	82	76	81	83
South East	96	91	93	89	90	88	90
South West	93	96	98	90	95	90	93
Wales	117	116	109	120	112	110	116
England and Wales	100	100	100	100	100	100	100

Fig. 5.13 Standardised mortality ratios by social class and region for males aged 15–64, England and Wales, 1970 – 1972

the elderly and the poor.

Differential accessibility to health care can itself lead to unequal use. Spatial factors may then exacerbate social factors affecting use. Spatial accessibility is restricted for many people when facilities are highly concentrated. So, for instance, the massive concentration of teaching hospitals in central London means that many patients have to travel long distances to use their specialist facilities. More specifically, the Great Ormond Street Children's Hospital draws clients from a national hinterland at no little inconvenience to the patients and their families.

Not only are patients restricted in their access to health resources by where they live, but access is constrained by socio-economic circumstances. Certain groups in society are better able to know about (awareness) and use public health care and better able to pay for private health care (financial access). Disturbingly, it is the lower socio-economic groups with the greater needs who often have less access to public health facilities (inverse care law) and use them less. The differences between socio-economic groups in levels of morbidity (illness) and mortality are combined with certain regional differences to give situations where the ideal of equality of opportunity of access to health care is shattered, such as the case of unskilled people living in the inner zones of a large northern city

(Figure 5.13). Their access to, and use of, health facilities both public and private, and their state of health can be unfavourably compared with those of the managerial and professional people (socio-economic groups 1 and 2) living just outside London. The latter types of groups seem to feel health care is more important and they make more intensive use of health services (higher utilisation rates). A good example of this is that more women have cervical smears from socio-economic groups 1 and 2 than from group 5, yet the latter has a greater incidence of cervical cancer. Also of social concern is the differential treatment of social groups by general practitioners. This is due mainly to the different demands of social groups, with groups 1 and 2 being more demanding of expert opinion. Consequently, people in groups 1 and 2 are more often referred to a consultant than other groups, who are more likely to be prescribed medicine and be satisfied by that alternative. So the need, provision, accessibility, use and treatment vary significantly for different socio-economic groups within the same region of a country. They also vary greatly among regions.

5.3c **Where you live and who you are!**

To an extent where you live brings along with it a range of positive and negative spin-offs, one being access to employment. If in the late 1970s you lived in Winchester, a town in southern England with almost full employment, you were in a favourable position to gain a job. On the other hand, people living in Consett, County Durham, after the decline of the coal and steel industries, were faced with few job opportunities and consequently many experienced periods of unemployment (Figure 5.14).

Where you live also helps or hin-

ders your access to private goods and services, for example finance. Credit for instance, is withheld from people living in certain 'problem' housing estates regardless of a particular individual's ability to repay such credit. Where you live can also directly affect your 'purchase' of insurance. Figure 5.15 shows how insurance premiums for cars, home contents and houses vary spatially.

Access to public services, other than education (Chapter 5, Section 3a) and health (Chapter 5 Section 3b), can also be much affected by where you live. For instance, near-

ness to open space, sports facilities, libraries and public transport is obviously an advantage, unless, in some cases, the facility is right next door. Such a house or area would therefore score highly on any ameni-

5.14 Where you live and access to jobs

Winchester	5.3% unemployed Jobs increased by 7% in five years 1976-1981
Consett	25% unemployed Jobs fell by 33% in five years 1976-1981

Postal Area	Car Insurance 1 – 6 (low – high)	Home contents insurance 1 – 6 (low – high)	Buildings insurance 1 – 4 (low – high)	Cumulative score
London W1 (Central London, South East)	6	6	4	(16)
Twickenham TW19 (West London, South East)	3	2	4	(9)
Warrington WA3 (Cheshire, North West)	2	2	3	(7)
Truro TR21 (Cornwall, South West)	1	2	1	(4)
Cleveland TW1 (North East)	1	3	2	(6)

5.15 Cost of insurance

ty index and make it more desirable. Where you live will also affect the nature, availability and cost (local taxes) of public services such as schools and refuse disposal. One local authority may well levy higher local taxes but offer considerable public services, whereas another may levy lower taxes but offer limited public services. Those households that are able to move may well consider as part of their locational decision the availability, quality and cost of services that they want in different local authority areas. In contrast, those who find it difficult to move, who live on some local authority housing estates on the periphery of cities or in some rural communities, may have limited access to goods and services. Overall, then, where you live does strongly influence your access to public and private goods and services.

Income obviously affects access to goods and services. People's income and status are determined largely by their occupation. Income, status and occupation, which are slightly different but related, can all affect access to social institutions and networks. Some social networks can be exclusive; for example, membership of golf clubs, rotary, freemasons and the formal and informal ties resulting from past attendance at schools and colleges give access to information and contacts and through them real influence and power may be exacted. They can also open up fur-

ther occupational opportunities. Who you are in terms of gender and ethnicity and their effects on access have already been discussed (Chapter 5, Section 2).

Knowledge is also power. It consists not only of the awareness and acquisition of information, such as via electronic databases and consumer associations journals, but also of the ability to use such information to achieve one's own objectives. A recent example of this is the use of the database established in 1987 listing places available at over 200 colleges and universities. This computerised Educational Computing and Credit Transfer Information Service (ECCTIS) is sponsored by the Department of Education and Science and is based at the Open University. Details of over 6000 courses with places left in August/September can be electronically accessed. If that information is used to contact admissions tutors then the result may be an offer on a desired course. However, without awareness of the existence of the data, as well as access to the relevant computer systems and appropriate subsequent contact with an admissions tutor, lack of such knowledge is equally lack of power. Potential students need to be aware of the existence of the data, need access to the appropriate computer systems and have to be able to make best use of their contact with admissions tutors in order to gain a place.

In an increasingly materialistic society, access to goods and services

and the finance to provide them may be over-valued and people may be tempted to employ dubious, even illegal means to pursue them. Access to restricted information and knowledge and positions of power represent opportunities for illegal as well as legal gains, with scandals about 'insider dealing' in the City of London indicating the financial power gained by those with such restricted and high-status information. The pursuit of material possessions and their conspicuous display sometimes leads to people being valued or categorised by what they have as well as what they do and who they are. The emphasis on material possessions may be questioned, partly because of the use of scarce resources and the deleterious environmental effects that can be associated with their production. Yet access to material goods, as well as services, has been included as a major aspect in definitions of 'social well-being' and 'quality of life', concepts that incorporate many aspects of everyday life.

Well-being can be measured at a variety of geographical scales. For instance, it can be analysed at a very local scale even to the level of the room plan arrangement of a high- rise office building (Figure 5.16).

Quality of working conditions is here equated with nearness to windows, more elaborate furnishings,

5.16 Power in the office

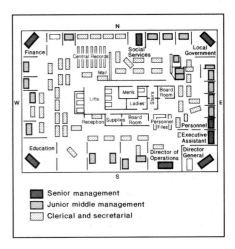

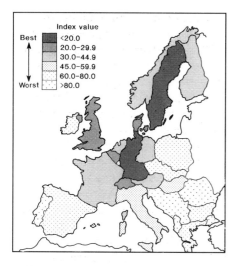

5.17 Well-being in Europe

Director General might lead to a greater access to power (the DG) for the Director of Operations than for the Head of Finance located at the other side of the building.

On another scale, one study analysed well-being across Europe. Originally it included twenty-seven variables, about half of which related to access to housing, health, education and private goods. These were reduced to six variables which represent the major spatial differences displayed by the original twenty-seven. Only two of these six relate to access.

It is interesting to note that no 'environmental' variables were considered as part of well-being in 1984, when the results were published. The map displays a pattern of marked inequality and a core-periphery relationship seems evident (Figure 5.17).

When different national groups of people are asked about their perceptions of their access to the 'good life', the results are interesting. Nearly 10,000 people were asked, from the ten member countries of the EEC at the time: 'On the whole are you satisfied, fairly satisfied, not very satisfied or not at all satisfied with the life you lead?' Three levels of satisfaction were identified. In group 1 Denmark and the Netherlands were most satisfied. Group 2 with still above-average levels of satisfaction were Eire, Luxembourg, Belgium, West Germany and the UK, whereas France, Italy and Greece formed a group of less-satisfied countries. These 'objective' and subjective measures of well-being are interesting to contrast, particularly in the case of Eire where the subjective view is higher than that measured from published data.

distance from lifts (elevators) and size of office. The privileged locations of senior management are the spatial manifestations of their power and status. Even within senior management a clustering around the

5.4   Alternative strategies

There is a variety of strategies that can be followed to improve access. Some involve changes in the service or industry itself, others target the individuals or groups for whom access is limited, while further ones reduce the spatial, financial and other constraints that these groups face. Some strategies involve combinations of these. Types of strategies range along a continuum of intervention from those that inform, educate and encourage; those that give incentives, usually financial; and those that involve legislation and elements of compulsion.

Improving availability

The differential availability of goods and services may be improved by new methods of resource allocation and location in the public sector, and

governmental intervention in the private sector to inform, induce or compel changes. The allocation of resources to the regional health services (RAWP in Chapter 5, Section 3b) is a good example of trying to produce a better match between need and provision. Unfortunately it has involved a relative decline in resources for some regions, rather than simply an increase in the others that would bring them up to the level of the better-off regions. The location of new hospitals, or new services in existing hospitals, in previously under-served areas also illustrates how differential availability may be improved.

The private sector may be provided with information about the possibilities in certain cities, regions or states that have hitherto not enjoyed an image that business relates to opportunity or success. The states in the USA have been producing such

marketing packages for many years. More recently local authorities in Britain, particularly in Scotland with the help of the Scottish Development Agency (SDA), have been investing in competitive marketing of their areas. Such *marketing of place* in Glasgow and Strathclyde has been relatively successful in helping to attract investment, and to create a more confident environment for both local enterprise and local well-being. There is an advantage in being first in the field. As more areas market their particular place, there is relatively less investment to compete for. There is also a possibility of overselling or 'hyping' your place beyond its potential and, perhaps even worse, believing your own 'hype'. This may only convince people that the differential availability of goods and services has been reduced, or the quality of life improved, for a

MYSTERI⁑US CRAFTS SEEN ALL ⁑VER GLASGOW.

7-HEADED W⁑MAN SIGHTED.

PANDEM⁑NIUM IN THE STREETS.

They've arrived. Beings from far-off lands. Everywhere you look around Glasgow this year you'll see them – artists, singers, athletes and dancers from all over the world.

They're here to take part in Glasgow's year as Cultural Capital of Europe 1990, adding to our own remarkable cultural heritage.

Hundreds of people will be running for their lives – to gain a place in the World Cross Country finals. As well as pedalling, rowing, tugging and throwing, in some of the many other sports events.

Some hideous creatures are being released in Glasgow's cinemaland, ten new horror films in fact, for the Horror Film Festival. With monster names in the theatre too, including the Bolshoi Opera and the Royal Shakespeare Company.

Prepare to make contact with many rather unidentified objects at our art & craft exhibitions. You'll be mystified by the ice carvings, Malaysian sculpture and Nigerian paintings. (Although you should recognise Henry Moore and Pissarro.)

And everyone will be taking to the streets, for all the music at the Chinese New Year festival. As well as taking to Glasgow's concert halls and stages for the many other music events such as the Leningrad Symphony Orchestra, German Folk, and all that jazz – from Dixieland to Belgian.

So send off the coupon opposite for a brochure. And you could be having a close encounter too – of the cultural kind.

MUSIC
21/24 FEB:* Scottish Opera: Die Fledermaus. Theatre Royal.
13/17, 20/22 FEB, 3 MAR:* Scottish Opera: La Forza del Destino, Theatre Royal.
20 MAR:* Cracow Philharmonic Orchestra, Conducted by Penderecki.
11·APR:* Scottish Chamber Orchestra: Conducted by Sir Peter Maxwell Davies.
12 APR:* Leningrad Symphony Orchestra: Conducted by Alexander Dimtriev.
13-19 MAY: Country Music Festival: Citywide. 15-30 JUN:* Scottish National Orchestra Promenade Concerts: Kelvin Hall.

COMMUNITY PROJECTS
15 DEC - 30 MAR: Get Knitted: Springburn Museum.
10 JAN-DEC: Keeping Glasgow in Stitches: Kelvingrove Art Gallery.
17 JAN-15 FEB: East End Banners, The Fabric of Glasgow: People's Palace. 29 JAN: Chinese New Year: City Hall. JAN-APR: Andrew Hay – Painting in the community: Touring various venues. 12 MAR-1 APR: 'Ma Mammy's Story: Clyde Unity Theatre, Touring Production.

DANCE
5 JAN-24 MAR:* New Moves: Experimental dance and movement from David Dorfman and company, USA; Sue McLennan and dancers; Truus Bronkhorst; Les Ballets C de la B; DV8 Physical Theatre in residence, Third Eye Centre, RSAMD and Tron Theatre.
27-28 FEB:* Gregory Nash Dance Group: 'Giant', Tramway.

THEATRE
13-17 FEB:* Mistero Buffo with Robbie Coltrane: King's Theatre.
3-5, 7-10 MAR:* Freaks: French Theatre, Tramway.
5-10 MAR:* The Comedy of Errors: English Shakespeare Company, Theatre Royal.
9-31 MAR:* Four Horsemen of the Apocalypse: Citizens Theatre. 19 MAR-21 APR:* John Brown's Body: A Wildcat Stage Production, Tramway.
4 MAY-2 JUN:* Mother Courage with Glenda Jackson: Citizens Theatre.

SPORT
4 FEB: Scottish Men's Cup Basketball: Kelvin Hall. 14-18 FEB: Ladies Curling Championships: Summit Centre.
10/11 FEB: UK and European Indoor Tug of War Championships: Kelvin Hall.
23 FEB: GB v. German Democratic Republic Athletics. 3-4 MAR: European Indoor Athletics Championships: Kelvin Hall.
11 MAR: World Cross Country Trials: Bellahouston Park.
30 MAR-1 APR: British Volleyball Men's Championships: Kelvin Hall.
14 APR: Slazenger National Badminton Finals: Cockburn Centre.

EXHIBITIONS
15 JAN-25 FEB: Degas' Images of Women: The Burrell Collection.
24 JAN-11 MAR: The British Art Show 1990: McLellan Galleries.
24 FEB-24 MAR: John Logie Baird: Collins Gallery.
10 MAR-5 APR: Philip Reeves, Recent Works: Compass Gallery.
10 MAR-21 APR: Steven Campbell, New Paintings and Drawings: Third Eye Centre.
27 MAR-9 MAY: Glasgow's Great British Art Exhibition: McLellan Galleries.

SPECIAL EVENTS
13 APR-5 NOV: Glasgow's Glasgow: An exciting multi-media event of Glasgow as a live city, Arches under Central Station.
31 MAR-1 APR: Glasgow Comic Art Convention: City Chambers. 4-26 MAY:* Mayfest: A key European festival of theatre, dance, music and performing arts – the biggest and best yet.
*Tickets are available now for these events – phone 041 227 5511. (No booking fee).

| THERE'S A L⁑T GLASGOWING ⁑N IN 1990. CULTURAL CAPITAL OF EUR⁑PE. | Please send me my free colour brochure about Glasgow 1990.
Return to Glasgow 1990, P.O. Box 88, Glasgow, or telephone: 041-204 4400.
Name
Address
Postcode   Tel No. |

The marketing of 'Glasgow City of Culture'

very short time.

Information may also be publicly provided about how certain institutions work, such as building societies (savings and loans) and redlining. This jolted some of them into considering alternative behaviour, such as consciously investing in inner-city areas, so that the differential availability of mortgages was reduced.

Incentives

Incentives or inducements may be offered by the local or national government. Some of the marketing of place is accompanied by local financial incentives. The national government may induce the private sector to relocate, set up new branches or factories by providing financial incentives in cities or regions which

have particularly high unemployment or high levels of poverty. In the 1960s and 1970s in Britain, regional policy provided such incentives as grants for relocating and relief on rents and property taxes. While it probably did create some jobs that would not otherwise have been available, the policy was criticised for, among other things, subsidising a number of developments that would have occurred anyway, and for not providing longer-lasting jobs because many of the branch plants set up under this policy were the first to close when the economy entered a recession.

More recently such inducements have been aimed at, or targeted, smaller areas, such as parts of inner cities. Between 1981 and 1984 twenty-five Enterprise Zones (Figure 5.18), for example, were designated in cities.

Originally these were conceived as areas where market forces would be allowed to operate without interference from local and national government. In the event, they were not such a major departure from previous policy. They became zones in which there was a reduction in the

5.18 Enterprise zones

amount of planning controls on development, but where considerable relief was given on land, building and property taxes over a period of up to ten years, and public money was invested in infrastructure development. Effectively, then, they became another example of spatially-focused state intervention rather than an example of 'non-planning' or 'a flagship for deregulation'. They were focused in the most disadvantaged areas of the country in such a way that they ended up combining industrial and welfare policy. Rather than local authorities being angered by the intended loss of planning controls, they used the zones as marketing tools to attract firms to their areas as well as to improve their opportunities of obtaining other forms of public support.

The idea was borrowed by the Reagan administration in the USA in 1982 but, although implemented by many states, federal legislation originally failed and was later overtaken by the general move to reduce federal involvement in programmes of urban redevelopment.

Much of the criticisms of this policy, in both Britain and the USA, have been similar to those of regional policies. Some of the businesses moving into the zones would have located there anyway and did not need the incentives, and some businesses had relocated there specifically in order to obtain the financial incentives. As a policy to create jobs, then, it has not been particularly successful because businesses and the associated jobs have been relocated locally in order to benefit from the incentives. In Britain many of the businesses and jobs have been in retailing and warehousing rather than manufacturing, as originally intended. In the USA the businesses involved have been mostly established ones rather than the new small businesses that were sought. These were expected to have a greater impact on job creation, but the financial incentives were more attractive to established

than to new small businesses. Small businesses would benefit more from risk or venture capital than from tax relief on profits, which often do not exist in the first year of operation.

Other incentives have been offered to the private sector to invest in British inner cities through Urban Programme money and various grants such as City Grant (Urban Development Grant and Urban Renewal Grant). Advocates of these policies argue that the national government uses the idea of 'leverage' (Chapter 4, Section 4) to offer the *minimum* amount of public money to attract private investment. Because private interests want the *maximum* amount of public leverage in order to reduce their risks and to increase profits, the first aim is not always realised in practice.

Controls

Forms of incentives are therefore not without difficulties. Neither are forms of control or compulsion that are used to improve differential availability. The controls, or sticks, which accompanied the inducements or carrots of British regional policy in the 1960s were to prevent industrial expansion in London and the South East, and Birmingham and the West Midlands, and office growth in London, and to act as encouragement for development elsewhere. Industrial Development Certificates (IDCs) and Office Development Permits (ODPs) were required for developments over particular sizes in designated areas. Companies found ways of overcoming the controls, for example by agreeing to build houses and shops, which local authorities wanted, along with the offices. Factories and offices were built just under the size that needed certification, while existing buildings were redeveloped and, given the controls, fetched high rents. The rapid rise in rents was

one of the reasons for the imposition of controls in the first place. Some industries and offices did relocate but not necessarily to regions and cities that were the objects of regional policy. The relocation of the government's own jobs and offices was more successful.

Spatial controls of these kinds suffer from the possibility of preventing development altogether rather than relocating it. Some companies may have located in other countries rather than locate in an area not of their choosing in Britain. In the controlled areas, developments that would have brought necessary diversification may have been prevented. The West Midlands, in particular, may to some extent have averted the decline that it experienced in the 1970s and early 1980s had development not been controlled in the 1960s.

Controls of this kind, like reallocation of resources, produce a levelling or equalising down in differential availability rather than an equalising up. Both controls and inducements that are spatially focused also produce artificial boundaries in space. On one side of the boundary a grant may be available or development is controlled, while on the other it is not. This point has been particularly felt by businesses located just outside Enterprise Zones. The alternative is some kind of spatial grading, whereby grants decrease in amount in zones away from the Enterprise Zone or targeted area, rather than cease completely. Both present problems of firms relocating locally in order to benefit from inducements.

Improving awareness

Improving people's awareness and information to reduce inequalities of access may operate in two major ways; one simply informs them about the opportunities, while the other allows them to experience them. People may be informed of their rights to certain benefits that are not fully taken-up by advertisements in the media or by advisory bodies such as the Citizens' Advice Bureau. Various kinds of businesses may come into schools and show pupils the opportunities of particular forms of employment. They may encourage women to enter those jobs in which women are poorly represented. In this way they may act as 'role models'. Representatives from higher education may go into schools in areas where the staying-on rate beyond the compulsory school leaving age is low, in order to encourage pupils to realise their full potential.

Alternatively awareness can be raised more directly by experiencing some of these opportunities through work experience or visiting institutions of higher education. Such experience may be especially important in offsetting the degree to which particular groups have been socialised to expect certain types of employment or roles in life. Visits by company directors to areas of the country they do not know may also change their images of such places and make them more aware of opportunities there.

Finally, awareness of new opportunities may be raised later in life by retraining for new employment or by continuing education for a more interesting and rewarding existence in and outside work. Such retraining may be subsidised. It might also be accompanied by financial assistance to relocate into areas of greater opportunity. Such *investment in people* is often contrasted with *investment in places* (investment in infrastructure and inducements to attract jobs).

Improving spatial accessibility

Spatial accessibility may be improved in a number of basic ways: changing the location of the services

or goods, even to the extent of providing them at the person's home, and reducing the friction of distance by providing better transport facilities or improving the mobility of the person. Relocating services is carried out to increase use. A number of local authorities have decentralised many of their services so that they are more accessible to the people they serve. Rather than one large central office in the town hall, there are a number of locally based offices. Not only are these more accessible spatially to the local people, it is intended that the proximity promotes a less impersonal and a better, more focused, locally informed service, whether that be in social services or housing. Sometimes there is insufficient demand for a permanent office so a mobile service is provided, as in a mobile library or an office that is opened on only a few occasions a week, as is the case for some rural banks. Some services may be delivered to the home, but this can be expensive and either the recipient will have to pay extra or the service will have to be subsidised. Mail order and direct marketing, however, may be competitive because they do not have the costly overheads of shops. Using new technology to shop and work from home by removing the need to travel may also reduce spatial inaccessibility.

Spatial inaccessibility may also be reduced by providing improved infrastructure: new roads, or new or extended public transport systems. The latter are most cost effective in densely populated urban areas. In rural areas alternative systems often have to be found, for example using a vehicle performing a delivery service such as mail also as a bus or taxi service. In other cases transport may be subsidised, either publicly or privately, to increase people's spatial mobility. The unemployed, for instance, may obtain very cheap fares to permit a wider area of search for jobs, while accessibility to hypermarkets can be improved by the retail companies running their

own buses from areas of low car ownership.

While all these methods improve spatial accessibility, they all involve costs. Since the least mobile are also often the ones who are least able to pay, there has to be either a public subsidy or a subsidy by other users to make the schemes possible. Otherwise, as in the case of new technology that allows shopping and working from home, those who have the greatest need may be those who can least afford the technology.

Improving access to finance

Access to finance, then, is again shown to be important. It can be improved in a number of ways. Indirectly any improvement in access to better-paid and more secure jobs improves access to finance. Given particular salaries/wages, people can be helped to become home owners by various low-cost schemes which are subsidised by central government (Chapter 4 Section 3c). Changing the rules that control access to mortgages (removing red-lining, treating women and men and their incomes similarly) may also help. These schemes and rule changes do not only improve people's access to housing. As home owners they are more likely to be able to obtain credit at more favourable terms. Since access to some credit and insurance is limited by address, any programmes that improve the area and its image, by reducing unemployment, crime rates and perceived social problems, may indirectly increase access to finance.

Improving access for particular groups

The access of particular groups to goods and services may be improved by better information and education, not just to the groups but also to the providers of the services. Quotas may be introduced to ensure equality of access, as is sometimes legislated for in the employment of the physically handicapped. Areal quotas may also be used, as in the allocation of new jobs in inner-city initiatives to a minimum percentage of inner-city rather than suburban residents. This sounds an excellent idea because too many of the jobs provided by these initiatives have gone to people from outside the inner-city and therefore have not improved inner-city life as intended. But there is an interaction between the labour and housing markets. Once the inner city residents had obtained the jobs by the quota, some of them moved to the suburbs as part of, and a sign of, their upward social mobility. Providing jobs is not enough. The inner-city housing and neighbourhoods also have to be made more attractive places in which to live.

Positive discrimination is another possible strategy. This may be introduced to change the present unequal system of allocation of jobs, housing or places in education. Women may be given preference to men in order to equalise the representation of gender in the workforce. This may be the only way to change deep-seated patterns of socialisation that are passed from generation to generation.

Improved access does not always occur for those most in need. Sometimes the treatment of a particular group presents ideas that are translated into opportunities for others in the group, for example the activities of local authorities and housing associations providing sheltered accommodation for the elderly (Chapter 4, Section 3c). Their activity and experience revealed a possible market for privately owned sheltered accommodation for the better-off elderly. These elderly were presented with a type of housing that was previously available only to the less well-off elderly.

Improving access to power

Improved access to power may be achieved by changing the political system; for example, proportional representation may be introduced so that a minority group within a constituency area has its own elected member. It will never be represented by its own nominee under a first-past-the-post system, as currently operated in Britain. Access may also be improved by increasing people's degree of participation in making decisions which concern their lives and their home area. Participation is more than consultation. Consultation is usually the decision-makers producing ideas and alternatives and the group of people choosing between them. In participation, the group plays its part in creating the alternatives in the first place. Communication is very much two-way: from the people upwards as well as from the decision-makers downwards. Such changes have occurred in some areas in the way local authority housing is managed. Tenants cease to be 'passive recipients of public welfare, dependent upon outside agencies for repair and maintenance and subject to petty rules and regulations concerning access, mobility, house upkeep and even trivial matters of day-to-day living such as the keeping of pets'. Tenants may be fully involved in the redesign and management of their homes.

Improvements may also be made to groups' access to information and resources for making cases at inquiries. Some opposition groups have relatively little resources compared with proponents that may be transnational or national business organisations. They may be granted money to make their case. In the same way, political parties may be granted equal amounts of money to spend at elections, so that wealthier parties do not have an unfair advantage.

Improving spatial justice

There are many strategies aimed at social and spatial justice. Positive discrimination and quota systems have already been mentioned. Some kind of areally based policies have already been discussed for improving access to jobs. Some areal policies have also been designed to improve access to services. Education priority areas were designated in the late 1960s in order to improve the education of children from areas that were seen as socially disadvantaged. More resources were given to the schools and teachers were paid somewhat higher salaries in order to attract and retain them. The difficulties of such area-based or spatially targeted policies are that the areas may include many people who are not socially disadvantaged and are not in need of extra help; that, though they may have concentrations of the socially disadvantaged, they may exclude the majority of socially disadvantaged people; and that designation gives the area a 'label' which can make matters worse through, for example, stereotyping and various kinds of discrimination based on address. The advantages of spatial targeting are that it is easy to deliver resources and that spatially concentrated inputs of resources may have a greater impact than those that are more widely scattered. They may contribute to changing the local social environment as well as directly affecting individuals within it.

Successful strategies to reduce inequalities of access in existing systems are not easy to find. Some therefore decide that only fundamental change of the existing systems will accomplish the aim.

5.5   Perspectives

Any discussion of improving spatial access and reducing social and spatial inequalities presupposes the different types of reasons or theories suggested to explain differential access and inequalities. Some explanations emphasise the inherent characteristics of the people, while some concentrate on the social and economic context in which the people live and have lived. The local and national environments, then, are used to explain the variations in access, and, as has been seen, some strategies involve changing various aspects of them.

Blaming the individual and social groups

One school of thought accounts for differential access of different social groups to educational qualifications and jobs solely by the characteristics of the individuals and social groups. They are not supposed to have worked hard enough at school or put enough effort into looking for jobs. This approach blames the individuals and the groups for their lack of access and any inequalities that may exist. The strategy for improvement then rests with the individuals and groups. It is their own responsibility to change their attitudes and increase their effort and improve their access. There is no need for any policy, except perhaps to encourage them to change or perhaps to assist them in that process. Sometimes it is even suggested that whole social and ethnic groups lack intelligence and because of that suffer poor access, particularly to education and subsequent employment. The associated strategy is to encourage the group to accept their lot.

For these explanations geographical considerations are not important. The locations of the groups can be mapped but their environments do not contribute to explaining their situation, so changing them will not affect it.

Blaming the environment

Other explanations differ markedly from this. Their proponents do not rely solely on the characteristics of the individuals and the group for explanations. They also study the local and national environments in which people live and have lived. The reason for men and women having differential access to particular types of jobs, for example, is not simply that they possess different inherent characteristics or skills because of biological differences, but that they have been socialised since birth into particular roles and role relations. Differences in aptitudes and skills may be socially or environmentally, not biologically produced.

While it may help if such institutions as the Manpower Services Commission (later the Training Agency and TEED) have, as one of their objectives, the increased entry of men and women into particular types of employment where they are respectively under-represented, it is not sufficient. There has already been much socialisation of the potential employees before they are sixteen and even more of the people operating the training schemes from private agencies to potential trainers or employers. More fundamental change is needed. Evidence from the youth employment training schemes suggests that despite the objective, the gender differences in job entry has increased rather than decreased.

Comparison of gender and employment shows that socialisation varies amongst nations. In some countries women dominate in jobs that are elsewhere performed by men, for example in heavy manual labour in the USSR and in agriculture in parts of Africa. Socialisation also occurs at the local scale. In certain areas in Britain, most children leave school immediately they have satisfied the compulsory years of schooling in order to enter local employment, as their fathers and mothers have before them. There is a demand for their labour from the major local employers and it has been expected of them that they will continue to do what the majority have done in the past. In other areas there is a much stronger tradition of 'staying on' and entering higher education. Although such differences are affected by social class and past education of parents, young adults

Women working in the USSR

with similar home backgrounds living in different areas will often conform to the norm of the area rather than that of the social class.

Types of equality

Any attempt to counter socialisation and other reasons for inequalities, and to improve access, should consider very carefully what is meant by equality. There are various kinds of equality that were hinted at in Section 5.3b. They include:

- equality of opportunity
- equality of use
- equality of expenditure
- equality of outcome.

Equality of opportunity to education, for example, may involve children from different areas of social, ethnic and ability groups having equal access to all schools. Equality of outcome may involve the same average educational attainment for all social groups and areas. There would be a range of attainment within the groups and areas reflecting individual differences, but no dissimilarity between the group or area means. At present educational outcomes vary by social group and area, even though steps have been taken to increase equality of opportunity. Equality of opportunity does not guarantee equality of outcome if the children start from different positions and some have more advantages and encouragement from their home backgrounds throughout their period of education. Indeed, to obtain equality of outcome there may have to be inequalities of expenditure and other inputs throughout their schooling in order to offset the unequal backgrounds. Such positive discrimination, as it has been called, may be objected to by some because not everyone is treated in the same way, and because it may equalise downwards rather than upwards. Thus in using the concepts of social or spatial justice or in applying strategies to

obtain them, the meaning of equality must be carefully considered.

So too must the concept of need, which forms the vertical axis of Figure 5.8a and Figure 5.8b, for spatial justice and the inverse care law. Need may be judged, for example, by professionals delivering the service, by politicians who are deciding on priorities of expenditure among services, and by consumers or clients themselves. They may all judge need in dissimilar ways. Even the same level of underlying need of clients may vary in the way it is expressed, according to the ability of individuals to articulate their needs. It is not easy, then, to measure need and therefore it is even more difficult to measure degrees of inequality.

Usually inequality is examined for a particular service. The ideas of social well-being and quality of life at the positive end of the spectrum, and multiple deprivation and social disadvantage at the negative end, include a concern for a whole series of services. Measures comparing these concepts across space and time effectively aggregate sets of indicators or measures, some of which are indicators of access. These include access to key elements of the physical environment, such as clean air and unpolluted water, and accessibility to areas of scenic beauty, as well as access to a range of jobs, housing, goods and services. They might also include access to attractive built environments, but, as with some other measures, there is not always a generally agreed idea of what is 'attractive'.

Such overarching concepts as quality of life are difficult to measure. The relationship between a particular indicator and the overall concept may be clear in one country or part of a country but not in another, or clear to one social group but not to another. Declining use of, and access to, public transport, for example, may be seen by some as a sign of increasing affluence and quality of life, because people can afford private transport (cars) and are more

spatially mobile. Others may view it as a sign of decreasing quality of life because private cars are a less energy-efficient way of transporting people and generally produce more pollution than public transport. Different values underlie the relationship between the indicator and the overall concept.

The concepts themselves also go in and out of fashion. During some periods concepts concerning wealth creation, economic efficiency and productivity tend to dominate public concern and/or governmental thinking. At other times concepts that are to the fore are concerned with quality of life rather than quantity of material possessions, and the (re)distribution of wealth between groups and areas rather than its creation. Just as the emphasis on the private and public sectors (Chapter 4, Section 5) is cyclical, there also seems to be another related cycle concerning wealth creation and wealth (re)distribution. Research and concern about access forms part of the emphasis on (re)distribution. It is part of Welfare Geography which studies who gets what, where, how, and why. (Chapter 1, Section 7). The concern for inequality and spatial justice are also fundamental to Radical Geography. (Chapter 1 Section 7). In the same way that there are cycles in public concern, approaches to geography also go in and out of fashion.

Those who are concerned with issues related to access may be divided into two major groups. There are those who wish to amend and improve the existing economic, social and political systems so that inequalities are reduced. There is another group who believe that inequalities between areas and groups of people are inherent to the existing systems and that only fundamental change of the systems will reduce inequalities. Many Welfare Geographers tend to fall into the first group, while Radical Geographers form part of the second group.

Underlying the debate is the root cause of inequalities. An economic system that involves the accumulation of profits to a few is bound to lead to inequalities between groups. One that creates and increases differences between areas by its operation will obviously produce spatial inequalities. If the social and political systems are used to support such an economic system, as well as to attempt to reduce social and spatial inequalities, then there are bound to be continuing conflicts and contradictions. Some inequalities between social groups and areas may be reduced only for others to emerge in other forms and other places.

Geographers are particularly interested in discovering whether there are major spatial differences in these overarching concepts such as quality of life, and whether the differences are increasing or decreasing. This may be at the scales of inner cities compared with outer suburbs, the so-called 'north-south divide' in Britain or 'east-west divide' in France, or the 'north-south gap' in development between sets of countries at a global scale.

Most of the discussion of this chapter has been at the scale of the individual, social group or area. Many of the headings could be discussed relative to business organisations or countries. Business organisations in one part of the country may have better access to finance for expansion than those in another part. Small businesses often find it more difficult to borrow money than larger ones. Similarly some countries find access to finance more difficult than others. Some countries have better access to resources than others and have the necessary 'know-how' to develop them. This is a very basic geographical difference between countries. Some have the resources but not the know-how. They find that they are too easily exploited by countries or transnational corporations (Chapter 8, Section 2) with the know-how. Profits from the extraction of resources, for example, often go out of the country. Problems of access and inequalities occur at different scales. Some of the processes are similar. Some are different.

At all scales geographers will be concerned about understanding the processes that produce the inequalities, and either accentuate or reduce them. They will also have their own ideas about reducing any inequalities between social groups within an area, between areas within a country and between countries. Some, for example, advocate a reduction in only one or two of these, rather than all three. For them it is important to consider why their aims vary with geographical scale.

The search for economic, social and political systems that reduce inequalities across social groups and areas within countries, and between countries, is for some a goal in itself. For others their main aim may be establishing environmentally aware and harmonious economic and social practices around the world. Countries which have already achieved high standards of living may more readily agree to such practices than those with much lower standards. The latter may be very conscious of the gap and perceive it as widening. Their priorities may be different. For those with this environmental aim, the reduction of inequalities between social groups, areas within countries and especially between countries may be a necessary means of achieving their environmental goals.

5.6 **Exercises**

1. (a) Identify any recent and/or planned shopping centre development in your local area and describe its location relative to other shopping facilities.
   (b) Describe the location of this new development relative to the geographical distribution of different types of people, for example, groups based on age, ethnicity and class.
   (c) Discuss the extent to which all groups have equal access to the new development.
   (d) Does the new development offer better opportunities for shopping and other activities than older shopping centres/ areas? If so, in what ways?
   (e) Are any groups further disadvantaged by unequal access to the new development?

2. The table (Figure 5.19) shows information about general practitioners (GPs, or general doctors) in England and Wales in 1987 by Regional Health Authorities.
   (a) (i) In which region are there most doctors relative to the number of people living there (i.e. the region with the greatest potential access to GPs or choice of GPs)?
       (ii) In which region is potential access to GPs least?
       (iii) Map the first column and comment on the differential availability of GPs across England and Wales.
   (b) The proportion of women GPs rose from 14 per cent in 1977 to 20.6 per cent in 1987.
       (i) Describe the regional variation in access to women GPs and suggest reasons for it.
       (ii) Suggest ways in which access to women GPs may be both generally and regionally increased.

Region	Population	Number per 100,000 % women	% overseas*
Northern	51.5	17.4	17.7
Yorkshire	52.2	18.5	21.3
Trent	50.0	19.0	22.1
East Anglian	51.8	16.0	11.0
North West Thames	57.0	29.2	30.4
North East Thames	53.6	23.6	41.3
South East Thames	53.2	21.5	38.9
South West Thames	52.9	25.4	20.0
Wessex	53.6	21.1	7.7
Oxford	52.0	21.6	15.1
South Western	55.2	17.5	6.4
West Midlands	51.8	19.0	30.3
Mersey	52.3	22.0	20.1
North Western	50.2	20.0	31.3
Wales	56.0	15.9	19.6
England and Wales	52.8	20.6	22.8

*From outside UK and Eire

5.19 Access to General Practitioners

(c) Describe and suggest reasons for the regional variation in GPs born overseas.

(d) Using the evidence from all three columns compare the provision of GPs for North West Thames, Wales and North Western and suggest the potential differential access of different groups of the population of these regions to GPs of their choice.

3. The table (Figure 5.20) refers to the percentage of the population staying on at age sixteen in education in selected local education authorities in two regions of England between 1979/80 and 1984/85. The recession at the beginning of this period resulted in many staying on to avoid the possibility of unemployment.

(a) (i) Describe the differences within each region in 1979/80.

(ii) Suggest reasons for the differences.

(iii) Describe the differences in staying-on rates between the two regions at the beginning of the period.

(iv) Suggest reasons for these differences.

(b) (i) Distinguish different patterns of change over the period among the LEAs.

(ii) Suggest reasons for these differences.

(c) (i) By 1985 have the differences within each region and between the regions increased, decreased or stayed the same?

(ii) Suggest the possible consequences of this growing or decreasing inequality within and between regions.

(d) Suggest ways in which the staying-on rate may be both generally and regionally increased.

4. Study Figure 5.21 which shows the housing of ethnic groups. Discuss the differential access of the ethnic groups to housing.

	1979/80	1982/83	1984/85
Greater London and South East			
Parts of Greater London			
Inner London (ILEA*)	43	51	49
Barking	255	38	31
Brent	57	66	58
Harrow	59	69	72
(ALL outer London LEAs)	47	56	52
Selected Counties in South East			
Berkshire	42	56	54
Essex	41	49	44
Surrey	53	63	62

* Inner London was abolished as an education authority in 1990

	1979/80	1982/83	1984/85
North East			
Metropolitan Boroughs			
Gateshead	26	38	39
Newcastle Upon Tyne	35	43	41
North Tyneside	35	48	48
South Tyneside	34	47	32
Sunderland	30	38	32
Counties			
Cleveland	32	44	44
Durham	28	37	36
Northumberland	39	52	47
All English LEAs	40	50	46

5.20 Staying-on rates in England

5.21 Housing of White, West Indian and Asian households

	% in flats	% in detached or semi-detached houses	% in dwellings built pre-1945	% lacking basic amenities	% with more than 1 person per room
All tenure groups					
Whites	15	54	50	5	3
West Indians	32	23	60	5	16
Asians	16	26	74	7	35
Owner occupiers					
Whites	5	67	56	3	2
West Indians	1	37	84	3	13
Asians	4	29	81	5	33
Council tenants					
Whites	27	39	27	3	5
West Indians	54	9	34	3	20
Asians	54	11	35	7	43
Private tenants					
Whites	32	33	87	27	2
West Indians					
Asians	24	21	83	32	22

5.7 **Further reading**

L. Bondi and H. Matthews (eds.) (1988) *Education and Society: Studies in the Politics, Sociology and Geography of Education*, Routledge

J. Cater and T. Jones (1989) *Social Geography: An Introduction to Contemporary Issues*, Edward Arnold

J. Le Grand (1982) *The Strategy of Equality: Redistribution and the Social Services*, Allen and Unwin

D. Harvey (1973) *Social Justice and the City*, Edward Arnold

D. T. Herbert and D. M. Smith (eds.) (1989) *Social Problems and the City*, Oxford University Press

K. Jones and G. Moon (1987) *Health, Disease and Society*, Routledge and Kegan Paul

J. Lewis and A. Townsend (eds.) (1989) *The North-South Divide: Regional Change in Britain in the 1980s*, Paul Chapman Publishing

Geography 16-19 Project Booklet (1986) *Superstores, Hypermarkets and the Environment*, Longman

J. Momsen and J. Henshall (1991) *Women and Development in the Third World*, Routledge

PART II

ENVIRONMENTAL 'BADS': HAZARDS AND THREATS

Chapter 6
Hazards

6.1 Case study: Alerte rouge! The fire hazard and its
    management in south-eastern France
6.2 General problem: key actors and processes
6.3 Other examples
    6.3a Impacts, responses and attitudes to hurricanes
        in two contrasting countries
    6.3b Landslide: the 'Shivering Mountain'
    6.3c Soil erosion above the Dungeon Ghyll Hotel
    6.3d Multi-hazard-prone area: Los Angeles
6.4 Alternative strategies
6.5 Perspectives
6.6 Exercises
6.7 Further reading

Chapter 7
External threats

7.1 Case study: the Canadian North under threat
7.2 General problem
7.3 Other examples
    7.3a Acid deposition
    7.3b Rabies
    7.3c Deflated Michelin Man
    7.3d Migrant labour
    7.3e Not here!
    7.3f AIDS: the modern plague
7.4 Alternative strategies
7.5 Perspectives
7.6 Exercises
7.7 Further reading

Welcome to
SOMEWHERE ELSE
Suggested site for
disposal of nuclear waste,
location of high security
prison, homes for the
mentally ill and hostels
for alcoholics

Chapter 6

HAZARDS

6.1 Case study: Alerte Rouge! The fire hazard and its management in south-eastern France

The department of Var in south-east France is accustomed to the fire hazard. Towards the end of August in 1982, however, the number and severity of fires experienced was more than normal. In particular, two massive fires raged in the Tourtour and Ste Maxime areas (Figure 6.1). The Tourtour area had 4000 hectares destroyed and the Ste Maxime area 3000 hectares. Nearly 300 fire engines were in action alongside 1155 firemen and 630 soldiers. As the ever literary and dramatic local newspapers put it, '*C'était l'apocalypse*' and '*Catastrophe écologique*'.

Although within Mediterranean Provence, Ste Maxime and Tourtour are quite different. Ste Maxime, part of the internationally renowned Côte d'Azur or 'French Riviera', is a densely populated and urbanised vacation and retirement area where large numbers of French people take holidays in August and a more select group live in retirement throughout the year. Tourtour, on the other hand, is in the Haut Var, an area of hills, brushwood and firs, limited agriculture and a small rural population living at low density. Both areas, however, supply the perfect physical prerequisites for fires. They both experience lengthy hot dry summers, making the vegetation tinder dry by the end of August.

This vegetation is predominantly brushwood and coniferous forest and, where cultivated, either vines or olives. The final prerequisite for devastating fires in the area is the Mistral, a notorious, powerful, drying wind blowing down the Rhone Valley and disastrously fanning any fire for days on end.

The 'triggers' for the fire hazard of 1982 were probably, as usual, a mixture of shorting electricity cables, natural combustion, arsonists and careless tourists or farmers. The situation was aggravated by a particularly dry year and the occurrence of the Mistral.

Various individuals and organisations (actors) were closely involved in the subsequent fires (Figure 6.2). Their knowledge and perception of the hazard varied. Some ended up as winners, others as losers. Some played an active and others a passive role; and the extent to which they

A plane spraying a forest fire

6.1 The fire hazard in SE France

had power to influence the situation varied. They adjusted to the hazard in a variety of ways before, during and after the fires (Figure 6.3).

Before the event, firemen helped to inform and educate the public of the danger, assisted in the development of a warning and evacuation system, practised their skills of firefighting, and looked out for fires. The local authorities also helped to develop a warning and evacuation system, insisted upon clearance of vegetation at set distances around buildings and caravans, cleared trees and dead growth and planned refuge areas. Some local residents cleared their own property of vegetation, bought insurance, and watered their properties and surroundings. Planners organised building and zoning regulations. Journalists and other media personnel kept the public informed and educated about the potential hazard. Some or all of the above probably prayed!

During the fires some local residents and holidaymakers left the

The actors		
The public (The vulnerable)	— residents	– permanent (retired or employed) – second home
	— holidaymakers	
Public employees (The managers)	— police — planners — foresters — public service eg gas, telephones, etc	
Fire fighters (Agents of management also vulnerable)	— firemen — soldiers — conscripted public — pilots of Canadair/helicopters/spotter planes	
The media (Communicators)	— TV announcers — radio announcers — pilots (airborne messages) — journalists	
Business (Profit makers)	— insurance employees — builders — hardware store owners — farmers	

6.2 Types of actors related to the fire hazard

6.3 Human responses to the fire hazard

Before	During	After
Clearance of trees and dead wood		Clearance of trees and dead wood
Creation of fire breaks and barriers	Emergency fire breaks and barriers established	Review system of fire breaks and barriers and create more where necessary
Warning systems developed	Warning systems in action	Review warning systems and possible change
Evacuation plans developed	Evacuation implemented	Evacuees return or permanently leave
Building/land use zoning regulations		New building/land use zoning regulation if felt necessary
Temporary refuge areas/buildings organised	Refuge areas/buildings used	Review of system of refuge areas/buildings
Education of children and public		Further education of children and public
System for informing public developed	Informing public	Review of system for informing
Fire fighters practice	Fighting fire	Review of fire fighting system
Watering of land and buildings to lessen fire risk	Watering of land and buildings	
Spotting fires	Spotting possible further fires Tracking existing fires	Spotting systems reviewed
Buying insurance		Paying out insurance and/or taking out of more insurance
	Looting	Offenders imprisoned
	Temporary fire control HQ set up	Dismantling of fire control HQ
	Road blocks	
Canadairs practice	Canadairs in use	Further practice
Rehabilitation (eg afforestestation) of previous ecology destroyed by fire		Permanent ecological damage possible (Clearance of resinous trees and replanting less fire-susceptible varieties). Further afforestation
	Some public services cut off	Public services returned
		Reconstruction of damaged buildings and farm land
		Meeting costs of reconstruction/losses

area; fire officers, army and foresters located and tracked the fires; the local authorities and fire officers activated the warning system; control headquarters, police and soldiers set up road blocks; and army, local residents and fire officers fought the fires. Not least, information on the fires was communicated by the employees of the media.

After the fires, some residents moved out and holidaymakers stayed away. Insurance salesmen sold more policies and paid out on others. Local authorities and fire officers modified the warning and

land use systems. Some local business people lost (tourist businesses) while others gained (local builders). Representatives of local services (water, telephone, electricity, in particular) reconnected supplies and householders met the losses (physical and psychological!).

The impacts were financial, ecological and human. Financial losses and gains were experienced by various individuals and organisations. Ecological impacts were negative since it can take three to five years for local ecosystems to recover, and bare hillsides in the meantime are

notoriously open to erosion. Human impacts included those on tourists (never to return), firemen (life and equipment) and residents (life and property).

The year 1983 was a similar if less disastrous one for fires in Var. It was noteworthy for the evacuation of thousands of holidaymakers in the Puget sur Argens – Fréjus area and the loss of a 'Canadair' with crew. Indeed, the Var in August 1983 suffered more damage from the serious flooding than from fires.

6.2   General problem: key actors and processes

The fire hazard in the south of France is just one example of the hazards that face people in that area. Every populated area suffers some kinds of hazards but the types of hazards, their frequency of occurrence and the human response to them usually vary from area to area. This spatial variation in hazards is due, on the one hand, to the different atmospheric, geomorphological, ecological and geological conditions that prevail in areas and, on the other, to the different combinations of social, economic and political activities that occur from region to region. The physical conditions produce so-called 'natural hazards' such as earthquakes, while the activities of people interacting with the physical processes may lead to such hazards as water and air pollution. Other hazards may arise from the built environment, such as gas explosions in high-rise flats, or from the human environment, such as crime and riots.

Definition of a hazard

A *hazard* may be defined as an event that is perceived as a threat to people, property and nature, and

which originates in, or is transmitted by, the physical, built or human environment. The processes operating in and between these varying environments, on occasions, lead to changes in conditions which constitute such a threat. Many of these changes are sudden and not easy to predict in time, duration, location, spatial extent or human impact.

Some areas are more prone than others to a particular hazard; for example, fires are a frequent hazard in southern France. A few areas are more prone than others to hazards in general, and so may be called 'multi-hazard prone'. Even within these areas, not every person, piece of land or property is equally likely to be damaged by the occurrence of a particular hazard. Some will be more vulnerable than others to damage: for example certain types of buildings to a hurricane or flood or certain types of people to a disease. The type of activities in which people engage may also affect their vulnerability. So depending on, among other things, where they live and what they do, people will live at greater or lesser risk. This means that there is a greater or lesser probability of them or their property being damaged by hazards. So there is *uncertainty* about the occurrence

of a hazard and about the impact it might have.

Statement of general problem

The general problem of this chapter, then, is how to cope with this uncertainty in the environment. How can people improve the predictions of hazards, prevent their occurrence, or reduce their impact?

Key actors and processes

A number of basic processes and types of actors associated with them may be identified (Figure 6.4).

First there are those living or working in the area, who are at risk, either knowingly or unknowingly. At worst they might lose their lives; at least they might be injured, or suffer damage to their property or land. Some of these people and possibly temporary visitors to the area, like the holidaymakers in the fire example, may act as triggering devices to the hazard by their activities or indeed be the agent of the hazard, such as a criminal or disease carrier.

There are researchers who try to understand the processes that lead to particular hazards, so that prediction, prevention and containment may be improved. Examples of these are the vulcanologist for volcanoes, the criminologist for crime, and the researchers into hazards like water pollution, motorway fog and cancer. These actors may produce results which may help warn people of the likelihood of hazards. The key processes of *warning* and generally *informing* both before and during the event, as in the fire example, involve further sets of actors such as the media and government. The latter may also implement *controls* on economic and social activities, particularly on land use and at extreme times movement, such as during an outbreak of foot and mouth disease, to prevent its spread within and outside the area. As Figure 6.4 shows, policy makers in local and national government may make the decisions as to what and how much information and controls should be provided. Various agencies and managers convey the information and implement the controls: beforehand to prevent or minimise the impact of an occur-

rence; during to warn and contain; and afterwards to reduce the indirect effects, repair the damage and bring relief to people to restore their quality of life. In so doing, further preventative methods may be employed, having gained general experience from the event.

Various business organisations may focus their activities on such hazard prevention, be it security systems to prevent burglary or monitoring systems to measure air pollution. Business may also be involved in insuring people and property against hazard, while public and voluntary organisations may meet the cost of hazard relief by providing compensation or aid.

Finally, there are the public movements which direct people and governments' attention to particular hazards. For example, there are the consumer movement, particularly in the United States, with its demands for greater car safety and the removal of lead from petrol, the environmentalist movement with its exposure of the ecological damage done by some inorganic fertilisers and pesticides, and anti-nuclear campaigners with their opposition to nuclear power plants as well as to nuclear weaponry. These movements inform and warn the public of

the hazards created by people's activities, some of which may complexly interact with natural processes to increase the danger, for example air pollution in fog prone areas forming smog.

The relationships between these sets of actors and processes are obviously complex, even for a single hazard. For example, there is the potential conflict between the people living in the area, who may well be aware of the hazard, and those visiting from outside who in their ignorance may trigger off the event. These visitors have to be informed and warned too. Information, preventative controls, management and relief all cost money. Should those who live in the area bear all the costs or should those outside the area also help to pay? To what extent do people listen to information and warnings, and abide by regulations? The further in time or space people are from the last occurrence of the hazard, the less attention they may pay, often to their eventual cost.

Similarly, governments and business may not wish to listen to public movements. Some businesses perceive that their costs would be increased and their profits decreased by controls advocated by the movements, for example water and air pollution controls. Other enterprising companies spot opportunities to make monitoring devices and less hazardous substitutes, for instance certain food ingredients and drugs. Government may bow to the movement's pressures or it may be more influenced by business interests, since it does not want transnational companies, for example, to move their business out to countries where there are fewer controls. Government may also attempt to play down a potential hazard as it may place public order ahead of public safety and see the disorder produced by the realisation of a hazard as presenting more danger to life and property than the hazard itself, for example inadequate civil defence

6.4 Actors and their roles in hazards and hazard management

Actors	Roles	
Inhabitants / Visitors	At risk and vulnerable to varying degrees / Triggering devices. Agents or carriers of hazard	
Researchers	Understand. Predict. Prevent. Contain	
Media	Inform. Educate	
Government – national / – local	Monitor. Inform. Warn / Provide incentives / Regulate. Control / Provide loans. Tax Relief / Compensate. Aid	Reduce direct and indirect impacts / Loss sharing
Public, private and voluntary implementation agencies	Manage. Monitor. Inform. Warn. Implement incentives, regulations and controls	
Insurers	Bear and share losses	
Public and voluntary relief agencies	Repair damage and restore quality of life / Reduce indirect effects, such as disease after major hazards	
Public movements / Pressure groups / Interest groups	Monitor new products and processes for hazard creation / Warn and inform. Put pressure on government and business for action to avoid hazard	

against nuclear attack. Government also has another basic set of decisions to make about hazards which affect the type of society in which people live. To what extent do they inform, warn and encourage people to act in a way that reduces hazard potential, as against implementing controls? Perhaps in the extreme, the latter may mean people are not permitted to live in certain hazardous areas.

The types of environments involved with hazards are varied from physical through to human, with all kinds of interrelationships along that spectrum. For example as well as the hazards like air pollution where human activities change the composition of the atmosphere making it potentially hazardous, there are human activities such as motorway driving which atmospheric processes like fog and ice may make very much more hazardous. Here the combined human (other drivers) and physical (fog) environments produce a greater hazard than the sum of the two if they occur separately.

The social context in which hazards occur and are managed affects the way they are perceived and the way people adjust to them.

Social context

In certain cultures, hazards are regarded as an act of God and people are simply in the hands of God. In other cultures, science and technology are applied to prevent and modify the hazards. Some are more exposed, therefore, to natural hazards, while others, in their application of science and technology, often unwittingly create further hazards which may be even more dangerous. The likelihood of such hazards being successfully brought to public attention through the environmental or consumer movements depends partly on the political system of the country. For example, the Ecology or Green Party has had greater impact and played a more active part in the political scene in West Germany with its proportional representation system than in Britain, where the first-past-the-post system makes it difficult for new parties to gain parliamentary seats (Chapter 11, Section 2).

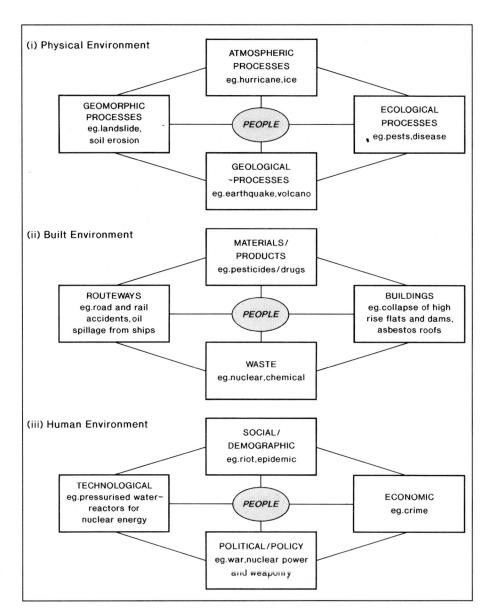

6.5 Types of environments and associated hazards
Examples of interactions between the environments
  a) Economic activities and technological processes producing waste materials which pollute the air, water and earth
  b) Fog and ice on motorways increasing the chance of road accidents
  c) Volcanic dust being sucked into aircraft engines causing stalling
  d) Tourism, forestry and agricultural activities leading to increased soil erosion

6.3   **Other examples**

As a means of introducing other examples of hazards, it is useful to classify them. This may be done in varying ways. It is helpful for us to categorise them first according to the elements of the physical, built and human environments, since this identifies their origins (Figure 6.5).

Classification of hazards

The diagrams display the elements of the three environments and associated hazards. They also show the interactions between the environments which generate, for example, pollution.

They may also be classified in ways which reveal various characteristics of the hazards or their impact (Figure 6.6).

Here we examine some hazards in more detail: hurricanes, which are spatially and temporally unpredictable, have devastating effects on life and property, are extremely difficult to affect, and are perceived in varying ways; an example of landslips, which at a more local scale present difficult transport problems with numerous side effects; and soil erosion produced by human activity and accentuated by physical processes. Finally, the example of Los Angeles is given as a multi-hazard-prone area where several hazards interact and where certain human activity increases the hazard danger.

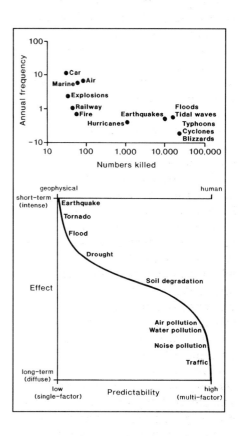

6.6 Ways of classifying hazards

6.3a   **Impacts, responses and attitudes to hurricanes in two contrasting countries**

Big differences exist between the peoples of the developed and developing worlds in their respective perception of and adjustments to hazards (Figure 6.7).

In the example, two severe storms had strikingly different impacts on

6.7 The Bangladesh and Camille hurricanes

Hurricane and date	GNP per capita in US $ 1977	Population affected in millions	Lives lost	Type of damage suffered	Damage cost in millions of U.S. $
Bangladesh, 12-13 November, 1970	79	4.7	300,000	Loss of crops especially rice Loss of cattle 400,000 peasant houses damaged or destroyed Small fishing boats destroyed Trees down	64
Camille, USA 17-20 August, 1969	6597	19	256	Houses destroyed or damaged Shipping damaged or destroyed; both fishing and cargo Shopping centres severely damaged Highways and railroads damaged Telephone cables down Cars and lorries damaged Trucking terminal destroyed Oil rigs damaged Parks/trees damaged Loss of cattle and ruin of crop land Schools and colleges damaged Community buildings damaged Cinemas/entertainment centres damaged	1422

the two countries in terms of damage and deaths. Interestingly enough, neither the majority of residents in the USA nor those of Bangladesh took precautions to avoid damage or death. So, for instance, only 20 per cent of the population of Miami, a high-risk urban area, had invested in protective measures and managed to put them into use during warnings. In Bangladesh during the disastrous storm of 1970, it is estimated that over 90 per cent of the people in the area knew about the storm, but only 1 per cent sought refuge. Clearly over-warning, lack of experience with such storms and lack of knowledge of what to do may account for much of the action or lack of it that people take when threatened by a severe storm.

> *Bangladesh attitudes:* Reluctance to leave homesteads and property in spite of warnings; 90% expected a future flooding, 70% of whom believed it would be soon; pessimism about recurrence of cyclones and flooding; unwillingness to leave good agricultural land and site of family house; perception of cyclone hazard uniform for a range of socio-economic groups.
>
> *US attitudes:* Better educated respondents were more likely to have a positive attitude toward damage prevention. The same was true with those who had experienced past hurricanes.

6.3b Landslide: the 'Shivering Mountain'

Mam Tor lies above the A625 west of Castleton on one of the main Sheffield to Manchester routes. Yearly, increasing numbers of locally and non-locally generated recreational and industrial traffic are using this route. The Mam Tor road was constructed by a Turnpike Company in 1902 to by-pass the existing route through the attractive limestone gorge Winnats Pass, with its severe 1:5 gradient. Since its opening, the road has been slipping below the 'Shivering Mountain' on an almost annual basis. The presence of interbedded gritstones and shales in the Mam Tor beds has resulted in complex rotational slipping, encouraged especially by heavy winter rainfall, which acts to lubricate the impervious shales. It is the fact that the rocks dip at a very low angle (away from the road – rotational slipping) which assists this particular type of mass movement. The great drought of 1976 followed by the winter rains caused the latest and most disastrous landslip on the road in 1977 and forced the Derbyshire County Surveyor to close the road and consider alternative routes.

The six alternatives are shown in Figure 6.8 and every one has different qualities. Route 1 (reopening the existing route) would be tempting providence yet again. Route 2 (the limestone route) is expensive, environmentally objectionable and geologically tricky. Route 3 (the

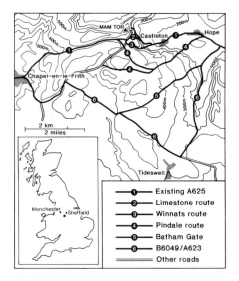

6.8 Alternative routes for the A625

Winnats route) is environmentally disastrous and has a steep gradient. Route 4 (Pindale route) allows the by-passing of Castleton and Hope but is expensive. Route 5 (the Batham Gate route) is used at present yet involves a detour. Route 6 (B6049, A623) allows the best traffic movement but has the longest detour. Various interest groups have different views on these alternatives. The geomorphologists and engineers dislike routes 1 and 2. The environmentalists dislike routes 2 and 3. The traffic consultants favour route 6 but are strongly against 3, as are local industrial and commercial interests. Farmers are most in favour of 1 which causes them least

Mam Tor: rotational slipping and the A625

	Geomorphological/ technical problems (the slipping hazard)	Environmental damage	Directness	Cost	Gradients	Traffic capacity	Impact of villages	Other factors
1 Existing A625 route	xx	✓	✓✓	✓✓	✓	✓	✓	Minimal disruption during construction
2 Limestone route	x	xx	✓✓	x	✓	✓	✓	Minimal disruption during construction
3 Winnatts route	?	xx	✓✓	✓✓	xx	xx	✓	Heavy traffic not suited to this route
4 Pindale route	?	?	✓	xx	✓	✓	✓✓	Two alternatives to this route (see map)
5 Batham Gate route	?	x	x	xx	✓	✓	✓✓	Much use made of existing A623.
6 B6049/A623 route	✓	✓	xx	xx	✓✓	✓✓	✓✓	Access to Castleton poor from west

✓✓ very positive   ✓ slightly positive   ? no influence either way   x slightly negative   xx very negative

6.9 An evaluation of alternative strategies for the Mam Tor road

disruption. The Peak Park planners are left with the difficult task of resolving the issue. They have consulted many of the above interest groups and produced evaluations of alternative strategies, such as those shown in Figure 6.9, which at first sight suggests that strategies 1 and 6 are the most satisfactory.

6.3c Soil erosion above the Dungeon Ghyll Hotel

In the Langdale Mountains in Cumbria (north-west England) there are two crags, called Middlefell Buttress and Raven Crag, which for years have been popular sites for rock climbers. Recently severe erosion of footpaths, loss of ground vegetation cover and extensions of scree have developed on the fell leading to and below these climbing crags. In places, ground level has dropped by 6 feet exposing 30 ton boulders. These were in imminent danger of sliding down the screes and crashing through the intake walls below (these are walls which separate the rough grazing of 'outfields' above and the more intensively farmed 'infields' below). In places scree was already spilling over the stone walls. The scars of eroded footpaths could be seen from miles away. The main causes were over-use of particular paths by climbers and hill walkers, a certain amount of scree running by the same people, and overgrazing by sheep.

The Countryside Commission, the British Mountaineering Council and the National Trust had to work together to formulate a plan to remedy the damage caused and hopefully lessen the chances of the erosion hazard recurring. The policy that was developed involved controlling access, informing the public, stabilising the scree and paths, implementing this policy and meeting the costs (Figure 6.10).

The successfully completed work, a pioneering venture in conservation, won a Civic Trust Commendation. This type of hazard from human activity has grown in its extent in popular walking areas in many countries as leisure time has become more available to a greater number of people.

Soil erosion at Stickle Ghyll, Langdale

6.10 A policy for managing the erosion hazard of Middlefell Buttress and Raven Crag, Langdale Valley (Lake District)

Element of Policy	Detail of Policy
Controlling of access	Three main access paths and three stiles were blocked off. Fences and stiles were erected to keep out sheep
Informing the public	There was a comprehensive way-marking for walkers and climbers. Notices at various points explained why the work was necessary and asked for walkers to keep to the marked footpaths and away from the scree runs
Stabilising scree and paths	Scree was stablised where necessary by tree planting. Indigenous trees planted included oak, rowan, holly and juniper. In all 35,000 trees were planted. In 1978 a further experiment was made with the seeding of birch
Implementation	Volunteer labour was directed by the National Trust's two wardens
Meeting the cost	The overall cost was £1600. In addition fencing was paid for by the Upland Management Experiment Scheme sponsored by the Countryside Commission

6.3d Multi-hazard-prone area: Los Angeles

Los Angeles is prone to a number of physical hazards including earthquakes, coastal storms, tsunamis, landslides, coastal subsidence, brush fires, flood, drought and smog (Figure 6.11).

The life style and economic activities of the inhabitants create or worsen some of these. Emissions from the many cars and industrial concerns, when combined with the fog to which the basin is naturally highly prone, create smog. The low-density residential development within the hills with their chaparral-type vegetation sets the scene for brush fire disasters which may be encouraged to spread by the drying Santa Ana wind. The use of high-pressure sprinkler systems to lower fire risk must be carefully monitored so that it itself does not lead to the soil erosion which often occurs in combination with floods when a slope is laid bare by fire. Seepage from sprinklers and irrigation channels (needed to counter problems of drought and to meet the enormous demand for domestic use of water), plus seepage from swimming pools associated with the people's life-style, removes the saline minerals which act as an adhesive to the

quickclays on which many recent residential suburbs have been built. Once removed the clays become unstable and may collapse during an earthquake, leading to catastrophic landslides on built-up areas (Figure 6.11). The undercutting of slopes to build roads has increased the probability of landslides while the extraction of oil has led to coastal subsidence, making it even more vulnerable to coastal storms and tsunamis. In addition to all these physical hazards there are many others related to the social and economic composition and life-styles of the area, such as the racial riots in Watts in 1965 and in east central Los Angeles in 1992, the crime rate, gang warfare, the expressway accidents, and the oil tanker spillages.

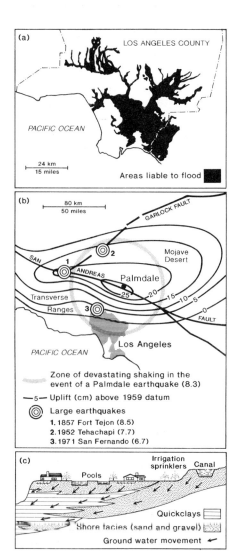

6.11 Hazards in Los Angeles

6.4 Alternative strategies

A number of approaches may be identified that people adopt in living with hazards. For example:

(a) fatalistic, that is regarding hazards as acts of God about which nothing can be done;
(b) problem solving (Figure 6.12);
(c) scrutiny, which involves monitoring change in human and physical processes in order to identify and publicise potential hazards (Figure 6.12).

This section examines the most commonly used one, problem solv-

ing, in order to illustrate the type of problems arising from, and strategies that may be adopted for hazard management.

The problem-solving approach

The degree to which the varying parts of the problem-solving approach are applied in any one area depends partly on the character of the hazard itself. It is also affected

by the people's perception of the hazard, the availability of capital, technical know-how and political will to implement policies, that is, the social, economic, technological and political environments. For example, it is difficult to affect the cause of hurricanes but possible to limit the creation of fire and soil erosion. Where people perceive the risk of a hazard to be slight, the policy adopted may simply be one of having disaster relief organisations and funds generally available, as in Australia for earthquakes, rather than having

Aims	Means	Examples	
		Hurricanes	Floods
Minimise the probability of hazard occurrence	Affect cause		Decrease run-off by afforestation, fire protection, and prevention of overgrazing
	Reduce intensity	Seed hurricanes to reduce pressure differences	Create small lakes to reduce peak flow downstream
Control extent of damage	Reduce vulnerability by eg building design	Anchor roof systems, increase window thickness and limit window size, increase resistance of roof to uplift pressures and lateral resistance to wind pressure	Flood-proof buildings to minimise damage eg water resistant flooring and carpets, keep water out eg coating on masonry to reduce seepage
	Warning and control eg identify and avoid hazard prone areas	Establish local severe wind areas and reduce density of exposed structure	Delineate floodway and flash flood areas in order to reduce number of structures subject to flooding
Adjust to losses	Individual bears loss	*For all hazards* No redistribution or sharing of loss	
	Insurance (optional or compulsory)	Reduces individual losses and redistributes economic loss, provides form of relief	
	Grants	eg to local government for preparing plans for hazard preparedness and prevention	
	Relief, rehabilitation, technical assistance and advice	Feeding and sheltering victims to avoid disease and social unrest, repairing and reconstructing	

6.12 A problem solving approach to hazards

major monitoring control and damage prevention systems, as in south-eastern USA for hurricanes where a high risk is perceived. The differential availability of capital and know-how is also illustrated by the example of hurricanes in the USA and Bangladesh (Chapter 6, Section 3a).

The choice of policies that will lessen the probability of hazard occurrence or damage range from simply informing to extensively controlling occupation of hazardous areas.

Degrees of intervention

Figure 6.13 reveals the problems of the degree to which local or national government is prepared or allowed to interfere with personal freedom. Are people to be controlled for their own protection or are they to be informed or advised and then left to make their own decisions? The compulsory or voluntary wearing of seat belts and the degree of warning against or control of cigarette smoking are good examples. Problems of spatial justice and spatial conflict are introduced when the strategies on loss and adjustment are considered.

6.13 Information-control processes for hazards

Process	Examples		
	Tanzania drought	USA floods	UK air pollution
Information	Advice provided by small-holders' irrigation advisory service	Deeds of new houses in California indicate flood hazard	Little or no information provided on levels
Incentives	Encouragement to plant early by political leaders	Subsidized flood insurance premiums	Subsidy for domestic heat conversion to smokeless fuel
Control on activities and land uses	Regional regulation for minimal planting of famine relief crops	Building elevation premiums	Factory emissions regulated by alkali inspectorate
Control by not allowing people to be exposed to hazard		Public purchase of flood plain to avoid settlement by people	Residential planning permission refused near heavy metal shelter at Avonmouth near Bristol

Entering neighbourhood watch area

on controls affects the degree of local autonomy (self-government). Whether it is local or national government that implements policies, such as communicating advice warnings or alerts, influences the extent to which the responsibility, accountability and financing of implementation is to be local. Within an area, the people monitoring the likelihood of a hazard or preventing it may be professional or volunteers or a combination of the two, as is advocated in neighbourhood watch schemes (Figure 6.14) to aid police in crime prevention. All these decisions affect whether jobs are created locally, nationally or at all, and influence the level of taxation locally or nationally depending on which finances the management schemes.

Who pays?

People can bear the loss themselves, be encouraged to take out insurance, have to take out insurance (as with car insurance), be given grants towards modifications that minimise loss, or be given local, national or even international aid during and after a disaster. In some cases they are paying themselves for living in hazard prone areas, as with higher car insurance premiums in large cities, whereas in other cases people living elsewhere are effectively also bearing the cost. People might even be indirectly encouraged and financed to live in hazardous areas, as for example income tax deductions for flood loss in the USA. The personal benefits from living in an area may well outweigh the costs or risks to individuals when they are backed by government aid, but it may be questionable whether the benefits to society as a whole outweigh society costs. This conflict between people living in hazardous areas and elsewhere becomes more obvious with open disputes arising when other areas are providing a resource much needed by themselves, for example water from Arizona to southern California to reduce the drought hazard.

Another dimension of spatial jus-

tice arises when subsidies are in effect being paid but not equally applied because there is no overall policy on hazard management. Thus farmers in an area affected by stormwinds may not be compensated for crop damage in the same way as those in another area where the harvest has been affected by floods. Few countries have a set of multi-hazard policies.

Who manages?

A further problem concerns which set of actors should manage the hazard. For example, whether it is local or national government that decides

Changing the geography

Hazard prevention and management may themselves, then, change the geography of areas, not only in employment and tax terms but in relation to land-use, resource use, technology applied, economic and social activities, human movement, consumption patterns and not least

6.14 'On the home beat'

On the home beat

The neighbourhood watch schemes announced by the Metropolitan Police on Thursday is an initiative which seeks to bind police and public together in the common cause of crime prevention. Making use of experience from the United States in such crime-prone cities as Detroit and New York, the aim is for an alert neighbourhood to deter crimes of opportunity, theft of an unlocked car, entry of an unprotected house or street,

crimes, robbery and violence against the person. This is the kind of thing a responsible citizen should be doing anyway. In return the police will advise on domestic security methods. Once 40% of a neighbourhood has joined, a sign will be erected to show that a watch is in operation.

For some elderly who are virtually housebound, not through infirmity but because they live in crime afflicted estates, a watch scheme is a potential godsend.

There may be a danger that the better heeled, more civic minded suburbs will make the running. American experience, however, suggests that inner cities, where the main victims of crime are concentrated can be the most enthusiastic and effective supporters of the scheme.

Some however, will see the scheme as either the beginnings of the busybody state or even the police state. *Adapted from* The Times, *September 8, 1983* the physical landscape. For this reason prevention and management should be considered in a wider context than its degree of success in managing hazards. For example building a dam for flood control may itself submerge farm land, replace edaphic with aquatic habitats, affect the stability of valley-side slopes and offer opportunities for recreation, perhaps attracting more traffic to the valley. Since these changes would be occurring in order that an area downstream would be less prone to floods, the potential for both spatial conflict and conflict over land use (Chapter 2) is great.

More dramatically, hazards can change the geography by prompting the removal of people from the area. The flight of the inhabitants of Tristan da Cunha after the volcanic eruption of the South Atlantic island in 1961 was for some only temporary as they could not settle down in Britain. The movement of the capital of Belize from Belize City to Belmopan (Central America) to reduce hurricane damage and the migration of the starving people from the semi-arid grasslands of the southern fringes of the Sahara away from the drought are more permanent. Less dramatically, the more vulnerable bronchitis sufferers may relocate to live in less polluted air.

Since different strategies to hazard management are practised in different places at different times, there is a continuously changing geography of hazard management which reflects and influences society changes.

6.5   Perspectives

In the past most hazards were viewed fatalistically. Gradually our understanding has grown so that some have been substantially reduced by improved living standards and applications of science. Given modern water provision and sanitation there is little chance of a repetition of 500 people dying from cholera within ten days in Soho, London as in 1848 due to polluted drinking water. There is a growing awareness, and more information and research about the hazards and their management. There has been a great boom in the insurance industry and growth in the involvement of both statutory and voluntary bodies concerned with disaster relief and prevention. These operate at the local, national and international level.

Hazard creation

There is, however, no room for complacency. The expanding population, the growing complexity of economic and social life, the increasing interference with biochemical systems and even the very management of hazards can themselves create further hazards, some of which are not yet known. The use of asbestos as a

fire-resistant material has put many at risk to cancer. The construction of a dam to prevent drought may by its weight trigger an earthquake. The increased movement of people and products has also increased the hazard of accidents. The movement of oil from producer to consumer countries has, due to spillage, led to ecological and economic disasters along coastlines as flora and fauna die and tourists are repelled, as in the Exxon Valdez incident off the south coast of Alaska, USA in 1988. The transport and storage of materials with inadequate knowledge of their properties has led to explosions and fires, as in urban depots at Stalybridge and Salford in Greater Manchester with

Attempts to clean up after the Exxon Valdez oil spill

consequent dangers to surrounding unsuspecting households.

The transference of risk and hazard

Sometimes the hazard or risk is just transferred; for example, coastal defences may reduce erosion on one stretch of coastline but intensify it elsewhere. Flood control in one section of a basin may transfer problems to other sections. Service-till machines outside banks, while convenient, transfer some of the risks of robbery from the bank to the individual who is extremely exposed in using them. More intensive policing in some areas and better-designed estates with perhaps more security systems may just deflect burglary to other areas. New technology with improved security against robbery may mean a change of hazard from bank robbery to computer crime. Therefore the hazard may be relocated or 'displaced', different people or institutions become more vulnerable or the hazard itself may change.

The result of hazard relocation often produces international conflict, which necessitates internationally agreed codes of behaviour.

International perspectives

The strategy of building taller chimneys has worked to reduce peak concentrations of SO_2 but has also dispersed it over a wide area, and through its conversion to a sulphate (SO_4) aerosol form has produced problems for countries by the acidification of rain and snow, as in Scandinavia. The problem is particularly bad where there is a snow cover, since accumulation occurs leading to a high concentration in the meltwater. Both international cooperation and implementation of controls are difficult to obtain in such circumstances. This problem is taken up in the next chapter (Chapter 7, Section 3a).

There is much need to contribute to the international sharing of information about hazards and their management. Poorer countries could benefit from the ways richer countries have tackled the management of natural disasters to which the poorer countries are still very vulnerable (Chapter 6, Section 3a). They could also learn to avoid the mistakes in their technology and life styles that have led to many hazards created by human activity in the richer countries. These mistakes have led to a re-evaluation of techno-

logical solutions to hazards and other problems. More research attention is being devoted to the human response to both hazards and their management, with perhaps relatively less emphasis on the hazards themselves and technological solutions.

Although in the richer countries there is still much to learn about natural hazard management, perhaps in the future the major approach to hazard problems is likely to be one of scrutiny – that is, monitoring developments in new products, new production processes, new information and communication technology and bio-chemical technology, and identifying and publicising any future hazards which may result. These hazards may occur at varying scales: in the home, for example, where the use of some polyurethane products when combined with improved insulation and reduced air flow may lead to air pollution within the house; at work, as new products or processes are created; or at an areal level, for example chemical explosions as at Flixborough (England) 1974, Seveso (Italy) 1976, Bhopal (India) 1984, and nuclear power leaks as at Three Mile Island (USA) 1979 and explosions as at Chernobyl (USSR) 1986, the effects of which were experienced across Europe.

Since there is enormous private and public investment involved with these new technologies, and since many individuals see their career chances linked to the introduction of these developments, there is considerable momentum created which is difficult for groups and individuals who have identified hazards to halt. Unless these identifiers of hazards are backed by government or substantial private funds it is very difficult for them to make their case. For example, in Sizewell's Pressurized Water Reactor Investigation the Central Electricity Generating Board spent £20 million publicising its view, whereas the opposing protest groups had only

The human inpact of the Seveso disaster, Italy, 1976

small private contributions with which to promote their case (Chapter 3, Section 1). Once legislation exists, government monitoring can be successful; for example, the Food and Drug Administration in the USA insists on prolonged tests before a new product is introduced and can remove it from the market if later evidence of hazard is shown.

Hazard or resource?

The conflict, of course, occurs because a particular event or thing may be regarded as a resource which leads to benefits as well as presenting a hazard. Sometimes the argument is about whether the benefits outweigh the risks. Sometimes it is that those people, organisations or areas that largely benefit are not necessarily the ones who are at risk.

The resolution of both types of conflict depends on the relative power of the groups and organisations involved as well as the logic and strength of their arguments. Sometimes the resource/hazard debate is simply a question of perception or vulnerability. To a small child snowfall may generate great fun; to a transport company it may bring its business to a halt.

The tendency for vested interest to underplay the hazard is often paralleled by government concern to minimise risks in order to maintain public order. In a minor way, both are classically illustrated in the film *Jaws*, where most of the local officials first refuse to accept that there is a hazard, then choose not to publicise it in order to maintain calm on the beach and retain their tourist industry. *Jaws* has its own solution.

Decision-makers concerned with hazard management face dilemmas in selecting the 'best solution', because as the Mam Tor example demonstrated there may not be a 'best' one for all of the actors involved. Their decisions are made all the more difficult when their area is multi-hazard prone, because not only do the hazards often interact, the solutions to some may adversely affect others. The social and spatial consequences of their decisions, in such terms as who benefits, who loses, who pays and who becomes less and who more vulnerable to future hazards, make them even more important.

6.6   Exercises

1. Is there any soil erosion in your school/college grounds? Where is it? Why has it happened? What can be done about it?

2. (a) What are the major hazards
      (i) natural
      (ii) built
      (iii) human
      in your local region?
   (b) Which areas within your region have the greatest hazard potential?
   (c) How are these various hazards managed?
   (d) Can you suggest improvements to this management
      (i) before
      (ii) during
      (iii) after the hazard event?

3. Examine one of the hazards from your answer to Question 2. Identify the major actors and discuss their roles in hazard occurrence and management.

4. (a) Select one of the following: earthquakes, tornadoes, droughts, floods, water pollution, riots, and discuss the spatial occurrence of the particular hazard in one continent over the last decade.
   (b) From this and other evidence sketch a map of hazard potential for this hazard over the continent.

6.15 'Storm rises over "controlled disaster" that went wrong'; Colorado flooding

---

"Storm rises over 'controlled disaster' that went wrong" – the Colorado flooding

After weeks of dithering over the timing of a massive release from swollen dams along the 1450 mile Colorado River – lifeline for seven states – federal offices realised they had waited too long. They had to unleash what they called a 'controlled disaster' which devastated vast stretches of the US South West and Mexico.

As a huge amount of water from melted snow, three times the annual average, flowed from the Rocky Mountains, the Colorado went on a rampage. Dam after dam in four states opened flood gates. 'If we hadn't done it, water from Lake Mead would just have poured over the top and the dam would have burst', said an official about the first crisis opening of the 725ft high Hoover Dam's great spillways.

Tens of thousands fled or lost their homes. Indian tribes and Mexican peasants near the delta on the Gulf of California were flooded out of their lands. At least seven have drowned. The property damage bill may top $100 million. Irreparable harm has been done to the Grand Canyon ecology. Wildlife galore and famous rapids have been wiped out. The tourist industry has lost millions.

Who is to blame? The Bureau of Reclamation in Washington, which runs the river's dams and hydroelectric system, and made the decision to release the flood, feebly points a finger at 'faulty computer models' both its own and those of the National Weather Service.

It opened the gates ten weeks too late for basically politico-economic reasons according to expert hydrologists. The Colorado is perhaps the world's most over-used, over-built river. A plethora of dams, reservoirs, and aqueducts divert its water thousands of miles from their natural course to the vast California businesses and to Los Angeles.

Fear of California's ever growing thirst led other western states to protect their supplies and maintain highest storage levels. As one bureau employee put it: 'The system's philosophy is simple: keep your reservoir full'.

This year, said Bob Gottlieb of the Los Angeles Metropolitan Water Board, the bureau has been under extra pressure from Washington to squeeze every kilowatt from the river's hydroelectric stations. The Administration, spending hugely on defence while cutting taxes, is pushing every government agency to increase revenue sources, the bureau being expected to produce more than most.

Influential tourist interests, with billions at stake, also want levels kept high on artificial lakes used for boating and watersports.

"Institutionalised greed, power politics and bureaucratic confusion worked together to create this mess' said a long time Colorado boatman and engineer. 'They've made the river into a piece of plumbing.'

Water supplies from Los Angeles to Utah have been polluted and health authorities warn of possible outbreaks of mosquito-borne encephalitis.

Worst hit are the Mexican poor, who see little of the Colorado's over-managed waters in normal times. Now 55,000 acres of farmland are flooded, thousands homeless and five dead.

Scores of civil law suits against the bureau are in preparation, including one from its sister agency, the National Park Service, whose chief is furious over the Grand Canyon disaster. A congressional investigation will apportion the blame.

Adapted from The Observer, 10 July 1983

5. (a) Classify the following hazards according to these varying criteria:
   (i) the origin of the hazard
   (ii) the spatial impact
   (iii) predictability
   (iv) frequency
   (v) duration.
   Chemical plant explosions, thunderstorms, oil tanker leaks, acid deposition (rain), avalanches, hurricanes, burglary, motorway fog accidents, cholera.
   (b) Suggest the value and possible uses of these classifications.

6. What factors affect people's perception of crime rates in different areas of a city?

7. (a) How do you think hazards that are produced or triggered by people's activities may best be reduced – by further information and warnings or by control of activities?
   (b) Indicate the reasons for your suggestions and discuss the possible consequences of your decision for personal freedom, spatial justice and employment creation.

8. After reading the press reports about the Colorado River (Figure 6.15), answer the following questions.
   (a) What processes led to the hazard?
   (b) What demands were put on to the use of the river and its water, and in what ways did these lead to the disaster?
   (c) What government policies were affecting the management procedures of the Bureau of Reclamation?
   (d) What were the direct and indirect consequences of the disaster?
   (e) Identify the groups of people most affected by the disaster.
   (f) (i) Indicate the conflicts, noted in the article, that arise from water being both a resource and at times a potential hazard.
      (ii) Using examples, suggest other ways in which water, in its varying forms, is both a resource and a hazard.
   (g) Using examples, indicate the hazards that may be associated with a major river that runs through a major city.

6.7 Further reading

I. Burton, R.W. Kates and G.F. White (1978), *The Environment as Hazard*, OUP, New York

I. Burton and A. Whyter (1980), *Environmental risk management, Scope Report*, 14 John Wiley

J.C. Chicken (1975), *Hazard Control Policy in Britain*, Pergamon

J.C. Chicken (1982), *Nuclear Power Hazard Control Policy*, Pergamon

R.N. Davidson (1981) *Crime and Environment*, Croom Helm

A.H. Perry (1981), *Environmental Hazards in the British Isles,* Allen & Unwin

W.J. Petak and A.A. Atkisson (1982), *Natural Hazard Risk Assessment and Public Policy*, Springer-Verlag

R.I. Palm (1990) *Natural Hazards: An Integrated Framework for Research and Planning*, John Hopkins University Press

K. Smith (1992) *Environmental Hazards*, Routledge

K. Smith and G.A. Tobin (1979), *Human Adjustment to Flood Hazard*, Longman

G. White (ed.) (1974), *Natural Hazards: Local, Natural, Global*, OUP

J. Whitton (1980), *Disasters: The Anatomy of Environmental Hazards*, Pelican

Chapter 7

EXTERNAL THREATS

7.1 Case study: the Canadian North under threat

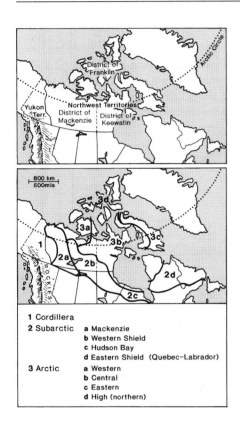

7.1 The Canadian North

1 Cordillera
2 Subarctic a Mackenzie
           b Western Shield
           c Hudson Bay
           d Eastern Shield (Quebec-Labrador)
3 Arctic   a Western
           b Central
           c Eastern
           d High (northern)

Recently the biggest challenge facing the Yukon and the Northwest Territories in the Canadian North (Figure 7.1) has been the proposed development of oil- and gas by consortia of transnational corporations primarily from the USA. The oil and gas-fields in the Beaufort Sea and Prudhoe Bay have proved very attractive to the USA, which yearns for secure energy sources. Two major routes have been proposed to transport the gas to the major con-

suming centres in the USA (Figure 7.2).

The projects have been called the biggest privately funded capital schemes the world has ever seen. The impact of such pipelines would be enormous on unique physical and human environments. They are regarded as an external threat to the Canadian North.

Here is a succession of wilderness areas in the Arctic and Subarctic, so far relatively undisturbed and unstudied. Because of the simplicity and fragility of the ecosystems and the slow regenerative pace of biological growth, any disturbance of one component of the ecosystem can cause long-term damage. Little is known of the likely impact of human activity on such systems; so, for example, it is not clear how the complex and long-distance migration routes of the Porcupine Caribou herds would be affected (Figure 7.3).

Certainly southern influences have already made themselves felt through the construction of the Dempster Highway, the first all-weather highway linking southern Canada with Arctic Canada, the emergence of a network of air services, and the increasing urbanisation of the population. The native Inuit and Dene peoples who have distinctive cultures and have partly land based economies have already proved highly vulnerable to these southern influences.

Many local people, particularly

the Dene (Indian), Inuit (Eskimo) and Metis (Indian/White), fear the effects of such huge pipeline schemes and through their increasingly articulate and vocal leaders have voiced their protest along with some liberals from southern Canada. They fear the so-called 'total intrusion effects', whereby the industrial development brings along with it all the other social and economic ways of the south, swamping the native culture. Similarly the 'corridor effect', whereby one pipeline is rapidly paralleled by further pipelines, cables and roads, is another legitimate fear. On the other hand some local whites, usually entrepreneurs and often newcom-

7.2 The proposed gas pipelines

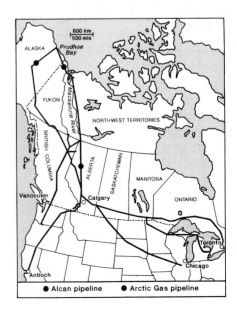

● Alcan pipeline   ● Arctic Gas pipeline

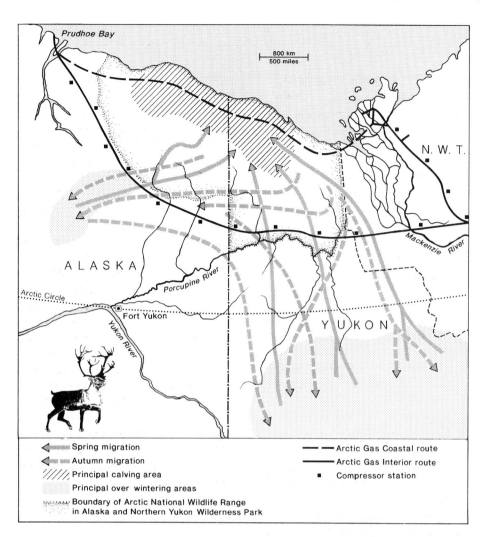

7.3 Migration routes of the caribou

Legend for map:

◁ Spring migration
◁ Autumn migration
///// Principal calving area
       Principal over wintering areas
······ Boundary of Arctic National Wildlife Range
       in Alaska and Northern Yukon Wilderness Park

– – – Arctic Gas Coastal route
——— Arctic Gas Interior route
■   Compressor station

Map labels: Prudhoe Bay · 800 km / 500 miles · N. W. T. · ALASKA · Arctic Circle · Fort Yukon · Porcupine River · Yukon River · Mackenzie River · YUKON

orable progress of such development is affecting the physical and human environments in many areas including the Amazon and Australia.

The choices for northern Canada amount to: rejecting the developments, proposing that they move elsewhere; suggesting the developments should be postponed; going ahead with cultural and environmental safeguards (or going ahead as planned). At present the likely future is for the Alcan route to be built when the price of gas has risen to make it profitable. The questions worth asking about this external threat imposed on human and physical environments include: What should be the economic and cultural future of the North? Who should wield the greatest power in the process of decision-making? What are the gains and losses associated with the decisions taken?

A Dene Indian in his summer camp

cro, in addition to some Inuit and Dene, loudly welcome the proposed development as a way of bringing the twentieth century (in their view money and jobs) to the North. This perspective is powerfully voiced and supported by the US government, the international gas consortia, the Canadian National Energy Board and many southern Canadians. As in other parts of the world, however, the environmental movement is becoming politicised through agencies and organisations such as the Friends of the Earth, the Sierra Club and Greenpeace. The case it is making is influencing public opinion.

The issue of large-scale industrial development, backed by huge industrial corporations and governments, is by no means restricted to northern Canada. The seemingly inex-

7.2 General problem

Types of threats

The case study demonstrates how the possible introduction of a gas-pipeline into northern Canada was perceived by some of the local people as a threat to their society, economy and environment. More generally, the source of a threat may be the entrance into an area of a new land-use, activity, set of events, group of people or some combination of these that it is perceived as producing negative effects on the physical, built and/or human environments. The local people, to some extent, see the activity as an invasion of their territory that will lead to change and instability.

Statement of the general problem

The general problem is, then, understanding why and in what ways some changes are perceived as threats. The section on alternative strategies discusses ways in which local people may respond to the threat and the ways that people and organisations associated with the threatening activity may counter their response.

External threat as a concept

External threat, as a concept, obviously has some similarity to the idea of hazard. The main difference that is drawn here is that the threat is originating from outside the area and may be kept out. A hazard is more likely to be associated with some characteristics of the area, for example its climate, geology or people. It is something that is not new to the area. There is already some

idea of its frequency of occurrence. The external threat, on the other hand, is not indigenous to the area and its newness is one reason for it being seen as a threat. As with hazards, people within the area may have different levels of awareness of the threat and different attitudes to it.

Threats to physical and built environments

The negative effects (negative externalities, Chapter 2, Section 2) associated with a threat may occur in one or a number of types of environments, for example the physical or built environments. The case study shows a threat to the physical environment because the pipeline is perceived as disturbing the fragile ecosystems of northern Canada, which will take years to recover. A further threat to the physical environment is represented by the output of sulphur dioxide and nitrogen oxides into the air in where one country presents a threat to the ecology of any country downwind of it through acid deposition (rain) (Chapter 7, Section 3a). The introduction of a chemical plant or nuclear power station is perceived as a threat not only for the potential hazard to life and property from its materials or technology, but also for the new built-form in the landscape which may be considered unsightly. Indeed, nuclear power plants have often received more objections on the grounds of the buildings and associated traffic than on being seen as a threat to safety. The introduction of a factory estate into a residential area may also be objected to on such grounds. Sometimes it is not so much the addition of something new but the removal or replacement of something that exists and is valued that is seen as a threat, for example some buildings of architectural and historical interest.

Slow recovery after a forest fire at Inuvik on the Mackenzie Delta

Threat to economic environment

The economic value of the built environment as well as its form may also be seen to be under threat from an anticipated reduction in property values. The building of a lower-priced housing estate in a high priced area or rented accommodation in an area of owner-occupation may produce such an effect. Apartment blocks in areas of two-storey housing may be viewed as a threat for both aesthetic and economic reasons. The economic environment may also be adversely affected by a threat to the amount or type of employment available in an area, if the employment is controlled by outside organisations such as foreign transnationals (Chapter 7, Section 3d). Such organisations are able to switch production to other areas and countries to benefit from lower costs (Chapter 8, Section 4).

Threat to technological environment

The introduction of new technologies to an area may also be regarded as a threat. They may affect the economic environment in reducing the need for jobs, and be regarded as a threat by unions. The introduction of nuclear technology in the form of a new power plant or some new chemical factory may also be regarded as a threat because it is viewed by some as a hazardous technology, even though it may increase the number of jobs available in the area.

Threats to social environment

The introduction of new types of residential property and new types of plants may also threaten the social environment through the potential occupants and employees. It may change the social mix of an area. This can be regarded by some as a threat in that their children may be educated alongside others who do not share the same set of values. They fear more vandalism and increased crime rates after the arrival of some groups. Often there are no grounds for these fears. Indeed, it may be argued that it is beneficial to be educated in a social mix so that children become aware of the values and attitudes of others and learn to understand them. This is particularly argued in the case of different ethnic groups and multicultural education, but it is often people of different ethnic background as well as people from a different class background that residents perceive as a threat (Chapter 7, Section 3e). Sometimes this prejudicial fear is overtly expressed in fear about house values. This is also the case for the introduction of community mental care centres (Chapter 7, Section 3f); the unfounded fears about the effect on children and increased crime are reflected in complaints about property values and increased traffic. The reactions of the existing population may produce a self-fulfilling prophecy when, for example, many simultaneously put their houses up for sale and in so doing immediately lower the likely price they will get for them.

Threats to political environment

The introduction of a new set of people into an area may also change the local political environment. If they have different values and interests they may vote for the opponents of the present elected representatives. This, in itself, may reinforce social opposition to entry and it may find support from the elected representatives as they see their position threatened. A change in political representation may result in a different emphasis of policy on the provision of public goods and services; for example, welfare services may be given greater priority in an area that has received an in-movement of poorer people.

The political environment may be changed in a different way by the more abstract threat of a policy introduced from outside the area which is seen as having adverse effects. This might be the threatened reduction of grants to an area from national government or a national directive about the organisation of its schools to which it objects. At another scale it may be a decision or policy of a body such as the European Community that a member state sees as disadvantageous to itself. The responses to these threats vary from reluctant acceptance to lengthy argument or even legal action.

Threats at the international scale

The problem of external threats may occur at varying spatial scales from the 'threatened' introduction of new housing or a factory estate into part of a town to the much larger scales of the pipeline example, the threat of rabies being introduced to Britain (Chapter 7, Section 3b), the arrival of polluted air over Scandinavia resulting in acid deposition (Chapter 7, Section 3a), and the possibility of a problem at a French nuclear power station affecting south-east England (Figure 7.4).
The last two cases, rabies and acid deposition, illustrate the overlap between the concepts of hazard and external threat. Both can be regarded as hazards. Unlike new housing or the pipeline there are very few, if any, positive effects associated with them by anyone. Both may also be regarded as external threats: rabies is prevalent in continental Europe but not in Britain and so is an exter-

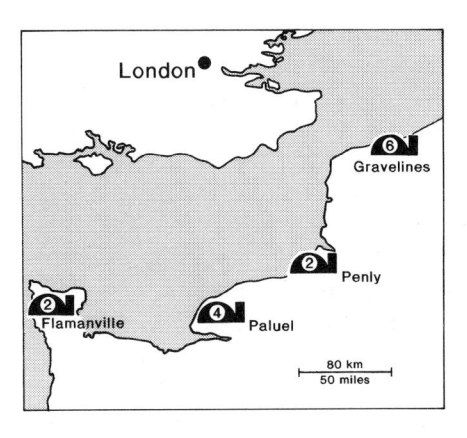

7.4 The threat of French nuclear power stations to south east-England - how do the French view this?

nal threat to Britain; the Scandinavians, in particular, argue that acid deposition arises from air polluted outside their territory by industrial and other activities located in other countries. They cannot keep out the polluted air in the same way that Britain can attempt to repel rabid animals but they can apply political pressure on the countries where the air is polluted. A further example of a similar external threat is to countries downstream receiving polluted water from countries upstream. In this case it is easier to identify the country which is the source of the pollution but not necessarily its specific source.

External threats and distance

Where there is a positive view of a development as well as a negative one, there is often a spatial difference in the number of people holding the opposed views.

Figure 7.5 shows that the negative views of a new motorway (expressway) development exceed the positive ones close to it, but decline very rapidly to a point beyond which positive views are dominant. There the advantages of increased accessibility to other places exceed the disadvantages of noise, air pollution and visual intrusion which decline rapidly with distance from the motorway. As the

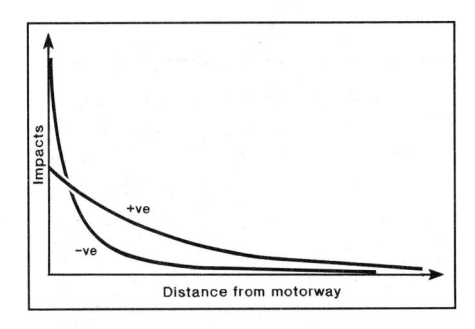

7.5 The distance decay of negative and positive effects (externalities)

spatial distribution of noise exposure around O'Hare International Airport shows, the distance decay of negative externalities may not be the same in all directions (Figure 7.6).

Any threatened expansion may be opposed more in some directions than others.

Threatened actors

So the area under threat can vary in size and the threat may be felt as greater at some distances and directions than others. There can also be varying elements of that area under threat. The people, households or residential community immediately come to mind but industrial or retail businesses may also regard themselves as threatened by the possible entry from outside the area of, for example, a major industry or hypermarket. The major industry may pay its labour force much higher

7.6 Noise exposure around Chicago's O'Hare International Airport

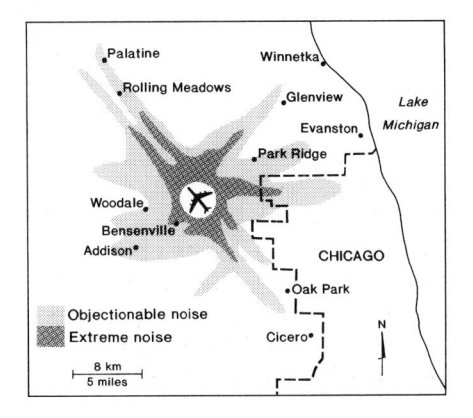

wages than are being received in the area at present, while the hypermarket may sell its wide range of goods at lower prices than are currently obtained. In the first case, increased competition for labour is feared, while in the second the fear is increased competition for customers. Of course, neither the employees nor the customers would see either entry as a threat.

Threats to individuals or the community

People may see a threat as affecting them as individuals or households, or they may see it as changing some wider more abstract entity such as the community or local economy of which they feel part. A community may be a set of people with shared values and attitudes but who have little interaction. It can also be an interacting set of people whose transactions with one another reinforce their feeling of being part of some whole that is bigger than the sum of its parts. Sometimes people claim that their community is threatened but in terms of a community of the interacting type, one can hardly be said to exist. Indeed, it has been suggested that in some instances of responses to external threat, such a community has been created, united in its opposition. The external threat in itself has produced the feeling of community that did not exist before. Some people suggested that this was the case in Covent Garden in London when people there opposed the proposed redevelopment in the 1970s.

Long-term threat, short-term gain

The threat to the local economy may be seen as quite long term. Sometimes in the short term there may be a boom in employment which acts to minimise opposition. Two types of examples may be given. The discovery of a resource may attract investment, develop the built environment and create new jobs, such as in north-east Scotland on the discovery of North Sea oil and gas. The investment may come from overseas and may be accompanied by an influx of foreign workers whose demand for homes may inflate the price of housing. The initial boost to the local economy may encourage many businesses to orient their products and services to the new demand. Old demand and connections may be ignored.

Resource development

If the resource runs out or becomes uneconomic to develop, the overseas investment and employees are withdrawn. It may then be too late for the already reoriented local economy to recover its more traditional markets. Decline may then set in. House prices may slump and people may find it difficult to sell and move elsewhere. Such a situation occurred in coal mining settlements when pits were closed. The over-reliance on a particular resource makes local economies and communities very vulnerable.

Tourism

A second situation of short-term gain which may be a longer-term threat is the advent of tourism to an area. The arrival of individual tourists and then packaged mass tourism and its hotel development may transform, for example, a Turkish fishing port. The local population may become almost totally oriented to the new source of income with the growth of restaurants and gift shops. Fishing may decline as other occupations become more attractive. A sudden drop in the

A Turkish fishing port transformed by tourist development

tourist trade may occur as other areas become more fashionable or as overdevelopment of hotels and apartments transforms the original physical and built environments that attracted people in the first place. Political instability within the country or dramatic changes in currency exchange rates that no longer make it affordable may be other reasons for such a loss of trade. The resort may find it very difficult to return to its old basis of economic survival. Those who foresaw the problems of over-reliance on one economic sector and uncontrolled development – that is, saw tourism as a threat as well as an opportunity – may have ensured the diversification of the local economy and restricted development so that the original 'resource' was not destroyed.

In the above cases, the development of resources or tourist areas elsewhere, the changes in exchange rates and the political instability may also be regarded as external threats. Some are very difficult for local people to counter.

Cash-cropping

A related example which may be even larger in scale of impact is the importation of a new form of economy to an area or country. In many countries their traditional agricultural production and methods have given way to cash cropping and monoculture for export, in order to gain the necessary foreign exchange for the importing of capital and consumer goods from more developed countries. These changes have been encouraged by corporations wishing to sell agricultural supplies and trade in the cash crops. In many cases agricultural methods by which the people have subsisted over centuries and that are harmonious with the physical environment have to be discontinued in order to produce sufficient quantities of the cash crop for export. Monoculture in itself changes the ecology and makes crops more susceptible to pests and diseases. Pesticides and other chemical materials may be eagerly marketed to combat them but this in itself means greater production in order to be able to afford the supplies. Often the gender roles and relations are changed as the women's previous agricultural role is taken over by men. Both the social and economic life of the area can be dramatically altered. The local economy may now be subject to world gluts in the particular commodity or poor harvests through climatic vari-

ability at home. It has now become more vulnerable to both external threats and internal hazards. Even more dramatically, the physical environment may be irreparably damaged by the new forms of production with, for example, desertification occurring and the people having to move elsewhere in order to survive. In these cases the threat posed by such development may have been poorly recognised or opposition may have gone unheeded in the push for modernisation and progress.

Summary

In summary, external threats may be perceived by different sets of actors, at different scales, both spatial and temporal, and may be seen as threats to individuals or to communities. People fear that these new events, land uses, activities and/or people may change the physical, built and/or human environments in detrimental ways.

7.3 Other examples

External threats, then, can be to the physical, built and/or human environment. They can be transmitted through physical and/or human processes. The first two examples involve physical processes and affect both the physical and human environments. Acid deposition may be locally caused and therefore in our terms is a hazard. The acidity may also be produced elsewhere and then be carried to other countries. As such it is a major external threat which some countries particularly suffer and wish to reduce. Rabies, a disease that affects the nervous system, is also a hazard to animals and humans where it is endemic, but it is an external threat to countries

where it has been eradicated. Both of these are viewed as threats to a nation. The third example discusses how the contraction or closure of a plant that employs a large number of people and is owned and controlled by a foreign corporation may also be viewed as an external threat to local economic life. The growth of immigration and the concentration of immigrants in particular areas, as discussed in the fourth example, is perceived by some as a threat to the social and cultural life of the area and to some extent the country. Similarly some see the establishment of a mental health centre or related institution as a threat to a community in various, often ill-

defined ways (example 5). The final example, AIDS, a disease in humans that is transmitted sexually and through blood, was originally perceived as an external threat to be kept out of countries to which it had not spread. More recently, having become established within a country, it is a hazard which is greater in some parts of the country than others.

External threats may be classified in a number of ways, for example according to the processes transmitting them, the environments they threaten, the scale at which they are perceived, and the degree of difficulty of combating them.

7.3a Acid deposition

Acid deposition, or 'acid rain' as it is commonly but misleadingly called, continued to hit the headlines throughout the 1980s (Figure 7.7). It was seen as a major hazard, created by human activity, and became the focus of environmental campaigns, especially in West Germany. It consists of dry deposition of sulphur

dioxide, nitrogen oxides and nitric acid, and wet deposition which includes sulphuric acid, nitric acid and ammonium in precipitation, mist and clouds (occult deposition). The deposition leads to the direct damage of plants, especially coniferous trees which are efficient in trapping acidic cloud droplets. In such

trees it produces yellowing needles and strange branching patterns and indirectly damages them by increasing their susceptibility to disease. Acid deposition also leads to the leaching of soils through metals being 'mobilised'. These toxic metals accumulate in lakes and rivers, many of which are also becoming

7.7 Acid deposition

increasingly acid. The toxicity and acidity lead to the death of fish. Acid deposition affects the built and human environments as well as the physical, by contributing to the corrosion of buildings and respiratory problems in humans.

There is still much debate about the causes of such phenomena as 'forest death' and the acidification of lakes. Some attribute them to other processes, such as poor forest management or in the case of lakes, afforestation with conifers in the catchment area, but much research points to a link with human activity that produces the air pollution causing acid deposition. The major sources of the increased amounts of sulphur dioxide and nitrogen oxides in the atmosphere are the burning of fossil fuels in power plants; industrial processes such as the smelting of metals; and the exhaust fumes of motor vehicles.

Acid deposition is regarded partly as an external threat because the geographical origins of such air pollution may be outside the country. Scandinavians in particular consider that much damage is caused by imported pollution. Since Scandinavia receives an airflow predominantly from the south-west, Britain is seen as a major cause of its acid deposition. As Figure 7.8 shows in the second to last column, Sweden (0.12) and Norway (0.07) contribute relatively little to their own deposition. Most comes from elsewhere. It is not easy to attribute the country of origin or emission source of the pollution. As is shown for Sweden (Figure 7.9), a third of its deposition is classified as of indeterminate origin. This is especially the case when parcels of air have trav-

7.8 Emissions are falling but is it enough?

Country	Sulphur emmissions ('000s tonnes)		Difference %	Promised reductions	Sulphur Deposition ('000s tonnes)		Difference %	Ratios I Own contr. total dep.	Export Import
	1980	1987			1980	1987			
Soviet Union	6,400	5,100	−20	30% by1993	5,101	3,584	−30	0.62	2.1
German Dem Rep.	2,500	(2,500)	0	30% by1993	963	979	+2	0.74	7.0
Poland	2,050	(2,270)	+10	–	1,443	1,492	+3	0.53	2.1
United Kingdom	2,335	1,840	−21	30% by1999	803	702	−13	0.81	9.7
Spain	1,625	(1,581)	−3	–	670	674	0	0.78	7.0
Czechoslovakia	1,550	1,450	−6	30% by1993	818	765	−6	0.50	2.8
Italy	1,900	(1,252)	−34	30% by1993	916	562	−39	0.63	4.3
German Fed. Rep.	1,600	(1,022)	−36	65% by1993	1,083	821	−24	0.40	1.4
France	1,779	(923)	−48	50% by1990	1,160	760	−34	0.44	1.4
Hungary	817	(710)	−13	30% by1993	416	337	−19	0.56	3.5
Yugoslavia	588	(588)	0	–	662	497	−25	0.39	5.0
Bulgaria	517	(570)	+9	30% by1993	293	235	−20	0.65	5.0
Belgium	400	(244)	−39	50% by1995	162	121	−25	0.41	2.7
Greece	200	(180)	−10	–	150	119	−21	0.29	1.8
Turkey	(138)	(177)	+22	–	209	210	0	0.29	0.8
Finland	292	162	−44	50% by1993	273	210	−23	0.23	0.7
Denmark	219	(155)	−29	50% by1995	110	83	−25	0.37	2.4
Netherlands	244	141	−42	50% by1995	175	139	−21	0.23	1.0
Portugal	133	(166)	−13	–	83	83	0	0.42	1.7
Sweden	232	(116)	−50	68% by1995	333	307	−8	0.12	0.3
Romania	100	(100)	0	–	405	330	−19	0.10	0.2
Ireland	110	(84)	−24	–	66	68	−3	0.31	1.3
Austria	177	(75)	−58	70% by1995	282	207	−27	0.09	0.3
Norway	70	(50)	−29	50% by1994	199	194	−3	0.07	0.2
Switzerland	63	(31)	−51	57% by1995	121	70	42	0.11	0.4
Albania	(25)	(25)	0	–	39	30	−30	0.14	0.8
Luxembourg	11	(6)	−45	58% by1990	10	7.	−30	0.14	0.8
Iceland	3	(3)	0	–	18	21	+14	0.0	0.1
Total	26,078	21,471	−18		20,484	16,695	−18		

*European part of USSR, within EMEP area of calculation

Indeterminate sources	33.6%
Sweden	12.1%
Poland	10.7%
German Dem. Rep.	10.7%
Soviet Union	7.5%
UK	4.2%
Denmark	4.2%
Czechoslovakia	4.2%
Finland	2.8%

7.9 Origins of sulphur deposition in Sweden, 1988

elled over the sea for a long time. Figure 7.8 does show, however, that despite major reductions in their own emissions, Sweden and Norway have still had only minor decreases in the amount of deposition. For them in particular, acid deposition is an external threat.

For the UK, the fourth highest emitter of sulphur dioxide in 1987, there is every reason to reduce its emissions because it is the nation with the highest contribution to its own problem. For the UK acid deposition is more of a hazard rather than an external threat. The UK is also, however, the nation causing the highest proportion of pollution beyond its own borders. It exports nearly ten times as much as it imports. It clearly has much to gain itself from taking action to reduce emissions as well as helping to reduce the degree of external threat for other countries.

This exporting and importing of pollution or trans-frontier pollution makes acid deposition a major international problem. Long-term solutions to it must involve international agreements that encourage research, advice, coordination and monitoring of reductions in emissions. There was a major leap forward in 1979 when the United Nations Commission for Europe initiated a major international collaborative step which included Eastern European countries among the thirty-four at its conference where the

'Convention and Resolution on Long-range Transboundary Air Pollution' was formally adopted. Later, in 1983 at the meeting of the Convention's Executive Body, the formation of the so-called 30 Per Cent Club (Figure 7.8) went some way to providing specific targets and a timetable for reductions. It involves twenty-one countries being committed to reducing their emissions of sulphur dioxide by 30 per cent by 1993, based on 1980 levels. Before 1982 West Germany was reluctant to sign agreements on targets but such was the pressure within that country to prevent the death of forests that its government changed its mind and became a leading advocate of such targets. As can be seen from Figure 7.8, the UK and USA are not members. The former argued that it had already reduced its emissions considerably before 1980. Its peak of emissions was earlier than those of its neighbours. As a member of the European Community, however, the UK is likely to come under further pressure to join the club.

In the 1980s the main aim was to reduce emissions by producing technologies such as catalytic converters for vehicles which would lower the amount of nitrogen oxides in exhaust fumes, and changing resources such as using fossil fuels with lower sulphur content. In Britain until 1990, there was also a policy of replacing coal and oil-fired power stations with nuclear ones. West Germany's conversion to targets for reduction in the early 1980s was accompanied by developments in abatement techniques such as Fluidised Bed Combustion systems and Flue Gas Desulphurisation. Such technological developments gave a boost to the economy and to trade, which partly offset the increased cost of electricity prices caused by the new pollution-reducing processes.

Alternative solutions to such pollution involve reductions in the demand for electricity and car travel. Both higher energy consumption and increased spatial mobility have been associated with development and progress in the twentieth century. Many arrangements that offer discounts to higher energy users and zoning practices that spatially separate industrial and commercial areas from residential ones are two such examples.

Acid deposition is a major environmental concern that affects many countries and because of its trans-frontier nature may affect the relations between countries. Canada looks to the USA, Scandinavia looks particularly to Great Britain, and Germany looks to Eastern Europe to reduce emissions so that less damage is done to their environments. Such remedial techniques as liming of lakes may contain the damage but they do not reduce the threat.

Acid deposition is just one form of trans-frontier pollution. Others include photochemical oxidant (ozone) episodes and accidental releases of large quantities of pollutants such as ionising radiation and toxic chemicals. The Chernobyl nuclear explosion in the USSR was the classic, most dramatic example yet of trans-frontier pollution. While much international concern and attention have been devoted to trans-frontier pollution, in the late 1980s and early 1990s more has been given to global issues such as ozone depletion and the build-up of carbon dioxide. The earlier agreements on acid deposition may have made discussions of these easier but there is a danger that political interest and environmental fashion will move on to these global issues, leaving acid deposition to be neglected as a familiar, relatively minor, already tackled but not solved hazard and external threat.

7.3b **Rabies**

At present all dogs and cats imported into Britain spend six months in quarantine. This regulation was imposed to prevent the external threat of rabies entering the country. Britain, Sweden and Norway are some of the few countries in the world that have succeeded in eradicating this virus disease in animals and eliminating the risk of human infection. It was originally stamped out in Britain in 1902 and quarantine measures prevented its reintroduction by imported animals until 1918. Following the illegal entry of an infected dog in the post-war confusion of 1918, rabies spread to seventeen counties in southern Britain; 908 animals were infected, 358 people were bitten and three years elapsed before the disease was again eliminated.

Although the immunisation of dogs, the major source of human infection, and the prompt vaccination of people after infection have reduced human deaths, rabies is still a threat to both animals and human beings. Although the risk of human death from rabies in affluent societies where rabies occurs in animals is slightly less than that of being struck by lightning, the presence of rabies does seriously disrupt public peace of mind. Its arrival in Britain would probably change the currently relaxed attitude towards wildlife which has permitted desirable changes in the approach to conservation.

In Britain there is a potential wildlife 'reservoir' of infection, particularly in its population of foxes, which inhabit cities as well as rural areas and therefore have easy access to domestic pets. Foxes have been shown to be the largest source of infection of domestic animals in Western Europe. Since infection spread rapidly after 1945 from the east across Germany to other parts of Western Europe (Figure 7.10), there is a continuing danger that it will cross the Channel into Britain and get re-established among its wildlife.

As a set of islands, the British Isles have an advantage that many countries do not have, a natural barrier to the spread of the disease.

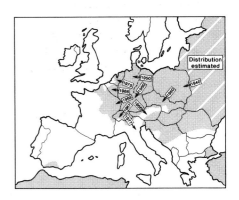

7.10 *The spread of rabies*

Whether the Channel Tunnel will physically break that barrier remains to be seen. Its presence, however, and the freer flow of people from 1993 onwards between European Community countries may reinforce pressure from pet owners for the abandonment of quarantine regulations. One of the indirect effects of the greater mobility of people between Britain and the continent may then be the re-establishment of a disease which in pre-vaccine days was the cause of death of on average forty-three people a year between 1876 and 1885.

7.3c **Deflated Michelin Man**

Michelin is a famous transnational corporation that specialises in the manufacture of tyres. Its international headquarters is located in Clermont Ferrand in France. Its main plant in the UK is at Stoke-on-Trent. The overall control of such a plant from another country is seen by some as *'external control'* with the threat to jobs, and more widely to the local economy, if decisions are taken to contract or to close. Such decisions may be relatively easier to make for plants outside the home country, thus protecting jobs in France.

The Michelin company alongside other large tyre makers has been faced with a contracting market for its product, increased competition and a worldwide glut of tyres. During the late 1970s and early 1980s the UK arm of the company had been losing about £1 million a week and drastic action began to be taken in 1981. At that time there were 6000 jobs at the Stoke plant and in spite of vociferous local opposition these were cut to 5500. Early in 1985, 2400 were made redundant and since then there has been a gradual reduction of numbers to below 3000. The negative spin-off effects of these job losses have been enormous, since some estimated that the 2400 made redundant in 1985 represented all told 4000 workers losing employment, if job losses in related industries and services providing for Michelin were taken into account.

Over this century, as some companies have grown into transnational corporations with many plants in numerous countries, the ties that often existed between a company and its local area when it had only one plant have been weakened. In the past the owners and managers of some companies and the representatives of the townspeople saw the need for mutual support between the company and the town. Indeed, sometimes owners and managers were very much involved in the town's as well as the company's affairs. One set of strategies to reduce the possible negative effects of 'external control' is to strengthen the ties between corporation and place. This may involve encouraging corporations to get more involved in civic affairs, sponsoring educational and recreational developments perhaps or establishing compacts with local schools (Chapter 5, Section 4). The town and the corporation could mutually benefit from joint promotion. A related but different strategy recognises the weaker position of the local area and involves its local government in maintaining and improving the locational advantages that it provides for the corporation. This may be through relaxing regulations or controls, giving financial incentives or developing infrastructure. Neither of these strategies will remove the external threat, they may only reduce it. A further set of strategies is to diversify the employment structure of the area by encouraging local companies and fostering new enterprise so that the local economy is not too dependent on externally owned plants and offices.

7.3d Migrant labour

As the economies of the European Community boomed in the 1950s and 1960s immigrant labour was sought to fuel the economic growth. France, with its long tradition of immigration, was no exception. By 1981 it had over 4 million immigrants. They came particularly from Portugal, Algeria, Italy, Morocco and Tunisia, in that order of numerical importance. In particular about 1.5 million came from North Africa. Most of these were unskilled, single males. In 1974 following the oil crisis the economic climate changed and immigrant labour was no longer sought after. Instead of the immigrants being seen as necessary labour for further expansion of the economy, to some they became perceived as a threat to French society and culture. Instead of filling jobs others did not want, they were then seen as competitors for the fewer job opportunities. As a result, during the 1970s immigration policy changed rapidly.

The perceived threat has been particularly felt and articulated, sometimes through acts of violence, in the three largest cities of Paris, Lyons and Marseilles where the immigrants tend to be concentrated. There they have much above average unemployment rates, poor health and poor housing. By 1980 few lived in *bidonvilles* (shanty towns) which had been mostly cleared, but most lived in segregated areas such as La Cage in central Marseilles where 22,000 North Africans were packed into slums.

As economic opportunities decreased, living conditions worsened and immigration policy changed and made their status uncertain. Some of the immigrants demonstrated and held strikes, such as that of the Metro cleaners in Paris in 1981.

Instead of seeing the immigrants as part of French society, some people saw them as a threat, an external element that could return to their countries of origin. In the late 1970s, the then conservative national government introduced a repatriation scheme which paid immigrants to return. In 1980 it established an Act which aimed to expel these immigrants without legal papers, despite their having been welcomed to the country in earlier years. This latter policy in itself produced demonstrations among the immigrants, which further inflamed some people's attitude towards them.

The change to a socialist government in 1981 brought a repeal of the Act and the introduction of a more humane approach to established immigrants while still controlling the entry of new ones. The issue still festers. The immigrant communities lag well behind many others in economic opportunities and well-being, so they continue to press for change. On the other hand, the emergence of an extreme right-wing group in French politics, whose policies have been called fascist, has built-up the issue and attracted the votes of some of those who see the immigrants as a threat. The very spatial concentration of the immigrants means, on the one hand, that by many they are rarely encountered and too easily stereotyped; on the other, it easily permits political agitators, from both within and outside the concentrations, to stir up unrest.

This issue, while being well illustrated by France, is by no means restricted to it. Similar situations occur in many countries of the world.

7.3e Not here!

This was the reaction of many local councillors and residents in Teignmouth when the proposal for a new school was made. It was a school with a difference, because it was to be a special boarding school for fifteen four-to six-year-old Downs Syndrome children. Somehow the community saw the conversion of a local hotel to this new use as a threat – perhaps to their quiet or perhaps house values! The proponents point to the modern trend to integrate the handicapped within society but have the task of either persevering with such schemes by educating the public and changing opinion or continuing to run such institutions physically and psychologically away from existing communities.

This response to the boarding school is typical of community responses to so-called community mental health centres in areas of cities which have become popular in North America and more recently in Britain as substitutes for large mental hospitals which, as asylums, isolated patients from the community. Community-based care is advocated by professionals as treatment changes, by civil rights liberals concerned by the deprivations of confinement, and by those alarmed by the rising costs of hospital maintenance. Unfortunately many communities have responded to such centres as though they were external threats.

In general, mental health centres have been regarded as 'noxious' facilities, that is, ones needed in neighbourhoods but not desired by the residents at any particular site. This also applies to such facilities as drug and alcoholic treatment centres, and board and care homes for discharged mental patients.

In such cities as Philadelphia, San Francisco and New York officials have responded to an anticipated resistance from certain communities and located such facilities in fewer areas, focusing often on low income neighbourhoods of deteriorating land uses, and areas where there is a high turnover of population and few children. Clearly these are not the stable communities in which patients are supposed more easily to recover and be rehabilitated. With little idea of the effects on the patients and the host communities, it is feared that such a concentration of facilities in certain neighbourhoods is creating 'an asylum without walls'.

7.3f AIDS: the modern plague

In the early 1980s AIDS (Acquired Immune Deficiency Syndrome) was regarded by some in Britain as an external threat. By the end of the 1980s it had spread into the country and was regarded as a major life-threatening hazard, though by no means all people considered themselves at risk.

AIDS results from a contagious virus, HIV. It was first detected and named in 1981 on the west coast of the USA. It was particularly associated with the homosexual community in San Francisco, but it was later recognised that there were parts of central Africa where the disease had also taken an early hold. There it was associated with heterosexuals. Its origin is unknown.

The breakdown of the body's immune systems leaves it open to attack and most people die within two years of being diagnosed as having AIDS. It is spread mainly through sexual intercourse with someone who is infected with the virus, transfusions with contaminated blood and injections using needles that have been used by another drug user who is infected. It is thought that the virus has an incubation period of about ten years. During that period, people carrying the virus may not suffer any symptoms of illness and thus may spread the disease unknowingly. It is possible to test to see whether the virus is being carried. If the blood has the antibodies to the virus HIV, the person is carrying the virus and may communicate it to others through blood or semen. Such people are said to be 'HIV positive'. The likelihood of them developing AIDS is not accurately known, but many do. At the time of writing, despite extensive research efforts, there is no known cure, but there are some drugs, such as AZT, which may help to delay the onset of symptoms and prolong life. Not surprisingly the disease has become to be regarded as a major modern social hazard.

In the early 1980s it was feared by some that the disease would spread from the USA into Europe through returning or travelling homosexuals, bisexuals or drug users, because these were the groups most affected in the USA. The fear of infection from heterosexual contacts in Africa was relatively little, partly because of less interaction with that continent and possibly because the disease was so horrible it was easier to regard it as a threat to only a minority of the population rather than more accurately to the whole population.

The usual strategy for restricting the spread of contagious diseases is by isolating infected people from the rest of the community. With the virus's long incubation period, this was not an option unless everyone entering the country was given a blood test. Even then isolation would not be acceptable because the disease may be spread in only very specific ways. It is quite possible to live with someone who is carrying the virus without contracting it, given suitable precautions if they are sexual partners, or if they bleed. The major strategy to limit the entry of disease into the country was education and increased awareness. Unfortunately there was much ignorance about the disease, and the rapidity with which it could spread was not matched by the speed of action to prevent it. Infected blood was imported and given to patients in transfusions. In this way haemophiliacs, who require many transfusions, became one of the groups at risk. Drug users desperate to get a fix became another. Through the North American contacts, the homosexual community in Britain also became a major group at risk. What had been an external threat, a mysterious disease happening to people elsewhere in the early 1980s, had become a rapidly expanding hazard within Britain and many other European Community nations by the mid-1980s (Figure 7.11).

At that time in the European Community the number of victims was doubling every nine months, and there were predictions of 100,000 cases by 1990.

An epidemic did take place but not quite at the rate predicted. This was due partly to changed behaviour by initially infected groups. The high initial infection of homosexuals and drug users and some of the publicity given to the disease in the popular

press meant that it became incorrectly associated with these groups. Too many people thought that they were not at risk because they did not belong to either of these groups. To some extent this was made worse by government campaigns that targeted so-called 'high risk groups'. They were high risk only because in the early years they were more likely to come in contact with infected people. In Africa, where the disease has been found mainly in heterosexuals, the same groups would not be considered high risk. In fact, anyone may contract the disease. It has no boundaries, not class, race, gender nor sexuality. Whereas campaigns by the government and by the homosexual community itself helped change behaviour so that 'safe sex' habits were adopted, there is not much evidence of such campaigns, on the use of condoms for example, having had as much effect on the behaviour of heterosexuals. Too many in Britain saw the disease as affecting others, not themselves. Such an attitude, 'it won't happen to me', is often found to such hazards.

Every area in Britain by 1990 contained people who had died from the disease and who had been diagnosed. It was suspected that there were many more who had HIV but did not know because they had not been tested. The map then, may show only the tip of the iceberg (Figure 7.12).

In some areas the hazard seems greater than others, but it should be remembered that the long incubation period very much under-emphasises the risk and that people, including infected people, are spatially mobile. Infected drug users have been traced who have shared needles from one end of Great Britain to the other. In some areas the hazard is particularly acute. In 1990 in Edinburgh, for example, one in 100 men between twenty-five and forty-four were infected with HIV, with the incidence slightly less among women. This was related to the large amount of drug abuse

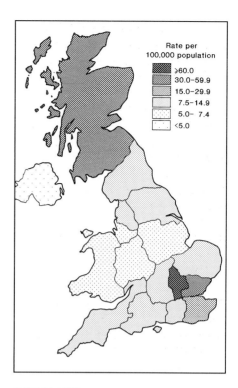

7.12 HIV, 1989

there in the early 1980s.

In 1990 experts feared that an epidemic might occur among heterosexuals in Britain in twenty to thirty years' time. In 1987 4 per cent of those contracting the disease had acquired it through heterosexual contact. In 1989 the proportion had increased to 8 per cent and was expected to rise further. Whereas homosexuals were aware of people whom they knew who had contracted the disease, few heterosexuals knew people who were HIV positive or had AIDS. As a result of this awareness and in response to campaigns, many homosexuals changed their behaviour. To many heterosexuals, the danger seemed too remote.

The disease has stimulated a number of other responses that have geographical consequences. The increased research effort into finding a cure has created some jobs, though, of course, resources have been deflected from other research activities. The drug companies are particularly active in trying to find a cure. National and local support groups have been rapidly built-up to help victims and their friends and

7.11 AIDS, 1989

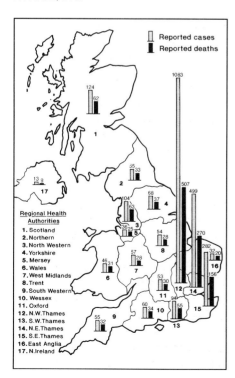

Regional Health Authorities
1. Scotland
2. Northern
3. North Western
4. Yorkshire
5. Mersey
6. Wales
7. West Midlands
8. Trent
9. South Western
10. Wessex
11. Oxford
12. N.W.Thames
13. S.W.Thames
14. N.E.Thames
15. S.E.Thames
16. East Anglia
17. N.Ireland

relatives, for example the Terence Higgins Trust in Britain. While such organisations help to inform, comfort and warn, there is still much ignorance about the disease and indeed much prejudice. Some people, for example, have not wished their children to attend a school where there is someone who is carrying the disease. More generally the public attitude to gays in Britain and North America has become less tolerant. Too few people see those with AIDS as victims. People attribute blame rather than realise that they may be at risk unless they change their own behaviour.

AIDS is a disease that has spread rapidly from its geographical origins in Africa and North America. Unlike rabies it has not been possible to keep the external threat out of Britain. It has rapidly become a hazard to us all, including you, yes you, the reader!

7.4 Alternative strategies

'Exit'

There are two traditional ways of responding to external threat: one is to 'exit' from the area under threat, while the other is to stay and exert some form of 'voice' or opposition to the intrusion. Exit solves the individual's or individual household's problem in that they move to a location which is not under threat. It does not, however, help the area or community because in leaving it, the household is likely to be replaced by one which does not perceive the event as a threat. Exit by some may also lead to others leaving, sometimes generating almost panic as a response. If many people leave, the community's response, if there is one, will be weakened and the event much more likely to occur.

Exit is possible only for those with the economic means available to move and for those whose social ties permit them to do so. Thus if exit is a major response, the social composition of the area may change very rapidly. The external threat, whether or not it occurs, will have been the triggering mechanism for geographical change.

Very occasionally a whole community feels under threat and responds by moving en masse. A community based on religious beliefs or a shared culture may be oppressed by other groups and seek a new territory in which to settle. Jewish communities have often moved out and relocated in such a way. In the nineteenth century the Mormons moved across the USA away from the attacks of other groups to establish themselves in what became Salt Lake City, while many religious groups seeking a new more tolerant world had arrived in the USA before them, escaping from the threatened existence that they had felt in their countries of origin in Europe.

'Voice'

The strategy of staying and using some form of voice may then depend upon the form and extent of the threat. Where it is a new land-use or activity then the strategy of voice may be more possible than if it is threatening to life. In such situations, voice may take the form of individual or community protest. People may individually write to their local or national political representatives. They may feel that a coordinated community response is more effective and hold meetings, organise petitions and/or lobby the representatives en masse. Their previous experience, the information they have and their ability to obtain useful information, their ability to mobilise resources and present a well-argued case all affect the success of their opposition (Chapter 5, Section 2). They need to develop or already know the lines of communication to obtain information and along which to convey their arguments to greatest effect. Access to representatives of appropriate national organisations may also help build a case. More affluent communities and ones with more professional experience may be better able to use voice successfully.

Tactics of voice

Typically, voice goes through a number of tactics over time. Opposition is to begin with simply a resounding 'no'. It may then be obvious that the threatened event or activity will take place. The next tactical stage is 'not here'. Such a response is obviously transferring the threat elsewhere and is a form of competition or conflict between areas, which is sometimes covert, at other times overt. When it becomes obvious that it will not be displaced elsewhere, then the next tactical stage is 'not here now'. The temporal postponement is in the hope that the situation may change and the threat may no longer be realised. If this fails, then the final tactic is modification, 'not like that'. These are the types of stages of voice followed in an attempt to keep out a large new housing development in an attractive rural area. The final stage may involve demands to lower the density of housing in order to reduce the number of people entering the area and to try to ensure that they are relatively affluent people with values and attitudes that are probably similar to those already living in the area. It may also involve trying to obtain some gains out of the development, such as new public facilities.

Communities that are better able to arouse and organise opposition may fail with the first tactic but be successful in the second in displacing the threat to another less well-organised community. This has happened with proposals for major new urban roads. The better-off areas are often able to deflect the route, for example into a more expensive, underpass tunnel or get an alternative route chosen that affects other less well-off areas.

Clearly the strategy of voice takes time and effort. Some people will be *free-riders*. They will not contribute any effort to a campaign. They will passively support it and be happy if it is successful. 'You'll be successful. You don't need me.' If it fails: 'If I had got involved, it would not have made any difference'. Others may have been alienated from the political process. 'You will not achieve anything. You are wasting your time. You always are.' If there are too many people like these in an area, it will be difficult to mount any successful opposition.

Formal participation

The presence of alienated people suggests previous failure or a breakdown of communications between local people and those who take decisions on their behalf. A longer-term strategy would be to improve the formal participation of local people in the making of decisions that affect them (Figure 7.13). This requires considerable political will from everyone involved. If the participation process is imposed from above, that is by the usual decision makers, it is too easy for them to manipulate situations to retain their control. When the local community agrees with the decision makers, it is taken as local support. When there is dis-

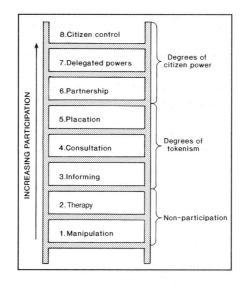

7.13 The ladder of participation

agreement, it is too easy to argue that any elected people from the local community or ones nominated by them are not representative. Not enough people may have been present at a public meeting. The opposition is discounted. This could easily be the case in areas where there is a lot of alienation or many free-riders. Full participation and representation cost money and need to be properly recognised by the usual decision-makers.

Illegal action

Where participation does not exist and voice is not listened to, alien-

ation may be so great that the response to a threat may be illegal action, that is action by the local community that breaks the rules and laws of the rest of the society. The particular threat may not be that great, but it may be the last straw for many. Such responses as riot and squatting are examples of this response. They are typical of relatively powerless groups in society who have, in their view, exhausted other legal alternatives. They attract attention and the protests increase their power because they are a threat to social order. So a threat to them is met by a threat of a different kind, an illegal response against society as a whole.

Such responses reflect great political divides in a society which may be based on economic, social and cultural differences that have grown over time. The riots in North American cities in the 1960s partly reflected the unfulfilled expectations of blacks who had moved into northern and western cities from the south and ended up living in poor ghettoes in the middle of general affluence that was easily visible to them. The riots in some British cities in the early 1980s again reflected social divides of poverty and ethnicity, which can often be

Armed forces called in response to squatting demonstration in Amsterdam

clearly recognised geographically.

In such situations, many of the people who serve the community, particularly the police, are regarded as being 'outside' the community. They are seen as representing the rest of society or a section or aspect of it, as threats in themselves. Hence the emergence of 'no go areas', where the police and other deliverers of services feel they cannot go or fear to go. The need for greater participation and less alienation is obvious. The means of achieving them is not usually so clear. One strategy operated by the rest of the society, not the local community, is a geographical one. The community is dispersed spatially, an enforced exit.

Responses to 'voice'

Such a consideration raises the question of response from the viewpoint of the people or organisation involved with the so-called threat. How do they reply to the voice of the local people? They can withdraw the proposal altogether and cut their losses, forgoing any money already spent. The opposition would have to be very strong for that. They can withdraw the proposal from that area and, having learned from the experience, try another where there may be less resistance. They can postpone the proposal in the original area, hoping that resistance will decline over time, perhaps as leaders of the opposition move out. They can modify the proposal to make it more acceptable. These are the responses to 'no', 'not here', 'not here now', 'not like that'.

Locate where least resistance expected

There are other variations on these. The first and most obvious strategy is to locate in areas where it seems there will be the least resistance in the first place. If an example of the development already exists there, there is likely to be less resistance. Applications for new nuclear power stations in Britain were made in locations such as Sizewell and Hinckley Point where plants already existed (Chapter 3, Section 1). Proposals for high- or medium-rise apartments blocks in both Canada and Britain tend to be focused on residential areas where they already exist. Such 'follow the leader' tendencies lead to spatial concentrations of activities and land uses, and, of course, increase the differences between places.

Attempts to minimise voice

Another strategy is to minimise any protest before it arises. This can be done in two main ways:
(a) by publicising the potential benefits to the local community from the development and anticipating the possible negative effects and taking action to reduce them or allay any fears;
(b) by introducing various benefits and gains to the community so that any perceived negative effects are offset.

The location of nuclear power plants in France is accompanied by reduced electricity prices and other direct financial incentives for the local people. There is also a policy of making the nuclear plant the focal point of a growth centre, so promising the area extra employment opportunities and economic development.

Postponement

The strategy of postponement can be very effective. A proposal to reorganise the education of sixteen-to-nineteen-year-olds in Stockport by the abolition of sixth forms in existing comprehensive schools and their replacement by sixth form colleges was met by much opposition. Parents and pupils defended their present schools. They saw the proposals as threats to their communities. There were three areas to be reorganised into three sixth form colleges. The area with greatest immediate need and least opposition was implemented immediately. For the other two areas, opposition was greatly reduced when the reorganisation was timed for a number of years in the future. Just as opposition to proposals usually declines with distance from their location, so too may it decline as the date of implementation recedes into the future.

The strategy of amending the proposal in response to the local objections might be genuine or it might have been anticipated. In the second case, the original proposal may have contained a part that could be dropped in the light of public opposition, so ending up with the intended development, for example a four-storey development being reduced to the three that were originally intended.

The form of amendment might be geographical. A large housing development of terraced and semi-detached housing in a detached area may be modified on its periphery so that there is a grading of housing density rather than an abrupt change. So some detached housing may be built on the periphery and then some larger semi-detached before the smaller semis and terraced properties towards the centre of the development. Another example might be a new factory estate being fringed with a line or zone of trees to reduce the visual intrusion.

The strategies of those perceiving the threat and those involved with the threatened activity have been examined and some of their geographical consequences noted. In the following section, among other things, the strategies of the organisations who have to make decisions about the threats are discussed.

7.5   Perspectives

Deciding on the threat and voice

Decision-makers, such as local authorities in Britain, have to listen to the 'voice' of a local community as well as that of the organisation responsible for the proposal that is perceived as a threat. Sometimes it is not within their powers to reject a proposal because the grounds on which protests are being made are not permissible ones for rejection. They have to consider that if they reject, say, a three-storey development the developer may go to appeal and the national government, through the Department of the Environment, may decide for the developer. That is costly for the local authority, so they must have reasonable grounds on which to reject.

The local authority may require modifications which may offset some of the local opposition, or they may negotiate it, indicating to the developer the extent of local opposition. In negotiations they may also obtain some help from the developers in providing other necessary facilities that otherwise the local authority will have to provide. The developers may pay for or build some recreational facilities or even a school, or a major road (Chapter 5, Section 1). These are called *planning gain*. Such gains may somewhat offset the negative effects of the threat and placate the local community. They may certainly put the local authority on the developer's side.

The local authority also has to consider the effects on all its local communities. If the development is seen as a threat to one community but as an advantage to many others, the local authority may put the many first. The positive effects or externalities for the wider area may be seen to outweigh the negative ones to the local area. In such situa-tions it may well be faced by the 'not here' response and become involved in competition between areas *not* to have a facility such as a refuse tip. The overall area needs such a facility but nobody wants it next door to them (the NIMBY, Not In My Back Yard, response). Local communities with the least powerful voice often receive such facilities. This can be cumulative so that certain areas have a concentration of noxious facilities. Each time the opposition becomes less strong, because past opponents have exited. Again spatial differences are increased.

Across their territory as a whole, local authorities will want to attract people, activities and developments that have positive effects or externalities and cost them little to service, and repel ones that have negative effects or externalities and cost them a lot.

They may also want to meet the needs of their population. This is not always straightforward. If they build or allow facilities such as drug abuse centres or houses for alcoholics because there is a need in their area, they may attract more people with such needs into their area because of the availability of the facilities. Meeting a local need may therefore increase the need, because the facilities do not exist elsewhere. Local people who saw such facilities as threats in the first place will be even less pleased if more people with need arrive and increase the demand for even more facilities.

Such cumulative developments suggest why some people exit from threatened areas. If people decide to stay and oppose, they may be forgoing their chance to exit or may be reducing their choice of alternative homes. Those who move out early may get reasonable prices for their homes. If property prices decline absolutely or relatively because of the threat, through the sudden exit of others or the arrival of the devel-opment/people, then they may not be able to afford to move or will have to move down-market. Staying to oppose may limit future options. People renting local authority housing who request a move immediately may succeed in getting out. Those who oppose the development run the risk of not being able to move because nobody else wants to exchange or move in because of the threat. On the other hand, if people stay and win, they may be better-off eventually than if they had exited.

Where it is the local authority that is responsible for the development that is perceived as a threat, then it is even more difficult to adjudicate. One of the difficulties with private-public partnerships (Chapter 4, Section 4) is that the responsibility of local authorities for development control and the need to listen to local people may be overridden. When the threat is to people in local authority housing, community opposition can be greatly reduced by the relocation of local leaders into local authority housing elsewhere. Moves that have been requested for years suddenly become possible. Such movement out of leaders has occurred, for example, where the refurbishment of local authority homes by private developers is proposed. These will be sold to people who can afford owner occupation. This does not usually include the existing tenants. The opposition to the transformation of the local community is thus muted.

Defence communities

One way of defending an area from unwanted developments and/or people is to set it up as the equivalent of a local authority. This occurs in the USA where small communities set themselves up in such a way and zone their land so that only large plots can be purchased and only single household dwellings may be built on them. In effect this keeps out everyone who is not rich. A proliferation of such small *defence communities* leads to a fragmented political organisation of space. It is not possible in countries like Britain.

Separate development

At a larger scale such defensive strategies are seen at their extreme in the idea of separate development or apartheid in South Africa. Under this system the blacks are separated spatially into territories and townships (Figure 7.14) because they are seen as a threat to what some of the white South Africans, particularly the Afrikaaners, regard as their own land. Their religious beliefs provide them with a justification for their claims. In such circumstances, international pressure through boycotts as well as voice and illegal actions from some of the blacks, the

A Vietnamese being forcibly ejected from Hong Kong and sent back to Hanoi

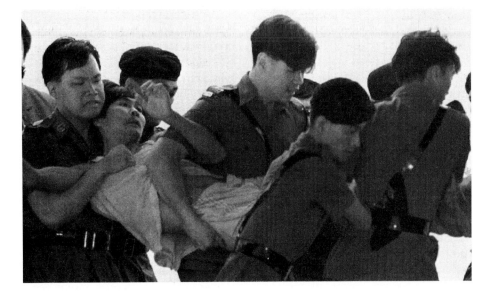

coloureds and the whites may not be enough to produce lasting change.

When one group of people sees another as a threat to their very survival, extremes of behaviour result, such as the imprisonment of whole groups of people in camps or their extermination, as with the Jews and, less publicised, the gypsies in Hitler's Germany. Such atrocities should continually remind people to seek understanding, to avoid stereotypes and to question why other human beings are regarded in any way as threats.

Need for international cooperation

Where the threats to countries are not human, as in the case of rabies and acid deposition, international cooperation is also needed. It is not always easy to obtain, because countries will not always admit to being the cause or origin of the threat. Extra research and publicity are often necessary, as well as much governmental activity to make the case. This is particularly difficult

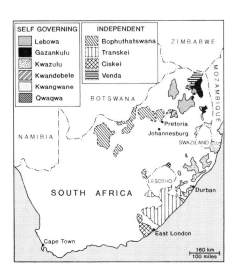

7.14 Territories and townships in South Africa

when there is much existing investment tied up in the practices producing the threat, as with acid deposition.

Some benefits are derived at this scale from international cooperation on developments that are perceived as being threats to the planet, such as the destruction of the ozone layer and the increase in the greenhouse effect. Once environmental issues are on the agenda and there are international agreements, then it is easier to make advances on other environmental issues that cross international boundaries.

From the local to the international level, there is still much to be done to improve the way that perceived threats to communities are resolved. The exit option becomes less of a possibility as the scale moves from the local to the international. Refugees exiting from a country where they feel threatened are too often regarded as a threat to other countries where they seek asylum. At all scales there is great need for political developments, so that there are channels for voices to be heard. Illegal action, whether riots or wars, may then be reduced.

7.6 Exercises

1. (a) From your knowledge of local TV news and local newspapers over the last year, identify issues that some local people have perceived as external threats.
   (b) Discuss the nature of these threats.
   (c) Identify the types of responses made to these threats and evaluate their success.

2. (a) From the viewpoint of those prepared to commit arson, why are second homes seen as a threat in rural Wales?
   (b) Based on the chapter, how would this form of response to external threat be classified?
   (c) For the local people in general, what are the advantages and disadvantages of second homes?
   (d) Where else in Great Britain and France are second homes viewed to some extent as an external threat?
   (e) Set up a parish council meeting in rural Wales to consider strategies to improve the access of local people to affordable housing.

3. Imagine that you are part of a consortium of developers who wish to apply for planning permission to build a new settlement for 10,000 people on the outer edge of the Green Belt in south-east England.

   (a) Whom would you be trying to attract to live in the settlement? In other words, what is your target market?
   (b) What arguments would you put forward to support your application?
   (c) How would you design your settlement to make it most attractive to existing residents?
   (d) What strategies would you adopt to counter any opposition from local people and their representatives?
   (e) If you were now playing the role of a local resident and/or a local planner, how would you respond to the consortium's proposal?

7.7 Further reading

K. Cox (ed.) (1978) *Urbanisation and Conflict in Market Societies*, Methuen

M. Dear and J. Wolch (1987) *Landscapes of Despair*, Princeton University Press (mental health)

A. Hirschman (1982) *Shifting Involvements: Private Interest and Public Action*, Blackwell (a follow-up to *Exit and Voice*)

A. Kirby (1982) *The Politics of Location*, Methuen

Geography 16-19 Project Booklet (1990) *The Challenge of Difficult Environments*, Longman

C. Park (1987) *Acid Rain: Rhetoric and Reality*, Routledge

S. Pinch (1985) *Cities and Services: the Geography of Collective Consumption* (ch. 3 *Externalities*), Routledge and Kegan Paul

G. V. Shannon, G.E. Pyle and R.L. Bashshur (1991) *The Geography of AIDS*, Guilford

PART III

CHANGING ENVIRONMENTS

Chapter 8
Changing economic actors and environments

8.1 Case study: transnational car producers
8.2 General problem
8.3 Other examples
    8.3a 'Big Blue' – IBM
    8.3b Worldwide leisure
    8.3c Boom in small firm sector
8.4 Alternative strategies
8.5 Perspectives
8.6 Exercises
8.7 Further reading

Chapter 9
Changing technological actors and environments

9.1 Case study: information technology
9.2 General problem
9.3 Other examples
    9.3a Developments in transport technology
    9.3b High-tech industry
    9.3c The geography of high-tech products
9.4 Alternative strategies
9.5 Perspectives
9.6 Exercises
9.7 Further reading

Chapter 10
Changing social actors and environments

10.1 Case study: the challenge of housing the elderly
10.2 General problem
10.3 Other examples
    10.3a Wider impacts of an ageing population
    10.3b The impacts on schools of a falling birth rate
    10.3c Migration: a component of social and demo-
           graphic change
    10.3d Urbanisation and counterurbanisation; two
           contrasting trends
    10.3e Geography of crime
10.4 Alternative strategies
10.5 Perspectives
10.6 Exercises
10.7 Further reading

Chapter 11
Changing political actors and environments

11.1 Case study: the rise and fall of metropolitan
      counties
11.2 General problem
11.3 Other examples
    11.3a The world as an arena of conflict or
           cooperation
    11.3b Degree of integration of states and
           separatism
    11.3c The green or environmental movement
    11.3d Urban Development Corporations
11.4 Alternative strategies
11.5 Perspectives
11.6 Exercises
11.7 Further reading

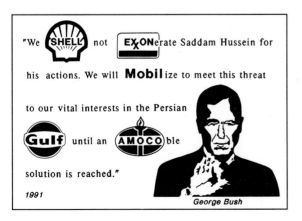

Chapter 8

CHANGING ECONOMIC ACTORS AND ENVIRONMENTS

8.1   Case study: transnational car producers

It has been argued that the Cavalier (Ascona in Europe, Holden in Australia) is the first 'global car'. The engines are made in the UK, Germany or Japan; the diesel engines and transmissions are made in Japan; the steel comes from Germany, and the gearboxes from the USA. The cars are assembled in plants all over the world. The manufacturer of the Cavalier, General Motors (GM), is the biggest car maker in the world and is still based around Detroit in the USA, its original location, but like many huge car makers has increasingly become international (Figure 8.1).

The advantages of international production are numerous. On the production side the breaking up of stages of production and the related geographical division of labour allows GM to gain from special qualities of places. So, for instance, Zaragossa in Spain was seen by GM as an attractive location for an assembly plant because of low levels of labour militancy, as was true of south-east Brazil where there are even lower wage rates. Production in branch plants can be shifted between established locations and to new ones whenever management wishes. Thus the branch plant in one country is then competing with branch plants in other countries to secure orders and consequently employment.

Further advantages of internationalisation include the extension of the market for cars, whereby a corporation has a 'home' advantage in any country where it possesses a branch plant. Also currency differences can work in favour of a transnational where manufacture or assembly in a country with a cheap currency can lead to a relatively cheap and competitive product in wider markets. Finally, the cost of research per unit (vehicle) can be spread through huge sales. On the other hand, such transnational policy presents some disadvantages to companies. Supply and communication lines are lengthened and delayed; language problems exist and different work traditions may be followed.

VAG and Renault are two major European-based transnationals with quite different policies and geographical organisations. VAG is based in Wolfsburg in Germany and produces VW and Audi motor cars. Twenty per cent of VAG is owned by the federal government, 20 per cent by the regional government of lower Saxony and the rest by shareholders. It is thus a private operation which has recently undertaken cautious international expansion. Both

8.1 The spatial organisation of General Motors

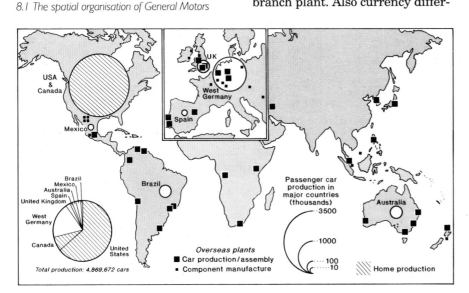

8.2 The production and sales of VAG and Renault, 1984

VAG		Renault
	Production	
71.4% ←	Home (W. Germany)	
	Home (France) →	83.8%
13.4%	Latin America	3.6%
11.8%	Spain	12.6%
3.4%	North America	
33.4%	Home % sales	39.7%

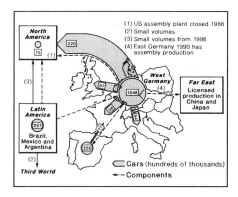

8.3 International production networks of VAG

its production and sales are less home based than those of Renault (Figure 8.2).

VAG has identified several advantages to such an international presence. Firstly, it is a form of insurance against currency fluctuations and/or imposition of tariffs. Secondly, it allows international flexibility whereby Germany with high cost and skilled labour can produce the luxury end of its line, such as Audis, while Spain, a recent low labour cost assembly location, can produce less sophisticated cars such as Polos. Research and development and the production of new advanced Audi and Golf GTI cars are concentrated on the homeland of Germany, whereas volume production is handled by branch plants across the world, giving 'insider' access to markets and benefiting from the advantages of low costs, particularly cheap labour (Figure 8.3).

The corporation therefore benefits from the differences between national economies; so, for instance, Brazil is used as a producer of cheap components.

Renault, on the other hand, is totally owned by the government and is seen as the national champion. Thus there has been a firm commitment to see that workers are not made redundant. In 1984, however, the company faced massive financial problems and under the guidance of a new chief has: rationalised the product line; withdrawn from peripheral activities so that plants in South Africa and Mexico have been closed; sold AMC to Chrysler in the USA; reduced the labour force with government support. This withdrawal to the home base of France in the face of these financial problems can be seen in Figure 8.4.

Again this shows the vulnerability of overseas activities of a transnational when such a company is faced with economic problems. Renault, however, has continued to support a range of Iberian plants, which are heavily subsidised by the Spanish and Portuguese governments, so that full advantages could be gained once these two countries had been integrated within the European Community. The Renault company hoped to break even by late 1987 but needed continued heavy subsidy from the national government to be able to do so.

This 'internationalisation' of large-scale automobile manufacturing is also well illustrated by the

8.5 Ford's changing spatial organisation of production in Europe

8.4 Renault's capital expenditure

1980		1986
75%	In France	85%
14%	Rest of Europe	10%
11%	Rest of World	5%

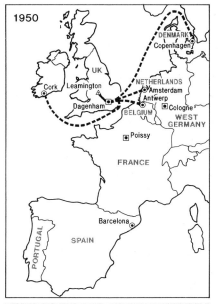

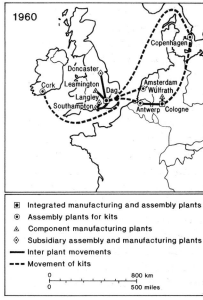

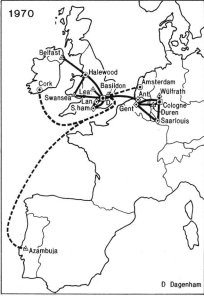

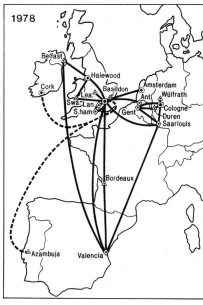

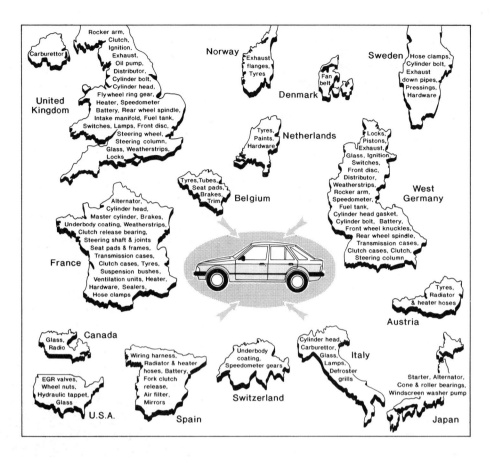

8.6 A global car, 1980

Ford Motor Company's changed organisation of production in Europe from 1950 to 1978 (Figure 8.5), and the component suppliers for the Ford Escort (Figure 8.6).

In 1983 Ford were second to GM as the leading transnational manufacturing corporation by sales but had a larger foreign component to their assets and employment (Figure 8.7).

The dominance of car producers in this list of transnational corporations, with five in the top twelve, shows their importance to the international economy. They are also extremely important to a national economy, so governments are anxious to retain and attract them. A good example in the 1980s was the attraction of the Japanese corporation Nissan to Britain, the first site being in Washington in north-east England.

Transnationals with their headquarters in different parts of the world are not just competing with one another, they are also cooperating to gain better access to markets, share research costs and benefit from each other's expertise. Honda's much-publicised agreement with Rover illustrates this very well. New Rover cars, jointly developed, allow the sharing of research and development costs and (in theory at any rate) open up the Japanese car market to Rover and the UK market to Honda.

Corporation	Country of origin	Total sales ($ million)	Foreign content as a percentage	
			of Assets	of Employment
General Motors	United States	57,728	12	31
Ford Motor Co	United States	37,086	40a	58
IBM	United States	26,213	46	43
Renault	France	18,958	46	24
Volkswagen	West Germany	18,313	46	38
Peugeot-Citroen	France	16,825	15	22
Volvo	Sweden	5,268	15	27

a 1976   *Source: based on UNCTNC (1983) Transnational Corporations in World Development: Third Survey, New York: United Nations, Table 11-31; UNCTNC (1978) Transnational Corporations in World Development: A Re-examination, New York: United Nations, Table IV-1*

8.7 Leading transnational manufacturing companies

8.2 General problem

The case study has illustrated some of the major recent changes in economic actors and their environments. The car manufacturing companies have extended their operations from their home countries into many others, so that they have become prime examples of *multinational* corporations. Some of these are extremely large economic units; of the largest 100 economic units in the world about half are nation states while the other half are multinational corporations. Multinationals are defined as corporations with operations in *many* countries. A more general term, used by the United Nations, is *transnational* which applies to corporations with operations in *more* *than one* country, so a corporation operating in two countries would be transnational but not multinational. Although the largest multinationals, such as General Motors and Ford, receive much attention, there are many smaller ones which should not be ignored.

The growth of multinational or transnational corporations is one of the major recent changes to economic actors or organisations. Most of these enterprises have grown from single-plant and single-product companies into *multi-plant, multi-product* ones which command enormous financial resources. Their development in itself has changed the economic environment of people as employees and consumers; companies as suppliers, competitors and consumers; and nation states as consumers and controllers of their economies.

Statement of the general problem

The general problem of this chapter is the ways in which the economic environment has changed, partly through the development of economic organisations like transnationals, the geographical impacts of these changes and the responses of various actors to these changes. The changes and their impacts will be reviewed in this section and illustrated by other examples in the next. The responses will be discussed under alternative strategies.

Growth of transnationals

Transnationals can be categorised in a number of ways, for example by major sector, size and country of origin. The car industry is a frequently quoted example of transnational enterprises in manufacturing that have emerged in the twentieth century. Many other transnationals based on manufacturing have grown since the Second World War. Many companies concerned with the extraction of oil and minerals and with commercial cultivation of, for example, tobacco, tea and rubber were transnational before then. The processing of these primary products, such as the petro-chemical industry, near to markets has led to

transnational enterprises which are concerned with both extraction and processing. The companies have integrated vertically (that is, they may develop their own raw materials, do their own processing, distribution and even retailing). This is in order to control their supplies. They have extracted or cultivated in more than one country in order to guarantee their supplies against exhaustion, weather and political instability. Processing takes place near to markets for reasons of cost, and sometimes to guard against nationalisation, which might occur if it was located in the country where extraction or cultivation took place. These companies, then, have controlled their marketing channels (Chapter 3, Section 5) which stretch across many countries.

The major geographical growth in transnationals which manufacture cars, electrical and electronic goods, clothing and other consumer goods occurred in the 1950s, 1960s and 1970s. In the 1950s world trade began to rise much faster than world production while in the 1960s foreign direct investment in developing countries showed rapid growth. Instead of producing in one country and exporting to others, many corporations became multinational during this time, expanding their operations into many parts of the world. The geographical growth of these 'invisible empires' has been achieved mainly by establishment of foreign subsidiaries, and merger.

Diversification

One mechanism of growth often associated with mergers is diversification, so it is less appropriate to categorise a corporation by product. Most are multi-product. Not only have they diversified into products, many have entered the service sector in which transnationals have appeared in their own right, for example in finance and

advertising and other so-called 'producer services' (ones which serve other companies rather than household consumers). Indeed, a major economic change in the core manufacturing countries (North America, Western Europe and Japan) has been the decline of the manufacturing sector relative to the service sector, especially in terms of employment. Part of the growth of the service sector has been through the rapid development of transnationals, such as Saatchi and Saatchi, a British-based advertising company which grew by merger and diversification (financial services, market research and consultancy) into the largest advertising company in the world within a twenty-year period.

From its launch in 1970, Saatchi and Saatchi was by 1988 handling 5% of the entire world advertising market, employing 14,000 people in 58 countries. It represented half of the world's 500 leading corporations and purchased nearly 20% of all commercial television air time in the USA, where 55% of all world advertising spending occurred. By acquisition of many regional companies, Saatchi and Saatchi were, by 1979, the leading advertising company in Britain. It went multinational in 1982 when it acquired Compton Communications, the American cousin of its first British partner. In so doing it obtained Compton's operations in 30 foreign countries. In 1985 it moved into management consultancy through its acquisition of the Philadelphia-based Hay group. It is noted for its aggressive expansion, its hard-edged advertising, called Mean Chic, and its campaigns for the British Conservative Party in the 1979, 1983 and 1987 elections. In 1989 it experienced some major setbacks, which may have resulted from too rapid growth and especially diversification.

There has also been an expansion of transnationals in retailing, property and tourism (Chapter 8, Section 3c). Although many corporations may specialise in extraction, agribusiness, manufacturing or services, the diversification of many of them means that they are involved in many sectors of the economy. Most are intricately connected with the banking and financial sectors which in themselves became international during the 1970s. These linkages are because transnationals increasingly depend on the financial system to raise capital and generate profits.

Classification of transnationals

In the 1980s many of these transnationals could be said to have developed into *global corporations*. They may be distinguished from other transnationals that are serving sets of particular national markets rather than a world market. They are competing at a world scale and not within individual countries. Their future decisions do not now concern expansion into new geographical production areas or markets. They have already expanded into them. Their future decisions involve the spatial organisation and coordination of their operations over the globe, for example into which areas they should invest more resources, reduce production or increase their marketing effort. In nearly all such cases, in recent years, the production in the corporation's own country has reduced relative to its overseas plants. The home base has thus become relatively less important. These globally organised corporations may be distinguished from other large transnationals which effectively serve many individual domestic markets rather than a global one. These transnationals are called *multi-domestic*. The competitive position of global corporations in one country is affected by their position in others, whereas for multi-domestic corporations competition within one country or a small set of countries is independent.

Countries of origin

The earlier manufacturing transnationals were dominated by those of US origins. Now there are many from Japan and Europe which rival this American influence and growing numbers from places like Canada, Australia and South Africa and the Newly Industrialising Countries (NICs) such as South Korea and Taiwan. Companies tend to reflect their country of origin in the way they are managed, so while it was possible to generalise about the early American ones, it is more difficult to do so for the larger, more heterogeneous present set. The American car manufacturers, for example, grew by having assembly plants in different regions of the USA. These regional operations, however, had centralised administration and research and development. Executives moved from one company to another and even when they became transnationals were almost always American. In contrast, European and Japanese companies emerged from very different business environments. Having assembly plants in different regions was uncommon because of the smaller size of the countries. Several European-based companies invested in overseas colonial territories. Indeed, research has shown that the locational strategies of American, British, French and German companies are different.

Thus transnationals can now be differentiated in many ways. It is therefore more difficult to generalise about them. So there are more types than before and yet, because of the diversification, mergers and interconnections with the international financial sector, they are more integrated than before.

Global products

Changes have occurred in products and production as well as organisa-

'The Real Thing' in China

tions. A trend towards global products as well as global corporations has also been noted, but there is more confusion over their definition. The products of car companies are assembled from parts that are manufactured in many countries, so in that sense they may be called *global products*. Yet they may be modified in various ways to suit local markets, so they are not usually exactly the same in all the countries in which they are sold. This would be the more usual definition of a global product. Their market has become a world market, so in that sense they have become global products, though none has penetrated world markets so extensively as the prime examples of global products, Coca Cola and Pepsi Cola. Coca Cola has the same brand name and the same ingredients wherever it is sold in the world. The company has been able to maintain over 50 per cent of the worldwide carbonated soft drinks industry, despite being in a product range which might seem particularly susceptible to local differences in tastes. So global products may result from production, the product itself or its markets.

Spatial organisation of transnationals

The example of the car industry demonstrates how the production process has been divided up with different stages taking place in different countries. There is then a *spatial division of labour* with, for example, production of parts in many different countries, assembly in one country, research and development in another and headquarters elsewhere. This spatial division of labour is facilitated by improved transport and communications. In some industries, production now takes place in the Newly Industrialised Countries (NICs), partly because their labour is cheap, less organised and more submissive.

Since manufacturing used to be concentrated in the developed countries with developing ones providing resources and a market for the manufacturing goods of the developed countries, this new location of manufacturing in the NICs, in particular, has prompted some writers to speak of a *'new international division of labour'*. This idea is substantiated by the case of Britain which until the 1980s used to export more manufactured goods than it imported. That position was then reversed. The importance of oil exports to Britain's balance of trade (value of exports to imports) together with this change in trade of manufactured goods superficially made Britain seem to have similar trading characteristics to many developing nations in the 1960s and before. The dominance of its invisible exports such as banking, insurance and more recently accounting and advertising, however, distinguishes its trading characteristics from those of developing countries in the past.

Explanations of growth

The growth of transnationals has been explained in a number of ways, not surprisingly since their diversity has already been noted. Some explanations emphasise the locational advantages of operating in various countries, such as the cost or degree of organisation of their labour, the availability of resources or the size or affluence of their markets. Others concentrate on the ownership advantages of large corporations: their greater knowledge about information, inputs (labour, natural resources, finance) and markets; their ability to gain access to inputs on favoured terms because of their size; their ability to spread their risks over different products and markets and take advantage of international differences in factors of production and markets. A further approach focuses on the advantages

gained from a whole series of transactions being internalised within the transnational rather than taking place within the market. Instead of buying or selling goods or services from or to other organisations, the corporation is able to obtain them from its own operations. It can thus protect against or exploit market failure. A set of decisions can be planned or coordinated within the organisation rather than rely on the unplanned, more uncertain operation of the market, where many transactions in themselves cost money. Indeed by setting its own prices for transfers within the organisation – 'transfer prices' – a transnational can avoid or reduce payments of tax and tariffs to governments. Greater control is gained over the price, quality and availability of supplies. One theory relates all three ideas (ownership, locational advantage and internalisation) together and is known as the OLI theory.

These theories focus on the advantages to the enterprises. Other writers depict the trends in the world system that facilitate global operations. There is a growing similarity between countries even in such phenomena as infrastructure, distribution channels and approaches to marketing which used to be very country specific. Capital is very mobile and fluid and there are forces which are equalising its costs among countries. There are falling tariff barriers and pacts to facilitate trade. Technological change has led to lighter more compact products which are less costly to transport, lower transport costs and easier communications and data transfer. Information technology has permeated production, distribution and research and development. In numerous ways buyers have become more aware and demand world-class products. All these changes have facilitated global competition in which global corporations can prosper and indeed in which new countries and corporations, those of

South East Asia being excellent examples, can emerge as they exploit the new conditions and new technologies to leapfrog well-established rivals.

Increasing interconnection of countries

The growth of transnational corporations and the development of an international division of labour within corporations has meant that countries and regions are more *interconnected* than before. A decline in the fortunes of Renault in France, for example, can lead to job loss or even plant closure in its operations in other countries. The desire of Japanese car companies to have easier access to the European market has led to the setting up and expansion of Nissan in Washington in north-east England. The foreign investment in Britain is mirrored by British investment abroad. Foreign investment, in general, has become more heterogeneous in that it comes from more nations. For any region within a core country (that is in North America, Western Europe and Japan), therefore, there is a much greater probability that foreign transnationals and investment will be present or even more dominant than in the 1950s or 1960s. Decisions about investment, operations and employment will be influenced, if not taken, by headquarters outside the region. Such *'external control'* illustrates the greater interconnectedness of regions and countries.

Government policies

The countries, and to a lesser extent their regions, have also been important, active rather than passive, actors. They represent part of the environment of transnational corporations but seen from a country's

Sony at Bridgend

viewpoint, transnationals and other countries are part of its economic environment. National governments may try to protect their own industry by tariff barriers or encourage it by awarding contracts. France, for example, tried to reduce the amount of Japanese imports of videos by an ingenious strategy of making all videos go through one location for customs, a time-consuming opera-

tion. On the other hand, they may try to encourage transnationals to locate in their country, perhaps in a region that needs new jobs, and offer incentives for them to locate there. In this situation, regions within the country may compete with one another to attract the corporation and the new employment that it directly and indirectly brings. The Japanese consumer electronic company Sony, for example, was attracted to South Wales. Transnationals may therefore benefit from the offers made to them by national governments and play them off against one another to extract the best deal for themselves. National government policies, then, are important components of the international economic environment.

NICs

One set of countries has emerged as new important actors in the international economy: the *Newly Industrialised Countries* (NICs).

Manufacturing is playing an increasing part in their gross national product and particularly in their trade. That trade is growing with both developing and developed countries, including Japan and the USA. It is particularly in clothing, leather, wood, cork, electrical machinery and textiles. The South East Asian countries of Hong Kong, Singapore, South Korea and Taiwan are especially important as newly industrialised areas. Together with Japan they are beginning to form a third major industrial area to rival North America and Western Europe. Their growth has been mainly by exporting their goods, though more recently their home markets have begun to grow. In contrast NICs such as Brazil and India have developed their manufacturing industry by substituting home production for imports (import substitution) to serve their much larger home markets.

	Share of world manufacturing output %			Average annual growth in manufacturing%		Share of total labour force in manufacturing %	
	1963	1970	1980	1960-70	1970-81	1960	1980
Hong Kong	0.08	0.15	0.27	n.a.	10.1	52	57
Singapore	0.05	0.06	0.16	13.0	9.7	23	39
South Korea	0.11	0.22	0.66	17.6	15.6	9	29
Taiwan	0.11	0.23	0.46[1]	15.5[2]	11.5[3]	16	32[1]
Brazil	1.57	1.73	3.01	n.a.	8.7	15	24
Mexico	1.04	1.27	1.95	9.4	7.1	20	26
Spain	0.88	1.18	2.24	n.a.	6.0[4]	31	40
Portugal	0.23	0.27	0.40	8.9	4.5	29	35
Greece	0.19	0.25	0.31	10.2	5.5	20	28
Yugoslavia	1.14	1.25	0.89	5.7	7.1	18	35
Total, 10 NICs	5.40	6.61	10.54				

[1]1977 [2]1961-70 [3]1971-1978 [4]1970-1980

8.8 Newly industrialised countries (NICs): the growth of manufacturing

Supra-states

The grouping of countries into *supra-states*, such as the European Community, is also of major importance. Relatively free trade may occur between member countries, that is, tariffs are removed or reduced. A single market of 322 million people will be open to companies located in member countries of the EC in 1993 when the remaining trade, travel and technical barriers are removed. The main reason for North American and Japanese transnationals (Figure 8.9) locating in the UK and other EC countries in recent years is to obtain access to the EC market, not simply that of the country in which they are located. These supra-states complicate the economic environment by adding an extra geographical tier, but simplify it by removing many barriers to trade within them and by standardising their barriers to non-member countries.

Summary of actors

So far a number of 'new' actors have been identified that have in themselves contributed to the changing economic environment: global corporations, multinational corporations, small multinationals (all of these are transnational), nation-states (new in their policies, not their existence), NICs and supra-states. Their organisation and behaviour respond to and affect the economic environment.

Effects of transnationals

The activity of the transnationals provides competition but also some opportunities for the large, medium and small national companies. Some become suppliers of goods and services. Indeed, some nations try to insist on a certain percentage of home-produced components being used by foreign transnationals based in their countries. Such 'local content', as it is called, is difficult to enforce. Local suppliers may also be squeezed to reduce costs as transnationals seek to survive downturns in the economy. Some local suppliers are small firms, a sector of the economy that has in many countries recently received renewed attention and exhibited growth (Chapter 8, Section 3c). It is too easy to treat transnational corporations and small firms independently. In some cases, though, they exist symbiotically, both benefiting from the presence of the other. In others the transnationals dominate because of their ability to transfer operations into other areas or to other suppliers and markets.

It is not easy to generalise about the impact of these changes on regions and nations. Transnationals are in themselves very varied now and their impact depends also on the time and the place. A number of key topics may be examined: *labour, linkages, capital* and *technological transfer*, with reference first to developed countries and then developing ones.

Labour

Since the discussion has been about the growth of transnationals, it would seem reasonable to assume that their demand for labour has grown and the location of new employment would be a major impact within a country; but this depends upon the state of the national and world economy. Between 1963 and 1975, a period with economic fluctuations but overall one of growth, foreign corpora-

8.9 Japanese manufacturing in the UK

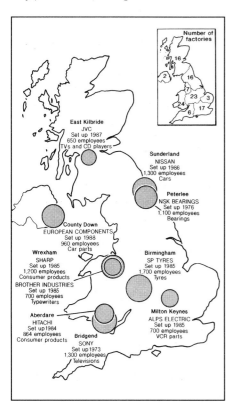

tions experienced a 72 per cent expansion in manufacturing jobs in the UK. Despite the feeling from other countries that such jobs would be concentrated in core regions, it was not the South East that was the most favoured destination. Scotland attracted nearly one third of the 34,000 jobs from abroad between 1966 and 1975. Indeed, it was the peripheral regions that grew, influenced by government regional policy, and the South East that relatively but not absolutely declined. This was not the case, though, for jobs associated with service functions of foreign enterprises. Manufacturing employment in foreign-owned establishments peaked in 1977 (1,013,800) and declined during the period of recession in 1979 and the early 1980s (858,100 in 1981). The amount of job loss varies by corporation, nationality, sub-regional location and date of occurrence. The USA-owned plants are more numerous and because of their greater age and more widespread regional distribution had a different pattern of job losses compared with other nationalities; the EC owned corporations' employment, for example, was concentrated in the South East and East Anglia. In general, relative to 1977 levels of employment in foreign-owned factories, the worst affected regions were Yorkshire and Humberside, the North, Scotland and East Anglia while the least were the South West, Wales and the East Midlands. The picture is therefore a complex one which does not neatly fit into the broad manufacturing regions of peripheral (Northern Ireland, Scotland, Wales, North), manufacturing heartland (East and West Midlands, North West, and Yorks and Humberside) and core (South East, East Anglia, South West) (Chapter 12, Section 1).

The job loss of this period does not seem to be accounted for by transfer of employment to other countries, but some transfer has taken place to other countries which offer lower cost and less organised labour, such as India.

Linkages between transnationals and other industries and services are again complex. One study of the Northern Region in England did, however, show the effect of external control.

Linkages

Between 1963 and 1978 there was a great increase in external control from just over 50 per cent to 80 per cent. Locally controlled companies had 77 per cent of their service linkages within the region while externally controlled ones had 77 per cent of them outside the region. In this case external control had little effect, however, on linkages involving materials. This may be peculiar to the area since a similar effect to that of services has been found elsewhere. If foreign ownership decreases the likelihood of local multiplier effects in services, then high external control in a region will downgrade its local service environment which will limit the growth of new and existing firms that increasingly need a developing local service sector.

Technological transfer

Technological transfer is of greater significance to developing countries, where the technological gap is wider. Yet even in developed countries, transnationals are often the source of new ideas. Sometimes these are guarded jealously so that they can retain their lead. Some, such as Japanese work practices, may be imitated or adapted more readily by the host nation, and thus the transnational can be an important agent of change in developed countries.

Impact on developing countries

The impact of transnationals on developing countries depends on the country, the transnational and the relationship between the two. Some NICs, for example, have their own transnationals and will benefit in many ways from them. The relationship between foreign transnationals and the host developing country depends partly on the reasons for locating there – for its resources, its market as in the case of Brazil and India, or as a base from which to export as in Singapore. Resource extraction is often exploitative, with the physical environment being devastated as there is little consideration of conservation or reclamation. The cultivation of cash crops for export has again often had major detrimental impact on the physical environment, as monoculture and the technology of cultivation have contributed to desertification, as in parts of Africa. Such cultivation has also had dramatic effects on the social organisation of developing countries, with changing roles for men and women and an orientation to western culture. Beneficially, the export of primary products has provided foreign currency for imports. Some would argue, however, that they are imports from the developed world which increase the dependency of the developing countries on the developed. They become both the market for their primary products and supplier of their capital and consumer goods. They may even be a dumping ground for products not permitted in developed countries, such as some drugs. Some products may be dangerous when used in the different conditions of developing countries, such as powdered milk for babies which requires the use of sterilised bottles.

Where transnationals serve the home market they replace imports, thus helping the balance of payments. They bring jobs and, through them, increased purchasing power, which itself produces multiplier effects, as indeed transnationals may through linkages with local companies. These linkages tend to be fewer than expected, as in developed countries. The concentration of many transnationals in the core of countries increases inter-regional inequalities and in itself encourages further polarisation, with resources, capital and people moving from the periphery to the core. The growth of the Sao Paulo-Rio core region of Brazil is a good example. The consequent demand for improved infrastructure in the core increases the inter-regional differences. Some argue that investment in infrastructure in the less congested periphery would bring better returns to the country as a whole.

The employees of transnationals may get higher incomes than workers in domestic industries. The difference between incomes of social groups, as well as regions, may also increase as workers become part of

the economy: the formal part which comprises transnationals and modern domestic industry and the informal part which consists of those in traditional crafts and various low level services.

Transnationals are one of the main means by which new technology is introduced to developing countries. It is suggested that indigenous companies imitate and apply the technologies. Some argue that this advances development; others that the technologies are often inappropriate for the level of development and that intermediate technologies would be preferable so that more people are employed and the benefits are spread more widely through the population.

Capital flows

Others argue that imitation is limited because, as in developed countries, corporations guard their technology and even where it is trans-

ferred, local people do not know how to apply it to other situations.

The inflow of capital from transnationals' investment is much sought after by governments, because its scarcity often limits the country's rate of development. Some transnationals, though, raise capital within the country and thus deflect it from use by home industry. Not all profits stay within the country and transnationals, through transfer pricing, often avoid taxes and tariffs. Thus the inflow of capital can be exaggerated.

Summary

This section has concentrated on how transnationals respond to and affect their economic and technological environments in developed and developing countries. Other more general effects will be explored in the perspectives section.

8.3   Other examples

The first two examples concern different types of transnational corporations, IBM, and Trust House Forte. They specialise in different

products and services. The final example analyses the growth of the small business sector in Great Britain, which represents a possible

change in the economic environment towards an enterprise culture.

8.3a   'Big Blue' - IBM

IBM, the leading computer system company, is one of the world's biggest and most powerful corporations (Figure 8.10).

From setting up its first foreign subsidiary in Canada in 1917 it has 'colonised' the world until it now bestrides the computer scene like a colossus!

Figure 8.11 shows how IBM is spatially organised at an international scale. It is of course an American company, but in 1951 IBM UK was established. Since then

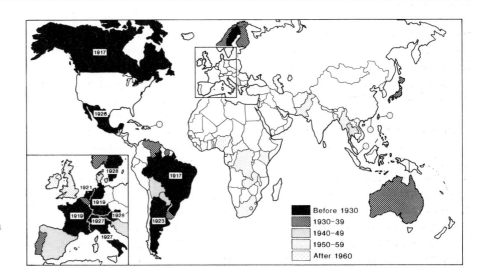

8.10 The global spread of IBM

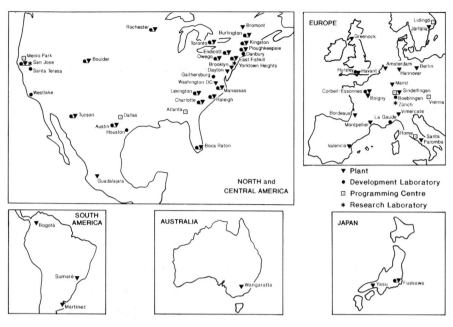

8.11 IBM's spatial division of labour

8.12 IBM's spatial organisation in the UK

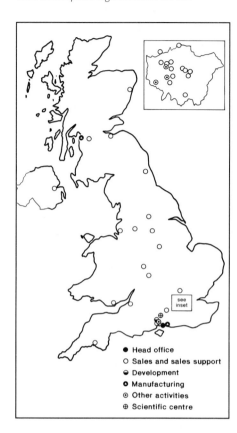

it has grown to become the UK's largest exporter. It employs 17, 506 people directly and 8000 people indirectly through IBM orders. In the UK it now has over forty locations (Figure 8.12) which serve a variety of functions.

For the UK the headquarters, for instance, is in Portsmouth, the scientific centre near Winchester and the manufacturing plants at Havant and Greenock. Some of these have key international roles; for instance, Hursley is part of IBM's worldwide research and development effort and has specialised in the field of interactive graphics.

8.11 IBM's spatial division of labour

8.12 IBM's spatial organisation in the UK

8.3b **Worldwide leisure**

Charles Forte began his own business in 1934 and has subsequently become the head of a large leisure-based corporation with an annual turnover in excess of £1 billion. This has been achieved by expansion, especially through acquisitions and mergers. For instance in 1970 Trust Houses Group Ltd merged with Forte Holdings Ltd; in 1973 the company took control of over 500 motels/hotels in the USA under the Travelodge trading name; in 1978 the company bought thirty-five Strand Hotels for a cost of £27.6 million. Although not the world's leading hotel chain (Figure 8.13), in 1984 it controlled 804 hotels worldwide, over 74,000 rooms, 3000 different catering outlets and provided in flight-meals for over 120 airlines.

Its staff numbered 56,000 and

2000 young people were taken on each year. Apart from expansion by buying into the lucrative US market and the emerging developing world's leisure industry, Trust House Forte has diversified into related sectors by setting up subsidiary companies; for instance, Puritan Maid supplies food products for its catering divisions, Lillywhites sells sport and leisure wear, and Sidgwick & Jackson are publishers.

Such diversification spreads the risk of possible collapse of one aspect of world tourism, or indeed an economic or political collapse of one nation. World travellers are also able to recognise and respond to a world-known leisure group name.

8.13 Multinational room service

The luxury hotel market around the world is dominated by American chains. This is the ranking of the largest corporations, 1983.

	Hotels	Rooms
Holiday Inn	1,740	312,428
Sheraton	447	118,584
Ramada Inns	613	85,188
Hilton Hotels Corp.	240	85,392
Trusthouse Forte (UK)	804	74,568
Balkantourist	658	61,207
Howard Johnson	515	60,390
Quality International	448	63,437
Marriot Corporation	115	48,406
Club Mediterranee (F.)	189	48,871
Novotel SIEH (F.)	362	46,253
Day Inns of Austria	322	45,530
Intourist (USSR)	173	41,562
Intercontinental	109	33,533
Hyatt Hotels	68	37,000
Hilton International	90	33,034
Westin Hotels	50	27,342
Hoteles Agrupados (Sp)	38	18,355
Rodeway Inns	152	18,600

Corporations based in US unless stated
Source: Hotels and Restaurants International

8.3c Boom in small firm sector

As transnationals widen their international power and networks, small firms too have witnessed a remarkable resurgence. The definition of a 'small firm' is open to debate but it is usually characterised by a small share of the total market; a personalised management structure; and independence, that is, not being a part of a larger enterprise. Nowadays in the UK it is generally regarded as a firm with 200 or less employees. The proportion of total manufacturing employment in small firms has risen since the early 1970s, especially in the USA. They have become popular with governments elsewhere because of the success of small firms in increasing employment in the USA. Governments have also become disillusioned with the performance of large companies as creators of jobs and indeed wealth. Possible reasons for the re-emergence of small firms include: workers made redundant by large and small companies having set up their own enterprises; increasing numbers of management buyouts and worker cooperatives; and greater popularity of franchising arrangements. Certain advantages of this scale of business also make it attractive, such as employees' job satisfaction, reward for bringing in new ideas and quick implementation of new ideas. Finally, small firms reflect and may have responded to the promotion of an enterprise culture and spirit or climate of enterprise by the

8.14 Small firms in the manufacturing sector of the UK 1935-79

Country	Year	Percentage of employment in small establishments	
		(a) 20-199 employees	(b) 1-199 employees
UK	1978	24	30
West Germany	1979	30	-
Austria	1980	33	35
USA	1977	34	39
Sweden	1978	37	-
Canada	1976	43	48
Norway	1979	54	62
Japan	1978	54	68
Spain	1978	52	64

8.15 Proportion of manufacturing employment in small establishments: an international comparison

Area	Time period	Size of firm (Employees)					
		0-20	21-50	51-100	101-500	501+	Total
		(% of employment change)					
East Midlands	1968-75	+2.7	+2.3	+1.5	-2.2	-5.9	-1.5
North of England	1965-78	+8.1	+3.0	-5.7	-4.9	-15.2	-10.7

Conservative government in the UK during the 1980s.

As well as providing a favourable climate, the government has introduced specific policies including information and advice, training and financial help. Examples include: the Department of Trade and Industry's small firm information centres; over 300 local enterprise agencies given government support; government funded training courses; government loan guarantee schemes; and reductions in red tape.

The changed contribution of small firms to the manufacturing sector between 1935 and 1981 can be seen in Figure 8.14.

Figure 8.15, however, shows how the UK, in spite of this trend of the re-emergence of the small business, is still dominated by large manufacturers in comparison with other countries. Still, the change in

8.16 Manufacturing employment change by size of firms for two English regions

8.17 Small firm competition winners, 1981-83

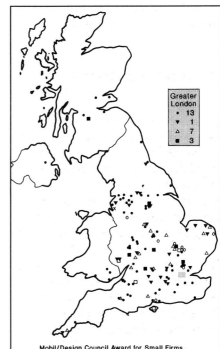

	Number of small enterprises	Percentage of total	Employment ('000)	Percentage of total employment	Percentage of total net output
1935	136,000	97	2,078	38	35
1963	60,000	94	1,543	20	16
1975	83,400	96.3	1,558	21.9	18.1
1979	86,800	96.8	1,498	23.1	19.5
1981	87,400	97.2	1,408	25.9	22.0

Note: the accuracy of the data, the methods of compilation and the definition of manufacturing have varied over time. 1935 and 1963 figures are from a different source than the rest

employment direction is marked, as is shown for two English regions (Figure 8.16).

Figure 8.17 shows the spatial aspects of one way of measuring the success of small firms. Such winners of recent small firm competitions (where the emphasis is generally on technical or design innovation) are concentrated in southern England (with 40 per cent in the South East alone). The areas with proportionately fewer winners are Northern Ireland, Scotland, Wales and the North. Small firms may be judged as financially successful if they appear on the Unlisted Securities Market (USM) which was created to provide smaller, more entrepreneurial businesses with access to a capital market. The distribution of such companies (Figure 8.18) shows a heavy weighting towards the South East (59 per cent of the total). The distrib-

ution of successful small firms, then, causes even greater concern to those who worry about the concentration of economic power and wealth in the South East.

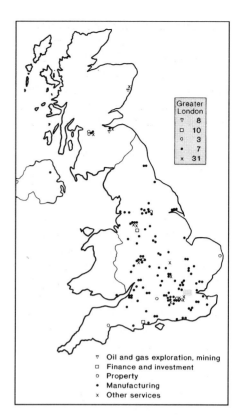

8.18 Companies on the Unlisted Securities Market, 1985

8.4   Alternative strategies

This section will examine the alternative strategies of both transnationals and the governments of countries. Strategic decisions that transnationals have to make include the scale on which to compete, whether to concentrate or disperse their activities, how to coordinate them and how to position their products in the markets of different countries. Governments have to decide whether and how to attract transnationals.

Transnationals

Scale of competition

One major decision for transnationals is whether they will compete globally or remain multi-domestic, that is, compete within countries independently of their activities in other countries. The advantages of

global competition include the economies of scale of production, marketing (including advertising) and research and development, and the ability to transfer rapidly the know-how derived from lead areas of technological development and lead markets, ones which first display significant changes in the demand for particular products. These advantages in themselves suggest two major considerations for successful global competition: obtaining the best *configuration* or spatial organisation of their operations, particularly research and development, production and marketing; and *coordinating* the operations in different countries and at different stages in the most effective way. The disadvantages of, or constraints on, global competition can be the differences in languages and cultures of countries that lead to varying tastes, different ways of operating marketing and sometimes different traditions of work. Some of these, however, can

be overcome to some extent, since new technologies can cope more easily with non-standardised products and allow greater tailoring to local conditions; computer-aided design, for instance, permits greater flexibility, as does automated order processing.

Concentration or dispersal activities?

For global corporations, alternative configuration strategies lie between concentrating or dispersing activities. Multi-domestic ones are by definition predominantly dispersed. A global corporation might concentrate each stage of operations in the most appropriate country or perhaps in a few countries, ensuring that there would be good coordination between stages. Research and development might then be located in the lead technological markets, for example Israel for defence systems and Japan for telecommunications. The advantage is both that of the location and the concentration in order to benefit from an accumulation of 'know-how' and a more rapid rate of learning. Production may be located in countries where there are comparative advantages associated with resources, the workforce or government incentives; in the computer industry, for example, the particular workforces encourage hardware assembly in Taiwan, the writing of computer software in India and research and development in Silicon Valley, California. Alternatively the most appropriate strategy may be to concentrate linked activities, such as research and development and production, in the same country so that there are advantages of close coordination. Complete concentration of all operations in one country returns to the strategy of a national company with exports rather than having a multinational presence.

Operations may be fairly dispersed to meet local production needs, facilitate marketing, ensure a build-up of local knowledge and reduce transport, communications and storage. Governments might encourage dispersal by their tariffs or their purchasing of goods made only in their own countries. Dispersal may also be advisable to reduce the risk of detrimental fluctuations in exchange rates, political changes or disruptions by strikes.

Coordination

Operations may be dispersed, but global competition may still be possible through good coordination between countries and activities. This may mean rapid transfer of technology, marketing techniques and knowledge. Marketing and coordination may involve standardising the brand name, the market positioning of the product, service standards, warranties and advertising

theme. It may also be learning from being present in the lead markets for particular products, monitoring and transferring information about shifts in buyer behaviour and life styles. The USA used to be the lead market for nearly all goods, but such have been the recent global shifts that new lead markets have emerged for some goods such as Israel for many agricultural goods and Japan for electronics.

Configuration and coordination

Figure 8.19 shows how different degrees of coordination and concentration and dispersal may be combined to form particular strategies. The position of the car corporations on the diagram indicates the diversity of approaches of corporations but, in these cases, they seem to be converging.

Some corporations mix their strategies in the way that the car corporations seem to be doing; for example, Xerox, the American copier corporation, until recently centralised their research and development (R and D) in the USA but dispersed their other activities, which were however highly coordinated. Now they have R and D in Japan for small copiers, in Europe for middle-sized ones and in the USA for high-volume ones. This way they can coordinate R and D, production and marketing more effectively, given the needs of the different markets. Typically manufacturers of glass and plastic containers have dispersed plants to minimise transport costs but centralised R and D to benefit from economies of scale and accumulated know-how. The camera and video industries have concentrated production but have local autonomy in sales and marketing so that they can respond better to local needs.

A comparison of car and marine oils in the lubricant industry neatly

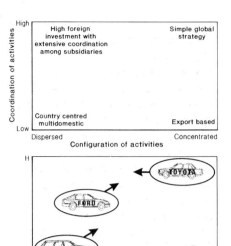

Toyota has achieved low-cost concentration production initially of simple small cars. A global scale allowed aggressive investment in new equipment and research and development. Now it is beginning to locate its activities in more countries as it produces increasingly differentiated cars. Ford has practised regional coordination while General Motors not only had separate manufacturing facilities, they also had separate brand names.

8.19 Transnationals: their coordination and configuration of activities

demonstrates the reasons for a global rather than a multi-domestic strategy. Car oil is multi-domestic. The products are different because there are different blends for different driving standards and weather, and indeed varying local laws. The distribution channels are particularly important and vary from country to country. Transport costs are high. Marine oil, in contrast, is global. The ships move worldwide and use the same oil everywhere.

Thus the configuration and coordination strategies used vary with the product, the industry and the corporation, and even for one corporation vary over time as the product range, technology, competition, demand and internal relations with in the organisation change.

The linkages between activities in the internal marketing channel (Chapter 3, Selection 5) of a corporation allow the organisation to change its environment. One strategy may be to encourage the development of a global product. The marketing department may provide the information needed for an appropriate design: its physical attributes and image. They may help to create demand for a universal product in areas where past demand has been more varied. They may therefore feed back information to research and development and production departments so that a global product may penetrate the market segments that have been identified in many countries.

Positioning the product

Sometimes the global product is aimed at the same segment of the market in every country, even though that segment may be of varying volume (Figure 8.20).

Usually the universal segment is the top end of the market, as for

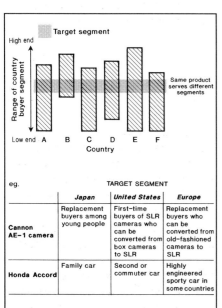

8.20 Transnational marketing: targeting different market segments in different countries

Mercedes cars which are positioned as a top-of-the-line, high-performance product in countries as varied as Japan, Zaire and Argentina. An alternative strategy is to aim at diverse segments across countries with the same product. So research and development and production are standardised, but marketing varies with the appropriate segment within the country. The Canon AE-1 camera, for example, was targeted towards young replacement buyers in Japan, up-market first-time buyers of 35mm lens reflex cameras in the USA, and older and more technologically sophisticated replacement buyers in West Germany.

Products that are tailored for every country or for sets of countries may also be aimed at universal segments or diverse ones. Telecommunications equipment and packaged goods, such as instant noodles, are both often tailored but the former are aimed at universal segments while the latter are targeted at diverse segments. Different marketing strategies are thus needed for different products.

There are constraints on the strategies of transnationals (Chapter 8, Section 2), government policies being one of them. One strategy which circumvents governments which want to have home production by home-based companies is to form coalitions with home-based companies. Such coalitions or alliances ideally combine the strengths and overcome the weaknesses of both companies. Governments often prefer these to mergers or to the prevalence of foreign firms in their countries. These are further examples of partnership, in this case within the private sector, that were more generally discussed in Chapter 4.

Governments

The strategies governments adopt to transnationals depend on their attitude to them and the state of their country's economy. Governments

cannot easily control transnationals because of their size and locational flexibility. Their withdrawal from a country may destabilise the economy or at least create substantial unemployment. While governments want to attract and retain investment, in a period of high unemployment they also want to attract and encourage job-creating enterprises. Transnationals and large companies have recently tended to shed jobs as part of rationalisation. Governments have thus become more favourably disposed to small firms (Chapter 8, Section 3d), which, at least in the USA, have produced more jobs. They are also part of the enterprise culture and operate more by market forces which in the 1980s were very much in vogue.

Most governments, however, have tried to attract transnationals. They usually want to encourage and facilitate the activities of their own transnationals, if for no other reason than that they do not want them to transfer too many activities abroad because they would lose their exports, taxes, jobs and multiplier effects. They try to attract foreign transnationals by marketing their country or regions within it with packages of incentives that include tax free periods, free rent on factories, grants towards buildings and development of infrastructure. Such national and regional marketing does not seem in itself to stimulate an increase in foreign investment. So competition between countries can be so great that they end up offering more than they are likely to receive from the presence of the investment. In those situations only the transnationals gain. The Andean countries actually set limits to their offers so that they did not lose out by competition between themselves.

Some countries have even set up *export processing zones* or *export enclaves*. These are relatively small, designated areas within countries, the purpose of which is to attract export-oriented industries. They offer necessary infrastructure, and concessions and incentives that do not apply outside the zones. The difference between them and freeports and free trade zones is that they are for manufacturing rather than simply warehousing and transhipment. Export processing zones have been established particularly in developing countries, especially those of Asia. They have developed mostly since 1970. They vary in size but in some over 30,000 people are employed. Electronic assembly, textiles and clothing are the dominant industries, while young women are the most common element of the labour force.

Import substitution

Such zones represent a more general strategy of developing countries, that of *export-oriented industrialisation*. The obvious alternative, called *import substitution*, has been less favoured recently. This is where the country tries to establish its own industries to produce once imported goods and protects them from foreign competition by imposing tariff barriers. Smaller countries, in particular, often lack a sufficient range of natural resources to follow the import substitution strategy. Even larger ones have turned away from the strategy as they still remained

dependent, for example, on foreign imports of capital goods to produce their own consumer goods.

Export-oriented growth

The export-based alternative uses the labour force of the developing country to attract foreign investment which it hopes will create new jobs and raise the level of skills and technology within the economy. The attraction of the labour force is not only its cheapness but also its adaptability and quiescence. Indeed, many countries control or ban trade unions. There are, of course, also incentives and concessions as described above. In return, some countries require from the transnationals a minimum percentage input of local materials (*local content*) or limit the degree of foreign ownership, but there is much variability in these controls.

Although many of the Newly Industrialising Countries have grown by this strategy, doubts linger over, among other things, the returns from all the incentives, the degree of technological transfer and the appropriateness of the technology for the rest of the economy. Most of all, the countries fear that the transnationals will relocate elsewhere, as others offer cheaper

and/or more compliant labour.

Whether by import substitution in the 1950s or export-orientation more recently, governments of developing countries have played a major part in their economies. Governments have also played a major part in developed economies, increasingly in attempts to retain or attract the investment of transnational corporations.

Finally, after reviewing some of the strategies of transnationals and nation-states, it is worth making some wider comments arising from the discussion in this section. The separation made earlier in the book (Chapter 2, Section 4) between market and planning strategies does not simply equate with the private sector and the public sector/governments. Although transnationals are very much part of the private sector, by internalising transactions they effectively operate planning strategies.

Markets and planning

By no means all of their activity is governed by market forces. On the other hand, the competition between regions and nation-states for the investment of transnationals means that governments are often very much part of the market.

8.5   Perspectives

This section discusses some of the characteristics of change in the economic environment. It also examines some of the effects that recent changes in economic actors and the economic environment have had on the physical, built and other types of human environment.

Change may consist of trends, cycles or periodic fluctuations and dramatic, sudden breaks or catastrophic events. These may all be

significant in the economic environment.

Business cycle

Most of this chapter has concentrated on the growth and increasing significance of transnational corporations as economic actors. This has been an obvious trend during the

twentieth century.

The chapter has only incidentally mentioned cyclical change, such as economic booms and recessions. These form what is known as the *business cycle*. These periods influence the behaviour of business organisations; for example, during recessions companies will tend to stop expanding their labour force and may well reduce it or cut costs in other ways. They may even close branch plants or in the extreme case close down altogether. Recessions may therefore trigger major changes that are not easily reversed. The transfer of operations to another country where costs are cheaper, might be the kind of restructuring or reorganisation that transnationals may make in a period of recession. It may be in response to longer-term trends, but the recession might have triggered the change.

The behaviour of business organisations in the aggregate may itself contribute towards an economic boom or decline. When organisations are confident about the future, they expand and invest, which contributes towards the economic upswing. When they foresee a slowing down in the economy they cease to expand, sometimes contract and often postpone investment plans. Again this behaviour, in itself, accentuates the economic decline. Geographically the business cycles are important, because some areas feel them earlier than others, and because they are not experienced to the same degree in all areas. A downturn in the economy of the USA, for example, may well produce major changes in the world economy because of its significance as a market. So it is a country that often leads the cycle. Even within a country, certain regions experience changes in the cycle earlier than others. This is usually because of the regions' industrial structures and their degree of interdependence with other countries. Areas with strong economic ties with the American market, for instance, may well feel the cyclical change earlier. Regions and localities that have a diversified economic base may feel the effects of the cycles less than ones with specialised activities. In the diversified areas, any industrial sector that is particularly hard hit by a recession may be offset by others that are less affected. In an area where such a hard hit sector is the dominant form of employment, the area will be especially affected, both directly by

Attempts to prevent leakage of poisonous gas from the Union Carbide factory at Bhopal

the loss of jobs from the sector and indirectly through the resulting loss in purchasing power that reduces demand for local services.

Dramatic change

Dramatic changes in the economic environment may be illustrated by the 400 per cent rise in oil prices in 1973 which had major effects on the global economy. More recently the interconnectedness of the global economy was vividly demonstrated by the dramatic fall in the financial markets on Black Monday in November 1987, when the major financial centres of New York, London and Tokyo in turn responded to the budget and trade deficit of the USA and to the reactions of each other, setting off a downward spiral in share prices. Underlying this collapse was the rapid shift during the 1980s of the USA from world creditor to world debtor. It had attracted foreign investment in order to expand its economy. Japan, in particular, needed a buoyant American market to permit the continued

expansion of its own goods, so was content to contribute to the US expansion. At the same time that very expansion and trade deficit threatened to produce a world recession, the fear of which triggered the fall in share prices. Japanese industries could not afford such a recession. This is a major example of the contradictions that exist within the global economy. It illustrates how fine the line is between stability and instability, and how the increased interconnectedness can contribute to instability as well as stability.

The remaining comments relate to the effects of transnationals on the various environments.

Effects on physical and built environments

Transnationals are often in a very strong position relative to national governments, particularly in developing countries, in their treatment of the physical environment. If there are too many restrictions on building or too strict pollution controls, they can transfer their activities to other countries. Knowing this, some governments permit detrimental effects on their physical and sometimes built environments in order to retain foreign investment. Some corporations may also operate less rigorous safety regulations in developing countries, so creating greater hazards, as illustrated by the chemical explosion at Bhopal, India in 1984 (Chapter 6, Section 5).

Effects on economic environment

The transnationals have, of course, greatly changed the economic environment. At the global scale their location of production in developing countries has contributed to what has been called 'Global Shift'. Whereas in the earlier part of the century manufacturing was concentrated in Western Europe and North America, in the 1970s and 1980s manufacturing plants were established in the Newly Industrialising Countries, with Western Europe and North America becoming much more service and research and development oriented and importing many manufactured products. Japan and the Newly Industrialising Countries of Asia became an important dimension to the global economy. Together with Australasia and the western part of North America they form the Pacific rim, which in many ways now challenges the economic supremacy of the Atlantic rim. Whether the Pacific Basin will take over from the Atlantic or whether the reunification of Germany and the opening up of Eastern Europe will produce a new land bloc that will rival both the Pacific and the Atlantic Basins are questions for the future change in the global economic environment.

Within a country, especially a developing one, the concentration of many transnationals' activities in one area, often the core, may exacerbate inter-regional differences. This will be reflected in the heavy investment in infrastructure in the core region which is needed to service the transnationals and which will in itself attract further activity and jobs into the core. This is often at the expense of the peripheral regions, which lose resources, investment and young people to the core – the so-called *backwash* or *polarisation effects*.

Disintegration

Transnational corporations have contributed to important changes in the economic environment in other ways. The standard strategy for reducing the uncertainty in their environments was to integrate both vertically (taking over suppliers and distributors) and horizontally (tak-

ing over competitors) so that they had more control. This was part of their growth mechanism and part of the way they escaped from some of the uncertainties of the market. During the 1970s and 1980s, in contrast, many corporations *disintegrated*. They sold off or closed parts of their activities. They preferred instead to contract out some of their work, in so doing contributing to and encouraging the growth of smaller businesses (Chapter 8, Section 3c). To some extent this passed the uncertainty onto the smaller companies which took on the contracts. In a recession it would be the smaller companies' order books that became thin. It enabled the transnationals to switch to other suppliers if their existing ones became too expensive or did not maintain the necessary quality. The large orders placed by a transnational give it power over its supplier and enable it to insist on high quality control. Although it does not own the smaller company, the transnational still exerts a considerable amount of control over it.

In many ways this is the kind of relationship transnationals have had with smaller companies. Some writers suggest that there can be a symbiotic relationship between large and small companies, so that both sets benefit equally. Even then there are many ways in which larger companies exert their power, for example delaying paying their bills or extracting higher discounts or better terms because of their bulk orders and larger-scale business. While many governments have encouraged the smaller companies as part of the development of an 'enterprise culture', they have not been able to change the power relations between large and small companies.

Effects on technological environment

The activities of transnationals have contributed much to the changing

technological environment. The alternative strategies of transnationals which involve decisions about the location and coordination of their activities imply a considerable amount of intra-corporation trade, that is trade, between one part of the organisation in one country with another part elsewhere in the world. Over a third of world trade is now intra-organisational rather than between different organisations in different countries, in itself a major change in the economic environment. This not only means flows of goods, the coordination of activities also involves flows of information and capital. Transnationals therefore comprise a significant demand for transport and communications just for their internal transactions, and have stimulated innovations in these in order to coordinate their activities more effectively. So in addition to the innovative techniques used in production processes, the new organisational structures of transnationals have in themselves led to changes in the general technological environment.

Effects on social environment

Transnationals may also spread a particular culture, based on acquisition of material goods. People's position in society is then determined by possession or even conspicuous consumption of particular goods. Their strategies, which seek both standardisation across countries and segmentation within them, substantiate this claim. The growth of transnationals from other than a USA home-base means, though, that the culture is more varied than it might have been when USA-based transnationals were more dominant. Although there are tendencies for transnationals to affect the social environments of different countries in the same way, the initial differences between countries and the particular interaction of corporations, home industry, government and civic society within countries ensure some variety of outcome between countries.

Segmentation of markets tends to accentuate social differences within countries, which in themselves may have been produced partly by the changing roles people play within the economic environment. Although this chapter reflects the literature in concentrating on the supply side of the economic environment, the development of the demand side should not be neglected. The chapter on demographic and social change (Chapter 10) illustrates some of the developments in demand. It is the interaction between social and economic change that is emphasised here.

Effects on political environments

Finally, economic changes have important effects on the political environment. The growth of transnationals has made them important political as well as economic actors. They negotiate with nation-states. Their pressure has been known to bring about political change in a country, replacing a government which is not well disposed towards the transnational(s) with one that is. A dramatic example of this is the replacement of Allende's democratically elected communist government of the 1970s in Chile. The possibility that they may withdraw their activities from a country gives them considerable power. This power has been used by other nation states as a means of exerting pressure on such countries as South Africa. They tried to convince the transnationals to withdraw as part of their sanctions on the country.

The power of transnationals is particularly strong in developing countries which are in great need of inward investment. In many ways a colonial dependency has been replaced by a new economic dependency on transnationals and a financial indebtedness that is in many cases crippling.

As the Second World, of once command economies, opens up its frontiers, there is a chance that transnationals will begin to look less at developing countries and more at the opportunities and potential of Eastern Europe. This may make development even more difficult for developing countries. In the same way that during the late 1960s and early 1970s there were many changes creating instability, including a new system of floating exchange rates and rapidly rising commodity prices which culminated in the oil price rise in 1973, it may be that the opening up of Eastern Europe and the former USSR and the political uncertainty in many of these countries may produce yet another unstable time for trade and production.

8.6   Exercises

1. With regard to your local area:
   (a) identify any manufacturing plants or offices owned by transnational corporations;
   (b) classify them according to
      (i)   their country of origin
      (ii) their product range and/or services offered;
   (c) discover whether they have experienced any recent job changes;
   (d) evaluate the impact of both the plants/offices in general and any recent changes in employment on the local area.

2. (a) Study the information about the spatial organisation of Cadbury-Schweppes in 1984 (Figure 8.21)
      (i)   Where is its main region of employment?
      (ii) Where are its headquarters and R and D located?
   (b) How would you explain the separate locations of headquarters, R and D and manufacturing plants?

3. (a) Study Figure 8.22 which shows the origin of foreign-owned transnationals in manufacturing in the UK during the 1960s and 1970s.
      (i)   Plot the changes in numbers of enterprises, establishments and employment separately on one piece of graph paper (with time as the horizontal axis).

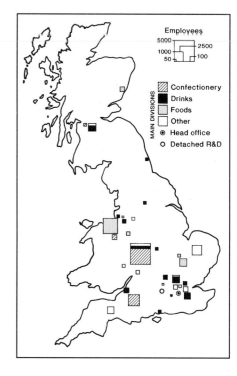

8.21 The spatial organisation of Cadbury-Schweppes, 1984

Country of origin	Enterprises			Establishments			Employment		
	1963	1975	1979	1963	1975	1979	1963	1975	1979
Total: numbers	502	1030	2042	1098	2121	2657	539,000	925,000	974,200
Percentage owned by:									
USA	73.5	64.5	60.4	74.0	62.5	57.9	75.3	71.1	67.9
Canada	3.8	3.7	3.6	3.7	6.3	6.0	6.4	6.5	6.5
France	3.8	4.75	3.7	2.7	3.6	3.3	2.9	3.4	5.0
Netherlands	3.4	4.1	5.4	4.8	5.75	6.3	4.2	6.8	6.0
West Germany	1.0	5.1	6.5	0.5	4.4	5.8	0.2	1.4	2.2
(Total EC	na	18.1	20.4	na	16.8	20.6	na	12.7	15.7)
Sweden	2.8	3.6	4.0	2.1	2.7	3.8	2.2	1.9	2.1
Switzerland	5.4	4.85	5.2	6.6	5.3	5.0	4.4	4.66	5.0

8.22 The changing origin of foreign-owned transnationals in manufacturing in the UK

(ii) Comment on the changes shown on the graph. (The comments should include a description of the relationships between the three graphs as well as a description of the separate graphs.)

(b) Compare the trends for transnationals from North America, the three EC countries, and non-EC European countries.

(c) Did the number of people employed by transnationals from the USA decrease or increase between 1963 and 1975, and between 1975 and 1979?

(d) Suggest reasons for the major changes in the origin of foreign-owned transnationals that you have observed from the table during this period.

4. Study one Newly Industrialised Country (NIC) and answer the following questions.
(a) What are the manufacturing industries that have been established in the country to warrant its classification as 'newly industrialised'?
(b) Are they based on local natural resources, labour, the home market or other factors?
(c) Are the products mainly for the home or overseas market?
(d) Have the industries been set up by home-based or overseas companies?
(e) If they are home-based companies:
(i) Have they become transnationals?
(ii) In what countries have they located?
(iii) Suggest reasons for the locations.
(f) If they are overseas transnationals, what has attracted them to the country?
(g) Which countries do you think will be the major competitors and which the major markets for the country's industries in the future?

8.7   Further reading

I.M. Clarke (1985) *The Spatial Organisation of Corporations*, Croom Helm

P. Dicken (1992) *Global Shift* (2nd ed.) Paul Chapman Publishing

A.G. Hoare (1983) *The Location of Industry in Britain*, Cambridge University Press

P. Knox and J. Agnew (1989) *The Geography of the World Economy*, Edward Arnold

W.E. Lever (ed.) (1987) *Industrial Change in the United Kingdom*, Longman

M. Taylor and N. Thrift (eds.) (1982) *The Geography of Multinationals*, Croom Helm

Chapter 9

CHANGING TECHNOLOGICAL ACTORS AND ENVIRONMENTS

9.1 Case study: information technology

Today the global volume of new information disseminated each year exceeds all the human knowledge accumulated over the ages from antiquity to the present day. The ever-increasing store of knowledge is overwhelming. However, this ever-increasing knowledge is of limited use unless stored and transmitted by information techniques. Information technology (IT), which is the technology to handle data of all types, has been transformed in recent years to provide knowledge to be stored and communicated and to allow near-instantaneous communications across the world. Advances in telecommunications, micro-electronics, information and computer communications have been at the heart of the so-called IT 'revolution'. It has been called a revolution because of the pace of change in the technology. It has been suggested that it is the third revolution after the agricultural and the industrial revolutions. In particular, telecommunications have been regarded as the electronic highways of this revolution, which could influence the economic geography of the 'information economy' as much as railways affected that of the industrial revolution.

It has been argued that in an industrial economy the key strategic resource is finance capital, but in a post-industrial society or 'information economy' knowledge becomes the strategic resource, that is the embodied and disembodied products of the education and research systems. To be of use knowledge has to be expressed in the form of information which can be exchanged, processed and applied. Collecting, codifying, verifying, accumulating and stocking relevant data is an expensive operation, but technical, legal, commercial and financial information is now a commodity of great value that can be traded. This has led to the increasing 'commodification of information', that is, information is no longer publicly available and has to be paid for. Increasingly economic activity is concerned with the generation, processing and exchange of information. The number of information workers (people whose job is primarily concerned with the generation, manipulation, transformation or processing of information) is growing rapidly in Western Europe. In 1981, 45 per cent of Great Britain's employed workforce were of this type – in London 58 per cent (Figure 9.1).

High-speed digital communications are part of the IT revolution and have had wide-ranging geographical effects. For instance, some technologies reinforce existing concentrations of human activity, whereas others have the opposite effect. Fibre optic cables, for example, tend to be established alongside existing transport routes, increasing the centralisation on existing nodes of networks, whereas satellites allow at least the potential of dispersal.

London	57.8
South East	47.3
Great Britain	45.0
North West	43.8
South West	43.7
West Midlands	42.0
East Anglia	41.5
East Midlands	40.9
Yorkshire and Humberside	40.3
Scotland	40.8
Wales	39.4
North	38.8

9.1 Regional variation of information workers

These communication systems may also have a variety of geographical effects at different scales. At the most local level, in the home, various aspects of IT allow the householder to be in direct contact with the outside world. In-home shopping, for instance, is now an established and growing element of the US economy. Over 11 per cent of total retail sales are achieved by telephone/computer in-house technology. Similarly, banking and other financial services are available through the use of the telephone system and/or a computer. Viewdata systems, such as Minitel in France and Campus 2000 in the UK, allow direct access to on-line databases, while electronic mail, fax and telex machines permit interpersonal communications. Thus IT makes much more possible the centring of work functions at home, reducing if not abolishing the need to commute to work. This is sometimes known as 'telecommuting'. Indeed, telephone and video conferencing reinforce this possibility. While it still seems that face-to-face interactions are necessary for many business liaisons, a proportion of such interactions being home based does allow the possibility of reducing the scale and expense of upkeeping a large central city office location. In Japan there is a trend for companies to rent, on a daily basis only, meeting/office facilities in the centres of cities, at airports and railway stations. Rank Xerox too gave retirement terms to many middle ranking executives only to rehire them on a contract basis giving them the technology to work from home.

At a local level too, certain modern office developments are 'high-tech' in that they have fibre optic cabling and satellite receivers already installed. These so-called 'smart offices' have been successful in attracting businesses with a need for such facilities at the expense of earlier, less well-served office developments.

9.2 The development of packet-switching networks

IPSS: International packet-switch service
NMC: Network management centre

Indeed, many of the more recent, sophisticated and therefore expensive elements of IT are available only to certain business users and in certain areas of a country. Transnational corporations, for instance, increasingly need rapid cross-continental communications to integrate their operations and thus have key offices located in teleports (high capacity optical fibres joining at collection points for onward satellite transmission to the whole world) in places such as Manhattan and London's Docklands. Major financial services clearly rely on these sophisticated communication nodes.

The world's money, stock and commodity markets rely on this technology and certain financial centres have emerged, not least because of twenty-four-hour trading across the world. The location of New York, Tokyo and London in distinct time zones, as well as their rapid uptake of the new technologies, has consolidated their importance as the three 'world' financial centres, where further major job opportunities have been directly and indirectly created.

Often the new technologies are brought into the core areas of developed world countries, further reinforcing the disadvantages of their peripheries. This is well illustrated by 'packet switching' networks, fibre optic cables which dramatically increase the volume of data or voice that can be transmitted (Figure 9.2).

Similarly, fully electronic telephone exchanges are usually started only in the biggest centres. Value added networks services (VANS) provided by private companies are a new feature of the now competitive telecommunications environment in the UK (Figure 9.3).

The substantial bias to the South East is obvious. Mercury's planned communication routes northwards (Figure 9.4) show again the spatial bias of such new IT in favour of large cities.

It seems that there are large regional variations in participation in the emerging information econo-

Companies:	164
Services (some companies provide more than one service):	
Automatic ticket reservation and issuing	54
Conference calls	10
Customers data bases	54
Deferred transmission	50
Long-term archiving	27
Mailbox	71
Multi address routing	49
Protocol conversion between incompatible computers and terminals	71
Secure delivery services	24
Speed and code conversion between incompatible terminals	43
Store and retrieve message systems	89
Telephone answering using voice retrieval systems Telesoftware storage and retrieval	24
Text editing	29
User management packages, e.g. accounting, statistics, etc.	46
Viewdata	49
Work processor/facsimile interfacing	40
Total	688

Location of companies	
London and Home Counties	125
South West	15
W Midlands	4
E Midlands	3
Yorks and Humberside	3
N East	-
N West	9
Scotland	4
Wales	-
N Ireland	1
Total	164

9.3 The nature of the private value-added network services (VANS) in the UK, 1985

my, as is shown by, for example, telex subscriber data (Figure 9.5).

New developments in technology are usually installed and taken up by organisations within existing core regions first, further reinforcing their economic superiority. So, in spite of the 'distance shrinking' potential of telecommunications and the possibilities of dispersal, these advances seem to be reinforcing existing concentrations of economic activity in the core regions of

9.4 Mercury's way north

Nation		Region	Telex subscribers per 100 inhabitants	As % of national average
United Kingdom	highest	London	0.41	256
	national average		0.16	
	lowest	Wales	0.08	50
Germany	highest	Hamburg	0.43	146
	national average		0.23	
	lowest	Kiel	0.12	48
Netherlands	highest	Amsterdam	0.47	204
	national average		0.23	
	lowest	Leeuwarden	0.10	57
France	highest	Ile de France	0.30	188
	national average		0.16	
	lowest	Bas Normandie	0.08	50
Italy	highest	Lombardie	0.14	175
	national average		0.08	
	lowest	Basilicata	0.01	13
Greece	highest	Athens	0.25	166
	national average		0.15	
	lowest	Thrace	0.05	33
Belgium	highest	Brussels	0.56	254
	national average		0.22	
	lowest	Libramont	0.06	27
Denmark	national average		0.20	-
Luxembourg	national average		0.52	-
Ireland	national average		0.15	-

9.5 Variations in the number of telex subscribers in the EC (1990-91)

European countries. On the other hand, within the cores some new areas of economic activity have emerged, for example the outer South East of England (ROSE).

At a local level various service occupations have taken up the new technology. Travel agents, for instance, rely heavily on viewdata systems to check on holiday/flight availability as well as being able to book directly with railway companies, holiday companies, hotels and the like. Estate agents also find computerised records a great advantage, particularly if offices are linked across the country bringing buyers and sellers more easily together. Building societies have rapidly taken on the new technology allowing speedier, often more efficient

customer services at the local level but offering links to a network of nationwide services. Mergers and acquisitions were a feature of the 1980s within the following services: travel agents, estate agents, building societies and solicitors. These have been partly justified by the expansion of their network and customer services made possible by the new technology. It was only larger organisations that could afford to invest in and obtain returns from such expensive technology.

There are, however, two viewpoints on the scale of uptake and effects of these new technologies. First there are the 'minimisers' who predict the least possible take-up.

They also point to the cost constraints on take-up and examples of unsuccessful adoption. They therefore suggest limited impacts. Secondly there are the 'maximisers' who foresee rapid and dramatic changes in ways of life and an extension of the 'global village'. Interestingly, in the UK each can claim support for their views. The maximisers can point to the dramatic adoption of home computers and video recorders (VCRs) and the minimisers can point to the limited success, so far, of cable and satellite television.

9.2   General problem

The case study has reviewed one area of technological change, information technology, which may have profound geographical effects. Information technology is basically the conjunction of computing and

telecommunications, once separate fields. Information technology, robotics and biotechnology have been some of the major areas of technological change in recent decades.

Statement of the general problem

The general problem is the ways in

which the technological environment has changed and the geographical effects these changes have had on economic activity and social life. The changes can affect where we work and at what we work. This section outlines the major technological changes, where and for whom they have been available and whom they have affected. There are organisations or actors directly associated with producing technological change, such as research institutions and universities. Their location within and between countries is significant for regional and national economies. Some of the research establishments are government funded. Others are privately funded and often part of transnational corporations. Both governments and transnationals are significant indirect actors in technological change and it is important to understand their role in how and why change has occurred.

This section examines technologies that change the way space is used and how movement across space occurs. It then examines technological changes in processes of production that may have indirect geographical effects.

Space-changing technologies

There are three major effects of these technologies: firstly by access to areas of space that have been little used in the past; secondly, more intensive use of space; and thirdly, shrinkage of space whereby places are brought closer together.

Developing new areas

One of the most significant ways that new areas of space have been opened up is through the search for natural resources. Technological advances in extraction techniques have made the sea-bed an area of resource development, particularly for oil and natural gas. The oceans

Technical adaptation to permafrost in Inuvik, Mackenzie Delta

are a potential resource of the future. Various technological changes have also made the polar areas easier to develop, for instance by insulating pipelines and improving living conditions as well as techniques for penetrating permafrost without causing melting. Such use of new areas presents problems of resource exploitation, conflict and environmental disturbance and even destruction (Antarctica, Chapter 2, Section 3e; the Canadian North, Chapter 7, Section 1). Mineral extraction on the sea-bed, for example, can involve changing the sea-bed landforms, coastal erosion, movement of biota, change in particle size distribution, oxygen depletion and release of sulphides.

New developments in biotechnology extend the areas in which crops can grow; for example, as well as the selective breeding (intergeneric hybridisation) of drought- and frost-resistant plants and ones that are tolerant to poor soils and saline conditions, there is now the alternative of inserting genes into bacteria that then protect plants from frost. Improved irrigation and drainage techniques also extend the boundaries of cultivation into arid areas, areas reclaimed from the sea and wetlands, producing opposition from environmentalists, especially in the last case.

The most obvious new territory, however, is outer space, 'the final frontier', with the advances in satel-

lites, rockets, shuttles and space stations. Most of this development has been for 'defence' purposes, such as the Strategic Defence Initiative, the so-called 'Star Wars' programme in the USA. Satellite developments have been part of the telecommunications advances which enable rapid transfer of information around the globe, but they have also been used to provide more information about the earth through remote sensing (such as LANDSAT). This has been used for defence, scientific and commercial purposes. It has aided the greater understanding of the climate and improved the prediction of violent weather. It can monitor the health of forests. It has assisted geological exploration for minerals, oil, coal and geothermal activity through a combination of rock type discrimination and structural analysis, based on the lines (or lineament) that such features as folds and faults make on the surface. It has allowed the exploration of the rock structures under the deep sand of the Sahara Desert. It can help the fishing industry locate fish by providing information on the changing spatial distribution of water temperature, salinity and chlorophyll concentration. The greater knowledge, understanding and ability to monitor the physical environment have permitted and will no doubt further allow the development and conservation of resources.

More intensive use of space

The second major effect of space-changing technologies is through the more intensive use of parts of space. In agriculture, intensification means greater yields per unit area per unit time. These have been derived over a number of years by increased inputs of machinery and water, applications of chemical fertilisers, pesticides and the development of resistant strains.

Agriculture

Many of these consume much oil-based energy and have had some major hazardous effects, especially through soil erosion and nitrates in ground and surface water. About 50 per cent of the nitrogen in chemical fertilisers is used by the plant and is transported through the hydrological system. This leads to eutrophication or over-enrichment which is characterised by algal blooms whose decay robs the water of its oxygen. New developments in biotechnology, such as the cloning of forest trees to produce more rapidly growing varieties, may increase yields. Recombinant DNA (the recombination of the genetic material of organisms, 'genetic engineering' as it is known) is a further example, which may increase nitrogen fixation in plants, improve photosynthesis and pest and pathogen resistance. A nitrogen-fixing bacteria, rhizobea, for instance, can be genetically engineered and the genes spliced directly into the plant. Chemical fertilisers and pesticides would not be needed, but yields would still increase. The danger of such engineered micro-organisms 'getting loose' and causing harm to other parts of the physical environment and to humans is

Container loading onto ship in Hong Kong

just one of the problems associated with this biotechnological change.

Manufacturing

More intensive uses of space may be made in manufacturing industry by increasing output per unit area per unit time. Some of the technologies which are employed in the manufacturing process that accomplish this are reviewed below. Their major effects concern capital, labour and satisfaction of markets rather than the use of space. They can, though, reduce the need for very large factories or plants, which is of geographical significance because a greater variety of plant size can permit a wider geographical spread of occurrence. The more intensive use of office and housing space has already been discussed in the case study (Chapter 9, Section 1). The house becoming a location for paid work and all kinds of entertainment that were once obtained in separate

places is an example of this intensification. The ability to build taller office blocks allows a more intensive use of a unit area of land, though it does not guarantee more intensive use of floorspace. Various developments in information technology mean that it is now less necessary for some functions to be carried out within the same building. Some that are less intensive users of space can now be relocated to cheaper sites leaving the higher-priced central-city locations for ones that need centrality and proximity to services.

Shrinkage of space

The third major effect of space-changing technologies is through changes in transport and communications technologies which reduce the frictional effect of distance on movement and permit the shrinkage of space or time-space convergence.

Transport involves the movement of goods and people, while communications include the transfer of intangibles such as information, ideas, images, financial agreements and transactions.

In transport, the increased size of vehicles and vessels has permitted reductions in the per unit cost of travel. Larger aeroplanes have allowed mass travel at relatively low prices, while giant oil tankers have meant fewer ships needed and larger harbours. The technological changes affecting ports have occurred in three principal areas: the development in materials and cargo handling methods; increasing ship size; and improved ship design and vessel specification. The 'unitisation' of cargo handling has been introduced by grouping individual items of freight into standardised units by packaging, the use of pallets, the use of containers and the roll-on/roll-off (RO/RO) methods of lorry and trailer movement. This leads to the much faster turn-round of ships in port and to the reduction in breaks of bulk. The ability to turn ships round much faster has removed the major constraint on the increased size of ships. In the case of the bulk and container trades, unit costs of handling can be reduced if throughputs are maintained at high levels. This and the high costs of ships and shore-side facilities argue for concentration, both within and between ports. The concentration within ports has released large areas of docklands that are now being developed for other functions, for example in London, Liverpool and Cardiff. Activities are also concentrated on fewer ports with specialisation occurring by part of the world served, for example Southampton with the Far East and South Africa, Tilbury with Australasia and India, and Felixstowe with East Africa and the Gulf. Following from this, such ports now serve the whole nation rather than their regional hinterland. The RO/RO traffic has grown rapidly but

has not been subject to concentration, partly because the technology has permitted dispersal. More ports have become involved and in this case the technology has encouraged the use of the nearest port to reduce land-haul costs. The changed orientation of Britain's trade from west to east, and from 'deep-sea' (ocean) to 'short-sea' (short-distance) traffic, has led to greater growth of small ports on the east and south coasts and the major decline of the general large west-coast ports, Liverpool, Manchester and Bristol (Chapter 9, Section 6, Question 2).

While there have also been improvements in land transport technologies (Chapter 9, Section 9a) that have reduced travel times, probably the most important change in transport in the 1970s and 1980s has been the reduction in energy use and pollution associated with various types of transport, especially the car. New materials and improved designs have decreased the amount of fuel required for a given distance travelled. Though there is still far to go in reducing the pollution created in both the manufacturing process as well as the use of the car, lead-free petrol (Chapter 6, Section 3d) and catalytic converters have cut some of it.

Communications

In recent decades the most dramatic changes have been in communications, as illustrated in the case study. Live transmissions via satellite of events taking place on the other side of the world are taken for granted. People in America sit and watch the women's Wimbledon tennis final over breakfast, while people in Britain stay up to see the closing holes of the US Masters' golf championship or the Superbowl. News programmes are broadcast live from Tiananmen Square in Beijing or from a bombed building in Beirut. The effects of political and environ-

mental disasters can be seen immediately in people's living rooms, from where they can vicariously experience the world. The effects of this immediacy on people's attitudes and interest in world affairs is not known. Transnationals' ability to transfer information and decisions so rapidly across the globe in order to coordinate their activities, and financial institutions' capacity to make transactions between Tokyo, London and New York in seconds have, however, more obvious effects (Chapter 8). The globalisation of activity and some organisations has been permitted by such developments. Their requirements, though, have in part brought about the innovations.

Global village

The idea of the 'global village' is, however, exaggerated. At various spatial scales there are major differences in the degree of time-space convergence. At the global scale, Tokyo, London and New York together with, to a lesser extent, other world cities are much more globally well-connected than smaller cities. Neither does such convergence occur uniformly over space

9.6 Satellite networks

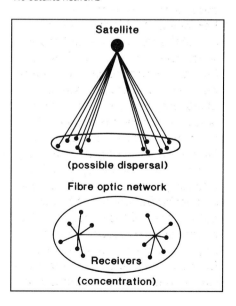

within a country. This is due partly to the *superimposition* of new *networks* on existing ones; optical fibre networks are following the rights of way of railways, waterways and highways, as the telegraph followed railways in the nineteenth century. In the north-east USA they go along, for example, the AMTRAK (railway) and the Ohio Turnpike. Mercury in Britain has been allowed to follow British Rail routes. Just as railways and canals favour point-to-point transport, the economics of fibre optic systems favour high-volume point-to-point communication from one hub to another and thus tend to go from one large city to another. Fibre optics are tiny strands of pure glass, carrying digitised data in the form of extremely fast streams of light pulses. Many strands form a bundle within a cable which is about one fifth the size of a conventional copper cable. They have the advantages of large carrying capacity, high-speed transmission, strength of signal and high security. They tend to shrink space between the large cities and within them on the local network. They therefore tend to accentuate existing concentrations of activity.

Some technological changes do favour general shrinkage and dispersal of activity. Satellite technologies favour traffic from one point to multiple points or vice versa (Figure 9.6).

Yet the receivers may be more

common in some areas than in others, reflecting the distribution of existing economic activity and wealth. Constraints on buying receivers may then limit the extent of dispersal of activity.

Continuing spatial separation of functions?

Although various forms of information technology have the potential to break down the spatial separation of home, work, education and leisure so that all may occur primarily in the home, there are other processes operating that in many cases keep the functions spatially separate. Much can be gained educationally from interactions with others in the process of education. Although people can sit at home and watch films on videos (VCRs), many still enjoy going out to the cinema to watch on bigger screens as part of a larger audience. Social interactions are important. Replacement solely by interactions with a machine omits an important dimension of work, education and leisure. So although telecommuting and teleshopping may increase, it is unlikely that they will become dominant. Employers prefer to have some control over their employees' work patterns and hours. Retailers and shopping centre developers have a major incentive to keep attracting people away from their homes into shopping environments that are conducive to pur-

chasing. Technological developments in retailing associated with point of sales technology (POS or as we prefer POST) through bar-coding and automatic financial transfers from bank accounts are making restocking, pricing and accounting more efficient. The use of videos within shops and various aspects of design are also making shopping environments more effective for selling. Such developments lower costs and increase sales so that there is even greater incentive to retain rather than replace shops and shopping centres. Workplaces, schools, shops and the like have their own momentum that will ensure their continuation as spatially separate organisations, though they too may change their form and perhaps location with the advent of new technology. The 'smart office' (Chapter 9, Section1) is an obvious change in form. The need for dust-free and temperature controlled environments for major computer facilities may also lead, indeed has already led, to relocations away from the city centre to avoid high floorspace rents as well as more easily controlled environments. In the 1960s and 1970s it was the routine clerical tasks that decentralised to cheaper sites. In the 1980s the computerised control centres of companies moved out, for example Barclays Bank to the site of a country estate outside Knutsford in Cheshire. From such control centres new communication networks emanate, for example the IP Sharp network from its Toronto base (Figure 9.7).

Geographers' interest in network analysis must now include these along with the more traditional transport networks. It is worth noting that some of these communications networks are less affected by political boundaries than are transport networks.

Changes in production processes

In addition to these space-changing technologies there have also been

9.7 The IP Sharp network

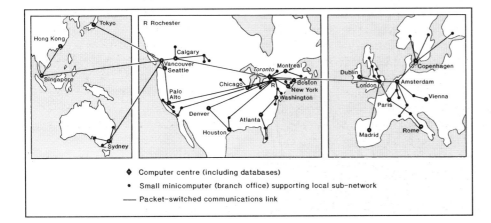

♦ Computer centre (including databases)
• Small minicomputer (branch office) supporting local sub-network
— Packet-switched communications link

major technological changes in manufacturing that have had more indirect important geographical effects. During the 1950s and 1960s automation had already been applied to the *process control* industries like chemicals, plastics, steel and rubber which produce materials, often in liquid form or extruded form, through a continuous process. The second type of manufacturing which involves making physical changes to solids (metals, plastics, wood and composites) with the aid of machine tools could be automated by the new technologies. In the early 1960s computer numerical control (CNC) machines could store data and design in their memory, making it possible to produce a range of goods on one machine.

Computer control

In the late 1960s the Japanese began to link sets of these machines to central computers which controlled their operation. This *direct numerical control* dramatically reduced labour because only one operator was required to control maybe a dozen linked machines.

The invention of the microprocessor chip in 1971 allowed rapid advances in robotics, the first generation of robots being ideal for dirty and repetitive tasks like welding and paint-spraying. They have also been used for dangerous work. By 1985 there were about 100,000 robot devices at work in the world (Japan 64,600, USA 13,000, West Germany 6600, France 3380, Italy 2850 and UK 2600). Sweden headed the European order on a per capita basis with nineteen robots per 10,000 production workers. By 1986, the USA had 20,000, West Germany 8800 and the UK 3200 robots, such was the pace of change.

Further technological developments allow computer-aided design (CAD) and computer-aided manufacturing (CAM) with testing of designs between the two processes (computer-aided engineering (CAE)). CAD/CAM have become established in the automobile and aerospace industries in companies like Chrysler, GM and Boeing in the USA and Ford and Rover in Britain. CAD/CAM is used particularly in routing the pipes of aircraft and oil rigs, and at another scale the optimum layouts for integrated circuits on microchips. It is also being used to simulate the entire operations of factories, warehouses and supermarkets before they are built. The potential is already being realised for doing the same for other parts of the built environment, such as large office blocks. Even whole new towns are possible.

Flexible manufacturing systems

Before analysing in more detail the geographical take-up of these advances and their effects, one further innovation in manufacturing needs discussing. This is *flexible manufacturing systems* (FMSs). These have received a lot of attention in the geographical literature and are regarded by some as a major sea change from previous forms of production. Flexible manufacturing systems enable a company to produce goods in small volumes as cheaply and efficiently as if it were using mass production methods which typically dealt in high volumes of one product. Small batches or variants of similar products can now be produced for different markets, whether for different segments in the same country or tailored for specific countries or industrial consumers. There are enormous savings in labour, particularly in assembly industries. It saves on plant space and on capital because less stock inventory is needed. Reduced lead times between orders and production enable the manufacturer to react much more swiftly to market trends. Some regard this not simply as a new technology but as a new way of thinking.

Robots welding a lorry cab

Economies of scope

Traditional mass manufacturing operated on economies of scale with large-scale plants and long production runs of standardised products. The advantages of FMSs are called *economies of scope* with economies possible at a wide range of scales. With such systems new entrepreneurs and countries can enter the field and compete successfully with older producers and nations. In many ways such systems result from the success of the marketing side of corporations in their internal conflict with the production side. For a long time marketing departments have wanted short lead times and short runs of adaptable products to meet changing market demand, while the production side has demanded long lead times and runs of standardised products. The new technology has emerged in response to the demand of the marketing departments as much as it has to save on labour costs, which is often the factor emphasised by many geographers. It can also produce great reductions in working capital. So the reasons for its implementation include savings on capital and labour costs and a faster, more effective response to market demand.

Take-up of FMSs

The first example of an FMS was in Britain in 1965 by Molins, a producer of cigarette-making machines. It was sold to Rolls Royce, IBM and Texas Instruments but it absorbed huge amounts of development money and by 1973 the entire machine division was closed down. At that time, though, the cheap micro electronics were enabling American companies to develop less costly flexible manufacturing systems. The Japanese followed suit in

1977 and rapidly took the technological lead.

By the late 1980s about half of the flexible manufacturing systems were in Japan, where the major suppliers were Yamazaki, Hitachi-Seiki and Fujitsu Fanuc. These systems combined with the inventory control concept of *just-in-time*, where parts are supplied when needed rather than being stockpiled, and the idea of preventative maintenance. One of Yamazaki's plants near Nagoya employs twelve workers during the day with one night watchman and manufactures as many machine tool parts in three days as a conventional equivalent would do in three months with 215 workers and nearly four times as many machines.

Generally FMS has been taken up more slowly in the USA and Britain than in Japan and Germany. The car industry has taken to FMS, with GM and Ford trying to keep up with their Japanese competitors. In Britain a number of companies have introduced FMS, for example Rolls Royce, the aero-engine maker, in their Derby works. Elsewhere in Europe, Volvo in Sweden and Renault in France use FMS.

Many of the examples are in the machine tool, car and aircraft industries. There is potential in many others, but FMS is expensive and has to be accompanied by successful management and marketing. The take-up of FMS may have been exaggerated in the fascination with new technologies and their potentials, but the Japanese lead in most of these technologies is well documented.

The effects of these new manufacturing technologies have been debated for some time. Much attention was drawn in the 1970s to the probable job losses and deskilling that would be produced by robotics and various uses of micro-electronics. In some cases the replacement of dirty, monotonous and dangerous jobs has affected ethnic groups and women more than white men. Many skilled jobs have been lost. Some jobs have

been created to oversee the machinery and to design it. In general, jobs have been lost where the technologies have been applied to manufacturing processes but new jobs have been created, of a different type, in the industries making high-tech products (Chapter 9, Section 3c). Some argue that more jobs would have been lost if manufacturing had been removed altogether from Japan, the USA and Europe into the areas of the world where labour was cheaper. By using the new technologies, it is argued, manufacturing remains in the developed economies. The increased flexibility of some production also permits, indeed encourages, greater market orientation. The just-in-time inventory systems also lend themselves to the greater clustering of suppliers around major producers using them. This may lead to renewed agglomeration, but there is little evidence as yet of this taking place. After all, it is only one of many locational factors.

Key actors

Some of the key actors in the technological environment are public and private research institutions and universities. The latter produce basic research that may well be applied later to particular uses; for example, Watson and Crick discovered the double helix structure of DNA which later permitted the developments in recombinant DNA. Most public research institutions are devoted to particular areas of applications of science, such as atomic energy or agriculture. Government money is seen as providing an important service to these industries and to the development of the nation. Much research is carried out for transnational corporations. Unlike that of the universities, this is mostly of a directly commercial nature, for example the research into new drugs. Both governments and transnationals are major providers of resources for research and not surprisingly control much of the direction of research and the resulting technological change. They therefore very much affect the technological environment.

R and D locations

Geographically they have a number of effects. First is the location of their research institutions or research and development centres, both within countries and, for transnationals, between countries. The clustering of research centres whether private or public can create synergy, where the overall effect is greater than the sum of the parts. Ideas can be transferred between institutions as key staff are lured from one to another, as in Berkshire, part of the M4 corridor. Freshly educated graduates from a university may be able to apply advances in basic research to commercial purposes, as at Cambridge (Chapter 9, Section 3b). These geographical concentrations of research activity, such as in the triangle in North Carolina around Charlotte, are usually areas in which key staff enjoy living. They are areas of high amenities. The areas benefit from the high salaries of key workers and the attraction they have for companies who want to benefit from rapid access to technological developments. This implies that proximity aids technological transfer between organisations, which is not always the case, but firms can benefit from the pool of research staff in the area. Countries can also benefit from the location of such research activities. They may then be effectively exporting ideas and applications rather than goods. Again they hope that their firms can benefit first from any advances. The adoption of new ideas, though, is not enough. There must be good management and marketing to see products successfully through production and the marketing channels. Proximity or location within a country, then, is not sufficient for successful development.

Areas of research interest

The second effect of governments and transnationals is in the area of research interest. Often private and public investment combine to push research in some countries in certain directions, for example nuclear research compared with research on renewable energy resources in Britain (Chapter 3, Section 1a). In much of the western world private and public investment has been devoted to curative medical development through drugs and surgery rather than to preventative medicine (Chapter 4, Section 2, Chapter 4, Section 3b). There is often a momentum to such research and the political relations surrounding it that ensures its continuation, despite perhaps better returns on investment from other research areas. Some writers have discussed the power of the industrial-military complex that has been sustained by wars and defence contracts and perhaps has sought to maintain tensions, cold wars and even active wars so that it can continue to make profits. Although many technological developments have been taken up and applied to commercial purposes from defence work, many more commercial and socially desirable technologies may have resulted from the same amount of investment of scientific effort and capital. Rapidly changing East-West relations in the late 1980s and early 1990s and the resulting relative decline in the military-industrial complex will show the extent to which investment is transferred into other research areas and the comparative technological progress. The success and commitment of the Japanese especially and Germans in the development of high-tech industries and their relatively small involvement in defence industries show the possibilities.

Government investment in research

The third effect of government and transnationals is the relative investments they make into research, both basic and commercial. Japanese government and industry are well linked and the government invests directly and indirectly in research and its development. In 1990 the USA, although traditionally a non-interventionist government, is considering better links with industry and investment in areas of high-tech so that its industries can keep up with, particularly Japanese, competition. The development of information technology in European countries has been hindered by desires to protect their 'national champions' which have led to a complex set of nationally varying technical standards, rules, regulations and charges. These have led to fragmented markets and massive duplication of R and D costs. Some argue that the large established national champions have been feather-bedded, living off regular work from national postal, telegraph and telephone organisations, lucrative government contracts and state R and D grants. The European telecommunication companies have seen the historical advantages of protected home markets and 'captive' sales to third world nations dwindling fast.

UK companies once held the world lead in robotics and numerically controlled machine tools, and had the first mainframe. Japan now leads. Some of the first applications of CAD were in Europe, particularly at Cambridge, but the USA now lead in CAD systems. Only Olivetti and Philips are among the world top ten companies in respectively computing and chip production, but both are connected with American companies. What was from 1945 to 1978 a positive trade balance in electronics, computers and telecommunications equipment for Europe has turned into a trade deficit. A number of factors have been suggested as reasons for this: rigid labour markets, state bureaucratic interference in business, conservative bankers and lack of venture capital and entrepreneurs. Whether or not these are important, in Britain too little effort is said to have gone into making the leap from the laboratory to the marketplace in translating research innovations into commercial applications.

The dropping of trade barriers within the European Community in 1993 may help to tackle the fragmented market, while the erosion of the policy of national champions may permit more successful cross-national cooperation. Most alliances, though, have so far been between European companies and American or Japanese companies in order to gain access to the US market or Japanese know-how. Such alliances of transnational corporations are more generally increasing, partly to reduce the uncertainty and risk of costly research and development. Whether alliances between governments such as the ESPRIT (European Strategic Programme for Research into Information Technology, jointly financed by the EC and industry from 1982) and EUREKA (European Research Coordination Agency, set up by the French in 1985 with eighteen participating countries, as an alternative to the American SDI programme) will also proliferate in the same way has to be seen.

On the one hand there are those arguing for more government involvement in developing all kinds of technology, and on the other those saying that governmental interference in the past has slowed progress. While state intervention may have restricted competition within countries, there are plenty of examples of state subsidy helping a nation to compete with other countries, such as in the higher subsidies of ports by European nations other than Britain, a factor that has contributed to the higher costs of British ports. Unlike many of their competitors, British ports pay for all the cost of their dredging and receive much less of the capital investment costs for port development.

Unions

A final set of actors who play a very significant role in the degree to which new technology is adopted are labour unions. It has been argued that failure to accept new technologies reduced the competitiveness of various sectors, particularly some British docks, with trade going to Rotterdam and Antwerp where union resistance was less and to private ports such as Felixstowe where there was no tradition of unionism. Such arguments often neglect the role of management in accepting innovations and their part in the relationships between managers and workforce. These relationships do vary from area to area and their geography does affect the adoption of new technology.

Much new technology requires multi-skilled workers rather than the traditional division of labour into separate specialised skills which formed the basis of unions and often apprenticeship training schemes. Such developments have either required the breakdown of traditional union boundaries with amalgamations and reorganisation or, as with the print industry, relocation into premises more suitable for the new technology with a much changed workforce. The move of many national newspapers from the Fleet Street area to Wapping in the London Docklands was accompanied by a transference away from many of the old print unions to less powerful or more pliable electricians.

Newspapers desert Fleet Street for the Docklands

Summary

The discussion of the geographical effects of the changing technological environments and actors can be summarised at a number of scales. While there are technological developments in transport and communications that are permitting decentralisation of people and jobs from cities, there are also other technological changes that encourage concentration and more intensive use of central city space. There are certainly many changes that are superimposed upon existing distributions and networks that increase centralisation within a country upon some cities and within the world on some major global cities. Some new specialist regions have emerged within countries as concentrations of high-tech industries, while older industrial areas may have been given new life by technological applications to their traditional industries. This may have produced what has been called 'job-less' growth, but it has stemmed the entire loss of the industries. Some nations, particularly Japan, have emerged as leaders in technological applications with many European countries losing their position and the USA struggling to keep up. Globally the world has shrunk, particularly for transnational corporations and financial institutions. Using new technology they can be aware of changes in markets and other conditions on the other side of the world almost instantly and can move investment and activities between countries in response extremely rapidly. Globally, too, individual people live in a new world. It took a year before people in Britain could read about the Russian Revolution of 1917, while now they can watch live coverage of the recent Russian revolution on their television via satellite. Our improved global awareness of political and social events is matched by that of environmental occurrences. There is now the possibility of governments and peoples being more rapid in their responses to all these events.

9.3 Other examples

Following on from the innovations in communications discussed in the case study, advances in rail and air transport demonstrate further space-shrinking effects. This section concludes with an examination of the new spatial concentrations of high-tech industries that have grown up within some countries and the emerging spatial organisation of the production of a high-tech product, semi-conductors, in the Newly Industrialising Countries (NICs) of South East Asia.

9.3a Developments in transport technology

Two broad advances in space-changing technology have occurred over the last few years. The first is the revolution in communications technology which was considered in the main case study (Chapter 9, Section 1). The second, which is the basis for this section, is the improvement in transport technology which allows people and goods to be moved more rapidly. Both changes have enormous impacts on the physical, built and human environments and these impacts vary considerably over space. Emphasis will be given here to railway technologies and, to a lesser extent, aircraft technology.

The *Train de Grande Vitesse* (TGV) heralded a new era for railways when in 1981 it set the world speed record at 237 mph. There are two elements to this innovation: firstly, there is a new generation of

9.8 Relative volumes of passenger movement on the French railway system

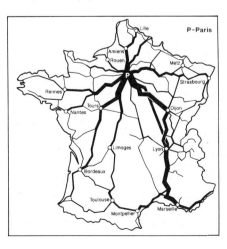

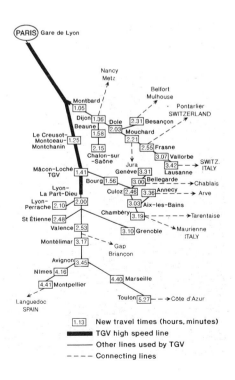

9.9 The Paris-Sud-Est axis

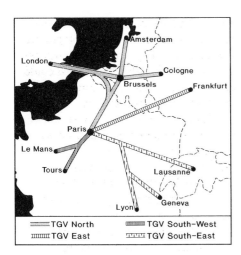

9.10 The proposed international TGV network

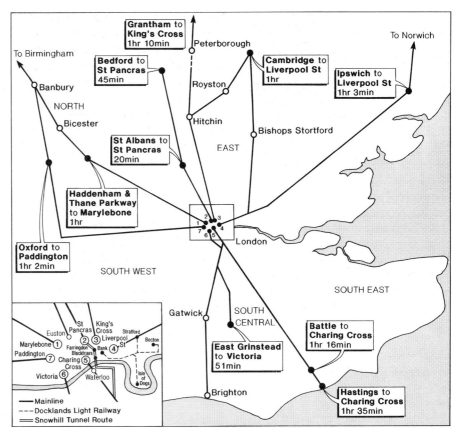

9.12 Space-time convergence through the electrification of Network South East

locomotives, and secondly a new network of tracks and overhead electric lines. The TGV has become an established part of the French communication system (Figure 9.8).

It began with the Paris-Lyon-Mediterranean axis, because this is one of the main arteries on the rail network and caters for almost 40 per cent of the French population (Figure 9.9).

This axis has particular significance because it links the three largest cities in France (Paris, Lyon, Marseilles) and provides access to the major resorts on the

9.11 Time savings for all regions after the Paris Lyon track was completed

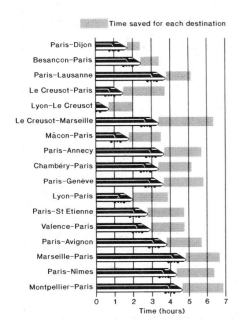

Côte D'Azur. High-speed track is still being laid and the network is being expanded to include international links, for example that linking France with the UK via the Channel Tunnel (Chapter 3). Journey time savings have been considerable (Figures 9.10, 9.11).

Impacts have included: greater numbers of passenger journeys including commuting; the easing of pressure on the Paris-Marseilles motorway; energy saving in a country where petroleum is at a premium and therefore expensive; and the re-building of several stations, for example the Gare de Lyon in Paris.

Another example of improved railway technology is the electrification of the network in the South East of England. This has led to the improved accessibility of areas around London, with the considerable shrinkage of travel times (Figure 9.12).

Such space-time convergence allows increased commuting: for example, on the Bedford to St Pancras BEDPAN line a journey of

over one hour is now just 45 minutes and this has permitted a 50 per cent increase in the number of commuters. Demand for housing increased along these newly electrified lines especially around certain nodes such as St Albans, with the consequent inflation of house prices. The new Brighton to Bedford direct-line, which will re-open the old Snowhill Tunnel under the Thames, may change the amount

9.13 Docklands' transport developments: the Light Railway and City Airport (STOLPORT)

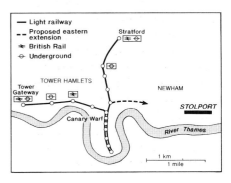

The Docklands Light Railway

and pattern of commuting but will allow people to travel from the north to the south of London without disembarking. This may increase the distance and change the areas to which people commute.

The final example of improved railway technology is the Docklands Light Railway opened in 1987. It is a new computerised railway linking the Isle of Dogs with the City and the East End of London. Initially it was geared to two wagons/cars per train and stations of a limited platform length. This has proved inadequate capacity, so the trains and the stations are being lengthened. The network is also being expanded. Housing, offices and the light railway were part of the same process of redevelopment of the Docklands (Figure 9.13).

Advances in aircraft technology enabled the opening of the City Airport (STOLPORT) in London's Docklands in 1987. The runway occupies a disused wharf between the Royal Albert and King George V docks (Figure 9.13) and is just 6 miles from the City of London and twenty minutes away by taxi. The new DASH 7 aircraft is quiet and requires only a short runway, and so enabled the UK to have its first STOL (Short Take Off and Landing) airport in a densely populated area. It cost £15 million to build and by 1992 it had a capacity of 1.2 million passengers a year. The development was supported by over 400 businesses in central London because it could cut journey times, for example by one hour from central Paris to central London. The airport may become a further commercial catalyst for that part of the Docklands and, if successful, it could cause pressure for other STOLPORTS to be built in nearby large European cities. Some local people in Docklands are concerned over the environmental impact of more flights being allowed each day and possibly other, more noisy aircraft being allowed to use the new facility. As yet such fears are unfounded since use of the airport has not expanded at the expected rates, local road access remains poor and it has not captured the attention of the business world.

9.3b High-tech industry

High-tech electronics-based industries have attracted much media attention since their emergence in the late 1960s. Particular attention has been paid to Silicon Valley in Santa Clara County in California where in the decade from 1968 to 1978 the electronics components industry generated 27,483 jobs. The extent to which similar localisation has occurred in Britain is open to question. While there is evidence of some high-tech industrial growth in the Thames Valley west of London (the M4 corridor), South Hampshire (M3/M27 corridors), around Cambridge in East Anglia and between Glasgow and Edinburgh in Scotland (Silicon Glen), they remain as yet only potential British versions of Silicon Valley (Figure 9.14).

Although there have been agglomeration economies, such as sharing facilities and face-to-face interaction, that have contributed to the growth of such areas, it has been argued for the M4 corridor, particularly west of Bracknell, that government-sponsored research establishments such as at Harwell, Culham and Aldermaston, as well as government aerospace contractors in the Bristol region, has been an important influence (Chapter 12, Section 1) (Figure 9.15).

Some argue that without substantial local sources of the investment capital that is needed to expand high-tech industry, the UK is unlikely to have its version of Silicon Valley. On the other hand, clear geographical advantages may have influenced the emergence of the M4 corridor. These would include: availability of modern sites with room for expansion; initially low rates and rents, together with offsetting grants in some locations; good links with main markets in the UK and abroad via Heathrow and Gatwick

9.14 High-technology manufacturing industry, 1981

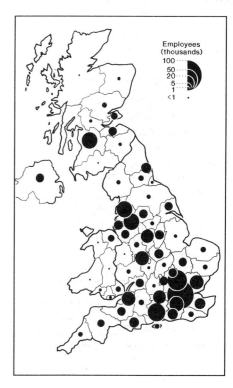

Employees (thousands)
100
50
20
5
1
<1

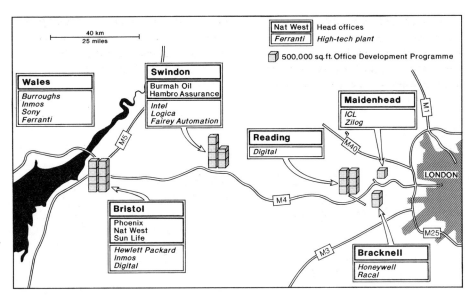

9.15 The M4 corridor

Airports; the proximity of suppliers, linked software houses, investors through the City of London; the availability of specialist labour such as analysts; and an attractive area to live for internationally mobile senior executives. 'Access. Good labour force. Railroads. Heathrow. Universities. Nice place to live' was the way the M4 corridor has been described by a director of Hewlett Packard.

The 'Cambridge Phenomenon' was a term used by a group of economic development consultants. They observed that since the early 1970s nearly 300 small new firms began operating in and around Cambridge in a wide variety of technologically advanced, research-based fields, namely computer hardware and software, scientific and industrial instruments and systems, lasers, micro-electronics and telecommunications, biotechnology and medical equipment, and applied research and development of many other kinds. This 'spawning' of new independent companies (Figure 9.16) is symbolised by the Cambridge Science Park set up by Trinity College in 1970 on an 82-acre site on the northern edge of the city.

It contains over sixty such companies employing 1500 workers, with a further 24 acres being developed in the late 1980s. The 'Cambridge Phenomenon' is much wider than the Science Park, since it embraces about 400 companies (1986) employing 16,500 workers in both new and older technology-based firms. On average thirty new companies have started up every year in the 1980s. Growing overseas and multinational investment is also now contributing to the phenomenon. Thus recent arrivals to the Science Park include IBM with a 'listening post', and US-based Napp Pharmaceuticals with a large R and D unit. Other new companies include Schlumberger's European R and D centre conducting custom-designed research for the world's oil industries, and Olivetti with its takeover of the Cambridge-based Acorn Computers. This concentration is a geographical reflection of the rapid world-wide change in micro-electronics, computer technologies and systems and biotechnology. This rapidly changing technological environment has been accompanied by explosive growth in demand for innovative products such as micro-computers, software, scientific instruments (incorporating micro-electronics and/or lasers) and new biotechnical applications. In turn, these changes have created a wide range of market opportunities for which small new firms set up research scientists or engineers have been able successfully to exploit.

Why has this happened in Cambridge? The university, as a major international centre of scientific research and education, has generated research ideas and scientific innovations. This has provided an important local environment of technological ideas and at the same time, for many of the researchers who have set up high-tech companies, it has provided a large local supply of highly qualified graduates as further entrepreneurs and employees of new firms. It has afforded a historic, architectural and cultural environment which is highly appealing to high-tech entrepreneurs and their staff as a place to live and work. Research has shown that 35 per cent of founders of new computer firms in the Cambridge region since 1975 have come straight out of the university and academic research. Other factors are the quality of local residential environments, and good transport links (the M11 and electrified rail). A further major suggested factor is the process of *synergy*. This is the relatively intense localised interaction between different firms and entrepreneurs, research institutions, local banks, financial agencies and business service organisations. The

9.16 The Cambridge Phenomenon

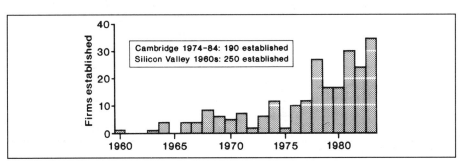

benefits of these links and relations generate outputs and outcomes the sum of which is greater than the sum of the individual parts. The ease of personal contact within a small geographical area has undoubtedly helped the continuing creation of new firms, the development of close links between firms on production and research and the general dynamism of the phenomenon. It has also made it easier to market the place through such phrases as 'the Cambridge Phenomenon'.

9.3c **The geography of high-tech products**

High-tech industry is by no means restricted to the developed world. With the international division of labour (whereby the skilled and technologically contrived labour tasks are usually assigned to the core countries of the international capitalist system whereas unskilled routine tasks, especially those that consume large quantities of labour, tend to be shifted out to the global periphery), transnational corporations have quickly identified the economic benefits of locating assembly plants across the developing world.

9.17 Growth of US-owned semi-conductor assembly plants in SE Asia 1964-1985

	Number of plants		
	1964	1974	1985
Hong Kong	1	8	8
Indonesia	-	2	2
Korea	1	9	5
Malaysia	-	11	14
Philippines	-	1	11
Singapore	-	9	11
Taiwan	-	3	8
Thailand	-	1	4
	2	44	63

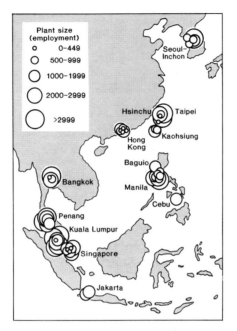

9.18 US-owned semi-conductor assembly plants, 1985

The semi-conductor industry is a good example of this trend. It can be broadly subdivided into four major clusters of activity:

- circuit design and mask-making
- wafer fabrication (diffusion)
- chip assembly
- testing.

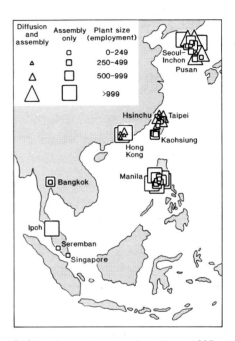

9.19 Locally owned semi-conductor plants, 1985

Most of this activity has been in South East Asia (especially Hong Kong, Indonesia, Korea, Malaysia, the Philippines, Singapore, Taiwan and Thailand). It started in 1962

9.20 Semi-conductor plants in SE Asia: number of plants and average employment, 1985

	US-owned plants			Locally-owned plants					
	Assembly			Diffusion and assembly			Assembly		
	Number of plants	Total employment	Average size of plant	Number of plants	Total employment	Average size of plant	Number of plants	Total employment	Average size of plant
Hong Kong	8	4,552	569	4	1,532	383	2	2,700	1,350
Korea	5	8,800	1,760	5	5,000	1,000	12	10,474	873
Malaysia	14	38,136	2,724	-	-	-	2	1,450	725
Philippines	11	13,112	1,192	-	-	-	14	18,046	1,289
Singapore	11	10,397	945	-	-	-	1	240	240
Taiwan	8	15,296	1,912	8	5,064	633	11	2,805	255
Thailand	4	6,470	1,685	-	-	-	2	900	450
Total	63	99,963	1,587	17	11,596	682	44	36,615	832

Sources: Industrial directories, field interviews, and mail questionnaire survey

when the Fairchild Corporation established an assembly plant in Hong Kong and since that time the expansion of the industry in South East Asia has proceeded apace. By the 1980s there had developed a sophisticated set of webs of intra-regional trade in finished and semi-finished devices. The growth and distribution of such US-owned semi-conductor assembly plants is shown in Figure 9.17 and Figure 9.18. Locational factors which attracted the US corporations to this region included: abundant cheap and compliant non-unionised labour; stable and highly reliable workforces; willingness to work long hours; political stability and accommodating forms of state intervention; and, not least, a positive business climate. Locally owned diffusion and assembly plants have subsequently been built (Figure 9.19).

Assembly depends on unskilled labour, whereas the other processes require more skills. Certain places within South East Asia have arisen as skill-based growth centres in this highly vibrant industry (Figure 9.20), notably Taiwan, Hong Kong and South Korea.

9.4 **Alternative strategies**

Business organisation

This section will concentrate on alternative strategies of business organisations and governments towards technology. Many of the alternative strategies of business organisations have been discussed in the last chapter (Chapter 8, Section 4) and previous sections. Just the major decisions will be outlined here.

9.21(a) % Workers	1972	1984*
West Midlands	43.4	31.0
North West	15.9	19.7
South west	14.5	17.6
South east	13.4	17.7
East Anglia	5.1	5.1
Scotland	3.2	4.8
Yorkshire and Humberside	2.2	0.7
Wales	1.6	2.3
North	0.6	0.5
East Midlands	-	0.4
Northern Ireland	-	0.3

* not strictly comparable

Technology and labour

New technologies in production may be introduced to reduce labour costs or to gain greater control over their labour, and/or to gain a competitive advantage in existing products in order to increase market share or to be the first with new products into new markets. One decision about lowering production costs may be between seeking cheaper labour or investing in new technology. The former may involve a new location. This may be within the country towards cheaper workers which may also be less organised, temporary or part-time and sometimes women (Figure 9.21a). Alternatively it may be outside the country to areas where there may also be governmental incentives to locate and weaker

9.21(a) Cadbury-Schweppes' early 1980s automation programme affecting product packaging and office work in the UK (b) their internalisation policy

regulations on health and safety and environmental pollution (Figure 9.21b). New technologies in themselves may also require new locations because of more space or more easily controlled environments.

Many geographers have emphasised moves related to labour costs and control but neglected other possible reasons for the moves and paid little attention to market-oriented decisions. Competition is not predominantly by price in many fields but by innovation in new products or product differentiation. Such competition means that R and D are needed in order to keep ahead of the opposition. Business has to decide whether it will attempt to lead in particular markets or play an imitator role, learning from the mistakes of the first in the field and not bearing their risks. Larger corporations can more easily bear the costs of R and D than small companies, but even they are entering *strategic alliances* with other major corporations in order to reduce their risks in such uncertain frontiers.

R and D and the rate of change

Decisions to invest in R and D in itself increase the rate of technological change, with products having shorter lives before they are replaced by other types of products

9.21(b)	1981	1982	Employment 1983	1984	Sales 1981	(£m) 1984
United Kingdom: numbers	23,384	22,897	21,587	20,089	710.7	920.8
percentage	64.1	60.0	58.1	56.7	57.8	45.7
Europe	8.3	13.0	14.2	14.0	8.7	11.5
N. America	6.6	7.7	8.2	8.5	14.2	24.1
Australia	8.6	8.0	7.8	8.9	12.4	12.9
Africa, Asia and New Zealand	12.3	11.7	11.7	12.0	6.9	5.8
Totals	36,463	38,148	37,140	35,455	1228.7	2016.2

Source: Cadbury-Schweppes, PLC, Annual Reports and Accounts

or, as it is termed, shorter *product life cycles*. This increases the need for further research into new products in order to keep ahead. The high costs of this research mean that a corporation must have some products that are yielding high returns without much present investment, or 'cash cows' as they are called. They can help finance R and D of other products which the corporation hopes will be future cash cows. At any one time a corporation needs to manage a portfolio of products, some cash cows and some newly developed which may be absorbing large amounts of investment but have the prospect of future high returns and low investment. It also needs to be using modern technology to keep it informed about changing market needs and the location of markets where a product is most likely to become a cash cow. The development of technologies involved in coordinating a global corporation's activities (Chapter 8, Section 2) and marketing its products may be as important as those concerned with the production process.

A corporation's locational decisions may also be affected by the technological policies operated by governments. It is these that will now be discussed. There has already been some discussion on supra and national governments (Chapter 9, Section 2). Clearly the effectiveness of governmental strategies is influenced by the degree of coordination there is between supra, national, regional and local policies.

Governments

Governments invest or not?

A national government first has to decide whether it is going to invest in technological development. Most governments invest in all kinds of ways but some, in seeking to reduce public expenditure, as in Britain in the 1980s, may cut back in various areas such as scientific research in universities or agricultural research stations. Some governments believe only that they must encourage the conditions in which private enterprise pays for its own research activity. Others see such research as of benefit to the nation, indeed part of its economic development, as is necessary infrastructure, which private industry will not pay for alone.

Investment in what?

The second question government has to decide is in which areas of technology it should invest. Limited resources are often targeted on key areas. One strategy is to invest in high-tech industries, the development of both new products and processes. One of Japan's policies was to identify key technologies for further resources, such as biotechnology, robots and the Fifth Generation Computer Project which could help develop artificial intelligence systems. The British government set up INMOS, a new company for microchip manufacture, and later in 1983 established the £350 million Alvey Programme of research into fifth-generation computers. Alternatively government can try to improve the technology used in traditional industries, which may otherwise run down further or disappear. These alternatives are sometimes discussed as investment in *'sunrise'* or *'sunset'* industries, with new high-tech industries being regarded as examples of sunrise, and textiles and steel being examples of sunset industries. This analogy with sunsets suggests that industries end like the day, but many can be revitalised by investment in new technologies, such has been the case in the textile and car industries. Failure to invest in the sunrise industries may mean that other countries obtain a lead and cannot be overtaken, while failure to invest in sunset industries may lead to even further job loss as foreign competition puts them out of business altogether. While sunrise industries at first created many new jobs, more recently technological developments within them have also led to job losses and *'job less'* or *'job loss'* growth.

The orientation to sunset or sunrise industries is important geographically because they are usually located in different regions. Crudely, sunset industries dominate the old manufacturing belt of the USA, now variously called the 'Rust Belt' or 'Rust Bowl', while the sunrise industries are mostly located in the so-called 'sun-belt' (as against 'frost belt') of the South and West. In Britain there is crudely a north-south division, but areas such as central Scotland and to some extent the North West have both sets of industries.

Defence?

Another key question for government is the degree to which to invest in defence and military technological development as against commercially oriented technology. Both can produce jobs and exports and both can produce technologies which are useful in the other. US and UK governments have been heavily committed to defence expenditure, even during the 1980s when other areas of public expenditure were relatively reduced. This has geographical effects. In the USA in the 1980s the high level of spending on defence, together with the dismantling of welfare programmes, was directly associated with the decline of inner cities and growth in new regions, particularly suburban locations in small and medium sized towns in California, Texas and some of the New England states. In the UK it has been argued that the development of much high-tech industry in southern England is based on government demand for military hardware (Chapter 12,

Section 1). This is to some extent true, though the South West, North West and central Scotland are important locations of military industry as well as the Outer South East. It is not just the contracts that generate economic development. Further impetus is given by the government research establishments involved in defence work, most of which are located in the South East. These include the Royal Aircraft Establishment at Farnborough and Pyestock in Hampshire, the Atomic Weapons Research Establishment at Aldermaston in Berkshire, and the Admiralty Marine Technology Establishment at Teddington. The main electronics research establishment is, however, at Malvern in Worcestershire.

Some defence expenditure is bound to go where the specialist plants are already located, such as British Aerospace in Manchester, Preston-Warton in the North West, British Aerospace and Rolls Royce in Bristol, Westlands in Yeovil and Smiths Industries in Gloucester. The most rapidly growing parts of the defence industry are those units concerned with high-tech research and development, not in massive factories as those above but in low-rise office laboratories. These units have been setting up particularly in the Outer South East where they can recruit scarce scientists and engineers who are attracted to the region. The disparities between regions can therefore indirectly influence the location of defence expenditure, as well as its location

9.22 UK regional assistance versus defence procurement

further accentuating the unevenness of development.

The scientists and engineers are scarce partly because at least one third of qualified scientists and engineers in the UK are employed on defence work, a measure of the orientation of the UK to defence rather than commerce. Whether they would bring greater returns to the country by commercial, non-defence work is a key question, particularly if the warming of East-West relations in the early 1990s continues. The overall orientation of national government to defence spending, then, may itself have important effects on technological development as well as have uneven spatial effects.

Defence versus regional assistance

One problem with national and indeed supra-national government is that there are so many departments concerned directly and indirectly with technology that often there is no overall policy and relatively little awareness of geographical impacts.

	Regional assistance		Defence procurement	
	1977/8	1983/4	1977/8	1983/4
North	144	92	154	139
Yorks & Humberside	27	36	51	139
East Midlands	2	18	180	346
East Anglia	-	-	103	208
South East	-	-	1077	3747
South West	8	12	385	763
West Midlands	-	-	180	278
North West	60	137	205	763
Wales	80	114	25	69
Scotland	117	222	180	416
Northern Ireland	50	108	25	69

9.23 Defence procurement and regional assistance by region, 1977/78 and 1983/84

In the UK, for example, the expenditure on defence contracts much exceeded regional assistance and their placing had greater effect on regional development. Defence procurement was four to nearly ten times as great as regional assistance in the years from 1974 to 1984 (Figure 9.22).

Many of the assisted regions were gaining more from this than from the regional policy. Only Wales and Northern Ireland got less. The main point from the position of regional policy, though, is that defence contracts very much countered the direction of regional policy. The South East received more in defence expenditure than the total regional assistance for all the areas (Figure 9.23).

Structure of technical industries

National governments also have to decide on the structure of industries where the adoption of new technology is especially important, for instance the postal and telephone authorities. Many European countries have maintained a policy of supporting a *national champion*, where one organisation has a public or private monopoly over services within the country and/or receives governmental support either directly

1974/5	1975/6	1976/7	1977/8	1978/9	1979/80	1980/81	1982/83	1983/84
Regional assistance:								
274	450	497	489	571	463	650	1062	738
Procurement expenditure:								
1302	1792	2138	2565	2984	3640	4885	6297	6939
Regional assistance as % of procurement:								
21	25	23	19	19	13	13	17	11

or indirectly in the form of contracts. National champions are protected from overseas competition in various ways, for example technical standards specific to that country. The British telephone service used to be organised as a public monopoly, while Britain's ICL and France's Bull were examples of supported national champions in computers.

Deregulation

One alternative to national champions and monopolies is *deregulation* in order to encourage greater competition. It is one form of privatisation (Chapter 4, Section 2). In the USA between 1913 and 1983, AT & T operated a private monopoly over the telephone network with the agreement of the federal government. In 1984 a new AT & T was established together with seven newly independent regional operating companies.

Local services are more expensive but there is now great competition over long-distance traffic between the new AT & T and alternative carriers, which has led to a faster introduction of new technology. Sometimes this has been done by major corporations setting up their own networks, partly as a response to the soaring local phone rates.

In Europe most telephone systems were state owned. There was a consensus that because of the economies of scale involved in operating a public network, efficient use of resources suggested a 'natural' monopoly. This led to pricing structures and cross-subsidisation practices that were based on social objectives rather than strict commercial ones, for example urban services subsidising rural ones. The partial privatisation of British Telecom and deregulation in Britain has allowed greater competition from Mercury (owned by Cable & Wireless), particularly on the provision of equipment and over long-distance business

traffic. As in the USA, the changes have not been without problems for residential users. Clearly there is a balance between the disadvantages of costly duplication of services and any inefficiency and higher prices induced by a lack of competition. Deregulation has, though, led to different geographies of services and industries and different geographical effects due to increased competition for particular types of customers, concentrated in certain areas and along certain routes.

Encouraging adoption of innovations

Governments have not been concerned only with the speed of adoption of new technology by their national champions. One other problem for governments of nations and supra-states is the slowness of the take-up of new technology by business organisations, particularly small and medium-sized ones, outside of the core regions. This differential take-up (Figure 9.25) increases regional disparities in development and prevents the more rapid growth of a home market for high-tech products, which home industries need. This has been a problem to Britain, other countries in the EC and the EC as a whole. Governments can inform managers and owners of possibilities but there is a crucial difference between awareness and adoption of innovations. A major set of alternative strategies then revolves around ways of improving the development potential of peripheral or less-favoured regions and the roles new technology may play in that.

Training

One policy is to make industry more aware of the potential. Making 1982 the year of information technology

9.24 *City Technology Colleges*

was one of the British government's attempts to do that. Improving training and retraining and introducing more technology-oriented education in schools are policies that can improve the skills of the labour force and make people more aware of opportunities and problems associated with new technologies. Although these may be national policies, they are not always implemented locally in the same way or to the same extent. Some schools and authorities obtained the extra resources from the Technical and Vocational Education Initiative (TVEI) earlier than others. Some schools use their micro computers, some of which were obtained through another government programme, more effectively than others, integrating their use into many areas of the curriculum rather than in maths or computer science only. The late 1980s policy of using government and private money to establish twenty City Technology Colleges, which would have a bias towards science and technology, will obviously produce uneven effects. Although they were supposed to be concentrated on inner-city areas, they have been established wherever private funding has been found, where a site has been available and where local government, which has been left out of this controversial education initiative, has not opposed too strongly (Figure 9.24).

Private money has not been sufficient and more central government capital has been invested than intended. Many argue that such capital should be spent on existing schools. The government argues that such a policy is needed to introduce innovation into the educational system.

Technology transfer

Sometimes there is quite a lot of research activity in a region but the *technology transfer* (Chapter 8, Section 2) to local industry is weak. This may be because there is a mismatch between the technological capacity of local firms and the ideas coming out of universities and research centres and there are poorly developed mechanisms for technology transfer. Such circumstances apply to much of Greece. One possibility is attempting to orient the research centres to the needs of the local region but if this is done it may mean that they forgo their international reputation and lucrative contracts from outside the region, move away from leading edge technologies and perhaps become locked into technologies and markets that are in decline. It is likely that the people being educated in the universities in such fields are leaving the region or nation in order to obtain jobs – the 'brain drain' – so as well as transferring technology, there is also a need to retain such labour in the region and nation.

One linked question is whether to put the emphasis on trying to generate or diffuse technology in the region. Some regions may benefit from the development of innovations by a small group of key enterprises. Others may benefit more by the diffusion of existing technologies to industry as a whole within the region. Innovations are usually products, while the diffusion idea is usually of processes.

Similarly, at a national level emphasis may be given to novel technologies, as in the early 1980s for the Alvey and ESPRIT programmes in the UK and Europe or to those technologies which have only immediately obvious applications and markets, as the British government favoured in the late 1980s.

Imported technology via inward investment

A further question is whether to try to develop indigenous technology or whether to import it. This can obviously apply to regions or nations. Inward investment has immediate impact via job creation and prestige and is much less long term than indigenous development. There is the possibility of technological dependency which may destroy what indigenous base there is. First, an externally controlled branch plant of a transnational may 'cream off' scarce scientific, research and technical staff and make it more difficult for indigenous industry to obtain it. Second, such branch plants may remain an island and not integrate with the local economy. This may be especially so for high-tech industry because their products have high value to weight ratios with transport costs being a small proportion of total costs. This makes them fairly free in their location relative to component suppliers and markets. Technologically sophisticated and high-value added production also requires specialised materials with more exacting technical specifications. Few suppliers can provide this, so input linkages are likely to be more wide-ranging and not local. However, 'technological isolation' does have an advantage.

Such branch plants can operate in environments that are not particularly well served with technological infrastructure because they bring so much with them, whereas potential indigenous units would be at a grave disadvantage in such environments. They may produce a more skilled local labour force and keep key workers in the region. They may also raise the profile of the region and improve its image. Both of these may attract further investment. Both Ireland and Scotland have been quite successful in attracting such inward investment. They were first into the competitive field and both have active development agencies. Ireland's success in attracting high-tech inward investment in pharmaceuticals is said to cast a shadow on surrounding regions, particularly England. There is not enough investment for all regions to adopt this strategy successfully.

Technological leakage

One danger of inward investment is that it increases '*technological leakage*', that is, indigenous companies being taken over and their research and development transferred to other parts of the transnationals' operations (Figures 9.25, 9.26) elsewhere or closed due to restructuring.

Some regions will have to rely mainly on their indigenous companies' technological development. Small firms may face barriers to entry in that R and D may be very expensive, as in pharmaceuticals. In other fields such as biotechnology, smaller firms may find entry less of a problem, though, as with any high-tech venture, there is even greater risk and many failures. Small firms are often related to and dependent upon large corporations, acting as subcontractors or suppliers of components of specialised services. In some cases the quality control of large corporations may insist on technological development in the

UK high technology firm	Activity	Location	Foreign firm	Activity	Nationality	Other comments
Columbia Automation	Automatic test equipment	Berkshire, South East	Zehntel	Automatic test equipment	USA	
Precima	Automated assembly equipment	Essex, South East	Emhart	Electronics and engineering	USA	
Applied Research of Cambridge	Computer aided design (CAD)	Cambridge, East Anglia	Mcdonnell Douglas	Aerospace/Computer systems	USA	Sold by the UK Government in 1982
Hoskyns	Computer systems and consultancy	London, South East	Martin Marietta Data Systems	Aerospace/Computer systems	USA	
Shape Data	CAD	Cambridge, East Anglia	Evans and Sutherland	Computer simulation	USA	Founders moved out and formed new company Three-Space
Acom Computers	Computer manufacture	Cambridge, East Anglia	Olivetti	Electronic business systems	Italy	Acom in severe financial difficulty before Olivetti takeover
General Computer Systems	Computer maintenance	London, South East	Bell Canada	Telecommunications	Canada	Company renamed – Bell Technical Services
Immediate Business Systems	Computer manufacture	Buckinghamshire, South East	Allied Signal	Computer/Communications	USA	
Remek	Robotics/vision systems	Bedfordshire, South East	Asea	Automation	Sweden	Remek acquired by VS Engineering which was then acquired by Asea
JK Lasers	Lasers	Warwickshire, East Midlands	Lumonics	Lasers	Canada	
Compeda	CAD marketing/ research	Cambridge, East Anglia	Prime Computers	Computers	USA	Founded in 1977 by UK Government's National Research Development Corporation (now part of British Technology Group)
Computer Interactive Systems	CAD	Cambridge, East Anglia	Computerisation	CAD/CAM	USA	Sold by UK Government in 1981
Sevcon	Micro-processor controls	Tyne and Wear North	Tech Ops Inc.	Electronics	USA	Sevcon was a division of Joyce Loebl; the division was acquired by Vickers then sold off to Tech Ops

9.25 Take-overs of UK high-tech firms by foreign companies

small firms which are supplying components. Technological transfer may then occur. Generally, though, small firms may need support mechanisms so that any technological development made by the company may be fully exploited commercially. Policy in Britain in the 1980s has been to set up advice centres for small businesses to help their marketing as well as their application of new technologies.

In England and Wales most policies related to technology are national or local. Locally most relate to providing property, in particular sci-

ence parks. Many local authorities have established these after the lead of Cambridge (Chapter 9, Section 3b) but there is insufficient development for every authority to be successful. There is also much competition between local areas, so making a regionally coordinated strategy extremely difficult. The local scale also rather inhibits the large aggregate funding necessary for technological development that is possible when there is some regional basis to government, as in Germany. There has been some local initiative in north-east England in demonstrating how new telecommunications technology can help small firms there, but most local emphasis in

Britain has been on science parks. In Denmark, in contrast, it has been in setting up research and development centres. The local initiatives vary from country to country. What rarely varies is the lack of coordination between central and local governments and horizontally between government departments.

Governments, business organisations and the physical environment

This section concludes by discussing the alternative strategies that governments may follow towards tech-

Name of HEI/PRE located in UK region which developed the innovation	UK region	Sector associated with the innovation	Name of foreign or UK core region manufacturer taking up the innovation	Location
Bristol University	South West	Pharmaceuticals	Sandoz AG	Switzerland
University of Birmingham	West Midlands	Biotechnology (Diagnostics)	Amersham International	South East, UK
Royal Signals and Radar Establishment, Ministry of Defence (and University of Sussex)	West Midlands	Chemical processing	Balzers AG and Etablissements Pieme Angenieux SH (+ OC LI Optical Coatings Ltd)	Liechtenstein St Heard, France (Dunfermline, Scotland)
University of Ulster	Northern Ireland	Electronic components	Boeing	USA
University of Leeds	Yorkshire & Humberside	Polymers	Celanese Corporation (owned by Hoechst, W. Germany)	USA
Health and Safety Executive, Sheffield	Yorkshire & Humberside	Gas detectors	Mine Safety Appliances	USA
Wolfson Unit (Cambridge Industrial Unit) at Cambridge University	East Anglia	Computer graphics	Control Data	USA

HEI – Higher Education Institute
PRE – Public Research Establishment

9.26 Technological leakages from UK regions

nology and the environment. Governments can let businesses operate in environmentally unfriendly ways, at least within limits, and encourage the development of technology to clear up and attempt to put right. Such a policy is similar to the economic policy towards the environment of 'the polluter pays'. On the other hand, they can insist by controls that technological processes that are harmful to the environment are stopped and replaced by environmentally friendly ones. The latter may be very costly to industry in the short term, prices would rise, and there would be much resistance to it. Transnationals may transfer their investments elsewhere. It would also be economically costly because, again in the short term, if such measures were carried out unilaterally industries in other countries would gain an advantage which may not be recovered. Many would argue that for the sake of the physical environment it is even more important that international action is agreed and that environmental values are given relatively greater emphasis than economic ones.

Government regulations

At present governmental regulations on new technological products and processes that detrimentally affect the physical environment vary considerably between countries. A country that is relatively strongly regulated in one field, for example Germany on air pollution, may be less environmentally oriented in another, such as allowing noxious effluents into the Rhine. Similarly there is considerable variation between countries in regulations on drugs, food and drink, and other products and processes that may be hazardous to health and safety. Part of investment in preventative medicine should include technologies that minimise health and safety hazards and consequent expenditure on surgery and drugs. Some would argue that environmentally oriented technologies are needed rather than ones oriented to increased productivity, efficiency and short-term profitability. They suggest that these may lead to longer-term profitability.

9.5   Perspectives

This section discusses the occurrence of technological change over time and space and some more general points about the relationship of technological change with the other environments and processes.

Long waves

Just as economic change consists of cycles as well as trends (Chapter 8, Section 5), so too does technological change. It has been noted by a number of writers that innovations tend to be clumped in time rather than occurring evenly.

The whole idea of technological

revolutions reflects this. One theory sees technological change and associated economic change as occurring in long waves, called Kondratiev waves after the Russian who identified them. Waves of about fifty years' duration, longer than business cycles, were observed (see Figure 12.4).

Their exact duration and correspondence with the historical record may be questioned, but if the description is approximately correct the question that must be asked is, why do innovations bunch in time? In the 1930s it was suggested that the bunching was caused by the activity of entrepreneurs. In a major recession such as occurred in the late 1920s and early 1930s, innovation is even more risky. In such periods, however, more adventurous entrepreneurs see the opportunity to make profit by investing in new ideas. Their success is then imitated by people who have a less favourable attitude to risk-taking and innovations follow in the same industries. Writers in the 1980s argued that the bunching was due to industries' response to the low level of profits coming from the last generation of innovations, which is thought to be characteristic of the end of waves. The search for greater profits shortens the time between inventions and their implementation. The varying levels of profits and lengths of time from invention to implementation are then the suggested reasons for bunching. It is not suggested that inventions are clumped in time, only their implementation as innovations.

Such theories are supposed to apply to all such waves. They apply at the international scale. Spatial considerations are not central to them; there is no attempt to show how innovations are diffused over space between national economies or how the changing spatial structure and organisation of the global economy has affected and been influenced by innovations.

Geographers have identified areas that play a greater part in generating innovations, and where new products and processes are first found. Such areas do not always decline at the end of a wave because they might also be centres of the next generation of innovations. The idea that geographical areas rise and decline with these waves is too simple. The interesting questions relate to why some areas and countries do decline while others adopt a further generation of innovations as readily as they had those of the past.

Past geographical theories suggested that technological innovations originate in very large cities and diffuse simultaneously both down the hierarchy of city-sizes and across space to neighbouring cities. In some theories the diffusion of information about the innovation is used as an explanation, while in others there is a spatial association made with the idea of the product life cycle. It is argued that there is much uncertainty attached to a new product and therefore it needs an entrepreneur who is very prepared to take risks, as well as adaptable labour and markets for success. Such entrepreneurs, labour and markets were concentrated in very large cities. As the product is accepted, becomes standardised and moves into mass production and consumption, less risk is attached to it and less skills are needed from the labour. Its production then occurs in medium-sized cities. Finally, during the period towards the end of the product's life cycle, when there is much competition, little risk but smaller profits, production may occur in smaller cities.

During the 1970s and 1980s, with the decentralisation and decline of manufacturing and the location of new high-tech industries outside cities, many innovations did not occur first in very large cities. Any theory of diffusion also has to take into account the dominance of transnationals and the intra-corporation movement of ideas across and between countries. The spatial diffusion of innovations is no longer as simple as the above model, if it ever was, though awareness, risk-taking and imitation are still important processes in understanding it.

Effects on other environments

Much of this chapter has reviewed effects on the economic and built environment and the interrelationships between technological, economic and political processes. The political processes that have major geographical effects are governmental incentives to particular technologies and governmental regulation of new products and processes. These vary between countries and over time. Some comments have also been made about effects on the physical and social environments. Some physical environments may be more prone than others to detrimental effects from a given type of technology, and there may be greater need for controls on its use. Some technologies have much greater detrimental impacts on the physical environment than others. Some societies may see the dangers of new technologies earlier than others; for example, the new technological capability of storing and transferring data presents problems of access to check the accuracy of personal records and invasions of privacy which were recognised through legislation earlier in some countries than others. In all these effects on other processes and environments, new opportunities are created that may be both beneficial and detrimental. Computers may be very helpful to the police in collating data and solving or preventing crimes (Chapter 10, Section 3e) but they also present opportunities for computer fraud and malicious 'hacking', that is, entry into private computer systems to cause damage to records and programs. New forms of technology transform the geography of crime; whereas most burglaries take place close to the home of the offender, such computer crimes may occur in areas or countries that the perpetrator has never entered. Such new technologies again increase the need for international cooperation, in this case between police forces and between governments over extradition.

Technical solutions

There are also some general points to emphasise between technological development and its relationship to other processes. It is not the neutral, autonomous, irresistible force that it is frequently made to seem. It often results from a need to reorganise production in the search for profits or the need for prestige. It is not an independent, external force. Secondly, the present dominance of technological solutions to problems such as world population and resources is not inevitable. Environmental and social solutions should not be ignored.

To some extent there is at present a technological imperative: we *can* do this too often becomes we should do it. Often other processes and environments are neglected at a cost. For example, it was possible to produce a so-called miracle rice as part of the perhaps inappropriately called 'green revolution' in Asia but the product of this technological revolution was not to people's taste. The social and economic organisation of agriculture also meant that only richer farmers benefited from the change. In a similar vein, the technical ability to build very large dams, as at Aswan in Egypt, or nuclear power stations in India, may not be the most appropriate scale or type of development of energy for Third world countries, or indeed First or Second. The technical solution or 'fix' is only one. Environmental and social solutions should also be considered. There is considerable momentum to the technical solution which is so closely linked to capitalism and the military-industrial complex that it is difficult to stop. Improved relations between East and West may lessen the drive of the latter but unless capitalism becomes more environmentally and socially orientated it is difficult to see the demise of the technological imperative.

9.6 Exercises

1. Figure 9.27 shows the distribution of 'substantial' innovations that have occurred in industrial sectors in the UK between 1945 and 1980. About 77 per cent of the substantial innovations that were identified by experts were products. About 17 per cent were major processes and the rest material innovations. The table also shows the share of innovations that were received by the transfer of foreign technology.
   (a) (i) Which area received the greatest share of innovations over the period?
       (ii) Which areas received a lower share than expected given their share of manufacturing employees and establishments?
       (iii) What do these answers suggest about the evenness of regional development within the UK?
   (b) Describe and suggest reasons for the distribution of the transfer of foreign technology.
   (c) Suggest ways in which some areas may be encouraged to be more open to the adoption of new ideas.

2. Study the table (Figure 9.28) of port rankings for England and Wales 1965-86.
   (a) Compare the rankings for total tonnage in 1965 and 1986.
       (i) Which ports have slipped down or disappeared from the rankings in 1986?
       (ii) Which ports have dramatically increased their position?
   (b) Which have emerged as specialist ports in 1986?
   (c) (i) To what extent does technological change rather than economic change explain these new rankings?
       (ii) Are there any other factors that might help to explain the changes?

9.27 The distribution of innovations in the UK, 1945-80

Years	South East	Non-assisted areas outside South East	Intermediate areas	Development areas	GB total
1945-59 regional share	36.7	27.5	19.1	17.5	
1960-69 regional share	31.2	28.4	24.8	14.8	
1970-80 regional share	34.0	24.9	30.3	10.6	
1945-80 regional share	33.7	27.0	25.5	13.7	2282
Foreign origin regional share	42.9	16.2	23.9	16.6	504
% of manuf. employees	24.9	30.6	24.6	19.9	
% of establishments	31.0	29.6	23.4	15.9	

(a) Total tonnage, 1965	(b) Total tonnage, 1986	(c) Non-oil imports, 1986
London	London	London
Liverpool	Grimsby/Immingham	Grimsby/Immingham
Southampton	Tees	Tees
Manchester	Milford Haven	Port Talbot
Tees	Southampton	Dover
Hull	Felixstowe	Felixstowe
Bristol	Liverpool	Medway
Tyne	Medway	Liverpool
Grimsby/Immingham	Dover	River Trent
Swansea	Manchester	Hull

(d) Non-oil exports, 1986	(e) RO/RO units, 1986	(f) containers (units), 1986
Felixstowe	Dover	Felixstowe
Tees	Fleetwood	London
London	Harwich	Southampton
Dover	Felixstowe	Hull
Grimsby/Immingham	Medway	Ipswich
Southampton	Grimsby/Immingham	Liverpool
Hull	Portsmouth	Grimsby/Immingham
Liverpool	Ipswich	Portsmouth
Ipswich	Ramsgate	Holyhead
Fowey	Hull	Tees/Hartlepool

9.28 Port rankings for England and Wales 1965-1986

(b) In what ways is tyre dumping a hazard?

(c) What alternatives are there to dumping tyres and what effects might they have?

4. Read the extract from the Intermediate Technology Development Group.
(a) Suggest why the large-scale, 'technical fix' solutions were unsuccessful for the people in Somalia.
(b) Summarise the suggested advantages of an intermediate technology approach.
(c) To what extent do you think that this is a biased letter?

5. Study the diagram (Figure 9.29) which shows the transformation process from an 'industrial soci-

3. Study the extract on 'Taking tyres off the scrap heap'

(a) Why were more tyres being dumped in 1990 than in 1980?

Taking tyres off the scrap heap

Burning rubber produces large quantities of smoke and oil containing carcinogens such as benzene, toluene, xylene, furans and dioxins.

The black smoke clouds can create a trail of poisonous fall-out several miles long, while the oil can seep through the soil and contaminate ground water and nearby water courses.

We are dumping almost of all our 20 million scrap tyres a year into an already rubbish-strewn landscape. Yet 10 years ago, we were recycling a larger proportion than we do now.

Tyres can be incinerated to generate heat and power; gas, oil and chemicals can be extracted from them, and some of the rubber can be re-used. The energy wasted by throwing these tyres away would provide enough electricity and heating for a large city.

Lack of enterprise, imagination and environmental concern on the part of industry and government lies behind the failure to tackle the problem. It has always been cheaper and more convenient to dump old tyres. Two United States companies have now arrived in Britain touting different solutions. They believe they can make profits from using waste tyres as fuel and a raw material.

The average car tyre weighs about 17lbs. The steel wire which reinforces it makes up a fifth of its weight. The rest is largely synthetic rubber which, when burnt, can produce about 20 per cent more heat than the same weight of coal.

Every 12 months Britain has to dispose of 23 million car and van tyres and two million larger truck tyres. About one fifth of the car and van tyres and half of the truck tyres are remoulded and retreaded to give them a second lease of life. Almost all the remainder are dumped – as are the remoulds once they wear out.

As environmental standards for rubbish dumps improve it is becoming harder and more expensive the find legal dumping sites.

Brian Lawton of the Retread Manufacturers Association says that 18 months ago the cost of dumping 100 car tyres was £5. Now it is about £35. This should make the tyre industry more interested in finding an environmentally sound solution, but it is leading to more illegal tipping.

Some 80 retreading firms, mainly in the Midlands, take old and worn tyres from the distributors free, pick out the best, scrape off the rubber and bond fresh material. Their produce sells at half the price of a new tyre.

The retreaders are left to dispose of the majority of old tyres which are too worn and damaged to remould. Manufacturers and distributors do not worry about the retreaders' problems.

Some manufacturers used to have tyre-shredding plants which produced rubber 'crumb' – tiny fragments used in carpet backing, traffic cones, mats, sports surfaces and roads. But 10 years ago most of these plants closed because of lack of demand and because it was cheaper to dump old tyres.

A Houston petroleum products company, MIC, is negotiating with Sheffield City Council for permission to build a £3m tyre-shredding plant next to a former steelworks site in Hillsborough. The machinery is already in Britain and Sashi Shojai, the company chairman, says the factory could be in full production within five months of gaining permission, chewing up 60 tyres a minute, 12 million a year.

The tyres' steel skeletons would become scrap metal. The rubber would be chopped into fragments for fuel. Mr Shojai says he has plenty of customers, such as cement manufacturers who use it in their kilns, lined up.

Within two years of starting up he hopes to have built a £5m pyrolysis plant which would heat the rubber fragments to extract oils akin to crude oil, plus methane gas and carbon black – a soot-like substance used as a pigment and filler in tyre manufacture and other industries.

'We've found a field called Britain full of old tyres,' he says. 'We believe we've got a bankable situation here.'

Another US company, ELM Energy, has senior staff in Britain promoting plans for a 30-megawatt power station which would use scrap tyres to generate electricity as well as providing steam and hot water for industry and housing. Burton-on-Trent, where Pirelli has a factory, is a possible location.

The Government's electricity privatisation legislation insists that the supply companies buy a small proportion of their power from generators which do not use fossil fuels. This obligation gives these generators economically favoured status, and a tyre-burning power station would qualify.

Burning tyres usefully should be an attractive energy option. But such proposals have run into stiff opposition from people worried about stench and dense clouds of black smoke.

However, in order to meet a European Community directive on combustion plants, any tyre-fuelled power station would have to burn at temperatures above 1,000C and include equipment to remove dust, pollutants and toxins from the exhaust gases.

intermediate technology

9 King Street,
London, WC2E 8HW

Lasting solutions to long-term problems – helping the poor work themselves out of poverty

December 4th 1985

'The gift of material goods makes people dependent.
The gift of knowledge makes them free.'
                 'Small is Beautiful'. Dr. Fritz Schumacher.

Dear Friend,

Some years ago when the last dreadful famine gripped the Horn of Africa, 40,000 nomads were airlifted from their barren land and set down in a fertile plain in Somalia.

They were provided with new brick-built homes and the most sophisticated farming machinery that money could buy.

Today ten years on, their 'model' village is deserted. Half the nomads slipped quietly away into the bush to go back to their old way of life. The rest built their traditional stick huts and began to farm the land using the methods of their ancestors.

In a vast four-acre compound, row upon row of tractors, bulldozers and combine harvesters lie idle, corroded with rust. A workshop the size of an aircraft hangar has barely been used since the day it was built.

This spectacular white elephant cost millions. Whatever went wrong?

These people who have always lived by the simplest means were suddenly faced with technology that was too complicated and too alien for them to accept.

The gap between their knowledge and Western technology was simply too great for them to make use of the 'help' that was offered.

Bridging that gap, matching technology to the needs and skills of people whose agricultural methods and tools have not changed for centuries, is a specialised job. It is the task that we, a small group of engineers, economists and advisers, have set ourselves and have been working on for 20 years.

The Work We Do

Our work concentrates exclusively on helping local people, wherever they may live, to become more independent, self-sufficient and better able to overcome their problems themselves; we are not involved in short-term relief work. So when we help the Turkana people in a remote desert region with a 'rainwater harvesting' project we don't just set it up and walk away. We teach the people how to use these techniques, then how to make the tools they will need and how to repair and maintain them. That way, we ensure that local people acquire the skills and technical understanding they need to become more self-reliant, creating employment as well as saving lives.

To give you just one example of the way we use technology to improve and even save the lives of people who live in the harshest, most brutal climates in the world:

A windpump, designed by Intermediate Technology and funded at first by Christian Aid, is hauling up much-needed water from hundreds of feet below ground in some of the driest parts of Africa.

Nearly 100 windpumps are already in use providing water for nomadic tribes, schools, clinics and villages. Thousands now have water for drinking, for irrigation, for their cattle and also for tree nurseries.

A single pump at Kaikor in Kenya, near the Ethiopian border, serves some 4,000 nomads, irrigating their crops as well as providing drinking water. Not only should this pump last for twenty years but it can be built, repaired and maintained by the local people. By making the design simple and teaching Kenyans basic engineering we can be sure that the pump will go on serving their needs. Again reducing their dependence on outside help and improving their self-reliance.

Without water we die. The windpump, a simple solution, has already saved thousands of lives.

But creating windpumps is only one small part of what we do. Throughout the Third World we have been involved in projects, all aimed at helping local people improve their living standards by making use of technology appropriate to their needs, their resources and their circumstances. So when we helped create a food processing and bottling factory in Sri Lanka we also helped local people understand how to distribute and market the product and how to manage the 'factory'. We gave them the skills and the confidence to carry on without further aid. This project for example is now being copied by other communities in Sri Lanka – and also in Africa.

Do please help if you can.

                        With grateful thanks

                        David Wright,
                        Director of Operations.

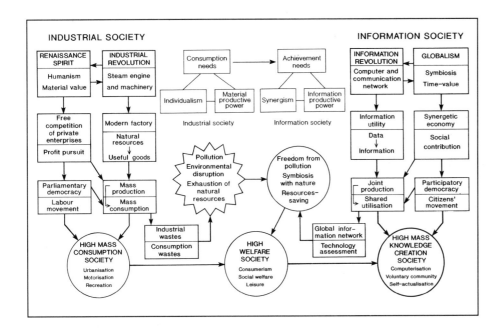

ety' to an 'information society'.

(a) What are the main industrial and technical differences between an industrial and information society as portrayed in the diagram?

(b) What are the main social and political differences between the two societies?

(c) To what extent do you think that your country has become an information society?

(d) Assess critically the description of an information society that is portrayed in the diagram.

9.7 **Further reading**

M. Castells (1989) *The Informational City*, Basil Blackwell

R.M. Cyert and D.C. Mowery (eds.) (1987) *Technology and Employment: Innovation and Growth in the US Economy*, National Academic Press

P. Hall, M. Breheny, R. Mcquaid and D. Hart (1987) *Western Sunrise: the genesis and growth of Britain's High-Tech Corridor*, Allen and Unwin

M. Hepworth (1990) *Geography of the Information Economy*, Guildford

A.R. Markusen, P. Hall and A. Glasmeier (1986) *High Tech America: the What, How, Where and Why of Sunrise Industries*, Allen and Unwin

M. Marshall (1987) *Long Waves of Regional Development*, Macmillan

J. Rees (ed.) (1986) *Technology, Regions and Policy*, Rowman and Littlefield

Chapter 10

CHANGING SOCIAL ACTORS AND ENVIRONMENTS

10.1 Case study: the challenge of housing the elderly

A recent and major demographic trend in the western world has been the rise in importance of the elderly.

The number and proportion of people who live beyond sixty have grown rapidly (Figure 10.1).

THE AGE OF AGEING
The stage is set for a unique population explosion. As fewer babies are born and people live longer we are beginning to witness the worldwide emergence of a new generation: the over–sixties. In the rich world the old are already one–fifth of the population. Soon this pattern will be repeated in the developing world.

Global Increase in the Number of People Aged 60+

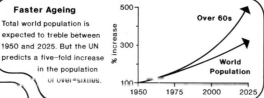

1950 2000 2025
North America
Europe
USSR
Eastern Asia
Africa
Latin America
Southern Asia
Oceania

300
100
20
Millions

Fewer Babies
World birth rate is slowing down. In 1950 there were over 36 babies born for every 1000 people. By 2025 the UN estimates there will be only half that number.

Faster Ageing
Total world population is expected to treble between 1950 and 2025. But the UN predicts a five–fold increase in the population of over–sixties.

% increase
500
300
100
Over 60s
World Population
1950 1975 2000 2025

Families of the Future
The parents of today are the grandparents of tomorrow. As younger generations decide to have fewer children and older generations live longer, so the structure of the typical global family is changing. By 2025 there will be relatively fewer young people to support a growing proportion of over 60s.

Industrialised Countries
Age		
20%	57%	23% 2025
25%	60%	15% 1975

0-14
15-59
60+

| 26% | 62% | 12% 2025 |
| 41% | 53% | 6 1975 |

Developing Countries

Average Life Expectancy at Birth
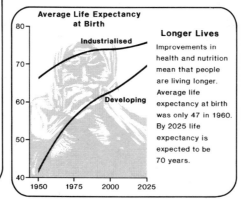

80
70
60
50
40
Industrialised
Developing
1950 1975 2000 2025

Longer Lives
Improvements in health and nutrition mean that people are living longer. Average life expectancy at birth was only 47 in 1960. By 2025 life expectancy is expected to be 70 years.

The Extra Years
Women's natural lifespan is up to 9 years longer than men's. But in developing countries the combined rigours of childbearing, hard work and poor nutrition narrow the gap. As living standards improve the gap will widen.

Industrialised
76 68
Developing
56 54

Going on Alone
In the industrialised world women in their sixties outnumber men by 10 to 7. By the time they reach their 80s women outnumber men by 2 to 1.

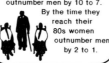

Two Steps Poorer
123 countries now offer a pension to retired workers but most developing countries only provide for those in formal employment. Up to 80% get no regular wage and cannot afford to retire.

Improvements in health and nutrition have led to longer and potentially more useful lives. In the rich world, sometimes referred to as 'the North', for instance, one in five of the population is over sixty, and men and women can expect to live on average sixty-eight and seventy-six years respectively. In 1981 elderly people in the UK numbered nearly 10 million, which represented about 17 per cent of the total population. Furthermore, the growth in the numbers of the very old and frail is even faster than the growth in numbers of the elderly population as a whole. Related to the increased demographic importance of the elderly is the trend towards smaller families which means there is a smaller proportion of children in the population as a whole. So the population structure of developed countries has therefore changed from a dependent population composed mainly of children to one composed mostly of the elderly.

Too often, however, this emerging group is stereotyped as frail, ill or at least in need of help. In reality they are a heterogeneous group and mobility is one characteristic which can illustrate that. On the one hand an elderly person may find difficulty in climbing the stairs, going out of doors or getting round the house without help, whereas another might be extremely fit. Mobility is

10.1 The age of ageing

just one measure devised to determine the extent to which elderly people need help. Figure 10.2 illustrates some of the dimensions including mobility which describe elderly people.

Social changes have influenced the lives and spatial distribution of the elderly. As society has become more spatially mobile, so children move away from their area of origin and leave parents without family support. As a result of this process and selective out migration, the group of elderly people who have remained in their original homes in inner suburban areas (Figure 10.3) and some rural settlements have become a major demographic group in these areas. Given the social trend towards smaller families, less children are available to support parents. As less adults, single, cohabiting or married, have children, in the future they will not have any children to support them.

So elderly people are concentrated in certain areas for a variety of reasons. People may stay in their original housing; or they may move locally into sheltered accommodation more appropriate to their needs; or they may move greater distances to 'Costas Geriatrica' such as the south coast of the UK and Florida in the USA. Other inland favoured

At least 20 per cent of persons over retirement age
At least 20 per cent of persons under sixteen
Combined characteristics
Wards with none of the above characteristics

10.3 The distribution of dependent population in Greater London, 1981

areas include spa towns such as Harrogate or climatically/scenically attractive towns such as Phoenix, USA. The growth of concentrations of retired people in England and Wales is shown in Figure 10.4 and the flows to such areas are shown in Figure 10.5.

Those elderly people who move to new areas do so at a variety of scales. They move at the most local level to more appropriate accommodation and at the regional and national level to live with or near relatives, or to live in one of the popular retirement zones. Good exam-

ples of the elderly moving at the international level are UK citizens who have moved to coastal Spain and Canadian citizens who have moved to the warmth of the Florida coast.

This heterogeneous population of elderly people means, of course, that their needs are equally variable. In particular, meeting their housing

10.2 Dimensions on which the elderly are differentiated

10.4 Growing retirement areas, 1951-71

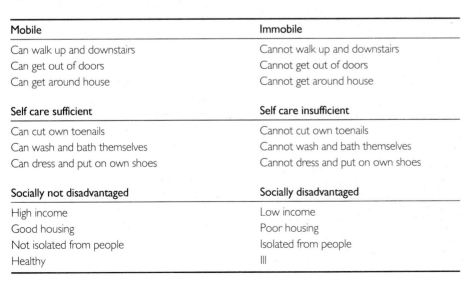

Mobile	Immobile
Can walk up and downstairs	Cannot walk up and downstairs
Can get out of doors	Cannot get out of doors
Can get around house	Cannot get around house
Self care sufficient	**Self care insufficient**
Can cut own toenails	Cannot cut own toenails
Can wash and bath themselves	Cannot wash and bath themselves
Can dress and put on own shoes	Cannot dress and put on own shoes
Socially not disadvantaged	**Socially disadvantaged**
High income	Low income
Good housing	Poor housing
Not isolated from people	Isolated from people
Healthy	Ill

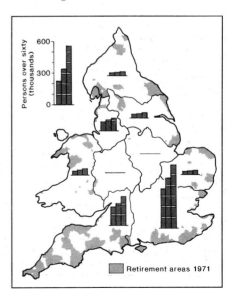

Retirement areas 1971

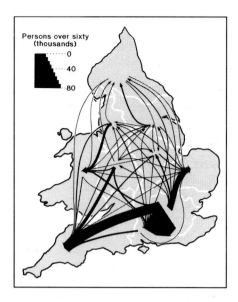

10.5 Net inter-regional migration flows of those aged 60 and over, 1966-71

Rented from state, housing association, private landlord	(Ownership continuum)	Privately owned
No service	(Health and domestic service continuum)	Service rich
All rooms communal including bedroom	(Privacy continuum)	Total privacy
Large unit	(Size continuum)	Small unit
All old people	(Age-mix continuum)	Mix of ages
Long distance move	(Movement continuum)	No move involved

10.7 The range of types of housing provision for the elderly

needs is quite a challenge (Figure 10.6).

Until relatively recently housing alternatives for the elderly in the UK were limited to almshouses, workhouses, living alone, living with their children or, indeed, children living with them. Nowadays the range of housing alternatives (Figure 10.7) is beginning to match their range of needs (Figure 10.2).

A specific example of the response of private house builders includes that of Independence Village in Rockford, Illinois, one of over 600 such retirement villages in the USA (Figure 10.8). One problem with such rather expensive homes is that they are available only to richer people.

Private sheltered accommodation for the elderly expanded in Britain later than in the USA. The earlier development of sheltered accommodation by local authorities and particularly housing associations (Chapter 4, Section 3c) had demonstrated that there was a potential demand. In the 1980s some developers established a specialist division concerned with private sheltered accommodation while other companies, such as McCarthy and Stone, set up based solely on the elderly market of fifty-fives and over. The greatest expansion was in the home counties, wealthy suburban areas of large cities and retirement resorts such as Southport in Lancashire.

Many developers established their own companies to manage the accommodation after it is developed, such as Peveril for McCarthy and Stone. Some housing associations manage both their own and private sheltered housing. Some companies have attempted to expand their market into periods later in life by developing private nursing homes, and earlier for the young more active retired where the accommodation has a swimming pool as well as the usual residents' communal lounge and launderette. The collapse of the general housing market in 1989, particularly in southern England, had a dramatic effect on the demand for such private sheltered accommodation because the elderly, not generally a risk-taking group, would not, or could not, sell their own homes.

10.8 The promotion of Independence Village, Rockford, Illinois

10.6 Housing problems of some of the elderly

Problems of:

Warmth "I have very bad circulation. I couldn't afford to use the electric fires and then I had to have them right on top of me to get warm." Widower, 80

Mobility "I have a plate in my hip and my left leg has been damaged. The doctor says I'm not to go up and down stairs too often." Widow, 70

House condition "I just couldn't cope with seeing the house and garden go to rack and ruin. The financial side of it is the problem. Everything seems to get more and more expensive and the pensions don't go up accordingly." Widow, 68

Here is what residents have to say about Independence Village.

'I moved to Independence Village, it's the best move I ever made.'

'To me, quality of life is more important than length of life. Here, my quality of life I much better than living a lonely life in my former home. Even my doctor was amazed at the improvement in my health now that I'm happy, eat good food and pal around with a group of active friends my own age.'

Ray Zimny,
Resident

'My family and friends love my new home, almost as much as I do.'

'I have a gracious dining room and card room to entertain my bridge friends, a library and game room where my son and grandchildren play monopoly with me, and even a pool room and theatre. It's like a mansion. Come over and I'll show you around.'

Naomi Vanden Brook,
Resident

10.2 **General problem**

Statement of general problem

The case study has examined one of the major recent changes in the structure of society, the growth in the number of the elderly. It also studied the ways in which one area of provision, housing, has responded to that change. The general problem of this chapter is to establish recent demographic and social changes, to examine the responses of various organisations and institutions to them, and to analyse their geographical effects. Social change can be viewed through changes in the number and type of actors and the organisations serving them, and through changes in the social environment. The social environment includes the changing relations between the actors, for example gender relations, and between the actors and organisations, for instance the degree of involvement in community groups.

10.9 Life paths, associated organisations and contexts

It also incorporates the changing social context of these relations, for example greater or lesser national interest in social inequality and varying relative reliance on individual or social responsibility.

The general problem can be discussed first by examining life paths/histories of individuals and households, and then by studying changes at a group level through the emergence of social movements.

Life paths

Figure 10.9 shows some key events that may occur through a person's life; some temporary or permanent alternatives from a general life path; organisations concerned with preventing, correcting or offering counselling for these alternatives; and the various environmental contexts that affect attitudes to the events, to the life paths and to the responses to them.

In relation to the case study, increased life expectancy and earlier retirement, both of which contribute to a longer period of retirement,

have led to changes at the end of the life path, particularly in developed countries. These have included an increasing diversity among 'the elderly' and 'the retired'.

The elderly and their effects

Many are very active and healthy while others are frail, immobile and in need of care. Some have large disposable incomes while others comprise one section of 'the poor' in western societies. The increased numbers and the diversity present opportunities for the market, particularly in housing and leisure, as well as needs that should be met by society, whether the mechanism is the market, public provision, voluntary organisations or the family (Chapter 4, Sections 2 and 4). The economic and social environments are then changed, because organisations respond to the new demands and needs of the elderly. The technological environment may also be affected through the discovery of new ways of responding to immobility and ill-health, for example the replacement of hip and knee joints. The increased number of the elderly in a nation also means that they are potentially an important political force and that their values and attitudes may have increased impact on society.

Geographical concentrations of the elderly mean that they are easier to target as a market and have potentially greater political force because they make up a greater proportion of the voting population. Concentrations may also lead to greater demands on the local health and social services. Such concentrations may emerge either where the elderly have been attracted to the area for retirement, such as in coastal areas, or where they have been left behind as younger people

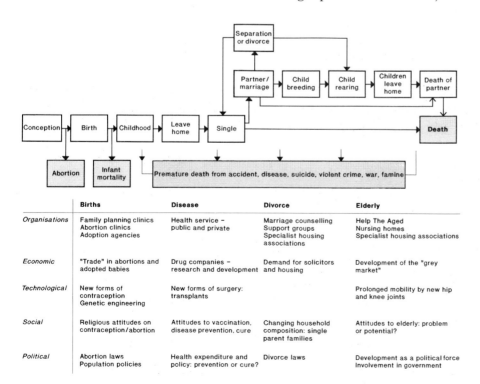

	Births	Disease	Divorce	Elderly
Organisations	Family planning clinics Abortion clinics Adoption agencies	Health service – public and private	Marriage counselling Support groups Specialist housing associations	Help The Aged Nursing homes Specialist housing associations
Economic	"Trade" in abortions and adopted babies	Drug companies – research and development	Demand for solicitors and housing	Development of the "grey market"
Technological	New forms of contraception Genetic engineering	New forms of surgery: transplants		Prolonged mobility by new hip and knee joints
Social	Religious attitudes on contraception/abortion	Attitudes to vaccination, disease prevention, cure	Changing household composition: single parent families	Attitudes to elderly: problem or potential?
Political	Abortion laws Population policies	Health expenditure and policy: prevention or cure?	Divorce laws	Development as a political force Involvement in government

have moved out, as in some inner-city and peripheral rural areas. Some retirement areas, such as Bournemouth, have tried to restrict the increased in-migration because of the load placed on health and social services by restricting the development of retirement homes. The inward movement of retired people increases the dependency ratio of the area, in the same way that a greater proportion of the elderly increases the national *dependency ratio*. Retirement moves may also produce gains for the area by what are called 'transfer payments'. These are the funds, such as state and private pensions, that accompany the retired into the area and increase the local purchasing power.

Changing birth rates

Changes have also occurred at the other end of the life path (Figure 10.9). Although fluctuations occur, the trend has been towards fewer births and smaller families in western societies. Increased use and efficacy of birth control techniques have facilitated the general decline in birth rates, though there are differing attitudes to their use. The Catholic Church, for example, advocates only natural methods of birth control and bans the use of the pill. In some countries legalised abortions have also reduced births. The differential availability of abortion has even led to the international movement of pregnant women, for example from Eire and the Middle East for abortions in Britain, thus contributing in a small, perhaps unfortunate way to international trade. The reduction in the number of unwanted births has reduced the possibilities for adoption in countries like Britain, so some people have sought adopted children in other nations, particularly developing ones, thus contributing in a small way to international migration.

There are numerous controversial issues, in addition to abortion and indeed related to it, that have recently arisen which concern this pre-natal period. Our understanding of biology and medical advances enable new ways of conception for previously infertile couples and ways of screening after conception so that the health and sex of the embryo may be discerned. These changes in the technological environment pose social questions about gender relations (the extent to which women have control over their bodies for example); about the family (the rights of a donor of an ovary or sperm to a child born to a childless couple for instance); and about genetic engineering (for example ways in which future generations can be modified). Many of these issues involve new legal thinking as well as ethical and political debate. The legal, religious and political systems all become involved. Many pressure groups form and are given exposure as the media highlight the debates. The outcomes of all these interrelated systems and processes vary from country to country and sometimes, in a political system such as in Canada, also vary from province to province.

Some people, usually the richer ones, are able to cross boundaries more easily to take advantage of practices that are legally or politically acceptable in other than their own country or state. Outcomes also vary over time as the social system changes. Some countries, such as India and China, have at times encouraged birth control to reduce the rate of growth of their population. China penalised families with more than one child by increased taxes. Some, such as France in the 1930s and Romania in the 1980s, have tried to encourage population growth because of their fear of a declining population. The geography of demographic and social change and the responses to it, then, vary from time to time as well as place to place.

Declining school rolls

One of the consequences of a reduced birth rate is a decline in school rolls, first in primary and then in secondary schools. Such declines do not occur simultaneously in space. Many inner city areas exhibited falling school rolls before outer metropolitan areas and counties (Figure 10.10).

Out-migration of women of child-bearing age from the inner cities exacerbated the decline in the birth rate. Some of these women were relocated in new towns or overspill estates due to redevelopment within the inner cities, while others suburbanised into owner-occupied housing. While inner areas of cities were closing primary schools in the early 1970s, some of the schools in the outer areas were suffering from overcrowding. The local political pressures may therefore be different at any one time. Falling rolls came later in most outer suburbs and so

10.10 The geography of falling rolls

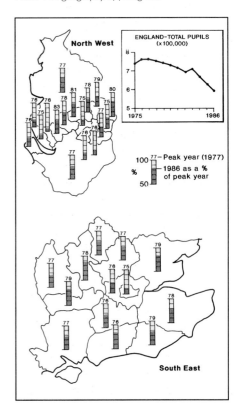

theoretically they were able to benefit from the experience of the varying responses of the inner areas to the demographic change.

Effects of birth rate at national level

At a national level there are three major consequences of a reduced birth rate. There are fewer young dependants, which in western societies somewhat counteracts the increased number of elderly dependants. There is then less demand for expenditure on education and the young, and more for health and social services for the elderly. Secondly, the declining pre-teen and teenage markets are relatively less attractive to the private sector than the expanding set of adults who formed the baby boom that ended in the mid-1960s. Indeed in North American terms the market is less interested in the 'pimplies' than the 'crinklies' and even the 'wrinklies'. The interest in the teenage market in the 1960s led to a much greater impact of teenage culture than before. In the 1980s, in contrast, the concern was more with young adults, particularly young urban professionals. Demographic change, then, has impacts on the demand for public and private expenditure and more widely on the social and cultural concerns of the period. Thirdly, a reduction in the birth rate will eventually lead to fewer young people entering the labour market, and fewer working people to support the dependent population. Some of the processes affecting the youth labour market are taken up in Chapter 12. Here it is worth indicating that the geographical distribution of youth (sixteen to nineteen) is not even, nor is the geographical distribution of job opportunities for them. Since the two geographical distributions do not match and youths travel relatively short distances to work, a complex, locally much differentiated

geography of youth labour markets, youth training and youth unemployment results.

Marriage

Another major recent change of life paths concerns marriage, separation and divorce (Figure 10.9). In many western countries the median age of marriage has increased. Later marriage, in itself, has been one of the reasons for fewer children. Couples are cohabiting more, instead of marrying or preliminary to marriage. This is due partly to social mores and partly to economic reasons; for example, a cohabiting couple until the late 1980s in Britain could each obtain mortgage tax relief on up to £30,000, whereas a married couple could only together receive up to that amount. With average house prices in the South East in excess of £50,000, it was not surprising that cohabitation rather than marriage was a growing trend. Some even divorced but continued to cohabit in order to receive the greater tax relief. In 1988 the Chancellor of the Exchequer changed the rules so that mortgage tax relief applied to the property, not to the people in it. The announcement of this financial change produced a surge in the housing market that year as people bought property in order to benefit from the higher tax relief before the rule changed.

Separation and divorce

The increased occurrence of separation and divorce has produced more work for solicitors and led to increased need for support groups, particularly for one-parent families and battered wives. Some of the separated and divorced join the single and the lone elderly to form a growing number of one-person households who have different housing,

food and social needs from multi-person households. Separated and recently divorced people who have left the former family home often need accommodation for a short period of time while they find something more permanent. Such individuals therefore tend to congregate in areas of rented accommodation towards the centres of cities, contributing to the high housing turnover and the transient nature of such areas.

Household composition

The social-demographic trends of more single young people living away from their parents and more separation and divorce have led to an increased number of households. This has meant a growing market for the housing industry, despite relatively little change to the total population. Household compositions have also changed. The increased number and diversity of single-person households together with single-parent families and the larger number of married or cohabiting couples with no children, or no children living at home, mean that the nuclear family of two parents with two children or indeed with any number of children is no longer the norm.

Urban change

Nuclear families still predominate in outer suburban areas but inner areas have many more non-nuclear households. The consequences of these distributions for the social life, demands for private goods and public services and related political activity of these areas are great. It is reasonable, then, to speak of increasing social polarisation between the inner and outer city.

This polarisation is being increased by the outward movement of nuclear families in particular, and the better-off elderly. The movement from the cities consists of suburbanisation and decentralisation beyond the built-up area to surrounding villages and small towns, from which people still commute to work in the city; movement out to rural areas from which there is no commuting; and movement to smaller towns, perhaps new or expanded ones where people also work. The process of urban to rural movement is called 'counter-urbanisation' (Chapter 10, Section 3d). It is one to which retirement moves may contribute. The move from larger to smaller towns is called 'deconcentration'. Both processes were dominant in many western countries during the 1960s and 1970s. There is a possibility that the trend slowed or for some cities reversed in the 1980s. The census results are eagerly awaited.

Many of the poorer elderly are left in the inner city areas. There are also some people moving inwards to offset out-migration. Young single people are attracted to the amenities of the central city and to the availability of low-cost housing though, in Britain, not in London. Some young professional couples also like access to the city centre where they work and perhaps do not care for suburban life-styles and houses with gardens. They have moved into many areas of London and some other British cities which were once occupied by lower income households. This process whereby areas change from lower- to higher-income people is called 'gentrification' (Chapter 13, Section 3c). It affects the demand for local goods and services and may produce social conflict between the new and the remaining population. The London Docklands is an example of such areas where new housing has been built, while Islington and Fulham are areas of older housing in London which have witnessed such a process.

Having examined the major recent demographic and household changes along the life paths and

Age	All causes	1st	2nd
Under 1	111	Perinatal causes 42	Congenital anomalies 30
1-4	5	Accidents 1	Congenital anomalies 1
5-14	2	Accidents 1	Cancer 1
15-34	6	Accidents 2	Cancer 1
35-44	15	Cancer 5	Heart disease 4
45-54	49	Cancer 18	Heart disease 17
55-64	132	Heart disease 49	Cancer 47
65-74	334	Heart disease 124	Cancer 95
Over 75	1001	Heart disease 339	Respiratory disease 195

10.12 Causes of death by age group

their associated geographies, some of the major alternative paths can now be discussed.

Early deaths

Many routes lead to early death. Abortion and miscarriages could be included as the first but certainly infant mortality (the rate of death within a year of birth) has a major impact on demographic change; so too may death through disease, accident, famine and war. In most western societies infant mortality has been gradually decreasing as general standards of health and living improve. In Britain in the early 1980s there was a brief increase, perhaps reflecting the increasing polarisation between rich and poor people and areas, with the children

10.11 Infant mortality in Detroit and other countries

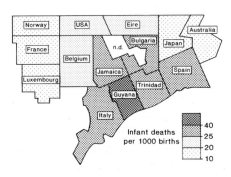

of the poor being more likely to die. Infant mortality is much higher in developing countries but in many it is decreasing (Figure 10.11).

Many childhood diseases are less likely to kill now because of vaccination, immunisation and treatment by drugs. Accidental death of children is now more probable than death by disease in most western countries (Figure 10.12).

Traffic and home accidents also account for many deaths of young people. Cancers of varying types and heart disease compose the biggest threat to the middle-aged, especially smokers. Such chronic diseases have replaced infectious diseases as the main causes of death. The geographical distribution of these diseases is complex and so are the changes in their distribution (Figure 5.12).

It is not an easy task for the health service and health education to respond to such complexity.

Disease and the environment

People's chances of dying from particular diseases vary according to where they live, because of social and physical variations in their environment. Research on Japanese migrants, for example, with controls for hereditary factors, reveals different rates of mortality from coronary heart disease in Japan, Hawaii and California, rising from first to last. The life-styles of the Japanese are different in the three places, as is shown by the differences in risk factors such as amounts of serum cholesterol, diet and uric acid (blood pressure and glucose did not differ). Similar mortality differences can occur within countries which may at least in part be due to life-styles. These are to some extent affected by social class, but even people of similar social class may live rather differently from one area to another because of regional influences on diet and stress. The physical environment may also vary, particularly in the quality of water and air. Research into geographical differences of ill-health and mortality may help identify possible causes and permit preventive action through, for example, dietary change. In the shorter term it also provides useful information on the need for health services.

Famine

Despite the global increase in food production there is enormous variation in the degree to which there is sufficient food to support local populations. In Western Europe and North America there is usually a surplus produced, though still within these regions some elements of the population suffer from malnutrition. In other parts of the world, for example East Africa, there have recently been frequent prolonged famines from which many people have died. The famines may be due mainly to climatic fluctuations or longer-term climatic change, leading to drought. They may also result from changes in agricultural practices where farmers have adopted western practices to provide cash crops for export. The new practices are often inappropriate for soil con-

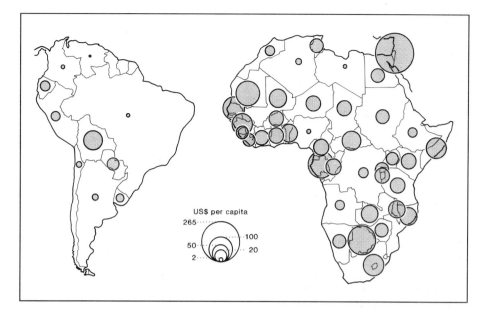

servation, with resulting desertification and famine. Some of these famines have been much publicised in western countries, which has generated major attempts at famine relief and longer-term prevention through such organisations as Oxfam, Save the Children and various popular movements such as Band Aid. All have raised the awareness of ordinary people in the generally affluent West to the plight of others elsewhere. New organisations have been formed and, new ways of giving aid have been found, producing a geography of aid (Figure 10.13).

Yet the task of reducing deaths caused by famine is a complex and major one. It highlights the general problem of matching the local supply of food, or its availability through trade, with local needs.

War

Although there has not been a major war involving so many countries since the Second World War, there have still been many, often long-lasting conflicts. Some receive major coverage in the western world because of direct involvement, such as the Korean and Vietnam wars, or indirect involvement through

10.13 The geography of aid: official development assistance, 1989

attacks on shipping and disruption to the oil trade, such as the Iran-Iraq war (Chapter 11, Section 3a) and conflicts between Arab countries and Israel. Other wars such as those in the Sudan and Angola have received less coverage.

Terrorism

Although West European countries have not experienced any wars within their territories since 1945, there has been a growth in terrorist attacks which have resulted in deaths and major injuries. These have been concentrated in areas where there are separatist movements, such as Northern Ireland and the Basque area of northern Spain (Chapter 11, Section 3b), and in major cities and their airports, such as London and Paris, where the terrorists may achieve greater publicity and disruption from their actions. Such attacks, or fears of them, may also affect international tourism, upon which many commercial activities now depend. The need to reduce the threat from terrorism has become nearly as important as the need to prevent war.

Crime

Police forces have had to respond to increased terrorist threats in addition to the growth in reported crime, particularly violent crime (Chapter 10, Section 3e). This has been another major trend leading to more deaths, more people injured and more damage to property. This increase in violence and crime in society is not understood, but there are major geographical differences in both the location of offences (Figure 10.14) and their victims, and the location of offenders (Figure 10.15).

There are also important, but not necessarily coinciding, geographical differences in the fear of violence and crime. Such fears can affect where people live, for instance not moving into certain areas or moving

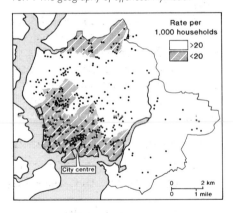

10.14 The geography of offences: Plymouth

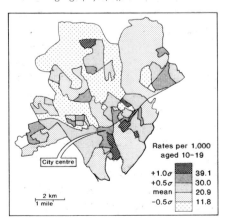

10.15 The geography of offenders: Swansea

out of them if they are able to. They can also influence people's behaviour, for example older people staying in after dark or women avoiding certain routes or areas.

Contextual and compositional effects

All these geographical differences and changes in the incidence of disease, famine, violence and crime that can be observed at various scales mean that the same type of people living in different places experience varying degrees of risk of being on an alternative shorter life path (Figure 10.9). This is a 'contextual effect', that is, it is the context or environment that is significant and not the type of person. In any one area, however, many of these risks are higher for, or particular to, certain types of people, whether this is associated with their age, gender, race, religion or social class.

The geography of some of these shorter life paths may simply reflect that some areas have more of some types of people; for example, particular illnesses may be more prevalent in an area because it has a larger proportion of female elderly. The composition of the population of an area, the 'compositional effect', is then one straightforward explanation of geographical differences. It is not the only one. As the above example of Japanese migrants shows, similar people in different areas may live in different ways and experience different degrees of risk. The Japanese were influenced by the dominant life-styles and diets of Japan, Hawaii and California and thus experienced varying risks in these three areas. In another example the differences between countries in crimes against the elderly may reflect varying societal attitudes to the elderly; in one country they may command and receive much greater respect, with their opinions and experience prized, and

consequently be less at risk and less afraid. Such differences in attitudes and styles of life in areas contribute to contextual effects. It means that the contexts of where people live are different. So two areas of similar composition (no compositional effect) may experience different risk to, say, disease and crime because of different attitudes and life-styles in the areas. These contextual effects may therefore be another explanation of geographical differences.

Changes in the social environment, then, may result from changes in the *composition* of the population of areas through, for example, migration, and from changes in the *contexts* of areas through changes in attitudes and life-styles. These may be triggered by immigration or by a variety of processes operating in the economic, technological and political environments as well as the social environment. Some of these effects will be highlighted as the geography of recent social movements and associated issues are discussed.

Social movements

Three of the major social movements of the late twentieth century are reviewed: feminists, blacks and gays/lesbians. The feminist movement has stimulated much thought about the contribution of women to society and relations between the genders, and some action on equal rights and pay (Chapter 5, Section 2, Chapter 12, Section 3). Geographers' interest revolves around the roles and relations between genders in different areas.

Feminist movement

The term, 'gender' refers to socially defined differences between men and women, as distinct from 'sex' which refers to biological ones. Different gender roles are acquired in different societies; for example, in much of sub-Saharan Africa women work in the fields growing basic subsistence crops for their families, whereas in much of Latin America women's agricultural work is confined to tending animals and food processing. What is defined as women's work in some societies, then, is done by men in others.

In many western countries, many more women follow careers and have full- or part-time employment than in the past. Some continue to be the main home makers while working full-time. In other households men take a more equal share of work in the home. The degree to which domestic tasks are shared varies between areas. In Britain it is generally less where fewer women are in employment, reflecting both a compositional and a contextual effect – that is, in these areas even the women who are employed still do most of the domestic tasks. It is also less where, given two areas of similar female activity rates, men rather than women are in positions of authority over women in their employment situations. Gender relations at work can therefore affect gender relations and roles in the home.

Career-oriented women may also affect the geography of the city. They, especially, tend to have fewer children and to return to paid employment sooner after childbirth.

This means that for some couples the ideal of suburban life, with the woman spending the daytime bringing up the family in a residential suburban area while the man commutes to work in distant employment locations, is replaced by one where the work and home are often less physically separated. With no children or a longer period before the first birth, many couples join single people in living much closer to the amenities and employment opportunities of the city centre. Such households contribute to the gentrification of inner-city areas (Chapter 13, Section 3b). Perhaps not surprisingly given the greater career opportunities, the feminist movement, like many other social movements discussed below, has been more to the fore in large cities.

Black movement

The move to obtain equal rights for women has been paralleled by that for ethnic (racial and religious) equality. Whereas there is relatively little difference between the numbers of men and women from place to place, there are often major ones between the numbers of different ethnic groups. A majority in one place may be a minority elsewhere or indeed at a different geographical scale. Race is a difficult concept to define. It has superficial biological associations with skin colour and even physique. It is also linked to area or origin. Probably the most important distinctions are cultural: differences in customs, traditions, social relations, life-styles, language and religion. Often immigrants enter particular occupations so that economic differences are superimposed upon cultural ones. Access to housing might also be constrained by income and perhaps prejudice, which may lead to residential differences. These may also result from people of a similar culture congregating together to maintain that culture, enabling access to religious buildings and to supplies of particular foods and clothes.

The waves of migration into Britain over many centuries (Chapter 10, Section 3c) brought together people from many different cultural backgrounds. Some have assimilated into the host society while others have maintained their identity, forming what has become known as a *multi-cultural* society. This has led to demands for a multi-cultural education, that is, one that reflects and informs about the many cultures making up present society rather than solely the original 'host' society. Such demands are obviously greatest in residential areas and schools where there is a mixture of cultures, so the introduction of such education has not been evenly spread across the country. Yet to achieve its ends, multi-cultural education should be carried out throughout the country.

Multi-cultural education has been rejected by some people because it does not tackle racism head-on. This is prejudice that is seen as operating overtly and covertly in employment, housing and many other areas of society. 'Anti-racist' education has been adopted in some areas in order to tackle prejudice directly. It is often accompanied by anti-sexist education. Though few can deny the differential access of some cultural groups and women to higher and further education, training and particular types of employment (Chapter 12, Section 3), some criticise the implementation if not the aims of many of these direct approaches, which can sometimes inflame rather than ameliorate social relations.

Unequal access and forms of prejudice remain problems which are unevenly distributed in themselves. Their geography is made more complicated by the uneven adoption of responses, such as multi-cultural education and anti-racism.

Gay and lesbian movement

A further major social movement emerging from the 1960s is gay and lesbian rights. Again, like feminist and black movements, it is international but has been more evident in some countries, such as the USA, and in some areas within countries, often (with gays) in very large cities. New organisations such as support groups, newspapers and meeting places have emerged for all these movements, creating a more varied geography of social amenities and social life in some areas.

Although sharing some similar characteristics, aims and geographies, these movements are separate. Even though they are categorised as 'movements' and in some cases 'communities', there are considerable social, economic and political differences within the so-called communities. It is also important to recognise that by no means every person regards themself in any way as belonging to a community. Just as with the 'elderly', it is very dangerous and misleading to class them as homogeneous groups and stereotype them in particular ways. Unfortunately the process by which a group combines to fight for a cause

in itself often encourages people outside the group to view it as homogeneous and, particularly if it uses publicity-attracting tactics, as 'a problem'. The problem is, of course, not the group but the structure and relationships in society that produce the need to fight for equal rights and the removal of prejudice in the first place.

The migration of people has brought different cultures into contact. The spatial concentration of people, by constraint or choice, has enabled cultures to be maintained or developed and given to social move-

ments both a geographical identity and sometimes a power base. These same concentrations have also often led to conflict as people outside the culture feel threatened (Chapter 7, Section 2) by what they do not understand. Societies can be enriched by additional cultures and sub-cultures. They can also be riven by conflict as in South Africa, where one culture has tried to remain dominant and to subjugate others. Tolerance of others is not equally distributed over space or time.

10.3 Other examples

The first two examples examine either end of the life path, first studying further geographical issues associated with the increased number of elderly people, secondly the effects on schools of changes in the

birth rate. The third and fourth examples concern migration both between countries and within them. Migration between countries involves some of the issues related to multi-cultural societies, while inter-

nal migration contrasts rural-urban and urban-rural movements within different types of countries. Finally, a range of strategies for reducing crime are reviewed.

10.3a Wider impacts of an ageing population

As elderly people have become an increasingly larger proportion of the population, they have become a considerable political force not least because of the work of Jack Jones in the UK (a former union leader and now a leading representative of the elderly's cause). Indeed, 25 per cent of the voting population of the UK is now at or beyond the usual retirement ages. Furthermore, the voluntary organisations Age Concern and Help the Aged, which act as pressure and support groups, are exerting increasing influence on public opinion. The impact of the elderly on public services has been considerable. Something like one seventh of all government expenditure in the UK in the 1980s was absorbed by retirement pensions and other related benefits. Similarly, elderly people consume 40 per cent of the total national budget for health and other

social services. These include night nurses and other medical support, nursing homes and meals on wheels. Elderly people are not just a cost to society, however; they also contribute positively to it. For instance, their present expenditure keeps many local retailers viable, they keep many post offices open and many voluntary bodies and committees are staffed by retired people.

Geographical concentrations of the elderly

In the 1960s and 1970s the elderly were seen more as a problem but in the 1980s increasingly they were seen as an opportunity, an expanding market to which the private sector has responded. So, for instance, private health facilities and nursing/residential homes boomed, as did the number and range of private

sheltered accommodation. SAGA, the over sixties' travel company, continued to expand. Certain financial services such as insurance broking and annuities on houses for the elderly have grown, and housekeepers/domestic helps have been increasingly employed by the wealthier elderly. Indeed, this 'grey market' is being targeted more and more by the business world as one where there is substantial demand and disposable income. As the elderly market has expanded, so too, sadly, has the criminal opportunity to exploit the old and helpless. This includes confidence tricksters, housebreakers, muggers and a few unscrupulous and exploitative nursing/rest homes.

A related social/demographic trend in western countries has been early retirement in both the public and private sectors, especially during the recession of the early 1980s. Employees or the self-employed either consciously opt for earlier retirement or they are given little choice but to retire early, to give way to younger people or not be replaced at all. In some cases the employees are very happy to accept early retirement which can be made highly attractive. The geographical impacts of early retirement are not dissimilar to those of the elderly since it can involve house moves and a need for certain goods and services to which the public and private sectors have to respond.

10.3b **The impacts on schools of a falling birth rate**

The other key demographic change in developed world countries is their striking reduction in birth rates. In the 1980s in North America the birth rate (number of live births per 1000 people per year) was seventeen and in Europe sixteen, whereas in Africa it was forty-six and Latin America thirty-seven. Whereas a hundred years or so ago in Britain there were many families with over four children, today the usual number per family is one or two. This demographic downswing is partly to do with fashion and social expectation – that is, a higher quality of life is increasingly expected and this cannot easily be achieved with many children. It is also partly related to couples postponing having children and to the conscious decision of some couples not to have children at all.

In the shorter term there are also fluctuations in birth rates which the public and private sectors have to adjust to. A good example of this is the need for the school system to adjust to decreased enrolment. In particular, it has meant closures and amalgamations of schools even though some would argue there was a lost opportunity to reduce class sizes. The desire in the 1980s to cut public expenditure ensured closure as against reduced class sizes. As the smaller cohorts of children passed through the system, this led first to primary and then to secondary schools being closed. Since 1981 on average about fifty schools per year have been closed in England and Wales. The decision as to which schools to close or amalgamate can be politically sensitive for local education authorities (LEAs).

This alongside recent restructuring and reorganisation of schools, particularly for the establishment of institutions for sixteen to nineteen year olds, has meant a great deal of local political ferment. In general, the over or fully subscribed schools have survived, as have those (often the same) which have middle-class and vocal parental support. The strength of community opposition has often swayed a political decision. In Manchester, for instance, in June 1982, 45 out of 162 primary schools were planned to close according to the City Council Plan. This amounted to a loss of 20 per cent of the then existing number of pupil places. After a period of public consultation and intense local political debate an amended plan was submitted to the Secretary of State for Education, who approved a reduction in the number of schools by 34. He allowed all but one of the schools to close. Interestingly, it appeared that the most disadvantaged parts of the city, the central and eastern areas, bore the brunt of the contraction. The local population in those areas participated less in the decision making process and when they did, they were notably less successful in preventing closure than the middle-class parents of the suburban schools (Chapter 7, Section 4).

At first sight this contraction in school places might appear to have been confined to inner-city areas where populations have certainly declined in recent years. However, even the expanding metropolitan ring around London faced the same phenomenon. Buckinghamshire, the fastest-growing local authority in the 1970s, is one such county. In 1983 it had permanent provision for 12,575 children in its seventeen secondary schools. However, only 10,700 children attended those schools and by 1997 it has been estimated that the secondary school population will be only 8800 pupils. This represents a decline in the secondary school population of 18 per cent. It has been argued that at least five schools have to be closed in the near future on cost grounds. A reduction of 2000 places, for example, would have saved £250,000 in teacher costs and £350,000 in building-related costs.

There are various implications of these trends on people and environments. The schools that close have to be sold or put to other uses. Some become offices, as Marylebone Grammar School has become the regional office of ASDA; some are sold to private schools, such as Cardinal Newman School in west London which has become a Japanese School; others are sold for housing development. The demographic downturn has also begun to affect the higher education sector and this alongside political factors has led to the closure of certain campus sites, for example Bedford College in Central London which has been sold to an American college. Similarly, many teacher training colleges have been closed and/or amalgamated and buildings/sites used for a variety of other purposes. The human impact of such closures has been considerable. On the one hand, staff have taken early retirement or have been encouraged to move away, and on the other hand pupils have had to travel greater distances to other schools and colleges. So the geography of education in this country is being rapidly transformed to the advantage of some and disadvantage of others.

This can be explained only partly by demographic factors, but a considerable concern is how the system will adapt to a birth rate upturn which happened in the mid 1980s. Readjustments in systems take

place slowly and it could well be that education has adapted to a population geography which has already changed and moved on!

10.3c Migration: a component of social and demographic change

Migration, that is the permanent or semi-permanent change of residence made by people for a variety of reasons, is a long-established geographical process. Migrants are important social actors who in themselves can change the demographic and social environment of areas. Over the centuries migrations have had massive global effects, particularly in North America, Australia, parts of Latin America and the Soviet Union. The long-term history of Europe and Asia is littered with large-scale movements of people including the Romans, Arabs and Saxons. In the nineteenth and twentieth centuries Western European migrations to colonial territories were most significant. Migration is also a contemporary phenomenon.

To make sense of the great variety of such movements in population, it is helpful to classify them.

Figure 10.16 shows some dimensions by which migrations may be

10.16 Dimensions on which migrations can be classified

classified. Local migrations can involve relocating one's household to a different but adjoining district, whereas international movements suggest a longer-distance relocation. Some migrations are temporary, for instance for work for a period, whereas others are permanent moves. Some moves are imposed and forced, such as the expulsion of some Jews from the Soviet Union. Others are of free will, such as emigration to Australia from Europe (apart from the earliest moves!). Some migrations are on an individual level where one person relocates to a new area or country, whereas others are whole family movements such as those for a new life in the 'New World' of Australasia. Some migrations are politically motivated, such as the forced movement of black people into the Bantustans of South Africa. Other movements are economically underpinned, such as when they are caused by the search for work, for instance within Britain to the South East in the early 1980s. There have been moves by highly

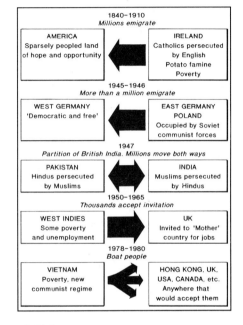

10.17 Great migrations

skilled people, such as the so-called 'brain drain' from the UK to the USA of doctors and scientists. In contrast, the movement of relatively poorly educated Afro-Caribbeans into Britain in the 1950s was encouraged to fill unskilled jobs in the public and private sectors (Chapter 12, Section 3).

Finally, some migrations can be of massive scale, such as the millions moving between Pakistan and India as a result of partition in 1947 (Figure 10.17). Others can involve just small numbers relocating to another district. Clearly a variety of motives underlies migration such as the movements of refugees (Figure 10.18). There can be 'push' factors such as poverty, war, religion, oppression and racism, or 'pull' factors such as demand for labour, higher standards of living and more

Temporal and spatial	Temporary _____ Permanent
	Contemporary _____ Historic
	Short distance_____ Long distance
	Intra-national_____ Inter-national
Nature of process	Rural-urban_____ Urban-rural
	Push dominated _____ Pull dominated
	Political _____ Economic
	Forced _____ Free-will
Characteristics of migrants	Individual (small nos.) _____ Mass (large nos.)
	Highly educated _____ Ill educated
	Young_____ Old
	Men _____ Women
	Women (of child bearing age_____ Women (beyond child bearing age)
	or younger)

Country	Number	Origin
Brazil	27 000	Europe
Argentina	30 000	Europe
Bangladesh	200 000	Burma
Pakistan	314 000	Afghanistan
Iran	135 000	Afghanistan
China	250 000	Vietnam
Thailand	720 000	Indo-China
Malaysia	42 000	Indo-China
Indonesia	41 000	Indo-China
Hong Kong	62 000	Indo-China
Algeria	52 000	Latin America, Africa
Djibouti	20 000	Ethiopia
Ethiopia	619 000	Sudan
Somalia	1 000 000	Ethiopia
Sudan	400 000	Ethiopia, Uganda, Chad, Zaire
Zaire	653 000	Angola, Burundi, Rwanda, South Africa
Mozambique	150 000	Zimbabwe
Botswana	20 000	Zimbabwe, Angola, Namibia, South Africa
Zambia	80 000	Zimbabwe, Angola, Namibia, South Africa, Ethiopia, Zaire, Uganda
Angola	160 000	Zaire, Namibia
Burundi	50 000	Rwanda
Uganda	112 000	Rwanda, Zaire
Cameroon	30 000	Equatorial Guinea
Gabon	80 000	Equatorial Guinea
West Bank (Israel)	318 000	Palestine
Gaza Strip (Israel)	363 000	Palestine
Lebanon	219 000	Palestine
Jordan	700 000	Palestine
Syria	203 000	Palestine
Honduras and Costa Rica	100 000	Nicaragua

10.18 The movement of refugees during the 1980s

attractive environments.

Different migrations involve contrasting actors, agencies, policies, motives and geographical impacts. Here the case studies will concentrate on migrant workers, and recent immigration to the UK and later rural-urban and urban-rural movements in the developing and developed worlds.

Migrant workers

Migrant workers, or guest workers as they are called in Europe, are a response to economic factors. The better-off European countries have since the Second World War required unskilled labour to staff essential services and manufacturing such as the car industry. People from the poorer parts of southern Europe and North Africa, where unemployment and underemployment are high, have been attracted to relatively well-paid work especially in West Germany and France. These people, often single and semi-literate men, occupied poor-quality housing and took on the lowest-paid jobs. They have become the focus for fascist, nationalistic and violent anti-immigrant campaigns which have at times led to riots such as those involving Algerians in Marseilles (Chapter 7, Section 7d). They were originally encouraged by the host countries (as well as by the manufacturing companies) to fill the employment needs of the time. Some of the greatest concentrations have emerged in Germany (over 7 per cent of the total population with mainly Turks, Yugoslavs and Italians), France (over 7 per cent of total population with mainly Portuguese, Algerians, Spaniards and Italians), and Switzerland (over 14 per cent of total population with mainly Italians). This movement has been slowed and even reversed in recent years as opposition to such immigration has grown and economies have less need for such labour. Social and political tension has been fuelled partly by racism and economic jealousies.

Similar semi-permanent, mainly male immigrants flocked to the industrial and mining cities in South Africa such as Johannesburg from the black homelands and neighbouring countries such as Botswana, to gain from the available employment and high wages. The social effects on the families they leave can be substantial, as can be the impacts, social and economic, on the areas of both origin and destination.

Recent immigration to the UK

Immigration to the UK is far from a recent phenomenon. The present population is a complex mixture derived from successive arrivals (indeed often invasions) of foreign peoples. The Saxons were a significant group but by no means the first. In turn Romans, Vikings and Normans have crossed the oceans to live here. More recent immigrations have been more peaceful and include a range of Europeans escaping war, persecution and intolerance (Jews and Poles) and poverty (Irish), and peoples from further afield, usually from former colonies such as the West Indies and the Indian sub-continent. Over time the amount of immigration has varied, partly as a result of changing governmental controls. Usually the new arrivals concentrated in particular parts of the inner areas of large cities, while others dispersed. In some cases the local moves have been distinctly sectoral. In the case of some Jewish people in London, for instance, in the early nineteenth century concentrations were in the east with later spread westwards and northwards particularly to Golders Green, and more recently further north-west well into the metropolitan ring (Figure 10.19).

Concentrations of nationals and ethnic groupings have emerged in London particularly since the war. Southall in west London has a concentration of people from the Indian sub-continent, whereas Brixton in south London has a concentration of Afro-Caribbeans. Other noteworthy concentrations are Irish in Kilburn, Australians in Earls Court and

10.19 The spread of London's Jewish population

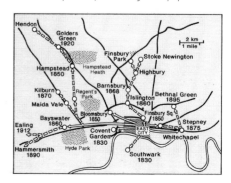

British Asians in Southall

Poles in Ealing. Understandably, once a concentration has become marked it attracts others of similar nationality and ethnicity. Most of the new groups recently arrived in Britain have located in large cities where many were employed in often unskilled jobs in the public sector and private industry (Chapter 12, Section 3c). The entrepreneurial skills of people from the Indian sub-continent and East Africa as shop-keepers, and Chinese, Greek, Italians and Indians as restaura-teurs, has aided the dispersal of these groups into smaller towns across the country.

Sadly these recent migrations have been beset with problems, resulting partly from the racial prej-udice, ignorance and intolerance of some of the host population. Newcomers in some cases have been trapped socially and economically in certain areas and walks of life, and ghetto-like concentrations have developed in some inner cities. Infamous incidents such as the riots in Brixton, St Pauls, Bristol and Broadwater Farm in north London speak loudly of racial intolerance and a divided society. Of particular concern has been the emergence of what some see as a cycle of depriva-tion in some of the UK's inner cities where migrants form a high propor-tion of the population. Fears of fur-ther large-scale immigration, fanned by the right wing, have been partic-ularly felt by the communities neighbouring existing concentra-tions who are afraid of invasion of their residential areas and competi-tion for jobs. Some people more dis-tant from immigrant communities are equally prejudiced and respond to stereotypes rather than personal interaction. However, too much can be made of the negative aspects of recent migrations. In many ways, as through the centuries, migrants have contributed positively to chang-ing society. British culture has been enriched by different languages, cus-toms, foods, clothes, music, festivals and the like. At the same time the economy has been supported by additional available labour. Many aspects of cultural life have also been boosted, including sport, enter-tainment, the arts, and religious and public life.

The tension for first- and particu-larly second-generation immigrants is the degree to which they are total-ly assimilated (their own culture is lost as they take on that of the host society), integrated (where they retain much of their culture but assume some of that of the host soci-ety) or segregated (where they remain almost completely culturally separated from the host society). Different members of a family may be in different positions along the continuum from assimilation to seg-regation. For example, women who do not speak English, may be subject to religious customs and home-bound by young children, may find themselves segregated from the men.

A recent and interesting group of semi-permanent immigrants to the UK have been the Japanese. In par-ticular, management has been attracted to work and live in differ-ent parts of the country wherever Japanese-owned factories and finan-cial institutions have been estab-lished (Chapter 8). Also, since the 'Big Bang' (the deregulation of the Stock Exchange in 1986) Japanese working in the financial sector have moved to west London where they can take public transport into the city and are near to the recently established Japanese School in London. Local and Japanese retail-ers have been quick to meet the new demands of this group by opening new shops and extending their range of goods sold at existing stores. Similarly, a special estate agency has been established to serve the housing, rental and ownership needs of the west London Japanese. The extent to which these recently arrived Japanese will remain dis-tinct and/or integrate with the host community is not yet known. Nor are the geographical consequences of migrants from member countries of the European Community, who are expected to increase after the removal of trade barriers in 1993.

10.3d **Urbanisation and counter-urbanisation; two contrasting trends**

Urbanisation is both the measure of the proportion of a nation's popula-tion living in urban places and the process by which it increases. It was especially rapid in developed coun-tries during the industrial revolu-tion and the first half of the twenti-eth century. Recently it has been much more characteristic of the developing world. Urbanisation can result from the differential natural increase in population in urban and

City	Period	Total increase in population (ooos)	Migrants as % of total increase
Bombay	1951-61	1207	52
Caracas	1960-66	501	50
Djakarta	1961-68	1528	59
Istanbul	1960-65	428	65
Lagos	1952-62	393	75
Sao Paulo	1960-67	2543	68
Seoul	1955-65	1697	63

10.20 Estimates of migration as a percentage of population increases in cities

rural areas and/or rural to urban migration (Figure 10.20).

This social and demographic process is of major significance in Africa, Latin America and Asia whose cities are growing much faster than those of Europe and North America (Figure 10.21).

Djakarta, for example, the capital city of Indonesia, is growing at over 200,000 people a year.

The push and pull factors can help our understanding of this process (Figure 10.22). Push factors encourage people to leave the land, and pull factors encourage out-migration, which is often selective consisting primarily of young, more able, single males. This move from rural areas to very large cities, often by-passing many small and medium-sized ones, is very important in understanding the changing geography of population in most countries of the developing world.

The environmental and human impacts of this rural-urban process

10.21 Populations of the top ten world urban agglomerations in 1900 and 1970 and estimates for 2000

are often seen as negative. There are shanty towns, some infested with disease and most lacking in adequate services. There is often a break-down of the urban infrastructure including water, sewage, sanitation, housing, power and transport. There are too few jobs in the formal economy to absorb the migrants, which leads to an expanding informal economy, under-employment and unemployment (Chapter 4, Section 2). These all paint a bleak downward spiralling picture. However, many recent studies warn against this one-sided view (Figure 10.23). For instance, the quality of urban life may well be better than the rural life the migrant left . Also, 'barriados' (Latin American shanty towns) are not always areas of deprivation, extreme poverty or disease. Many tend to be well organised and not the first destination of recent immigrants, which tends to be rented accommodation in city centres where there are even greater problems.

On the other hand, many countries in the developed world have experienced a quite different social and demographic process. This was first observed in the USA where, after 200 years of urbanisation when

cities in general had grown in size, large cities began to decline in population and more people were moving out of them than were moving in (in the 1970s, for every 100 moving in 131 moved out). Since the cities were declining and many people were moving to rural areas, this was termed 'counter-urbanisation'. In addition to the urban to rural movement, there were two other significant trends. Many people continued to decentralise from the cities. For some this involved a move from the central cities to the suburbs. For others it meant a move from the outer suburbs beyond the continuous built-up area to small towns that were functionally connected to the large city, where they often continued to work. The other significant trend was towards small towns and cities that were independent of large cities. The growth of small towns and decline of large cities is called 'deconcentration' but is often, rather confusingly, included within the umbrella term of counter urbanisation.

This change from urbanisation to counterurbanisation did not occur suddenly. Decentralisation has been going on for many years. The move towards rural areas from which there is no or little commuting to large cities, however, is relatively new. For the first time for many decades, these areas grew faster than the national average during the 1970s. Some regard this move to rural areas as a search for a bucolic ideal (Arcadia). In the USA writers refer to a return to the frontier and backwoodsman ideal of the eighteenth and early nineteenth centuries. Others point to the activity of developers buying up cheap rural land and greatly increasing its value by creating prestigious low density residential areas for rich people. Some writers therefore emphasise demand factors, while others concentrate on those of supply. In demand-based explanations, people respond to differences in space, escaping the cities for the rural

1900		1970		2000	
London	6.48	New York	16.3	Mexico City	31.6
New York	4.24	Tokyo-Yokohama	14.9	Tokyo-Yokohama	26.1
Paris	3.33	London	10.5	Sao Paulo	26.0
Berlin	2.42	Shanghai	10.0	New York	22.2
Chicago	1.72	Rhine-Ruhr	9.3	Calcutta	19.7
Vienna	1.66	Mexico City	8.6	Rio de Janeiro	19.4
Tokyo	1.50	Paris	8.4	Shanghai	19.2
St. Petersburg	1.44	Los Angeles	8.4	Bombay	19.1
Philadelphia	1.42	Buenos Aires	8.3	Peking	19.1
Manchester	1.26	Sao Paulo	7.8	Seoul	18.7

Push factors	Pull factors
Imbalance between resources and population numbers ie overpopulation, underemployment and unemployment	A range of perceived job opportunities including those in transnationals
Poverty and low wages	Opportunity to earn better wages
Unfavourable physical environment for agricultural production	Better provision of housing, education and other community facilities
Agricultural change, including declining markets for exported cash crops, modernisation and land reform	The 'lure' of the cultural, recreational and intellectual activities of a large metropolis
Break-up of traditional communities and social ties, partly produced by selective out-migration	
Lack of social services such as education and housing	

10.22 Push and pull factors in rural to urban migration

ideal; in supply-based explanations, differences in space are created in order to increase profitability, and to some extent demand is created by marketing that emphasises the pastoral nature and the prestige of the area.

Large cities have declined in terms of employment as well as population. Again, small towns and some rural areas have seen marked increases in employment opportunities. Characteristically population decentralised first, later followed by employment. The growth of small towns that are not connected by commuting to larger cities, however, may have seen employment growth that was simultaneous with or even preceded population growth.

In the USA there was also a regional shift from the cities of the North-East and Mid-West which tended to decline, to those of the South and West, many of which rapidly expanded. Some of their expansion represented retirement moves, for example to Phoenix and many parts of Florida. Some was due partly to the scenic attraction of the areas, such as the mountains of Colorado. The resources of Colorado and Southern Texas were further reasons for growth. To highlight the migration change, it is worth noting that the number of blacks moving to northern cities from the South in the 1970s was exceeded by the number moving south out of the northern cities.

Counter urbanisation and particularly deconcentration have also been observed in many European

countries. In Britain the government policy of creating New and Expanded Towns in part accounts for decentralisation and deconcentration into smaller towns. Retirement moves have also contributed to the growth of small towns and coastal areas. Employment has also expanded in smaller towns (Chapter 12, Section 2) stimulating further population growth. This has particularly been the case for the metropolitan ring around London.

While such rings have continued to grow around London and other cities, such as Paris, there are signs that counter urbanisation slowed during the 1980s. This may be due partly to the revitalisation of some inner parts of cities, a process which was carried out in order to reverse the decline of the cities as a whole, not just their inner areas. Again some writers argue that such revitalisation is due to the search for higher profits, while others see a swing back to the appeal of urban life styles. The marketing of place, which both creates and reflects demand, has emphasised the cultural opportunities, the social activities and the employment possibilities of cities. The 1980s' image of the young urban professional living in the converted warehouse apartment summarised the appeal.

Whether large cities permanently halt their decline or whether they can only reduce its speed remains to be seen.

10.3e **Geography of crime**

Earlier retirement and greater longevity in the developed world can be seen generally as social 'goods' whereas the widespread increase in crime can be seen as one of society's 'bads'. Unravelling the components and complexities of the spatial and environmental elements of crime can help to reduce the problem.

Broadly, most crime can be classified into two major types: crimes against the person which can involve physical and sexual violence, and crimes against property such as arson and burglary. 'White collar' crime is another type which has often been neglected in geographical studies. It includes financial fraud which has

occurred over share dealing in the City of London.

The spatial incidence of most types of crime is uneven at whatever scale it is analysed. Certain housing areas are notoriously crime ridden at the most local scale, whereas at the national level certain regions and cities experience more crime

Johnathan Dimbleby reports from Sao Paulo

Brazil's 'miracle' crushes the poor

We walked through the children's hospital in Sao Paulo. We had driven there from the centre past great international banks and glossy shopping centres, along crowded freeways which criss-crossed South America's biggest and richest city.

The doctor turned back the covers on the cot. At once we were back in Third World: Ethiopia, Bangladesh or Biafra: emaciated bodies, wide eyes in wizened faces, starving children. Yet this was Brazil, not a disaster, but, according to the legend, a miracle.

Risk of arrest

The astonishing economic progress has been largely financed by foreign investment which flourished in the industrial atmosphere which only generals can create – free from strikes which were illegal, free from political activity which was eliminated, and free from free speech.

Why were the children in this condition? The doctor lowered his voice, and asked that we not mention his name: 'The root cause of 90% of the sickness in this hospital is poverty. Economic miracle? It's a human disaster.'

In Sao Paulo, which has accumulated wealth beyond the imagination of most of Brazil's people, a small élite lives in bliss while at least half the population – perhaps seven million – live more than 50% below the minimum subsistence level as defined by the State itself.

They live in rough, homemade houses on the outskirts of the city or in the slums and shanty towns that cluster like warts around the factories where, in the years of the miracle, more wealth has been created than almost anywhere else on earth.

Today a labourer must work twice as many hours to earn the same real wage as 15 years ago.

Then it took 40 minutes' labour to buy a kilo of beans; now it takes more than four hours. Then, it took three hours to buy a kilo of meat; now it takes eight hours.

And in Sao Paulo, poverty kills; each day in the city's largest cemetery they bury 40 children in rows of specially prepared miniature graves: each year they bury more children than adults.

In desperation, thousands of families are forced to abandon their children. In Sao Paulo alone, some 600 000 boys and girls, ranging in age from six to sixteen live rough on the streets, begging, stealing or prostituting themselves to survive.

The reply from the Brazilian Ambassador in London the following week

Flocking to live in squalor

Your article deals with the problems of poverty, squalor and destitution in the biggest Brazilian conurbation – Sao Paulo – which now encompasses about 12 million people.

If I did not know Sao Paulo and had not devoted many years of my life to study its development, the article would have made upon me an impression like that caused in their time, by the writing of Engels, Dickens and Disraeli on mid-nineteenth-century Manchester, which was then at the peak of its industrial revolution, just as Sao Paulo is now the throbbing core of Brazilian industry.

The population of this metropolitan area more than trebled between 1950 and 1970; only one third was due to natural growth and the rest to internal migration.

More than half a million people have headed each year for Sao Paulo from rural areas – this is the equivalent of adding almost one Manchester or two Southamptons.

Staggering investment in the urban infrastructure of housing, sanitation, schools and hospitals would be required to prevent poverty and squalor.

The average national indicators, which include areas much poorer than Sao Paulo, show that the proportion of families earning not more than one minimum wage fell from 16 million in 1970 to 12,700,000 in 1976. And the average life expectancy, which is a good overall measure of social improvement, rose from 59 years in 1973 to 63 years in 1978.

This is not to deny that unacceptable social and income inequalities remain in Brazil, and they are particularly poignant and visible among the migrants that flock to the big conurbations, lured by the lights of the city and the 'satanic mills' of industry.

I am reminded of the saying that 'one of the best ways of telling a lie is to select the wrong truth'.

10.23 Two views on the growth of Sao Paulo

than others (Figures 10.24 and 10.25).

Knowledge of the spatial incidence of crime is useful for policing strategies such as neighbourhood watch schemes (Chapter 6, Section 5). Some researchers think that the areas of high crime incidence may

10.24 Regional crime rates in England and Wales, 1981

Region	Property crimes per 10 000 households	Personal crimes per 10 000 people
Wales	3876	1061
North	5728	735
North West	4294	1872
Yorkshire/Humberside	5156	1090
West Midlands	3706	1346
East Midlands	5163	1350
East Anglia	1776	1294
South West	3159	1120
South East	3606	1212
Total	4038	1266

Crime type	Inner city[1]	Elsewhere	Proportion of victims resident in inner city[2]
Property crimes			
Vandalism	10.2	9.2	7.6
Theft from motor vehicles	7.3	5.4	9.0
Burglary	8.4	3.1	16.9
Theft of motor vehicles	2.7	1.3	13.2
Bicycle theft	1.5	1.1	9.3
Theft in dwelling	0.6	0.5	7.8
Other household theft	7.1	5.5	8.7
Personal crimes			
Common assault	2.5	2.3	7.3
Theft from persons	3.1	0.9	20.6
Wounding	1.1	0.7	10.2
Robbery	1.9	0.2	44.2
Sexual offences	0.3	0.1	27.3
Other personal theft	5.2	3.1	10.5

1 As defined by a classification of parliamentary constituencies given in Webber (1978)
2 Overall 6.8% of respondents (victims and non-victims together) live in inner-city locations
Source: First British Crime Survey, weighted data

10.25 The inner cities and crime: percentage of households/persons victimised by property/personal crimes

benefit from modifications of the built environment to reduce opportunities for crime, such as the removal of overhead walkways which can act as escape routes and increasing the degree to which entrance ways may be overlooked.

Sociologists, criminologists and others have been grappling for years with the causes of crime, which are many and complexly related. Contributory factors include: personal and family distress and unhappiness; alcohol; high unemployment; poor housing; social mores and alienation in general. Particular places and people (as both victims and perpetrators) seem more at risk than others.

The impacts of crime are of course felt directly by the victims whether it is financial (loss of property), psychological (fear) or physical (injury), and also indirectly by the wider community, such as the residents of an area through increased fear and perhaps declining property values or the various employees of the social services serving that area. The environments in which crimes are committed can also be affected via damage or vandalism and can contribute to or simply reflect a downward spiral of neglect and decline.

Various individual and community responses can be made to the threat of occurrence of crime. These can be reactive, protective or preventative, as Figure 10.26 shows.

Unfortunately some measures,

such as neighbourhood watch schemes, can suffer from declining effectiveness over time. There may also be displacement whereby the problem is shifted to an adjoining area which is less well protected, or other types of crimes are committed.

A good example of one way in which geographical information can help fight crime is illustrated by the case of North Tyneside. In particular Killingworth New Town and Longbenton on the eastern fringe of Newcastle-upon-Tyne have been the locations for a Home Office project. Longbenton, with 33 per cent unemployment in 1987, is a traditional post-war council estate of about 400 dwellings which has always had its share of crime, mainly property offences. Killingworth was completed in the early 1970s but has a central area of housing blocks which have already gone through a process of urban decay usually associated with much older developments. It is an unpopular housing area and new tenants have found themselves in an increasingly impersonal and hostile environment. Crime, social disorder and solvent abuse have flourished, increasing fear among the inhabitants and the burden of work on

10.26 Examples of individual and collective responses to crime

	Individual	Collective
Reactive	Report to police Victim retaliation Bystander intervention Move from area Write to MP/councillor/local paper	Victim support groups Petitions to local MP and press
Protective	Self defence courses Alarms Security system Night watchmen Insurance Avoidance behaviour	Neighbourhood Watch Creation of defensible space/territoriality Vigilantism Community policing: police walk around area/change policing
Preventive	Support and join local action group Support law and order moves	Improve social and economic environment Broadly based neighbourhood organisations Change policing

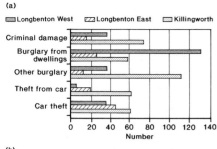

(a)

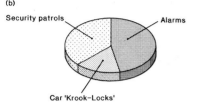

(b)

10.27 *Longbenton's crime profile and possible solutions*

agencies such as the police and social services. The crime reduction project adopted a 'protective' approach, that is the removal of the opportunity to commit local crime by quick, cost-effective measures, as against longer-term preventive social measures. A key first step was to develop a geographical information system (GIS) which was based on detailed social and commercial surveys as well as questionnaires

completed by offenders (Figure 10.27). Then a much more detailed crime profile of the area was compiled than was possible from the usual police crime reports. So, for instance, although it was realised that residential burglary was a problem at Longbenton, it had not previously been realised that 70 per cent of burglars entered premises through ground-floor windows and doors, many of which had been left open. A comprehensive computerised GIS was created for residential burglary; burglary in other buildings; theft of and from cars; and criminal damage. The GIS became a forceful tool in persuading bodies to invest in crime protection in the area; for example, the local authority housing committee immediately allocated sums towards the protection of ground-floor flats at Longbenton. Geographical targets for crime, such as the new commuter car parks servicing the Tyneside Metro rapid transit system, were revealed to agencies, together with a demographic breakdown and a full description as to the nature, timing, targets of offences and prospective offenders. The net effect over eigh-

Crime	% reduction
Burglary from dwellings	23
Non residential burglary	51
Theft of vehicle	13
Criminal damage	19
Theft from vehicle	11

10.28 *Effects of protective measures in Longbenton*

teen months of having protective measures and a comprehensive geographical database was a reduction in crime (Figure 10.28). Other factors, however, have been involved such as a greater presence of police in the areas.

This project's particular success has been in helping to pinpoint some obvious problems of crime within a community and thereby to focus on effective short-term solutions. It will be interesting to discover if any 'displacement' of such crime takes place to nearby areas and whether such policies have longer-term effects. They do not tackle the question of why people are prone to offend. They only reduce the opportunity to offend.

10.4 **Alternative strategies**

Three major strategies are reviewed in this section. The first concerns individuals and households and their mobility; the second the degree to which certain types of people are concentrated or dispersed, or segregated or mixed, within the population as a whole; and finally the type of response to various social issues which may vary from reaction or protection to prevention.

Move or stay?

One of the key geographical deci-

10.29 *Move or stay?*

	Move	Stay
Growing family	To larger house with extra bedroom and/or playroom To area where better schooling available	Add an extra bedroom and/or playroom on to the existing house (where physically possible and planning permits); older children like present school and have good friends locally
Widowed person over 75	To more suitable accommodation (eg easier to care for garden and home or sheltered accommodation with warden care); present home is difficult/costly to maintain (house and garden); preferred area of retirement (eg coastal, rural)	Can adjust present home to make more suitable; contains good memories; established local friends and neighbours; accustomed to and likes physical and built environment
Divorcee	Mixed memories of present home; cannot afford present house; new start in new area	Moving itself is another traumatic experience; needs available local support and friendship; children well settled in school

sions which people take affecting their and other people's lives is whether to move from or stay in their homes. This can be associated with a change in personal circumstances, such as retirement. Here the decision is between staying in the family house or moving to a different kind of dwelling, perhaps in a new area. It can be associated with a loss of job, with the decision being either to stay and search for a new one in the same area or to move to an area or even country where there are greater job opportunities. The decision may have been prompted by a threat to the local environment (Chapter 7, Section 2), with the possibility of staying and opposing the change (voice) or moving (exit) to avoid it (Chapter 7, Section 4). The local environment may have become more intolerant of, say, religious differences, perhaps even becoming threatening. In such cases, mass rather than individual movement might occur. The opportunity to make a choice and the range of choice are not the same for everyone. Some have little income or accumulated wealth and cannot afford to move. Some live in areas where it is difficult to sell their house or it would sell at a price too low to allow access to housing in a preferred area. Others cannot afford to own their house and cannot obtain suitably priced rented accommodation in other areas.

Where there is some possibility of choice, the factors affecting the decision to move or stay include those associated with the house itself as well as with the local area. Figure 10.29 gives examples associated with decisions to move or stay for families that are growing, divorcing couples and widowed individuals who are over seventy-five. For example, can the house be modified to fit changing circumstances? The house might have great meaning to the person, embodying a collection of memories which would be lost if that person moved. Similarly an individual might have particular attach-

ment to the place, to the physical environment, the rolling hills and valleys modified by farming practices over the centuries perhaps, or the social environment of family and friends. They might enjoy the access to particular amenities which are present in that area.

Controls on mobility

The above decisions concern individual people or households at some point along their life paths. The following strategies involve various organisations, some of them governmental, and their treatment of individuals and social groups at different positions along their life paths. One such strategy relates to whether people move or stay, or more generally their spatial mobility. Can they move freely or will their

movement be controlled? Some governments at particular times have controlled people's movement. In the USSR in the 1930s under Stalin there was forced migration to Siberia and the Arctic. Later in the 1960s and 1970s there were unsuccessful attempts to limit the size of Moscow and Leningrad by controlling immigration. Even in Britain, during the miners' strike of the mid-1980s Kentish miners were not allowed to drive through the Dartford tunnel to travel to the northern coalfields.

Concentrate or disperse?

A second major geographical strategic question is whether to develop policies that concentrate people or

10.30 Concentrate or disperse?

	Concentration	Dispersal
Elderly	Mutual care and support; easier monitoring of welfare eg sheltered accommodation, mobile warden; efficient service delivery; specialised services and amenities possible given concentrated local demand	Able to stay in own homes which may be amended to make more suitable; support from local community of mixed age; can play active role in mixed community through voluntary sector involvement
Mentally ill	Easily monitored and easy to give specialist care; if mentally ill are seen as a threat to the rest of the community, then separation reduces the threat. Against – institutionalises people making it more difficult to rehabilitate back into society.	Integrated within the community and part of it; mental illness seen as any other illness, not as something that carries a stigma; instills greater understanding in the community; easier rehabilitation Against – seen too often as cheaper option, when service not fully delivered, but if properly carried out may be as expensive as asylum typ
Petty criminal	Obvious punishment in prison, used as deterrent to others; potential to retrain and change ideas; easy monitoring and control Against – centre of learning of other criminal behaviour, sharing of criminal skills; more difficult to rehabilitate; institutionalisation; greater likelihood of re-offending	Punishment within the community to fit the crime; easier to work on rehabilitation; less chance of re-offending or learning criminal skills Against – more difficult to monitor or control (electronic tagging regarded by some as dehumanising; probation service would have to control in addition to rehabilitate, making the latter more difficult; seen as soft option by some; some say advocated because cheaper rather than better.

those that disperse them. This is associated with ideas about isolating them from or integrating them within the community; for example, the non-violent mentally ill may be isolated in mental homes or integrated through community health facilities (Chapter 7, Section 3e), and petty criminals may be put into prisons or rehabilitated within the community. The policy is also related to whether people live in segregated or socially and demographically mixed areas. This applies, for example, to social classes, ethnic groups and the elderly. It is also connected to whether ethnic groups are assimilated into the dominant culture or whether society becomes one characterised by cultural pluralism.

As Figure 10.30 suggests, the types of situations associated with concentration and dispersal are very different. In the case of those elderly who need care, it is a question of whether it is provided by one form of private/public/voluntary service in some kind of residential home, sheltered housing or retirement community, or by individuals within the community where the elderly person lives. Concentration allows efficient service delivery, easier provisions of amenities specifically for the elderly and easy monitoring of their welfare by some responsible individuals. Dispersal implies that relatively younger people will help the elderly and keep an eye on them. Again it must be emphasised, this is only if they need such care. Dispersal also allows the elderly to contribute in varying ways to numerous communities through their experience, expertise and enthusiasm. As long as the opportunities exist and they have the means, the elderly may make their own decision about where they live.

Such decisions are more difficult for the mentally ill, who have to be advised. As professional ideas have evolved and financial pressures have grown, there has been a trend towards community-based mental health facilities and away from the large 'asylums', the sites of which are attractive to developers (Chapter 7, Section 3e).

The treatment of petty criminals is also under review. Some would emphasise punishment, while others concentrate on control or close monitoring while attempting rehabilitation. The avoidance of prisons or similar institutions is advocated by some because they can be centres of learning about other ways of committing crimes. They also argue that prisoners can become institutionalised and unable to return successfully into the outside world. *Institutionalisation* can also be a problem with the mentally ill and indeed the elderly. Others argue for treatment away from the prison because, like mental hospitals, prisons are very expensive to run. They want cheaper methods for control and monitoring and are often not interested in rehabilitation.

Social mix or social segregation?

More generally, people from different social classes have different degrees of freedom to choose where they live but their choices can be affected by the supply and marketing of housing, and by more general social attitudes. Recently people have probably become more socially segregated in residential areas of large western cities. To counteract this, some attempts have been made to produce socially mixed areas by building varied houses. There has also been an introduction of different forms of tenure into areas originally dominated by one form for example, public housing. Where varied housing has been built in desirable areas, the effect has often been for the small property to be bought by relatively well-off small households rather than by lower-income people. The result is then not a set of families of varying incomes but a set of varying sized households of similar per capita income. This is because the market and social value of a house is affected by the surrounding property and occupants.

Mixed tenures

It is too early to observe the effects of mixed tenure in Britain. In inner-city areas where owner occupation has been introduced into an area previously consisting of all public housing, the people from the two tenures have not interacted socially, so there is little sense of a 'mixed community'. It is possible, though, that an external threat (Chapter 7, Section 2), such as major road construction, could bring the people together in order to repel it.

Mix or segregation in schools?

In both the USA and Britain there has been more social engineering in education than in housing. Residential segregation of social classes and some ethnic groups has almost been taken for granted but there have been attempts at producing a social and ethnic mix in schools. This has been associated with the desegregation movement of blacks and whites in the USA and comprehensive education in Britain. Different strategies have been tried in order to produce schools with an ethnic or social class mix from segregated residential areas, bussing of pupils between areas and re-zoning of catchment areas being the most common. In the USA the rapidity of change in some residential areas, particularly from white to black, has led to a further need to re-zone, as once desegregated schools have rapidly become segregated. The policy of busing between largely black inner suburbs and the white outer suburbs, in the case of one city in the southern USA, led to many white households moving out beyond the city limits to avoid the policy. The education policy had affected the residential patterns, making it even more difficult to achieve the policy goal. In Britain, the introduction of comprehensive education in at least some areas where more socially mixed schools would have resulted led to some of the higher social classes withdrawing from state education and entering private education, effectively reducing the potential social mix in the state schools. To produce social or ethnic mix when some element of the population does not want it is, then, extremely difficult.

More recently there have also been pressures for greater segregation of children in schools both by sex and by religion. Some argue that the only way to ensure a balance between genders in the further study of science and technology and associated careers is by educating girls and boys separately. Others such as Muslims require separate education of the sexes for religious reasons. Some advocate separate schools for ethnic groups so that they can be educated about their culture in an environment where their values dominate. Others, such as some Afro-Caribbeans, prefer multi-cultural schools with separate Saturday schools to enhance children's understanding of their ethnic backgrounds. Whereas the 1960s in Britain was a period in which integration in schooling of social classes, sexes and ethnic groups was advocated, the late 1980s saw relatively more pressure for segregation of social classes, ethnic groups and, to a lesser extent, sexes, both directly and indirectly through the extension of parental choice, opting out and increased use of private education. Some fear that a combination of residential areas and schools that are increasingly segregated by social class and ethnicity will lead to an even more divided society.

Reaction, protection or prevention?

The third set of alternative strategies is not in itself geographical but it has geographical effects. Figure 10.26 showed three responses to crime: reactive, protective and preventive. A similar set of responses could be identified for ill health. Reactive responses occur after a crime is committed or someone is ill. They attempt to catch the criminal, help the victim or treat the patient. The police service is concerned mainly with the first and the health service the last, though it could be argued that both might be more oriented towards prevention. Considerable resources that are used by hospitals for treatment might be better employed on promotion of such changes as more healthy diets (though it is not always agreed what these are), better fitness, reduced smoking and more moderate consumption of alcohol, all of which are thought to reduce future ill-health. There are two major barriers to change from reaction to prevention: the need to catch present offenders and to treat present patients, meaning that additional rather than substituted resources are necessary for future prevention; and the lingering doubt as to whether resources used for prevention will in fact be successful in leading to reduced crime and ill-health.

New forms of crime and illness may emerge if prevention works on present ones. A change to prevention might entail a redeployment of police and health professionals with different duties and greater involvement in and interaction with the community. Becoming much more part of the community may be seen as a change in status, because the mystique of jobs may be reduced as ordinary people learn more about them. Drug companies and manufacturers of surgical equipment, for example, who have vested interests in retaining growth of reactive policies, would have to find new markets, probably using different resources. These sets of changes in themselves would have geographical effects on the type and location of employment, on the day-to-day involvement with the community, and on resource use. There might also be an increased need for education both in schools and through the media.

Synthesis

The three major strategies discussed in this section are not unrelated. For example, a preventive approach to health and crime may increase the chances of an elderly person feeling that they are able to stay in their home in a mixed community rather than move, for instance, to sheltered accommodation where they are segregated in often well-protected units. Decisions over the most appropriate strategy or combination of strategies vary between groups and over space and time. This variation contributes to creating ever-changing geographies.

10.5 **Perspectives**

This section discusses ways in which changes in the demographic and social environment occur and the ways in which these may affect people's life chances and quality of life. It also shows the effect of demographic and social change on the other types of environment. It concludes with a review of the debate over the importance of the environment's effect on people's behaviour.

Birth rate cycles

There are trends and cycles in the demographic and social environment as well as in the economic and technological ones. Increased longevity is an example of a trend, while fluctuating birth rates in western nations is an example of a cyclical change. The downturn of such a cycle may be due to technological change such as the introduction of the pill, or social change through later marriage and/or child bearing. The effect of economic changes on social ones is not clear cut. An economic recession may influence some to delay having children, while for others an economic boom may encourage more women to continue working longer before having their first child. An upturn in the birth rate may occur at the end of a war or even be stimulated by the birth of a royal baby! Unlike economic and technological cycles an earlier cycle of births influences, in twenty or so years, time, a future cycle, as babies grow up to have their own children. Although much is known about the geography of demographic trends, less is known about the geography of demographic cycles: whether there are lead and lag areas in upturns of a nation's birth rate; whether these are consistent across cycles; and what reasons account for them.

Effects of fluctuations

Demographic and social changes affect people's lives considerably. Someone who has been born during a 'baby boom' may face a different future of opportunities and problems than one born during a trough

in the birth rate. The first will probably experience an expanding education system in which overcrowding may be a problem in areas of particularly rapidly rising enrolment, and perhaps more difficulty in finding employment as many enter the youth labour market, especially if this coincides with an economic recession and is in a badly hit part of the country; but they will benefit from the generation having a relatively large impact on society and attention from business as it represents an important segment of the market. The second will experience a contracting education system in which schools are amalgamated or closed, often lowering the morale of teachers and a greater chance of obtaining employment as fewer enter the youth labour market, particularly if this coincides with an economic boom and is in an economically expanding area; but they will belong to a generation which will have less impact on society, and probably be part of the economically active when there are relatively more economically inactive to support. As indicated, the differences will be heightened or reduced by the state of the economy and the part of the country in which the person lives.

Social changes, such as the movement towards equal rights and opportunities for the two sexes, mean that women who were born later in the century and are living in particular areas probably have more chance of obtaining these than those born earlier or living in other areas where gender relations are much more male dominated. Similarly those living at times or in areas where there is considerable conflict between generations, religious groups, ethnic groups or social classes may be affected in different ways to those living in periods or areas where social relationships are more harmonious. Contrast, for example, growing up in Belfast or Beirut with Edinburgh or Cairo.

Changing social environment and social values

The social environment also changes as relations between individuals and organisations develop. If housing or care for the elderly is provided mainly by private companies seeking profits rather than public or voluntary organisations, access to that housing or care will be by ability to pay rather than need. This suggests rather different ranges in the quality of life in the two situations. Access by ability to pay will probably produce a greater range than access based mainly on need. The latter usually has more effect on increasing the quality of life of the poor.

Such changes in relations contribute to and reflect modifications to the social environment or context. Private provision often reflects greater reliance on the responsibility of individuals for themselves. Public provision represents collective rather than individual consumption with much greater reliance on the state, through national or local government, to be responsible for the provision and its management. Voluntary provision places greater responsibility on communities. The trend in the 1980s away from public provision and collectivism towards private provision and individualism has been accompanied by moves to try to focus on community involvement, for example in mental health provision and care for the sick elderly. The emphasis has been on individual and community self-help, but the former, with its orientation to the individual or household, tends to counter the latter, which necessitates effort on behalf of others. These changes have not been geographically uniform. There are some indications from voting behaviour, attitudes to privatisation and the take-up of private rather than public services that individualism has been more accepted in the South East of England than elsewhere.

Effects on other human environments

Changes in the social environment in the behaviour and attitudes of people also influence the other environments. Changing desires of where to live, and a trend from passive to active involvement in sport and leisure, affect the built environment, which both responds to and influences such changes; for example, the rapid spread of recreation centres in Britain during the 1970s both reflected demand and encouraged further participation. Demographic and social change not only affect the economic environment through changing market composition and demand, they also influence it through the labour market; for instance, the bulge in the number of youths entering the labour market in the early 1980s in Britain produced a greater need for youth training schemes in order to reduce unemployment rates and to retain the work ethic. The dip in the number entering in the early 1990s has already produced greater competition for graduates and a re-evaluation of the need for married women and the elderly to be employed. This trend, however, has been tempered by a recession. The technological environment is also affected, as already illustrated through the needs of the elderly for hip and knee replacements. The social trend towards small families has increased parents' desire to have healthy children, so lending extra impetus to research into genetic disorders, genetic engineering and screening. Finally, there is a major interaction between the social and political environments, with inward and outward migration sometimes altering the composition and voting patterns of constituencies for instance, and people from different ethnic backgrounds to the ruling élite occasionally demanding political independence as in the southern Soviet republics during the early 1990s.

Effects of environment on behaviour

Underlying much of the above discussion is the assumption that the social environment at various scales affects how people live and behave, that it influences their quality of life both directly and indirectly through its effects on the other environments. This assumption involves a wider debate about the effect of inheritance and genetic make-up as against that of the environment on people's behaviour. The debate is termed 'nature versus nurture'. In education there is an argument about the extent to which education in the family and school contributes to attainment compared with innate intelligence. If innate intelligence is all-important then policies that try to mould the environment, for example, by mixing pupils of varying abilities in schools in order to improve overall achievement, are doomed to failure. On the other hand, a belief that the social environment in and outside schools has important effects on attainment, over and above innate intelligence, make such policies well worth while. In health the argument revolves around the degree to which genetics makes some people more susceptible to disease and whether it is more or less important than the way that people live and the environment in which they live. In crime, again some argue that individuals' make-up is all important and that the local and more general social environment in which they live is of little concern. While arguing that there are marked individual differences in intelligence and personality, susceptibility to varying diseases and latent propensity to commit varying types of crime, one can still support the view that the environments in which people live considerably affect their educational attainment, health and chance of committing crime. Environments present and limit opportunities. Within these, individuals vary considerably in the choices they make.

10.6 Exercises

1. Read the insert below on the elderly in the UK.

An ageing population
The population of the United Kingdom was 55,767,381 in 1981. 9,673,476 people (3,226,298 male and 6,447,178 female) are over pensionable age which is 60 for women and 65 for men.
8,163,241 are aged 65 or over.

3,117,981 are aged 75 or over. 563,805 are aged 85 or over. 17.3% of the population of the United Kingdom are elderly people. Between 1981 and 2001, the total number of people of pensionable age will have increased overall by 3.3% having peaked in 1991. The proportion aged 75 and over will, however, steadily increase by 27.6% and those aged 85 and over by 79%.

Over two thirds of people aged 75 and over are women: 2,100,097 women compared to 1,017,884 men. This imbalance is even more pronounced in the 85 and over age group: 430,891 women to 132,914 men.
On retirement a woman can expect to live to 80.6 and a man to 77.4. Either from choice or because they cannot find employment, people are

retiring earlier. In 1983 in the five years before the basic state retirement age only 59.5% of men and 50.8% of women were working. Almost half pensioner households depend for at least 75% of their income on state pensions and benefits.

Many pensioners have to claim supplementary benefit because of their low income. In 1985 1,720,000 pensioner households claimed.

In Great Britain 35% of pensioners who were entitled to supplementary benefit did not claim.

The proportion of weekly expenditure per person spent on housing, fuel and food is greater in households where the head is aged 65 and over (58%) than it is in those where the head of household is aged under 65 (43%).

Proportionately pensioners spend nearly twice as much as the rest of the population on fuel.

The most severe deprivation is experienced by pensioners living alone who are mainly dependent on state pensions. In all, 70.1% of their expenditure goes on housing, fuel and food.

Amongst households with people over 60, 68% have no car, 50% no central heating, 34% no telephone, and 39% have no washing machine.

Living alone

70.4% of men of pensionable age are married, but only 44.2% of women. Widowhood is very common; of the women of 75 or over, 64.2% are widows and of those 85 or over, 72%.

34.8% of households have one or more pensioners living in them. This is 6,947,163 households of which 2,825,269 are pensioners living on their own (1,239,459 aged 75 or over).

1,965,319 are pensioners living with one or more pensioners.

2,156,575 are pensioners living with people under pensionable age.

29.2% of pensioners live on their own.

39.8% of old people on their own are aged 75 or over.

About 25% of old people in Scotland have no children and 22% have no brothers and sisters.

In a 1977 study in England, 30% of the over 75s had never had children and 7.5% had outlived their offspring.

Services at home

In a year amongst those aged 65 and over:

605,426 are seen by Health Visitors.

1,632,881 are visited by Home Nurses.

1,732,452 receive NHS chiropody services.

In 1980 765,754 received the services of a home help.

Health

In 1980 55% of all elderly people aged 65 and over had a long standing illness which limited their activities.

36% had hearing difficulties.

12% could not go out of doors and walk down the road on their own.

A study in England in 1972 found that about 5% of people aged 65 or

over and 20% aged 80 or over had senile dementia.

In 1984, the deaths of 857 people aged 65 or over involved hypothermia according to their death certificates. A 1972 study indicated that 10% of old people are at risk of hypothermia.

(a) Describe the circumstances of the elderly living alone who are dependent mainly on state pensions.

(b) Suggest the likely effects on the health and social services of future changes in the elderly population.

(c) In what geographical areas are these effects going to be most experienced and to what extent can these areas afford to provide the required services?

2. (a) What images do you have of rural areas?

(b) Is there a particular rural place that has special meaning to you? If so, describe the place and the meaning that it has for you.

(c) By examining advertising material of various kinds, suggest the images on which developers draw in order to market housing in semi-rural and rural areas.

10.31 A comparison of crime rates: criminal statistics (CS), 1981, and the British Crime Survey (BSC), crime rate per 10,000 people

Region	All crimes		Violence against persons		Burglary		Robbery		Theft/ handling		Criminal damage	
	CS	BCS	CS	BCS	CS	BCS	CS	BCS	CS	BCS	CS	BCS
Wales	508	2883	19	428	130	138	1	0	266	1375	71	942
North	685	3577	23	371	188	216	2	0	363	1751	90	1200
North West	708	3999	22	143	196	227	4	20	363	1573	89	754
Yorkshire/ Humberside	616	3657	25	563	163	213	2	38	321	1714	86	1120
West Midlands	584	3099	23	606	158	230	3	38	303	1575	78	654
East Midlands	583	3915	27	820	134	211	2	13	319	1800	75	1068
East Anglia	454	2172	116	1023	89	38	1	0	277	816	51	296
South West	433	2691	15	609	88	93	1	0	253	1348	51	628
South East	623	2935	18	490	139	228	8	47	346	1383	82	724

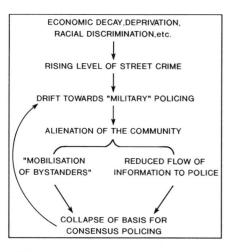

10.32 From consensus to military policing

	All cities	Northern cities	Southern cities	Western cities
Total population	4.9	− 9.8	20.1	13.2
White population	− 6.3	− 18.7	7.4	− 5.2
White families*	− 20.4	− 25.8	− 8.4	− 24.8
Black families*	− 16.2	− 22.0	14.5	− 13.5

* Families with children

Source: US Census – quoted by C. D. Judd, Public Schools and Urban Development, Journal of American Planning Association 51 (1985) 74-83

10.33 Percent population change in US central cities 1970-80

(d) To what extent do these correspond to your images of such areas and to the place that has particular meaning to you?

(e) How realistic are the images conveyed by the developers?

(f) To what extent are people:

(i) moving to semi-rural and rural areas still connected to cities;

(ii) living similar lives as they might in cities?

g) In what ways may rural lives be less than idyllic?

3. Figure 10.31 shows regional comparisons of reported and surveyed crime rates. Reported rates are those crimes reported to the police. Surveyed rates are those crimes said to have been experienced by people when they answered questions in an official survey.

(a) To what extent are there differences between the two rates shown for all crimes?

(b) Which crime is less reported? Suggest reasons for this.

(c) What are the differences between regions in rates of reporting?

(d) Which set of statistics should be considered when studying the geography of crime and strategies for crime prevention? Give reasons for your choice.

4. Figure 10.32 shows the collapse of 'consensus policing'. Consensus or community policing attempts to encourage the preventive and non-conflictual aspects of policing such as crime prevention and community liaison. 'Military policing' involves saturation policing or 'swamp' tactics to combat a perceived rise in actual crime, use of 'stop and search', specialist units and much greater use of surveillance technology. Military policing is seen as characteristic of Northern Ireland. This is one view of a vicious circle occurring in some areas of cities.

(a) Suggest how this vicious circle may operate.

(b) Discuss whether there are areas of your country where such a vicious circle may have occurred.

(c) Suggest strategies that may be adopted to break this vicious circle.

5. Study Figure 10.33 on population change in the 'central cities' of the USA in the decade of major counter-urbanisation. Central cities are approximately equivalent to the inner cities and inner suburbs of British cities.

(a) To what extent was counter-urbanisation a northern phenomenon?

(b) To what extent was it a white phenomenon?

(c) To what extent was it a family phenomenon?

(d) What group would explain the rise in population in western cities?

10.7 **Further reading**

L. Bondi and H. Matthews (eds.) (1988) *Education and Society: Studies in the Politics, Sociology and Geography of Education*, Routledge

J. Cater and T. Jones (1989) *Social Geography: an Introduction to Contemporary Issues*, Edward Arnold

A.G. Champion and A.R. Townsend (1990) *Contemporary Britain: a Geographical Perspective*, Edward Arnold

D. Herbert (1982) *The Geography of Urban Crime*, Longman

P. Jackson (ed.) (1987) *Race and Racism*, Allen and Unwin

P. Jackson (1989) *Maps of Meaning*, Unwin Hyman

P. Knox (1987) *Urban Social Geography*, Longman

J. Little, L. Peake and P. Richardson (eds.) (1988) *Women in Cities*, Macmillan

P.E. Ogden (1984) *Migration and Geographic Change*, Cambridge University Press

S. Smith (1986) *Crime, Space and Society*, Cambridge Unviersity Press

A.M. Warnes (ed.) (1982) *Geographical Perspectives on the Elderly*, Wiley

Chapter 11

CHANGING POLITICAL ACTORS AND ENVIRONMENTS

11.1 Case study: the rise and fall of metropolitan counties

Since the 1960s there has been a continuing debate on the restructuring of English and Welsh local government. In particular the old local authorities set up in the late nineteenth century, and largely unchanged since, were proving to be inadequate in both size and resources to deal with the increasingly complex and heterogeneous problems of England's conurbations. The conurbations had spread spatially and needed political boundaries that reflected that.

Figure 11.1 shows a comparison of the various structural local government reform proposals between

11.1 Local government reform proposals for England, 1969-72

1969 and 1972. In particular, it was felt that the emerging functional city regions needed a corresponding metropolitan authority able to create and implement policies on housing, services and employment. It was argued that such a conurbation level authority could coordinate conurbation-wide and local planning. It should be able to integrate and coordinate both policies and areas within the conurbation.

By the 1972 Local Government Act, the proposed spatial extent of the metropolitan authorities had been reduced and it was generally felt that there should be two tiers of elected councils in major conurbations, a county and a district level rather than a unitary body, one that

Metropolitan county	City or district
Consumer protection	Education
Fire services	Environmental health
Highways and traffic	Housing
Police	Libraries
Public transport	Local planning
Strategic planning	Local streets
Waste disposal	Social services
	Waste collection

11.2 The main functions of metropolitan councils and district councils after the 1974 reorganisation

covered all functions. The Act legislated that for each metropolitan area there must be a metropolitan authority responsible for the planning, transportation and major development group of functions

	Redcliffe-Maud Report, 1969	Labour government White Paper, 1970	Conservative government White Paper, 1971	Local government bill, 1972	Local government act, 1972
Metropolitan areas and districts	3 (20 districts)	5 (28 districts)	6 (34 districts)	6 (34 districts)	6 (36 districts)
Councils outside the metropolitan area	58 Unitary authorities	51 Unitary authorities	38 two-tier counties + districts; a boundary commission to recommend district areas	38 two-tier counties + districts, but changes in boundaries	39 two-tier counties + 296 districts
Provincial councils	8 Indirectly elected	No decision	No decision	No decision	No decision
Local/parish councils	In unitary areas existing authorities to become local councils	As Redcliffe-Maud, except that large cities allowed to subdivide	Existing parish councils to continue	Existing parish councils retained new parish councils in urban areas possible	Existing parish councils retained 300 municipal boroughs and urban district councils to become urban parishes

Source: B. Wood (1974)

throughout the whole area. Alongside the Greater London Council (GLC) there were to be six metropolitan counties (Greater Manchester, Merseyside, South Yorkshire, Tyne and Wear, West Midlands and West Yorkshire). There was also to be a two tier system of county councils and district councils with a different division of responsibilities; for instance, within the metropolitan areas it was the districts which controlled education, while in the shires it was the county not the district councils. This reorganisation finalised and rationalised the effective planning responsibilities which were passed to county councils and metropolitan authorities (Figure 11.2).

The reorganisation of local government is illustrated for Manchester Conurbation (the Greater Manchester Metropolitan County) which came into existence in April 1974 (Figure 11.3).

It involved much debate, with Wilmslow and Poynton, areas to the south, successfully arguing to remain outside Greater Manchester

11.3 Reorganisation of local government in Greater Manchester (also showing the past changes to accommodate the growth of the built-up area)

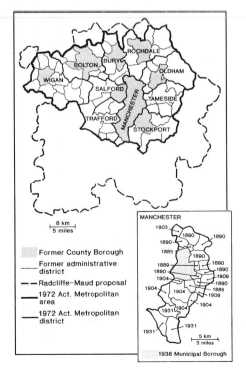

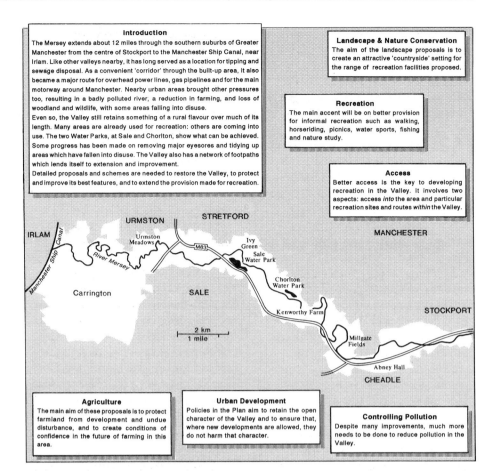

Introduction
The Mersey extends about 12 miles through the southern suburbs of Greater Manchester from the centre of Stockport to the Manchester Ship Canal, near Irlam. Like other valleys nearby, it has long served as a location for tipping and sewage disposal. As a convenient 'corridor' through the built-up area, it also became a major route for overhead power lines, gas pipelines and for the main motorway around Manchester. Nearby urban areas brought other pressures too, resulting in a badly polluted river, a reduction in farming, and loss of woodland and wildlife, with some areas falling into disuse.
Even so, the Valley still retains something of a rural flavour over much of its length. Many areas are already used for recreation: others are coming into use. The two Water Parks, at Sale and Chorlton, show what can be achieved. Some progress has been made on removing major eyesores and tidying up areas which have fallen into disuse. The Valley also has a network of footpaths which lends itself to extension and improvement.
Detailed proposals and schemes are needed to restore the Valley, to protect and improve its best features, and to extend the provision made for recreation.

Landscape & Nature Conservation
The aim of the landscape proposals is to create an attractive 'countryside' setting for the range of recreation facilities proposed.

Recreation
The main accent will be on better provision for informal recreation such as walking, horseriding, picnics, water sports, fishing and nature study.

Access
Better access is the key to developing recreation in the Valley. It involves two aspects: access *into* the area and particular recreation sites and routes *within* the Valley.

Agriculture
The main aim of these proposals is to protect farmland from development and undue disturbance, and to create conditions of confidence in the future of farming in this area.

Urban Development
Policies in the Plan aim to retain the open character of the Valley and to ensure that, where new developments are allowed, they do not harm that character.

Controlling Pollution
Despite many improvements, much more needs to be done to reduce pollution in the Valley.

11.4 The Mersey Valley plan

and within Cheshire while Cheadle and Gatley lost its case. Cheshire also campaigned to maintain its area and county status. This raised the general issue of the most appropriate delimitation of a metropolitan administrative area. Many people commute from Wilmslow and Poynton to central Manchester. Should a metropolitan county be limited to the continuous built-up area or to some definition based on the functional area? There was also a debate about the size and form of districts within the conurbation. In 1969 it had been proposed that Manchester and Salford be combined as the centre of the conurbation, and that Bury and Rochdale should also form one district. In these cases the pressures to maintain their historical independence resulted in their separate designation as four district level authorities.

The GMC covered an area of 49.7 square miles, a reduction of one third on the original proposal for SELNEC (South East Lancashire

and North East Cheshire) in 1969. This represented a major truncation of its spatial extent to the south in Cheshire and Derbyshire. It had a total population of 2,730,000, a drop of one-fifth on the original size. It comprised ten metropolitan districts each of which had specific responsibilities with regard to the administration of local affairs. It incorporated eight county boroughs, fifteen municipal boroughs, forty-three urban districts and parts of two rural districts, a reflection of the fragmentation of political organisation that had resulted over years of incorporation and annexation.

One of the examples of the coordinating and innovative work of the Greater Manchester Council after 1983 were the developments in the Mersey Valley. The Mersey extends 12 miles through the southern suburbs of Greater Manchester from the centre of Stockport to the Manchester Ship Canal near Irlam.

The GMC, alongside Manchester City Council and Stockport and Trafford Metropolitan Borough Councils, put forward in 1983 the Mersey Valley Local Plan (Figure 11.4) with the intention of improving the valley and guiding the development of recreation within it. The valley-wide proposals provided guidance on landscape and nature conservation, recreation, access, agriculture and measures to control pollution and urban development.

In July 1985 a public local inquiry was held. The developments over five years included the construction of a visitor centre, improved land management and an increase in Mersey Valley staff from 7.5 to twenty permanently there to improve the environment and educate the people. Examples include a news sheet 'Mersey Valley News', the creation of Broad Ees Dole Nature Reserve, and 'Operation Countryside' geared to involving children. The valley is now regarded as a forerunner of urban environmental improvement schemes. The Chief Warden felt these initiatives would not have occurred without the GMC. He disputed whether ten districts could have coordinated the developments.

The system of metropolitan counties established in 1974 was abolished on 1 April 1986. They had been set up to play mainly a strategic role but they had not been given the territory or powers to accomplish that. In 1983 the Tory Party manifesto pointed to the 'wasteful and unnecessary tiers of government. We shall abolish them and return most of their functions to the boroughs and districts. Services which need to be administered over a wider area will be run by joint boards of borough and district representatives'. The main arguments for abolition were: they were an unnecessary layer of bureaucracy; and their abolition would save public money and 'streamline the cities'. It was suggested that they lacked real functions and that the GLC in particular

trespassed into inappropriate spheres of policy, such as involvement in Northern Ireland. It was argued that the new system would be 'simpler for the public to understand in that responsibility for virtually all services would rest in a single authority', the metropolitan district, and would be more 'local, democratic, and accountable'.

The arguments for retention included a conurbation wide perspective for planning and policy making concerning such issues as shop and office developments and Green Belts. This also involved being large enough to achieve economies of scale for creative policy making and implementation, and to coordinate cross district schemes such as the Mersey Valley Project.

Although the overt criticisms of the metropolitan counties were about comprehensibility, democracy, accountability and economy, there were criticisms of some of their policies which may well have contributed to their abolition, for example: the GLC's grant-aiding activities for a variety of minority groups; South Yorkshire' public transport policy (Chapter 4, Section 1); and

Merseyside's relations with its police authority.

Because of their size, they were able to establish and implement policies such as those on job creation and public transport which were alternatives to national government's policies. Since these policies were reasonably successful and presented as alternatives to a national government which did not believe there was an alternative policy, there was bound to be political antagonism particularly because national government and the metropolitan counties were under the control of different parties.

The impact of abolition is not fully known but one is the complexity of the succeeding system, such as that in Greater London (Figure 11.5).

More generally the new division of functions for England and Wales may be seen in Figure 11.6 where it is compared with that for Scotland. There have already been problems of coordinating policies on new developments where metropolitan dis-

11.5 The redistribution of the functions of the old Greater London Council

Function	Transferred to	Centralized?	Category
Education	ILEA	D*	CS/SE
Fire services	QUELGO	D*	SE/SC/SI
Housing	Bs, QGAs, LRB, U	D*	SC/SI
Transport (roads and bridges)	CG, Bs, LRB, U	C+D	SI
Transport (rail and buses)	QGA	C	SI/SC
Waste disposal	QUELGOs, Bs, QGA, U	C+D	SE/SI
Flood control, drainage	QGAs, Bs, U	C+D	SE/SI
Arts and recreation	QGAs, LRB, U	C	SC
Entertainments	QGAs, Bs, U	C+D	SC/SE/SI
Sports	QGAs, Bs, U	D*	SC
Parks	Bs, CCs, U	D*	SC
Museums/buildings	QGAs, ILEA, U	D*	SC
Records	City of London	D	SE
Architects	GQGAs, QUELGO, ILEA, Bs	C+D	SC/SE
Computer services	LRB	U	SE
Greater London training	QGA? (MSC?)	C	SC/SI
Judicial services	Bs	D	SE
Industry and employment	BS, GLEB, LRB, U	C+D*	SI
Research and intelligence	LRB, U	C	SE
Voluntary grants	Bs, LRB, U	D*	SC
Valuers	LRB, U	C	U
Supplies	ILEA	D*	SI/SE

Key: QGA – Quasi-Governmental Agency, eg Thames Water Authority; QUELGO – Quasi-Elected Local Government Organisation eg Fire Board; Bs – London Boroughs; CCS – County Councils; LRB – London Residuary Body; CG – Central Government; C – Centralisation; D – Decentralisation; D* – Ambiguous Decentralisation (Central Government has reserve powers); SI – Social Investment; SC ° Social Consumption; SE – Social Expenses; U – Unknown.

	England and Wales Metropolitan		England and Wales Non-Metropolitan		Greater London Borough Councils	Scotland		
	Joint Authority	District Councils	County Councils	District Councils		Regional Councils	District Councils	Island Councils
Social services		●	●		●	●		●
Education		●	●		●¹	●		
Libraries		●	●		●	●	●²	●²
Museums and art galleries		●	●	●	●	●	●	●
Housing		●	●	●	●		●	●
Planning – strategic		●⁴	●		●	●		●
– local				●	●		●²	●²
Highways		●	●		●	●		●
Traffic management		●	●		●	●		●
Passenger transport⁶	●	●	●		●	●		●
Playing fields and swimming baths		●	●	●	●		●	●
Parks and open spaces		●	●	●	●		●	●
Refuse collection	●⁵	●⁵		●	●		●	●
Refuse disposal		●	●		●		●	●
Consumer protection		●	●		●	●		●
Environmental Health⁷		●		●	●		●	●
Police³	●		●			●		●
Fire³	●		●			●		●

1 Outer London = London boroughs; Inner London = Inner London Education Authority. (From 1989 education throughout London becomes the responsibility of the London boroughs.)
2 Except in Highlands, Dumfries and Galloway and Border regions, where the function will be regional.
3 There are joint police forces and joint fire brigades in some areas. In London the police authority is the Home Secretary and the Fire and Civil Defence Authority controls the fire brigades.
4 Strategic planning in metropolitan districts is co-ordinated by a joint committee of the districts in each former metropolitan county area.
5 In metropolitan areas, refuse disposal may be either a joint authority or a district council function.
6 Passenger transport in London is carried out by a separate body, London Regional Transport.
7 Regional and Island councils in Scotland control water and sewerage, in addition to the usual environmental health duties.
Source: Chartered Institute of Public Finance and Accountancy, Local government Trends, CIPFA, 1987, p6.

11.6 The principal functions of local authorities in Great Britain after 1986

tricts within a conurbation have had opposing views. (See Chapter 5, Section 1 for the dispute over shopping centre developments in Greater Manchester.)

A more general observation of any political reform is that it may be partly inspired by political self-interest. Certain organisational arrangements tend to give some interests, some perspectives, more effective access to those with decision-making authority. Such self-interest may be geographically demonstrated through gerrymandering, whereby local government and constituency boundaries are drawn in such a way as to maximise the electoral impact of support for one party and diminish that for another. Edward Heath, a former Conservative Prime Minister, even declared the 1980s redrawing of ward boundaries to be 'the greatest act of gerrymandering in the last hundred years of British history'. Self-interest may sometimes underlie the reform of local government. The Conservative Party's reorganisation of both Greater London (1963) and the rest of England and Wales (1972), for example, placed nearly 58 per cent of the population in local authority areas that were likely to be under continuous Conservative control and only 17 per cent in those likely to be under continuous Labour control.

The case study demonstrates the changing central/local political tensions in a western developed nation, which can lead to geographical changes in political units. It also illustrates the debates about the appropriate sizes, functions and geographical delimitations of political units, particularly for metropolitan government.

11.2 General problem

Statement of the general problem

As the rise and fall of metropolitan counties demonstrates, political units or actors can change rapidly, with major impacts on the geography of a country. The general problem of this chapter concerns recent changes in the geographical organisation of political units or actors, such as local, national and supra- national governments, political parties and pressure groups and changes in their policies which have direct and indirect geographical effects. The changes in the actors both influence and are affected by wider changes in the political and policy environments. In order to illustrate some of the most important changes, this section is divided into two parts: the rise of state intervention and its possible fall, and changes in the international arena.

The rise of state intervention and its fall?

At the national scale in numerous countries, it is possible to observe first the expansion of government activities and then very recently a reassessment of government's role. The forms that these have taken vary from country to country but the general trend is similar. The changes in the relationships between central and local governments, however, display greater variation. The expansion and reassessment will be illustrated by Britain, which in many ways is an extreme case of both expansion and reassessment.

There was a great expansion in both central and local governments' activities in Britain after 1945. This was due partly to the reconstruction that was needed to recover from the Second World War. It was also due to a major change in ideology which the reconstruction in part permitted. The 'welfare state' had been initiated early in the century but many of its major components were established in the late 1940s, including the National Health Service. Public expenditure on housing, education and social services, as well as health, greatly expanded from 1945 to 1975. The foundations of the present planning system were also established with, on the one hand, new local government planning powers and, on the other, specific pieces of legislation which set up the New Towns, Green Belts and National Parks. The latter very obviously affected the geography of Britain but so too did the expenditure on council housing, schools and hospitals, and the planning controls which limited private development.

Government as employer

As government activities expanded, so too did the number of people directly employed. Local government employment, by definition, is spread widely throughout the country, even though within local government administrative areas it is often spatially concentrated. National government jobs, however, have been highly centralised in London. This has meant that the South East has benefited from the spending power of these employees, as well as from the expenditure of the staff who work at company headquarters, which are attracted to the capital partly for reasons of prestige but also to be near to the government (Chapter 8, Section 2). It was to off-set the regional imbalance that some governmental jobs were decentralised to the Development Areas as part of regional policy in the 1960s and early 1970s, for example the National Vehicle Licensing Centre to Swansea and the Department of Health and Social Security to Newcastle. More recently, the headquarters of the Manpower Services Commission (TEED) was set up in Sheffield. The major decision-making departments of government, though, still remain in London.

Government as customer

The growth of governments as major employers has been paralleled by their development as significant customers. With the advent of the Cold War between East and West in the late 1940s, for example, defence spending became particularly important and the placing of defence contracts became especially significant as an indirect geographical effect on employment growth. As Figure 9.22 shows, expenditure on defence was much greater than that on regional assistance, even at its peak. It also conflicted with the spatial effect and intent of regional policy (Figure 9.23) which was directed towards reducing regional inequalities in employment opportunities, infrastructure and standard of living. Government incentives to manufacturing industry, and later to services, to relocate or set up in development areas, where traditional industries were declining, were accompanied by restrictions on the expansion of floor-space of factories and offices in the South-East and, to a lesser extent, the West Midlands. These direct efforts at influencing regional geography were to some extent off-set by the government acting as a customer and placing defence and other contracts (Chapter 9, Section 4). The conflict results partly because governments paid little attention to the indirect geographical effects of their policies and activities.

The impact of federal contracts to the defence and space industries has also been very significant for regional economic growth in the USA. The electronics industry of New England, for example, benefited, which helped part of the region to withstand the decline of its textile industry. Such a spatial coincidence of old and new industries did not occur to the same extent in Britain. California and south Texas have also been beneficiaries. This helped them to become lead industrial areas, rivalling the manufacturing belt of the North-East, the relative decline of which in the 1970s and early 1980s resulted in its renaming as the 'Rust Belt'.

These are a few examples of the direct and indirect effects of the expansion of national government activities in Britain and, for comparison, in the USA. Until the early 1970s, the political environment in Britain was dominated by increased governmental involvement and spending or, as it has been called, the 'growth of the state'. The public

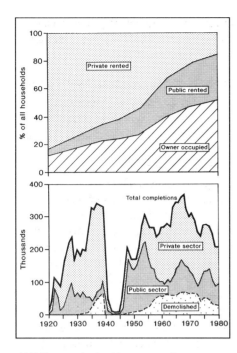

11.7 The growth of public renting and owner occupation up to 1980 and the fluctuations in new provision

sector grew in size, influence and prestige. In 1975 30 per cent of those employed in Britain were part of local or central government. The state not only regulated the economy, it owned various sections of it, from the utilities to the traditional industries such as steel and coal that had been nationalised and, in some cases, denationalised and renationalised by successive governments of different political complexions. It was also concerned with social welfare and the quality of people's lives, and with individual, group and regional equality. Many more people lived in local authority housing (Figure 11.7).

Most children were educated in comprehensive schools, which were introduced in part to permit equality of opportunity. The social services and social security system had expanded to help those in need. Regional policy was well developed to help areas where there were concentrations of poverty, unemployment and environments of poor quality. The state was therefore involved in many aspects of life.

A change in government's role

The political climate was beginning to change at the start of the 1970s, but change was accelerated after the oil crisis of 1973, which triggered a major world recession. There was a major reassessment of economic and political thinking. Until then, as the national economies went into recession, governments would increase their spending in order to prime the market sector by increasing demand. This reflected the dominance that Keynesian economics had had over government policy in the USA and UK. In this recession, though, unemployment and inflation were rising simultaneously, an unexpected and new set of circumstances. Monetarist policies that controlled the money supply eventually replaced Keynesian thinking, at least for a time. This economic reassessment coincided with greater favour being shown to New Right thinking about the role of the state: less dependency on the state was needed with greater responsibility given to the individual and family; bureaucratic intervention was thought to be inefficient and alienating and needed to be replaced by greater reliance on private initiative and enterprise; the state should remove itself from many areas of life. All these ideas were encapsulated in the phrase, 'rolling back the frontiers of the state'.

This new thinking resulted in policies directed towards reducing public expenditure (in contrast to Keynesian-based policies), particularly on welfare services such as housing, education and health. By cutting public expenditure, governments could reduce taxation of the private sector and encourage its expansion (though in doing so, the private sector would receive less demand for its goods and services from the public sector). Economic growth and *wealth-creation* became

of prime importance. Interest in the distribution of wealth, social welfare and individual and regional inequality waned. Economic growth then became dominant while social justice receded as a governmental goal.

Changes in public expenditure

In Britain the reductions in public expenditure became significant in 1976 under a Labour administration and continued apace under the Conservative governments from 1979 throughout the 1980s (Figure 11.8). Not all sectors suffered reductions. Some generally increased, such as services related to law and order and defence. Since unemployment climbed very rapidly in the early 1980s, spending on benefits also increased. Because these increases offset many of the cuts, overall public expenditure did not decrease in absolute terms, but it did decline as a proportion of the gross domestic product (GDP). Certain services were especially affected. Housing expenditure was particularly hit, storing up future problems in the housing stock (Chapter 13, Section 2). Building of local authority housing was greatly cut back. Housing improvement of all kinds of stock was reduced. The

11.8 Changing government expenditure in the UK (a reclassification occurred within the period)

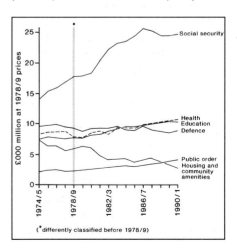

allocation to local government for their housing investment programmes (HIP) dropped dramatically, for example for Salford from £33 million in 1979 to £13 million in real terms by 1986. Whereas a falling birth rate had led to declining rolls in schools and it could therefore be argued that education could withstand a reduction in expenditure, the number of households and the demand for housing were growing, and the need for improvement of various parts of the housing stock was increasing (Chapter 13, Section 2). The demands on the health service were also growing, as the number of old people increased (Chapter 10, Section 1), the services it could perform expanded and people's expectations rose. Expenditure did not rise at a rate that could meet this demand. Expenditure on hospitals, as distinct from general practitioners, was particularly controlled and decreased through part of the period. In some regional health authorities this was especially acute as health resources were being redistributed to other regions which historically had lower resources relative to their health needs (Chapter 4, Section 3b, Chapter 5, Section 3b). Such reductions and controls on expenditure for local authorities and health authorities began only a few years after they had been reorganised (Chapter 11, Section 1). Reorganisation had been associated with expansion in services and new ideas of how they might be provided. Controls reversed that momentum and during the 1980s the relationship between central government and local authorities and the roles that they both played were changed.

Finance of local government

First we will examine the changed relationship between local authorities and central government, through the way they are financed,

and secondly the new roles that local authorities are being expected to play. Housing and education are two of many services provided by the local authorities out of funds coming from national government and the community charge or poll tax (pre-1990 domestic rates and possibly from 1993 a council tax) which is set and collected locally. The national government grant, the equivalent of which was called the rate support grant, is raised from taxes and distributed to the local authorities according to their assessed needs. The percentage of local government expenditure that was provided by the national government in the form of the rate support grant rose from 50 per cent in the mid-1960s to about 65 per cent in the early 1970s and declined to about 45 per cent in the late 1980s. This was one of the major ways that national government sought to reduce public expenditure. Where local government tried to maintain their level of expenditure on services, by raising local rates for example, national government passed legislation to reduce local and increase national powers.

Centralisation of power in the UK

It produced penalty clauses so that if a local government spent more than national government felt was necessary, its rate support grant was reduced. Some authorities also had their rates capped, that is, the extent to which they could increase local rates was limited. Such moves have changed the balance of power between local and central government. They have reduced the autonomy of local government and increased central government's power.

There are many geographical points to be made about such a change. Firstly, the relations between central and local govern-

ment vary from country to country as well as from time to time, as has been illustrated for Britain.

Decentralisation of power in the USA

In the USA, for example, it is more complex because of the federal system. Local governments there receive funds from both the state and federal level, so there are more sets of relationships that can vary: local and state, local and federal, state and federal. In the 1980s under the Reagan administration, the federal role was generally reduced, as national government's role was supposed to be in Britain. In education, for example, the federal government had decreasing influence, as did local school boards which continued their declining role. The states began to take much greater interest and make greater financial contributions. Many state governors saw improved education as a way for states to compete with one another economically. More generally, decreasing federal intervention in the USA led to a decentralisation of power and activities to the states. In Britain, in contrast, the forms of central government intervention changed and power was centralised.

Geographical allocation of finance

Secondly, the allocation of central funds to local areas is important geographically. At the time when Britain's central contribution to local expenditure was 65 per cent, the American equivalent was 45 per cent. The greater the central contribution, the greater the potential for redistributing funds between local authorities. So in Britain that potential was reduced and the rate support grant became a less powerful means of contributing towards spatial social justice (Chapter 5, Section 2). In the 1970s in Britain, national governments changed the formula of the rate support grant so that different dimensions of need were included or were given greater weight; for example, the number of single-parent families was considered and unemployment given more or less weight. In one period these changes had the effect of directing proportionately more money to the inner cities at the expense of the outer metropolitan boroughs and the shire counties. This was a period of Labour government. During Conservative administrations, the shire counties were more generously treated relative to the metropolitan boroughs, especially the inner-city ones. Such changes can be interpreted as reflecting either different attitudes and definitions of need or, more cynically, the distribution of political support.

In the 1980s the Conservative administrations changed altogether the way the grant was calculated. Less went to high spending authorities, many of which were inner-city ones, and also Labour controlled. Such authorities argued that they were providing the services that were needed in their areas and that they had been elected to do so. The national government, on the other hand, argued that it had been elected to reduce public expenditure and make public services more efficient. Here there is an immediate conflict between local democracy and national democracy. By passing additional legislation, national government was able continually to reduce local powers.

The rate support grant was an allocation of general funds to authorities. They had more control over how it was spent within their areas. Earlier in the 1960s, grants were more specific. In the 1980s national government reduced these general funds but increased special funds for which local authorities had to bid. This means that national govern-

ment decides the priorities of spending by introducing particular grants and it decides which authorities will receive the funds. Both increase its power.

Though other resources were targeted at the inner cities in the form of urban partnership (Chapter 4, Section 4) or programme money, urban development grants (Chapter 4, Section 4) and so on, these extras were offset – often more than offset – by reductions in the rate support grant. Sometimes projects would be set up under partnership funds but later run into trouble as their running costs became part of normal local authority expenditure. With reduced overall funds, inner city local authorities could not afford them. Claims that governments have spent more money on inner cities, or some other particular areas or services, have to be carefully interpreted. Sometimes they are spending more on special funds while spending less on general ones, or spending more on particular parts of a service and less on others, so that overall there may be a decline in the resources going into an area or service.

Declining local authority provision

There have been further reductions in local authority power through changes in the services they provide.

11.9 The decline in public rented housing since 1980, through council house sales and fewer completions

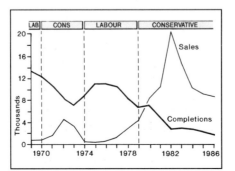

The encouragement and then later the command to sell local authority houses to their tenants at subsidised prices have meant a reduction in council-owned stock. Councils now have less stock to manage and the stock they are left with is generally the least popular and most in need of repair. There have also been controls on the degree to which they can use receipts from council house sales to build new stock (Figure 11.9). Councils may also lose the management of their stock, because tenants on estates may now choose whether they want to have as their landlord the council, a housing association or a private landlord.

Similarly parents with pupils at local authority controlled schools may now vote to 'opt out' of that control and be directly funded by the national government as grant maintained schools. This has so far occurred where there has been threat of closure to the school, or its selective nature is under threat, or it is felt that it is not sufficiently resourced. The threat to close a school is the result of local authorities carrying out central government's policy and instruction to run education in a financially efficient way. A further result of the 1988 Education Reform Act is that local authority schools will now be managing their own finances. Instead of the local authority giving the school a set of budgets for a number of separate areas of spending, it will give each school an overall budget and the head will decide how that sum is allocated within the school. Governing bodies of schools have been given increased responsibilities and parental representation upon them has been augmented. This is an example of power being devolved downwards from the local authority to the school. Allowing council estates to manage themselves is an example of the same trend, but often in these cases the pressure came from below (Chapter 4, Section 2), that is from the tenants themselves rather than from above from the national government, as in the case of the schools. The local authorities have lost power to groups and institutions within the authorities, and to the central government. Many of these changes have not occurred in a geographically uniform manner.

From public to private provision

There has been much criticism of public service provision, whether it be housing, education, health or social services. This has been aimed at improving their efficiency and sometimes their effectiveness. Financial criteria have usually dominated measures of both. Some would argue that criticisms have in part been used to justify the reductions in public expenditure and to encourage use of private services, thus reducing the need for public provision. Others would argue that criticisms are part of 'voice' to improve services and not there to encourage 'exit' (Chapter 7, Section 2). It is fair to say that for public services in general, and housing, and to a lesser extent education, in particular, reductions or controls on public expenditure were accompanied in various ways by encouragement to people to take-up private provision. Two examples are sales of council houses to tenants at subsidised prices and assisted places by which able children may have their fees at private schools paid in full or in part by the state.

From 'provider' to enabler'

The local authorities have had their functions changed not only by acquiring some extra services from the abolition of metropolitan councils, but by a change of emphasis in their overall role. One function they have is development control. They receive applications from developers for changes in land use or new buildings and decide whether or not to grant permission (Chapter 2, Section 4). In declining areas in a recession, applications fall. Local authorities were encouraged to enter into various forms of partnership with private developers, assemble various grants and enable development to take place. The public monies were used to 'lever' private investment into the area (Chapter 4, Section 4). The local authorities were then becoming *enablers* or *facilitators* of development rather than controllers of it.

From controller to entrepreneur

They were also trying to promote their own areas, to attract jobs and investment. American states had performed this marketing role for many years but only during the 1970s and especially the 1980s did some British local authorities develop this *entrepreneurial* and *marketing role*. Both the partnership schemes and promotion were ideas borrowed from the USA, particularly the revitalisation schemes of cities such as Boston and Baltimore. Strathclyde, the largest local authority in Britain by population, has been very much to the fore in promoting its success at revitalising some of Glasgow's poor areas. Although many of these changes occurred in declining parts of the country, partnerships with the private sector and the marketing of place were also adopted elsewhere, even where there were plenty of applications from developers (Chapter 2, Section 3b). In both types of areas, the involvement of local authorities in partnerships for development often led to less strict application of development control functions. So there has been a change in their roles and their relations with private developers and a greater emphasis on private rather than public provision of services.

Local authorities, then, have acquired new roles as enablers and entrepreneurs, though not all authorities to the same extent or in the same way. Some authorities, led by some of the now abolished metropolitan counties, tried to create jobs and bring about change with much less emphasis on the private sector. Controls on their spending have made such strategies more difficult to follow, and after abolition the metropolitan district councils could not operate on the scale the metropolitan counties had. These had adopted an alternative economic strategy, especially on job creation (Chapter 12, Section 4), to that of the national government, which was one of the political reasons for their abolition. The enabling and promotional roles have also been taken up by Urban Development Corporations (UDCs), which are national government bodies that have been set up to coordinate development in defined areas of large cities (Chapter 11, Section 3d). Such roles and activities of local authorities, financed mainly by national government grants, and UDCs have tended to fill the void left by the much reduced role of regional policy. It is important to note that the geographical scale of these activities changed from the region in the 1960s and early 1970s to the locality in the late 1970s and 1980s – the local authority or, in the case of most UDCs, part of a local authority. This suggests a higher degree of spatial targeting (Chapter 11, Section 4) on particular areas than under regional policy and the potential for much more variability across space.

Summary of the UK in the 1980s

The controls on public expenditure and the encouragement of private sector provision are two major elements of the political environment in the 1980s which in Britain weakened local government and changed its roles. At the same time central government's powers were increased and to some extent local groups and institutions within authorities acquired more control over their affairs. The same elements have dominated the political environment of many western countries but, as indicated in the discussion about education in the USA, have not necessarily had the same effect on the political actors.

The international arena

At the international level the discussion is divided into:

(a) important changes in political units;

(b) political conflicts;

(c) major changes in the political climate, which include the reduced tension between the western and eastern blocs, the political emergence of Islam and the rise of the green movement.

The emergence and subsequent growth of the European Community from the original six countries linked together by the Treaty of Rome in 1957 (Belgium, France, Germany, Italy, Luxembourg and the Netherlands) to twelve (Denmark, Eire, Great Britain, Greece, Portugal and Spain) has been a major political change. Although based originally on an economic union, it has a major political dimension. The constituent countries or member states can adopt a common policy to world events which gives them much more influence, particularly relative to the so-called superpowers, the USA and the former USSR. The government of the Community is split into a number of elements. There are elections to the *European Parliament* with its assembly in Strasbourg. There are also seventeen commissioners appointed from the twelve

countries to the *Commission* in Brussels, and the *Council of Ministers* (members of the national governments of the twelve) often meets in Luxembourg, where the Parliament's general secretariat is located. The geographical separation of these three institutions has its disadvantages but was seen as being more politically neutral in that the activities were not centred in one country. While there may be tensions between member states over particular issues, competition for the location of EC agencies such as the European Environmental Protection Agency, and debates about the loss of national autonomy or sovereignty, the Community has contributed to Western Europe as a whole being dominated by cooperation in the second half of the twentieth century rather than the conflict that characterised much of the first half.

The European Community is one of many examples of attempts at cooperation between countries. Some have a military purpose, such as NATO, SEATO and the Warsaw Pact, while others like the European Community are predominantly economic in origin. Whether they be military or economic groupings, they still wield political power.

Economically such groupings may somewhat change the balance of power between countries and global corporations (Chapter 8, Section 2), since the latter are often larger than an individual country in financial terms. The groupings have certainly caused a major change in the environments of such corporations, as they can present great market opportunities to which the companies want access (Chapter 8, Section 2).

Military alliances

Military groupings are usually for defensive purposes but they can also form during wars. Again there may

well be tensions within the groupings over the relative contributions of finance or manpower, or on the location of military bases or over policy on missile deployment. Each country occupies a different geographical position relative to some foreseen threat which may influence its view on policy. Western Germany, for example, occupied a front-line position relative to the perceived threat of the Warsaw Pact and in the late 1980s it was eager to establish an agreement on the withdrawal of short-range nuclear weapons since it would be the battlefield where they would be used. Other NATO countries in less potentially perilous positions were less convinced of the arguments.

Political conflicts

While there has not been any military action between NATO and the Warsaw Pact in Europe, there have been conflicts in other parts of the world where some of the constituent countries have backed, advised or even fought alongside opposing forces. Many of these wars and conflicts were entered into by the West to prevent the spread of communism, which was seen as the great threat to freedom. Political thinking was dominated by the 'domino theory', which suggested that if one country tipped over into communism, that would tip the next and so on, in the same way as dominoes will knock one another over if set up in a row. The Korean War in the early 1950s and the Vietnam War in the late 1960s and early 1970s were fought on that basis. Involvement of the USA in Latin America has also reflected the same fear. Each country, however, tended to adopt communist ideas in its own way because they were influenced by their own history and culture, as in China and Vietnam. Countries, unlike dominoes, are very different.

Economic dependency

While some feared communism, others feared the spread of what they regarded as capitalistic imperialism, a new form of colonialism. Although many European countries gave up or lost their colonies after 1945, it was feared that new empires were being built through the activities of transnational corporations. Political independence from the colonial power may have been won or freely granted but a new economic dependence seemed to be emerging, a dependence on western multinational investment. In countries where governments came to power which were not well disposed to these corporations, too often they were seen as threats to western democracy, even though they may have been democratically elected. The corporation represented capitalism, which is the economic system of the West. Perhaps to threaten one was seen as threatening the West in general. Most evidence supports the view that the violent overthrow of the Allende regime in Chile in the early 1970s, for example, was supported by American corporations and the CIA. Such defence of Latin America from communism, in this case a democratically elected regime, rather than from a revolution, as in Cuba, has to be juxtaposed with the Soviet Union's intervention in Hungary (1956) and Czechoslovakia (1968) to reinstate strong communist states on what it saw as its borders. Both superpowers have been involved in areas near their borders to maintain or put into power regimes that are friendly to them (Afghanistan by the USSR and El Salvador by the USA). Both have also attempted to gain the greater influence in the Middle East, which both see as an important strategic area because of its geographical position between the East and the West and its oil. Some Middle Eastern nations have played off one against the other, being sometimes friendlier to the USA, then to the USSR. Egypt fits such a picture. Syria and Saudi Arabia on the other hand have both been respectively pro-USSR and pro-USA and have received much backing from the superpowers. This has inflamed disputes within the area, particularly the Arab-Israeli conflicts. Yet at the same time the USA helped to set up the accord which restored peace between Israel and Egypt in the late 1970s and played a leading part in bringing about the United Nations coalition which forced the Iraqi army out of Kuwait in the Gulf War in 1991. Superpower involvement is therefore multi-faceted.

Relations between superpowers

The improved relations between the superpowers during the late 1980s is one of three major changes in the international political environment that may be identified, the other two being the emergence of religious fundamentalism in political form and the expansion of the green or environmental movement.

The cold war between the East and West has eased. This is reflected in proposed reductions in nuclear and conventional arms and much greater interaction and trade. The easing may be explained by their desire to secure a more peaceful or less threatened world, or by their need to reduce expenditure on weapons because it is wanted for the production of goods and services in their own countries. Internal pressure to improve the standard of life in the former USSR may well account for the Soviet initiatives. Greater openness (*glasnost*) and restructuring of political and economic life (*perestroika*) may mean that the USSR has become more inward-looking at itself and the eastern bloc. Equally, the transition of the USA from a world creditor to a debtor during the 1980s may have produced a change of thinking. American internal policies are certainly aimed at improving their economic position relative to Japan and Germany. Changes in the economic environments may have important effects, therefore, on the political environments. While the military-industrial lobby that has kept up pressure for defence spending and benefited from it (Chapter 9, Section 4) will no doubt continue to do so, it is much more probable than at any time since the late 1940s when the Cold War began that defence spend-

The dismantling of the Berlin Wall

ing may see a relative decline with consequent effects on companies and areas that have previously received contracts.

The contribution of the peace movement to this easing of tension is unclear. Those who argue that the threat of nuclear weapons has kept Europe free from war since 1945 may be committing the fallacy of associating two events in time and concluding that they are necessarily causally related. It may be equally fallacious to argue that recent rising pressure from the peace movement has led to the rapprochement between the East and West.

Islam

While tensions have lessened between the East and West, they have mounted elsewhere. The overthrow of the Shah and the instatement of Ayatollah Khomeini as leader of Iran in 1979 highlighted the emergence of a very significant trend, the politicisation of what has been called Islamic religious fundamentalism. Khomeini sought to rid Iran of western cultural imperialism, which he perceived as displacing Islam. Islam is not a religious culture that is part of a wider culture, which is how Christianity might be seen in Britain. It is a comprehensive religious philosophy or culture which teaches specific things such as that production should satisfy needs and that material wealth and growth are not necessarily good. Given this, it is easy to see why Khomeini and his followers were antipathetic to capitalism with its emphasis on consumption, satisfaction of wants and economic growth. He also wanted to reduce sharply the dependence of Iran's economy on the western-led capitalist system because western firms were managing or financing Iranian business. Iran, however, was still selling oil to finance its own, mainly consumer goods industries which were based

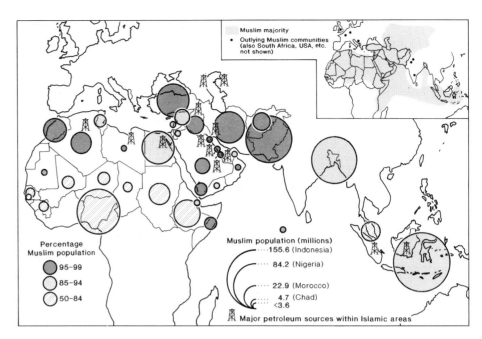

11.10 The Islamic world

largely on imported inputs.

Khomeini encouraged other Islamic countries to follow the Iranian revolution. Since one in five people in the world is a Muslim – one who follows the Islamic faith – such encouragement may have a significant effect on global stability. There are about thirty countries from Morocco to Indonesia, the most populous, that are Islamic or predominantly so (Figure 11.10).

There are sects within Islam, with 'orthodox' Sunni Muslims accounting for nearly 90 per cent and most of the remaining number belonging to the Shi'ah or Shi'ite sect. Iran is about two-thirds Shi'ite and while many Islamic countries may share its distrust of both the West and the East, they may also be wary of its own nationalism. From 1980 until 1989 it was at war with Iraq, another Islamic country but with a Sunni majority and an Arab rather than Persian national tradition (Chapter 11, Section 3a).

The Islamic resurgence has been used to justify terrorist actions by extreme groups in such areas of conflict, or 'hot spots', as the Lebanon. The capture of hostages from one country by groups in another has emerged as a common tactic which is used to exert political pressure on or extort a ransom from

the hostages' country. It allows relatively small political groups to wield considerable power over very large nations. Other extreme political groups such as the IRA in Ireland have also adopted such tactics. Care must be taken when discussing these extreme and violent aspects of Islamic fundamentalism. They are by no means typical of Islam. Such a connection would be similar to equating the IRA with Catholicism. Islamic resurgence does mean that greater understanding will be necessary both between Islamic and other countries, and within countries where there is an Islamic minority.

Green movement

A further major political movement of a very different kind, the green or environmentalist movement, is not associated with any one faith and as yet does not dominate the government of any one country (Chapter 11, Section 3c). Its emergence in the form of a political party has been particularly marked, however, in Germany, where the Greens received 8.3 per cent of the vote in 1987. Acid deposition (Chapter 7,

Section 3a) has been a major issue there, as westerly winds bring pollution from other western nations and easterly winds bring highly polluted air from the eastern bloc neighbours where pollution control had very low priority, at least until 1989. There are also Green members of parliament in Belgium and Italy. In the 1989 European election the Greens achieved a high per cent of the vote, almost 15 per cent in the UK. That election highlighted divisions within the movement that had been evident long before. Some are very left wing and socialist in their politics and have been called 'Red Greens', such as many in Germany. Others are more centralist as in France. Some are more to the right – the 'Blue Greens'.

In many countries where the electoral systems are based on some form of proportional representation, it is easier for new parties such as Green parties to obtain parliamentary seats and even to be in a position of holding the balance of power between parties. In Britain the 'first-past-the-post' system of electing Members of Parliament makes it very difficult for new or small parties to enter parliament unless they have geographically concentrated support, as do the Welsh and Scottish Nationalists (Chapter 11, Section 3b). Although there is some geographical variation in support for the green movement within countries, variation is much greater between countries. This reflects their different electoral systems as well as the extent of people's concern for the environment.

In this section the discussion has examined the changes at the national and international scales separately. There are, of course, important interactions between the two scales, as illustrated by the effect of the national electoral system on the success of the green movement. Further interactions will be discussed in the section on perspectives.

11.3 Other examples

Some of the developments mentioned in the previous section are discussed more fully here. At the international level, contrasts are made between the world as an arena of conflict and as a stage for cooperation. At the national scale, the difficulties of integrating countries politically is examined, with particular attention given to separatist movements. The green movement is discussed at national and international scales with national and international organisations identified which, together with green political parties, are important actors in the movement. Finally, a national policy is reviewed on a new form of organisation at the local level. Urban Development Corporations are new actors which both reflect and affect the changing relationship between central and local government.

11.3a The world as an arena of conflict or cooperation

For many years the politics of the world have been dominated by the interests and policies of nation-states. Each nation-state may be seen to have certain short- and long-term goals. Some of the more important ones are: to secure vital resources; to maintain favourable trade relations; and to defend the country. These and other goals can engender conflict or stimulate cooperation with other nation states. Particularly influential 'players' in this world political arena are the 'superpowers'. Until recently these were the USA and the former USSR. They have a global capacity to influence events. There are also the major powers who have strategic and/or commercial interests throughout large parts of the world and are either on the way up, such as Japan, or on the way down, such as Great Britain after the loss of its Empire. Lastly come the minor powers who have very limited direct role or influence on the world stage. The arena has been viewed as a chess board, with the superpowers as the queens, the major powers the knights, bishops and rooks and the minor powers the pawns.

The relationship between states can vary along a continuum with conflict and cooperation as the two poles. Sometimes there is a history of conflict, such as between France and Germany or England and France. These three countries have now moved along the continuum towards cooperation. The relationships between powers can swing between the two extremes over short periods of time. The so-called 'cold war', for example, between the Soviet Union and the western 'blocs', has done exactly that since the Second World War. The first cold war was between 1954 and 1963 – 1964 and was followed by a period of detente between 1964 and the late 1970s. The second cold war was between the late 1970s and 1987. Gorbachev's internal policies of *glasnost* and *perestroika* and his disarmament proposals have led to a distinct warming of relations since

1987. Conflicts can be short-lived and local, such as the Falklands/Malvinas conflict between Britain and Argentina in 1982, but on the other hand can be long-lasting and extensive in spatial impact, such as the Second World War. Other conflicts are localised but long-standing, such as the troubles in the Lebanon and on the borders of Israel. Often conflicts have underlying economic and/or religious as well as political bases and can be between alliances of countries based on common interests. The world is sadly full of local conflicts or 'hot spots' where human and environmental damage is caused. The Persian Gulf was a classic example of this where petroleum, religious fervour and tangled international relations made a deadly brew. In 1979 religious fundamentalists took over in Iran and the new leadership installed Islamic law. Iraq felt threatened by its neighbour and invaded in September 1980, striking at refineries and an oil-loading terminal at Kharg Island. Iran responded in October by taking Iraq's Gulf oil terminals and preventing Iraqi tanker shipments from passing through the Gulf. The attacks and threats on oil tankers led to the involvement of the USA and other nations which were concerned over the security of oil shipments and they began to escort tankers sailing under their flags. The conflict drew in both superpowers and major powers to safeguard their interests. The danger was that the situation would lead to a wider conflict. Within the Gulf region, nations took actions to avoid that. Within a year of the Iraqi invasion, Saudi Arabia, Kuwait, Bahrain, Qatar, the United Arab Emirates and Oman established the Gulf Cooperation Council to strengthen economic and cultural ties but with security of the Gulf region as a top priority. Although the Iran-Iraq War ended in the late 1980s, further major hostilities rapidly ensued as in 1990 when Iraq invaded Kuwait

and the Gulf War between Iraq and the United Nations force, led by the USA, resulted. In a very short time, in western eyes, Iraq had turned from almost an ally into an enemy. The geographical impacts of such conflicts are wideranging. Clearly, the effects on the peoples and environments of Kuwait, Iraq and Iran have been devastating, but in the longer term there is likely to be less investment in the Gulf since it is regarded as an unstable area and transnational oil companies will be looking for alternative supply areas.

International cooperation, like conflict, is underlain by strategic, commercial and political influences. So the North Atlantic Treaty Organisation (NATO) set up in 1949 (including Canada and the USA and most West European countries) and the Warsaw Pact in 1955 (including the USSR and its Eastern European satellites) had clear strategic goals. On the other hand, international groups such as the European Community in Western Europe and Comecon for Eastern Europe had initially economic objectives. Similarly, commodity cartels have emerged such as OPEC (oil) set up in 1960, COPAL (cocoa) set up in 1962 and ITC (tin) in 1971 and they dominate the world supply of their respective products. Other alliances have political goals. The African National Congress (ANC), for instance, represents the front-line African states in their fight against apartheid in South Africa.

The geographical impacts of all these alliances are extensive. The European Community's policies on agriculture, the Common Agricultural Policy (CAP), and on the regional problem (the Regional Fund), for example, have had wide-ranging impacts. The CAP's main aims, for instance, are:
* to increase agricultural productivity
* to ensure thereby a fair standard of living for people involved in agriculture
* to stabilise markets

* to guarantee regular agricultural supplies
* to ensure reasonable prices in supplies to consumers.

The impacts of these goals are open to debate but some include overproduction in wheat, sugar, milk, butter and wine. CAP subsidies have led, for instance, to much greater areas of land in the UK being given over to arable farming and a transformation of its rural landscape, for example rape seed and its striking yellow colour. Countries with larger agricultural sectors have tended to gain at the expense of those with smaller agricultural sectors. For instance, France and Denmark benefit much more than Britain. Within Britain, greater CAP support to cereal farmers has led to larger farms reinforcing existing specialisation based largely on physical factors, of cereals in the South East and livestock farming, which is less generously supported by CAP, in the North and West. This has added to the general North West/South East divide in farm prosperity in Britain. However, the effects of the CAP are not felt only by farmers. It has indirect effects on many other aspects of society: on employment in farm-related industries, on consumers of food, on planning; and on recreation. Agricultural development of large arable farms in areas like the Norfolk Broads has consequences for recreation and other land uses in the area as well as the local farm-related industries.

The changeover in Britain from imported cane to home-grown sugar beet has affected the operations of Britain's major sugar refiner, Tate and Lyle. By 1979, 2000 refining jobs had been lost, mainly on Clydeside and Merseyside; in 1981 their main Liverpool refinery was closed with more job losses. In this case the CAP was a key element affecting the pace and direction of change, and with particular geographical consequences.

11.3b **Degree of integration of states and separatism**

Integration of regions within states, and disintegration, cause pressures within states or groupings of states. The former USSR, for instance, since the Second World War effectively 'bound in' its own periphery both within its national boundaries and in Eastern Europe by a combination of economic and military pressures. Military pressure was applied to achieve the continued integration of Hungary in 1956. Economic and political pressure was used to tie together the constituent republics of the USSR until the late 1980s when various separatist movements began on its periphery, such as in Tadzshikistan, Armenia, Uzbekistan, Lithuania, Latvia and Estonia.

Regional nationalism or separatism is common throughout the world. Separatist movements vary from underground, violent, illegal organisations to overtly peaceful political parties. The degree of political integration within a state varies over time and from country to country. Some Basques, Quebecois, Bretons and Scottish are to different degrees and with different tactics trying to achieve greater autonomy, indeed ideally independence, from a central government from which they feel alienated. Such areas often have distinct languages and culture and are peripheral geographically to the core within the nation state. These factors underlie the regional separatist movements. However, the success of such movements has been limited since they have already been largely integrated into their nation states economically and culturally as well as politically. This is particularly true for the areas within the regions that border the rest of the nation. These areas are often less supportive of the movement than the peripheral areas within the region. Often internal political, cultural and language divisions within such regions also hamper the movement's progress. Whereas Scotland, for example, had its own independent existence before becoming part of Great Britain, the Basque Country never had.

Thus the Basque nationalists had to invent a Basque word for the four Spanish and three French provinces which make up the whole of the Basque country – 'Euskadi' – and the separatist slogan '4 + 3 = 1' was taken by some to indicate the unlikelihood of a separate Basque state comprising all seven provinces ever emerging (Figure 11.11). Such

Country/ Political Parties	1945	1959	1970	1974 October	1979
Scotland:	%	%	%	%	%
Nationalist	1.3	0.8	11.1	30.4	17.3
Conservative	41.0	47.2	38.0	24.7	31.4
Liberal	5.6	4.1	5.5	8.3	9.0
Labour	47.5	46.7	44.5	36.3	41.4
Wales:					
Nationalist	1.1	4.8	19.7	10.8	8.1
Conservative	23.9	32.6	27.7	23.9	32.2
Liberal	15.0	5.5	6.8	15.5	10.6
Labour	58.4	56.4	51.6	49.5	48.5

11.12 Scottish and Welsh nationalist votes

separatist pressures can have indirect and different geographical effects. It may be argued that in order to off-set the separatist pressure of the Scottish nationalists, British governments have given Scotland a greater share of the national cake than would otherwise have been the case.

On the other hand, the province of Quebec with its still active 'Quebec libre' movement has lost investment and resources to the neighbouring rich but stable Ontario where Toronto has especially gained at the expense of Montreal and perhaps Quebec City. Similarly, outbreaks of violent Welsh nationalism have probably caused a slowdown in English people purchasing cottages and thereby engaging in expenditure in certain Welsh mountain areas. This violence represents a minority of the Welsh nationalist movement, which is represented politically by Plaid Cymru (Figure 11.12).

11.11 The Basque country and provinces: 4+3=1

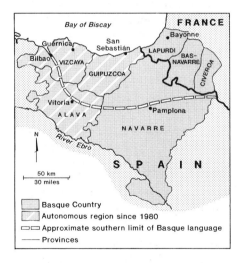

- ▨ Basque Country
- ▧ Autonomous region since 1980
- ▭▭ Approximate southern limit of Basque language
- —— Provinces

11.3c **The green or environmental movement**

A political movement of relatively recent history but of rapidly growing power is the green movement. Arguably it can be traced back to the 'prophet of environmentalism', John Muir, who in 1892 in California initiated the Sierra Club. The environmental movement has been very prominent in the USA and in many ways has taken a leading role. National Parks, for example, were first set up there at Yellowstone in

1872 with the National Park Service established in 1916 to manage eleven parks. The movement, though, has had periods of quiescence before emerging again, often triggered by particular events or issues. Rachel Carson's *Silent Spring*, for instance, aroused much concern over the uses of pesticides and insecticides during the 1960s, when the environmental movement re-emerged as a strong force. In some ways the USA has been ahead of other countries, for example in the introduction of lead-free petrol and in concern over ozone depleting gases, which were removed from many aerosols in the late 1970s. Britain followed in both cases about a decade later. The Friends of the Earth was established as a radical wing of the movement in the USA in 1969. Radicalism and a new style of campaigning based on the complementary tactics of solidly based academic research and conscious publicity seeking gestures became the order of the day.

The environmental movement gained momentum in Britain when Sir Frank Fraser Darling delivered his Reith lectures on the environment, pointing to the 250,000 acres of dereliction in Britain which 'are just the bare bones of our degradation' and warning of 'the more subtle effects of air and water pollution [which] have not been presented in any national balance sheet but [which)] are dreadful in the real meaning of the word'. In 1971 came the founding of the UK Friends of the Earth (FoE) which in its short history has made a significant contribution to making people aware of environmental issues, giving evidence at public inquiries, affecting legislation and opposing potentially environmentally damaging proposals. These include whaling, acid rain, Windscale (Sellafield) and Sizewell Inquiries, Royal Commissions on environmental pollution, endangered species legislation, and Rio Tinto Zinc's plans for the Mawddach Estuary.

At the international level, World Wide Fund for Nature (WWF) and Greenpeace are similar and related organisations, while in Britain Friends of the Earth work together with a network of environmentally concerned groups such as the Royal Society for the Protection of Birds (RSPB) and the Council for the Protection of Rural England (CPRE). Certain personalities give a higher profile in the media to environmental issues, for example Jacques Cousteau (French) on marine life, David Attenborough (British) on wildlife in general, and the ecologist David Bellamy (British).

Greenpeace has been particularly active, radical and successful in its campaigns. Action has included drawing attention to the plight of North Sea seals and the pollution in the Irish Sea from Sellafield. Major world attention was drawn to the *Rainbow Warrior* incident in New Zealand when the ship was blown up during protests against French nuclear tests in the Pacific.

Present campaigns are:
- To save the whales.
- To protect seals, dolphins, porpoises and sea turtles.
- To reduce the trade in endangered species.
- To stop tests of nuclear weapons.
- To stop the disposal of radioactive waste and dangerous chemicals at sea.

Jacques Cousteau

David Attenborough

David Bellamy

- To close down nuclear power stations and nuclear processing plants.
- To stop acid rain and protect the atmosphere.
- To declare Antarctica a World Park, free from all military and industrial exploitation.

Their campaigns have been supported by the role of environmental education in schools, which agencies such as RSPB and WWF support. They produce a level of public concern that politicians can ill afford to ignore. In early 1989, for example, Mrs Thatcher, the British Prime Minister, who had previously not been known for her interest in environmental issues, made a key-note speech that focused particularly on the global issues of ozone depletion and the increase of gases that contribute to the 'greenhouse effect'. This gave added impetus to media attention on environmental issues which raised awareness and perhaps contributed to the Green Party's 15 per cent share of the vote in the mid-1989 European election. The green movement has changed party politics in many western countries. In some countries the green movement has been represented mainly by green parties, such as De Grunen in West Germany. In others, many parties have incorporated green elements into their manifestos. Some of the environmental concerns are local or national, but many are global. This has meant that western countries which have contributed in a very significant way to environmental damage are now pressing LDCs to adopt environmental policies which they feel they can ill afford. Global environmental issues have now formed one of the major focuses for debate between the Western and Third World countries, or the 'North' and 'South' as the divide is more widely known.

11.3d Urban Development Corporations

During the 1980s when the government in the UK was dismantling the metropolitan counties, it began creating Urban Development Corporations (UDCs) as a cornerstone of its inner-city policy. In 1980 the then Secretary of State for the Environment, Michael Heseletine, set up the London Docklands Development Corporation (LDDC) and the Merseyside Development Corporation (MDC). They were given four main aims to achieve regeneration: to bring London buildings into effective use; to create an attractive environment; to encourage the development of new industry and commerce; and to ensure that housing and social facilities were available to encourage people to live and work in the area. They were a form of state intervention where the corporations had a coordinating and promotional role, using public money to 'pump prime', 'lever' or attract considerably more private investment. They were seen by their opponents as anti-democratic agencies because locally elected bodies had no representation on them. Their supporters put them forward as models of what strong involvement by the private sector can achieve.

The MDC for instance is a small and simple organisation that was given the task of physically regenerating 865 acres of redundant dockland (Figure 11.13).

It consists of a chairman and a board of thirteen, appointed by the Secretary of State, which meets at monthly intervals. There is a small permanent core staff of about sixty including three architects, four engineers and two planners. These professional staff act essentially as project managers and encourage schemes designed by private consultants and implemented by private contractors. Two advantages of UDCs have been suggested: administrative simplicity and speed of implementation. Proponents suggest that these have been amply demonstrated by 'bringing land and building into effective use' and 'creating an attractive environment'. The speed of implementation was permitted because the planning and consultation procedures of local authorities were by-passed. Much

11.13 The Merseyside Urban Development Corporation

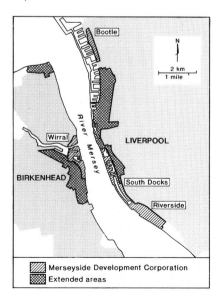

The refurbished Albert Dock, Liverpool

land was purchased including the Albert Dock which was refurbished to contain shops, restaurants, flats, museums and art gallery, in all attracting about 3 million visitors a year. The International Garden Festival was also completed. A new tourism/leisure-led strategy was developed for the Liverpool waterfront, after the failure to attract sufficient industrial interest. This rapid activity was seen by supporters as boosting confidence in Liverpool's future, while opponents viewed it as superficial and not tackling the real problems. While much has been achieved in a short time,

the MDC has yet to generate the significant levels of private investment which the government expected, or a significant number of jobs. Only 1500 jobs had been generated by 1988 and arguably at great public cost. The MDC was also accused of poor management, by a House of Commons Public Accounts Committee, in letting the Liverpool Garden Festival site to a company which went into liquidation owing £2.6 million on festival activities. Despite the extension of the MDC area in 1987, it is having an impact on only relatively small areas of a city where deprivation is still wide-

spread. Some fear the creation of a 'waterfront oasis in the middle of a Liverpool desert'.

Other UDCs have been established since 1987: Bristol, Cardiff, Black Country, Trafford/Salford, Central Manchester, Sheffield, Leeds, Teesside and Tyneside. Some argue that UDCs achieve results faster and more assuredly than local authorities. Critics argue that local authorities would achieve similar results, be more accountable and be more oriented to the needs of local people if they had the same financial resources as the UDCs.

11.4 Alternative strategies

Three major sets of strategies will be discussed, all of which apply at various geographical scales. The first involves whether to centralise or decentralise political control and the related question of whether to organise government by area or by economic or service sector (Chapter 4, Section 4). The second concerns the degree to which political units should be integrated together. In many ways these two are related issues. The difference depends on the scale from which you are looking. In the first, one political unit area decides the extent to which power should be decentralised within it. In the second, a political unit decides the extent to which it wants to be integrated with others. Both are partly a question of the geographical distribution of power. The third set of strategies relates to the scale and degree of targeting of policies. To what extent should policies be targeted spatially? What scale of areas should be used for particular policies? All these strategies can apply to various scales: within a local government area, within a region or state, within a nation or within a supra-state such as the European Community.

Centralise or decentralise power?

The degree to which power is centralised at a national level can often be seen by the size of the capital city relative to other cities and by the degree to which national government functions are concentrated into one city or region of the country. In federal systems, the capital city has often been chosen so that no one state capital or largest city becomes the centre of power; Washington DC in the USA, Canberra in Australia,

Ottawa in Canada and Brasilia in Brazil are such examples. Washington DC was even designed so that the physical arrangement of its political institutions reflects the checks and balances that control the distribution of power between them. The choice of capital and its design may, then, reflect the distribution of power and is one dimension to the centralisation/decentralisation strategies.

Wherever the national government's functions are located, there is

11.14 The advantages and disadvantages of decentralisation

Some national level powers decentralised to local government.		
powers	advantages	disadvantages
policy making	based on detailed local knowledge, can fit local needs	non-uniform national policy, possibility of too parochial a view or too extreme views
raising revenue	control over amount raised and spending priorities (if national government permits)	less national control over public expenditure
redistribution	can redistribute within area (eg tax rich more than poor)	limited tax base, not obtaining redistribution between areas of country
Some local government powers decentralised to local areas		
policy making	area-based priorities rather than priorities reached within divisions/ departments which do not consider overall outcomes for local areas	too parochial view perhaps with too little attention to minority groups
service delivery	close to people in receipt of service, more responsive, easier access	lacks economies of scale

also a question of the amount of power that is concentrated at the national level relative to regional/ state or local levels. Figure 11.14 shows the possible degrees of decentralisation and the advantages and disadvantages for this question. It also displays similar questions for local government and decentralisation within its area. (Readers should refer back to Chapter 4 for a more general discussion of the organisation of private and public services which complements the discussion here.)

Power may be decentralised or devolved to varying degrees. Regions or local areas may have their own assemblies or councils which raise their own finance and make decisions about their own geographical areas. Some would argue that such powers should be devolved to Scotland so that it remains in the Union but enjoys a much greater control over its own affairs. This would counter the argument that it is controlled from London, often by a party in government with a minority of the Scottish votes. Clearly the call for devolution will be greater in countries where there are clear geographical cultural divides that are reinforced by different patterns of voting. Central governments often find it difficult to decide whether to agree or resist such pressure, because they fear that either course may lead to the area seeking an independent existence. They also often try to limit any loss of central power.

In a lesser form of decentralisation, finances may be raised centrally and the devolved institution decides how the allocated budget is spent on services within its area. Local management of schools within local authorities in England and Wales under the 1988 Education Reform Act set up a similar system where the school was the equivalent of the geographical area and the head and governing body the equivalent of the assembly. Some local authorities, such as Rochdale and

Walsall, have set up decentralised area offices so that they can try to meet local needs more efficiently and allocate their budgets within areas to meet local priorities. Sometimes there is no local budget allocation but services are organised and delivered locally. This aims at better coordination between services. In an even lesser form, local offices may exist simply to inform the local people and receive requests or complaints about services that are centrally organised and delivered.

A major aspect in the above degrees of decentralisation is the inclusion of some local political representation. If there is no locally elected body which makes decisions on either locally set or allocated budgets, then decentralisation is simply a management technique for the delivery of services.

The advantages of decentralised power lie around the potential to respond to local needs and demands. Local 'voice' can more easily take the full form of participation rather than consultation (Chapter 7, Section 4). It permits greater local democracy and accountability.

Centralised power, where democratic, depends on representative democracy and a bureaucracy which takes and conveys central decisions for local implementation. Decisions are taken more remotely from the areas they affect, yet the expertise available to the decision-makers may be much greater. Though they may not be so familiar with particular local circumstances, they have wider experience upon which to draw from many different kinds of areas. Such wider understanding may offset the potential parochialism of decentralised systems.

Degree of integration

The second set of strategies concerned with degrees of integration is well illustrated by the debate over the future structure of the European

Community. Full integration might involve a federal system, as in the USA and India. Every country would become the equivalent of a state in the USA. Even though Europe might adopt a similar constitution to the USA which carefully balances power between its various constituent bodies and between the federal and state governments, countries would lose a considerable amount of their present autonomy. Their identity and people's loyalty to them may still remain but people may also identify with and be loyal to the European Community. In many ways this is no different from someone in Lancashire feeling Lancastrian, English and British. They could also feel European. This is identity at different scales.

Full integration would entail, for example, major economic, social, environmental and defence policies being made at a European level. All of the countries would belong to one monetary system and indeed might share the same currency. There may be many advantages to this in political relations with the rest of the world. Europe would have greater economic and political power.

Within Europe such full integration may be less popular because countries would have less control over their internal affairs. Decisions may be taken that are for the good of the Community as a whole but they may not affect every country in the same way and may be to the detriment of a few in order to be for the good of the many. Countries that think they will find themselves too often in the 'few' may decide against full integration. Countries that see themselves as peripheral to the Community, perhaps geographically, economically or culturally, might also see less advantage than those which perceive themselves as central in these ways. Those which see themselves as becoming less powerful within the Community by full integration may also prefer a more cooperative structure that permits greater self-determination. Such decisions may be made on the basis of imagining future geographies, whether they be idealistic or realistic. Once made, they certainly affect future geographies.

This discussion has been at the scale of nation- and supra-state. A similar analysis could be carried out at the level of an area on the urban fringe and a metropolitan authority into which it might be integrated, as indicated in the case study (Chapter 11, Section 1). The first question is whether to be included and, if so, how the responsibilities would be shared between the local area and the metropolitan authority. In Britain, at least, these decisions are finally made by national rather than local government.

To target or not?

The third set of strategies concerns the targeting of policies. Many policies have been made in the past which involve achieving a minimum level of quality of life for everyone, for example levels of nutrition and standards of housing. Some of these have been applied universally so that everyone within the population receives them. In Britain the provision of free school milk is a good example of this in the recent past, while child benefit is a present example. In order to ensure that every child received a minimum level of nutrients a day, everyone was given a free third of a pint of milk. Many children would already have received sufficient calcium and other nutritional requirements, so did not need the milk. Such policies are obviously expensive. The idea of targeting policies on to those who require them may superficially seem more sensible. The idea is similar to the private sector targeting market segments for particular kinds of goods and services that they demand.

Targeting of policies, as with targeting of market segments, requires finding out who and where are the people who need the services. Need, though, is not the same as want. People may need the service but they may not want to be identified or labelled as such. Some may regard the service as a form of charity and refuse to accept it. Many will not want to complete forms that permit the government to determine whether they qualify for the service, as they see such a process as a form of means testing and degrading. So the target population may be difficult to identify or difficult to reach. Many in need may not receive the service. Such targeting of individuals may, then, be costly to administer and not as effective as universal provision at reaching those in need.

Spatial targeting

Spatial targeting is an alternative strategy which has often been used (Chapter 13, Section 4). Certain areas are identified that contain many of those in need for a particular service or benefit, or that have a much higher proportion of people in need of a whole range of services or benefits (these are called multiply deprived areas). Implicit in the approach is the idea that living in an area where there is a concentration of people in need is more difficult and in itself magnifies the level of need. Extra resources are therefore necessary for those areas. During the late 1960s, when such area-based policies were very popular, it was thought that there were cycles of poverty or deprivation that extended from generation to generation and prevented people in these areas from realising their potential. Targeting extra resources into the areas was meant to break the cycle. Such thinking partly underlay the idea of Education Priority Areas (EPAs) which were set up after the Plowden Report (1967) on primary education in Britain. Extra resources were put into schools in these areas and teachers were paid more in order to attract and retain better teachers. They modelled themselves on similar thinking in the USA for the Headstart educational initiative, part of the Johnson administration's poverty programme in the 1960s.

Criticisms of area-based policies

Such *area-based policies* were criticised because they neglected many people in need who lived outside the areas, and indeed included many within the areas who were not in need. In the then Inner London Education Authority (ILEA) only 28 per cent of multiply disadvantaged children went to EPA schools. Half the schools in the authority would have had to be designated as EPAs in order to include, even then, only 74 per cent of such pupils. Such criticisms miss the point that concentrations of such children may make it even more difficult to progress. They do, however, show one of the major difficulties of spatial targeting.

A further criticism concerned the idea of cycles of poverty which tended to suggest that the reasons for the deprivation or disadvantage lay with the people and the area. Many argued that wider social and economic forces produced the problems and that concentration on the areas ignored these. The 'blame' lay not with the people or the area but outside. Other criticism suggested that such compensatory policies would not work in the face of stronger societal processes. Others criticised the idea because it labelled areas, suggesting that there was something wrong with them. Such labelling may have encouraged movement out and discouraged movement in. It was further observed that some areas are subject to rapid change and that designation at one point of time may not be justified a short time later.

Such policies became less favoured. Education Priority Areas became Social Priority (1975) schools aimed more at positive discrimination for special groups or needs rather than areas. Their status received less publicity because of the labelling issue. Yet area-based policies continued to be used in housing where attempts were made to improve whole areas. A series of programmes and initiatives directed at the inner cities continued to use the strategy. Some had social objectives. Others were to improve the local environments.

They were given greater prominence again in the 1980s, during which time the term 'spatial targeting' began to be used. At that time the initiatives were more economic than social. They were aimed at creating jobs and developing property. They targeted areas in order to attract more investment into them. Sometimes they removed planning controls and offered financial incentives, such as in Enterprise Zones. They promoted the areas and coordinated activities within them so that

they could be revitalised. Urban Development Corporations (Chapter 11, Section 3d) and Urban Task Forces are two such examples. The reasons for the initiatives were different but they were still area-based. They still diagnosed area-based problems, but the criteria for designation were different and the indicators of success had changed. Increased land values became a measure of success.

Criticisms of spatial targeting

Such spatially targeted policies have been criticised for ignoring social issues. The people who lived in the targeted areas have often received little from the initiatives. Many have been displaced and replaced by higher income people. Many of the jobs created have gone to people from outside the area, increasing commuter traffic. Some of the jobs have not been created but have simply been moved from other local

areas where financial incentives are not available. The built environment has been improved, so land values and property prices have increased. The emphasis has been on *property and place*, but *not people*.

Spatial targeting, then, is criticised again for not hitting the right people and for including some that do not need the incentives, in this case higher-income people, property developers and companies that have transferred rather than created jobs.

There are some criticisms that are inherent to spatial targeting. These are including within areas people, land uses and activities that are not in need of assistance; and, by designating an area, either attracting people or activities that do not need incentives, or, through labelling it, repelling people or activities that might otherwise have moved in. Although labelling is often associated with social issues, there have been instances when an area has refused to be designated to receive economic incentives because such labelling may have discouraged inward investment.

11.5 Perspectives

As in the other types of environments, there are different forms of change in the political environment: trends, cycles and sudden changes. As with the other changes, it is not always easy at the time to distinguish between an upward trend and the upturn in a cycle, or to realise whether the present period is one of major change to a different system or a period of instability within the same system. For example, the emergence of the Alliance between the Liberals and the Social Democrats in the 1980s seemed to have ended the period of two-party politics that had characterised Britain for most of the century. The collapse of the Alliance after the 1987 election and the disruption caused by the merger of the two parties may herald a return to a

two-party system or a short-term lull in the fortunes of the third party.

Cycles

Cycles may be identified, such as the electoral ones, where governments introduce what may be controversial or unpopular policies in the earlier part of their term and more popular ones in the later part when they are seeking re-election. Such cycles often have effects on the economic environment, with mini-booms appearing just before elections. There are also longer cycles, such as those identified in Chapter 4 on the relative emphasis between the public and private

sectors. Such a cycle can be illustrated by the diagnoses and solutions of inner-city problems. In the 1960s and early 1970s they were viewed as problems created by disinvestment of the private sector, and public solutions were proposed that changed the social and built environments. In the 1980s, in contrast, some saw the problems as being created by the inefficiency and overspending of local government and inappropriate public education. A private solution involving property development was followed. A related cycle is the swing between wealth creation and economic growth on the one hand, and redistribution of real income and social justice on the other. Such cycles have indirect geographical effects through the type of policies that are followed, as the inner city example demonstrates.

These cycles are also reflected to some extent in the changing geographical distribution of party political support. Between elections in Britain, for example, support will usually harden for the main opposition party in its geographical heartland while in the heartland of the party of government, its support may dwindle and be threatened in mid-term by-elections by the main opposition party or a third party. The latter often gains its greatest success at such times when its party workers and resources can be concentrated in one place rather than spread across the nation as in a general election. Mid-term by-election losses, which are characterised by protest votes, are often won back at the next general election.

Many of the other cycles are also reflected in the changing geography of party political support. A national swing away from the support of the public sector and redistribution of real income may be more strongly opposed in areas where public sector employment is relatively high and/or where there is much greater need for redistribution from wealthier regions. During such a swing any economic and social divides which have a spatial expression will probably be accentuated. This will generally be reflected in even greater spatial divisions in voting behaviour.

As the spatial distribution of support changes, through either population movement or a switch of party allegiance, there is sometimes a tendency for parties in power to restructure the spatial organisation of constituencies in order to maximise their chances of electoral success. This biased adjustment of constituency boundaries is called 'gerrymandering'. The changing spatial distribution of population offers the opportunity to gerrymander because in Britain boundary changes are needed to retain constituencies of similar population size. It is therefore very important that such alterations are made in an unbiased, open way.

Voting systems

In Britain the first-past-the-post voting system clearly identifies a Member of Parliament with a spatially defined constituency which only he or she represents. At the same time such a system can yield a distribution of seats in parliament that does not correlate very much with the distribution of votes. It is also difficult for minority parties to gain seats unless their support is spatially concentrated, as are the nationalist votes of the Scottish and Welsh. Critics argue that the first-past-the-post procedure maintains a two party system and the confrontational politics that that so often involves. Supporters note its simplicity and the clear identification of an MP with an area. Other countries employ some form of proportional representation, where the number of seats is related to the number of votes. In such systems Members of Parliament usually represent larger areas and are not the sole representatives of their constituency. Critics suggest that such systems produce coalition governments which too often give too much power to minority parties whose support is necessary for the coalition. Supporters note that there is greater continuity of government and cooperation and negotiation are the main political processes rather than confrontation and rhetoric.

The effects of centralisation/decentralisation

There are other differences between countries and over time within a country in the spatial organisation of political and administrative control. As discussed in Chapter 11, Section 4, a major one is the degree of centralisation/decentralisation. Centralised systems encourage top-down decision-making in which, even though lower levels may be consulted, the idea and decision come from the top. Decentralised systems can be more open to bottom-up decision-making where the idea has come from lower levels and the decision may even be made there. Decentralised systems allow more local diversity and innovation, while centralised systems allow greater spatial coordination of policies and perhaps an easier introduction and diffusion of innovations.

The permissive nature of the relationship of political organisation to the above effects is important. Such forms of organisation are similar to technology (some would say they are a form of technology) and they have permissive rather than deterministic effects. The degree of decentralisation is not usually imposed on the nation as a whole. It has grown out of political and other processes operating within the nation over many years. Decentralisation therefore might exist because the particular nation has a tradition of bottom-up decision-making. Another that is centralised may have experienced and generally accepted such government over many years. There can be some fluctuation between the two, however, within a country. Indeed at times, there may be a dramatic change from one to the other as there is a revolution in the political system.

Effects on other environments

The effects of the political processes, structures and strategies discussed in this chapter on the other environments and processes are numerous and varied. Some of them have already been discussed in this chapter and the preceding three chapters under governments' strategies towards the environment, economy, technology and society. Political decisions on energy policy, for example, affect the physical environment in terms of which resources are used and the amount of pollution emitted. They also influence the direction of technological development – for instance whether it involves nuclear, fossil-fuel or renewable resources.

Political decisions also very much affect the economic and social environments. For example, the strategies of spatial targeting, area-based and regional policies with their incentives and concessions can affect the costs of business organisations and to that extent change their economic environment. Targeted rather than universal welfare policies can accentuate distinctions between people, and so in a similar way to segmented rather than mass marketing can increase social differences.

Most importantly, political decisions and processes affect both the type of physical environment in which we shall live in the future and the chances of our living in peace.

11.6 **Exercises**

1. (a) By examining the newspapers and other media over the last three months, identify the current 'hot spots' in the world.
   (b) Are they spatially concentrated or dispersed?
   (c) What are the possible causes of the conflicts within countries? Are other countries involved in these conflicts?
   (d) For all conflicts, discuss the extent to which the following are involved:
       (i) resources
       (ii) economic disputes
       (iii) religious differences
       (iv) separatism
       (v) any other factor you consider important.

2. For each of the following issues, discuss whether decisions should be made at the local or national levels:
   (a) (i) the curriculum and
       (ii) the organisation of schools;
   (b) types of policing;
   (c) abortion;
   (d) health care.

3. Examine the changes in voting in the tables (Figure 11.15).
   (a) Using the information on the three Scottish regions:
       (i) indicate the major trends apparent for Scotland as a whole, relative to the changes in Britain as a whole;
       (ii) indicate the major differences between the Scottish regions.
   (b) Using the information for the four SE regions:
       (i) indicate the major trends for them as a whole, relative to national changes;
       (ii) indicate the major differences between the four.
   (c) From this evidence, what are the major differences between the changing patterns of voting in Scotland and the South East of England?
   (d) Suggest reasons for these differences.
   (e) Compare the changes in the voting of the three conurbations (Figure 11.15).
       (i) Which two of the three are more similar?
       (ii) Which of the three is more similar to the South East?
       (iii) Which is more similar to Scotland?
   (f) From this partial evidence, is there any basis for saying that the nation's voting became more spatially polarised during the 1980s?
   (g) If so, suggest reasons for this polarisation.

11.15 Changes in the percentage of the electorate voting for each party, comparing the 1979, 1983 and 1987 elections

	Conservative			Labour			Alliance		
	79-83	83-87	79-87	79-83	83-87	79-87	79-83	83-87	79-87
National	− 1.7	1.1	− 0.6	− 7.2	4.1	−3.1	8.3	− 1.4	6.9
Scotland									
Strathclyde	− 3.3	− 2.4	− 5.7	− 3.9	10.5	6.6	11.2	− 4.0	7.2
East Scotland	− 0.9	− 0.9	− 1.8	− 4.6	7.9	3.3	11.0	− 3.3	8.6
Rural Scotland	− 0.3	− 0.3	− 0.6	− 4.0	5.2	1.3	8.1	1.0	9.1
South East England									
Inner London	− 3.8	2.6	−1.2	− 7.4	3.2	−4.1	7.8	−0.1	7.7
Outer London	− 3.2	3.7	0.5	− 9.0	1.6	− 7.3	8.3	− 2.3	6.0
Outer metropolitan	− 0.5	2.9	2.4	− 8.4	1.1	− 7.3	8.5	− 1.2	7.2
Outer South East	− 0.4	1.8	1.4	− 7.7	1.3	− 6.4	8.1	0.4	8.5
Merseyside	− 5.0	− 3.5	− 8.5	− 4.5	7.7	3.1	6.8	0.7	7.5
Greater Manchester	− 4.0	0.8	− 3.1	− 6.3	4.6	− 1.7	6.9	− 1.8	5.1
West Midlands	− 3.4	1.4	− 2.0	− 6.2	2.9	− 3.3	8.7	− 1.9	6.7

11.7 **Further reading**

M. Campbell (ed.) (1990) *Local Economic Policy*, Cassell

R.J. Johnson, C. Pattie and J. Allsop (1988) *A Nation Dividing? The electoral map of Great Britain*

R.J. Johnson and P. Taylor (eds.) (1989) *World in Crisis? Geographical Perspectives*, 2nd ed.

J. Mohan (ed.) (1989) *The Political Geography of Contemporary Britain*, Macmillan

R. Paddison (1983) *The Fragmented State: the Political Geography of Power*, Basil Blackwell

D. Pepper (1984) *The Roots of Modern Environmentalism*

J. Short (1989) *Introduction to Political Geography*, Routledge

P. Taylor (1989) *Political Geography: World-Economy, Nation State and Locality*, Longman

C.H. Williams and E. Kofman (eds.) (1989) *Community, Conflict, Par
tition and Nationalism*, Routledge

PART IV

SYNTHESIS: HOME AND WORK

Chapter 12
The changing geography of work

12.1 Case study: sectoral shifts in employment
     and spatial ramifications
12.2 General problems
12.3 Other examples
     12.3a Coventry: striving to adapt
     12.3b Gender and employment
     12.3c Ethnic employment
12.4 Alternative strategies
12.5 Perspectives
12.6 Exercises
12.7 Further reading

Chapter 13
Urban renewal policies and access to housing

13.1 Case study: from redevelopment to rehabilitation in
     Birmingham
13.2 General problem
13.3 Other examples
     13.3a New developments in the metropolitan ring:
           Saint-Quentin-En-Yvelines
     13.3b Rehabilitation: a GIA and an HAA
     13.3c Gentrification in London's Islington and
           Battersea and some American cities
     13.3d Housing stress: the London borough of Brent
13.4 Alternative strategies
13.5 Perspectives
13.6 Exercises
13.7 Further reading

The recession has badly hit the South... but has hardly affected the North

Based on *The Guardian*, Saturday–Sunday June 1–2 1991

Chapter 12

THE CHANGING GEOGRAPHY OF WORK

12.1 Case study: sectoral shifts in employment and spatial ramifications

Economies are constantly changing and the UK's is no exception. Throughout much of the nineteenth century the UK's economy was driven by the highly dynamic coal and iron and steel related industries. These have declined dramatically since the 1920s, with a new boom period for consumer goods production occurring in the post-war period. Since the mid-1970s there has been a rapid growth in employment in parts of the tertiary sector and high-tech-related industry. The main sectoral changes post-war are shown in Figure 12.1.

The most extreme examples of growth and decline in manufacturing are highlighted in the late 1970s (Figure 12.2), a period of very rapid

Manufacturing output index 1981	(1975=100)
Electronic computers	253.5
Radio and electronic components	144.7
Radio, radar and electronic capital goods	124.3
Plastic products	122.4
Pharmaceutical chemicals and preparations	115.9
Iron castings	55.5
Leather, leather goods and fur	65.5
Shipbuilding and marine engineering	68.5
Textiles	71.3
Other metal goods	73.3

12.2 The extremes of growth and decline

employment change.

The general spatial effects of these sectoral changes are displayed in Figure 12.3. This shows how the South East has overtaken the old manufacturing heartland in manufacturing employment while maintaining its dominance in service employment.

These sectoral shifts have occurred while the economy has experienced long-term and short-term cyclic changes. The long term changes have been called *long waves*

(Chapter 9, Section 5). They are of about fifty years' duration. The beginning of each wave is associated with a set of innovations and since these have often been spatially concentrated, certain regions are associated with the initial growth (Figure 12.4). When the regions have not attracted the new set of innovations associated with the next wave, they may also have experienced decline during the downward part of the wave.

The relative decline of the manufacturing heartland and the industrial periphery has contributed to the so-called North-South 'divide' which is illustrated by maps showing manufacturing employment decline (Figure 12.5) and service employment growth (Figure 12.6).

The marginal position of the West Midlands is clearly demonstrated

12.1 Sectoral change in the UK: employment as a percentage of total employment

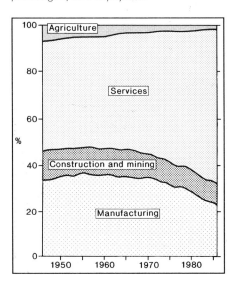

12.3 Changes in regional shares of sectoral employment (100% = total GB employment in manufacturing/services/all industries and services)

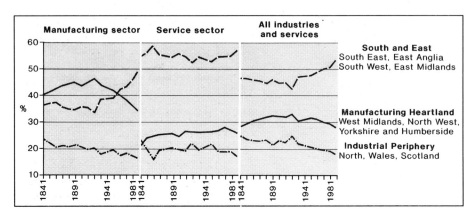

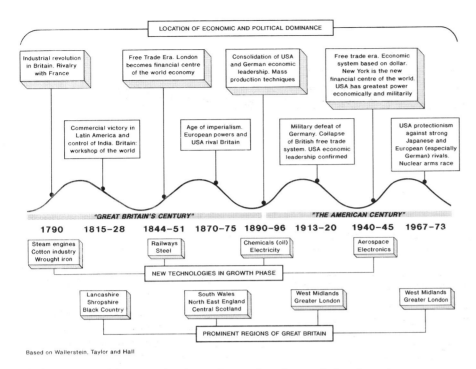

12.4 *Long waves and their national and regional significance*

Based on Wallerstein, Taylor and Hall

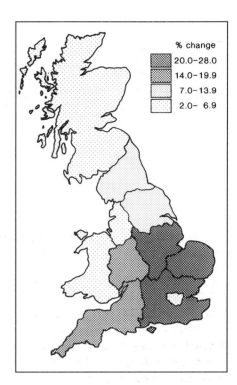

12.6 *Increase in service sector employment, 1976-86*

because it belongs to the 'North' in manufacturing decline and to the 'South' in service growth. The complexity of the regional divide is illustrated through the loss of manufacturing employment in Greater London and the changing percentage shares of the regions of the UK's manufacturing employment (Figure 12.7).

The South West, East Anglia and the East Midlands were going up from relatively low levels; the North West and Yorkshire and Humberside were declining from high levels; Wales and the North were first growing, then declining; the South East was first declining and then rising. The changes in the South East represent the rapid decline in Greater London which slowed in the later years, and the rise of the Rest of the South East (ROSE).

The overall effect of severe reduction in manufacturing jobs, particularly in the 'North', and at the same time a boom in the manufacturing and service sectors in much of the 'South' can be shown by figures for total employment by region through the 1980s (Figure 12.8).

This shows a clear pattern of net job gain in all component regions of the 'South' and job loss at rates of 5 per cent or more throughout the 'North'. This pattern has been somewhat reinforced by the striking recent growth of certain newer and notably high-tech industries in the

South East, East Anglia and the South West but offset by their emergence also in the North West, West Midlands and central Scotland

12.7 *Regional percentage shares of UK manufacturing employment, 1965-85*

12.5 *Industrial employment decline, 1976-86*

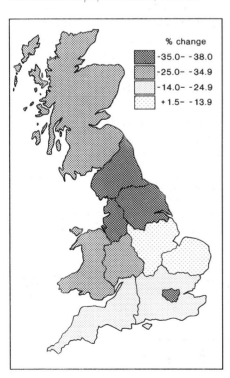

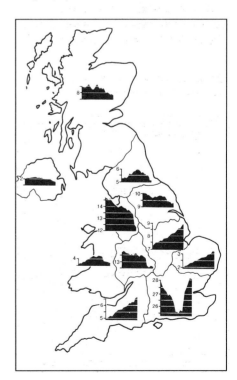

Region	1979 '000s	1987 '000s	Change, 1979-87 Nos.	Change, 1979-87 %
South East	8.124	8,480	+356	+4.4
East Anglia	781	922	+141	+18.1
South West	1,744	1,870	+126	+7.2
East Midlands	1,671	1,717	+46	+2.8
Sub-total, South	12,320	12,989	+699	+5.4
West Midlands	2,382	2,260	−122	−5.1
Yorkshire and Humberside	2,145	2.038	−107	−5.0
North West	2,890	2,541	−349	−12.1
North	1,325	1,198	−127	−9.6
Wales	1,157	1,011	−146	−12.6
Scotland	2,262	2,080	−182	−8.1
Sub-total, North	12,161	11,128	−1,033	−8.5
Great Britain	24,481	24,117	−364	−1.5

Sources: *Employment Gazette*, 1988, March, p162; May, Table 1.5; Historical Supplement no.1, pp28-40

12.8 Total employment change

(Figure 9.14). Figure 9.14 maps seven unequivocally high-technology systems, broadcasting and sound-producing equipment, aerospace and electronic computers, components and capital goods.

These sectoral shifts in the UK economy have the geographical effect of generally accentuating the divide between the relatively wealthy 'South' and the relatively

12.9 The North-South divide: personal disposable income 1985

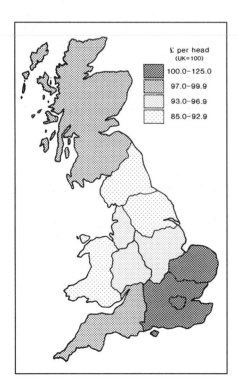

impoverished 'North' (Figure 12.9) where more people are unemployed (Figure 12.10) and more are on supplementary benefits (Figure 12.11).

These spatial generalisations are, of course, crude since there are pockets of personal and economic wealth in the 'North' (for example north Cheshire and the southern edge of Manchester) and there are large areas of disadvantage in the 'South' (for example inner London and the north Kent coast).

Some writers have described this patchiness as the 'Swiss Cheese' effect – that is, there are holes. Others have noted the metropolitan ring around London and spoken of it as the 'dough' part of the doughnut.

The exact location of a North-South boundary is debatable, with doubts about the allocation particularly of the West and East Midlands at different times. This broad economic divide, however, has been reinforced by the voting behaviour of the 'North' and 'South' (Figure 12.12), the 'South', including much of the Midlands, becoming the heartland of the ruling Conservative government through the 1980s whereas the 'North' is relatively disaffected, having lent much greater support to the Labour opposition.

There are many interpretations as to why this North-South divide has been accentuated in the UK in the 1980s. The increasing concentration of key decision-makers in the

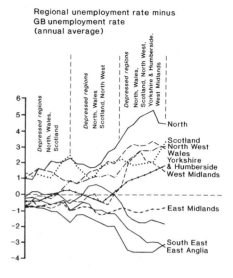

Regional unemployment rate minus GB unemployment rate (annual average)

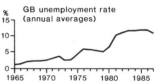

12.10 The North-South divide: unemployment

headquarters of companies in the South East (Figure 12.13) leads to higher incomes there.

Leading-edge, high-tech-related research establishments have a sim-

12.11 The North-South divide: expenditure on supplementary benefits, 1984-5

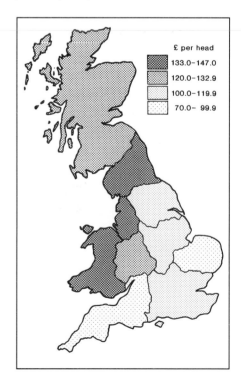

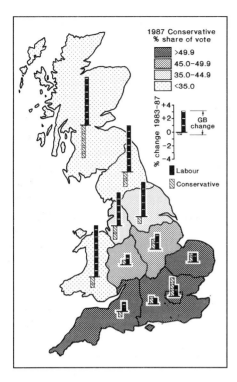

12.12 The North-South divide: voting behaviour

12.13 The North-South divide: the location of company headquarters

ilar distribution (Figure 12.14) and have transferred technology more readily into southern small industries.

Other factors probably contribute to this spatial imbalance. They include a perceived high environmental and cultural quality of life in the 'South', and accessibility to government and to the financial sector of the City. The international importance of London particularly for finance and the location of transnational headquarters is both affected and reflected by Heathrow's position as the leading international airport in the world. Finally, much underplayed is the role of government investment in defence-related research, development and manufacturing. Throughout the M4 corridor this has arguably underpinned the success of the high-technology sector. For instance, in the Bristol region technologically advanced activity and employment are dominated by aerospace which represents over 7 per cent of total employment compared with under 1 per cent in the country as a whole. This includes a major concentration of specifically electronics-based R and D and production at the leading edge of a range of technologies. It also includes a major concentration across these activities of scientific and technological expertise. This pool of labour has helped feed both small and large high-technology-related industrial newcomers such as Hewlett Packard and thereby helped add momentum to that type of industrial growth.

Bristol is just one part of the 'South' but there does seem to be a major regional bias in the pattern of government spending on defence equipment and the spatial distribution of defence manufacturing. This favours, in particular, the South

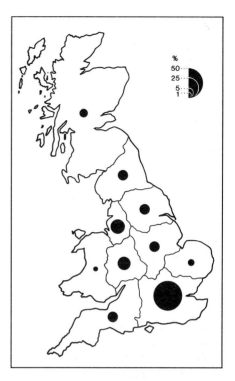

12.14 The North-South divide: the location of research establishments

East and the South West regions with less prosperous parts of the country losing out – Wales, Yorkshire and Humberside and Scotland being the most conspicuous examples. So, arguably, massive expenditure by government on defence equipment has had quite the opposite effect to the aims of 'regional' policy in the 1960s and 1970s which tried to balance out economic wealth across the country (Chapter 9, Section 4).

This new regional economic polarisation between the 'doughnut' of affluence around London with its 'doughnut' people, predominantly professional, especially engaged in financial services, engineers, scientists and technologists, and the economically disadvantaged 'North' was reinforced by a governmental approach in the 1980s which was overtly non-interventionist.

12.2 General problem

Statement of the general problem

The case study has shown how the geography of paid employment in the UK has recently changed. Other western countries have experienced broadly similar sectoral trends but the degree of change and their detailed geographies have been different. This chapter examines manufacturing decline and service sector growth. It also analyses cyclical changes in the economy affecting employment and their geographical effects. These are both the short-term booms and recessions (Chapter 8, Section 5) and long waves in the economy (Chapter 9, Section 5). The chapter ranges wider than paid employment. It examines training for employment as well as analysing changes in unpaid work. The general problem of the chapter concerns the geographical influences on, and the geographical effects of, changes in all forms of work.

The case study and other parts of the book (Chapter 8) have shown that there are major structural changes occurring in the UK: a shift in the economy from manufacturing to service-based employment; with 1983 as the pivotal point, a reversal in trade from a net exporter of manufactured goods to a net importer; the decline of the very large cities as the prime foci of production; the growth in the dominance of transnational corporations in the economy; and the shifting emphasis from full-time to part-time employment. Many of these changes are interrelated. Part-time work, for instance, is an integral part of the rise in employment in some of the service sector, while transnationals have a growing influence in the service sector. Any understanding of the changing geography of work has to be based around these structural changes in the economy.

Deindustrialisation at the national level

It is not always clear what the term *deindustrialisation* means, but it is said to be characteristic of the UK in the 1970s and 1980s. Sometimes it refers to an absolute decline in manufacturing employment. At other times it is used to indicate a relative decline. For some, it concerns output rather than employment, while for others it has a wider meaning, namely that the economy is no longer able to achieve full employment. The precise definition affects the timing of its occurrence in the UK. Manufacturing was in relative decline in employment from the mid-1950s to the mid-1960s but only declined absolutely after the peak of 1966. Even after 1966 manufacturing output grew until 1973, so 1966 to 1973 was a period of jobless growth. Output rose again during the latter half of the 1980s.

The trade balance in manufacturing goods did reverse in 1983 but the trend had been developing for some time as the world economy became more integrated and open to more competition. The changes in the position of the UK economy reflect processes occurring both in the UK itself and in the global economy. The latter has experienced *internationalisation*, that is, each country's economy has become less self-contained and more a part of the global process of change. A self-contained economy might have trade characteristics based on internal surpluses and deficits, such as Britain in the early part of the century when it was the 'workshop of the world', exporting manufactured goods and importing primary products. By contrast, in an economy that is internationalised there would be strong two-way flows in all categories. This is much more characteristic of the UK now. Although there was this reversal in trade in manufactured goods, it was against a background of increased trade in manufacturing with exports in 1980 being nearly double what they were during the 1960s. Two-way flows were also characteristic of trade in food, with the UK exporting much more after the post-war recovery, almost halving its net import of food between 1958 and 1983. Much of this general two-way flow of trade was carried out by the expanding transnationals, much of that being trade internal to the corporation, between parts of the same organisation located in different countries.

The global economy was also experiencing *multi-lateralism*, the emergence of trade agreements between sets of nations, rather than bilateralism, between two. The UK economy experienced a change from an orientation to Commonwealth trade to exchange within the EEC. This opening up of trade also offered the markets that countries such as South Korea and Taiwan needed to become major competitors to the UK in various fields ranging from clothing to shipbuilding.

Such international changes affected all national economies but they responded in different ways according to their own economic structures and the processes operating within them. These international changes provide the context for intra-national change.

Uneven deindustrialisation within the country

The changes in manufacturing employment have been spatially uneven across the country. The spatial changes have also varied over time (Figure 12.15).

	Manuf. employment 1971 ('000)	Employment change 1971-77 (%)	Manuf. employment 1977 ('000)	Employment change 1977-84 (%)	Manuf. employment 1984 ('000)
South East	2,173	−14.6	1,856	−15.2	1,574
Gt London	1,049	−26	776	−22.8	599
Rest of SE	1,124	−3.9	1,080	−9.7	975
East Anglia	190	6.8	203	−11.8	179
South West	439	−3.2	425	−13.4	368
West Midlands	1,104	−10.1	992	−28.1	713
East Midlands	618	−3.6	596	−17.3	493
Yorkshire and Humberside	777	−8.0	715	−28.1	514
North West	1,131	−11.1	1,005	−30.9	694
North	461	−5.9	434	−33.2	290
Wales	324	−4.6	309	−31.4	212
Scotland	669	−8.1	615	−28.1	442
Northern Ireland	170	−16.5	142	−29.6	100
United Kingdom	8,056	−9.5	7,292	−23.5	5,579

Note: 1984 manufacturing employment is defined according to the 1980 Standard Industrial Classification (SIC). This adopts a wider definition of manufacturing than the previous 1968 SIC, and 1984 figures are to that extent 'inflated' relative to those for previous years (by an average of +3.6%, comparing CB 1983 estimates for the two SICs).

12.15 Regional trends in manufacturing employment, 1971-84

From the mid-1960s there was a reversal of the concentration that had previously been characteristic, with one writer describing it as *spatial dispersion* to the relatively unindustrialised sub-regions and to some of the old industrial regions. In the steep decline of the late 1970s and early 1980s this was again reversed, with rural East Anglia and the South West still doing well but the old industrial areas showing very rapid decline while the South East relatively recovered. The 'South' was receiving much more of the new employment in high-tech industry (Chapter 12, Section 1, Chapter 9, Section 4).

It was not just the numbers of jobs that were regionally different; it was also the *quality of employment*, with many more high-status jobs, especially in the professional and managerial occupational groups, being concentrated in the 'South'. This meant that for manufacturing there were relatively greater employment opportunities, the possibility of greater social mobility and higher incomes in the 'South'.

There were also different opportunities between different sizes of cities and between urban and rural areas (Figure 12.16). In fact, some writers saw these differences as more significant than regional ones. They suggested that the regional differences reflected the regions' settlement sizes. For example, East Anglia and the South West have no large conurbations and had fared relatively well, while the North West and Yorkshire and Humberside each have two major conurbations and had suffered great job losses.

Regional change: locational explanations

The explanation of these regional and settlement size differences varies according to the timing of the change and the geographical approach taken. In short, the explanations are debatable. In the 1960s some of the variations between regions were produced by relocating firms rather than by differences in birth and death rates or differential expansion and contraction. This is when the so-called dispersal from the South East and West Midlands took place. Some looked for locational factors that would explain why certain areas had declined faster than others. They argued that the key factor causing the moves in the 1960s was regional policy with its

12.16 Urban-rural shift in manufacturing employment, 1981-87

District type	1981-84 % change	Differential shift	1984-87 % change	Differential shift
	Total	shift	Total	shift
South				
Inner London	−14.9	−6.4	−20.5	−18.8
Outer London	−18.2	−6.9	−11.7	−8.2
Industrial areas	−10.0	1.9	1.0	3.8
Non-metropolitan cities	−10.5	1.9	−8.1	−3.7
Districts with New Towns	−7.1	4.0	−4.5	0.2
Resort, port + retirement	−5.0	5.4	−0.6	2.8
Urban + mixed urban-rural	−4.2	6.3	−3.4	−0.3
Remoter, mainly rural	−3.2	7.8	0.1	3.4
Total	−9.3	−0.5	−5.8	−2.6
North				
Other metropolitan cities	−20.5	−7.0	−10.1	−6.0
Other metropolitan districts	−15.0	−2.5	−2.9	1.5
Industrial areas	−12.9	0.2	2.5	8.0
Non-metropolitan cities	−9.7	0.9	−6.1	−0.3
Districts with New Towns	−11.7	1.9	2.1	6.4
Resort, port + retirement	−19.6	−8.1	9.6	14.7
Urban + mixed urban-rural	−8.2	4.3	−4.1	0.4
Remoter, mainly rural	−5.9	5.7	3.9	7.6
Total	−13.4	−0.4	−2.6	2.4

(differential shift = the difference between actual employment change and expected change, where expected change is calculated by applying the appropriate national rate of change to every one of the industries of the district) variety of incentives, while in the 1970s most significance was attached to *agglomeration diseconomies* (the costs of being located in large cities outweighing the benefits). It was suggested that the high cost of land and buildings, the age of buildings and congestion outweighed the *agglomeration economies* that had made cities attractive much earlier in the century. These writers considered locational factors associated with the areas of greater and lesser decline and interpreted them as causes. They can be called the 'locational school'.

Restructuring explanation

Other writers examined the processes involved through case studies rather than statistical analysis. They argued that statistical analyses could not disentangle factors; for example, available labour may be attractive to firms but since regional assistance was given based partly on unemployment rates, it was impossible to distinguish whether it was the available labour or the assistance, or both, that influenced the move. They also argued that the same factor may affect firms in different ways and it was necessary to understand the competitive pressure that industry was under and the varying ways in which firms responded to it in order to understand first why they might move and then where they moved. Some firms that were labour-intensive or in areas where labour costs were rising fast might have decentralised in order to find cheaper labour. Regional assistance might have been a contributory factor accounting for where they located but not an explanation of why they considered moving in the first place. Other companies in sectors where technological change was more possible may have automated their production processes. Regional assistance may have subsidised this.

The technological change may have led to new labour needs, often from traditionally skilled and well-unionised labour to cheaper and less well-organised labour elsewhere. This was often also a change from men to women. People were writing about the *feminisation* of manufacturing in the early 1970s, a short-term trend that was not to last. In these cases, the reasons for moving were complex and could not be put down simply to regional policy.

The changes that industry was making to retain or increase its profitability, some of which may have involved locational moves, are known as *restructuring*. Those advocating case studies and qualitative analysis in order to understand the processes operating for different sectors of industry are called the 'restructuring school'.

Urban change

The explanations of the differences between settlement sizes also show some differences between approaches. The major difference between the sizes related to the expansion of existing firms, not to births or deaths, the age of firms or their ownership. Having established this, one set of writers suggested that the availability of land was the crucial factor, because over a long period of time in manufacturing, the space needed per worker had increased. Firms in large cities could not easily expand their employment. Those elsewhere did not have the constraints on space. This accounts for the differences over a long period of time. It reflects a trend rather than a dramatic decline, such as that characteristic of the late 1970s and early 1980s. These writers explain change over a longer time scale than the restructuring school. They also treat labour problems as technical problems of availability and cost whereas the restructuring school sees the search for cheaper, less

well-organised labour as a reflection of the continuing struggle between capital and labour under capitalism.

Services and growth

Parallel to the idea of deindustrialisation is the *growth of services*. There is a problem of definition here too. Services are usually viewed as work where there is no tangible product and where consumption and production occur simultaneously. There are problems with these definitions; for example, hairdressing is a service but there is a visible end product which is enjoyed or consumed for some time.

Service sector

It is helpful to suggest a number of elements of services. There are *service industries* which make up the service sector and are defined in industrial classifications. It is employment in these that is referred to in models of stages in development and in the analyses of sectoral shift. Not all service industries have experienced employment growth. Public transport and personal services as a whole (including hairdressing, laundries, dry cleaning, shoe repairs, private domestic services) declined throughout the 1960s, 1970s and 1980s. Retailing remained static. In the 1960s and early 1970s in Britain, public services such as health, education and welfare services grew rapidly, but slowed or even declined as public expenditure cuts increasingly took place. It was financial and business services that experienced greatest growth, especially during the 1980s which they dominated. The service sector has also apparently grown because manufacturing industry has bought services from outside firms rather than providing them in-house. This *externalisation* of corporate services has meant a reclassification of jobs rather than a growth of new jobs. The boundaries of the manufacturing and service sectors have changed. At the same time, much of the growth in the service sector has been part-time, low-skilled and often poorly paid. Of the 4.9 million employed part-time in Britain in 1984, almost 90 per cent were in the service sector. Many of the jobs have also been performed by women, though these have dominated certain sectors such as retailing and public services rather than financial and business services.

Service occupations

There are also *service occupations*, such as clerical work, which can take place in manufacturing and mining as well as in service industries. They can occur in all sectors. While those employed in transport services have declined, the number of people employed in transport occupations has remained about the same because there has been a growth in the number employed in transport occupations within manufacturing industry. There has been a general growth in service occupations. 'White-collar' workers have increased in their proportion of the workforce, particularly within manufacturing. There has also been a professionalisation of the workforce, with more administrative, professional and technical workers. This has been seen by some as a marked change from the past, a part of a new emerging type of economy and society, the *post-industrial society*. At the same time, however, some service occupations have also been 'industrialised', with increased automation of service delivery, the standardisation of products and the growth of part-time casual labour. Examples include fast food and industrial cleaning. Although there has been a change, this could be viewed as the widening of the indus-trial society rather than a totally new one.

Sector model explanation

Here there is a hint that the growth of the service sector and service occupations at a national level are rather differently explained. Three types of explanation may be identified, the best known of which is the sector model or Clark-Fisher thesis. This suggests a natural set of stages through which economies pass and the evidence used is percentages employed in the primary, secondary and tertiary sectors. The percentage of employed is largest first for the primary sector, then the secondary sector during the industrial stage and finally the tertiary sector in the post-industrial stage. Such an observation can be made for many economies.

The key processes that are supposed to underlie it involve increases in productivity per employee and elasticities of demand for goods and services. Productivity is said to increase faster in agriculture, which releases people for manufacturing employment. Increases in productivity then follow in manufacturing, which releases workers for the service industries where productivity is more difficult to improve. As people's income increases they are said to demand proportionately less agricultural goods than manufactured goods and then in turn less goods than services. It is, however, difficult to gauge productivity in many services and the greater elasticity of demand for services than goods may be questioned. Certainly, not many of the workers released from manufacturing have entered the service industries, with predominantly full-time men losing their manufacturing jobs while part-time women obtain ones in services. Evidence on output and investment might show a rather different picture from that of employment, and in any case not all service industries have expanded their employment.

Such a model also ignores the international context of the economy. Much demand for manufactured goods in Britain is now satisfied by imports from abroad, partly from the newly industrialised countries (NICs) to which some of Britain's manufacturing has been transferred, and much of the recent growth in services has been in financial and business services which in part are servicing global manufacturing production.

'Self-service' economy explanation

A second explanation, the *'self-service' economy*, focuses more on the interaction between the sectors and the changing technological and organisational structure of production. Technological changes have allowed goods to be substituted for services. As productivity has increased less rapidly in some services, such as laundries, and costs have increased, people have found it easier to buy goods, such as washing machines, and perform the services themselves – hence the self-service economy. This is not simply a demand process. Manufacturing companies in search of wider markets have seen the potential and marketed such goods heavily. Many service functions are now performed in the home (Chapter 4, Section 4), ranging from entertainment to decoration and repair. Such self-services also demand services from outside the home, such as the repair of televisions and domestic equipment, and DIY stores. These intermediate consumer services have been part of recent growth in the service sector.

In order to make these and other goods for consumers and industry, manufacturing companies have sought to be more efficient. This process has involved a greater number of white-collar workers, that is

there are more in service occupations within manufacturing, such as
managers and research and development people. Their attempt at
increased efficiency has also led to
the contracting out of specialist services such as advertising, market
research and accountancy, and to
the consequent growth of what have
been called 'producer services'.
According to this theory, the greater
number of people in service occupations has resulted from structural
change in searching for greater
efficiency within manufacturing
industry, not from different elasticities of demand or increases in productivity.

'Search for profitablility' explanation

The third explanation, the capitalistic *search for profitability*, emphasises economic processes that give
direction to technological and organisational change and produce
changes in types of occupation. It
notes the diversification of many
manufacturing transnational corporations into services and the growing concentration of ownership in
many service sectors with the
growth of large service-based national companies and transnational corporations (Chapter 8, Section 3).
These changes are explained by the
opportunities for relatively greater
profitability in some services than
manufacturing. For example, it is
argued that many services are, by
their local character, protected from
foreign competition, although this is
increasingly debatable. With the
move of large-scale capital into the
service sector, various services such
as health, education, recreation,
leisure and culture come to be treated as commodities. *Commodification*
of services occurs as corporations
introduce marketing techniques
from manufacturing and advertise
services, or commodities, such as
packaged holidays. In this explana-

tion the expansion of services is seen
to be very much part of the restructuring process of big business.

Regional differences in service growth

These three explanations of a
national-scale phenomenon have different degrees of applicability to geographical differences in the changes
in services within a nation. The case
study demonstrated the inverse
relationship between deindustrialisation and service growth (Chapter
12, Section 1). Where manufacturing
jobs have been least lost, there has
been much service employment
growth, as in the south of England.
Where they have been most lost,
there has been least growth in services, as in most areas outside the
south. The impacts of these two
changes on regional economic development have therefore been reinforcing. It shows again that the people losing manufacturing jobs are
not those going into services, as the
sector model of Clark and Fisher
would suggest. There has not been
that great a migration from the
'North' to the 'South'.

The difference between regions in
employment change in the service
sector is not so great as that in manufacturing employment change. This
is in part because some types of services have a national coverage.
Public services such as education
and health are spread throughout
the country and these tend to dominate the service employment of
regions like Scotland, Northern
Ireland, Wales, the North and the
North West. In the late 1970s there
was a time of rapid change when
employment in private services
increased much faster than that in
public services. The growth in private services was concentrated in
the 'South' and the 'East', while
some regions even lost employment
in public services (Figure 12.17).

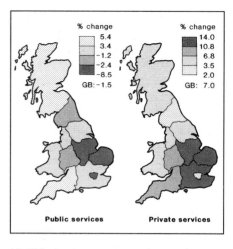

12.17 Regional percentage employment change in
public and private services, 1976-81

In the 1980s the service gap
between the 'North' and 'South'
widened, with about two-thirds of
the service sector jobs created being
located in the South East, East
Anglia and the South West.

Producer services

The private services that are especially concentrated in the 'South' are
those in *producer services*, the ones
that serve manufacturing and other
service industries. These include
advertising, market research, insurance, accounting, financial services
and research and development.
Many of these services decentralised
from London and added to the general expansion of services in 'free-
standing' towns. Much growth
occurred along the M4 corridor and
the M25 and M11 motorways, with
service employment being numerically even more important there
than high-tech employment.
Although London lost some service
employment, it continued to grow as
a major centre of international
finance and commerce and as a centre of consumer-oriented services. It
also has a very high proportion of
service occupations, a characteristic
of world cities.

Explanations of regional differences

Again there are differences in explanations of these changes. Some writers account for the concentration of producer services in the south by the demand from existing service activities concentrated there, such as the headquarters and research and development, and the consumer-oriented services that high-income occupations have stimulated. They also point to the expansion of the export market for services in which insurance, banking, accountancy, advertising and legal services have been prominent, especially the London-based companies. So the 'South' has been able to benefit more from the export market because it already had a concentration of internationally known companies. In addition to these factors, these writers argue that manufacturing has been more dynamic in the 'South' and has externalised services more, with demands ranging from contract cleaning to consultancies. This is a market-oriented approach based on the location of demand.

Other explanations emphasise the organisation of companies and the way they restructure to increase or maintain profitability, in a similar way to the deindustrialisation explanation. One mechanism is their use of space. For example, routine clerical work in insurance was decentralised from London to locations where office space was less costly but clerical workers were still available, perhaps at lower wages than in London. Decision-making functions remained in the capital. Such explanations emphasise the growing concentration of ownership in many service industries and the location of their and other headquarters in London and the South East. This concentration of control, whereby decisions are made in the South East that affect production and employment in other areas of the country, is seen as particularly important. It is implied that decisions will favour the South East rather than other areas.

The 'City'

A final point relates to the 'City', the centre of financial services in London. It clearly has international significance. Its expansion after deregulation and subsequent dramatic collapse on Black Monday in 1987 had significant impacts on employment growth and decline and related multiplier effects on other services, including housing. More generally its dealings in the control of financial assets has an important effect on the restructuring of the spatial economy; for example, at times its preference for investment in property as against manufacturing industries in Britain has had significant impacts, firstly on the built environment, including counter-urbanisation and its effects on services, and secondly on the economic environments where it may have advanced the rate of deindustrialisation. Whatever the explanations of deindustrialisation and growth in the service sector, there is no doubting their differential geographical impacts on work in Britain.

Types of employment

The above discussion of sectoral shifts in employment has involved comments on the changing types of work people do, for example the increasing polarisation between well-paid, full-time, 'career' professional and administrative jobs and low-grade, often part-time, routinised or industrialised service jobs. More generally, some writers have described the emergence of the flexible manufacturing firm with a differentiated workforce, while others have argued that the labour market has been segmented or dual for a long time but the segmentation becomes more marked or obvious in times of recession.

Segmented labour markets

The idea of *dual or segmented labour markets* applies to an economy and involves primary and secondary segments, while the concept of the *flexible firm* involves core and peripheral workers in manufacturing. The primary or core segment consists of full-time, permanent employees who have good job security and high incomes. These increasingly perform a wide range of tasks and possess a similarly wide range of skills. The high incomes and job security reflect the desire of the companies to retain these employees. The secondary or peripheral segment includes a number of different groups. One group is the semi-skilled workers who perform fairly routine tasks for lower pay and less job security. The company, it is argued, may reduce these in bad times and increase their number in periods of recovery. Another group are the part-time and temporary workers who are on short contracts or training schemes. These are even more easily taken on and dismissed as economic circumstances change. Finally, as part of the periphery there is a group who are self-employed or do sub-contracting work for larger companies. Some authors argue that in recent times companies have tried to restructure to produce a more flexible labour force, relocation being one method that they may have used to trigger such a process. So some see the above descriptions as referring to the internal structure of a firm's labour market, and suggest that this has been changing towards greater use of *flexible labour market strategies*. Others do not see much that is new. They perceive changes to the labour markets in general that reflect some of the above sectoral changes.

There is little evidence of such internal strategies of flexible work-forces within manufacturing indus-tries as a whole, although there are important instances which may be leading a future trend. These are often in plants owned by overseas corporations and it is suggested that governments have welcomed these companies because their practices may stimulate change in other com-panies. Here, then, there is a hope not so much of technological transfer but of the diffusion of labour man-agement processes.

Part-time employment

It is useful to describe the changes in the labour force in more detail. *Part-time* work has risen mostly in services, not manufacturing, and has been used to meet changes in demand during the week or year as much as between recessions and booms. Fast-food chains in particu-lar very carefully estimate the changes in the customer-flow during a week and allocate staff according-ly. Part-time work has generally fol-lowed the geographical changes in service employment, being concen-trated in the South East and South West, although the North West and Scotland have higher than expected growth rates.

Self-employment

Self-employment grew dramatically in the 1980s to become about 10 per cent of the workforce, but it again has been concentrated in the service sector and has been more clearly concentrated in the South East, East Anglia and the South West than part-time work, with just over half of all self-employed being located in these regions. The growth in the self-employed is complicated. In part

it reflects the governmental encour-agement of an enterprise culture through its help for the unemployed to set up in self-employment. Some companies and some past employees have preferred to substitute self-employment which is contracted back in place of having or being employees. Finally, there are tempo-rary workers who again have been more prominent in the service sec-tor, with recent growth especially within the public services of health and education. Here, though, there is some evidence of manufacturing firms taking on temporary rather than permanent labour because of the uncertainty of future conditions.

Youth employment

The role of youth employment in these segments is worthy of study. The recession of the late 1970s and early 1980s roughly coincided with the peak entry of youths (sixteen to nineteen) into the labour market (Chapter 10, Section 5). As many of the youths who do not go on to high-er or further education become part of the secondary segment of the labour force, there were bound to be great problems in finding employ-ment. This was particularly so in the deindustrialising North where ser-vices were not growing so fast. The introduction of youth training schemes, YTS, managed by the Manpower Services Commission (later the Training Agency and then TEED), served a much greater pro-portion of youths in the 'North' than in the 'South'. Youths with exactly the same qualifications from school got employment in the 'South', some-times in jobs with career prospects,

| | Recruitment into regular jobs through YTS | |
	(a) as a % of YTS entrants	(b) as a % of all 16-year-old labour market entrants
Middlesbrough	18.8	15.9
Wolverhampton	26.5	18.6
Nottingham	28.5	15.7
South West London	36.7	8.9

12.18 Recruitment through YTS in contrasting localities, 1985-86

while they had to go on training schemes in the 'North'. They may have had similar skills, but the local job opportunities were very differ-ent.

Youth labour markets

Youth labour markets are very local because young people are often tied to public transport and cannot travel far from their parental home. Consequently, if there are differ-ences in opportunities on either side of a very large city, youths living on one side may not be able to benefit from the better opportunities on the other. Such limits to distance trav-elled produce very local variations in labour markets, as well as the broad differences between 'North' and 'South'. The importance of the uneven geography of job opportuni-ties at both the local and regional scales certainly brings into question the dominant idea of occupational choice, as a way of understanding the process by which youths eventu-ally enter employment. Their choice is highly constrained, in some areas much more so than in others.

The spatial variability in the buoyancy of the youth labour mar-ket is shown for four localities (Figure 12.18).

A much higher percentage of youths entered YTS in Middlesbrough than south-west London because of fewer job oppor-tunities there. Yet a higher percent-age of those entering YTS in south-west London obtained regular jobs, despite their covering a narrower and lower-ability range than in Middlesbrough.

Youth training schemes

There were also major variations in the operation of youth training schemes from one area to another, even where there was little difference in rates of unemployment. In some areas union opposition to such schemes, which were regarded as providers of cheap labour without any real training component, reduced opportunities. In others, the fears of unions proved well founded and very few jobs or well-trained youths emerged.

The schemes were divided into two types, employer-based and college- or project-based schemes. The first, called 'mode A' and later 'basic' places, tended to channel young people into the mainstream of the youth labour market. Many trainees eventually obtained jobs with their trainee employer. In many ways, in previous times, the YTS places would have been jobs. In effect, the schemes allowed firms greater time to evaluate or screen the youths. The second type, 'mode B' and later 'premium' places, were effectively sheltered provision for disadvantaged trainees who would otherwise be unemployed and who after YTS had less chance of employment.

Inequalities from school tended to be reinforced by the schemes. Better-qualified youths in any one area got into mode A/basic places and once there had still better future chances of employment. There were, however, other means of discrimination. The premium funded places needed the endorsement of the Careers Service. Some of the criteria for this endorsement were educational sub-normality, frequent truancy and area of residence. The last was a further example of red-lining, in this case of inner-city and peripheral council estates. These often had

their own schemes which were seen as the 'natural' places to go. Future employment prospects for premium-endorsed trainees were less than for others, just as they were for mode B as against mode A people. Youth opportunities therefore varied with the local area in which they lived as well as the local labour market and the region.

Unpaid work

Finally, it is necessary to note that by no means all work is paid work. Most domestic labour is performed without payment, much of it being carried out by women. This gender difference within the home has continued to be the case even where women have entered full-time paid employment. There are, however, signs of change in younger generations, perhaps as the feminist movement increases its impact. Whether the adoption of greater equality within the home varies between regions and/or different settlement sizes remains to be seen. At present motherhood limits job opportunities for women. In many cases careers are interrupted in major ways. The introduction of a reasonable length of pregnancy leave and the greater availability of crèches in workplaces and other forms of pre-school provision may allow greater opportunities

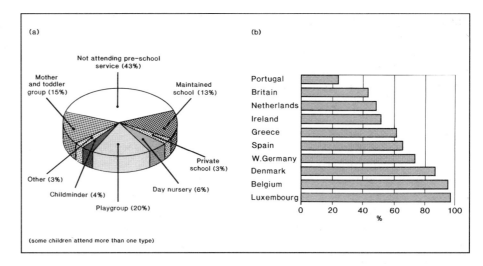

12.19 Pre-school provision a) types within GB b) the percentage of children attending pre-primary school in some European countries

for women. The amount of pre-school provision, which overall is much lower in the UK compared with many countries in Western Europe, varies within the country from area to area, as does the proportion that is provided publicly (Figure 12.19 and see Figure 5.10).

With the dip in the number of youths entering the labour market in the early 1990s, there will no doubt be greater pressure and perhaps greater provision for women to enter the labour market. If, however, they are to fill the gap left by youths, many will be entering the secondary lower-paid segment. This will not help women to gain equality of income with men. It may, however, help to break down the gender separation that sees women as occupying the private or domestic domain while men operate in the public domain of paid employment and political decision-making. This in itself may begin to change the way the sexes are viewed, and eventually give more equal opportunities to women.

Summary

In summary, there have been very

significant changes in work in the last few decades which some see as revolutionary. Undoubtedly people's place of residence will have influenced the types of changes that they have experienced and the opportunities that have been open to them.

12.3 Other examples

The national and regional analysis of the changing geography of employment in Britain in the case study is given greater depth by the following examples. The first focuses on changes at the locality level by examining Coventry. The last two return to the national scale but concentrate on how changes in work have affected particular groups, namely women and ethnic groups.

12.3a Coventry: striving to adapt

The changing structure of the British economy and the related impacts on employment are reflected not only at the national/regional level but also at the level of particular towns. Coventry in the West Midlands, more than most towns, has swung from boom to bust. In the Middle Ages, agriculture and specifically the wool industry gave it great prosperity. Indeed, at the time, by population, it became the fifth-largest city in the country. Ribbon weaving, watch and clock making, sewing machines, bicycles, motorbikes and cars have all had their time as the leading industries of the local economy.

In the case of cars, it was just over a hundred years ago when Daimler-Benz decided to set up a car manufacturing plant there. On the back of that rapidly expanding industry, Coventry boomed in the era between 1945 and 1965. The population increase at the time, from 250,000 to 350,000 made Coventry the fastest-growing city in Britain. However, the general relative decline of car making since then and Coventry's continued reliance on it have caused severe unemployment problems. Between 1974 and 1982, 6200 manufacturing jobs were lost and the rate of unemployment rose to nearly 19 per cent in December 1981, having been only 7.7 per cent in January 1980. The reasons for the decline of car making were complex and probably related to: the ownership of the car plants being from beyond Coventry's boundaries (absentee ownership); high wage settlements; a reputation for industrial unrest; increased automation, a worldwide malaise in car making, and foreign competition especially from Japan.

During the 1980s further decline was experienced in metal goods, engineering and vehicle industries. Some expansion occurred in transport and communication, banking, finance, insurance and business services. Figure 12.20 shows the employment structure in 1987 for the top hundred employers who account for 73 per cent of total employment. It shows Coventry's continuing reliance on a very narrow range of activities and on a few organisations. Public services dominate with Coventry City Council being the largest overall employer (18,680). Only 40 per cent of employment in Coventry was in the service economy (28 per cent in the public sector), a good deal below the national average. So Coventry was still relatively dependent on manufacturing industry, with vehicle manufacture, although much reduced, still dominant. Jaguar's and Peugot-Talbot's employment levels seemed to have stabilised by 1988 but came under threat again in the 1990-91 recession. Furthermore, 44 per cent of all Coventry's jobs were with transnational corporations (TNCs) whose headquarters were mainly in south-east England. For such employers, Coventry's activities are only a minority interest and events external to Coventry will determine the future role of these corporations in the Coventry economy.

Various initiatives have recently been undertaken by the local authority (allied with Warwick University in some instances) to increase employment and to diversify the city's economic base. In particular, a department of economic development and planning has been established with an annual budget of £3 million. Possibly the best-known initiative has been the establishment of the University of Warwick Science Park – a joint university/local authority initiative taken in 1984. Generically this had

12.20 Coventry's top 100 firms, 1987

Sector	Employees	Firms
Public sector	30,646	7
Vehicle manufacture	19,832	8
Telecommunications	10,370	3
Specialist engineering	8,404	8
Vehicle components	3,966	14
Retailing	3,685	11
Plastics manufacture	3,069	1
Financial services	1,808	7
Domestic/ Household goods	1,767	6
Machine tools	1,625	6
Coal mining	1,621	1

its roots in the Silicon Valley developments in California with the strong functional links which grew up between Stanford University and rapidly growing high-tech industries. Successful and complex links grew up between people, products and research. Britain's first two science parks were established by Trinity College in Cambridge (Chapter 9, Section 3) and Herriot-Watt University in Edinburgh in 1972. There are now about fifty such science parks around the UK, some much more successful than others.

Within a few years, Warwick's Science Park has become one of the most successful in attracting companies.

It covers 42 acres of landscaped area, with 250,000 square feet of built space and forty firms employing 700 people. Companies from North America and other parts of Western Europe now make up 40 per cent of all companies there. 'Technology transfer', that is, direct linkages between university and the science park firms, has been a success. This has especially been the case in the fields of pure science and technology. Indeed, it has become a leading centre in the field of automation technology. More recently the

Park has been pioneering the concept of 'knowledge transfer' by which is meant linkages between the companies and university departments outside of pure science and technology. The Barclays Venture Centre, offering as it does small workshops, has proved a successful seedbed for many new enterprises; when established they move on to larger premises. The momentum of growth in the Science Park has been maintained with acquisitions of more land and the recent creation by English Estates of 30,000 square feet of speculative floorspace.

An adjoining and related, local-authority inspired development has been the creation of Westwood Business Park in 1988. Here, a 74-acre green-field location adjoining both university and Science Park has attracted half a million square feet of buildings and 3310 jobs. As the local authority puts it, they have provided 'high specification multi-purpose buildings and serviced development sites'. Links with the university and polytechnic are stressed, as is the availability of university sports facilities for recreation of employees. The advance buildings have been set up by a variety of developers anxious to benefit from

accessibility both to the rest of the country and to local higher education, technological excellence, low density of developments and a highly landscaped campus. 'Quality of life' is stressed heavily in all publicity materials.

In addition to the adjoining employment sites of the Science Park and Westwood Business Park, Coventry's department of economic development and planning has recently (1989) succeeded in attracting the National Grid Company which will bring 700 further jobs and 100,000 square feet of offices to the city. That company claims that Coventry's good communication links nationwide, the permission and space to develop their own purpose-built offices and the quality of life for staff were what brought them there.

Overall, Coventry still has a problem of overdependence on a narrow range of manufacturing industry but has shown that local authority initiatives, among others, can create a more positive spirit and environment for modern growth when ten years ago the economic and employment prospects for Coventry were depressing.

12.3b Gender and employment

Gender inequalities, especially in employment. are present across the world. Although in the UK women represent 52 per cent of the population, they comprise only 45 per cent of the labour force. In general,

12.21 Gender and earnings

	£ per week			
	1970	1975	1980	1986
Men	29.7	60.8	121.5	205.5
Women	16.2	37.4	78.8	136.3
Differential	13.5	23.4	42.7	69.2
Women's earnings as % of men's	54.5	61.5	64.8	66.3

women are in lower-grade and lower-paid jobs since, for instance on average women get paid only two-thirds of men's pay (Figure 12.21), although there is legislation on equal pay for men and women for doing the same job.

There is a particularly strong concentration of women in a relatively small number of industries especially in education, health, retail and personal and financial services. During the 1980s the reduction in public sector jobs particularly affected women. Another setback for job opportunities for women was the recent trend towards a de-feminisa-

	Manufacturing + primary + const. 000	Services '000	Total '000
1974			
Total	8,617	13,681	22,298
Male	6,220 (72.2%)	7,144 (52.2%)	13,364
Female	2,397 (27.8%)	6,537 (47.8%)	8,934
1984			
Total	7,416	13,334	20,750
Male	5,577 (75.2%)	6,125 (45.9%)	11,702
Female	1,839 (24.8%)	7,209 (54.1%)	9,048

Source: Employment Gazette

12.22 Gender and employment sectors

tion of manufacturing industry. In northern cities, where manufacturing has traditionally comprised a

June (millions)	1971	1976	1979	1981	1983	1986
Employees in employment	21.6	22.0	22.6	21.4	20.6	21.0
All male	13.4	13.1	13.2	12.3	11.7	11.6
All female	8.2	9.0	9.5	9.1	8.9	9.4
FT female	5.5	5.4	5.6	5.3	5.0	5.4
PT female	2.8	3.6	3.9	3.8	3.9	4.0
Total unemployed	0.7	1.2	1.2	2.3	2.9	1.2
Women as % of all employees:						
All women	38.0	40.9	42.0	42.5	43.2	44.8
FT women	25.5	24.5	24.8	24.8	24.3	25.7
Total working population	24.6	25.5	24.8	26.1	26.9	27.3

12.23 Gender and employment trends

large proportion of available job opportunities, this has been a particular problem. Women in the 'South', on the other hand, have been able to participate more in an expanding service sector (Figure 12.22).

Indeed, overall in the UK the growth in working population has been made possible through an increase of women in the workforce (Figure 12.23).

Many women are employed on part-time contracts, possibly a vanguard of a future more 'flexible workforce'. To an extent, however, this has been forced on them, partly by companies' policies and partly by a social system that expects women to bear the greater responsibility for raising children and other unpaid domestic tasks. At home women are primarily responsible for 88 per cent of the washing and ironing, 77 per cent of the cooking and 72 per cent

of the cleaning. Furthermore, 89 per cent of all single-parent households are headed by women.

In spite of this clear exploitation and the unequal employment picture, employment prospects for women are now a little brighter than before the Second World War. It was the war, with the need for women to work in munitions factories and to join the armed forces and public services, which changed society's attitudes to women working. Another more recent, trend has been the emergence of a new group of women professionals and managers especially in major urban areas who are in turn employing others to undertake domestic and child-caring tasks. Yet the overall employment picture for women remains the same – a narrow range of less skilled and lower-paid opportunities in addition to society's expectations of burdensome unpaid domestic roles.

12.3c Ethnic employment

The UK economy in the 1950s was expanding rapidly and that expansion was made possible partly by the considerable migration of people from the Caribbean and the Indian sub-continent. The economic opportunities were there and so was the legal opportunity (British passports) for residents of former British colonies where standards of living were low and unemployment/underemployment high. This was a predominantly 'black' immigration of Caribbeans in the mid 1950s and early 1960s. The 1962 Commonwealth Immigrants Act severely curtailed migration, but dependants continued to arrive. Not all the immigrants came from poor backgrounds. Many of the Asians from East Africa who were pushed out of Kenya and Uganda during the 1960s and early 1970s had occupied relatively well-paid, often profes-

sional positions. Since they were not allowed to take any of their accumulated wealth out of their East African country, however, they entered Britain as poor people. Many were initially forced to take jobs well below their positions in Africa. For immigration as a whole, the people were mainly young and because fertility rates were high, Britain's black and Asian population grew from 25,000 in 1951 to 1.4 million in 1970 to 2.38 million in 1985. Of this latter figure 689,000 were Indians, 547,000 West Indians, 407,000 Pakistanis, 102,000 Africans and 99,000 Bangladeshis.

In the 1950s two types of jobs needed filling. First there were jobs in fast-growing manufacturing industries like engineering and vehicles. These had a quite inadequate supply of labour. Secondly there were poorly paid, low-status jobs

that few other people wanted, often with poor working conditions, such as in public transport, cleaning and textiles . There were also industries where black labour was viewed as a temporary measure by companies, either as a substitute for restructuring and modernisation or to fill occupations degraded by such restructuring and modernisation. In the 1950s West Indians gained jobs in engineering, metal goods, chemicals, metal manufacturing, vehicle building and public transport. Indians and Pakistanis filled similar jobs. Indians were also working in the clothes industry, while both sets were involved in textiles where Asian women were employed as well as men. Many of the types of jobs available were spatially concentrated, so this encouraged the spatial concentration of these immigrant groups.

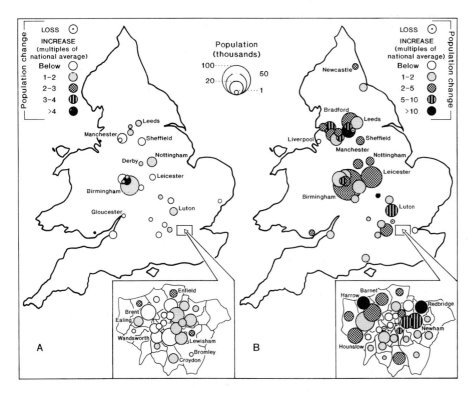

12.24 The urban concentration of a) West Indians and b) South Asians in 1981 and the change 1971-81

Over time the newcomers adapted to British life and work and moved to other parts of the country (Figure 12.24).

Some were socially mobile and moved to the suburbs of cities. However, a large proportion of UK black people still live in the core of inner cities to which they originally moved. Some have consequently become trapped in a downward spiral of decline typified by UK inner cities, out of which it is difficult to break. The familiar elements of job loss, selective population loss, obsolete infrastructure and inadequate investment have had a particularly hard impact on black communities. Poor employment and life-chance opportunities of both blacks and poor whites underlay the inner-city riots of 1981. All the post-event analysts pointed to the extreme economic marginalisation and political powerlessness of Britain's black population together with the blockage of potential escape routes and pathways to progress. Many found themselves in those parts of the economy which have borne the brunt of recession and deindustrialisation. Not surprisingly some have developed an understandable alienation, a sense of estrangement and non-belonging.

They have faced two major social handicaps – racial discrimination and racial disadvantage. Discrimination, explained partly by white people's prejudice and perception of threat from the black population, is still clearly rife within society in spite of legislation. It takes the familiar forms of blocking availability of employment, slowing speed of promotion, giving poor conditions of work and limiting access to some housing. Racial disadvantage, on the other hand, relates to problems caused by cultural and linguistic differences, concentration in environmentally deprived areas and difficulties with the British educational system.

There are many differences between the ethnic groups. Religious and language differences among the Asians are reflected to some extent in occupational differences and locations. More from the Asian communities than the Afro-Caribbean have become entrepreneurs and set up their own businesses. Some, for example to the east and north of Manchester city centre, have replaced the Jewish textile and clothing firms. Others have become shopkeepers, serving either predominantly Asian communities, such as in the shopping strips to the south of Manchester city centre and to the north of Leicester city centre, or areas away from concentrations of Asians working as newsagents and restaurateurs. Although not well represented generally in higher education, some Asian students are successfully penetrating courses such as medicine and computer science. They are also showing higher achievement levels than most other groups in secondary education in some parts of the country, which promises even greater future social mobility. While there are some positive signs of reducing social inequalities between groups, there are still many differences which have to be faced by society as a whole.

In this section some strategies of workers, companies and governments are examined under different economic circumstances.

12.4 **Alternative strategies**

Workers' strategies

At a time of recession when employment opportunities may be few, a number of possible strategies are open to those seeking work. The first is to move to an area which is not being so hard hit by the recession, for example in Britain in the 1979-82 recession a move from the 'North' to the 'South'. The higher cost of housing in the 'South' and the inability to sell their own houses restricted this as an option for many in the 'North,' however. For others, social ties were too great. The families of some remained in the 'North' while work was found in the 'South', with the workers commuting home at weekends and living in as cheap accommodation as possible during the week.

There are other possibilities, such as self-employment and job sharing. The first depends upon the availability of capital and indeed expertise in setting up a new business. Redundancy pay funded many self-employed during the early 1980s but many did not succeed in their new ventures. The growth of advisory services for small businesses and various government schemes encouraged such a choice. A more buoyant economy presents greater opportunities for new businesses and not surprisingly there was greater growth in self-employment in the 'South' than the 'North'. There may have been a greater orientation to such a strategy there, too, because people seem to have more readily accepted the enterprise culture and privatised solutions. Seeing others in their home area take that route may also have further encouraged people to adopt this strategy.

Job sharing depends upon people already in work and companies' policies. More generally earlier retirement of those in work may allow younger people to obtain jobs, but often those who retire voluntarily during a recession are not replaced.

Another possibility for households where a woman is not in paid employment is for her to enter the labour force. Often this is difficult in a recession but the expanding service sector of the 'South' during the early 1980s provided opportunities especially for part-time employment, while the earlier movement of manufacturing into the development areas (Chapter 12, Section 2, Chapter 9, Section 4) and peripheral areas of cities allowed many women to obtain jobs. In some of the development areas there was a complete household reversal, with the male manual skilled worker made unemployed and women entering often semi-skilled manufacturing employment that was not very well paid. The availability of kin and friends to mind children or of free pre-school provision or paid help to live in may be possible if the occupation being followed is highly paid. Such highly paid jobs for women are relatively more available in the South East.

Company strategies

Many of the strategies for companies have been indirectly reviewed in this chapter on the flexible firm (Chapter 12, Section 2) and in the chapters on economic and technological change. Firms can restructure in many ways. Some may involve substituting capital for labour in the form of investment in technology.

Labour relations

Many companies located in central cities where labour is highly priced or strongly organised have followed such a strategy and remained in the city. Others have moved towards cheaper or less well-organised labour elsewhere, sometimes changing their technology so that less skills are needed as part of the move. Some of the plants established by overseas investment have introduced different work processes, such as multi-skilled workers instead of people being restricted to particular tasks, and working in teams. These are ideas that are supposed to enrich the labour process as well as to make it efficient and effective. Without restrictive trades or skills there is no need for many labour unions to operate in the same plant. Companies have tried to obtain single-union plants which may make negotiations easier. Sometimes they have made no-strike agreements. For multi-plant firms they have also tried to obtain single plant agreements rather than national ones. Such a fragmentation of labour negotiations is also being attempted in the public sector where unions still remain nationally relatively strong, because of the geographical spread of public service employment. Some regard these moves as attempts to break down the power of unions. Others see it as negotiating wages and conditions that are appropriate to the local labour market and to local costs of living. Since such moves have been accompanied by legislative reductions in union power, it is difficult not to associate the two as a combined move of government and employers.

Changing the labour process or labour management relations, however, are just two elements of a much wider set of possible organisational strategies of a company. Those writers who see labour-management relations as part of a continuing class struggle have tended to emphasise the importance of labour-oriented strategies of the firm, to the neglect, for instance, of market-oriented strategies in explaining their changing spatial organisation. Their emphasis, though, has been reinforced by the attention of governments to labour relations, though often the writers and the governments have very different values and beliefs.

Internal labour markets

Some large companies have developed strategies that retain their core workers or key staff. They provide career structures for them within the company and try to obtain their loyalty. So that they do not become too attached or loyal to a place, they move their key workers from branch to branch at regular intervals, paying relocation fees and helping with house purchases. Such mobile employees form an important part of the 'mobile elite' who characteristically move from the outer suburbs of one city to those of another at frequent intervals, having an important effect on the housing market. Companies operating such a strategy have effectively *internalised* the labour market, that is, there are few people entering or leaving the company into core or primary employment except at the bottom end of the hierarchy.

Government's strategies

Governments have a set of questions to decide about policies on work. The first is the degree to which they should intervene in the economy. They may decide that their main or even only task is to try to encourage the overall conditions for wealth creation and employment, such as by following policies that keep down inflation and interest rates. Other governments may intervene further to encourage job creation and/or job relocation.

Relocating jobs

In times of rapid economic growth when companies are expanding and forming, it is easier to encourage relocation. During recessions there is little expansion and few new jobs to move. In these times, job creation is a much more suitable policy and more politically acceptable. If there were going to be new jobs in an area in times of poor employment prospects and a government helped move them to another part of the country, this would not be very popular with the area losing the jobs, even if it had a lower rate of unemployment than the other area. The policies concerning relocation and their problems have been discussed elsewhere (Chapter 5, Section 4). They were associated with the regional policies of the 1960s and early 1970s in Britain. The costs per job were often high, and many were branch plants that were the first to close or contract in recession. There was also too great an orientation to manufacturing as against service jobs, the potential of which was recognised very late on. The new jobs, however, did have some multiplier effects and undoubtedly raised the morale of areas that would otherwise have declined more dramatically.

Job creation

Job creation policies may be followed by local as well as national government. In the early 1980s the job creation policies of the metropolitan counties offered an alternative strategy to economic recovery from that of national government, a factor that may well have contributed to the abolition of the counties because the national government did not appreciate alternative policies (Chapter 11, Section 1). A number of authori-

ties, for example, set up *Enterprise Boards*, which were to create and preserve jobs by intervention in the local economy, in most cases providing venture capital. Four were set up by metropolitan counties (Greater London, West Midlands, Merseyside and West Yorkshire) and two by county councils (Lancashire and Derbyshire). All were Labour controlled. Greater Manchester also had an Enterprise Board but this was set up before the 1980s by a Conservative controlled-council and was concerned mainly with property rather than finance. The boards varied. For Greater London investment was to create high-quality long-term jobs that mirrored the social priorities of the GLC, especially the needs of women and ethnic minorities, and the requirements of workforce participation. In West Yorkshire investment in industry had the more pragmatic concern of ameliorating unemployment and arresting economic decline. Its board was complementary to the economic development unit of the county. In Lancashire its unit became the board, Lancashire Enterprises Limited (LEL). While West Yorkshire, until abolition, only provided corporate finance, LEL also handled property, training, promotion, sponsorship, the Lancashire Cooperative Development Agency and the county's application for grants from the European Regional Fund and the European Social Fund. The revitalisation of the Leeds-Liverpool Canal Corridor, for which EEC funds were obtained, was one of the major projects that LEL coordinated. LEL, unlike West Yorkshire, combined subsidy-oriented with commercial activity.

The boards of the metropolitan counties carried on after abolition but with much-reduced funds and new names. The national government introduced more and more controls on what authorities could do. Although it promoted partnerships between the private and public sectors, it did not look favourably on such initiatives of the metropolitan counties.

Economic Development Units of other authorities learned from these initiatives and moved away from just providing land and factories and promoting their areas. They also became involved in the labour market, particularly the nature of jobs and access to them, with attempts to help ethnic minorities and women. Some also turned to cultural activities in order to create jobs. Liverpool, Birmingham and Nottingham followed Glasgow's lead in this. Sheffield attempted to create a 'cultural industries quarter' next to its science park, with municipally and privately owned music and recording studios and a music, dance and arts centre. In general by the late 1980s, there was a broader view being taken by local authorities, moving from the narrow view of an industrial policy to a wider economic one. There was also much more attempt to link social policy objectives to employment ones. These changes in strategy were made against a background of national government control and limitation of local authorities' strategic roles.

Targeting sectors

National government may help to create jobs in particular sectors such as the high-tech industries or in particular types of firms such as small businesses. Both strategies have been followed, the latter being part of the late 1980s approach to job creation in Britain as part of the drive towards an enterprise culture. This policy was based on the observation that most employment growth in the late 1970s and early 1980s in the USA was due to small businesses. It was a time when large corporations were restructuring and either shedding labour or sub-contracting. The adoption of such a policy demonstrates an ideological commitment to small firms as much as to job cre-

ation. The success rate of small firms is not too high. There are always many closures, particularly at times of high interest rates. The fact that they were the main form of new employment during one period in one country does not mean they would be at another time in another place. Many small business jobs grew in the USA in services rather than manufacturing, again a point that was somewhat ignored. Help to small firms comes in the form of cheap or rent-free buildings, relief from certain taxes and free advice and training services. Some schemes have been particularly targeted at ethnic groups in inner cities, for example in St Pauls, Bristol where there was a major riot in the early 1980s. One problem has been that help ends abruptly after an initial period, at the end of which some of the businesses are just getting going and are entering a make-or-break period of establishing a market. The removal of assistance at such a time leads to the collapse of many enterprises, or in some cases a return to unemployment, because the assistance was seen only as a short-term alternative to unemployment pay. Risk-taking is not easy to learn.

Training

Another government strategy sometimes going under the heading of job creation is training, particularly of youths. This has a number of aims. One is to ensure that the work ethic is not lost by too long a period of unemployment after leaving school. More generally it is to keep young unemployed off the streets and out of crime. Another is to improve the disciplines associated with some work, such as time-keeping. Too often in the earlier forms of youth training in Britain, that was all that was accomplished. Few specific skills were acquired. In theory such schemes were to improve school-leavers' skills, which were seen by

some writers and politicians as the reason why they had not got jobs in the first place. This account ignored the varying states of the local economies that were discussed earlier (Chapter 12, Section 2). In many areas where youths were well qualified, there were not any jobs to obtain. In these cases it was not lack of skills but lack of jobs that produced such unemployment. The other aim of training was to improve the pool of skills so that when there was an economic upturn there would be adequate supplies of labour to meet the demand. Some young people gained jobs through these schemes and learned new skills.

Many of the schemes improved over time. For many young people it was a better prospect than unemployment. Some preferred unemployment. Many critics of the schemes saw them simply as ways of reducing the unemployment figures, obtaining cheap labour, accustoming young people to low pay and reducing the chances of social unrest.

In many ways such strategies are short-term ones. In the 1990s the aim in many countries is to make the education system more oriented to the needs of the economy, producing a narrowing of the aims of education. Such longer-term policies on work are difficult to apply because there is so much uncertainty about future employment needs. Governments' planning of the labour supply has never proved very successful in limited fields such as teaching and nursing, let alone the economy as a whole.

An economy based on manufacturing or services?

There is a wider question for governments and more generally the people of a country, city or region to decide or, to the extent that they can, influence. Do they want an economy based on manufacturing or one based on services? Some think the latter is impossible and regard manufacturing as basic to any successful economy. They see it as the primary way of wealth creation. Services are seen as almost parasitic. This is not to say that they think more people should be employed in manufacturing than services, but that manufacturing employment, investment and output should grow absolutely and provide the necessary engine of growth.

Perhaps in some situations only investment and output will grow, producing jobless growth. In either case there may be indirect or multiplier effects of increasing employment in related supply and service industries. In jobless growth there may be less multiplier effects from the increased purchasing power of the manufacturing industry's employees. Even this may be debated because much-increased incomes for the same number of employees over time may yield as great a multiplier effect as an increased number of employees on relatively low incomes. It is not just the number employed in the manufacturing or indeed service industry that is important for multiplier effects but the type and/or quality of employment. Unemployment may be reduced through the multiplier effect rather than directly by the new industry or service.

Propulsive firms

The increased purchasing power and the increased demand for supplies and services from propulsive firms (ones that have very significant multiplier effects) are of little use to the local or national economy if demand goes out of the area or country. The geography of the multiplier effects matters. If supplies and services are imported and imported goods are purchased by employees, there will be little local or national indirect growth generated. The key questions for an economy, at the local,

regional or national scale, based on manufacturing or services are:
(a) Is manufacturing industry or services more propulsive?
(b) Which set of multiplier effects, that of manufacturing industry or of services, is generated more within the local area, region or country?

Some manufacturing industry is very propulsive. It generates many linkages with suppliers, customers and services. It is easier, however, to know retrospectively which are more propulsive. It is not always easy to predict for the future. The degree to which the linkages or multipliers are local varies with the type of plant and its ownership. Where transport costs are not a significant element within assembly costs of parts, suppliers may be located in other areas or countries. The example of the global car (Chapter 8, Section 1) is evidence of this. Where suppliers are already located in the area, they may be used, but where a new plant is located and it is hoped that suppliers will be attracted to locate around it, expectations may often not be met.

Growth centres

Such an agglomeration of linked industries is the idea underlying the strategy of *growth centres*, which were a major method of attempting to stimulate regional economic development in the 1960s and 1970s. The idea of just-in-time inventory control (Chapters 8 and 9) may encourage a greater clustering of suppliers, as seems to be the case around the Nissan factory in the north-east of England, but other countervailing factors may prevent such concentrations. Regional linkages to both suppliers and services are also often low when the factory is a branch plant controlled from outside the region or country. Both sets of linkages are often decided at headquarters, which tend to be ori-

ented to linkages in other regions or countries. In the North East, locally controlled companies had 77 per cent of their linkages within the region while externally controlled ones had 77 per cent outside the region.

Some services are propulsive. They generate demand from manufacturing industry as well as other services. It has been estimated that 7 per cent of manufacturing jobs are supported by the demands of the service industries, while 20 per cent of service jobs are supported by demands from manufacturing. This two-way interaction between the sectors is sometimes forgotten, such as when expenditure on public services is cut in order to give various forms of encouragement to private industry. Public services demand goods from manufacturing, such as medical equipment, drugs and books.

Producer services

The most propulsive and geographically significant services are probably producer services. They generate demand for other services and attract manufacturing industry into regions where they are well represented. Manufacturing companies are then able to contract work out to them. They represent an *external economy* to the manufacturing companies. Part of the growth of manufacturing in the 'South' has been attributed to the presence of producer services. Equally, their growth has increased as the demand from regional manufacturing firms has expanded. This is an example of cumulative growth. Producer services in the 'South' have also benefited from demand from the headquarters of manufacturing companies located there, whose plants, however, are located in other regions of the country or outside the country.

Trams, and old style traffic control, part of the artificially created 'charm' of Lowell, Massachusetts

Exported services

It is the producer services that are mainly quoted as supplying the exports necessary if a country is to survive on a service base. The rapid growth of some advertising firms into global companies is cited as an example. The concept of the information economy (Chapter 9) relies partly on the idea of a service base, with knowledge as the most significant commodity. Services oriented to tourism are also seen by some as attracting income into a country, region or city. Many old industrial cities have decided to base new jobs on what has been called the 'heritage' industry, where, for instance, old mills and factories are turned into industrial museums and canal-boats link the sites of interest, as in Lowell in Massachusetts, USA, one of the leaders in such developments. More generally cities are investing in leisure, recreation and cultural activities that will attract people from elsewhere in the country and abroad. They are trying to become 'cities of spectacle'. The more there are that compete to do so, the more difficult it will be for any to make major advances. As with many other ideas, the first in the field often gather momentum that others find difficult to match.

Other authors state that exports have to be based on manufacturing goods, because services will never provide sufficient income. In the new internationalised economies (Chapter 12, Section 2) it seems there will be major flows of exports and imports in all sectors, and that the idea of specialising in one or two sectors is past. As stated elsewhere, the distinction between manufacturing and services is blurred and perhaps becoming more so. Perhaps the debate between manufacturing and services as a base is becoming outdated. The important decisions may be in which combination of primary products, manufactured goods and services to specialise at any one period for export, rather than whether it is manufacturing or services. If major corporations have diversified across these sectors, it would be strange if countries and regions were not also to do so.

Summary

Whatever set of decisions are made for any one country in order to influence the future base of its economy, to the extent that it can in such an interdependent world, the decisions will have geographical and social effects within the country. In Britain an emphasis on producer services would benefit the 'South', while a push towards tourism may be more widely spread between regions, even though certain centres within regions would be favoured. At present an emphasis on manufacturing would benefit men, while a drive on the service front may be more beneficial for women in terms of employment opportunities. These are decisions for the future that you should be participating in making.

12.5 Perspectives

Changes in work

Employment has changed much in the last few decades. Its inverse, unemployment, has also increased and fluctuated. The post-war goal of full employment came under pressure during the 1970s and was clearly out of reach in the following decade. A high rate of unemployment began to be accepted as part of the new economic circumstances of the time. Unemployment, though, has been unevenly spread across the country and has been one feature of the growing North-South divide in Britain. Women seeking to enter the workforce are not counted within the official figures, so those wanting paid work are under-estimated. Indeed, the method of counting the unemployed changed during the 1980s in a way that reduced the numbers still further, even though no more people had found paid work.

The proportion of women in unpaid work (See figure 12.31 question 4 in Chapter 12, Section 6) also varies across the country.

The greater opportunity that this reflects of having two employed people in the household in the South East has been an important contribution to the expansion of home ownership and the inflation in house prices there. The spatial variation of women already in employment also means that the pool of potential labour is unevenly spread. With fewer young people entering the labour market in the 1990s (Chapter 10), there is therefore a spatial variation in the extent to which their decline can be easily made up by more women becoming economically active. The provision of child-care is also uneven, so women in some parts of the country will find it easier to take on paid work than others.

Effects on changes in work

These changes in work in one country have been influenced by international changes, such as the growth of manufacturing in South East Asia, the emergence of global corporations and the internationalisation of trade. They have been affected by company policies, technological change, labour-management relations and government policies within the country. They have also been influenced by movements such as feminism and campaigns such as the one for equal pay. The effects of these and other factors have not all been evenly felt across the country.

Decline of industrial regions

One major change has been the decline of the industrial regions. The agglomeration economies and close spatial linkages between firms that characterised them no longer operate to the same degree. This has led

some geographers to argue that the concept of the 'industrial' region is no longer an appropriate description of the real world. They suggest that smaller areas, such as towns, based on the idea of the *local labour market*, have become a more appropriate scale to study economic geography and its relationships with social and political geography. This scale of the local labour market, the town or semi-rural industrial area, has also been called a *locality*.

'Rise' of localities

Others argue that new industrial regions have emerged, such as Silicon Valley in California. Generally, though, most economic geographers now study labour markets or localities, corporations, types of investment, nations and the global spatial economy, rather than industrial regions. The scales of study have changed to reflect the dominant economic processes operating.

Effects on social and political environments

Work, employment and unemployment have all become more than simple economic issues. They have become social and political too. The gender and ethnic differences in employment (Chapter 12, Sections 3b and 3c) are some aspects of the social. The concentrations of unemployment in parts of inner cities and peripheral local authority estates have major social and political importance. Inner-city areas are more visible and have received much more political attention than the peripheral estates. Even though, in any one city, unemployment in total in peripheral estates often exceeds that in the inner city, it is scattered around the city while the central concentration is more easily

identified and more associated with unrest.

Urban-rural change

Changes in work have also affected the other environments. The new locations of industry in rural and semi-rural areas have helped to blur the difference between town and country. Employment change has both contributed to counter-urbanisation (Chapter 10, Section 3d) and been affected by it. As people moved out of very large towns to smaller ones and to some rural areas, new jobs were created to serve them. The new homes of key workers led to decentralisation of companies in their direction, for example to the south-west of Greater London. The built and social environments have therefore been changed. The changes in work have also stimulated new technologies as well as been affected by them. The new locations of employment and the growth of women in paid work have also changed the political environment, with changed attitudes and voting patterns in affected constituencies.

The changes in geography

Finally, it is worth noting how the study of geography has changed in its view of work. In the 1960s economic geographers were interested primarily in manufacturing growth and relocation. The three Ms dominated writing: male, manual, manufacturing. In the late 1970s and early 1980s economic geography was characterised by discussions about job loss, manufacturing decline and job creation. The feminisation of manufacturing in the early 1970s had been noted, so women at long last began to be considered. As the growth of services, the decline of manufacturing employment, the relative increase of women in the workforce and the defeminisation of manufacturing were analysed in the 1980s, there began to be a broader discussion of sectors and gender, but still too often work is seen as employment, male and manufacturing.

12..6 **Exercises**

Region (thousands)	1930	1940	1950	1960	1970	1980
New England	1099	1158	1381	1479	1541	1606
Middle Atlantic	2950	2995	3902	4235	4274	3814
East North Central	2682	2909	4167	4664	5361	5120
Manufacturing Belt	6731	7062	9450	10378	11176	10540
South Atlantic	1087	1248	1623	2134	2789	3222
East South Central	470	489	685	930	1277	1437
West North Central	745	550	818	1035	1250	1450
Mountain	187	101	161	295	385	597
Pacific	692	586	1019	1788	2172	2722
Other US	3747	3373	4950	7097	9159	11198
Total Mfg Employ.	10478	10435	14400	17475	20335	21738
Total US Employ.	47402	49625	60203	64374	76581	96947

12.25 Manufacturing employment in US regions, 1930-80

1. (a) Study Figure 12.25 on the changes in manufacturing employment in the USA between 1930 and 1980.
   (i) What changes have there been in manufacturing employment as a proportion of total employment for the USA as a whole?
   (ii) Graph the regional changes in manufacturing employment and comment on the most significant changes.
   (b) Study figure 12.26 on types of employment in manufacturing in the USA.
   (i) Compare the changes in types of employment in manufacturing for the manufacturing belt and the rest of the USA for the period 1947-82.
   (ii) Suggest reasons for the differences.
   (iii) What evidence is there to support the hypothesis that changes in types of employment in manufacturing occurred earlier in the manufacturing belt?
   (iv) What do these changes in types of occupations in the manufacturing sector suggest about the validity of the distinction between the manufacturing and service sectors?
   (c) Figure 12.27 shows the regional differences in closures and layoffs in the USA in 1983-84.
   (i) Suggest ways in which the data may be represented in other forms.

12.27 Regional differences in closures and layoffs in the USA, 1983-84

Region	Number of establishments (a)	Percentage of total	Rate of occurrence(b)	Number of employees	Percentage of total
Total	7790	100	7.8	1049000	100
North-East	1880	24	7.6	227000	22
New England	640	8	9.3	80000	8
Mid Atlantic	1240	16	6.9	147000	29
Midwest	2190	28	9.0	312000	29
East North Central	1690	22	9.6	227000	21
West North Central	500	6	7.4	85000	8
South	4260	32	7.4	299000	29
South Atlantic	850	11	5.2	76000	7
East South Central	310	4	5.5	48000	5
West South Central	1300	17	12.0	175000	17
West	1260	16	7.0	211000	20
Mountain	320	4	7.2	36000	3
Pacific	940	12	6.9	175000	17

Notes: (a) Establishments with 100 or more employees experiencing closure, or permanent layoff (of 20% or more of the workforce, or over 199 employees). (b) Percentage of all establishments per region with 100 or more employees experiencing closure or permanent lay-off

12.26 Changes in types of employment in the US manufacturing sector, 1947-82

Region		1947-67			1967-82	
	Total employment change(000s)	Production worker change (000s)	Non-production worker change (000s)	Total employment change(000s)	Production worker change(000s)	Non-production worker change(000s)
Manufact. Belt	1396.0	−144.3	1540.3	−2175.7	−2323.4	146.7
Other US	3535.2	2155.9	1379.3	1973.9	778.9	1195.0
Total	4931.2	2011.6	2919.6	−201.8	−1544.5	1341.7

Region	Self-employed	
	(000's)	%
South East	+389	+55.3
Greater London	+132	+48.2
Remainder	+257	+59.8
East Anglia	+52	+59.1
South West	+80	+35.6
East Midlands*	+61	+41.8
South	+582	+50.0
West Midlands	+80	+46.8
Yorks & Humb.	+75	+45.5
North West	+78	+35.8
North	+31	+36.5
Wales	+34	+29.3
Scotland	+69	+45.1
North	+367	+40.4
Great Britain	+948	+45.8

The East Midlands is increasingly included within the 'South', but traditional classifications include it alongside the West Midlands.

12.28 Growth of self-employment, 1981-89

(ii) What evidence is there to suggest that the recession of the early 1980s had a differential regional effect?

2. (a) Map the distribution of increases in the number of people who were self-employed in Britain between 1981 and 1989 (Figure 12.28).

12.29 Employment change in inner and outer areas of conurbations

City	Total	Manufacturing	% change 1981-87 Services	Distribution	Transport & communication	Business services
Birmingham	−9.0	−27.3	+3.1	−8.1	−12.6	+21.2
Glasgow	−7.8	−27.7	−1.2	−14.2	−28.4	+46.7
Liverpool	−20.4	−44.2	−13.2	−28.4	−34.7	+50.3
Leeds	−2.3	−15.0	+5.4	+4.8	−8.5	+25.9
Manchester	−4.1	−17.9	+0.0	−8.5	−7.6	+69.3
Newcastle	−0.4	−43.7	+15.0	−10.3	−18.0	+93.5
Sheffield	−16.1	−38.2	−2.7	−16.9	−9.3	+14.6
Seven cities	−8.7	−28.6	+0.3	−10.9	−18.8	+38.7
London	−1.6	−29.6	+6.9	+0.6	−14.7	+70.9
Eight cities	−4.2	−29.1	+4.7	−3.5	−16.0	+64.4
Great Britain	−0.2	−15.7	+9.4	+3.7	−8.4	+80.6

(b) Describe and suggest reasons for the national and regional changes.

3. (a) Study Figure 12.29 which shows employment change in the conurbations.
   (i) Describe the changes in employment for the central and inner areas over time.
   (ii) Describe the changes in employment for the outer areas over time.
   (iii) Compare the changes in the two types of areas.
   (iv) Suggest reasons for the changes that you have

12.30 Employment change for eight large cities

observed over time and between areas.
   (b) Study Figure 12.30 which shows employment change for eight cities during the 1980s.
   (i) Compare the changes for London with those for the other seven cities as a whole.
   (ii) Describe the variation among the seven cities.
   (iii) Suggest reasons for the variations in decline of manufacturing employment and the variations in growth of business services among the eight cities.

4. (a) Study Figure 12.31 which shows the regional change in female economic activity rates.
   (i) Draw one map showing both the 1971 rates and the changes from 1971 to 1987.
   (ii) Describe and suggest reasons for the variation in rates among regions in 1971.
   (iii) Describe and suggest reasons for the variation in the changes from 1971 to 1987.
   (b) (i) Describe the changes in rates between 1979 and 1983.

Period/sector	Central and inner areas		Outer areas		Overall conurbations		Great Britain
	000s	%	000s	%	000s	%	(%)
1951-61							
Total employment	+43	+1.0	+231	+6.0	+274	+3.4	(+7.0)
of which:							
Manufacturing	−143	−8.0	+84	+5.0	−59	−1.7	(5.0)
Services	+205	+6.7	+164	+9.3	+369	+7.7	(+10.6)
1961-71							
Total employment	−643	−14.8	+19	+0.6	−624	−8.3	(+1.3)
of which:							
Manufacturing	−428	−26.1	−217	−10.3	−645	−17.2	(−3.9)
Services	−272	−8.5	+262	+13.6	−10	−0.2	(+8.6)
1971-81							
Total employment	−538	−14.6	−236	−7.1	−774	−11.0	(−2.7)
of which:							
Manufacturing	−447	−36.8	−480	−32.6	−927	−34.5	(−24.5)
Services	−183	−6.8	+272	+12.7	+89	+1.8	(+11.1)

Note: the conurbations are London, West Midlands, Greater Manchester, Merseyside, Tyneside and Clydeside.

	Economic activity rate (%)				Change (%)
	1971	1979	1983	1987	1971-87
South East	46.2	48.2	48.4	52.5	+6.0
East Anglia	39.6	45.1	47.4	50.0	+10.4
South West	38.5	44.0	44.7	49.9	+11.4
East Midlands	44.1	47.4	48.1	50.2	+6.1
West Midlands	46.4	49.5	47.0	49.8	+3.2
Yorkshire & Humb.	42.7	46.8	47.2	48.4	+5.7
North West	45.3	48.6	47.2	50.1	+4.8
North	41.1	45.7	44.8	48.8	+7.7
Wales	36.7	49.8	47.0	47.8	4.2
Great Britain	43.9	47.4	47.0	50.0	+6.1

Note: Rates expressed as percentage of home population aged 16 or over who are in the civilian labour force
Source: Regional trends 23 (1988), Table 9.5 and 24 (1989), Table 10.5

12.31 Regional change in female economic activity rates, 1971-87

  (ii) Compare the changes in rates between 1979-1983 and 1983-1987.
  (iii) Suggest reasons for the differences between the two time periods.
 (c) From other sources:

(i) Describe the major types of employment that women have entered since 1971.
(ii) What constraints have there been on women entering paid work?
(iii) Suggest ways in which these have been or can be overcome.

(d) Describe and suggest reasons for the changes since 1971 in:
 (i) unpaid work carried out in the home;
 (ii) the share of unpaid work in the home carried out by women and men.
(e) (i) What evidence is there to suggest that unpaid work in the home is shared between genders in different ways in different parts of the country?
 (ii) Suggest reasons for any such differences.

5. (a) For an area near you, discuss the extent to which recent immigrants have taken up particular occupations.
(b) Suggest reasons why, in the nation as a whole, recent immigrants are often concentrated in specific occupations and areas.

12.7 **Further reading**

J. Allen and D. Massey (eds.) (1988) *The Economy in Question: Restructuring Britain*, Sage

A G Champion and A R Townsend (1990) *Contemporary Britain: a Geographical Perspective*, Edward Arnold

P. Cooke (ed.) (1989) *Localities: the Changing Face of Urban Britain*, Unwin Hyman

R.J. Johnston and V. Gardiner (eds.) (1991) *The Changing Geography of the UK*, Routledge

R. Martin and B. Rowthorne (eds.) (1986) *The Deindustrialisation of Great Britain*, Macmillan

D. Massey and R. Meagan (1982) *The Anatomy of Job Loss*, Methuen

A. Scott and M. Storper (eds.) (1986) *Production, Work and Territory*, Allen and Unwin

Chapter 13

URBAN RENEWAL POLICIES AND ACCESS TO HOUSING

13.1   Case study: from redevelopment to rehabilitation in Birmingham

Saltley is a residential area just outside the inner ring of East Birmingham (Figure 13.1).

Its rows of terraced houses were built between 1860 and 1910 to house the families of skilled men working in local factories, railway yards and gasworks. Unlike the back-to-backs built for unskilled labour, these houses were well constructed. A few local builders had purchased leases from two landowners, who had placed conditions on the density and future use of housing. Originally most of the houses had been sold leasehold to private

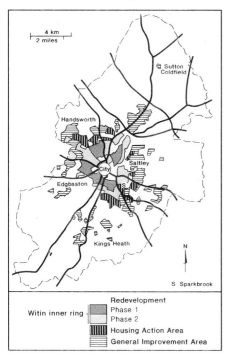

13.1 Urban renewal in Birmingham

landlords who then rented the properties. From 1920 onwards, and especially during the 1950s, the building society gradually replaced the rent collector, because the increasing restrictions of Rent Act legislation triggered the landlords to sell their houses and invest their capital where it received better returns. Estate agents bought them and canvassed sitting tenants to see whether they wanted to become owner-occupiers. For those that did, they arranged finance with a local building society.

The increasing burden of maintaining and repairing the now deteriorating houses thus passed from landlords to owner-occupiers. The inhabitants of Saltley, however, were changing and the new owners were less able to maintain their houses. After 1945 the better-off skilled workers had begun to move out to the newer, semi-detached houses in the suburbs. First Irish immigrants, and later, in the 1960s, West Indians and Pakistanis replaced them. Many had low-paid, unskilled jobs and Saltley was an area of cheap housing that they could just afford. The loss of the traditional skilled jobs from Saltley, 10,000 from 1964 to 1974, led to further outmigration of the skilled. As the area declined, building societies stopped lending mortgages (redlining) because many houses needed major repairs and most had only a short period of their leasehold

remaining. Estate agents organised alternative finance for mortgages from banks and finance companies, but the interest rates were higher from these sources. Between 1972 and 1974 over 60 per cent of the houses purchased in Saltley had mortgages from these sources. Only 15 per cent were from the then conventional sources of building societies and local authorities, compared with a national level of 94 per cent. Borrowing at higher rates of interest left even less for repairs.

This short history of Saltley illustrates some of the roles of the key actors in the housing market, the interaction between the housing and labour markets, and, most importantly for this case study, the reasons for housing decay and the need by the 1970s for some kind of renewal. In order to examine some of the alternative types of renewal, and to set Saltley's problem in a wider context, other programmes within Birmingham will be reviewed.

Like many old industrial towns, Birmingham inherited many old houses. Even in 1981, nearly 30 per cent of its housing had been built before 1919 and 46 per cent of that was classified as unfit. Nearly 40 per cent of its housing was built after 1945, of which 2 per cent was unfit. In 1981 in all, 17.6 per cent of its housing was classified as unfit. This is in spite of considerable efforts over a long period to renew its housing.

By 1970 Birmingham City Council had already completed much of a very large redevelopment programme in the inner ring, just outside of which Saltley lies (Figure 13.1). This involved pre-1919 housing that had decayed to the extent of being classified as slums. The programme had begun before 1939 when the council was one of the first to realise that piecemeal clearance and rebuilding were unsuitable and that comprehensive redevelopment was needed. In 1946 it had created five redevelopment areas under Phase 1 (Figure 13.1) which involved buying 32,000 houses, but by 1954 only 3000 had been demolished. This was due partly to the slow rate of new house building and partly to the great housing shortage during this immediate post-war period. The council had to renovate some of the properties because people continued to live in them. In Phase 2, in 1954, it purchased another 30,000 to complete its slum clearance programme. The housing shortage and slow building rate, however, continued and the council faced a conflict over the allocation of its new housing between those on the waiting list and families who had to be rehoused after clearance. The council also had difficulties in finding space for new housing, so some new development took the form of high-rise flats. The space problem was alleviated when national government at last permitted two new towns, Telford and Redditch, to be designated (to the north-west and south of Birmingham respectively) and a large peripheral overspill estate, Chelmsley Wood, to be built in the Green Belt. These developments allowed some of the people from the inner ring to be relocated outside Birmingham. In the second half of the 1960s 39,000 council houses were built, 23,000 houses in the inner ring were demolished and 18,000 renovated. At last, redevelopment seemed to be going at the required rate.

Over the period of redevelopment, however, the middle ring in which Saltley is situated had become the area of cheapest private housing in the city. As in Saltley, low-income people, including ethnic groups, began to be concentrated in many parts of the middle ring. Some moved there because they were unable to obtain council housing or were ineligible for rehousing after clearance. Some were home owner-occupiers and, as in Saltley, borrowed at high rates of interest. Others rented the villas (large detached or semi-detached houses) in the inner parts of the middle ring, such as at Sparkbrook. These had been vacated by middle-income families who had suburbanised. They were replaced by a number of households in each villa as the houses were converted into multi-occupancy. These inner parts of the middle ring, adjacent to the redevelopment areas and characterised by multi-occupancy, were regarded as next in line for clearance. The policy was to leave these areas alone but to contain multi-occupancy within them.

In the outer parts of the middle ring, grants were given for improvement to 20,000 properties between 1954 and 1969. It was in these areas that General Improvement Areas (GIAs) were designated (Figure 13.1) from 1969 when national policy moved away from redevelopment to improvement or rehabilitation. People in these GIAs, which consisted of about 400 houses, were encouraged to take up grants towards improving their homes. Up to 50 per cent of the approved cost was given for eligible property which would have to be improved so that it would last for at least another thirty years. Local authorities could also obtain some money from national government to improve the areas environmentally, which was indirectly another encouragement for people to invest in their own homes. Improvement meant that communities could be retained, unlike in the redevelopment areas. The policy also sought to involve local people in participating in the decisions about their areas.

Local authority management, however, was often a problem. Environmental Health Officers had previously dealt with improvements, while Housing Officers had been concerned with local authority housing and redevelopment. Planners began to be involved as the policies became area-based and required traffic management and environmental work. In Birmingham interdepartmental conflict occurred and the ideal interdisciplinary approach did not take place.

The GIAs were concentrated in the outer parts of the middle ring where the houses were better and people somewhat better-off. In 1973 a Labour-led Birmingham Council decided to do something about the worst housing and social conditions in the inner parts of the middle ring. They designated twenty-eight renewal areas which included Saltley and which combined improvement and clearance. In 1974 the new Labour national government implemented another area-based policy, Housing Action Areas (HAAs), which the previous Conservative government had devised. HAAs were directed at areas of housing stress for which GIAs were not catering. This was the turning point nationally when improvement replaced redevelopment rather than accompanied it. So in 1975 part of Saltley became one of Birmingham's first HAAs, Havelock HAA, in which grants were now 75 per cent of approved costs and only fifteen years' further life was expected. At the end of five years the work of an HAA was supposed to be complete. This seemed unlikely because the take-up of grants was lower than hoped and the uneven take-up gave a 'pepper-pot' pattern of improved houses. Some did not obtain grants or improve their property themselves because either they were satisfied with it or there was insufficient return on their investment in the revised valuation of

HAA	Declaration date	Envelope date	Average no. of grants paid per year between declaration and enveloping	Average no. of grant applications per year since enveloping
Little Green	4.3.75	20.2.78	17	70
St. Silas (a)	19.3.76	5.1.80	17	70
St. Silas (b)	19.3.76	8.9.80		
Conway	23.4.76	7.1.80	5	33
Balsall Heath	16.1.76	7.4.81	16	55

The overall number of grants paid per year has been taken as an indication of the degree of success of an HAA. The rate of grant applications per year has increased dramatically since the commencement of the Envelope Schemes (column 4).

13.2 The enveloping effect

their property after improvement. For example, for an unimproved pre-1919 property with a market value of £6-8000 the improvement costs would have been £10-12,000 and the market value after improvement only £13-14,000. This 'valuation gap', as it is known, is still a problem hindering improvement in some inner-city areas. It is not restricted to individuals as it is also faced by housing associations which began to be major actors in rehabilitation by acquiring property for improvement and sale in the declared areas (GIAs and HAAs).

In 1978 with the help of national government's Inner City Partnership Funds, the then Conservative local government spent £1.5 million on 'Operation Facelift' in Havelock and one other HAA. These schemes, which renovated the exterior of houses free of charge to owners, proved so successful that they were extended (Figure 13.2).

Since all the houses in an area were completed, the scheme was known as 'enveloping'. Its aim was to bring the areas 'up' and by doing so encourage owners to apply to improve their interiors. In Havelock, most did. Those who had improved before the envelope scheme, however, would already have contributed

much of their own money and lost out on obtaining help.

Urban renewal policy in Birmingham went from redevelopment to envelopment. The city was often innovative, yet its problems demonstrate those of urban renewal. Concentrating on redevelopment in the inner ring precluded preventive action in the middle ring, which deteriorated badly. Subsequent improvement in the middle ring was unlikely to be completed before the condition of suburban local authority housing reached crisis point. Housing deterioration continues (Figure 13.3) and is a continual problem.

In 1984 it was estimated that the West Midlands had received only half of the sum it needed in that year to check the increasing deterioration of the region's housing. In the later 1980s public initiatives were limited because of the lack of funds, so Birmingham and the rest of the West Midlands did not in any way catch up with this housing problem.

The case study illustrates some of the problems associated with housing decay and some of the policies or strategies of urban renewal that have been adopted locally and nationally to solve them. Incidentally it has also shown how the housing in an area can be home to different sets of people over time, how the tenure of the housing may also change and how access to the housing may vary for different types of people. It has also demonstrated the roles of some of the key actors in the housing market and in urban renewal.

13.3 1980 projected deterioration

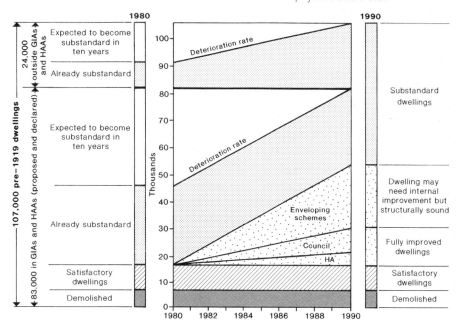

13.2 General problem

Statement of the general problem

The case study illustrates some of the changes in housing over recent years and demonstrates some of the problems underlying those changes. They involve the built environment with its decay and renewal. More specifically they include the design, layout, mix, density and location of housing, its quantity and quality. They also involve: the social environment with the match of households to housing, the social mix or segregation of neighbourhoods and the stability of change in neighbourhood status; and the economic environment with the tenures, prices and rents of housing, and their rates of change. The general problem of the chapter is to maintain and improve the overall housing stock while at the same time improving for all households their quality of life and their access to the stock. This problem involves a number of types of actors and institutions whose viewpoints and aims are summarised in Figure 13.4.

The extent and form of the problem are affected by the social and economic contexts of the time, while varying attempted solutions to it have far-reaching consequences, particularly to the built, social and economic environments. These will be examined in the section on alternative strategies. This section will study the characteristics of housing and governments' involvement with it, the influences on demand and supply, the reasons for decay, differential rates of decay over time and space, and the effects of housing change and the institutions associated with access to housing on the structure of cities.

13.4 Actors and their viewpoints on housing

Actors	Viewpoints
Demand Household type eg single(s) nuclear family, lone parent family, elderly, homeless	varying views on housing depending on • socio-economic status • life-cycle • life-style
Owner-occupiers	• maintain house as investment • enhance value • want available mortgages, low interest rates, tax relief on mortgage interest and capital gains • want stable or improving neighbourhood
Tenants	• security of tenure • low rent and rent increases • good maintenance of service by landlord
Supply Builders (large scale)	• economies of scale in land purchase, production technology and marketing • profit and rapid sales • more cheap good land • less planning • joint ventures, with LAs to obtain cheaper land, with building societies for mortgage finance, with HAs for rapid sales
Builders (small scale)	• rapid sales and profit • cheap land • area of high demand

Characteristics of housing

The relationship between supply and demand of housing is obviously fundamental to this chapter, and in order to understand this it is useful first to consider some of the characteristics of housing. It is more than just a simple commodity to consume, because for some it can be an investment to which people add by extension and improvement. Sometimes consumers can therefore also be in part producers of housing. Housing is also immobile and takes up a piece of land, so that its value is affected not only by housing demand and supply factors, but also by the land uses and activities around it and by those that might be competing for its space. This leads to variation in price both locally and regionally. Housing is durable, usually beyond the life of its first occupants, and thus much housing is inherited from past times when demand, building design, fashion and standards were different. Probably most importantly, it is a home providing not only the basic need of shelter but also security, comfort, health and more abstractly status. The location of your house and your ability to move have important consequences for access to jobs (Chapter 5, Section 3c), and conversely the type of job you have affects your ability both to move and to obtain finance for housing. Where you live may influence your life chances and social mobility.

Housing and governments

Because it is so basic to life, most governments view housing as worthy of much attention. It is often given its own ministry or department. Some governments see it as a mechanism for redistribution, as part of their policies on social justice (Chapter 5, Section 2). Others emphasise property rights, especially the right of ownership, and may encourage a 'property-owning democracy', while others may aim for 'state housing for all'. It can thus be the focus of ideological disputes. It is also used as part of governmental economic policy as a regulator since, on the one hand, it is part of government expenditure and can be cut, and on the other, increased provision of new housing can stimulate demand for consumer products such as furniture, carpets and electrical goods. When British governments found that they wanted or had to reduce their spending, as in 1967-69 (Labour) and 1979-90 (Conservative), housing expenditure was cut. When governments seek to expand the economy, public money is often pumped into housing. In the late 1980s with nearly two-thirds of households in Great Britain being owner-occupied, general interest rates were used partly to lower and then to raise mortgage interest rates in order to influence the amount of consumer demand in the economy. With all these functions of housing, it is perhaps not surprising that demand and supply of housing are rarely in equilibrium in a country as a whole, let alone within particular regions.

Influences on demand and supply

Figure 13.5 shows the different influences on the demand and supply of new buildings. Building new housing is obviously one means of improving the stock as well as meeting demand. Net migration, if it is selective in age or occupational type, affects not only the number but also the type of housing demanded. Recent changes in the rate and type of household formation and dissolution (Chapter 10, Section 2) with more single, separated and divorced

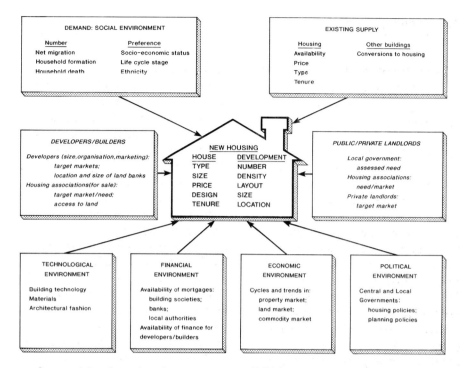

13.5 Influences on housing demand and supply

people requiring housing, have increased demand at a time when population is static or even falling. If there is conversion of buildings from one function to another, such as offices taking over houses adjacent to existing commercial centres, this stimulates a demand for houses elsewhere. Policies of local and national governments concerning demolition, usually applying to inner areas of cities, may also lead to increased demand elsewhere, since redevelopment may be at lower densities. Overspill, decentralisation and new towns may thus be encouraged, while government policy at the same

time through planning controls attempts to contain the spatial extent of cities and limit the availability of building land through Green Belt policies. On the other hand, government subsidies to private developers to use derelict land and inner-city sites have partially offset the high land values of inner-city areas, and via joint venture schemes brought the private developer back into the inner cities in both Britain and the USA. Finally,

13.6 Reasons for housing decay

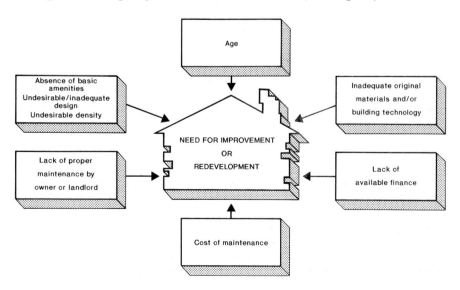

the economic and technological contexts of the building industry, via the cost of materials and building technologies together with land prices, affect whether developers will build and be able to sell new houses, given the competing prices of existing housing. The state of the property market influences whether developers find housing less profitable than alternative opportunities such as building offices, factories or shopping centres. Developers will be especially interested in other alternatives if potential house purchasers are finding mortgages difficult to obtain because of the low flow of funds into lending institutions, or because they cannot afford high interest rates. Since there are business cycles producing fluctuations in the cost of materials, cost of land, profits from other types of property, and the availability of mortgage finance, it is not surprising that even without government intervention, the amount of new building fluctuates markedly.

Reasons for decay

A further diagram (Figure 13.6) shows the reasons for housing decay and the need for housing improvement.

Housing does not decay at the same rate. In fact, some argue that if property is properly maintained it need not decay at all. The quality of the original building and the amount and quality of its maintenance obviously affect its length of life. Building standards have varied over time, with for example in Britain high standards of state housing insisted on immediately postwar, while quantity not quality became more important in the mid-1950s and late 1960s. Therefore it is not just the rate of past house building but its quality which affects present need for improvement or demolition. The need for major repairs to housing that is a hundred years old,

Back-to-back housing where each house shares a back wall

fifty years old and as little as twenty years old may therefore coincide. Very old housing usually lacks amenities now considered essential, or was built at densities or in designs now considered undesirable, such as back-to-back. More recently-built housing may suffer from the unforeseen inadequacies of: materials, such as alumina cement; building technology, such as industrial systems of the 1960s and timber-frame houses of the late 1970s; and design, such as flats with deck access. Some of these problems arose for some public housing built in the 1960s. The resulting deterioration contributed to the emergence of 'difficult-to-let' or 'problem' estates.

Lack of maintenance and investment may result from

- private landlords not getting sufficient returns in rents because of rent controls;
- local authorities not receiving sufficient national government grants for housing and not wishing or being allowed to increase local taxes or rents;
- owner-occupiers not having sufficient income to spend or not seeing the point of spending on improvement;
- governments not giving sufficient improvement grants in numbers or amounts;
- landlords, local authorities and owner-occupiers failing to take up the grants that are available.

Economic and social effects

Maintenance and improvement are also affected by the economic environment. In a recession, incomes may be stretched and borrowing may be difficult and expensive, so maintenance may be postponed by owners, landlords and councils until there is an economic upturn. This economic cycle, together with building cycles and the periodic lowering of housing standards, means that there are fluctuations in the overall need for renewal. These may be accentuated or deflated by variations in the perception or assessment of that 'need' by professionals or government.

The social environment also affects the amount of maintenance and improvement. This adds a spatial variation to the temporal fluctuations. If a neighbourhood or even a street is perceived as being stable or going up in social status, house values are likely to remain steady or rise, and maintenance and improvement seem worth while. If the area is viewed as 'going down' in social status or is 'blighted', because of the planning of a new motorway for instance, people may see little reason to invest and consequently property deteriorates. In both situations the perception is, in part, a self-fulfilling prophecy. The refusal of many building societies (savings and loans) to lend money on old properties in inner-city areas (red-lining) because they were not seen as sound investments was a good illustration of institutions' contribution to such self-fulfilling prophecies. Other borrowing institutions charged higher rates of interest so less investment was possible and areas declined (Chapter 13, Section 1). However, when higher-status people moved into some of these areas, replacing lower status-ones (gentrification) (Chapter 13, Section 3c), the building societies lent money, old houses were improved, often with the help of government grants, and house values rose substantially.

Policy effects

The above discussion hints at the complexities of housing change. It involves changing rights to property and security of tenure; for example, the Rent Act of 1965 gave tenants in private rented accommodation greater security and freedom from rent increases that were too rapid or too high. Such controls were necessary partly because those tenants received less help with their housing than the other tenure groups. At that time, council tenants benefited from national and local subsidies on rents and owner-occupiers received tax relief on mortgages. Both groups tended to be better represented locally by tenants' associations and residents' groups. Such legislation, however, led to many private landlords either selling their properties (disinvesting) because other types of investment could provide better returns than housing, or doing less maintenance of their properties. Disinvestment resulted in a decline in the amount of rented accommodation available, which in itself led to

higher rents for that remaining. It also meant less flexibility and choice in the housing market overall, since rented accommodation is easier to move into and out of than owned housing, and is therefore useful for short-term stays in an area. Less maintenance led, in the longer term, to increased need for government policies on improvement grants. So one policy, that of rent controls, it is argued, had unforeseen consequences that created a need for further government policy on improvement.

The above illustration also demonstrates the importance of changes in tenure and the variety of choice available. This can affect mobility rates. It also shows that supply responds to many factors other than demand. For example, the growing number of single, separated and divorced people seeking homes may well have suggested that the supply of rented accommodation would have increased rather than decreased, because such people sometimes need rapid access to accommodation and require it only for short periods of time (Chapter 10, Section 2).

Institutional effects

Generally changes in demand, if met at all, may be met by new building or by conversion or extension of existing buildings. Usually households have to, or choose to, move as their demands change, thus involving the transfer agents, such as estate agents (realtors) and conveyancing solicitors, and the financial institutions such as banks and building societies. These organisations each have their own goals which means that they are not neutral agents in the housing market. They control access to information and finance and they can actively influence the housing market. In so doing they can help neighbourhoods retain and increase their status and

house prices by channelling higher-income people into them, or encourage decay by restricting finance, as in red-lining. These transfer and financial institutions are called 'urban managers' and 'gatekeepers' of the housing system because they control access to information and finance (Chapter 5, Section 2).

Effects on cities

The location of converted property and new homes, which is influenced by both builders' demand and planning controls, greatly affects the spatial structure of cities and the rate of decentralisation from cities. Much new housing has been built on the periphery and encouraged decentralisation. More recently the growth of new private housing, the slowdown of comprehensive public redevelopment and the availability of private and public funds in the inner areas of cities ('green-lining') may lead to a reduction of population loss and slow decentralisation. If accompanied by increased job opportunities this green-lining may also lead to an overall revitalisation of inner city areas. This may, however, be at the expense of the original occupants. These may find that they are displaced from their housing to make way for higher-income people, through either gentrification of older housing, demolition and new building or private refurbishment of council housing for sale to somewhat better-off households. The housing stock of the inner cities may have improved but the people who used to live there have moved elsewhere and do not benefit from the improvement. Equally, new jobs in inner cities may go to the commuters who live outside them. Any new, lower-status jobs that indirectly result from these, such as office cleaning, may be less accessible to those inner city residents that have been displaced elsewhere.

Summary

The construction of new housing occurs unevenly over time and space. Housing decay also occurs unevenly through time and space. Therefore the need for redevelopment and/or improvement also varies over time and space. The housing system is complex. Demand and supply are influenced by many factors external to housing and are rarely in equilibrium. Gatekeeping institutions affect access to housing, as does the labour market. This complexity makes it very difficult to solve the general problem of the chapter: to maintain and improve the housing stock while at the same time improving for all households their quality of life and their access to the stock.

13.3 **Other examples**

This chapter emphasises changes in the built environment. It shows the cycles in the building of new houses of different types. The first example of St Quentin, a new development to the south-west of Paris (Chapter 13, Section 3a), illustrates some of the new building beyond the built-up areas of large cities on green-field sites. This extends the functional areas of these cities and facilitates the decentralisation of population. Other new building may occur on the edge of the built-up area or within it, as infilling between existing housing or on demolished sites, so-called brown-field sites.

Rehabilitation or improvement has become an alternative strategy to redevelopment and has complicated the build-decay-rebuild cycle. It is illustrated by a General Improvement Area in Macclesfield in the north-west of England and a Housing Action Area, Havelock, in the case study area of east Birmingham (Chapter 13, Section 3c).

Although the focus of the chapter is on the built environment, this cannot be divorced from the economic, technological, social and political or policy environments. The change from redevelopment to rehabilitation, an adaptation of policy in itself, involved economic and social factors in addition to the reaction to the new built form of high-rise dwellings that had been made possible by technological change and which characterised much redevelopment. Economic and social factors are also involved in the movement of people of different socio-economic statuses within the housing stock. Some moves accelerate the rate of decay because the new occupants cannot afford to maintain the property. Other moves, such as those of higher socio-economic status into housing previously occupied by people of lower status, known as *gentrification*, may lead to housing improvements. This again alters the build-decay-rebuild cycle. Gentrification of areas of London and some American cities (Chapter 13, Section 3c) illustrates the associated improvement process as well as other changes produced within the areas.

Finally, the spatial, economic, social and political problems associated with housing decay, and access to housing of varying tenures and states of fitness, are demonstrated for the London Borough of Brent (Chapter 13, Section 3d).

13.3a **New development in the metropolitan ring: Saint-Quentin-En-Yvelines**

A major recent trend in developed countries has been the rapid population increase in the 'metropolitan ring', the area or zone 15 miles and more out from the city centre (Chapter 2, Section 3c). Formerly rural areas have been transformed by expanded or new communities which have attracted people and employment from the nearby city or cities. Surrounding London is a series of early new towns, such as Stevenage and Crawley, and the more recent large-scale development at Milton Keynes. Saint Quentin-en-Yvelines is an equally large and recent development to the south-west of Paris.

In 1972 Saint Quentin was designated a new town and put under the control of SCAAN, the French planning organisation for new towns. Thirty kilometres out of Paris and 21 minutes by train from Montparnasse station, the new town rapidly gained population and local employment. A sleepy rural area with only 23,000 people was transformed into a new town with 154,000 by 1983 and a proposed tar-

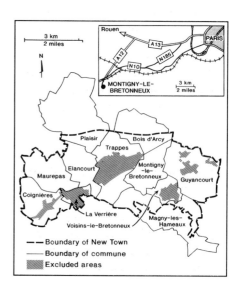

13.7 The eleven communes of St. Quentin

Square Fraganard, Voisins-le-Bretonneux

get population of 239,000. The eleven communes or villages that make up the town (Figure 13.7) were given genuine identity by markedly different architectural styles, size and price of accommodation. Small areas, closes or squares within each commune have meant that at the local level the developments have been at a human scale.

For instance, in Square Fraganard in the commune of Voisins-le-Bretonneux there live twelve families in a residential cul-de-sac reminiscent of the cheek-by-jowl living of older French towns.

Most of these families were first-time buyers and moved recently from rented apartments in Greater Paris. Most couples were in their thirties with young children. Occupations varied but in this square all were within occupational groupings 3 and 4 (Figure 13.8).

The managers and professional people commute by rail into Paris and most wives work locally to pay for their new homes. Early on they all anxiously awaited the many services and facilities promised by SCAAN but these did not arrive until the population had grown con-

siderably. The town has been considered as one of the most successful new towns and a good place to live. This is due partly to an emphasis on the provision of recreational facilities and imaginative architecture. By 1983 the new town had attracted 30,000 jobs in secondary and 25,000 in tertiary industry. High-technolo-

gy businesses were well represented and generally Paris-based firms moved there; in some cases these were head-quarters.

Saint Quentin represents a trend in the western world of a growing metropolitan ring, attracting its own employment but still needing to depend on commuting. Furthermore, the trend towards home ownership in France was represented here even though house prices were relatively high. Not only people in professional, managerial and skilled occupations had access to such desirable private homes, because lower-income groups were also given considerable government financial assistance to buy their own homes.

13.8 A demographic profile of Square Fraganard, Voisins-le- Bretonneux

Professional group of husband	Husband	Wife	Children
4	Demographer working for central government	Museum worker	2
3	Freelance carpet fitter	Housewife and childminder	3
4	American Express executive	English teacher	2
4	Partner Paris-based accountancy firm	Housewife	2
3	CRS policeman	Agency for employment	2
4	Engineer working for French army	Housewife	3
3	University scientific researcher	Housewife	3
3	Electrical engineer for EDF	Bank clerk	1
3	Salesman for heating equipment	Clerk	2
4	Engineer for company	Child psychologist	
3	Assembly worker in car industry	Secretary	
4	Engineer in aircraft industry	Medical student	

13.3b Rehabilitation: a GIA and an HAA

In 1971 an architect bought a house in Black Road, Macclesfield. His house was built in 1815 and like 300 or so in the immediate area had

been declared statutorily unfit and designated for slum clearance. He formed a local action group and managed in 1973 to get an area of

thirty-two houses designated as a General Improvement Area (GIA) (Chapter 13, Section 4). As a result the local authority provided funds for environmental works; gave maximum improvement grants where possible; carried out necessary legal work; supplied mortgages; relaxed standards and public health by-law controls; and made available temporary accommodation for residents while improvements to their houses were being made. The residents contributed the remainder of the money needed and as a self-help group acted as general contractors. The work was completed in 1974 and later the group of houses became designated as a conservation area.

GIAs were made possible by the Housing Act of 1969. The Act widened the scope of house improvement grants, increased their value and gave local authorities the power to declare GIAs. They were intended to be areas of fundamentally sound houses capable of providing good living conditions for many years to come and unlikely to be affected by redevelopment and other major planning proposals. By December 1979 there was a total of 1,208 GIAs in operation containing nearly 400,000 houses spread through the country.

Black Road was not a typical GIA since it consisted of a small group of residents who initiated the drive to give it GIA 'status' and they also did much of their own building work. The architect was a quite unusually strong single influence there, and that was reflected in his use a little later of one of the houses as his office. His work consisted mainly of designing and advising on improvement areas.

The reasons for such legislation on housing improvement included a

---

The Havelock Housing Action Area

The Havelock Housing Action Area was declared by the City Council of 4 March 1975, along with three other areas in Birmingham: Nechells, Sparkbrook East and Little Green. Previously four other declarations had taken place in London, Manchester, Liverpool and Newcastle. It is bounded in the north west by the Saltley Trading Estate and in the north east by the post-war Hutton Council Estate, in the east and south by other terraced properties of the same age which are in declared General Improvement Areas, and in the west by the Adderley Road Clearance Area, now laid out as open space.

At the time of declaration it consisted of 457 dwellings, with the following tenants:

Owner-occupied	294	65%
Private landlord	130	29%
Housing Association	5	1%
Council	28	6%
Total	457	100%

Dividing the residential area is Saltley's main shopping street, the Alum Rock Road. Although it is decaying fast, it supports one large supermarket, several small grocery, drapery and butcher shops, two banks and Saltley Market. The Old Rock cinema has been bought up by Ladbrokes and turned into a bingo hall; next door is the St. Saviours Primary School. In the same road there is a disused nightclub, and a neighbourhood Law and Resource Centre (the Saltley Action Centre) where the local housing association COPEC, the Family Planning Clinic and the Minorities Resource Centre are also based.

In George Arthur Road there are swimming baths, a Baptist Chapel and Asian Prayer House, and in Havelock Road and Washwood Heath Road there are two builder's yards. The only other industry in the area consists of two car repair yards in Havelock and Adderley Roads and a waste paper merchant on the corner of Phillimore and Wright Roads. None of the industry is large scale or noxious.

The population of the area is predominantly middle aged or elderly white people and young immigrants, mainly from Mirpur, a rural district of the Pakistani part of Kashmir. There is a small Bengali community in George Arthur Road. All of these groups are owner-occupiers. Younger whites tend to live in the tenanted property, now mainly owned by the Housing Association.

---

rejection of the large scale developments of the 1960s where community spirit was lost. It was also a cheaper alternative. Such legislation acknowledged that one third of British housing stock was built before 1919 and presented therefore a formidable improvement task for householders alone. Government support was necessary.

The Housing Act of 1974 established Housing Action Areas (HAAs) (Chapter 13, Section 1). These were smaller areas than GIAs where poor housing was combined with social stress and deprivation. The aim was to secure an improvement in living conditions in existing houses as

13.9 The Havelock Housing Action Area (HAA)

quickly as possible within a five-year period while at the same time keeping the local community together. Each HAA usually had a local office located within it to provide information about grants, to help people to complete application forms and generally to promote the idea of improvement. By 1980 there were over 400 HAAs in operation containing over 100,000 dwellings. One of the earliest HAAs to be declared in the country was the Havelock HAA discussed in the case study (Chapter 13, Section 1) (Figure 13.9).

13.3a Gentrification in London's Islington and Battersea and some American cities

In the 1960s, Islington in north London was the oft-quoted example of the process of gentrification. This process occurs when lower-income groups are displaced by more affluent people usually in professional or managerial occupations. On the one hand, it is attacked as a mechanism which can drive working-class households particularly private renters into poorer-quality accommodation as the privately-rented housing sector shrinks, thus increasing urban deprivation. Yet on the other hand, it means the bringing of higher-income households into inner-city areas, thus contributing to 'social balance' and increasing residents' purchasing power and hence the general prosperity of those areas.

More recently this process took place in Ellington Street in another part of Islington. Two families are typical. They both moved into the street in the mid-1970s and steadily improved their properties. The houses were large, four-storey terraces with the basements used as kitchen areas and dining rooms. The husbands were barristers who found the journey to the Inns of Court on the edge of the City very easy, and the wives were former teachers who stayed at home to look after the young children. The top floor in one case was let to students to help pay for the mortgage and improvements to the house. The street is an island among many others which remain to be improved. The island analogy also holds true for the social mixing of the residents. The gentrifiers keep very much to themselves, sending their children to private schools, though for some attendance at church and a local comprehensive school has brought them active participation within the local community. However, the street and its residents are very much a gentrified element within a generally run down working class area. One of the families recently moved to a large country house south of London and their house in Ellington Street fetched a great deal more money than was paid for it. This massive rise in house values caused one local middle-class resident, an architect, to remark that nowadays even he felt as though he was an outsider in an

area which required very high incomes for people to be able to afford the properties.

Since the 1960s, other areas of central London have undergone gentrification. Stockwell and Victoria Park were involved in the 1970s and in the 1980s parts of Battersea were undergoing such changes. London Road, Battersea was a good example where large Edwardian houses were gutted and improved. Even the gentry in a literal sense moved in from across the river in Chelsea! Although usually these owners are spatially and socially divorced from the areas within which they reside, they have been active in lobbying for the improvement of local services such as street cleaning and traffic management. Indeed, it has been known for some local retail outlets and services such as restaurants to be established to serve the newcomers.

Some managers of the local housing market have been shown to play a key role in initiating and maintaining gentrification of an area. Red-lining by building societies has been replaced by green-lining whereby building societies, developers and estate agents act in concert to encourage and lubricate the process. For instance, estate agents have bought up property and negotiated home improvement grants. Such actions are aimed at profit-making rather than social concern. Certain requirements need to be met by an area to allow the process to succeed. These include relatively large houses and access to a range of service facilities and to the city centre for

work and leisure.

Similar processes have been observed in the USA. The early 'pioneers' in some gentrified neighbourhoods, such as the Soho section of New York, tended to be young people just starting in the professions. These people moved into a run-down commercial and industrial area where considerable loft space was available. Indeed, many newcomers were artists. These were displaced by more typical gentrifiers. These seem to be young adults in the 25-34 age bracket, without children and often divorced, separated or cohabitants. They tend to be dissatisfied with the suburban housing choice and attracted by the area's relatively low-priced housing and convenience to work. Such gentrifiers tend to be white, highly educated, economically secure urbanites. In time a neighbourhood can change so much that it becomes accessible only to persons with high incomes. Society Hill in Philadelphia and Georgetown in Washington are two examples of long-established revitalised neighbourhoods where houses sell for well over $100,000 (1980 prices).

Certain problems accompany the gentrification of neighbourhoods in the USA. These include a decline in the social quality of neighbourhood life for the original residents affected by the influx of newcomer-gentrifiers; in some cases increases in traffic, noise and litter; and displacement of the long term residents once rents, rates and taxes become too high for them.

13.3d Housing stress: the London Borough of Brent

Nominally Brent is an outer London borough but in reality it shares many elements of deprivation with the inner London boroughs (Figure 13.10).

In 1983 the Department of the Environment published 'Urban

Deprivation' which made direct comparisons of relative deprivation between authorities, and Brent was given the eighth-highest score in England. Apart from Brent the top ten boroughs were all in inner London.

Some of the indicators of deprivation for Brent are shown in Figure 13.11. Items 2, 3 and 4 relate directly to a series of housing problems in the borough. As one recent council document put it in 1984: 'The housing problems described in earlier

a) Number of households with more than 1.5 persons per room
b) The number of sharing households
c) The number of sharing households with three or more persons per room
d) The number of households with no bath
e) The number of households without extensive use of hot and cold water, bath and w.c.
f) The number of households of three or more persons, with more than 1.5 persons per room
g) The number of sharing households without exclusive use of a stove and sink

13.10 Greater London Council's housing stress index

submissions remain, and in some instances are demonstrably worse.'

Figure 13.12 shows the details of housing fabric under stress in Brent in addition to particular categories of people under stress.

It shows how the three sections of housing stock each have their own problems. There is the huge and mainly future problem of inter-war owned-occupied property to the north and west becoming unfit and in need of major repair as well as lacking basic amenities. Half of Brent's housing stock is inter-war.

The housing register or waiting list for local authority accommodation was 12,792 households in mid-1982; 15,115 in mid-1983; and 16,819 in mid-1984. The shortage of public sector housing became worse.

13.11 Indicators of deprivation for Brent

	Percentage	Rank[1] position
1 Ethnic origin	33.5	1
2 Overcrowding	8.7	3
3 One parent families	7.8	10
4 Lacking basic amenities	8.1	17
5 Population change	–9.8	19
6 Unemployment	10.1	95
7 Pensioners living alone	12.5	235
8 Mortality rate[2]	0.86	317

Notes: 1 Rank position out of 365 English local authorities
2 Mortality rate is the only variable not from 1981 Census
Source: Census Information Note no.2: Urban Deprivation, Inner Cities Directorate, Department of the Environment

A total of 839 units of accommodation were sold by April 1984 and many more since that date. In addition, the rate of new housing construction by the local authority was limited by the lack of national government funding. In any case, Brent started from a position of having a relatively low percentage of public sector housing compared with other boroughs.

A particular problem in Brent was that the majority of local authority accommodation was in large estates dominated by flats.

Of the 21,778 council housing stock in 1984, about three-quarters were flats. Some of the estates were large, high rise and vandalised. Disadvantaged families were given little choice but to concentrate there (Figure 13.13).

Many households in Brent relied on the rented sector because house purchase was so expensive. However, the private rented sector was declining, expensive and deteriorating. Therefore much of the demand had to be met by the public rented sector.

Alongside shortage and decay, homelessness was the most severe single problem which worryingly was intensifying. This was due partly to an increase in demand caused by married couples who were living with their parents having their own children and being asked to leave by their parents, or indeed, wanting to leave of their own accord. It was also because of newcomers to the borough, the younger than average population of Brent creating many new households and the modern development of smaller family units such as one-parent families, single people

Owner occupied
(54% of stock)
- 63% of Brent's unsatisfactory* dwellings
- deteriorating
- expensive (very little below £25,000)

Public sector
(26% of stock)
- problem estates
- concentration of ethnic minorities
- increasing number of temporary units eg B&B
- stable number/marginal decline
- low % compared to other London boroughs
- inefficient heating systems (38% of all tenants)

Private sector
(20% of stock, 10% furnished, 10% unfurnished)
- declining supply (was 39% of stock in 1971)
- expensive £45 per week for 1 bed flat (1980)
- spatially concentrated in north
- deteriorating (27% of Brent's unsatisfactory* dwellings)

People under stress in Brent (from housing and other factors)
- homeless unemployed
- single parent families
- battered wives
- on housing register
- high-rise dwellers
- residents in problem estates
- households in temporary accommodation

** Unsatisfactory because unfit, lacking amenities or in serious disrepair*
NB some major council estates have a much higher than average proportion of the above

13.12 Housing fabric and people under stress in Brent

13.13 The composition of the major estates in Brent, 1981 (see Figure 13.14 for locations)

Estate[1]	Unemployment (%)	Ethnic origin[2] (%)	Under 5s (%)	One-parent households (%)	Households over one p.p.r. (%)
Chalkhill	19.0	49.0	12.7	24.0	15.0
Kilburn	20.5	29.5	8.7	13.1	8.1
Stonebridge	13.2	44.0	8.3	12.2	13.1
Church End	13.0	57.3	11.4	18.3	14.3
St. Raphaels	18.6	51.6	12.1	16.2	13.9
Brent average	10.1	33.5	6.1	3.2	8.7

Notes: 1 Estates approximated by E.D's with over 90% Local Authority households.
2 Ethnic origin is percentage of persons in households headed by someone born in New Commonwealth or Pakistan.
3 These are one-parent households as a percentage of all households. Households containing a one-parent family are of course higher still.

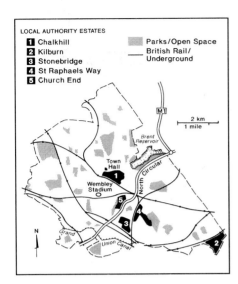

LOCAL AUTHORITY ESTATES
1 Chalkhill
2 Kilburn
3 Stonebridge
4 St Raphaels Way
5 Church End

Parks/Open Space
British Rail/
Underground

13.14 Brent

and elderly people living alone. This serious homelessness problem is illustrated by the fact that in May 1984 there were 847 families in temporary accommodation of some sort and 527 families in bed and breakfast accommodation. The numbers in such accommodation were increasing. Sadly, 'temporary housing is literally becoming a substitute for permanent rehousing'.

The overall housing scene in Brent was dominated by a range of interrelated housing problems which in the most part were getting worse. This was aggravated by a relatively less crowded, less deprived and more owner-occupied north and west. To the south and east (Figure 13.14), crudely south of the North Circular Road, is an area of crowding, with social and physical problems getting worse by the year.

Many of the enumeration districts in this area scored highly on the GLC's Housing Stress Index (Figure13.10). Most people under housing stress were located in this part of the borough and often in large problem estates.

13.4 Alternative strategies

Figure 13.15 shows the key questions concerned with intervention in the housing market, some of which are discussed below.

The market solution

There are a number of possible strategies for improving the housing stock in general and improving the houses in which poorer people live in particular. Some people would recommend letting the market operate without interference. Private developers would build new houses for higher-income people, who vacate their houses for people with somewhat less income. By moving they, in turn, allow even lower-income people to move into their housing. This process, by which any one house is occupied by successively lower-income people, is called *filtering*. The house filters down the socio-economic ladder. Since similar types of housing are often grouped in space, this process will tend to lead to neighbourhood change as poorer people replace richer people. It also implies that the location of new housing and the behaviour of the rich very much influence the residential structure of cities and regions. The problem with this strategy is that, if developers build mainly for the rich, then not enough housing is released for the poor, because there are fewer rich than poor. If there are tenures in the area other than owner-occupation, there are often financial barriers to movement from those tenures to owner-occupation and thus the filtering process does not penetrate sufficiently into the poorer set of households.

Improved access to owner-occupied housing

Other strategies are needed. One policy has been to improve the access of lower income people into

- What goals are desired?
  - eg   – stabilisation of the economy
         – investment in the built environment
         – social justice
- What level of state intervention is needed?
- What priority does housing have relative to other sectors such as education, health, defence?
- What type of state intervention should it be?
  - eg   – information and encouragement
         – legislation on rights
         – tax relief, grants and subsidies
- To whom should any subsidies be given?
  - eg   – consumers or suppliers?
         – which consumers or which suppliers?
- To what kind of housing should assistance be directed?

tenure?	age?	location?	design?
owner-occupied	pre-1919	individual properties	high rise or low rise
rent - local authority	inter war	designated areas	cul-de-sac or street
private rented	post war	only certain parts of city	mixed housing
housing association	new	overall	or standardised

- Whether to build new? if so, private or public?
- Whether to renew old by redevelopment or rehabilitation?
- Whether to mix or separate tenures within areas?

13.15 Strategic questions about housing

owner-occupied housing, which is necessary if an increase in the proportion of property owners is desired. In Britain in the late 1970s and early 1980s large-scale developers were encouraged to build for this first-time buyers' market, with building societies or local authorities linking with them to provide mortgages which were not normally available to these people. Economies of scale in production and marketing, and rapid turnover because of available mortgages, made these lower price homes possible. In the USA the Federal Housing Authority guaranteed the repayment of mortgages for people who were good risks but who did not have sufficient funds to qualify for loans from the banks and saving and loans institutions. This policy was criticised for giving preference to middle-income whites for single-family dwellings and for encouraging suburbanisation. Recently in Britain, so-called joint ventures with local authorities, who subsidise the cost of the land in various ways, have encouraged large private developers back into the inner cities to build new homes or to rehabilitate older ones. Some of these are for middle-income people, particularly the young professionals who work in the city centres, but

others are for lower – although not the lowest-income people. These recent trends attract higher-income people back into the inner areas and increase the mix of people and tenures there. In general the policy of helping first-time buyers has been criticised for distorting the market, because by increasing demand it may increase prices and so make it even more difficult for other non-owner-occupiers to enter the system. As these first-time buyers trade up in the future, it may also inflate the value of middle-priced housing. The policy is also criticised for indirectly subsidising developers, whose risks are much reduced.

Public (council) housing

Another strategy is to subsidise the building of housing for poorer people. Private developers may not derive sufficient profit from building low-priced housing and so may have to be encouraged to do so by state intervention. In Britain, local government gave contracts to builders for public or council housing which, with the local authority as landlord, was rented to lower-income people at rents subsidised by national government and other local tax-payers. By controlling access to this housing,

local government was another manager or 'gatekeeper' of the housing system. Access to such housing depends on length of residence in the authority and the composition and circumstances of the household. The poor who do not qualify for council housing on these criteria end up either in private rented accommodation, which can be expensive, less secure and not subsidised, or homeless. The amount of council house building declined rapidly during the 1980s because national government cut housing funds. National government also made local authorities sell some of their stock at heavily subsidised rates to tenants who wanted to buy them (Chapter 4, Section 3c). In 1990 it also prevented council house rents being subsidised from the taxes of other people in the area, so removing the possibility of the local redistribution of real income.

Housing Association housing

A more general increase in the choice of tenure occurred recently in Britain with the expansion of housing associations (Chapter 4, Section 3c). These non-profit-making organisations of varying size provide accommodation for rent and for sale (Figure 13.16).

The housing association movement is promoted, controlled and financed by the Housing Corporation which was set up in 1964 and given increased powers in 1974 to act as an instrument of central government housing policy. In the 1970s housing associations helped to fill the gap between public renting and owner-occupation, and during the 1980s almost replaced local authorities in housing provision. In the late 1980s and early 1990s the national government's encouragement to them to find private finance changed their structure, the people they served and the areas in which they operated, as they sought to gain

13.16 The goals of housing associations

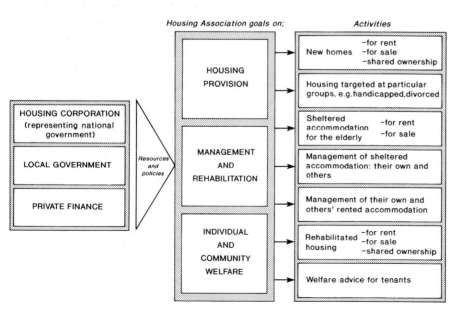

returns for the private finance.

All these ways of providing homes for people with lower incomes or specialist needs may still not meet the goals of social justice. Various kinds of rebates and benefits have therefore been given to those who do not have sufficient income or capital to meet their rents or local taxes (community charge/rates). Although these lessen the cost of housing to the individual, they mean completing forms and having personal and financial circumstances investigated. This is not liked by many people and some consequently do not apply. Others are not aware of their eligibility.

Employers' provisions

Another strategy of providing homes for poorer people was more prevalent in the past. Employers built or obtained housing for their workers. This helped provide a healthier labour supply, but also tied the worker to that employment. Similarly, until legislation in 1976, agricultural workers in Britain would have lost their tied cottages if they lost their jobs. Nowadays employers are more likely to provide housing for their key personnel or to help them with housing finance. A job, however, was also instrumental in being allocated a house in the early British new towns. This link of housing to employment was one reason why a disproportionate number of unskilled and semi-skilled were left in the inner cities, because they could not obtain jobs and therefore houses in the new towns.

Squatting

In some places and at some times, demand greatly exceeds housing supply for some sections of society. To draw attention to their plight, some take illegal action and squat in any housing to which they can get physical access. Squatters in Amsterdam in the 1970s also demonstrated in the streets in order to stimulate some action (See page 135).

Improvement and the market

There are also a number of strategies for the maintenance and improvement of the housing stock in general. One is the market. The emergence of double-glazing and cavity wall insulation companies is one sign of this. The expansion of DIY shops and superstores over Britain is another, linked to the self-service economy (Chapter 12, Section 2). Some households cannot afford or do not wish to improve their homes. Others, because they rent, are not permitted to do so. National and local government may intervene to encourage or inform, particularly on insulation, where energy saving rather than improvement is the main goal. They may give grants for improvement, from loft insulation to re-roofing and repointing, to provision of basic amenities such as inside toilets and bathrooms. They may also compulsorily purchase and redevelop the house.

Redevelopment

Demolition and redevelopment were much favoured in Britain during the 1950s and 1960s, rising to a peak in 1967 with 70,000 houses cleared with an associated completion rate of 400,000 new houses, over half of which were for local authorities. Comprehensive large-scale redevelopment was encouraged, which meant a very different built environment, often with new street plans and high-rise flats, and markedly changed local social and economic environments because communities were disrupted or destroyed and back-street workshops were demolished. High-density redevelopment was linked with the policies of urban containment which were to save agricultural land and prevent urban sprawl. High-rise flats seemed to meet this aim, which coincided with the emergence of a few dominant large firms in the building industry. These had the capacity to employ capital-intensive and highly profitable system-building technology. This could be applied to high rise-building and could increase the rate of construction. Local authorities were encouraged to adopt high-rise building by informal central government pressures, increased subsidies for multi-storey flats, the marketing techniques of the large building companies, and architectural fashion. In consequence, nearly a quarter of new council housing built between 1960 and 1968 was of at least five storeys. The gas explosion and partial collapse of one multi-storey block at Ronan Point in east London in 1968 (page XXX), the subsequent removal of the subsidy, the complaints about the social upheaval and life in high-rise dwellings and the realisation that low-rise housing could give similar densities at less cost led to a marked change in policy. Attitudes also changed. Early redevelopment had involved the dispossession of landlords, whereas in later times it was increasingly owner-occupied housing that was being compulsorily cleared, and this seemed to impinge more upon personal freedom.

Rehabilitation

Improvement or rehabilitation should be a complementary rather than an alternative strategy to redevelopment because they are suited to housing in different degrees of decay, but in Britain as redevelopment became unpopular, rehabilitation gained favour. It was less expensive, retained communities and did not lead to population loss through overspill estates or new town development. In 1964 improvement grants were made available and powers given to compel landlords in designated Improvement Areas to improve their property. The government also encouraged coordination of measures to improve the environment, with smoke control and better traffic management as well as improvement in the quality of the built environment via provision of street furniture, tree planting, more parking facilities and more attractive open space. There were not subsidies available for this environmental improvement, however, until the 1969 Act when improvement grants were increased and improvement began to have more of an impact. At this time, General Improvement Areas (GIAs) were designated, an area-based policy directed at improving a whole area rather than individual isolated homes. In 1974 grants were increased again from 50 per cent to 75 per cent of the approved costs of improvement in Housing Action Areas (HAAs) (Chapter 13, Section 1 and 3b). GIAs seemed to have avoided the worst housing and the lowest income areas. HAAs were designed to combat poor housing in areas of social deprivation. As with other area-based policies (Chapter 11, Section 4) there can be problems in delimiting the areas, and in including houses not in need of repair while excluding other properties which may not be spatially clustered that do need repair.

Poor take-up

Despite the grants and the encouragement within HAAs, the take-up rate was not as high as desired. Indeed, more grants were approved outside these areas than within them. 'Pepper-potting' too often resulted, with some improved and

some not. One problem of pepper-potting is that an improved house does not increase in value as much as it would if all houses around it were also improved, so the incentive to improve is less (an example of negative spatial externalities) (Chapter 2, Section 2). The 'envelope' scheme introduced in Birmingham was an attempt to avoid this conclusion (Chapter 13, Section 1). It certainly improved the image of areas and increased house values. Although enveloping helped, it was not applied in every city and the take-up rate was still insufficient. Older people were often happy with their home and saw no reason to invest the little money they had in a property they would not occupy for long.

Who took up grants?

There were other major problems. Relatively more applications were from the better-off, some of whom could afford to improve without grants but obtained them because their property was eligible and perhaps they were better informed of the availability of grants. One half of the grants to owner-occupiers in 1973, before HAAs were introduced, went to professional and managerial people, while only 13% went to the semi-skilled and unskilled. The availability of grants and the proximity to central cities, attractive outer suburbs or rural areas sometimes led to gentrification, with higher-income people displacing the poorer, who particularly if they were tenants often ended up in worse accommodation. Finally, improvement could decrease the mobility of labour, since a move within five years of improvement necessitated some repayment of the grant. The last point was particularly important in areas like inner cities where improvement occurred at the same time as job loss (Chapter 12, Section 2). Some of these points suggest that

grants can help the better-off rather than the poor, counter to views of social justice and the aims of the policy.

Although redevelopment and improvement are not alternatives, the economic argument between them is affected by interest rates, the future length of life of renovated property and the difference between the running costs of modernised property compared with rebuilt ones. The spatial and social arguments involve population loss from cities and the retention of communities, but even improvement does not guarantee this because of the possibility of gentrification.

Although trends can be identified at the national level of favouring one strategy then another, local authorities within Britain have not adopted strategies uniformly. Some, like Birmingham, acted rapidly in setting up HAAs and established a large number; others have relatively few. So improvement to the housing stock varies between towns as well as within them.

Private rehabilitation of council housing

The 1980's policy of involving the private sector in the rehabilitation of council housing for sale as low-cost home ownership units has been popular in some districts, such as Salford. Even there it was originally regarded as a last resort, because of the lack of housing finance. It has been one way of attracting national government funds. It has usually meant the relocation of existing tenants who can rarely afford access to the rehabilitated homes, even though they are low-cost units. A range of one- or two-person households has been attracted to them, mostly from outside the inner areas. Some have good incomes and did not need the subsidy. Some, who have just managed to enter owner-occupation, find the service charges on the flats an

Council housing in Salford (top) that has been privately rehabilitated for sale (bottom)

not available on rehabilitated property that has already had one or more owners, while any free goods originally included have become second hand. Mobility may not be as great as desired.

On the positive side, such developments may improve the image of an area, help to restore confidence and attract further public and private money. They help to bring somewhat better-off people back into the inner cities, but replacing rather than joining the original tenants. On the negative side, they may break-up communities in the same way as redevelopment did, not produce improved quality of life for the original tenants who have not been the recipients of the public subsidy, and in some cases the rehabilitation may not have been of a high standard, 'repackaged rather than improved' as some have said.

Summary

No strategy has successfully solved the general problem of maintaining and improving the housing stock while at the same time improving for all households their quality of life and access to that stock. This is because each strategy has been applied to only part of the housing system. An overall approach which takes into account the relationships between employment and housing seems to be needed.

additional burden and end up with the building society repossessing their property because they are not making their repayments. Repossessed property tends to be put back on the market at its original price. Too many of such properties in one development can deflate the price of other units and make it difficult for their owners to trade up. This is a problem with any scheme

involving people for whom owner-occupation is marginal.

As with other strategies, activity in surrounding areas may affect their success. The rehabilitation of further blocks nearby may make it difficult to sell the originally rehabilitated ones because the new ones are packaged to include carpets, white goods, mortgage finance and even free legal services. The last two are

13.5 Perspectives

Building cycles

Just as in the economic, technological, social and political environ-

ments, there are fluctuations or cycles of activity in the built environment, in particular in the housing system. Booms and slumps in house building have been observed with cycles of about thirty years in

duration being reflected in the built environment, as successive booms are represented by large areas of building on what were the edges of towns. These are separated in space by less extensive areas associated with the slumps and clearly distinguished in time by their styles and layouts. More recently Green Belt policies have limited this building in Britain with resultant leap-frogging beyond the Belt and often lower-quality housing within the built-up areas of the city, at higher densities than would have occurred without the policies. This is because increased demand within the built-up area leads to higher land values, and cheaper housing is built to keep house prices within the reach of households.

As new houses are built in the booms, filtering will be the dominant process. In the slumps when demand is increasing, conversions from single to multiple occupancy of larger dwellings may become more profitable, with poorer people replacing richer ones, usually in the inner suburbs. Invasion, with higher-population densities, is then the main process of neighbourhood change during times of slumps. Filtering and this form of invasion are both market processes.

Cycles also occur in state housing. Figure 13.17 shows how the need for new council housing varied from being mainly to solve an overall shortage to being largely to rehouse people from slum clearance. It also indicates how central government

13.17 Fluctuations in housing provision and policy

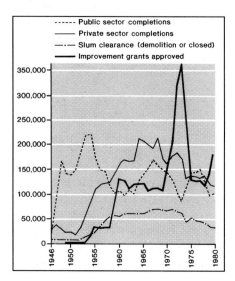

has vacillated between encouraging council housing or private housing to meet the needs of overall shortage. The cycles in state housing, as with private housing, have not been just in numbers built but also in quality. Again the booms are reflected in design, density, quality and location. The high-rise blocks of the inner area redevelopment schemes of the 1960s and the inter-war housing estates are two obvious examples within British cities, and the three phases of new towns with their increasing percentage of private homes over time is another. The huge private estates recently built by the large developers such as Tarmac, Wimpey and Barratt beyond the Green Belts, especially around Greater London, are almost mark four new towns, but private not public, and with fewer employment opportunities within them. These like Saint Quentin (Chapter 13, Section 3a) are part of, and an encouragement to, decentralisation.

The location and type of new housing are, then, important for the spatial structure of cities and regions. Decentralisation, whether in the form of new or expanded towns, or the suburbanisation into private or public overspill estates creates demand for new infrastructure such as roads, shops, schools and hospitals. The supply of these often lags behind house building in Britain, which increases the difficulties of settling down in a new environment. Construction that encourages decentralisation, especially of the richer and the skilled, means that cities are left with the problems of declining population and declining tax bases on which to raise money for services for the remaining people, an increasing proportion of whom are in need. Consideration has to be given to the spatial, social and economic consequences of housing policy as well as to those concerning built form.

The problem is not just in meeting need, however that is defined, but also 'wants', sometimes individual wants that may not in the aggregate yield 'societal wants' (Chapter 3, Section 5). For example, individual wants for a house on the urban-rural fringe in the aggregate produce continued urban sprawl. Planning controls in this case try to favour what are viewed as societal wants.

Political beliefs and housing

There are a number of perspectives involved with people and housing. Some blame the occupants of decaying housing for the state of the houses or their presence in such housing. The individuals are seen to be at fault for not taking proper care of the house or not working hard enough in order to occupy better housing. Others blame the structure of the economy and society, pointing to unequal opportunities and unequal incomes. These mean that for some there is little choice about where they live, and not enough money for repairs, or not enough power to get landlords to do repairs. Supporters of these two extremes would offer different reasons as to why better housing or different tenures have not solved social problems and changed attitudes and behaviour as many hoped. One extreme would say the individuals are responsible for their behaviour and changing where they live will not alter it. The other extreme would argue that interfering with one part of the system is not enough and that unemployment or low incomes and poor life chances still remain. Indeed, these may not allow people to live properly in the better housing, for example not being able to afford to run expensive electric underfloor heating which featured in much of the redevelopment of the late 1960s and early 1970s.

Other perspectives involve goals of social justice, personal freedom and the efficient use of resources.

Policies that effectively subsidise accommodation by rebates on property taxes may encourage continued occupation of homes which are larger than needed and are more suited to larger families. This raises sensitive issues. Should an elderly widow who has brought up her family in her house but now lives alone be encouraged to move to somewhere smaller so that another growing family can use the accommodation? Since homes contain memories, involve much past work and care, and are more than just living spaces, it is not an easy question to answer.

Many elderly people cannot afford to maintain their houses properly so the growing number of elderly (Chapter 10, Section 1) and the extension of owner-occupation down the scale of socio-economic status is producing an increasing problem of low income owner-occupation where there is inadequate maintenance and so increasing obsolescence. Today the need for renewal is no longer mainly a problem of private and public rented accommodation. Changing people's tenure does not necessarily offset problems associated with low incomes. Nor does government intervention via improvement grants, because many houses improved in the 1970s were already in need of improvement again in the 1980s. This was due to lack of maintenance and/or in some cases poor-quality rehabilitation. Housing cannot be treated in isolation from other issues.

Redistribution of real income

It is more difficult than it first seems to use housing as a means of redistribution for purposes of social justice or, as some would argue, social control, in that better housing can keep the lower paid quiescent. In Britain mortgage tax relief has favoured high-income people within owner-occupation. Subsidised rents have tended to favour higher-income people within council housing, and mortgage relief together with capital gains from house sales has outweighed rent subsidies. Redistribution has then been upwards, to higher-income people both within and between tenures. Even improvement grants until recently involved no redistribution downwards, because they were based on the eligibility of the house, not the income of its occupants. If gentrification accompanies improvement, redistribution may again effectively be upwards.

Changing approaches to housing

Gentrification, however, in parts of inner cities can be viewed positively, because it may increase the tax-base for public goods and services and the local market for some private goods and services. Whether these offset the problems of the displaced poor is an open question.

The reason for and the ways of providing better housing, especially for poorer households, have changed over time. In the nineteenth century the worst housing was improved for health reasons, not so much for the poor as for the rich, who feared the epidemics that emerged from housing with poor sanitation. In 1919 state housing began to be an important alternative to the worst private rented accommodation, the dominant tenure of the time. Some say this higher-quality housing was built for charitable reasons. Others argue that it was to prevent social unrest after the First World War. In the 1930s, home ownership expanded for the better-off during rapid suburbanisation. More recently it has been seen by some as the goal for all people. Since it is the tenure most favoured by the British tax system, its popularity is not surprising, and of course the transfer agents, financial institutions and private developers have a vested interest in its growth. Even the British new towns, which were planned from the late 1940s onwards, have become progressively more owner-occupied through increased involvement of developers and through council house sales. New towns and associated public comprehensive development in old towns have given way to population retention and improvement within the cities, and increasingly to joint schemes between various combinations of developers, financial institutions, housing associations and local government.

Changing institutions

The increasing interdependence of these institutions has been accompanied by a diversification of their functions. Building societies, for example, are operating more like banks and have set up their own housing associations and even building companies. Merger activity in recent years has also led to larger and fewer building societies and estate agents as they seek economies of scale, especially from information technology. Insurance companies have taken over estate agents in an attempt to increase their market share of insurance related mortgages. Similar mergers have occurred in the building industry as companies seek to acquire land held by small builders and to obtain economies of scale of finance, production and marketing. The institutional context of housing provision and the structure of the building industry are rapidly changing.

Changing geographical approaches

Just as the form of the problem, the strategies and the institutions have changed, so too have geographers' approaches to housing. In the 1960s and before, most research was dominated by the demand side, with an emphasis on filtering, invasion, residential mobility and social areas within the city. In the 1970s much attention was given to policy, to managers or gatekeepers of the housing system, and to the social justice problems of differential access to housing. In the 1980s there was increasing interest in developers and the relationships between them and other institutions involved in joint ventures, and the interrelationships between housing and labour markets.

The form and the geographical emphasis may change, but the basic problems of housing decay and access to housing remain. Given the relative decline in public expenditure on housing in Britain, it seems that its priority has declined along with the political will to tackle the problems, which consequently will worsen in the future.

13.6 **Exercises**

1. During the 1980s there was a rapid increase in house prices in Great Britain. The boom began in London and gradually spread to other parts of the country in what has been known as a 'ripple effect'. The decade ended with a slump in prices in London and much of the rest of the South. Figure 13.18 catches much of the period of the boom in the South.
   (a) Describe the major differences in prices in 1979 and the major differences in the inflation rates of house prices between 1979 and 1988.
   (b) Suggest reasons for the regional differences in prices in 1979 and the differences in inflation rates between 1979 and 1988.
   (c) (i) Giving examples of easier and more difficult moves,

suggest how easy it was for labour to move between regions in 1979.
   (ii) During the 1980s, did it get easier or more difficult for labour to move between regions?
   (d) (i) What do the 1988 figures suggest about differences in the cost of living among regions?
   (ii) What do they suggest about the effects on spending among the regions of the following changes in the interest rates on mortgages
      – a 1% increase
      – a 1% decrease?
   (iii) What do the figures suggest about changes in the distribution of wealth inherited on the death of parents who owned their houses?

   (e) In 1984 national house prices were rising at double the rate of earnings. What effect might this have on the rate of entry of first time buyers on to the market?
   (f) The prices given in Figure 13.18 are average house prices. Discuss the limitations of these data.

2. Some housing policies, such as comprehensive redevelopment schemes, General Improvement Areas and Housing Action Areas, have been targeted at particular areas. Others have been aimed at particular properties or people.
   (a) What are the advantages and disadvantages of area-based policies?
   (b) What are the advantages and disadvantages of policies aimed at particular properties?

3. Between 1978 and 1988 the percentage of people owning their home in Great Britain rose from 54 to 65 per cent.
   (a) Using Figure 13.19, describe the variation and rate of change in ownership among regions.
   (b) (i) Using Figure 13.19, comment on the regional variation in council house sales.
   (ii) Discuss the advantages and disadvantages of the policy of council house sales.
   (c) Between 1979 and 1984 the

13.18 Changing house prices in the UK

| | House prices (£) | | Change in house prices (%) |
	1979	1988	1979-88
Outer Metropolitan Area	28 570	95 320	234
Greater London	27 640	92 160	233
Outer South East	24 060	80 230	233
East Anglia	20 560	74 620	263
South West	22 200	70 950	220
West Midlands	20 110	55 740	177
East Midlands	16 460	53 460	256
Wales	18 720	47 860	157
Yorkshire & Humberside	16 620	43 520	162
North West	18 270	40 910	124
Scotland	21 400	36 310	70
North	16 740	35 590	113
Northern Ireland	22 450	28 850	29
UK average	21 540	62 470	190

Department of the Environment region	All sales	Sales as % of council stock[1]	Owner occupation as % of total stock	
			1979	1985
South East (excl. Gt. London)	140 468	16.7	63	70
Eastern	36 844	15.5	58[2]	66[2]
South West	54 305	15.0	63	69
East Midlands	63 658	15.6	59	66
West Midlands	78 379	12.5	57	63
North West (incl. Cumbria)	84 234	11.1	59[3]	65[3]
North (excl. Cumbria)	46 291	11.0	47	55[4]
Yorkshire & Humberside	59 290	9.7	56	62
Greater London	86 954	9.6	48	55
England	650 414	12.5	57	64

Notes
1 Stock is taken as stock of dwellings in 1985 plus sales
2 East Anglia standard region
3 North West standard region
4 North standard region

13.19 Changing tenure and council house sales by region

number of people in arrears with mortgage repayments tripled to 32,000, while between 1979 and 1987 the number of repossessions of properties by building societies rose from 2530 to 22,630. After a fall in repossessions in 1988 and 1989, they rose again to over 75,000 in 1991.

(i) Suggest reasons for these trends.
(ii) When building societies put repossessed property back on the market they often do so at below market prices. What effects may a relatively high per-centage of repossessed property have on an area?
(iii) What other problems may be associated with owner occupation by households with low incomes?

4. Study Figure 13.20 and the following extracts on homelessness. 'In 1990 the fastest growing reason for homelessness was mortgage repossessions. One in ten people presented themselves to local authorities as homeless for this reason.
The number of households that local authorities in Britain are prepared to accept as 'homeless' rose from 53,000 in 1978 to 126,000 in 1989. These figures are for households not people and they do not include single homeless people.
Thirty-eight thousand households were living in temporary accommodation, 23,500 of them in London. The cost of bed and breakfast accommodation for these households cost £143 million. Between 1984 and 1987 the cost of such accommodation in London rose ten times more than the retail price index.'
(a) Discuss the extent to which official homelessness statistics reflect the problem.
(b) Suggest reasons for the rise in homelessness.
(c) Suggest reasons why London features so prominently in the news on homelessness.
(d) Suggest ways in which homelessness may be reduced.

13.20 Official homelessness, 1989

Region	Number of officially homeless
North	7 800
North West	20 690
Midlands	22 090
East Anglia	3 160
London	29 320
Rest of South East	16 540
South West	7,630

13.7 Further reading

M. Ball, M. Harloe and M. Martens (1988) *Housing and Social Change in Europe and the USA*, Routledge

T. Barnekov, R. Boyle and D. Rich (1989) *Privatism and Urban Policy in Britain and the United States*, Oxford University Press

D. Donnison and A. Middleton (eds.) (1987) *Regenerating the Inner City*, Routledge and Kegan Paul

M.S. Gibson and M. Langstaff (1982) *An Introduction to Urban Renewal*, Hutchinson

B.T. Robson (1988) *Those Inner Cities*, Oxford University Press

J. Short (1982) *Housing in Britain: the Postwar Experience*, Methuen

N. Smith and P. Williams (eds.) (1986) *Gentrification of the City*, Allen and Unwin

Chapter 14

OVERVIEW

This final chapter contains reflections, summaries and new thoughts. It urges readers not only to look deeper and read further in order to expand their observations and extend their understanding of the complex world around them, it also exhorts them to act in the light of their observations and understanding. It advocates an active rather than a passive discipline of geography. The chapter includes some reflections on the framework of 'people and changing environments' that has been used throughout the book to make readers aware of its possible limitations and stimulate them to consider other less overt frameworks and analogies that are adopted by other writers. The range of changes that have been identified is then summarised. First they are analysed at the varying scales at which issues have been discussed throughout the book: global, international, national, regional and local. Secondly, changes resulting from the interaction between these geographical scales are examined. Lastly, after observing other changes that have been identified as occurring at varying scales, the problem of establishing the significance of any change is discussed. With these summarised ideas, which are intended to shed 'light' on a complex world, the book ends, and it is the turn of the reader for 'action'.

Reflections on the framework: people and changing environments

Actors and roles

In future reading and thought, readers might consider the differing views there are of people and society. We have referred to people as actors, which emphasises their roles and their relations with others. People are obviously more than the set of roles they play and relations they have. Even then, there may be complex conflicts or contradictions between some of the roles they play. Local councillors, for example, may support their political party in making the organisation of education more efficient by closing some schools where there are too few pupils for the schools' capacities. On the other hand, they may support the parents and teachers in their local constituency who wish to retain the school as an effective focus and asset of the community (Chapter 10). Their party and constituency loyalties are opposed. How they resolve their dilemma may depend upon the relations they share with their party and their constituents. Indeed, their position may be more complicated because they may also be parents with children at the

school. Identification of roles and relations helps our understanding of situations, but it is important to recognise that people playing the same roles may have a range of views.

Other analogies

Our analogy of actors has limitations. So too do other commonly-used analogies of people, societies or related geographical entities, such as cities. Biological analogies in geography, for example, often reflect Darwinian thought, with such ideas as competition being assumed, frequently misleadingly, as an underlying basis of most human behaviour. Societies and economies are often viewed as passing through stages, as though they were human beings passing inevitably from youth to maturity and old age. The city is often regarded as an organism with attention given to its growth, and its relationship to the surrounding countryside. The latter is often seen in biological terms, such as 'symbiotic' or 'parasitic'. At other times the city is treated as though it were a machine. Such an analogy emphasises the ways in which it functions, the relationship between the parts and its efficiency. It tends to ignore change that may be introduced from outside. Readers should be aware of the limitations as well as the advantages of such analogies.

People and environment as a framework

We have adopted a framework where people or organisations interact with their environment, being constrained by them and adapting to them but also partially selecting them and changing them by their actions. This is to some extent another biological analogy. It is more than that, though, because in our identification of actors and roles we are also seeing society as analogous to a play or, more generally, a text, another more recent common analogy. Scale is important to this framework. At one scale, for example, part of the environment of managers and operatives in a manufacturing plant is the transnational corporation to which it belongs. At another scale that same transnational corporation may be regarded as the organisation with the global economy as part of its environment. Thus the environment at one scale may form the organisation at another. In the latter case the transnational partially selects its environment by choosing the countries where it will operate. By extending its activities to a country it may also contribute towards changing that country, as has the recent influx of Japanese corporations into Britain with their new work processes and management-employee relations (Chapters 8, 9 and 12). In the former case, although the transnational corporation may give its manufacturing plant some degree of autonomy, its overall corporate plan may constrain the activities of the plant.

This separate identification of people (or organisation) and environments seems very helpful, but as with all frameworks of thought it can produce difficulties. For example, in relation to the physical environment, it may encourage the idea of viewing people as separate from and outside nature rather than as part of nature. Our diagram (Figure 1.1) saw people as central to the surrounding four major components of the physical environment, and demonstrated the interactive form of the relationships. Similarly, an emphasis on physical hazards (Chapter 6) to the exclusion of the opportunities provided by the physical environment (especially Chapters 2 and 3) may present the idea of conflict with nature rather than harmony. Our inclusion of hazards from the built and human environments (Chapter 6) should also have offset this possibility of seeing people only in conflict with their physical environment.

Harmony and conflict, cooperation and competition are just some of the processes that may produce change. It is the changing environments to which we now turn, discussed first of all at the varying scales featured within the book.

Changes at the global and international scales

The global scale has become increasingly important as a level of analysis. This has been the case, for example, in the study of the physical environment, where global warming has become a central concern. There are fears that the destruction of the ozone layer and an increase in the greenhouse effect, resulting from air pollution and the destruction of forests, may change the atmospheric circulation system. It is suggested that these processes will produce new regional climates, including a warming of the polar regions and consequently an increased rate of melting of ice caps and glaciers. The resulting change in sea-levels could then mean that low-lying areas would be covered by water and the land area of the planet would decrease. The degree of warming, its permanence as a trend and the extent of any change in sea-levels are all much debated, but they are central geographical issues at the global scale.

Human activities, it is argued, have been the major cause of any warming, and changes in climates and sea-levels would have significant consequences on a range of human activities, including agriculture and tourism. The processes involved, however, with atmospheric and climatic change and other physical processes, which are central to understanding the mechanisms of global warming, are not the subjects of this book. The book does, though, discuss the hazards that are produced by human activities, which modify the physical environment, such as flooding due to changes in sea-level. It also examines the responses that groups of people make to these hazards, from methods of prevention to reactions (Chapter 6). The issue is highlighted here partly to illustrate the importance of the global scale but also to demonstrate the need for further reading in order to develop a greater understanding of the links between physical and human geography.

Another related global issue is the relationship between the earth's resources and its population, which was discussed in Chapters 2 and 3 where the contrasting optimistic and pessimistic views of the future were considered. This has been a major concern for many centuries, but the details of the arguments and the ways they are viewed have changed over time. So too have the geographical areas which have been the focus of the debate. The famines in East Africa have particularly aroused concern about food deficits. The rapidity of population increase in countries such as India and Mexico has highlighted demographic issues related to high birth rates relative to death rates, while acid deposition in European and North American countries (Chapter 7) has reinforced concern about the long-term damage to the physical environment, seemingly caused by industrial activities and certain ways of harnessing energy.

A more recent set of changes, which like global warming have moved the level of geographical interest to the global scale, has been the growth of global corporations, global products, global marketing and international financing. These changes in the economic environment (Chapter 8) have all been assisted by the space-shrinking developments in transport and communications technology and advances in information technology, discussed in Chapter 9.

International scale

There have also been some significant changes that have attracted the attention of geographers to the international scale. These involve parts of the world and the relationships between different parts and nations of the world, as against changes at the global scale, which tend to affect the whole world. There have been some international trends that have been identified for many nations, although they may affect them in somewhat different ways and thus have often been analysed at the national level. Examples include an ageing population (Chapter 10), counter-urbanisation (Chapter 10), growing environmental awareness and politics (Chapter 11) and, to a lesser extent, privatisation (Chapters 4 and 11). These have been identified mostly in western countries.

There are also international cultural trends that are reflected in such activities as advertising which saw the 1980s as the 'me decade' and predicts the 1990s as the 'us decade'. These designations suggest a move from individualism, with an emphasis on economic advancement and social mobility, to a greater sense of belonging to family, community and society (Chapter 10). Such a cultural change is identified particularly for the USA and the UK but is given wider spatial extent by the world-wide advertisements of transnational corporations and advertising companies based in those countries (Chapter 8).

Growing interest has also been shown towards international relations, between the East and the West, and between the North and the South, as the developed or First World and the developing or Third World have become loosely known. The phases of the Cold War between the East and West have been dramatically highlighted in Berlin, where the blockade and air lift of 1947 marked its beginning and the construction of the wall enclosing West Berlin in 1961 denoted a worsening of relations, which had warmed somewhat during the mid-1950s. The breaking down of the wall in 1989 symbolised the warming of East-West relations and the fall of Eastern European communist regimes, and heralded the reunification of the Germanies. The events of the late 1980s and early 1990s have thrown into question the continued existence of the international defence organisations NATO and the Warsaw Pact, the forces and missiles of which had faced one another for over four decades (Chapter 11). The strategic map of Europe and to some extent the rest of the world is in a state of change with the warming of the relations of the super-powers and what some have called 'the collapse of the Russian empire'. These events of the late 1980s have also produced a rethinking of the economic and political maps of Europe, as the European Community (Chapter 11) may seek to become exactly what its name implies rather than a grouping of mostly Western European nations.

The warming of super-power rela-tions may have important consequences for the Middle East, the centre of so much recent conflict in which the super-powers have become involved because of its strategic position between East and West and its oil resources (Chapter 11). Whether the removal of one dimension of the conflict in the Middle East will be enough to lead to peace is open to question, because of the complexity and the intensity of the Arab-Israeli conflict.

The changing relations between East and West may have significant effects on North-South relations. The economic opportunities that have been opened up in Eastern Europe and the need for support from western governments to enable a transition from command to market, or at least more mixed, economies may deflect First World investment from the Third World. The move towards a wider European Community may accentuate this possibility. If capital sees greater returns nearer at hand, it will usually be attracted there. Eastern Europe also now provides another possible area of cheap labour, an attraction to corporations that previously would have gone to Third World countries. The threat of relocating production from Western to Eastern Europe also becomes a powerful tactic when corporations are negotiating wage levels and conditions with their workforces. In short, the new relations between East and West may widen the gap between North and South still further unless positive action is taken to avoid the eventuality. A further development complicates North-South relations. The concern over global warming and the environment has been led by the First World which, along with the Second World, the old communist bloc, has contributed most, so far, to world pollution. The further development of the Third World to the current position of the First World is seen as posing an environmental threat to the globe. World-wide controls on pollution may make it more difficult for the Third World to catch up and may add a further dimension to the dependent relationship between the First and Third Worlds, as the Third World relies on the First for its pollution control technologies. International agreements are necessary for pollution control because of cross-boundary effects (Chapter 7), but much of the Third World has been imbued with the necessity of economic growth by the First World and not surprisingly sees economic priorities as greater than environmental ones (Chapters 2 and 3). So, while at the beginning of the 1990s East-West relations and events in the former Soviet Union and Eastern Europe dominate the headlines, North-South relations should not be forgotten.

Changes at the national, regional and local scales

Changes at the global and international level have great impacts on nations. The nation itself has become somewhat under threat. Economically, transnationals and economic groupings transcend national boundaries and together with the globalisation of the economy make it increasingly difficult for a nation to control its own economy (Chapter 8). Politically, too, the emergence of supra-states such as the European Community causes concern about a possible loss of national sovereignty (Chapter 11), yet offers rather stronger counterbalances to global corporations than do single nations.

Within nations, there are continual tensions and sometimes changes in power-relations between central and local government and, both politically and economically, between core and periphery. Pressure for devolution, or even separatism, has occurred in the periphery of many countries, particularly when this is fuelled by ethnic and cultural differences between the core and the periphery (Chapters 10 and 11).

Regional scale

Economically and socially the peripheries of many western countries have become more differentiated. They were nearly all areas characterised by out-migration. Now some are growing as people retire there and some move to work there as part of the trends of counter-urbanisation and industrialisation of rural areas (Chapter 10). Some peripheral areas have been economically strengthened through tourism based on attractive environments and/or heritage industries, while others (sometimes the same) have experienced booms from the development of natural resources. Both kinds of change have produced local conflicts (Chapter 2).

In a number of countries some old industrial regions were part of the periphery, such as the North East of England. In others the major old industrial regions formed part of the core, as in the USA with the Manufacturing Belt and the former West Germany with the Ruhr. Such areas declined, and some parts of them have been recovering faster than others, such as the more rapid rate of recovery of the southern part of New England in the USA. The decline of these large areas and their subsequent spatially differentiated rates of recovery have led some observers to suggest that the spatial economy is no longer organised at this large regional scale. Areas within an industrial region used to be connected by having similar industries and/or linked industries which benefited from the external economies and agglomeration economies afforded by spatial proximity. Improved communications and transport technologies (Chapter 9) and the changed size and organisation of corporations (Chapter 8) have reduced the importance of proximity. The new high-tech industries that have emerged (Chapter 9), where they have concentrated spa-

tially, form regions of different scale and shape, often called 'valleys' or 'corridors'. Even here, the interest of economic geographers has still tended to focus on a different regional scale based on labour markets, usually demarcated by journey-to-work regions. These are functional regions based around towns or cities. Such journey-to-work areas have been the major geographical units by which the changing spatial economy has been observed and the scale at which 'regional' processes have been thought to be operating. These smaller regions, based around towns or small cities, have been referred to as 'localities' (Chapter 12).

This change in scale of interest is reflected in government policy in Britain, where the old large scale regional policy has been reduced and policy inputs have been more spatially targeted (Chapters 5 and 12). The form of political intervention has also changed, with greater attention being focused on training, which has been seen to be more sensibly organised at the scale of labour markets and journey-to-work areas. The greater interest of towns and cities in Britain in promoting themselves and taking their own economic development initiatives has reinforced this attention to a different scale, particularly that of the local authority (Chapter 11). Thus economic and political processes combine to make the locality a suitable scale of geographical interest in the 1980s and 1990s.

Urban scale

As the discussion of regions suggests, the city-region and the city have become greater focuses of economic and political interest. Identification of counter-urbanisation trends of the 1970s and earlier, presented additional reasons for the large and medium cities that it affected to promote themselves and arrest their feared decline. Attempts at regeneration of cities, particularly their inner areas, have attracted much geographical attention, because the built environment often changes dramatically (Chapter 13) and, though often less visibly, so too does the social environment (Chapter10). Gentrification and attempts to increase the mix of housing tenures has often led, not to greater social mix, but to social segregation at a finer spatial scale (Chapter 13). Therefore, in addition to the social segregation between the inner city, inner suburbs, outer suburbs and metropolitan ring (Chapters 2, 10 and 13), there is now, in many cities, greater social segregation within the inner parts of the city. These differences are reflected not only in types of housing but also in occupations and types of employment (Chapter 12).

Local scale

Although a city or town may be regarded as the local scale, a residential area within a city, or a village in a rural area, more often represents what we think of as the local scale. It is the scale with which many readers will be most familiar and for which they feel most 'sense of place'. It may also be the scale to which the reader feels most attachment, though that may be the city or region or even nation. Generalising about change at this scale is very difficult. There are so many more local areas than cities or regions. There was, however, a move to encourage people to be more involved in local issues in the 1970s. Such greater *participation* is costly of time, of both the residents and the local officials. During the later 1970s as local governments became pressed for resources, there was little to spare on participation exercises and still less to provide for any recommendations arising from them. The message changed to greater *self-help* at the community

scale. This also became the national political message for the household and individual scale: greater personal responsibility and self-help and less dependency on the state. The degree to which local areas have adopted this political message has varied greatly.

Community self-help suggests cooperation, but there has often been greater conflict. The shortage of resources at the local government level has led to greater competition between areas for service provision or more often fewer reductions in service. This has often been between communities of similar social composition. With less possibility of providing extra services to areas to offset them, there has been perhaps even greater feeling about the location of noxious but necessary facilities such as refuse disposal tips. Such external threats (Chapter 7) produce great conflict between areas as they seek to avoid having the facility near their homes. In the 1980s at the local scale, there was perhaps an emphasis on *protection* of the area rather than participation in issues concerning it. Neighbourhood watch schemes provide an excellent example (Chapters 6 and 10).

Where greater participation is advocated, as in more parental involvement in schools, other proposals, such as parental choice of schools, mean that there may be a reduction in the identity of institutions with their local communities. In this case, greater power to the individual may lead to less integrated spatially-defined communities.

The relationships between geographical scales

Changes at the global scale have both triggered change and formed the context for change at more local scales. They have also accentuated the growing interconnectedness and interdependence of places.

Global change can affect nations and other scales, though, in different

ways. One nation, for example, may have an economic, social and political structure that may be more able to adjust or respond to global changes in a positive way. Another may have structures that are less adaptable and are more negatively affected. For instance, a country that has its own energy resources is less affected by a global shortage or rise in price of oil, while one with an energy policy that emphasises varied sources of supply is less likely to be hit by an international move away from one type of energy than a nation that concentrates on one source, such as nuclear or coal.

Change, however, is not all top-down. Some research over-emphasises the influence of global or national changes on regional or urban ones, and under-emphasises the influences on global change of national, regional and urban developments, and on national changes of regional and urban innovations. For example, the technological and organisational innovations in Silicon Valley, California have had dramatic impacts on global technology and been a model for locality/regional change elsewhere (Chapter 9), while experiments by local authorities, such as Cambridgeshire on the local management of schools, have been taken up and applied as national policy by central government in Britain (Chapter 11). Local areas may therefore produce new geographies that are taken up as models for others to attempt to emulate, or produce ideas that are nationally applied but often implemented differently from place to place. Although there may be a standard national policy, its local interpretation and application may be different. The effects of a policy may also be locally variable, such as the degree of 'colonisation' of jobs by YTS schemes (Chapter 12). This may be the case even if a policy is uniformly applied.

Thus the relationships and interactions between different geographical scales are both upwards and downwards, complex rather than simple, and thus, despite the increased influence of global change, do not necessarily produce a greater similarity between places.

Other major changes

There have also been some major changes that have occurred at a number of scales, particularly ones that may be regarded as reflecting interactions between the types of environments that have been identified in the book.

Economic priorities

The first represents the dominance of economic priorities and particularly the prominence of the capitalistic organisation of production, distribution and consumption in many parts of the world. It has led to many structures, processes and relations being increasingly treated as products or commodities. Parts of the physical environment, such as lakesides and beaches, to which there was free access, have been parcelled up as pieces of land with high amenity value and sold to private owners who then control or restrict access to them (Chapter 5). The processes of relaxing and enjoying the sun and scenery in certain physical environments have been turned into packaged holidays which have been mass marketed and consumed (Chapter 8). In such ways the physical environment has been *commodified*.

The built environment has also been treated as a product to be marketed and consumed. The whole idea of the 'heritage' industry with its reconstruction and packaging of the past has commodified history and with it the relict features from the past that remain in the built landscape of the present. Many of the newly constructed parts of the built environment have also been packaged and sold, not just as individual

homes or offices but as much larger communities or developments, being part of which is promoted as being advantageous. In these cases, such ideas as rurality and status for housing developments in metropolitan rings, and prestige and success for office parks or science parks, are being commodified along with the built environment. Such commodification of the built environment accentuates differences between places at a local scale but increases similarities at regional and even national scales because such residential and office developments may be very similar in design from one area to another.

Commodification also extends to the human environments. Technology is often treated as though it were a commodity. Information certainly is (Chapter 9). Information is produced, acquired and often sold. When the characteristics of the so-called 'post-industrial society' were first described, knowledge was designated as its most central and important product. Access to it was seen as all-important (Chapter 5). Thus the processes of informing, innovating and learning have been commodified. So too have personal relations, with the establishment of dating services and telephone chat lines turning social processes into products. Political processes have also gone the same way, as politicians, parties and policies are marketed in a similar way to products, indeed often by the same advertising agencies.

Such changes have a number of consequences. First, it means that the environments and the sets of processes that are included within them are becoming more interlinked. Just as it is becoming increasingly difficult to distinguish an advertisement for a product or company from a party political broadcast promoting a politician or a party, so too it is becoming less easy to draw neat lines demarcating what is economic and what is political. Second, it means that economic

ways of thinking become more natural and people are less surprised when processes that have not previously been regarded as economic are treated in economic terms. Education, for example, has been discussed in terms of value for money and returns on investment rather than as a right or a social and cultural necessity. Health has been similarly commodified and health care increasingly discussed in economic terms, while economic solutions have also been suggested for problems of pollution of the physical environment.

Technological solutions

Parallel to this elevation of the economic way of thinking is the dominance of technological solutions or 'fixes' (Chapter 9). This is particularly the case for issues relating to economic development. Improved technology has also been increasingly seen as the solution to such diverse issues as population and resource use, illness, surveillance of offenders (electronic tagging) and peace. Some people argue that the overemphasis on technology has been part of the problem in many of these areas in the first place. They also see the continued allocation of human and capital resources into many of the technological solutions as hindrances to progress, preferring changes in social and political attitudes and thought (Chapter 3). Again the argument is that technological processes are given higher priority than social, political and environmental or ecological ones.

Blurring of town and country

Thus there has been a growing intertwining of these sets of processes and a debate about their priority in our thoughts and actions. There has also been a blurring of a number of opposites or dichotomies, and observations have been made on the need to re-evaluate them. 'Town' and 'country', or urban and rural, for example, have become more difficult to differentiate. There has been counter-urbanisation (Chapter 10) and rural industrialisation on the one hand, and the 'greening' of some cities on the other. There has also been the spread of urban thought and ways into rural areas, with few rural areas remaining in western countries that are not heavily influenced by cities. The rural idyll is used to attract people to live in the countryside (Chapters 2 and 10), but the housing created and the residents so attracted bring the city to the countryside.

Blurring of manufacturing and services

'Manufacturing' and 'services' is another dichotomy that is being challenged. As Chapter 12 argues, the differences are becoming very blurred. For example, service occupations have risen in the manufacturing sector as processes such as marketing and management assume a greater importance relative to those of production; manufacturing corporations have diversified into services while service companies have diversified into manufacturing; and services are treated in many ways as products.

Blurring of private and public sectors

The distinction between the 'public' and 'private' sectors has also been blurred, as discussed in Chapter 4. For instance, in the 1980s many public services were fully or partially privatised or were managed with much more emphasis on the practices of the private sector and the operation of market forces. Various

kinds of public-private partnerships (Chapter 4) were also established.

Blurring of private and public spheres

To some extent the distinction between the 'public sphere' of employment and politics and the 'private sphere' of the home has also been eroded, in that relatively more people work from home. The association of the public sphere with men and the private sphere with women has also been reduced and, indeed, seems set to be further weakened as more women enter or re-enter paid employment and men are increasingly involved in sharing domestic work.

More distinct public and private spaces

On the other hand, the distinction between 'public space' and 'private space' may have intensified because of the trends towards greater protection of private space against crime ('target hardening', Chapters 6 and 10) and towards a greater degree of private ownership of housing (Chapter 13). Certainly the greatest investment in private space is greatly contrasted with the lack of investment in public space in such places as the redeveloped British docklands of the 1980s (Chapter 11).

Mass production and consumption versus flexible production and segmented markets

New distinctions arise, however, that pose questions about the direction of change. Two related examples are between mass and 'flexible' production and between mass and 'segmented' marketing. In the 1950s

and before, mass production and mass marketing were the rule. From the 1960s onwards there have been moves towards more flexible production (Chapters 9 and 12) and segmented marketing (Chapters 5, 8 and 10). New technology has made it possible and profitable to have small runs of products amended to customers' specifications or to particular market segments, while companies have improved their marketing methods, including better selections of marketing channels (Chapter 3) for targeted market groups based on such characteristics as socio-economic status, age, stage in the life cycle, ethnicity and life-styles (Chapters 5 and 10). For example, holidays are packaged for eighteen to twenty-five-year-olds where the product offered is opportunities for new relationships, social or other! The readers of this book are likely to be targeted for such holidays, while the authors, somewhat envious of the readers, await the lure of SAGA holidays for the elderly, hoping that by then the rejuvenating powers portrayed in the fantasy film *Cocoon* may have become a reality.

Some researchers have regarded flexible production, in particular, as a change to a new system, seeing it as a replacement of mass production. Others see it as new but as an additional form of production rather than as a replacement of mass production. This raises the whole question of how we distinguish significant change and establish its degree and scale.

Establishing change

New 'isms'

This book has been written during a period when people have been highlighting significant changes in the structure of societies, such as from industrial to post-industrial, from 'modernism' to 'post-modernism', from 'organised capital' to 'disorganised' or 'fragmented capital', from 'Fordism' to 'post-Fordism' or to 'flexible accumulation'. These observations of changes in societies and capitalism have been given much promotion. They catch the eye. 'Isms' become 'wasms'. Only some have been discussed in this book. They are mentioned here to provoke further reading and also to raise questions about the significance of any change.

Every generation seems to like to think that it is living in an important period of change, so it is quite common to search for it. Establishing such a key change also attracts considerable academic prestige, so it is a rewarding activity. Both of these factors tend to inflate the significance given to any changes observed. For instance, what turns out to be an upward curve in a cycle is sometimes purported to be a major trend, or is even identified as a dramatic change that marks a new structure to the system, a complete change from what went before.

Actual or wished-for change

Sometimes such published changes reflect the direction in which the observers think society *should* go, rather than where it is going. Their values should be considered when evaluating their suggestions. Welcoming the advent of the 'enterprise culture' or the 'global village' are examples of particular forms of economic, technological and social ideals as much as observations of realities. Thus it is often difficult to assess the significance of observed change.

Selective data

Even if the readers want to try to collect data over time and make

observations themselves, there are problems with the data they may use as evidence. If geographers want to describe and analyse change in places, they find that more and more of the evidence that is available has been collected to promote the places. The growth within Britain of the marketing of place (Chapter 11) seems a significant change in itself, but it has meant that data are published to demonstrate how attractive a location a place is for economic activity or for tourism, or how well developed it is economically or culturally. The data are often one-sided. Some are collected and published while others are neglected. Again the motives and values of those producing or interpreting the data have to be assessed.

Blurring real and false

It is therefore often difficult to distinguish the real from the false, or the real from the image. Real – false is another dichotomy that has been blurred. Data are manipulated, but changing definitions, for instance so that they present a better image of the success of the government in power. This has happened in the UK to unemployment figures and data on the homeless. Information is given about government policies which often reflects the promised effects rather than the real impacts, which to be fair are very difficult to observe. In short, sometimes data about places, companies and government policies are more persuasion than information. It is therefore very important to be aware of the sources of the data.

Other evidence

There is a tendency for some of this marketing of place and policy to hide unwanted factors, such as poverty and homelessness. Indeed, one

unfortunate geographical strategy for such problems is to conceal them in less visited or observed parts of the city or to hide them by dispersal. The problems do reappear, though, in other images presented in such forms as books, plays, paintings, films, pop songs and advertisements. Consider, for example, the images of cities portrayed in films and advertisements. Some are go-getting, fast-moving, striving cities of tall buildings glinting in the sun. Others are of threatening, oppressive back alleys full of garbage and rodents. They are images of decline, disease and disorder. These cultural forms to some extent offset the one-sided marketing of place. They provide other sources of data for observing change, though of a less conventional kind.

Image creation

The marketing of place is part of a wider trend of creating images, in which geography plays a number of roles. The media create or accentuate stereotypes of people and places. Because some social groups have little contact with others who live in another part of the city and have different jobs and life-styles, the stereotypes in the media are their main source of knowledge. For some people it is difficult to distinguish a soccer fan from a 'soccer hooligan'. The only contact many people have had with a 'young urban professional' has been through advertisements. In a similar way, lack of personal experience means that places often remain as stereotypes, for example the Spanish coastal resort, the 'North' and the 'South' of Britain, and New York. Even if people visit these places, they often arrive with the stereotypical image and find it difficult not to view them from that perspective. Even our personal experience of reality is filtered in many ways, which makes it difficult enough to observe what an area is

The Hovis 'delivery boy' advertisement

like, let alone how it has changed.

Companies and political parties in their advertising often create imaginary communities to which people are invited to belong. Buying the product or voting in a particular way supposedly allows you to adopt certain life-styles and to belong to certain groups. Some of these, such as the 'jet set', are suggested as natural goals, even though by definition they are exclusive. Geography plays a part in this creation of such communities and groups, for example the Caribbean beach, the French Mediterranean resort and the converted warehouse apartment.

Some researchers argue that we buy products less for their qualities than for the images associated with them. Geography also plays a role in creating these images. In times of uncertainty and a declining economy, for instance, many long-lasting branded goods are repositioned so that they are associated with stability and the past. This is achieved by showing the goods in such rural scenes as depicted by the paintings of Constable or in old cobbled streets. A voice from northern England, a so-called 'brown voice', may be heard, which is to convey reliability, important for basic goods such as bread. So scenes of past geographies, real or imagined, and voices from particular regions help to create the images to be associated with the products.

Not only is it difficult in some situations to distinguish image from reality, it may be argued that image is reality or at least part of it. In many people's eyes the East End of London and Miami are as they appear in the television series *Eastenders* and *Miami Vice*. Citizens may also become more like the image that is directly or indirectly promoted of them. For instance, perhaps more people want to live in converted warehouses after seeing them in advertisements for things such as financial services. In such ways image and reality become blurred.

Sometimes a life-style or social group from one area or country is adopted and depicted as part of a national trend and thus imposed on other regions; for example, the idea of the 'young urban professional',

originated in the USA, was applied to people especially in the City of London and then aimed at people in other regions. This does not mean that other regions accepted the term or idea. Again there are geographical variations. People in some regions positively rejected and derided the idea. There may be resistance to such ideas and images that may in itself be geographically differentiated. Thus there may be different views and images of social groups from one area of the country to another, and indeed there may also be varying images of places from one social group to another.

Views of reality

Whether you live inside or outside an area may well affect your view of how it has changed. Both views may be equally important in influencing the future geography of the area, even though they may not be the same. The first, for instance, may affect whether a young person stays in the area to seek employment. The second may influence whether someone from outside decides to invest in the area, perhaps providing greater opportunities for the young person. Neither view may coincide very much with data available on the area. It is not easy to say which of the three is the best reflection of reality.

Indeed, it raises the question: 'What is reality?.' Some thinkers view it as existing, as an objective world, outside of the people viewing it, while others consider it as something that is subjective, constructed by individual people or groups of people.

If the real world is said to be changing, in whose eyes or from what viewpoint is that change seen? If there are differences in view as to what it was like before, there may well be varying opinions of how it is changing. Different sets of data may reflect contrasting trends, in the same way as one political party uses a particular selection of economic data to indicate the improving state of the economy, while its opponents recount another set to demonstrate a worsening situation. Much is left to the voters to make their own conclusions. In the same way, you as geographers need to develop a critical awareness of data and ideas, an awareness that allows you to detect any bias in the data and to determine the underlying values in its interpretation.

Epilogue

In the same way, it is important to note that significant change has been discussed and indicated in this book and portrayed within a particular geographical framework. The values of the authors and the influences on them throughout their lives have no doubt affected both the framework adopted and their perception of geography and change.

The success of the book will not be measured just by the extent to which people accept the authors' reading of geography and change, but also by the degree to which it makes the readers think about their own values and develop their own geographical viewpoints and their own views of reality and change.

We would not only like readers to be aware of the ideals and goals that may influence the thinking and writing of others, we want them to evaluate the present, decide what is wrong with it and consider their own visions of the future, their own future geographies towards which they wish society to move.

This is obviously challenging. It is difficult to unravel the complexities of the present world. It is not easy to achieve visions of the future. Interventions often fail to achieve their goals because of complex interactions between sets of processes. However, these are the challenges of being modern geographers.

In short, we have tried to unravel some of that complexity. We have

tried to encourage readers to observe present and recent geographies, develop an understanding of how and why these came about, consider present and predicted problems, and evaluate possible strategies for them. This is clearly not just an academic exercise. We also hope the readers' understanding of geography will inform their future actions in contributing to the achievement of societal goals which underlie the strategies they have chosen.

At the beginning of the book we said 'look around you'. As you are observing the world, identifying problems, understanding the key processes affecting them and evaluating alternative strategies for them, we encourage you to act and to get involved in the issues that concern you at varying geographical scales. We hope that this book helps to inform that action and involvement, and makes you aware of the ways you will be affected by, and be helping to change, the physical, built and human environments that are around you.

14.2 Further reading

P. Cloke, C. Philo and D. Sadler (1991) *Approaching Human Geography: an introduction to contemporary debates*

D. Harvey (1989) *The condition of Postmodernity: An Enquiry into the Origins of Cultural Change*, Basil Blackwell

A. Kobayashi and S. Mackenzie (eds.) (1989) *Remaking Human Geography*, Unwin Hyman

A. Rogers, H. Viles and A. Goudie (1992) *The Student's Companion to Geography*, Blackwell

E. Soja (1989) *Postmodern Geographies: the Reassertion of Space in Critical Social Theory*, Verso

J. Wolch and M. Dear (1989) *The Power of Geography*, Unwin Hyman

More general reading for the whole book:

J. Chaffey and S. Warn (1992) *Decision Making Exercises 1 and 2*, Collins Educational

K. Cowlard (1990) *Decision Making in Geography: a Manual of Method and Practice*, Hodder and Stoughton

P. Franks and P. Guinness (1992) *People and the Physical Environment*, Hodder and Stoughton

R.J. Johnston and V. Gardiner (eds.) (1991) *The Changing Geography of the UK*, Routledge

N. Law and D. Smith (1991) *Decision Making Geography*, (2nd ed.) Stanley Thomas

Open University Course D205 (1985) *Changing Britain, Changing World, Geographical Perspectives Units 1-32*, Open University Press

F. Slater (ed.) (1986) *People and Environments: Issues and Enquiries*, Collins Educational

F. Slater (ed.) (1991) *Societies, Choices and Environments*, Collins Educational

APPENDIX

ORGANIZATION OF BOOK AND TRADITIONAL BRANCHES OF GEOGRAPHY

Branches of Geography	CHAPTERS													
	1	2	3	4	5	6	7	8	9	10	11	12	13	14
Physical Environment	1.1 1.7	2.1 2.3 2.3a 2.3d 2.3e	3.1 3.2 3.3a 3.4 3.5	4.5		6	7.2 7.3a 7.3b	8.5	9.4		11.2 11.3c 11.5			14
Agriculture, Fishing & Forestry		2.2 2.3e 2.4 2.5	3.3b			6.1	7.1 7.2		9.2		11.3a 11.3c			14
Mining/Quarrying		2.1 2.2 2.3a					7.1							
Manufacturing			3.3e				7.3c	8	9.2 9.3b 9.3c			12		14
Services: Public & Private		2.3b 2.5		4.2 4.3b 4.4 4.5	5	6.1	7.3f	8		10.3b	11.2 11.3d	12	13	14
Leisure/Recreation/ Tourism						6.1 6.3b 6.3c	7.2	8.3b						14
Transport/ Communications		2.4	3.2 3.3c	4.1 4.3a		6.3b	7.1 7.2		9.1 9.2 9.3a					14
Energy/Power		2.3a	3.1 3.2 3.3a 3.3d 3.4 3.5				7.1 7.2				11.3c 11.5			14

Branches of Geography	CHAPTERS													
	1	2	3	4	5	6	7	8	9	10	11	12	13	14
Population	1.2	2.5	3.4		5		7.3d 7.3e 7.3f			10	11.3a 11.3b	12.1 12.3c 12.3d	13.3c	14
Settlement		2.2 2.3b 2.3c 2.4 2.5	3.3d 3.4	4.3c	5.1	6.3d				10.1 10.3d 10.4	11.1 11.3d		13	14
Urban		2.3b 2.3c 2.5	3.3d 3.4	4.1 4.3a 4.3c 4.4	5.1 5.2 5.4	6.3d	7.3d		9.3a	10.2 10.3d 10.3e 10.4	11.1 11.3d 11.4	12.2 12.5	13	14
Rural		2.1 2.2 2.3a 2.4 2.5	3.3b			6.1	7.1					12.2 12.5		14
Regional		2.1 2.3e 2.5	3.1 3.2 3.3e 3.5	4.1 4.2 4.3b 4.5	5.1 5.2 5.3a 5.3b 5.3c	6.3a 6.4	7.1 7.3a 7.3d 7.3f 7.5	8.1 8.2 8.3a	9.1 9.3a 9.3b 9.3c 9.4	10.2 10.3c 10.3e	11.2 11.3a 11.3b 11.4	12.1 12.2 12.3a 12.5	13.3a	14
Economic	1.1	2.2	3.2 3.3e 3.4 3.5	4.1 4.2 4.3c 4.4 4.5	5.2 5.4	6.2 6.4	7.2 7.3c	8	9	10.3c 10.5	11.2 11.4 11.5	12	13.2 13.4	14
Social	1.1 1.2			4.2 4.3c 4.4 4.5	5	6.2 6.4	7.2 7.3d 7.4	8.5	9.5	10	11.4 11.5	12.2 12.3b 12.3c 12.5	13	14
Political	1.1	2.3e	3.2 3.5	4	5.1 5.2 5.4	6.2	7.2 7.4 7.5	8.2 8.5	9.2 9.4	10.2 10.5	11	12.4 12.5	13.2 13.4 13.5	14

INDEX

A

Ability to pay 62, 72, 91
Access 87-109
Accessibility 5, 90, 91, 103
Accountability 65, 66, 77
Acid deposition (rain) 42, 129, 130, 133, 134, 145, 239
Age 92, 199-202
Ageing 196-198, 220, 221
Agglomeration diseconomies 254
Agglomeration economies 254
Agribusiness 45
Agriculture 19, 29, 31, 46, 132, 172
Aid 203
AIDS 138, 139, 140
Allocation of resources 63, 71
Area-based policies 104, 242
Antarctica 27
Availability 87, 88, 89, 95, 100
Awareness 87, 89, 102, 103

B

Backwash 165
Barriados 211
Base load 42
Basque country 237
Battersea 282, 283
Bay of Fundy 38
Birmingham 273-275
Birth rates 200, 201, 207, 219
Black movement 205
Brent (Housing) 283, 284, 285
Bryce Canyon 22
Building cycles 289, 290
Built environment 1, 18, 33, 51, 116, 129, 164, 220
Bus travel 58-60, 68, 69
Business cycle 163, 164

C

Cambridge Phenomenon 182, 183
Canadian North 127, 128, 171
Cantril Farm 74, 75

CAP 236
Capital flows 157
Capital intensive 52
Cars 48, 49, 53, 148-150
Centralisation 63, 64, 240, 241, 244, 229
Channel Tunnel 45, 46, 47
Chernobyl 37, 51, 135
Coastal land, conflict 26
Colorado River 125, 126
Command economies 81
Commodified 299
Competition 63, 160, 163
Compositional effect 204
Concentration 160, 206, 216-217
Configuration 160, 161
Conflict 16-19, 22-26, 28-30, 63, 232, 235, 236
Conservation 50
Consumer involvement 67
Consumer movement 68
Consumer rights 67
Contextual effect 204
Controls 102, 121
Cooperation 144, 192, 235, 236
Cooperatives 66, 67
Coordination 160, 161
Corporate management 64
Corporate sector 93
Council Housing (local authority) 74, 286, 288, 293
Counter-urbanisation 202, 210-212
Coventry 260, 261
Crime 130, 192, 204, 212, 213, 214, 215, 222
Crime prevention 122, 214, 215, 218
Cultural views of land 33
Cycles 163, 164, 191, 243, 244, 248, 249, 289, 290

D

Death 138-140, 199, 202

Decentralisation 63, 64, 202, 229, 240, 241, 244
Deconcentration 202, 211
Defence industry 185-186
Deindustrialisation 252
Demographic environment 2, 116, 196
Deregulation 60, 76, 187
Developing countries 154, 156, 157
Disease 133, 136, 138-140, 199, 202-203
Disintegration 165
Diversification 151
Divorce 199, 201
Docklands Light Railway 181
Domestic economy 78
Doughnut effect 250, 251

E

Ealing Broadway Centre 23, 24
Ecological marketing channel 52, 53, 54, 56
Economic dependency 233
Economic environment 19, 116, 130, 164, 184-185, 220, 245
Economies of scope 176
Education 95, 96
Elderly 196-200, 206, 207, 220, 221
Employment 248-251
Enterprise zones 101, 102
Enveloping 275
Environmental good 52
Environmental priorities 83
Environmentalism 12
Equality 106, 107
Ethnic employment 262, 263
Ethnic groups 92, 96, 106, 108, 130, 205, 209-210
Exchange value 30
Exit 140
Export enclaves 162
Export processing zones 162
Exported services 268

Externalities (positive & negative) 20, 31, 129, 131
External control 154
External economy 267
External threats 127-145
Exxon Valdez 123

F
Falklands 27
Famine 203
Fares Fair 58
Feminisation of manufacturing 254
Feminist movement 204, 205
Filtering 285
Finance 64, 65, 87, 91, 103, 229
Financial organisation 64
Fire hazard 112, 113, 114
Flexible manufacturing systems 175, 176
Floods 121, 125, 126
Footpath erosion 119
Forest fire 112, 113, 114
Free riders 141
Friction of distance 90

G
Gas pipelines 127, 128
Gatekeepers 90, 279
Gay movement 205, 206
Gender 10, 92, 204, 205
Gender and employment 261, 262
General Improvement Areas 274, 281, 282, 288
General Practitioners 107, 108
Gentrification 202, 282, 283
Glasnost 78, 235
Global products 152, 153
Global scale 10, 295
Global shift 11, 164, 165
Global village 173, 174
Government 27, 79, 223-226, 227-232
Government policy 28-29, 33-34, 49, 154, 162, 177, 185-190, 265, 276
Greater London Council 225
Green Belt 25, 29
Green movement 234, 235, 237-239
Greenhouse effect 42
Greenpeace 34, 35
Growth centres 267

H
Haggett, P 5
Harrisburg 37
Harvey, D 8
Havelock Housing Action Area 281, 282
Hazard 112-126

Health and health systems 70, 73, 97, 98
High-tech industry 181-184
Home 1, 2, 3
Homelessness 293
House prices 292
Household composition 92
Household economy 78
Housing 47, 48, 73-76, 83, 107, 108, 196-198, 273-293
Housing Action Areas 274, 275, 281, 282, 288
Housing Associations 73, 74, 79-80, 286, 287
Humanistic Geography 8, 9
Hurricanes 117, 118

I
IBM 157, 158
Illegalisation 141
Image creation 301, 302
Immigration 209, 210
Import substitution 163
Incentives 101, 102
Inequalities 86-100, 105-107
Informal economy 78
Information Technology Education Centres 78
Information technology 168, 169, 170
Insurance 99
Integration 241, 242
Intensity of use 31, 32
Interconnected 154, 298
Interdependence 11, 54, 55, 298
Intermediate Technology 194
International cooperation 144
Internationalisation 252
Intervention 27, 121
Islam 234
Islington 282, 283

J
Job creation 265, 266
Just-in-time 176

K
Kanab 22

L
Labour 48-49, 155-156, 184, 264
Labour intensive 52
Labour markets 257-258, 265
Land 21, 22, 32-34
Landslide 118, 119
Lesbian movement 205, 206
Lever 79
Life cycle 92

Life paths 199
Linkages 156
Local authority housing 74
Local government 223-226, 227-232
Localities 11, 269
Location 5
Locational analysis 5
London transport 58, 59
Long waves (kondratiev) 191, 248, 249
Los Angeles 120
Linkages 156

M
Mam Tor 118, 119
Management 63
Manchester 224, 225
Manufacturing 61-68, 148-166, 172, 175, 248-270, 300
Market economies 81, 82
Marketing 42, 52-54, 67, 162
Market share 63
Marketing of place 100, 101, 301
Marriage 201
Mental health care 71, 138
Merseyside 239, 240
Merseyside Development Corporation 239, 240
Metropolitan counties 223-226
Metropolitan ring 24, 25, 280, 281
Michelin 136, 137
Migrant labour 137, 209
Migration 208, 209
Military alliances 232
Miners strike 41
Minimize costs 63
Mobility 216
Modal split 56
Mortality rate 97, 98
Multi hazard prone 114, 117, 120
Multi-lateralism 252
Multinationals 148-167
Multiplier effects 18
Mutliply disadvantaged 91

N
National Express 68, 69
Need 62, 68, 69, 71, 87, 91-94, 199
Negative externalties 20, 129, 131
Neighbourhood watch 122
New Right 12
NIC's 152, 154, 155
NIMBY 143
Non renewable resources 50
North - South 249, 250, 251, 257
Nuclear cycle 53
Nuclear industry/power 36-37, 56, 129, 239

O

OLI theory 153,
Office, power 99, 100
Optimists 50
Organic farming 45
Organisations 3, 4
Ownership 61

P

Part-time employment 258
Participation 141, 298
Partnerships 79, 80
Peak District 17, 18, 19
Peak load 42
People 3, 4
Perestroika 78, 235
Permaculture 45
Pessimists 50
Physical environment 1, 18, 116,
  129, 164, 189-190, 245
Planning blight 24, 30
Planning gain 143
Plogoff 38
Polarisation 165
Political beliefs 62
Political conflicts 232
Political environment 1, 18, 130,
  166, 220, 269
Power 87, 93, 104
Power relationships 54
Prison 83, 84
Private consumption 82
Private health systems 70, 72, 73,
  80, 81
Private monopoly 62
Private ownership 61, 78
Private sector 61, 70-73, 76, 80,
  231, 300
Privatisation 76, 77, 78, 84
Process control industries 175
Processes 13
Producer services 256
Protection 214, 218, 298
Public consumption 82
Public health 70, 71, 72, 73
Public goods & services 61, 70, 71,
  76, 78, 88, 89
Public sector 61, 70-73, 78, 80, 231,
  300
Public transport 58, 59, 60, 65
Pump priming 79
Push and pull factors 212

R

Rabies 136
Radical Left 8, 31, 106
R and D (Research & Development)
  50, 153, 158, 160, 177, 184, 185
Rank Xerox 25

Recycling 51
Red lining 91
Redevelopment 287
Regional change 253, 254
Regional differences 270, 271, 272
Rehabilitation 287, 288
Renewable resources 50
Resources 18, 20, 21, 27, 28, 30-35,
  124-125, 132
Restructuring 254
Retail decision making 88
Retail developments 85, 86, 87
Retail provision 88, 89

S

Saltley 273-275
Scales 19, 295-298
School closure 93, 94, 207, 208
School rolls 200, 201, 207, 208
Sector model 255
Self employment 258
Self interest 52
Self-help 298
Self-service economy 255
Semi-conductors 183, 184
Separation 201
Separatism 237
Segmented labour markets 257
Services and service sector 58-83,
  85-109, 248-270, 300
Severn Barrage 38
Shopping centres 85, 86, 87
Shrinkage of space 17, 173
Site of Special Scientific Interest
  17, 32
Sizewell 36, 37, 38
Small firms 159, 160
Smith, D 10
Social class 92, 93
Social distance 90
Social environment 2, 19, 116, 130,
  165, 192, 219, 245, 269
Social good 52
Social justice 94, 95, 104
Social ownership 78
Social segregation 217-218, 298
Social status 93
Soil erosion 119
Solar energy 43, 44
South Yorkshire 60
Space-time budget 91
Space-time process 91
Spatial dispersion 253
Spatial distribution 5
Spatial division of labour 153
Spatial interaction 5
Spatial justice 94, 95, 104
Spatial scales 19
Spatial targeting 242, 243

Speculative gains 30
St Quentin En Yvelines 280, 281
Stockbridge village 75, 76
Subsidies 59, 60, 65
Sunrise or sunset industries 185
Superpowers 233, 234
Supra-states 155
Swiss cheese effect 250
Synergy 182

T

Targeting 242
Technical fix/solution 32, 192, 299
Technological environment 2, 116,
  130, 165, 245
Technological leakage 188, 189
Technological transfer 156, 188
Technology 168-195
Teignmouth special school 137, 138
Terrorism 203
TGV 179, 180
Three Mile Island 37
Tillingham Hall 29
Time scales 19, 131, 163, 190, 218,
  243
Topley Pike 17, 18, 34, 35
Training 187, 258, 259, 266
Tourism 132, 158
Tragedy of the Commons 32
Transnationals 148-167
Transport 41, 46, 58-60, 68, 69,
  118, 127-128, 131, 179, 180, 181
Trust House Forte 158
Tuan, Yi Fu 10
Tyranny of small decisions 54

U

Unions 66, 178
Uniqueness of place 54, 55
Unpaid work 259
Unenumerated economy 78
Urban Development Corporations
  239, 240
Urban managers 279
Urban renewal 273-293
Urbanisation 210, 211
Use value 30

V

Values 9, 10, 12, 82, 219
Voice 140, 142, 143
Voluntary sector 79, 80
Voting systems 244, 245

W

War 30, 203, 236
Wind 43, 44
Worker involvement 66